W9-CFC-665

The Call to Write

The Call to Write

brief fifth edition

John Trimbur

EMERSON COLLEGE

WADSWORTH
CENGAGE Learning™

Australia • Brazil • Japan • Korea • Mexico • Singapore • Spain • United Kingdom • United States

WADSWORTH
CENGAGE Learning™

The Call to Write, Brief Fifth Edition
John Trimbur

Executive Editor: Monica Eckman

Senior Publisher: Lyn Uhl

Acquisitions Editor: Margaret Leslie

Development Editor: Kathy Sands-Boehmer

Assistant Editor: Amy Haines

Editorial Assistant: Elizabeth Ramsey

Media Editor: Cara Douglass-Graff

Marketing Manager: Jennifer Zourdos

Marketing Coordinator: Ryan Ahern

Marketing Communications Manager:
Stacey Purviance

Content Project Managers: Corinna Dibble;
Margaret Park Bridges

Art Director: Jill Ort

Print Buyer: Sue Spencer

Senior Rights Acquisitions Account Manager,
Text: Margaret Chamberlain-Gaston

Senior Rights Acquisition Accounts Manager,
Image: Jennifer Meyer Dare

Production Service: Pre-PressPMG

Cover Designer: Steven Schirra

Cover Image: © Daniel Jaeger Vendruscolo /
Stock Exchange

Compositor: Pre-PressPMG

©2011, 2008, 2005, Wadsworth, Cengage Learning

ALL RIGHTS RESERVED. No part of this work covered by the copyright herein may be reproduced, transmitted, stored, or used in any form or by any means graphic, electronic, or mechanical, including but not limited to photocopying, recording, scanning, digitizing, taping, Web distribution, information networks, or information storage and retrieval systems, except as permitted under Section 107 or 108 of the 1976 United States Copyright Act, without the prior written permission of the publisher.

For product information and technology assistance, contact us at
Cengage Learning Customer & Sales Support, 1-800-354-9706

For permission to use material from this text or product, submit all requests online at **www.cengage.com/permissions**
Further permissions questions can be emailed to
permissionrequest@cengage.com

Library of Congress Control Number: 2010920686

ISBN-13: 978-0-495-89753-8

ISBN-10: 0-495-89753-1

Wadsworth
20 Channel Center Street
Boston, MA 02210
USA

Cengage Learning is a leading provider of customized learning solutions with office locations around the globe, including Singapore, the United Kingdom, Australia, Mexico, Brazil, and Japan. Locate your local office at:
international.cengage.com/region

Cengage Learning products are represented in Canada by
Nelson Education, Ltd.

For your course and learning solutions, visit **www.cengage.com**

Purchase any of our products at your local college store or at our preferred online store **www.CengageBrain.com**

Printed in Canada
2 3 4 5 6 7 14 13 12 11 10

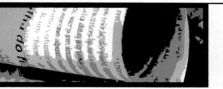

brief contents

v

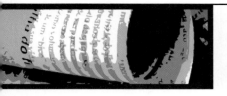

contents

vii

PART 2   WRITING PROJECTS 89

■ **CHAPTER 4**

LETTERS: THINKING ABOUT THE GENRE 91

■ CHAPTER 6

PUBLIC DOCUMENTS 172

■ **CHAPTER 7**

PROFILES 214

PART 3   WRITING AND RESEARCH PROJECTS   375

■ CHAPTER 13

WORKING WITH SOURCES 413

■ **CHAPTER 14**

A GUIDE TO PRINT, ELECTRONIC, AND OTHER SOURCES 442

■ **CHAPTER 15**

FIELDWORK AND THE RESEARCH REPORT 449

PART 4   WRITERS AT WORK   475

■ CHAPTER 16

THE WRITING PROCESS: A CASE STUDY OF A WRITING ASSIGNMENT   478

■ CHAPTER 17

THE SHAPE OF THE ESSAY: HOW FORM EMBODIES PURPOSE   495

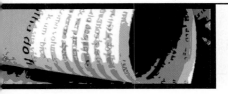

guide to visual design

PAINTINGS

PHOTO ESSAY

POSTERS AND BILLBOARDS

POWERPOINT

WEB PAGES

preface

The Call to Write, Brief Fifth Edition, offers students a broad introduction to writing so that they can learn to write with flexibility and influence in a variety of settings. Many of the assignments in the following chapters are typical of the writing college students are called on to do. A central aim of this book is to help students become effective writers in their college coursework. At the same time, *The Call to Write* takes as its starting point the view that writing is much more than a school subject. Writing is an activity individuals and groups rely on to communicate with others, organize their social lives, get work done, entertain themselves, and voice their needs and aspirations. Accordingly, this textbook presents a wide range of situations that call on people to write—in everyday life, in school, in the workplace, and in the public sphere.

Just as the situations that give rise to writing differ, so do the tools available to writers. Writing can no longer refer simply to the traditional forms of print literacy. It also involves the visual design of the page and screen and the new digital media that enable the integration of text, graphics, sound, and video. Although *The Call to Write* cannot teach many of the skills needed to operate the new writing technologies, it takes into account how writers use these new means of communication and how many forms of writing combine words and graphics to deliver a message.

One of the main premises of the book is that writing should belong to everyone in the various roles people play. *The Call to Write* offers students an education in writing with the goal of enabling them to see how writing connects individuals to others and to the cultural practices and social institutions that shape their lives. In this regard, the call to write—the felt sense that something needs to be said—presents writing not just as a skill to master but as a means to participate meaningfully in the common life and to influence its direction.

DISTINCTIVE FEATURES OF *THE CALL TO WRITE*

The goal of *The Call to Write* is to offer teachers and students a range of activities that are grounded in rhetorical traditions and the accumulated experience of successful writing instruction. It has been enormously gratifying that teachers and students who used the first four editions of *The Call to Write* have confirmed the practical value of its approach. The fifth edition builds on—and seeks to refine—the basic features that give *The Call to Write* its distinctive character:

- **An emphasis on the rhetorical situation.** *The Call to Write* begins with the idea that writing doesn't just happen but instead takes place in particular social contexts. Throughout the textbook, students are provided with opportunities to analyze how rhetorical situations give rise to the call to write. A wide array of writing—from news stories, reports, and op-ed pieces to posters, graffiti, ads, flyers, and newsletters, as well as academic articles, literary essays, and student work—illustrates the range and richness of situations that call on people to write.

- **Genre-based writing assignments.** To help students understand the choices available to them when they respond to the call to write, the "Writing Projects" in Part Two use the notion of genre as the basis for guided writing assignments. Each chapter includes individual and collaborative writing assignments based on familiar genres; extensive treatment of invention, planning, peer commentary, and revision; samples of student writing; and an opportunity for students to reflect on the process of writing.

- **Integration of reading and writing.** Chapter 2, "Understanding the Rhetorical Situation: The Choices Writers Make," emphasizes the kind of reading students are called on to do in college courses. This focus continues in Part Two, with For Critical Inquiry questions that ask students to read closely and carefully to understand their response as readers and the decisions writers make when they take up the call to write.

- **A focus on visual design.** *The Call to Write* emphasizes not only how many types of writing integrate text and graphics but that writing itself is a form of visible language. Chapter 19, "Visual Design," explores how visual design is used for purposes of identification, information, and persuasion; the chapter also provides instruction in effective page design. Chapter 20, "Web Design," considers how Web pages integrate word and image, and Chapter 21, "Oral and PowerPoint Presentations," includes guidelines on designing PowerPoint slides.

- **An emphasis on ethics and the writer's responsibilities.** *The Call to Write* presents boxes on the ethics of writing that raise issues concerning writers' responsibilities toward their readers and their subjects. Chapter 3, "Persuasion and Responsibility: Analyzing Arguments," includes extensive coverage of how writers can deal responsibly with disagreements and negotiate their differences with others.

- **An emphasis on collaborative learning.** *The Call to Write* includes many opportunities for group discussions as well as guidelines for peer commentaries in each of the chapters in Part Two. Chapter 16, "The Writing Process: A Case Study of a Writing Assignment," traces how a student used peer response to write an academic paper, and Chapter 18, "Working Together: Collaborative Writing Projects," offers information and advice about group writing projects.

NEW TO THE FIFTH EDITION

The fifth edition includes new and revised features to help students understand and respond to the call to write. These additions come in large part from discussions with writing teachers who used the first four editions of *The Call to Write*.

- **A new emphasis on global and transnational issues,** with current readings and visuals

- **Updated readings and visuals** in the genre chapters in Part Two, including an extended discussion of scholarly and popular articles in Chapter 8, "Reports"

- **Completely rewritten Chapter 2, "Understanding the Rhetorical Situation: The Choices Writers Make,"** emphasizes how writers encounter rhetorical situations and the choices they make as they define and respond to the call to write.

- **New MLA guidelines for citation and formatting**, based on MLA's 2009 update, appear in Chapter 13, "Working with Sources."

- **Completely revised book design** has improved the usability of *The Call to Write*, making features easier to identify and enhancing readability.

USING *THE CALL TO WRITE*

The Call to Write is meant to be used flexibly to fit the goals and local needs of teachers, courses, and writing programs. While there is no single path to follow in teaching *The Call to Write,* for most teachers the core of the book will be the Writing Projects in Part Two—the guided writing assignments based on common genres. Teachers can choose from among these genres and assign them in the order that best suits their course design.

A rich array of material appears in the other sections of *The Call to Write,* and teachers may draw on the various chapters to introduce key concepts and deepen students' understanding of reading and writing. It can be helpful to think of the organization of the book as a modular one that enables teachers to combine chapters in ways that emphasize their own interests and priorities.

The following overview of the organization of *The Call to Write* describes the six main parts of the book.

- **Part One, "Writing and Reading,"** introduces students to the notion of the call to write, offers strategies for critical reading and rhetorical analysis, and presents methods for identifying disputed issues, planning responsible arguments, and negotiating differences with others. These chapters can serve to introduce central themes at the beginning of a course, or they can be integrated throughout the course.

- **Part Two, "Writing Projects,"** presents familiar genres of writing, with examples, For Critical Inquiry questions, and individual and collaborative writing assignments. Assignments call on students to write for a number of different audiences and in a number of different settings, ranging from everyday life to the academic world to public forums. These chapters form the core of *The Call to Write*.

- **Part Three, "Writing and Research Projects,"** explores the genres of the critical essay, the research paper, and the fieldwork report. It considers what calls on people to do research, how they formulate meaningful questions, and the sources they typically use. Part Three provides an overview of the research process, introduces students to library and online research, and includes information about research projects that use observation, interviews, and questionnaires. This section is particularly appropriate for writing courses that emphasize writing from sources and research-based writing.

- **Part Four, "Writers at Work,"** presents a case study of a student using peer commentary to complete an academic writing assignment, explores the genre of the essay and the meaning and purpose of form in writing, and looks at how writers work together on collaborative writing projects. These chapters can be integrated into a course at a number of points—to initiate discussion of how writers manage individual writing projects, to enhance students' understanding of peer commentary, to prepare students for collaborative writing projects, and to deepen students' understanding of form.

- **Part Five, "Presenting Your Work,"** looks at how writers communicate the results of their work to readers. It includes information on visual design, Web design, oral presentations, essay exams, and portfolios. These chapters can be integrated into a course at many points, depending on the teacher's goals.

ADDITIONAL RESOURCES FOR *THE CALL TO WRITE*

Instructor's Resources

Multimedia eBook *The Call to Write* is now available as an eBook! Students can do all of their reading online or use the eBook as a handy reference while they're completing other online coursework. The eBook includes the full text of the print version with user-friendly navigation, search, and highlighting tools, along with links to videos that enhance the text content.

Book Companion Web site Visit the book companion Web site to access valuable course resources. Resources for students include an extensive library of interactive exercises and animations that cover grammar, diction, mechanics, punctuation, research, and writing concepts, as well as a complete library of student papers and a section on avoiding plagiarism. The site also offers a downloadable Instructor's Manual.

Online Instructor's Manual Available for download on the book companion Web site, this manual contains valuable resources to help you maximize your class preparation efforts. Included are suggested assignments, discussion starters, and sample syllabi.

Enhanced InSite With Enhanced InSite for *The Call to Write,* instructors and students gain access to the proven, class-tested capabilities of InSite—such as peer reviewing, electronic grading, and originality checking powered by Turnitin®—*plus* resources designed to help students become more successful and confident writers, including access to Personal Tutor, an interactive eBook handbook with integrated text-specific workbook, tutorials, and more. Other features include fully integrated discussion boards, streamlined assignment creation, and access to InfoTrac® College Edition. To learn more, visit us online at www.cengage.com/insite.

Student resources

Multimedia eBook *The Call to Write* is now available as an eBook! You can do all of your reading online or use the eBook as a handy reference while completing other online coursework. The eBook includes the full text of the print version with user-friendly navigation, search, and highlighting tools, along with links to videos that enhance the text content.

Book Companion Web site Visit the book companion Web site to access valuable course resources. Resources include an extensive library of interactive exercises and animations that cover grammar, diction, mechanics, punctuation, research, and writing concepts, as well as a complete library of student papers and a section on avoiding plagiarism.

Enhanced InSite With Enhanced InSite for *The Call to Write*, you gain access to the proven, class-tested capabilities of InSite—such as peer reviewing, electronic grading, and originality checking powered by Turnitin®—*plus* resources designed to help you become a more successful and confident writer, including access to Personal Tutor, an interactive eBook handbook with integrated text-specific workbook, tutorials, and more. Other features include fully integrated discussion boards, streamlined assignment creation, and access to InfoTrac® College Edition. To learn more, visit us online at www.cengage.com/insite.

ACKNOWLEDGMENTS

Preparing *The Call to Write* has made me acutely aware of the intellectual, professional, and personal debts I have accumulated over the years teaching writing, training writing teachers and peer tutors, and administering writing programs and writing centers. I want to acknowledge the contributions so many rhetoricians and composition specialists have made to my thinking about the study and teaching of writing, and I hope they will recognize—and perhaps approve of—the way their work has influenced the design of this book.

The unifying theme of the "call to write," as many will note immediately, comes from Lloyd Bitzer's notion of "exigence" and the "rhetorical situation." My treatment of argument and persuasion is informed by Aristotle's appeals (by way of Wayne Booth's sense of "rhetorical stance") and stasis theory (as articulated in Dick Fulkerson's *Teaching Argument in Writing*), and my understanding of reasoning in argument is altogether indebted to Stephen Toulmin (though the terminology I use differs somewhat). The influence of Carolyn Miller's seminal work on genre as "social action" should be apparent at every turn. I learned to teach writing from two great mentors, Ken Bruffee and Peter Elbow, and their mark is everywhere in the book.

I want to thank the lecturers and graduate instructors in the First-Year Writing Program at Emerson College for the work they've done redesigning the first-year writing curriculum and turning what had become a more or less moribund second-semester term paper class into an exciting and innovative genre-based research writing course. Their teaching, the writing assignments they developed, and their students' work shaped many of the changes that appear in the fifth edition of *The Call to Write*. Working with these wonderful colleagues since 2007 has been one of the best experiences in my professional life, and I am happy to note in particular the contributions that Aaron Block, Kara Mae Brown, and Steve Schirra made to the preparation of this edition. I also want to note the writing from Emerson students and from students at Worcester Polytechnic Institute, where I developed and taught early versions of *The Call to Write*. Some of the student writing, I should note, has been edited for this book.

To the many reviewers who provided valuable feedback at many points, my thanks: Kevin Brooks, North Dakota State University; Sidney I. Dobrin, University of Florida; Carol H. Grimes, Florida Community College; William Lalicker, West Chester University; Robert Lively, Truckee Meadows Community College; Mursalata Muhammed, Grand Rapids Community College; Phyllis Mentzell Ryder, George Washington University; Nancy A. Shaffer, University of Texas, El Paso; Kathleen M. Smith, Merrimack College; and Amy Rupiper Taggart, North Dakota State University.

Finally I want to acknowledge the contributions to *The Call to Write* made by members of my family—Lundy Braun and Clare, Lucia, and Catherine Trimbur. They not only provided emotional support; they were coworkers, contributing samples of their writing, suggesting readings and assignments, and locating Web sites and online resources. This has been, in many respects, a joint venture, and I am gratified by their presence in the book.

JOHN TRIMBUR

The Call to
Write

writing and reading

© Dan Jaeger/stock.xchng. Image altered for design purposes.

1

INTRODUCTION: THE CALL TO WRITE

The call to write may come from a teacher who assigns a paper, someone who wants to friend you on Facebook, or a supervisor at work. You may feel called to write an email to your congressman or sign a petition about an issue you care about. Or you belong to a campus organization or community group and want to publicize its aims and activities. In any case, as you will see throughout this book, people who write typically experience some sense of need that can be met by writing. Accordingly, what a person writes will be shaped by the situation that gave rise to that need.

By thinking about these various occasions for writing, you can deepen your understanding of your own and other people's writing and develop a set of strategies that will help you become a more flexible and effective writer. The three chapters in Part One offer a way of looking at why and how people respond to the call to write:

- Chapter 1 "What Is Writing?" looks at four contexts in which writing occurs—everyday life, the workplace, the public sphere, and school.

- Chapter 2 "Understanding the Rhetorical Situation" analyzes how writers identify and respond to situations that call for writing.

- Chapter 3 "Persuasion and Responsibility" considers what makes writing persuasive and how you can build a responsible argument.

■ REFLECTING ON YOUR WRITING

The Call to Write

1. Choose a piece of writing you've done at some time in the past. Think of something other than a writing assignment you did in school. The piece of writing could be an email to a friend, a blog, a Web page, something you wrote at work, a diary entry, a letter, an article for a student newspaper or community newsletter, a petition, a flyer, or a leaflet for an organization you belong to. Whatever the writing happens to be, write a page or two in which you describe what called on you to write and how you responded.

   ■ What was the situation that made you feel a need to respond in writing?

   ■ Why did you decide to respond in writing instead of taking some other action or not responding at all?

   ■ What was your purpose in responding to the call to write? Who was your audience? What relationship to your readers did you want to establish? What tone of voice did you use? How did you make these decisions?

2. With two or three other students, take turns reading aloud what you have written. Compare the situations that gave rise to the call to write and the way each of you responded. What, if anything, is similar about the ways you identified and responded to the call to write? What was different? How would you account for the differences and similarities?

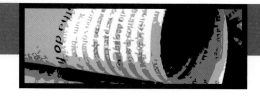

what is writing?
analyzing literacy
events

Learning to write involves an understanding of your own experience as a writer—seeing how various situations have called on you to write, how you have shaped your writing tasks accordingly, and how your writing has involved you in relationships with people in various social contexts. In this chapter, we look at how people respond to the call to write in everyday life, the workplace, the public sphere, and school.

The goal of this chapter is to enable you to analyze how writing actually takes place in the world and how you and others make sense of the writing you encounter and produce. The writing assignment at the end of the chapter— "Analyzing a Literacy Event"—calls on you to examine an occasion in which writing played an important role in people's interactions and the social context in which the writing took place.

Analyzing a literacy event can help you understand the role writing plays in your life—as a private individual, worker, citizen, and student. And it can help you become a more flexible writer who understands the effects writing has in the wider social world.

WRITING IN EVERYDAY LIFE

The call to write in everyday life emerges from a range of situations. People write notes for roommates or family members and send letters of condolence and congratulation. They write emails, post on Facebook, and send text messages to maintain relationships and organize their social life. Some people keep diaries to record their experiences—and to let off steam, put their feelings in perspective, and cope with the stresses of life. Others write poetry, raps, songs, and stories for similar purposes and for the pleasure of using language to create imaginary worlds.

The purposes of writing in everyday life tend to be personal, and intended readers are often people we know well or encounter in our immediate surroundings. Not surprisingly, the tone is characteristically informal and familiar. And although these writings are personal, they are, like everyday life itself, tied to the larger social context.

MAKING LISTS

Nothing could be more ordinary than making a list—to remember class assignments, to keep track of chores and errands, to plan events, to make a wish list of things you'd like to buy or get as a gift. As the anthropologist Sidney Mintz suggests, one of the primary functions of lists is managing time. "Making lists," Mintz says, "must be connected to thinking of time as finite and limited, and we live in a society that gets its power partly from telling us that everything is scarce—even time." Do you make lists? What functions do they perform? How do they help you organize time?

Making lists reveals one of the most powerful aspects of writing: it frees us from having to commit everything to memory. In fact, the Greek philosopher Plato worried that with the widespread use of writing, people's capacity to store things in memory would diminish. Consider Plato's concern in light of the incredible storage capacity of computer memory. What memories do you keep in your head? What memories do you store on paper? What memories do you keep digitally?

Do laundry

Email Mom

Go to drug store

Read history assignment

Start paper for WR101

Go to gym

Invite Martha and Tim
    to dinner on Saturday

Do food shopping

Lists are generally written for an audience of one person, the list maker. Notice, for example, how this shopping list shows that only the writer could bring home from the store exactly what he or she intended to buy. Someone else wouldn't know, for example, how many apples or what kind of meat to buy. This type of writing is a kind of private code that works when you want to talk to yourself. How would this list have to be rewritten if someone other than the writer were going to do the shopping?

apples	Windex
vacuum cleaner bags	spaghetti
hot dog rolls	butter
bananas	bread
milk	paper towels
meat for Sunday dinner	chicken
cat food	two cans of tomatoes
	salad stuff

This list may be written in a private code for an audience of one, but, it also connects the list maker, as writing typically does, to a complex network of social relationships—from the larger economic order of food production and distribution to the everyday activities of preparing meals, caring for pets, and managing a household.

WRITING IN THE WORKPLACE

The call to write emerges repeatedly in the workplace. For financial and legal reasons, companies need to keep careful records of all their transactions, their inventory and sales, the contracts they enter into, and their dealings with unions and federal and state regulatory agencies.

Equally important is written communication among the members of an organization. Such writing serves to establish a sense of shared purpose, a common plan, a clear chain of command, and procedures to evaluate performance. Writing helps manage the flow of work.

Writing in the workplace is often specialized. Many professions have their own genres of writing—for example, legal briefs of lawyers; case histories of doctors, psychologists, and social workers; and the proposals of engineering, marketing research, management consulting, and other professional firms. So crucial has specialized writing become that the ability to master the genre of a profession is crucial to success in the world of work.

KEEPING A LITERACY LOG

To get a sense of how writing is part of your everyday life, keep a literacy log for four hours. Carry a notebook with you so you can record every time you read or write something. Note the time, place, and type of written text involved. Here's an example of the first couple of hours.

Marcie Chambers, December 2, 2009

8:02 a.m.	Dorm room	Checked email and Facebook. Wrote email to my sister Lucille.
8:25 a.m.	Walking from dorm to classroom	Noticed sign about stopping gentrification in Olneyville. Text message from Dave (really sexist).
8:30 – 9:45 a.m.	Sociology 121 lecture	Took notes on lecture. Doodled on handout (is that writing?).
9:52 a.m.	Walking from class-room to Starbucks	Passed homeless man with a sign.
9:54 a.m.	Starbucks	Looked at menu. Took free MP3 download card. Text-messaged Sean to meet in library.

Meet with two or three classmates to analyze your logs. Group types of writing into categories according to their purposes. What patterns emerge from your analysis?

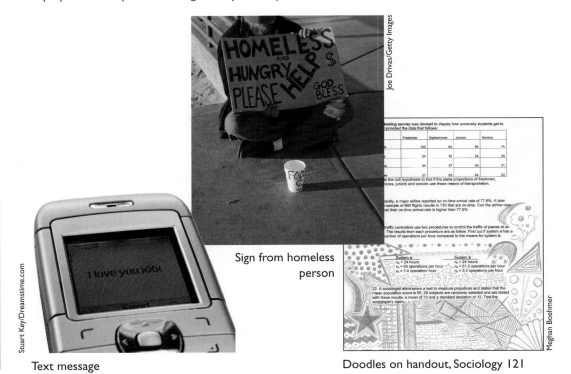

Sign from homeless person

Text message

Doodles on handout, Sociology 121

IN THE OFFICE

Compare the series of emails written by and to Michael Brown, who was director of the Federal Emergency Management Agency (FEMA) when Hurricane Katrina hit on August 29, 2005, to the memo written to coworkers (but addressed to "The thief that has been stealing pens from the IBM"). Consider what the call to write seems to have been in each case.

FEMA AND KATRINA

EMAILS FROM AND TO MICHAEL BROWN

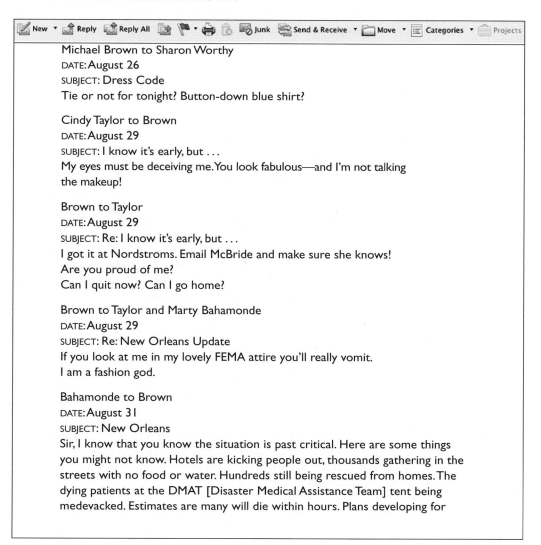

Michael Brown to Sharon Worthy
DATE: August 26
SUBJECT: Dress Code
Tie or not for tonight? Button-down blue shirt?

Cindy Taylor to Brown
DATE: August 29
SUBJECT: I know it's early, but . . .
My eyes must be deceiving me. You look fabulous—and I'm not talking the makeup!

Brown to Taylor
DATE: August 29
SUBJECT: Re: I know it's early, but . . .
I got it at Nordstroms. Email McBride and make sure she knows!
Are you proud of me?
Can I quit now? Can I go home?

Brown to Taylor and Marty Bahamonde
DATE: August 29
SUBJECT: Re: New Orleans Update
If you look at me in my lovely FEMA attire you'll really vomit.
I am a fashion god.

Bahamonde to Brown
DATE: August 31
SUBJECT: New Orleans
Sir, I know that you know the situation is past critical. Here are some things you might not know. Hotels are kicking people out, thousands gathering in the streets with no food or water. Hundreds still being rescued from homes. The dying patients at the DMAT [Disaster Medical Assistance Team] tent being medevacked. Estimates are many will die within hours. Plans developing for

dome evacuation but hotel situation adding to problem. We are out of food and running out of water at the dome, plans in works to address the critical need. Phone connectivity impossible. More later.

Brown to Bahamonde
DATE: August 31
SUBJECT: Re: New Orleans
Thanks for update. Anything specific I need to do or tweak?

Worthy to Brown
DATE: September 4
SUBJECT: Your shirt
Please roll up the sleeves of your shirt . . . all shirts. Even the President rolled his sleeves to just below the elbow.
     In this crisis and on TV you just need to look more hard-working . . . ROLL UP THE SLEEVES!

MEMO TO A THIEF

memorandum

To:	The thief that has been stealing pens from the IBM.
From:	A very angry phone receptionist who is constantly putting more pens near the IBM and who is perpetually frustrated with the fact that whenever he/she goes to use them they are missing.
Re:	A way to remedy this situation.
Date:	The summer

Over the course of the summer it has come to my attention that pens were mysteriously vanishing from the IBM computer. The action causes significant trouble when one tries to take a PHONE MESSAGE or attempts to take a START and commit it to memory. Instead of philosophizing about the possible criminals who insist on making my life harder (I know who who are!), I simply ask that if you, per chance, notice the absence of a pen or pencil near the IBM that you take it upon yourself to correct this mishap and replace one immediately.

I thank you for your time and efforts in this matter.

WRITING IN THE PUBLIC SPHERE

Writing in the public sphere includes writing that defines the landscape we live in—traffic and street signs, billboards, murals, the names of stores, restaurants, libraries, schools, parks, and churches. This kind of public lettering may be engraved on monuments and architectural edifices, written in neon lights, or rendered by commercial artists. Other types of writing in the public sphere are mobile, circulating in the form of posters, flyers, leaflets, newspapers, books, and magazines.

Writing in the public sphere identifies places, provides information, advertises goods and services, deliberates on social and political issues, expresses cultural identities, and seeks to shape the direction of society.

ETHICS OF WRITING

Graffiti has become an omnipresent feature of contemporary urban life. Spray-painted or otherwise pasted on walls and subway cars, graffiti can perform a number of functions: marking a gang's turf, putting forth political messages, expressing the individual writer's

©Martha Cooper

Martha Cooper

identity, expressing grief for someone killed or anger at an enemy. Our reactions to graffiti differ dramatically. Some see it simply as a crime—an antisocial act of vandalism—while others see it as a form of artistic expression and political statement by the disenfranchised. What ethical issues are raised for you by such examples of graffiti as the two printed here? Do you consider graffiti a justified form of writing even though it is illegal? Why or why not? ◼

Frank Mullin

GALLERY OF SIGNS

Assembled here are a range of signs you might encounter in any urban environment. Consider the purposes these signs serve. Are they meant to identify, inform, or persuade? On whose behalf do the signs speak? What sort of relationship do these signs seek to establish with the people who read them?

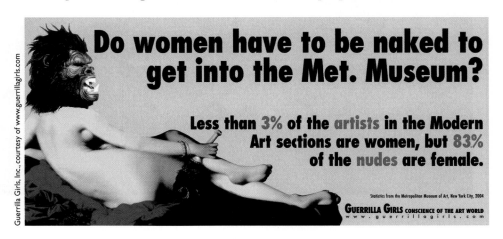

Guerrilla Girls, Inc., courtesy of www.guerrillagirls.com

Charles Gullung / Getty Images

Digital Vision/JupiterImages

iStockphoto.com/Dan Moore

© Bruno Medley/Alamy

WRITING IN SCHOOL

At first glance it may appear that writing in school is relatively uncomplicated—a call to write, from a teacher who is also the audience, with the purpose of showing how well the student understands the material. From this perspective, school writing fits into the social context of schooling, in which students are in the role of performers, teachers are in the role of evaluators, and writing serves as the basis for ranking students according to the prevailing reward system of grades.

Writing in school, however, is more complex than this description allows us to see. First, students do lots of writing for their own purposes that is not directly evaluated by teachers—taking notes in lectures, for example, or writing summaries of textbook chapters to study for tests. And papers that students turn in to teachers for grades may not include all the writing—for example, research notes, outlines, first drafts, and false starts—a student has done to complete the assignment.

Second, even when students are writing for grades, they are not just displaying knowledge of the material. They must also take into account how the different academic fields call for different genres of writing—a lab report in chemistry, a critical essay on a poem for English, or a case study in psychology. For this reason, learning a subject is in part learning how chemists, literary critics, psychologists, and others use writing to communicate in their respective fields.

HIGH SCHOOL AND COLLEGE WRITING

The following two pieces were both written by the same student. The first is a high school research paper. The second was written in college as a response to an assigned reading.

As you read, compare the two pieces:

- How does the writer seem to understand the assignments? What does his purpose seem to be in each instance?

- What kind of relationship does he establish with his reader and his subject?

- What features distinguish the college writing from the high school writing? Does the college writing seem to be more "mature" or "advanced" than the high school writing?

SAMPLE 1: HIGH SCHOOL RESEARCH PAPER

Davis 1

Zack Davis

English 3

Mrs. Tanner

1 May 2007

Politics and the Olympic Games

The revival of the modern Olympic Games was influenced by the politics of
the late nineteenth century. The Baron de Coubertin had two motives in reviving
the Olympic Games. After France lost the Franco-Prussian War, a gloom set over all
of France. The Baron wanted to revive the games to inspire the youth of France. In
the lycées of France, the intellectual aspects dominated the school. There were no
physical education classes and very little, if any, athletic training. The Baron
wanted both athletics and education in the schools. When creating these perfect
schools of France he used the ephebes of ancient Greece and the public schools of
England as examples when education and athletics played a major role in the young
boy's lives; there would be a perfect school. The Baron's other purpose in recreating
the Olympics was to promote world peace by gathering all the countries together.

Though the Baron's intentions were to produce world amity he did the
opposite. Instead of peaceful relations the games created many conflicts. In
1936, for example, there was much conflict at the summer games in Berlin. The
problem of the games was racism. Adolf Hitler wrote the following in *Mein
Kampf,* while in prison in 1924. "Americans ought to be ashamed of themselves
for letting their medals be won by Negroes. I myself would never even shake
hands with one of them." Adolf Hitler, the leader of Germany at the time, was
clearly very racist. When Jesse Owens, a black American, won the gold medal in
the 100 meter dash, Hitler was infuriated. Hitler refused to congratulate him.
Political incidents like these increased over the course of the Olympic Games.

In 1968 the politics shifted from racism to protests against racism. Before
the games sprinter Tommie Smith and other students suggested to boycott the

Davis 2

Olympics because of the racial conditions in the United States. Although Tommie Smith went to Mexico City, he expressed his feelings on racism there as well. During the ceremony for the two hundred meter dash the "Star Spangled Banner" was played. At that time, both Tommie Smith and John Carlos staged a protest by giving the black power salute. They were suspended by the International Olympic Committee and ordered to leave the country.

Another incident that politics played a major role in was the boycott of the Moscow Olympics in 1980. After Russian troops were sent into Afghanistan in 1979, President Jimmy Carter proposed that the games be rescheduled and moved to another location. The response of the International Olympic Committee was that "politics should be of no influence in the Olympic Games." After failing to reschedule and move the games to another location, the President and sixty-four other countries boycotted. Of the one-hundred and forty-five nations that were invited to take part in the games, only eighty-one entered. Some nations that boycotted the games were West Germany, China, Japan, Canada, Kenya, Australia, New Zealand, Great Britain, France, and Italy. Though many athletes within the United States protested that politics should be of no factor in the games, Carter refused to reconsider. By boycotting the Olympics, Carter did not get the troops out of Afghanistan, but simply increased the tension between the United States and the Soviet Union.

In 1984, in response to the boycott four years earlier, Russia, along with East Germany, Czechoslovakia, Poland, Hungary, Bulgaria, and Cuba, declined the invitation to participate in the summer games in Los Angeles. The Soviets denied the boycott was revenge, but argued that the publicity and ten billion dollar cost of the games were outrageous. They also argued that the security in Los Angeles was not sufficient.

In the most recent games, politics as usual influenced the games. The games were held in South Korea. Though the bid was won fairly by South Korea, North Korea felt they deserved to be the co-hosts. Fearing what North Korea might do out of jealousy, South Korea had 120,000 specially trained antiterrorist fighters,

Davis 3

700,000 men of the Republic of Korea's armed forces, 40,000 permanently stationed United States soldiers and marines, and 100,000 United States sailors aboard aircraft carriers patrolling the Korean shores. In addition, there was 63 armed personnel for each of the 13,000 athletes. Both the United States and South Korea had to take drastic measures to secure the safety of the athletes. If politics played no role in the Olympics none of those measures would be necessary.

When Baron de Coubertin revived the Olympic Games he had nothing but good intentions. His hope was that the Olympics could be a place where people from all over the world could gather together in peace doing what they all had in common. Though his intentions were good, politicians took advantage of the Olympics. They used the games as chances to boycott what they thought was wrong and, in other cases, as revenge. Jesse Owens and all the athletes that were not able to go to the 1980 and 1984 Olympics suffered from politics. The purpose of the Olympics has changed into something that is not right. Let's leave the politics to the politicians and competition to the athletes.

SAMPLE 2: COLLEGE RESPONSE PAPER

Assignment: What is the role of popular religion—as portrayed through the worship of the Madonna—in defining the ethnic identity of the Italian community of East Harlem?

Davis 1

Zack Davis

English 120

Prof. Oboler

1 May 2009

Popular Religion and Ethnic Identity

As I read through *The Madonna of 115th Street: Faith and Community in Italian Harlem, 1880–1950,* and the important role that popular religion played

Davis 2

in the role of defining ethnic identity in the Italian community of East Harlem, I could not help but think of my hometown, Cranston, and the similarities that popular religion played there as well. As I read about the feasts of the Madonna of 115th Street I was reminded of the Feast of St. Mary in Cranston and the almost identical origins of the feasts. In Cranston, the feast of St. Mary was started to honor La Madonna della Citta or the Madonna of the city, who was from a small village in southern Italy where many of the first Cranstonians originated. It also served as a distinguishing feature from other Catholics in the area and a marker of ethnic identity. Both of the creations of the Madonnas and the feasts in their honor were popular religion. Popular religion was an important role in shaping ethnic identities in Italian communities.

Both of the feasts in Cranston and East Harlem's purpose were to honor the Madonnas, each from a specific place in Italy, where many of the honorees were from. The Madonna served as a shared history in the new world and gave immigrants something to serve as a reference point. Each immigrant could relate to the Madonna and trusted her with their most sacred prayers. The Madonna listened to the needs of the newly arrived immigrants. As quoted from the work, *The Madonna of 115th Street*, the author says of immigrant Italians, "the Italian feels safer when he plays homage to the patron saint of his hometown or village who in the past was considerate to the people."

The feast of the Madonna of 115th Street began in the summer of 1881 when immigrants from the town of Polla formed a mutual aid society. One of the functions of the mutual aid society was to give unemployment and burial benefits to immigrants. But a larger function of the mutual aid societies and the feasts that it started was to gather immigrants and preserve as well as observe traditional customs in the new world. Because mutual aid societies were unique to Italian Roman Catholics they served as a model for ethnic identity. Furthermore, Catholics of other ethnic backgrounds, such as Irish Catholics, were hostile to feasts of the Madonna of 115th Street. Orsi speaks of an attack published in the *Catholic World* in 1888. The attack criticized the shrines, holy cards and pagan superstitions and "devotions" of the Italian Roman Catholic and the ignorance for "great faith of religion." These attacks on Italian Catholics served to further separate Italians from other Catholics and create a stronger ethnic identity.

In addition the building of certain specifically Italian churches (chiesa), which, again, is popular religion, in East Harlem served as another ethnic identity. Italians as a group gathered to build their own churches. The building was a gathering of everyone, of an ethnic group to create something that they could call their own. As the book noted, junkmen and icemen donated their carts and horses to help manage the burden of building materials as people prepared refreshments for the workers. This act was substantial in the creation of ethnic identity.

During the late nineteenth century, popular religion served as an ethnic identity for Italians in East Harlem, Cranston, RI, as well as in other parts of the eastern seaboard. The creation of Madonnas from hometowns as well as feasts for their honor were the most unique feature and distinguishing characteristic. The separation of Italian Catholics from other Catholics such as Irish Catholics provided further ethnic identity in America.

ANALYZING A LITERACY EVENT

The term *literacy event* gives us a way to think about how reading and writing enter our lives and shape our interactions with others. All the samples of writing in this chapter, for example, can be considered literacy events, because they focus our attention on the role that particular moments of reading and writing play in our experience. These literacy events take place in different social contexts, but each of them, in one way or another, reveals an aspect of what writing does in the world.

When analyzing a literacy event, you are asked to examine how people make sense of their encounters with reading and writing—how they understand what writing is and what it does. You will need to focus on a particular moment in which writing takes on a meaningful role in your life or in the lives of others. The three reading selections that follow provide further examples of literacy events. As you will see, each example concentrates on a specific encounter with writing and the social relationships involved.

- The first selection is from *Narrative of the Life of Frederick Douglass,* the account of Douglass's life as a slave and his escape from slavery.

- The second selection appears in Eudora Welty's memoir *One Writer's Beginnings,* about her childhood in Jackson, Mississippi, in the early twentieth century.

- The third selection comes from Margaret J. Finders's *Just Girls: Hidden Literacies and Life in Junior High,* a study of how junior high girls used reading and writing to establish personal identities and social networks.

FROM *NARRATIVE OF THE LIFE OF FREDERICK DOUGLASS*

FREDERICK DOUGLASS

Very soon after I went to live with Mr. and Mrs. Auld, she very kindly commenced to teach me the A, B, C. After I had learned this, she assisted me in learning to spell words of three or four letters. Just at this point of my progress, Mr. Auld found out what was going on, and at once forbade Mrs. Auld to instruct me further, telling her, among other things, that it was unlawful, as well as unsafe, to teach a slave to read. To use his own words, further, he said, "If you give a nigger an inch, he will take an ell. A nigger should know nothing but to obey his master—to do as he is told to do. Learning would spoil the best nigger in the world. Now," said he, "if you teach that nigger (speaking of myself) how to read, there would be no keeping him. It would forever unfit him to be a slave. He would at once become unmanageable, and of no value to his master. As to himself, it could do him no good, but a great deal of harm. It would make him discontented and unhappy." These words sank deep into my heart, stirred up sentiments within that lay slumbering, and called into existence an entirely new train of thought. It was a new and special revelation, explaining dark and mysterious things, with which my youthful understanding had struggled, but struggled in vain. I now understood what had been to me a most perplexing difficulty—to wit, the white man's power to enslave the black man. It was a grand achievement, and I prized it highly. From that moment, I understood the pathway from slavery to freedom. It was just what I wanted, and I got it at a time when I the least expected it. Whilst I was saddened by the thought of losing the aid of my kind mistress, I was gladdened by the invaluable instruction which, by the merest accident, I had gained from my master. Though conscious of the difficulty of learning without a teacher, I set out with high hope, and a fixed purpose, at whatever cost of trouble, to learn how to read. The very decided manner with which he spoke, and strove to impress his wife with the evil consequences of giving me instruction, served to convince me that he was deeply sensible of the truths he was uttering. It gave me the best assurance that I might rely with the utmost confidence on the results which, he said, would flow from teaching me to read. What he most dreaded, that I most desired. What he most loved, that I most hated. That which to him was a great evil, to be carefully shunned, was to me a great good, to be diligently sought; and the argument which he so warmly urged, against my learning to read, only served to inspire me with a desire and determination to learn. In learning to read, I owe almost as much to the bitter opposition of my master, as to the kindly aid of my mistress. I acknowledge the benefit of both.

FROM *ONE WRITER'S BEGINNINGS*
EUDORA WELTY

1   Jackson's Carnegie Library was on the same street where our house was, on the other side of the State Capitol. "Through the Capitol" was the way to go to the Library. You could glide through it on your bicycle or even coast through on roller skates, though without family permission.

2   I never knew anyone who'd grown up in Jackson without being afraid of Mrs. Calloway, our librarian. She ran the Library absolutely by herself, from the desk where she sat with her back to the books and facing the stairs, her dragon eye on the front door, where who knew what kind of person might come in from the public? SILENCE in big black letters was on signs tacked up everywhere. She herself spoke in her normally commanding voice; every word could be heard all over the Library above a steady seething sound coming from her electric fan; it was the only fan in the Library and stood on her desk, turned directly onto her streaming face.

3   As you came in from the bright outside, if you were a girl, she sent her strong eyes down the stairway to test you; if she could see through your skirt she sent you straight back home; you could just put on another petticoat if you wanted a book that badly from the public library. I was willing; I would do anything to read.

4   My mother was not afraid of Mrs. Calloway. She wished me to have my own library card to check out books for myself. She took me in to introduce me and I saw I had met a witch. "Eudora is nine years old and has my permission to read any book she wants from the shelves, children or adult," Mother said. "With the exception of *Elsie Dinsmore*," she added. Later she explained to me that she'd made this rule because Elsie the heroine, being made by her father to practice too long and hard at the piano, fainted and fell off the piano stool. "You're too impressionable, dear," she told me. "You'd read that and the very first thing you'd do, you'd fall off the piano stool." "Impressionable" was a new word. I never hear it yet without the image that comes with it of falling straight off the piano stool.

5   Mrs. Calloway made her own rules about books. You could not take back a book to the Library on the same day you'd taken it out; it made no difference to her that you'd read every word in it and needed another to start. You could take out two books at a time and two only; this applied as long as you were a child and also for the rest of your life, to my mother as severely as to me. So, two by two, I read library books as fast as I could go, rushing them home in the basket of my bicycle. From the minute I reached our house, I started to read. Every book I seized on, from *Bunny Brown and His Sister Sue at Camp Rest-a-While* to *Twenty Thousand Leagues under the Sea,* stood for the devouring wish to read being instantly granted. I knew this was bliss, I knew it at the time. Taste isn't nearly so important; it comes in its own time. I wanted to read *immediately.* The only fear was that of books coming to an end.

FROM *JUST GIRLS: HIDDEN LITERACIES AND LIFE IN JUNIOR HIGH*
MARGARET J. FINDERS

1   As school years draw to a close, students across the nation anticipate the biggest school-sanctioned literacy event of the year: the sale and distribution of the school yearbook. Like students elsewhere, Northern Hills Junior High students anxiously awaited its arrival.

2   Produced by 65 students working together with the help of two staff advisors, the yearbook, a 48-page soft-bound document, captured the year through photographs, student-produced artwork, and captions. Sports held a prominent place in the pages of the yearbook: photos of football, track, basketball, and wrestling events for the boys and

track, tennis, volleyball, and basketball for the girls filled the pages. The book also contained photos of Soda—a drug and alcohol awareness club—and drama club.

3 I believe that most teachers would agree with one of the yearbook's faculty advisors, the media specialist, who described the importance of the yearbook this way:

4 > If you can find your mug in here [yearbook], it gives you a tremendous sense of belonging. We tried to cover all the major events, and it's important to find yourself. We took a lot of pictures. If you and your mom can find yourself in here, then everything is just A-OK.

5 At Northern Hills Junior High, the yearbook had become a central part of the end-of-the-year curriculum. . . . For the most part, teachers described the yearbook as a celebration and well-earned reward for hard work. They allocated class time for signing and sharing yearbooks. Perceived as a way to control the behavior of the 531 seventh and eighth graders who in late May may not be eager to participate in discussions or complete end-of-semester projects, signing time was a tool for negotiating with students, often appearing as a bribe. Teachers told students: "If we get all our work done . . ." "If you are all good . . ." "If you cooperate, and we can hurry through this . . ." The following teacher comment received several nods and "me-toos" from staff in the teacher's lounge: "I give them the last five to ten minutes to write depending on how the class goes. It's a reward. It's a privilege. It's their reward for good behavior."

6 The yearbook played such a large role in the end-of-school activities because the teachers and administrators all believed, as the media specialist articulated, that it gave a tremendous sense of belonging. The discourse of adolescence that privileges peer-group allegiances constructed filters, it seems, that prevented school personnel from seeing the yearbook as exclusionary. Although the yearbook was viewed as a symbol of solidarity for all students, only a particular population of students was made to feel as if they belonged to this club. Other students remained outsiders.

7 Constant comments from Northern Hills staff that "Everybody gets one" and "Everyone loves them" reveal that Cleo and Dottie [social outsiders from poor families who did not buy yearbooks] and many others were invisible to school personnel. Current enrollment was 531; 425 books were ordered. Eight were sold to adults, 10 distributed as complimentary copies, 10 were mailed to students who no longer lived in the district, and 5 remained unsold. 397 copies were sold to students, which left 134 students without yearbooks. That figure represents 25% of the total student population. While students may not have purchased a yearbook for a variety of reasons, the socioeconomic status of families

may have been a critical issue. For whatever reason, when teachers rewarded students with "signing time," one out of four students was not able to participate.

8   Katie: Can I sign your yearbook?

9   Barb: No.

10   A quick glance at the yearbooks shows row after row of white faces ordered by alphabetical arrangement. The seeming homogeneity conceals diversity: invisible barriers such as attitudes, beliefs, economics, and experiences separate these young people into at least two camps. The girls created markers to maintain the borders between them. Allegiances became visible in both the act of writing and in the messages themselves. What is written and to whom is controlled by one's social status. Yearbooks circulated across social boundaries, yet those with the greatest social status stood in judgment of those less powerful. Students carefully monitored who could sign their yearbooks. To allow one of lesser status to mark one's book appeared to lower the status of the book owner. Students often asked for and were denied signing privileges. . . . Some students were in fact told "No," after asking, "Can I sign your yearbook?" In the same way, some students refused to sign yearbooks of those perceived to be outside the circle of significance. Who had the right to write was clearly an issue of entitlement. . . . If one was perceived as an outsider, then one was not entitled to write. Likewise, one might or might not be entitled to even view the message. Students guarded their written texts and controlled who had the right to see them.

11   Students with the greatest status were freed from judgment, and their written comments became models for others to copy. As I watched, one student carefully moved her finger across the page, working cautiously to transfer a phrase exactly from one yearbook to another. Because a particular phrase was perceived as carrying more currency in this arena, this teen appropriated the words of another student as her own in order for her voice to contain that power. Students shared texts and at times took another person's message for her own, copying the same phrase from one yearbook to the next to the next. In such borrowing of texts, one, in a sense, borrowed the social status of another. In taking another's message as her own, each girl had to be careful not to overstep her boundaries and write . . . what she was not entitled to write.

12   In the act of writing, students inadvertently may mark themselves as outsiders by writing a message judged inappropriate by others. If one was not savvy enough to create an appropriate text or powerful enough to forgo judgment, often, out of fear of marking oneself as an outsider, one just scribbled safe messages such as "Have a good summer" or "See ya next year."

13   Some students, in order to preserve their social position, asked a friend, "What should I write? What do you want me to say?" Students took this opportunity to exert their position of authority and made such playful comments as "Say I'm 'just too cool' " or "Say 'she's always got a taco' " (a current description for shorts or jeans that were considered too tight across the seat of the pants) or "Write, 'BFF ASS' " (a code for best friends forever and always stay sweet or sexy). Many comments were so highly coded that only those few insiders could translate them.

14   In order for students to demonstrate that they were with it, comments carrying the current pop jargon taken from movies, television, and local sources become etched into this school-sanctioned document, creating an unusual juxtaposition of sanctioned and out-of-bounds literacies. Dark, graffiti-like messages boldly cut across the white-bordered layout and quite literally "defaced" students and teachers alike. With big pink erasers, students rubbed out the faces of outsiders.

15   In all of this signing, the [social] queens [a group of the most popular girls] demonstrated a tremendous sense of play. Signing yearbooks had the feeling of recess, providing playtime away from the institutional demands of schooling, away from adult supervision. Similar to the playground, who could play was controlled by the peer dynamic. The yearbook was used to stake out territory and control social interactions.

16   Conceived as an opportunity for all to celebrate the completion of another successful academic year, the yearbook provided much more. For Tiffany and all the other social queens it reaffirmed their position in the school arena and in the larger community. They measured their status by the number and size of their pictures and by the number of requests to sign books: "Everybody wants me to sign their book." For Cleo and her friends, it also reaffirmed their position: "None of my friends are in there anyway."

17   The role of the yearbook in the institutional context remains central to the closing of the school year. The yearbook stands as an icon. Unknowingly, some are allowed to speak while others are silenced, some to write while others are written upon.

■ FOR CRITICAL INQUIRY

1. The literacy event Frederick Douglass recounts involved a "new and special revelation, explaining dark and mysterious things." What is the literacy event to which Douglass refers? What exactly is this revelation?

2. What insights does Eudora Welty gain from getting a library card and access to books? What roles do her mother and the librarian, Mrs. Calloway, play in this literacy event? Explain how each makes sense of Welty's encounter with

literacy and how their interactions shape the literacy event. What role, if any, does Welty's gender play?

3. Margaret J. Finders begins by describing the end-of-school ritual of the junior high yearbook from the perspective of teachers and staff. How do school personnel make sense of the yearbook? How do their views differ from those of students? How does Finders analyze and explain the interactions among students that take place around signing yearbooks?

WRITING ASSIGNMENT

Analyzing a Literacy Event

Now it's your turn to analyze a literacy event. Your task is to identify a particularly meaningful encounter with writing—whether those involved are in the role of a writer, a reader, or both. Then you need to explain how the people involved made sense of the event and the role that writing played in their interactions.

Directions

1. Select a particular encounter with writing in which you were directly involved or that you observed. Look for encounters with writing that reveal powerful feelings or strong responses on the part of the people involved. Look for misunderstandings, conflicts, resolutions, or alliances in which writing plays a key role. Look for instances of writing that had an effect on people's sense of themselves as individuals or as part of a group. If you have time, discuss with a partner three or four literacy events that you are considering for this assignment. See what seems most interesting to another person. Use this information to help you make a decision about the literacy event you want to analyze.

2. Analyze the literacy event. Here are some questions to take into account:

   ■ Describe what happened. What is the social context of the encounter with writing? Who was involved? What did they do?

   ■ What type of writing did the encounter center on? What were the specific features of the writing? What was its purpose?

   ■ How did the participants make sense of the literacy event? Did they share the same perspective or differ? How would you account for these differences or similarities?

   ■ What were the relationships among the participants? What role did writing play in their interactions? What were the results or consequences of these interactions?

3. Write an analysis of the literacy event. You will need to describe what happened and to explain how the participants made sense of the literacy event and how this particular encounter with writing shaped their interactions. ■

chapter 2

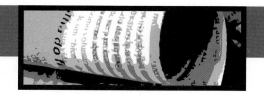

understanding the rhetorical situation
the choices writers make

A major theme of this book is that writing doesn't just happen. It occurs when people encounter a situation that calls on them to write, when they experience the sense that something is lacking, something needs to be paid attention to, something needs to be said. This can happen in a relatively simple and straightforward manner—when we realize, for example, that it's the right thing to send a note of condolence to the family when a friend or relative dies or a thank-you card for a birthday present. In these cases, the situation seems to dictate the appropriate response. If anything, the situation is so conventional that you can buy appropriate cards for the occasion.

In other situations, things are more complicated, and it's not as clear-cut how to respond. Let's say there is a proposal to cut financial aid at your college or university, and you want to do something about it. There is a sense of urgency—a realization that something needs to be done—but it doesn't automatically dictate what to write. You've got to make sense of the situation first, to develop an orientation toward it in order to clarify what you want to say and who you plan to address. There are multiple options about how you could locate yourself in the situation. You could appeal directly to college officials to cancel or reduce the cuts, write to the student newspaper protesting the cuts, or rally other students to join you in opposing the cuts. How you position yourself will determine what type of writing is appropriate for your purposes, and the possibilities range from a formal letter of appeal that seeks to persuade college decision makers to flyers, petitions, and posters that publicize the issues in a student campaign to roll back the cuts.

The purpose of this chapter is to investigate what leads people to recognize the desire to write—to have their say, to influence the course of events, to exchange ideas and feelings with others. This is where the motivation to write takes place, what we will call the rhetorical situation.

This chapter is an introduction to analyzing rhetorical situations to understand the choices writers make when they respond to the call to write. In the first section, we define the rhetorical situation. Next, we present a case study that asks you to analyze a rhetorical situation and present reading strategies useful in your analysis. Finally, in a writing assignment at the end of the chapter, we ask you to use these strategies to look closely at a commentary in a newsmagazine and to analyze its rhetorical situation.

THE RHETORICAL SITUATION

Rhetorical situations begin with a felt sense of need or urgency, an exigence that motivates people to write. In this chapter, we examine how three factors work together to constitute rhetorical situations that produce writing.

- **Writer's orientation**. As you can see in the example of the financial aid cuts, complex social situations don't generate appropriate responses automatically. The writer has to locate himself or herself in the situation by making sense of what is urgent or pressing and what needs to be done in order to identify the call to write and how to respond to it. Writers have choices about how they wish to position themselves in relation to the situation and the people involved. They have to figure out how to represent what's at stake for them and others and to construct a sense of themselves and a tone of voice that fits their orientation toward the situation.

- **Audience**. Audience depends on how writers position themselves and how they clarify their own motivation in writing. The audience consists of the intended readers, who may be more or less diverse in their interests and attitudes according to the circumstances. At times writers may be addressing what seem to be multiple audiences. In the case of the financial aid cuts, for example, a letter to the student newspaper would likely have a diverse readership, of students, certainly, but also faculty, administrators, and staff. The financial aid cuts example also reveals another sense of the term *audience* that may factor in the rhetorical situation—namely, that there are times when writers not only address an existing audience, such as the college officials responsible for the aid cuts, but also may, through the act of writing, try to organize and bring into being an audience that is only in the process of formation, as in the case of students joining together in a campaign against the cuts.

- **Genre**. Genres are the different types of writing people draw on to respond to the call to write. The financial aid cuts help us see how genres are not simply the written form that carries the writer's message but offer distinct strategies that shape and respond to the rhetorical situation. Consider the difference, for example, between writing a polite and well reasoned letter of appeal to campus officials and writing slogans on posters (which can also be well reasoned but in a different way) to use in demonstration in front of the president's office. Genres, from this perspective, are social and rhetorical actions that embody writers' purposes and motivations, shaping and responding to situations that call on them to write. An understanding of how various genres of writing work and when they are appropriate is part of a writing repertoire that enables writers to have choices and respond flexibly. (Part Two in *The Call to Write* presents a range of genres of writing.)

The point here is that the three factors—writer's orientation, audience, and genre—are really a way of naming the choices writers make based on their knowledge of the strategies of writing available to them to define and deal with the rhetorical situation. These choices can be analyzed separately, but they mutually influence each other to constitute the rhetorical situation as the grounds for producing writing.

ACORN KATRINA SURVIVORS ASSOCIATION

In the aftermath of Hurricane Katrina in 2005, the ACORN (Association of Community Organizations for Reform Now) branch in New Orleans helped set up the ACORN Katrina Survivors Association (AKSA) to deal with the devastation of the storm and the struggle of local residents to rebuild and return home. This two-page flyer presents the AKSA platform, written in 2005, a few months after the storm.

Hurricane Katrina unquestionably produced a sense of urgency on the part of New Orleans residents, but as a complex situation it didn't dictate a single response. Rather, the rhetorical situation that emerged from the storm led to a variety of responses from individuals, government agencies, and community groups. Consider how AKSA defines and responds to the rhetorical situation in the wake of Katrina. Take into account here the three factors—writer's orientation (or, in this case, AKSA's orientation), audience, and genre. How do these factors combine to produce this document?

ACORN
Katrina Survivors Association

The **ACORN Katrina Survivors Association** is the first nationwide organization of displaced New Orleans residents and other Katrina survivors. The Survivors Association unites members of our displaced communities in order to demand more effective relief efforts and a voice for survivors in the rebuilding process.

The ACORN Katrina Survivors Association uses public pressure, direct action, and dialogue with elected officials and public policy experts to win respect and a voice for survivors, the resources needed for families to survive, and a rebuilding plan that builds stronger communities for all.

The Platform of the ACORN Katrina Survivors Association

Right of return – The people of New Orleans will not be kept out by deliberate attempts to change the make-up of the city, or by neglect, which gives the richer and more powerful first access to choices and resources.

The means to take care of ourselves and our families – Survivors need help with housing, healthcare, income from unemployment, and assistance for those who've helped us.

Rebuilding the right way – Reconstruction should include affordable housing, living wage jobs, and good schools for our children.

Recovering together – The Hurricane should not be used as an excuse to cut health care and food assistance programs that help families across the country.

Accountability and honesty – An independent investigation is necessary so we can understand what went wrong and how to protect ourselves in the future.

ACORN Organizing and Direct Action

The Survivors Association will continue and expand the organizing that local ACORN chapters have accomplished since Katrina first hit, which has already resulted in some notable actions and victories.

- On October 7th, the Houston ACORN Katrina Survivors Association confronted Houston FEMA Director about a lack of response to the needs of the survivors. After negotiations, ACORN members won a shuttle bus to their service center, translated materials, and extended benefits to Rita survivors.

Courtesy of ACORN Survivors Association

Courtesy of ACORN Survivors Association

SAVE OUR NEIGHBORHOOD
No Bulldozing!
Contact ACORN
1-800-239-7379

Courtesy of ACORN Survivors Association

o Louisiana ACORN members staged a caravan into the Lower 9th Ward on October 15th to claim their right to return and to placard hundreds of homes with signs stating "No Bulldozing!"

o A thousand people gathered on the steps of the Louisiana State Capitol for the October 28th Rally to Rebuild Louisiana, to demand job priority, training, and good wages for Louisiana's displaced working families.

ACORN Community Forum on Rebuilding New Orleans

o The Survivors Association sponsored the ACORN Community Forum on Rebuilding New Orleans, which convened in Baton Rouge, Louisiana on November 7th and 8th.

o The conference brought together low-income and minority residents of New Orleans and top urban planning, architecture, and development professionals from around the country.

o Forum participants took a bus tour of affected areas and held discussions on how to rebuild New Orleans to speak to the needs of all New Orleans' residents.

o More than 130 participants at the forum site were joined online by participants from all over the globe, who took part via webcast.

Katrina Survivors Continue to Fight to Return Home

o On November 22nd, 100 ACORN members marched to the Houston FEMA office to deliver a letter demanding that FEMA rescind its recently announced decision to stop paying bills for roughly 150,000 hurricane victims still in motel rooms come December 1st.

o Later that same afternoon, FEMA rescinded the unpopular policy and said that it would extend its hotel-housing program by a month in 10 states.

o Advancement Project obtained a favorable settlement on November 22nd in a lawsuit filed on behalf of ACORN and other groups in response to evictions that had been proceeding without notice to the tenants.

o The agreement requires FEMA to turn over to the courts in Orleans and Jefferson parishes the addresses of tenants facing evictions, and requires that hearings be scheduled no sooner than 45 days after notice is mailed to the evacuees.

The ACORN Katrina Survivors Association members are continuing the fight for the practical resources families need to return home: access to trailers on or near their property; water and electricity back all over New Orleans; federal dollars dedicated to rebuilding individual homes; assistance in Texas to find safe, quality rental housing; and assistance with furniture and transportation.

Courtesy of ACORN Survivors Association

CASE STUDY: THE SOMALI PIRATES

U.S. Navy photo by Mass communication Specialist 2nd Class Jason R. Zalasky/Released

As a case study for analyzing the rhetorical situation, we will use two commentaries on the Somali pirates. Fred C. Iklé's "Kill the Pirates" appeared in the *Washington Post* on April 13, 2009, while Johann Hari's "You Are Being Lied to About Pirates" appeared in the *Independent,* a British newspaper, on January 5, 2009. These commentaries offer typical examples of the kind of reading on complex and contested issues that you'll be asked to do in college courses. The aim of this section is to help you develop reading strategies to come to terms with the commentaries and to analyze how the two writers defined and responded to the rhetorical situation. But first a little background on the Somali pirates.

By early 2009, the Somali pirates had become a hot news item in the American and international press for hijacking ships in the Gulf of Aden and holding them for ransom. The pirates' activity was a growing source of concern to governments and the multinational corporations who depend on the twenty thousand or more cargo ships that pass each year through the Gulf of Aden on their way to the Suez Canal. In 2008, the pirates attacked 111 ships and successfully hijacked 42 of them. The number of attacks increased dramatically in early 2009. Then, in April 2009 the pirates captured an American ship, the *Maersk Alabama,* and held its captain, Richard Phillips, for ransom, leading to a dramatic confrontation between the United States and the pirates holding Phillips in a lifeboat. Phillips was rescued by Navy SEALS, who killed three of the pirates. This map gives a picture of where the Somali pirates' activity was taking place in 2009 and the location of the *Maersk Alabama* when it was hijacked.

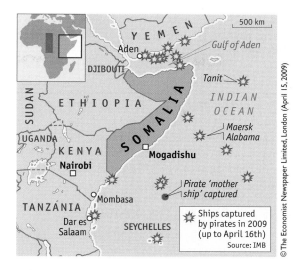

© The Economist Newspaper Limited, London (April 15, 2009)

Even before the hijacking of the *Maersk Alabama,* the Somali pirates had prompted a good deal of news reporting, news analysis, commentary, and other types of writing, including a Wikipedia entry and a Friends of the Somali Pirates group on Facebook. The meaning of the Somali pirates was a contested one, with some commentators viewing them as dangerous criminals, while others represented the pirates in more complicated terms by putting them into the context of recent Somali history, where the breakdown of the Somali state and the toxic dumping and overfishing by international fleets have

Courtesy Steve Schirra

weighed heavily on coastal communities. The two readings that follow were part of the writing that responded to the notoriety of the Somali pirates from very different perspectives.

STRATEGIES FOR READING

To analyze how the two commentators, Fred C. Iklé and Johann Hari, defined a rhetorical situation to write about the Somali pirates, we'll first present a number of reading strategies that will help you come to terms with each commentary.

FIRST QUESTIONS TO ASK OF THE READINGS

Background information about the context of issues, the writer, and the publication where the writer's work appeared is useful in understanding how the writer identifies the call to write.

Context of Issues

What do you know about the particular topic the writer is treating? If your knowledge is limited, where can you get reliable background information? What have people been saying about the topic? What do they think the main issues are? What seems to be at stake in these discussions? Do people seem divided over these issues? If so, what positions have they taken?

The Writer

What do you know about the writer? What authority and credibility can you attribute to the writer? Is there reason to believe that the writer will provide informed accounts and responsible arguments, whether you agree with them or not? What political, cultural, social, or other commitments is the writer known for? How are these commitments likely to influence the writer's argument? How do these commitments relate to your own views? How is this relationship likely to influence your evaluation of the writer's argument?

Publication

What do you know about the publication? Who is the publisher? Is it a commercial publication? Does it have an institutional affiliation—to a college or university, an academic field of study, a professional organization, a church? Does it espouse an identifiable political, social, cultural, economic, or religious ideology? If the publication is a periodical, what other writers—and types of writing and topics—appear in the issue? Who would be likely to read the publication? If the site of publication is the Web, consider whether the site is .edu (educational), .org (nonprofit), .gov (government), or .com (commercial). What is the purpose of the Web site? When was it last updated? Does it have links to other Web sites?

Use these questions to develop background information on the Somali pirates, the two writers—Fred C. Iklé and Johann Hari—and the two publications—the *Washington Post* and the *Independent* (UK). You should be able to get this information through a Google search.

DOING A CLOSE READING

You have probably used some or all of the following strategies while reading textbooks and other course material. It's useful nonetheless to review them—to consider what each strategy enables you to do and to refine your overall approach to reading texts like Iklé's commentary.

Underlining

Underlining the writer's key points helps you identify main ideas, keep track of important information, and return to marked phrases to reconstruct the writing's meaning quickly. Underlining should be done selectively, to enable you to recall quickly where the writer presents important information, claims, evidence, interpretations, and conclusions.

Annotation

Annotations are comments that readers write in the margins of a text. Annotation can help you read actively and create a record of your experience as you come to grips with a text's meaning. There are no rules about annotation, but here are some suggestions: Write brief notes on major points. Agree or disagree with what the writer is saying. Refer to what the writer is doing at a particular point (for example, making a claim, giving an example, presenting statistical evidence, or refuting an opposing view). Raise questions or voice confusion about something you need to clarify. Draw connections to other things you have read or know about.

SAMPLE UNDERLINING AND ANNOTATION

KILL THE PIRATES

FRED C. IKLÉ

Links pirates to terrorists

Is there any evidence that terrorists have forced pirates?

With the rescue of American Richard Phillips from the hands of pirates yesterday, there was a blip of good news from the Indian Ocean, but it remains a scandal that Somali pirates continue to routinely defeat the world's naval powers. And worse than this ongoing demonstration of cowardice is the financing of terrorists that results from the huge ransom payments these pirates are allowed to collect.

It is naive to assume that the millions paid annually in ransom to pirates merely enables them to purchase villas and fancy automobiles. Somalia is a country without government, where anarchy is being exploited by terrorist organizations. Although the threat that pirates pose to commercial ships is increasingly known, little is being done to combat it. And we must consider the bigger picture: Terrorists are far more brutal than pirates and can easily force pirates—petty thieves in comparison—to share their ransom money.

Check background info on Somalia

We already know that Somalia is an ideal fortress and headquarters for global terrorist activity. The United States has learned the painful lesson that Somalia is not an easy place for our military to establish law and order; two of our interventions there became embarrassing defeats—in 1993 and more recently in support of Ethiopian forces.

Uses rhetorical questions. the language seems overheded

So why do we keep rewarding Somali pirates? How is this march of folly possible?

Start by blaming the timorous lawyers who advise the governments attempting to cope with the pirates such as those who had been engaged in a standoff with U.S. hostage negotiators in recent days. These lawyers misinterpret the Law of the Sea Treaty and the Geneva Conventions and fail to apply the powerful international laws that exist against piracy. The right of self-defense—a principle of international law—justifies killing pirates as they try to board a ship.

States his main point

Disputes ship owners' reasons for not arming crews

Nonetheless, entire crews are unarmed on the ships that sail through the Red Sea and the Gulf of Aden. Shipowners pretend that they cannot trust their crews with weapons, but the facts don't add up. For one thing, in the United States most adults except felons are allowed to have guns, and the laws of many other nations also permit such ownership. Even if owners don't want everyone aboard their ships to be carrying weapons, don't they trust the senior members of their crews? Why couldn't they at least arm the captain and place two experienced and reliable police officers on board?

When these pitifully unarmed crews watch pirates climb aboard their vessels, they can do little to fight back. And while the United States and many other naval powers keep warships in the Red Sea, the Gulf of Aden and the Indian Ocean—deployments that cost millions of dollars—these ships cannot keep pirates from boarding commercial ships that have unarmed crews.

Lists other measures that should be taken

The international right of self-defense would also justify an inspection and quarantine regime off the coast of Somalia to seize and destroy all vessels that are found to be engaged in piracy. These inspections could reduce the likelihood that any government will find itself engaged in a hostage situation such as the one that played out in recent days. Furthermore, the U.N. Security Council should prohibit all ransom payments. If the crew of an attacked ship were held hostage, the Security Council could authorize a military blockade of Somalia until the hostages were released.

Takes a hard-line position— accuses anyone differing of being a coward

Cowardice will not defeat terrorism, nor will it stop the Somali pirates. If anything, continuing to meet the pirates' demands only acts as an incentive for more piracy.

Summary

A summary condenses clearly and accurately what you have read. Like underlining, a good summary identifies the main idea and important supporting material. But it also calls on you to explain the connections between points. To write an effective summary, follow these steps:

1. Review your underlinings and annotations. Start your summary with a statement in your own words that identifies the writer's purpose and expresses the main point. If the writer didn't explicitly state his or her main point, write the main point as you see it. (The main point is often tied to the writer's purpose, so thinking about purpose might help in stating the main point.)

2. Consult your underlinings and annotations to identify the most important supporting details. Rewrite these details in your own words, combining ideas when you can.

3. Check your summary to see if it holds together as a coherent piece of writing and is not simply a series of unconnected statements. Add transitions where needed to make connections between parts of the summary.

Sample summary of "Kill the Pirates"

In "Kill the Pirates," Fred C. Iklé responds to the Somali pirates' success in hijacking ships in the Indian Ocean by suggesting that ransom money is going to finance terrorists in Somalia. He proposes that much more needs to be done to stop the pirates, including arming the crews of the ships that pass through the Gulf of Aden and recognizing that the right of self-defense justifies the crews killing pirates. Iklé also argues that any ships involved in piracy should be seized and destroyed and that the UN should ban ransom payments as a matter of policy and instead apply a military blockade to Somalia to free hostages. Iklé closes by saying that bargaining with the pirates only encourages further hijackings.

Describing the Writer's Strategy

The summary gives an account of what the writer is saying. Describing the writer's strategy asks you to identify what the writer is doing, to explain how paragraphs or groups of paragraphs function in a piece of writing. Focusing on what the writer is doing—for example, defining a problem, providing background information, proposing a solution, explaining causes or consequences, giving reasons, offering examples—is a way to analyze how a piece of writing is constructed and how the parts are connected to form a whole.

To describe a writer's strategy:

1. Write a statement that describes the writer's overall purpose.
2. Explain what the writer is doing in each paragraph. If a sequence of paragraphs forms one unit in the writing, explain what that group of paragraphs is doing. (It is particularly helpful to divide longer pieces of writing into sections by grouping sequences of paragraphs together.) Label the writer's strategy in each paragraph or section to explain how it functions in the writing as a whole. Try to do this, as much as possible, by using terms that express strategies and functions instead of referring to the content of the writing.

Sample Description of a Writer's Strategy

Overall purpose: To propose a change in policy toward Somali pirates.

¶1–2: Establishes the existence of one problem.

Argues that failure to deal with the problem has produced a bigger problem.

¶3: Provides brief background information on the situation.

¶4: Poses rhetorical questions that ask why the problem is allowed to persist.

¶5: Gives one explanation for the problem and proposes a change in policy.

¶6–8: Provides support for change in policy by (a) refuting reasons for not adopting policy, (b) showing weakness in current policy and, (c) explaining further implications of changing policy.

¶9: Closes by explaining negative consequences of continuing current policy.

WRITING STRATEGIES

What a Writer Does

- ❏ Narrates, tells a story, relates an anecdote or incident
- ❏ Describes things, people, places, processes
- ❏ Illustrates by using examples, details, data
- ❏ Defines key terms, problems, issues, trends
- ❏ Compares and/or contrasts things, ideas, persons, places, processes
- ❏ Classifies things, ideas, people, places, processes into categories

- ❏ Explains causes and effects
- ❏ Gives reasons
- ❏ Offers evidence (statistics, established facts, expert testimony)
- ❏ Cites other writers
- ❏ Makes concessions
- ❏ Refutes opposing views

EXERCISE

DOING A CLOSE READING OF JOHANN HARI'S "YOU ARE BEING LIED TO ABOUT PIRATES"

Now it's your turn to use the reading strategies we've just reviewed. Underline and annotate Hari's commentary. Then write a summary and a description of the writer's strategy.

YOU ARE BEING LIED TO ABOUT PIRATES

JOHANN HARI

Who imagined that in 2009, the world's governments would be declaring a new War on Pirates? As you read this, the British Royal Navy—backed by the ships of more than two dozen nations, from the US to China—is sailing into Somalian waters to take on men we still picture as parrot-on-the-shoulder pantomime villains. They will soon be fighting Somalian ships and even chasing the pirates onto land, into one of the most broken countries on earth. But behind the arrr-me-hearties oddness of this tale, there is an untold scandal. The people our governments are labelling as "one of the great menaces of our times" have an extraordinary story to tell—and some justice on their side.

Pirates have never been quite who we think they are. In the "golden age of piracy"—from 1650 to 1730—the idea of the pirate as the senseless, savage Bluebeard that lingers today was created by the British government in a great propaganda heave. Many ordinary people believed it was false: pirates were often saved from the gallows by supportive crowds. Why? What did they see that we can't? In his book *Villains Of All Nations*, the historian Marcus Rediker pores through the evidence.

If you became a merchant or navy sailor then—plucked from the docks of London's East End, young and hungry—you ended up in a floating wooden Hell. You worked all hours on a cramped, half-starved ship, and if you slacked off, the all-powerful captain would whip you with the Cat O' Nine Tails. If you slacked often, you could be thrown overboard. And at the end of months or years of this, you were often cheated of your wages.

Pirates were the first people to rebel against this world. They mutinied—and created a different way of working on the seas. Once they had a ship, the pirates elected their captains, and made all their decisions collectively, without torture. They shared their bounty out in what Rediker calls "one of the most egalitarian plans for the disposition of resources to be found anywhere in the eighteenth century."

They even took in escaped African slaves and lived with them as equals.

The pirates showed "quite clearly—and subversively—that ships did not have to be run in the brutal and oppressive ways of the merchant service and the Royal Navy." This is why they were romantic heroes, despite being unproductive thieves.

The words of one pirate from that lost age, a young British man called William Scott, should echo into this new age of piracy. Just before he was hanged in Charleston, South Carolina, he said: "What I did was to keep me from perishing. I was forced to go a-pirateing to live." In 1991, the government of Somalia collapsed. Its nine million people have been teetering on starvation ever since—and the ugliest forces in the Western world have seen this as a great opportunity to steal the country's food supply and dump our nuclear waste in their seas.

Yes: nuclear waste. As soon as the government was gone, mysterious European ships started appearing off the coast of Somalia, dumping vast barrels into the ocean. The coastal population began to sicken. At first they suffered strange rashes, nausea and malformed babies. Then, after the 2005 tsunami, hundreds of the dumped and leaking barrels washed up on shore. People began to suffer from radiation sickness, and more than 300 died.

Ahmedou Ould-Abdallah, the UN envoy to Somalia, tells me: "Somebody is dumping nuclear material here. There is also lead, and heavy metals such as cadmium and mercury—you name it." Much of it can be traced back to European hospitals and factories, who seem to be passing it on to the Italian mafia to "dispose" of cheaply. When I asked Mr Ould-Abdallah what European governments were doing about it, he said with a sigh: "Nothing. There has been no clean-up, no compensation, and no prevention."

At the same time, other European ships have been looting Somalia's seas of their greatest resource: seafood. We have destroyed our own fish stocks by overexploitation—and now we have moved on to theirs. More than $300m-worth of tuna, shrimp, and lobster are being stolen every year by illegal trawlers. The local fishermen are now starving. Mohammed Hussein, a fisherman in the town of Marka 100km south of Mogadishu, told Reuters: "If nothing is done, there soon won't be much fish left in our coastal waters."

This is the context in which the "pirates" have emerged. Somalian fishermen took speedboats to try to dissuade the dumpers and trawlers, or at least levy a "tax" on them. They call themselves the Volunteer Coastguard of Somalia—and ordinary Somalis agree. The independent Somalian news site WardheerNews found 70 per cent "strongly supported the piracy as a form of national defence."

No, this doesn't make hostage-taking justifiable, and yes, some are clearly just gangsters—especially those who have held up World Food Programme supplies. But in a telephone interview, one of the pirate leaders, Sugule Ali: "We don't consider ourselves sea bandits. We consider sea bandits [to be] those who illegally fish and dump in our seas." William Scott would understand.

Did we expect starving Somalians to stand passively on their beaches, paddling in our toxic waste, and watch us snatch their fish to eat in restaurants in London and Paris and Rome? We won't act on those crimes—the only sane solution to this problem—but when some of the fishermen responded by disrupting the transit-corridor for 20 per cent of the world's oil supply, we swiftly send in the gunboats.

The story of the 2009 war on piracy was best summarised by another pirate, who lived and died in the fourth century BC. He was captured and brought to Alexander the Great, who demanded to know "what he meant by keeping possession of the sea." The pirate smiled, and responded: "What you mean by seizing the whole earth; but because I do it with a petty ship, I am called a robber, while you, who do it with a great fleet, are called emperor." Once again, our great imperial fleets sail—but who is the robber?

ETHICS OF READING

BOREDOM AND PERSISTENCE

Going to college means that you will encounter a wide range of academic and professional writing, some of which may be specialized and technical. You may find at times that the reading you're assigned is intimidating and hard to follow. You may wonder what the writer is trying to prove, or you may think the writer is splitting hairs. The writing may seem abstract, detached from the real world.

These are all symptoms of boredom, and the danger is that you will give up at this point and say you weren't really interested in the first place. What is often the case, though, is not that you aren't interested but rather that you are unfamiliar with the particular type of writing, its forms, specialized vocabularies, and ways of reasoning.

To act responsibly in college, the workplace, and the public domain, you need to read writing that is pertinent and carries weight. An ethics of reading holds that readers need to give difficult material a chance. It's not simply a matter of being fair to the writer. By working on new and difficult material, you also, in effect, refuse to be alienated from it. In this regard, you avoid the threat of boredom leading to the premature closure of communication. ■

ANALYZING THE RHETORICAL SITUATION: THE SOMALI PIRATES

Analyzing the rhetorical situation builds on the reading strategies just presented, as steps that have already begun to suggest how we might understand the choices these two writers have made to define and respond to the call to write. In this section, we examine how Fred C. Iklé and Johann Hari make sense of the Somali pirates by identifying their orientation as writers, their audience, and their genre of writing.

WRITER'S ORIENTATION

The way in which the two writers establish the sense of urgency calling on them to write differs dramatically. Interestingly, both of them, in their opening paragraphs, identify a "scandal" that motivates them to write.

For Iklé, the scandal is the "cowardice" of the "world's naval powers" and how their failure to stop the pirates is enabling ransom money to finance terrorist activities. Iklé's orientation is changing what he sees as a failed policy that has had dangerous consequence. So, he calls for sterner measures and argues that self-defense, including shooting to kill the pirates, is justifiable and legal. Basically he's proposing a solution to a problem, which he defines in terms of national security. He's positioning himself as someone called to write by the dangers of Somalia as a "headquarters for global terrorist activity."

For Hari, on other hand, the scandal is the pirates' "untold" story that has not gotten out to the public. This lack is what Hari experiences as calling on him to write. Notice that Hari is proposing a change in understanding more than a change in policy, as Iklé does. Accordingly, he looks at the history of pirates, who "have never been quite who we think they are." He's positioning himself as a revisionist, to change our view of what piracy has meant historically and to rethink who the Somali pirates are by examining the context of nuclear dumping and overfishing in which they emerged.

AUDIENCE

The differences in how the two writers identify the call to write lead to differences in the way they approach their audiences.

Iklé's stance is hard-line, and his language is at times heated, when, for example, he implies that opponents are "cowards" on a "march of folly." In this sense, Iklé is consolidating an audience of readers who share his desire for a strong military response. Other readers may feel bullied by his approach but at the same time worry about the dangers he says the Somali pirates represent. The fact that he doesn't really provide any evidence for the link between pirates and terrorists suggests that Iklé assumes his readers, or at least those he feels he has the best chance of reaching, will accept the connection.

Hari approaches his readers as people who are interested in getting the story behind the news and government's representations of the Somali pirates as a "great menace." There is a good deal of research in Hari's commentary, but he doesn't come off as pedantic. His tone is rather breezy and informal, and he seems to invite readers to join him in examining piracy, past and present. Like Iklé, Hari faces a diverse readership and seems to be looking for an audience among his readers who are interested in rethinking things. He is more personal in his approach, addressing readers as "you" and treating them as people who can think for themselves, whereas Iklé uses "we" to posit an imagined group of people (who know Somalia is a terrorist fortress yet who keep rewarding the pirates) that is meant to include the reader and on whose behalf Iklé is speaking.

GENRE

It shouldn't be surprising, given the situation, that the two writers have turned to the genre of commentary as it appears on op-ed pages in major newspapers like the *Washington Post* and the *Independent* (UK). The genre and the places of publication are particularly well suited to the writers' goals of influencing public opinion concerning the Somali pirates. (See Chapter 9 "Commentary" for more on the genre.) Some of the strategies both writers employ, such as rhetorical questions ("So why do we keep rewarding Somali pirates?" "Did we expect starving Somalians to stand passively on their beaches?"), are characteristic of genre. But more important is that the genre of commentary has long been part of the public forum, where writers offer opinion and analysis, to shape public understanding of the events and issues they feel compelled to write about.

A CHECKLIST: ANALYZING THE WRITER'S LANGUAGE

Words and phrases carry powerful associations that can sway readers to share or reject what a writer is saying. It is one thing to refer to business executives as "corporate leaders" or "entrepreneurial visionaries" and quite another to call them "fat cats" or "robber barons." The choice of terms reveals the writer's orientation and the perspective readers are invited to share. Paying attention to the writer's language, as the two commentaries reveal, is a useful reading strategy in analyzing the rhetorical situation.

Tone

We've already noted the hard-line, sometimes bullying tone in Iklé's commentary ("It is naive to assume," "Cowardice will not defeat terrorism") and the breezier tone of Hari's ("Who imagined that in 2009, the world's governments would be declaring a new War on Pirates?"). Tone projects attitude and helps define the writer's orientation.

Denotation/Connotation

Words have *denotative* meanings that you can find in the dictionary. For example, the denotative meaning of *terrorism* is "violence or the threat of violence, especially bombing, kidnapping, and assasination, carried out for political purposes." Denotation is meant to be the specific, precise, literal meaning of a word, but, in practice, as writers use words they inevitably release *connotative* meanings as well that contain additional senses, associations, and emotional charge—evoking in the case of the word *terrorism* images of Al Qaeda, 9/11, and threats to the homeland.

One of Iklé's key rhetorical moves is to associate "terrorism" with the Somali pirates, while Hari, on the other hand, seeks to redefine the term *pirate* altogether by associating it with sailors rebelling against injustice.

Figures of Speech

Figures of speech include simile, metaphor, analogy, overstatement, and personification, among others. Hari uses a figure of speech when he says that we still think of pirates "as parrot-on-the-shoulder pantomime villains." The most commonly used are simile and metaphor—figures of speech that compare one thing to another. Similes use the words *like* and *as* to make a comparison. ("My love is like a red, red rose." "He is as happy as a clam.") Metaphors make an implicit comparison, as though one thing is actually another. ("She was a thin reed of a girl." "The long arm of the law grabbed him and brought him to trial.")

Stereotypes

Stereotypes are oversimplified representations that fit people into unvarying categories. These broad generalizations break down under careful scrutiny but carry powerful (and often self-serving) explanations. "Women are more emotional than men" is a classic stereotypical statement that a writer might use to argue that women won't do well under the stress of positions of authority (and therefore shouldn't be promoted over men). Along the same line, stereotypes of poor and working-class people and racial and ethnic minorities have created popular images (of "white trash," "drunken Indians," "welfare queens") that make subordination of one group to another seem necessary and inevitable.

SAMPLE ANALYSIS OF A RHETORICAL SITUATION

The following analysis draws on a number of reading strategies presented in this chapter to examine how the writer Kevin Powell identifies and responds to the call to write in his commentary "My Culture at the Crossroads."

"My Culture at the Crossroads" appeared in the October 9, 2000, issue of *Newsweek,* as part of its special feature cover story "The Rap on Rap."

Following Powell's commentary is a sample rhetorical analysis with annotations.

Newsweek

My Culture at the Crossroads

A rap devotee watches corporate control and apolitical times encroach
on the music he has loved all his life. BY KEVIN POWELL

I am a hip-hop head for life. I have tagged my moniker—
"kepo1"—on walls; break-danced on cardboard; bumped
elbows with fellow hip-hoppers at legendary clubs like The
Rooftop, Union Square and Latin Quarter in New York
City, and done everything from organizing rap shows to
working as a hip-hop journalist and managing music
producers. This culture has not only rescued the lives of
countless masses who look like me, but it has empowered
more young, working-class black and Latino cats than the
civil-rights movement.

Yet something peculiar erupts when you've been around
hip-hop for a while. Although you still love it, you look at its
culture from a more critical perspective, particularly if you
have studied other music genres, traveled widely and
reflected intensely. You realize that what began as party
music has come to be the soundtrack for post-civil-rights
America. You realize that hip-hop is urban folk art, and as
much an indication of the conditions in impoverished areas
as bluesman Robert Johnson's laments in the 1930s.
Naturally, you see a connection between the lives of
Johnson and Tupac Shakur, not to mention a not-so-funny
link between the mainstream hyping of Elvis and Eminem as
innovators of black music forms. And, for sure, you wonder,
loudly, if what happened to rock and roll will happen to
hip-hop, if it hasn't already.

That is the external battle for hip-
hop today: corporate control and
cooptation. But there is also a civil
war going on within the hip-hop
nation. Part of it, unquestionably,
has to do with this corporate stran-
glehold. Part of it has to do with the
incredibly apolitical times in which
we live: for some white Americans
the current economic boom has
created the myth that things are
swell for all Americans. Not the
case; 20 years after the Reagan
backlash on civil rights, the influx of
crack and guns and the acceleration
of a disturbing class divide in black
America, hip-hop has come to
symbolize a generation fragmented
by integration, migration,
abandonment, alienation and, yes,

self-hatred. Thus, hip-hop, once vibrant, edgy, fresh and
def, is now as materialistic, hedonistic, misogynistic,
shallow and violent as some of the films and TV shows
launched from Hollywood.

It wasn't always that way. But, unfortunately, the golden
era of hip-hop—that period in the late '80s and early '90s
when such diverse artists as Public Enemy, N.W.A, Queen
Latifah, MC Hammer, LL Cool J and De La Soul coexisted
and there was no such thing as "positive" or "negative"
rap—has long been dead. Gone as well is an embrace of
hip-hop's four elements: graffiti writing, the dance element
(or what some call break-dancing), DJing and MCing. The
MC or "rapper" has been singled out to be his own man
in this very male-centered arena, and the formula for a hit
record is simple: fancy yourself a thug, pimp or gangster;
rhyme about jewelry, clothing and alcohol; denigrate
women in every conceivable way, and party and b.s.
ad nauseam.

None of this would matter much to me if videos didn't
pump visual crack into the minds of young people across
the planet. Of if "urban radio" actually played something
other than the same 10–12 songs every day. Or if some
of our fabulous hip-hop magazines didn't make constant
references to marijuana, liquor and "niggas" under the
guise of keeping things real. The above notwithstanding,
I am not a hater, or someone who disses
for the sake of dissing. Nor do I feel
hip-hop has created urban misery,
racism, sexism, homophobia or
classism. That said, what I do believe
is that hip-hop is at a crossroads,
struggling for control over its creativity,
while truly creative artists like Mos Def,
Bahamadia and Common wonder
when they will get the attention they
deserve. In other words, Jay Z's "Big
Pimpin" would not bother me so much
if Dead Prez's "Mind Sex" received as
much notice. Perhaps Chuck D is
correct in stating that the Internet is the
great equalizer for would-be artists. But
what does it matter if homeboys are still
screaming "nigga" or "bitch" for global
consumption, with no regard for who is
inhaling those sentiments?

© Erica Berger/Corbis

Powell is the editor of "Step Into a
World: A Global Anthology of the New
Black Literature," to be published in
November (Wiley), and is guest curator
of the Brooklyn Museum of Art's "Hip-
Hop Nation: Roots, Rhymes & Rage."

ALLISON NADEAU, SAMPLE ANALYSIS

Nadeau 1

Allison Nadeau
English 101
Prof. Malek
15 October 2006

Rhetorical Analysis of "My Culture at the Crossroads"

Identifies publication

"My Culture at the Crossroads" by Kevin Powell appeared in the *Newsweek* issue of October 9, 2000, as part of a special feature in the Arts and Entertainment section on the current crisis in rap music and hip-hop culture. In

Summarizes the commentary

Powell's view, there is a "civil war going on within the hip-hop nation," caused in part by corporate control of the music and in part by an apolitical climate in post-civil rights America. The result, as Powell sees it, is that hip-hop is now as "materialistic, hedonistic, misogynistic, shallow, and violent" as Hollywood movies and TV shows. Powell points out that hip-hop was not always this way. In the "golden age" of the late 1980s and early 1990s, hip-hop was a vital "urban folk art" that included graffiti writing, breakdancing, DJing, and MCing. Since that time, however, the single focus on the MC or rapper as a thug, pimp, or gangster has brought hip-hop culture to a crossroads. The issue for Powell is whether the most creative artists can gain control of the music and take it in a positive direction.

Explains the context of issues

Powell's commentary is part of a larger debate about the current status of rap. Hip-hop culture has always been controversial, but for many people, black and white, inside and outside the hip-hop nation, rap music now seems to focus exclusively on money, sex, and violence. The murders of Tupac Shakur and Biggie Smalls have heightened concerns about rap's "gangsta" image, and the constant preoccupation with guns, expensive jewelry, fancy cars, drugs, and partying worry many that rap is feeding racist stereotypes and has turned the music away from its original promise to tell the truth about black America. As Michael Eric Dyson is quoted in another article in *Newsweek's* coverage of rap. "There's a war going on for the soul of hip-hop."

Identifies the call to write

Describes writer's credentials

Describes writer's orientation to the rhetorical situtation

The term "war" that both Dyson and Powell use gives the commentary its sense of urgency and enables readers to see what was calling on Powell to write. He appears to have excellent credentials to speak on the topic. As he notes in the opening paragraph, Powell has a lot of experience in the hip-hop world and, despite recent trends that bother him, he is a "hip-hop head for life." In fact, it is his devotion to hip-hop culture as creative and empowering that defines his purposes in this commentary. He wants first to explain what has gone wrong and then to call for change within the hip-hop nation. It would not make much sense to call for reform unless there was something worth preserving, and Powell describes rap as an "urban folk art" and discusses the "golden age of hip-hop" to establish the positive possibilities.

Analyzes relationship to one intended audience

Powell's relationship to his readers is a complicated one because he has a number of intended audiences. One audience is the broad readership of *Newsweek* and includes many people who know very little about rap and may have negative feelings about it. For these readers, it might come as a surprise that someone within hip-hop is so critical of it, and Powell seems to use this fact to explain the power of hip-hop for "young, working-class black and Latino cats" and to provide readers with a way of understanding how corporate control and an apolitical times have brought out the worst in hip-hop culture. Powell's criticism of hip-hop may well increase his credibility with these readers and encourage them to see that hip-hop did not create "urban misery, racism, sexism, homophobia, or classism" and that its glorification of money, sex, and violence is no different from what Hollywood and the TV networks put out.

Analyzes relationship to second intended audience

These mainstream readers, however, are not the people who can change the hip-hop nation. If Powell's goal is to educate *Newsweek* readers about the crisis in rap (and perhaps to neutralize feelings of hostility toward it), he has another goal in addressing intended readers within hip-hop culture, namely to acknowledge the crisis and do something about it. Powell must have been aware (and may be worried) that these readers might be skeptical about his

Nadeau 3

publishing criticisms of hip-hop in a mainstream magazine. This perhaps accounts for the way Powell lists his own roots in hip-hop and proclaims his devotion to it. He also tries to make it clear that he is not "someone who disses for dissing sake." But he must also know that he is unlikely to convince those MCs who are making millions rapping about pimps, "niggas," and "bitches." Instead, his commentary seems to seek out those readers within hip-hop who might join with him to turn things around.

Analyzes language use

Tone

Powell's language is one technique he uses to establish his allegiances to hip-hop and a common ground where progressive forces can join together. The commentary has an informal, conversational tone that emphasizes Powell's sincerity and makes it seem he is speaking directly to his readers. Powell sprinkles his commentary with rap terms such as "tagged," "def," and "DJing" and the names of rap artists, not so many that mainstream readers will lose the train of thought but enough to ensure Powell's authenticity for his hip-hop readers. The use of the term "fresh," for example, will probably just go by many readers as denoting something new, while hip-hop readers will recognize its connotative use as a key term in rap vocabulary. Finally, Powell's most powerful figure of speech—the phrase describing videos that "pump visual crack into the minds of young people"—provides all readers with a striking image of what he sees as wrong with the current rap scene.

Denotation/ connotation

Figure of speech

My analysis suggests that Powell's commentary is rhetorically effective, given the constraints of space and the fact that we cannot assume that Powell's argument will actually rally progressive rappers and produce genuine change. The commentary does, however, make available to many readers what may well be a new and more complicated understanding of hip-hop, and it clearly offers points of identification for "positive" rappers. For some readers, Powell's argument that "the current economic boom has created the myth that things are swell for all Americans" may be too brief and lacking in evidence, but this in part is a problem of space. Those predisposed to share Powell's view

Evaluates rhetorical effectiveness

Nadeau 4

that there is an accelerating class divide may just be glad to see this idea put forward in a major mainstream publication like *Newsweek*. In all, Powell has done a skillful job of conveying the sense of urgency that called on him to write this commentary and a skillful balancing act in establishing the authority to address two very different audiences.

WRITING ASSIGNMENT

Analyzing the Rhetorical Situation

Your task is to select a piece of writing to analyze its rhetorical situation. Use the sample rhetorical analysis as a flexible guide—not as a rigid model. How you organize your analysis will depend in part on the writing you choose and in part on the decisions you make about how to arrange the parts of your analysis.

Directions

1. Select a short (five to ten paragraphs) written text that takes a position on an issue. Newspaper editorials and op-ed pieces, featured columnists published in newspapers and magazines, magazine commentary, political ads, and ads from advocacy groups are all good sources for this assignment. It helps if you know something about the topic and the issues involved.

2. To prepare for your analysis, use the reading strategies presented in this chapter to come to terms with the reading you've chosen.

   ■ Do a first close reading that uses underlining, annotation, and summary to make sure you understand what the writer is saying. Go back to any sections that need clarification.

   ■ On a second reading, pay attention to what the writer is doing by describing the writer's strategy.

3. Use your close reading to analyze the rhetorical situation. Here are some questions to guide your analysis:

   ■ What is the context of issues? What do you know about the topic? What issues does the topic raise? Is there a larger debate, discussion, or controversy already going on? What seems to be at stake?

- Who is the writer? What do you know about the writer's background, credibility, knowledge of the topic, beliefs, and social allegiances?

- What is the publication? What do you know about its intended readers, reputability, political slant, and the topics it covers?

- How does the writer define the rhetorical situation and identify the call to write? What is the writer's orientation toward the issues involved? What is at stake for the writer?

- Who is the intended audience? Is the writer addressing one group of readers or more than one? Is the writer trying to bring an audience into being? What kind of relationship is the writer trying to establish with readers? What assumptions about readers does the writer seem to make?

- How does the writer use language? What is the writer's tone? What does the writer's word choice show about his or her assumptions about readers? Does the writer use specialized terms or slang? Are there memorable figures of speech? Does the writer stereotype?

- What is your evaluation of the rhetorical effectiveness? Does the writer accomplish his or her purposes? What constraints, if any, qualify the writing's effectiveness? ■

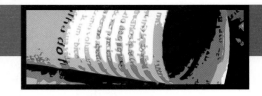

persuasion and responsibility
analyzing arguments

Imagine you are taking a walk and encounter an elderly man whose car has broken down. His request "Can you give me a hand?" requires no explanation. What makes it persuasive is the shared belief that people should help each other in times of need.

You can probably think of other occasions when persuasion takes place as a spontaneous meeting of the minds. A friend suggests that you go to the basketball game together on Friday night, and you agree. Neighbors ask if you can feed their cat when they are away for the weekend. Woven into the fabric of social life, persuasion refers to moments when people reach agreements and join together on common purposes.

Moments such as these require no elaborate explanation. In other instances, however, we do need to make explicit arguments—to give reasons and explanations—to persuade others. Here are two situations that call on people to make explicit arguments:

- A Muslim man and a Christian woman want to get married. Both families are very devout and always imagined that their children would marry someone of their faith in a religious ceremony. Grandchildren, of course, would be raised in the family religion. The couple, however, decide that the best way to handle their different religious backgrounds is to get married in a civil ceremony and let their children make their own decisions about religion. Since the couple are of legal age, they could just go ahead and get married, but they want their parents' blessing. Clearly, they have a problem of persuasion and need to come up with some good arguments.

- As part of a campaign to increase childhood immunization, a group of health workers has been commissioned to develop public service announcements for television. They have some decisions to make about the pitch of their publicity. What is the most persuasive approach? Should they emphasize the health risks and what can happen if children are not inoculated? Or should they appeal instead to positive images of good parents taking care of their children? Should they target mothers as the primary audience?

As you can see, situations that call for explicit arguments to persuade others can be complicated. Part of learning to write is learning how to deal with such situations. That is precisely the purpose of this chapter.

ETHICS OF WRITING: UNDERSTANDING ARGUMENT

People often think of arguments as heated moments when tempers flare and discussion degenerates into a shouting match. There is no question such arguments can be found in the political arena and the media, on radio and television talk shows, for example.

For our purposes, however, such images of argument are not very useful. Part of the problem is that arguments in politics and the media are often cast in simplistic, pro/con, liberal or conservative terms, where polarized speakers or writers are trying to defeat each other. This winner-take-all mentality is hardly conducive to the responsible investigation of complicated issues, where there may be more than just two positions and the task is to identify how and why people differ in their views.

Another problem is that restricted adversarial notions of argument can lead people to give up altogether on the hope of negotiating their differences with others. Some just say, "What's the point? Everyone has their own ideas, and there's nothing you can do about it." While such a statement does, in an important sense, acknowledge the validity of others' perspectives, it is often based on a sense of powerlessness in the face of differences and can end up leading to a refusal to take others seriously enough to engage with them about issues facing us all.

Genuine argument (as opposed to a shouting match) is devoted to understanding the reasonable differences that divide people and using this understanding to clarify the issues. This view of argument does not mean that you can't hold strong positions or find weaknesses in the views of people who differ with you. It means that you need to take others seriously—to see them not as obstacles to your views but as reasonable human beings. In this sense, arguments involve working with as much as against others. Exploring and negotiating reasonable disagreements through argument amount to a collective effort to understand what divides people and what the best course of action maybe.

WHAT IS ARGUMENT? DEALING WITH REASONABLE DIFFERENCES

Some disagreements among people are not, properly speaking, reasonable ones. Two people might disagree, for example, about the driving distance between New York City and Buffalo, New York, or about the chemical composition of dioxin. These are not reasonable disagreements because they can be resolved by consulting a road atlas or a chemistry book. There are sources available to settle the matter, so there's really no point in arguing.

On the other hand, people might reasonably disagree about the best route to drive to Buffalo or about the best policy concerning the production and use of dioxin. In disagreements such as these, there are no final, definitive answers available. One person may prefer a certain route to Buffalo because of the scenery, while another wants only the fastest way possible. By the same token, some may argue that policy on dioxin needs above all to take environmental and health risks into account, while for others the effect of policy on the economy and workers' jobs must also be a prime consideration.

DARCY PETERS AND MARCUS BOLDT: EXCHANGE OF LETTERS

Following is an exchange of letters between Darcy Peters, a homemaker from Camas, Washington, and her representative in the state legislature, Marcus Boldt, a recently elected Republican. As you will see, Peters wrote to Boldt asking him to oppose a plan to eliminate the state's Readiness to Learn program, which supported the Family Learning Center, an adult education and preschool program that Peters and her three sons attended in Camas. Included here are Peters's letter and the response from Representative Boldt.

Representative Marcus Boldt:

1   Please do not cancel funding for the Readiness to Learn Family Learning Center.

2   Our family came to the learning center frustrated. Barely self-supportive, we were struggling but living with no outside assistance. My husband was frequently laid off from work, and I was a full-time mother, not working outside the home. With four-year-old twins and another child, age three, we couldn't afford to pay for a preschool program. When I went to the Head Start program, I was told that we were ineligible because we made too much money. I felt like a victim of the system.

3   I was thrilled to find out we were eligible for the Readiness to Learn program. My children could all attend, and so could I. My sons, Caleb, Zachary, and Nathan, have learned so much at the center. They constantly surprise me with skills I didn't even know they had. I am so proud of their success. I myself have learned a great deal as well. Being challenged academically has sparked a thirst

for learning that I never knew existed in me. I have seen the world open up before me, and I feel capable of meeting any academic challenge. Furthermore, using one of the agencies I learned of at the center, my husband is making a career change, having decided to leave the construction business to become an electrician.

4

This has been such a valuable experience that I hope many other families are able to attend the center. Abolishing Readiness to Learn might rob another family of the chance to improve itself and reach its long-term goals. We need this program in our area.

Sincerely,
Darcy Peters

Dear Ms. Peters:

1

Thank you for writing to me about your concerns regarding funding for the Family Learning Center. Your letter goes to the heart of the matter in the area of budgetary reform. My positions on budget expenditures are well-known, and served in large measure to assure my election to this office.

2

I see that you have three children, ages three and four. You wrote that your husband is subject to frequent layoffs. You indicate that you are a "full-time mother, not working outside the home."

3

The concerns expressed by the taxpayers over your situation are as follows:

a. If your situation was subject to so much financial instability, then why did you have three children?

b. Why is your husband in a line of work that subjects him to "frequent layoffs"?

c. Why, in the face of your husband's ability to parent as a result of his frequent layoffs, are you refusing to work outside the home?

d. Since there is no state or federally mandated requirement that children attend these programs, why should the taxpayer foot the bill for them?

e. Since your family apparently makes too much money for assistance, why should you receive subsidies of any kind?

f. How much of the situation outlined in your letter should be the responsibility of the people of this state?

g. What arrangements have you made to repay this program at some future date?

4

I do not necessarily agree with all of these perspectives. But I must contend with the expectations of a constituency that is tired of paying for so many programs without any discernible return.

5   The voters have made it clear that, in this era of personal responsibility, life must become a more "pay-as-you-go" proposition. To put it bluntly, the taxpayers' perspective says, "This program is something that Darcy wants to have, and not something that she must have."

          Thank you for your time.

Marcus Boldt
State Representative

■ FOR CRITICAL INQUIRY

1. What argument is Darcy Peters making? What differences are at issue in the two letters? Do they seem to be reasonable ones? On whose behalf is she writing? How does she seem to imagine her relationship to Representative Boldt? How can you tell?

2. How does Boldt seem to identify differences? On whose behalf is he writing? How does he seem to imagine his relationship to Peters? How can you tell?

3. Peters's letter, clearly, did not persuade Boldt or lead to a meeting of the minds. By the same token, it is not likely that Boldt's letter persuaded Peters either. Here, then, is a situation in which arguments have failed to achieve their intended aims. How would you explain this failure? Does the exchange clarify the differences that divide the two? Can you imagine some common ground on which agreement might take place? Why or why not?

WHAT DO READERS EXPECT FROM ARGUMENTS?

In high school and college courses, you've probably been assigned papers that call on you to take a position and back it up. Thesis and support, after all, are common features of written academic work. This is also true of persuasive writing in everyday life, in the workplace, and in the public sphere. But whether the writing is for a class assignment or a petition circulated to increase state funding for the arts, readers expect successful arguments to have a number of features in common.

Readers justifiably expect that the writer's line of thinking will be easy to identify and to follow. Otherwise, they will have a hard time evaluating the writer's argument, and that defeats the whole purpose of taking a position on matters where there are reasonable differences. Accordingly, arguments typically provide the following things:

■ A clear statement of the writer's position on the issue at hand. This statement is the writer's central claim (or *thesis*) in the argument.

■ Evidence that supports the claim. As noted in Chapter 2, the main types of evidence are statistics, research, expert testimony, and examples.

■ Clear explanations of how this evidence actually supports the main claim. These explanations are the reasons in the argument—the statements that show how the writer's evidence is linked to the claim.

■ A sense of the larger implications of the main claim.

The annotated student essay that follows offers a good illustration of how Katie DiMartile makes a claim by taking a position in a controversy, explains how her evidence supports the claim, and finally proposes a compromise in the controversy. (You will find a fuller treatment of how Katie wrote this essay in Chapter 16, "The Writing Process: A Case Study of a Writing Assignment.")

Notice how the ideas in the essay relate to each other and make the essay easy to follow. Because the essay meets readers' expectations about the presentation of ideas, readers don't have to spend a lot of time trying to figure out what the writer is saying. Instead, readers can engage with the writer's ideas to see if they make sense and offer a persuasive point of view.

DiMartile 1

Katie DiMartile

American Pop Culture

Prof. Brown

November 14, 2008

Roadside Memorials

Establishes the context of issues by describing a controversy

Our culture has always made a point of remembering the dead. For example, in Washington D.C. there is the Tomb of the Unknown Soldier, the Vietnam Memorial, and many others. Additionally, there are memorials at Columbine, Ground Zero, Oklahoma City, and Virginia Tech honoring those who lost their lives in those tragedies. While all these memorials are accepted by the public without question, roadside memorials, small monuments marking the sites of fatal car accidents, are plagued by controversy. Some argue that such

Main claim: takes a position in the controversy

memorials should be banned because they often contain religious symbols that should not be displayed on public property. Others think that the memorials could distract drivers and become safety hazards. However, such proposals to ban roadside memorials ignore the important functions they serve.

DiMartile 2

One important function that roadside memorials serve is that they can help the victim's loved ones get through the grieving process. When someone is killed unexpectedly in a car accident, loved ones are left with a tragic loss. Coping with such a dramatic loss can be hard and going to the site and seeing the memorial gives the family closure. By putting a cross, or another symbol, at the site of a fatal car accident the victim is being remembered. One of my friends lost his brother in a car accident during our freshman year of high school. I went with him several times during that year to put flowers at the site of his brother's accident. More than visiting his brother's grave or talking to his family, visiting the memorial seemed to bring my friend peace. I believe standing where his brother lost his life helped my friend feel closer to him.

Roadside memorials are not just important to families or loved ones, but they can act as warning signs to other drivers. Roadside memorials make the danger of driving much more real because they remind drivers of the serious consequences of reckless behavior on the road. When I drive down the road and see a memorial it reminds me to check my speed and become more aware of my surroundings. It is easy to ignore speed limit and other warning signs because they are so familiar. But when you see a small cross you know someone actually lost their life, they didn't just get a speeding ticket.

Perhaps the best way to compromise between the different sides of the controversy over roadside memorials is to enforce regulations on the form of these monuments. Memorials could feature pictures of the deceased or meaningful personal items instead of religious symbols. There could be rules for where memorials could be safely erected. Such regulations would still allow roadside memorials to provide important services to loved ones and drivers while also respecting the views of others and maintaining proper safety.

Supports main claim by explaining one function in general terms

Explains function by personal example

Supports main claim by explaining second function

Proposes a compromise to resolve controversy

ENTERING A CONTROVERSY

The idea that argument takes place when there are reasonable disagreements among people means that writers do not just start arguments from scratch. Rather, they enter a field of debate—or a controversy—where some positions have already been staked out and people are already arguing.

Entering a controversy is like coming into a room where a heated conversation is taking place. You may know some of the people talking, but not all of them. You need to listen for a while to find out what the various speakers are saying and what the issues seem to be. You may find yourself drawn toward some of the views argued, and skeptical about others. Some speakers may be throwing out facts and figures, but you may not be quite sure what they are trying to prove. Some may be taking jabs at other speakers' reasoning.

Gradually, as you listen, you find you agree with some of the speakers' views but oppose others. The controversy begins to make sense to you, and you start to speak.

Entering a controversy, as this scenario reveals, is a matter of coming into the middle of something, and it takes some time to learn your way around and figure out what is going on. It might well be considered rude or presumptuous if you started arguing the moment you entered the room. You need to listen first to see how you can fit your own views into the stream of debate.

A second point this scenario illustrates is that people enter controversies through their relations to others. As the scenario reveals, your sense of what the debate is about depends on what others have said, what they value, what they propose to do. For this reason, when you do step forward to speak, you are also articulating your relationship to others—whether it is agreement, qualified support, or counterargument. Entering a controversy inevitably draws a person into alliances with some people and differences with others.

ANALYZING ISSUES

Listening to and reflecting on the heated conversation going on around you amounts to analyzing the issues. To take part in a controversy—to have your say—you need to first understand why speakers disagree and what they have at stake. This can be complicated—and sometimes confusing—because people do not always agree on what they are arguing about.

Take the following argument about baseball superstar Manny Ramirez's suspension in 2009 for taking performance-enhancing drugs:

- One person says that now we know why Manny Ramirez was such a productive home run hitter with the Boston Red Sox and Los Angeles Dodgers.

- A second person responds that the Ramirez incident just goes to show how corrupt all sports have become, that athletes will do anything to be successful, whether in pro sports or the Olympics.

- A third person chimes in, claiming the real point is that Major League Baseball has for years failed its fans and its players by not developing and enforcing a league-wide policy on steroids and other performance-enhancing drugs.

These people might argue all night long, but their argument will be fruitless and unproductive unless they can agree on what they are arguing about. In fact, one person could hold all three of these views and agree with each of the speakers, though we sense that some real differences divide them. The problem is they have not sufficiently clarified the nature of the disagreement.

To enter a controversy and argue responsibly, your arguments must respond to the issues already posed in dispute. Otherwise, you cannot possibly engage with others. You will simply be left with a sequence of claims but little productive debate about how and why people differ.

But let's not give up on the three people in our example. They may still be able to engage each other and find out where and how they differ. But first they need to agree on what the issues are. They need to do some work, some sorting out, to understand what is at stake in the various claims they have made.

TYPES OF ISSUES

Issues are arguable points that people make when reasonable differences exist. For example, the statement "Barack Obama was elected president in 2008" isn't an issue because no one would dispute it. Instead, most people would agree that the statement is an established fact. On the other hand, the statement "Obama's use of taxpayers' money to bail out the banks rewards greed and incompetence at the expense of ordinary people" raises an issue because, in this case, the point can be reasonably disputed. Some will say that Obama's bailout prevented the wider collapse of financial markets and a deepening economic recession, while others might argue that the federal government should have thrown out the scoundrels, nationalized the banks, and put in people to run them in the public interest.

To return to our three speakers, we can see that there are three different and distinct types of issues in their argument about the case of Manny Ramirez's suspension—issues of substantiation, evaluation, and policy. Each of these issues offers a place to begin a productive argument.

Issues of Substantiation

Issues of substantiation are questions of disputed facts, definitions, causes, and consequences. They involve asking whether something actually happened, what it is, what brought it about, and what its effects are. The first speaker raises an issue that can be substantiated by asserting that performance-enhancing drugs gave Manny Ramirez extra strength and an edge in hitting. This is an issue that asks us to look at the evidence available to establish such a cause-and-effect relationship. What are the effects of these drugs? How do they work?

Issues that call for substantiation occur regularly in ongoing arguments:

- How widely are amateur and professional athletes using steroids? (question of disputed fact)

- What kinds of actions amount to sexual harassment? (question of definition)

- Are environmental carcinogens responsible for the increase in breast cancer? (question of cause)

- Has expansion of pro football into new cities increased teams' profits? (question of consequences)

Issues of Evaluation

Issues of evaluation are questions about whether something is good or bad, right or wrong, desirable or undesirable, effective or ineffective, valuable or worthless. The second speaker addresses an issue of evaluation when he focuses not so much on the effects of performance-enhancing drugs (in running faster times or hitting more home runs) but on a moral judgment about athletes' decision to use drugs.

Issues of evaluation appear routinely in all spheres of life:

- Is a Macintosh or a PC computer system best suited to your computing needs?

- Is *American Idol* a cruel display of untalented performers or an old-fashioned talent show that everyone can enjoy?

- Is affirmative action unfair to white males?

- What novels should be included in an American literature course?

Issues of Policy

Issues of policy are questions about what we should do and how we should implement our aims. The third speaker takes on a policy issue when he finds fault with how Major League Baseball has handled its drug problem. Support or refutation of policy issues will typically focus on how well the policy solves an existing problem or addresses a demonstrable need.

Issues about policy are pervasive in public discussions. Typically, they use the terms *should, ought,* or *must* to signal the courses of action they recommend:

- Should the federal government ban late-term abortions?

- Must all students be required to take a first-year writing course?

- Should there be a moratorium on capital punishment?

- Should schools provide bilingual education?

Identifying what type of issue is at stake in a speaker's claim offers a way to cut into an ongoing controversy and get oriented. This does not mean, however, that controversies come neatly packaged according to type of issue. The three types of issues are tools of analysis to help you identify how and why people disagree. As you prepare to enter an ongoing controversy, you are likely to find that the three types of issues are connected and lead from one to the next.

Here is an example of how the three types of issues can be used to explore a controversy and invent arguments.

Sample Exploration of a Controversy

Should High Schools Abolish Tracking and Assign Students to Mixed-Ability Classrooms Instead?

1. Issues that can be substantiated: How widespread is the practice of tracking? When did it begin? Why was tracking instituted in the first place? What purposes was it designed for? What are the effects of tracking on students? What experiments have taken place to use mixed-ability groupings instead of tracking? What are the results?

2. Issues of evaluation: What educational values are put into practice in tracking? Are these values worthy? Is tracking fair to all students? Does it benefit some students more than others? What values are embodied in mixed-ability classrooms? How do these compare to the values of tracking?

3. Issues of policy: What should we do? What are the reasons for maintaining tracking? What are the reasons for implementing mixed-ability groupings? Can mixed-ability classrooms succeed? What changes would be required? What would the long-term consequences be?

TAKING A POSITION: FROM ISSUES TO CLAIMS

The point of analyzing the issues in any ongoing controversy is to clarify your own thinking and determine where you stand. Taking a position amounts to entering into the debate to have your own say. Determining your position means you have an arguable claim to make—an informed opinion, belief, recommendation, or call to action you want your readers to consider.

Look at the following two statements:

Tracking was recently dismantled in a local school district.

Tracking has become a very heated issue.

As you can see, these sentences simply describe a situation. They aren't really arguable claims because no one would reasonably disagree with them. They don't tell readers what the writer believes or thinks should be done. Now take a look at these two statements:

> For the dismantling of tracking to be successful, our local school district should provide teachers with in-service training in working with mixed-ability groups.

> Tracking has become such a heated issue because parents of honors students worry unnecessarily that their children won't get into the best colleges.

Notice that in each statement you can see the writer's stand on the issue right away. The first writer treats an issue of policy, while the second is trying to substantiate the cause of the tracking controversy. What makes each claim arguable is that there can be differing views regarding the issue. Readers could respond that in-service training is a waste of money because teachers already know how to teach different levels of students, or that the real reason tracking is so controversial is because it holds back the brightest students. To make sure a claim is arguable, ask yourself whether someone could reasonably disagree with it—whether there could be at least two differing views on the issue on which you've taken a position.

Both writers have successfully cued readers to their positions, in part by using key words that typically appear in position statements. Notice that in the first sentence, the writer uses *should* (but could have used similar terms such as *must, ought to, needs to,* or *has to*) to signal a proposed solution. In the second, the writer uses a *because* statement to indicate to readers that there is evidence available to back up the claim. Writers also use terms such as *therefore, consequently, thus, it follows that, the point is* to signal their positions.

■ **EXERCISE**

Steps Toward a Tentative Position

Take a current controversy you know something about, where reasonable differences divide people. It could be the death penalty, drug testing for high school or college athletes, censorship of lyrics, curfews for adolescents under eighteen. The main consideration is that the controversy interests you and that you believe it is important.

1. State the controversy in its most general terms in the form of a question: "Should colleges routinely conduct drug tests on varsity athletes?" "Do we need a rating system for television shows similar to the one used for movies?"

2. Then use the three types of issues—substantiation, evaluation, and policy—to generate a list of more specific questions: "How do drug tests work?" "Why were drug tests developed in the first place, and what are their consequences?" "Do drug tests violate constitutional freedoms?" "Is drug testing sound policy?"

3. Pick one set of questions from your list of types of issues. For example, you might pick the interrelated questions "Do drug tests actually work?" "Are they

reliable?" "Can they be circumvented?" Develop a tentative position that responds to the question or questions. Make sure it presents an arguable claim.

4. Consider whether your tentative position is an informed claim. At this point, you may need more information to analyze the issues responsibly and develop an arguable claim with sufficient evidence.

DEVELOPING A PERSUASIVE POSITION

WHAT ARE THE RHETORICAL APPEALS?

Once you have a tentative position in mind, you can begin to think about how to present it to your readers in the most persuasive way possible. One powerful set of persuasive strategies is known in classical rhetoric as *the appeals*. The three appeals—*ethos, pathos,* and *logos*—offer three different but interrelated ways to influence your readers by appealing to their ideas and values, sympathies, and beliefs.

- Ethos: *Ethos* refers to the writer's character as it is projected to readers through the written text. The modern terms *personality* and *attitude* capture some of the meaning of ethos and how readers build an impression of the writer's character—how credible, fair, and authoritative.

- Pathos: *Pathos* refers to the readers' emotions and the responses a piece of writing arouses in them. Pathos should not be associated simply with emotional appeals to readers' fears and prejudices. Instead, it offers a way to analyze their state of mind and the intensity with which they hold various beliefs and values.

- Logos: *Logos* refers to what is said or written. Its original meaning was "voice" or "speech," though the term later took on an association with logic and reasoning. For our purposes, the term offers a way to focus on the writer's message and the line of reasoning the writer develops.

The term *rhetorical stance* refers to the way writers coordinate ethos, pathos, and logos as interrelated components in persuasive writing. To see how this coordination of the three appeals works in practice, let's look at a passage, shown on the next page, from one of Malcolm X's most famous speeches, "The Ballot or the Bullet," delivered to a largely black audience in 1964. At the time Malcolm X gave his speech, the U.S. Senate was debating the Civil Rights Act of 1964, which passed later in the year, following a filibuster by its opponents.

ANALYSIS OF PERSUASIVE APPEALS IN "THE BALLOT OR THE BULLET"

Ethos

Malcolm X identifies himself first by explaining what he is not—a politician, a student of politics, a Democrat, or a Republican. In fact, he does not even consider himself an American. Instead, he identifies himself as "one of the 22 million black people who are victims of Americanism."

Malcolm X presents himself as someone who is willing to look at the racial situation in America without illusions. "I am one," he says, "who doesn't believe in deluding myself." Just being in America, he argues, doesn't make black people Americans. Otherwise, black people would not need civil rights legislation to achieve equality.

The tone and attitude Malcolm X projects are militant and unrelenting, chosen in part to distinguish his appeal from the appeals of civil rights leaders such as Dr. Martin Luther King Jr., who emphasized racial reconciliation and working through the system. For Malcolm X, there is no point in appealing to American democratic values, as King often did, because the system has always been hypocritical—not a dream but a nightmare.

FROM "THE BALLOT OR THE BULLET"

MALCOLM X

Malcolm X banner by Mike Alewitz

1   I'm not a politician, not even a student of politics; in fact, I'm not a student of much of anything. I'm not a Democrat, I'm not a Republican, and I don't even consider myself an American. If you and I were Americans, there'd be no problem. Those Hunkies that just got off the boat, they're already Americans; Polacks are already Americans; the Italian refugees are already Americans. Everything that came out of Europe, every blue-eyed thing, is already an American. And as long as you and I have been over here, we aren't Americans yet.

2   Well, I am one who doesn't believe in deluding myself. I'm not going to sit at your table and watch you eat, with nothing on my plate, and call myself a diner. Sitting at the table doesn't make you a diner, unless you eat some of what's on that plate. Being here in America doesn't make you an American. Why, if birth made you American, you wouldn't need any legislation, you wouldn't need any amendments

3   to the Constitution, you wouldn't be faced with civil-rights filibustering in Washington, D.C., right now. They don't have to pass civil-rights legislation to make a Polack an American.

No, I'm not an American. I'm one of the 22 million black people who are the victims of Americanism. One of the 22 million black people who are the victims of democracy, nothing but disguised hypocrisy. So, I'm not standing here speaking to you as an American, or a patriot, or a flag-saluter, or a flag-waver—no, not I. I'm speaking as a victim of this American system. And I see America through the eyes of the victim. I don't see any American dream; I see an American nightmare.

Pathos

By locating a stance outside the system, Malcolm X invites his audience to join him in rejecting the moderation of civil rights leaders and to share a new, more militant politics.

He seeks, on one hand, to mobilize his black listeners' feelings about what it means to be an American. By offering an explanation of how blacks have been systematically excluded from the American dream, Malcolm X seeks to redirect the intensity of his black listeners' emotions—away from the hope of racial integration and toward a new identity based on the power and self-reliance of black people united in struggle. He is offering them a way to see themselves not as humble petitioners to the white power structure but as a power in their own right.

On the other hand, it may well appear that Malcolm X has written off white listeners. For some, his use of ethnic slurs such as *Hunkies* and *Polacks* are offensive and can hardly have endeared him to his white audience (many whites did indeed reject his message as antiwhite and potentially dangerous). But for others, Malcolm X's unflinching analysis of race relations in America brought with it the shock of recognition that white-skin privilege is a pervasive feature of American life. In fact, Malcolm X did gain a wide audience of whites who came to admire his unyielding insistence on "telling it like it is" and who were thereby led to rethink the consequences of racism in America.

Logos

As you have just seen, Malcolm X established a relationship with his listeners by projecting an attitude and a message that elicited powerful responses. If anything, the way he presents himself (ethos) and his listeners' responses (pathos) are inseparable from the form and content of his message (logos). Still, it is worth noting how cogently reasoned this message is.

Malcolm X's reasoning is simple yet devastating. It all revolves around the issue of how people get to be considered Americans. According to Malcolm X, people who came from Europe are already considered Americans. They don't need civil rights legislation. At the same time, the fact of being born in America is not necessarily enough for a person to be considered an American; otherwise black people born in America would not need civil rights legislation. Put these two propositions together and you get the unavoidable conclusion: the fact that black people need civil rights legislation proves in effect that they are not considered Americans, and the implication is that they are therefore something else—not the inheritors of the American dream but the victims of an American nightmare.

CONSTRUCTING AN APPROPRIATE RHETORICAL STANCE

Experienced writers know that to make persuasive arguments they need to construct an appropriate rhetorical stance. Whether the rhetorical stance you construct is appropriate will, of course, depend on the situation that calls for writing, your purposes, and the beliefs of your readers. Arguments that are appropriate and persuasive in one situation may not necessarily be appropriate and persuasive in another.

The following letters were written by a student applying for a summer internship at a cable television station—Greater Worcester Media Cable Company. As you read, notice that the student is making an arguable claim, namely, "you should hire me as an intern." The question is whether the rhetorical stance he develops is appropriate to the occasion.

Sample Letters of Application

Letter 1

I would like to apply for a summer internship at Greater Worcester Media Cable Company. I've just switched my major from pre-med to mass communication, and I'm really excited about getting out of those boring science classes and into something that interests me. I just finished this great video production class and made a short documentary called "Road Kill," about all the animals that get run over on Highway 61. It was pretty arty and punk, with a sound track dubbed from Sonic Youth.

I want to learn everything I can about television. I'd love to eventually be an anchorman on the national news, like Dan Rather or Peter Jennings or Tom Brokaw. I've always known that television is one of the most influential parts of American life, and I think it would be awesome to be seen nightly by millions of viewers. Think of all the influence—and fun—you could have, with everyone watching you.

Of course, if I do get the internship, I won't be able to go home this summer, and that will be kind of a bummer because my parents and girlfriend are pretty much expecting I'll be around. But still, it would be worth it to get into television because that's where I see myself going long-term.

Letter 2

I would like to apply for a summer internship at Greater Worcester Media Cable Company. As my résumé indicates, I am a Mass Communication major in my sophomore year, with course work in video production, mass communication theory, and the history of television. In addition, I have a strong background in the natural sciences.

I believe that my studies in Mass Communication have given me skills and experience that would be valuable in a summer internship. In my video production class, I filmed and edited a short documentary, and I am eager to gain more experience in production and editing.

A summer internship would be a wonderful opportunity for me to learn how the day-to-day world of cable television works. This kind of practical experience would be an invaluable complement to my coursework in the history and theory of the media.

■ WORKING TOGETHER

Rhetorical Stance

You have probably concluded that the first letter is inappropriate as a letter of application to Greater Worcester Media Cable Company and that the second letter has a greater chance of success. Your task now is to explain why. Work together with two or three other students. Follow these directions:

1. Compare the two letters in terms of the rhetorical stance the writer has constructed in each case. Be specific here and point to words, phrases, and passages that reveal how the writer coordinates ethos, logos, and pathos.
2. Think of a situation in which the first letter would be appropriate to the writer's purposes and the interests of readers. It may be inappropriate when applying for a summer internship, but that doesn't mean it is not as well written as the second. Notice that in certain respects it has more life, more telling details, and more of a sense of the writer's personality than the second letter.

MAKING AN ARGUMENT

Good arguments aren't found ready to use. They have to be made. To make a persuasive argument, you need to develop an effective line of reasoning. To do that, it is helpful to look at the parts that go into making an argument. In this section, we draw on a model of argument developed by the philosopher Stephen Toulmin, although we use somewhat different terms.

What Are the Parts of an Argument?

Here is a quick sketch of the parts of an argument that we'll be considering in more detail in this section:

Claim	Your position, the basic point you want readers to accept
Evidence	The supporting material for the claim
Enabling assumption	The line of reasoning that explains how the evidence supports the claim
Differing views	Disagreements with all or part of your argument
Qualifiers	Words that modify or limit the claim

Claims, Evidence, and Enabling Assumptions

As you have seen, you can't have a responsible argument unless you have an arguable claim, and you've looked at some ways to develop claims by analyzing issues and constructing an appropriate rhetorical stance. In this section, we look in detail at the three basic parts of an argument—claims, evidence, and enabling assumptions. Taken together, these terms give us a way to think about the line of reasoning in an argument. Readers justifiably expect writers to provide evidence for the claims they make. Moreover, they expect the evidence a writer offers to have a clear connection to the claim. As you will see, enabling assumptions are explanations of how the evidence supports a writer's claim.

To see how these connections work, take a look at the following two evaluations that students wrote of their composition instructor.

Sample Evaluations

Evaluation 1

Ms. Smith is probably the worst teacher I've had so far in college. I've never been so frustrated. I could never figure out what the teacher wanted us to do. She didn't grade the papers we turned in but instead just wrote comments on them. Then we had to evaluate each other's writings. How are students qualified to judge each other's writing? This is the teacher's job. We had to revise some of our writing to put in a portfolio at the end of the term. How were we supposed to know which papers were any good?

Evaluation 2

Ms. Smith is probably the best teacher I've had so far in college. I really liked how she organized the work. By not grading our papers, she gave us the opportunity to select our best writing and revise it for a portfolio at the end of the term. The comments she offered on drafts and the evaluations we did of each others' papers really helped. I found this freed me to experiment with my writing in new ways and not worry about getting low grades. This system made me realize how important revision is.

In one sense, both evaluations are persuasive. It's hard not to be convinced, at the level of lived experience, that the first student did not like the class, while the second student did. But what are we to make of these differences? What do they tell us about the teacher and her way of teaching writing?

In this case, to understand why the two students differ, it will help to see *how* they differ. Each has made an argument, and we can analyze how the arguments have been made. Each consists of the same basic parts.

Claims

In the two student evaluations, the competing claims are easy to find: Ms. Smith is either the best or the worst teacher in the student's experience. Each claim, moreover, meets the test for writing arguable claims.

- **Reasonable differences:** Both claims are matters of judgment that can't be decided by referring to an established, authoritative source. The question of whether Ms. Smith is a good teacher is worth arguing about.
- **Plausibility:** Both claims could be true. Each has a certain credibility that a claim like "An invasion of flying saucers will take place next week" doesn't have.
- **Sharable claims:** Both claims can be argued on terms that can be shared by others. In contrast, there's no reason to argue that blue is your favorite color or that you love the feel of velvet. Such a claim refers to a personal preference based on subjective experience and can't really be shared by others.

Evidence

Evidence is all the information available in a particular situation. Like detectives in the investigation of a crime, writers begin with the available evidence—data, information, facts, observations, personal testimony, statistics, common knowledge, or any other relevant material.

QUESTIONS TO ASK ABOUT EVIDENCE

To make a persuasive argument, you need evidence for your claim—and you also need some guidelines to evaluate whether the evidence you turn up will work for your argument. Here are some questions to ask yourself:

1. **Is the evidence clearly related to the claim?** As you plan an argument, you are likely to come up with lots of interesting material. Not all of it, however, will necessarily be relevant to the claim you want to support. For example, if you are arguing about how Darwin's theory of evolution influenced fiction writers in the nineteenth century, it doesn't make sense to give a lot of biographical details on Darwin. They may be interesting, but it's unlikely that they will help you explain the influence of his theory.

2. **Do you have enough evidence?** Basing a claim on one or two facts is hardly likely to persuade your readers. They are likely to dismiss your argument as hasty and unjustifiable because of insufficient evidence. The fact that two people in your neighborhood were laid off recently from their construction jobs is not enough evidence for claiming that the construction industry is in crisis. You would need to establish a pattern by showing, say, a decline in housing starts, the postponement of many major building projects, layoffs across the country, or bankruptcies of construction companies.

3. **Is your evidence verifiable?** Readers are likely to be suspicious of your argument unless they can check out the evidence for themselves. For instance, to support an argument for campaign finance reform, you might use examples of how corporate donations influenced politicians' voting, but if you don't tell readers who the politicians and corporations are, they will have no way to verify your evidence.

4. **Is your evidence up-to-date?** Readers expect you to do your homework and provide them with the latest information available. If your evidence is dated, readers may well suspect that newer information has supplanted it, and may therefore find your argument unpersuasive. If you are arguing for gender equity in medical education, citing figures on the enrollment of women in medical schools in the 1960s (around 10 percent) will be quickly dismissed because women currently represent around 50 percent of students entering medical school classes. (You might build a better case for gender equity by looking at possible patterns of discrimination in residency assignments or at the specializations women go into.)

5. **Does your evidence come from reliable sources?** You would probably not make an argument based on the *Weekly World News*'s latest Elvis sighting. As mentioned in Chapter 2, evidence needs to be evaluated and interpreted in light of its sources. Scientific studies, government reports, and research by academics, professional associations, and independent research institutes are likely to carry considerable authority for readers. Partisan sources—magazines such as the conservative *National Review* or the liberal *Nation*—often contain important evidence you can use persuasively, especially if you acknowledge the bias and ask readers to consider the merits of the information in the context of your argument.

Writers use this evidence to construct a sense of what happened and what the unresolved issues are. Notice in the two evaluations of Ms. Smith that the students do not seem to differ about what happened in class. Both describe the same teaching strategies: students wrote papers that were not graded; they received comments from the teacher and from other students; they were required to revise a number of the papers for a final portfolio. The difference is in how each uses this evidence.

Enabling Assumptions

Consider how the two students move from the available evidence—the facts that neither disputes—to their differing claims. This is a crucial move that each argument relies on. For an argument to be persuasive, readers need to know how and why the evidence cited by the writer entitles him or her to make a claim. This link—the connection in an argument between the evidence and the writer's claim—is called the *enabling assumption* because it refers to the line of reasoning that explains how the evidence supports the claim. Such assumptions are often implied rather than stated explicitly.

Notice that the enabling assumptions in the two student evaluations are implied but not directly stated. To find out how the two students connect the evidence to their claims, let's imagine we could interview them, to push them to articulate this missing link in their arguments:

Sample Interviews

Interview with Student 1

Q. How was your writing teacher?

A. She was the worst teacher I've had so far [*claim*].

Q. What makes you say that?

A. The teacher never graded our papers. We had to evaluate each other's papers and then revise a few and put them in a portfolio [*evidence*].

Q. So why was that so bad?

A. Well, because good teachers give you lots of graded evaluations so you know exactly where you stand in a class [*enabling assumption*].

Interview with Student 2

Q. How was your writing teacher?

A. She was great, best I've had so far [*claim*].

Q. What makes you say that?

A. The teacher never graded our papers. We had to evaluate each other's papers and then revise a few and put them in a portfolio [*evidence*].

Q. So why was that so good?

A. Well, because good teachers help you develop your own judgment by experimenting without worrying about grades [*enabling assumption*].

Of course, we could push each writer further to explore the assumptions that underlie the one he or she has articulated. If we push far enough, we are likely to find fundamental beliefs that each holds about the nature of education and learning. For example, in the case of the second student, an exploration of assumptions might look like this:

> Assumption 1: Good teaching helps students develop judgment by experimenting and not having to worry about grades.
> Assumption 2: Too much emphasis on grades can get in the way of developing judgment through trial and error.
> Assumption 3: Education should emphasize the development of individual judgment as much as or more than the learning of subject material.
> Assumption 4: Students naturally want to learn, and will do so if given the chance.

This process could continue indefinitely, and exploring the assumptions underlying assumptions can be a useful exercise. The practical question in making an argument is to decide which of these assumptions—or some combination of them—are likely to be shared by your readers and which ones can best clarify differences you have with others.

■ WORKING TOGETHER

Analyzing Claims, Evidence, and Enabling Assumptions
To work with the terms introduced here, analyze the statements that appear below. Identify the claim each statement makes. Identify the evidence that each statement relies on. Finally, explain how an enabling assumption, which may or may not be stated explicitly, connects the evidence to the claim.

1. Ultraviolent video games will inevitably lead to more school shootings.
2. The current increase in cases of tuberculosis can be attributed to new strains of the disease that are resistant to treatment by antibiotics.
3. The fact that both parents have to work just to make ends meet is destroying the American family.
4. It is reasonable that the CEOs of American corporations make over one hundred times in salary and bonuses what the average worker in the company earns.

DIFFERING VIEWS

To argue responsibly, you can't pretend that no one disagrees with you or that there are no alternative perspectives. To note these differences does not, as students sometimes think, undermine your own argument. In fact, it can strengthen it by showing that you are willing to take all sides into account, that you can refute objections to your argument, and, when necessary, that you can concede the validity of differing views.

Summarize Differing Views Fairly and Accurately
Readers often detect when writers handle differing views in a distorted way. In fact, their impressions of a writer's credibility and good character—the writer's ethos—depend in part on how reasonably the writer deals with differences. For

that reason, the ability to summarize fairly and accurately is quite important to the success of your argument. By summarizing fairly and accurately, you can show readers that you have anticipated reasonable differences and intend to deal with them responsibly.

This can help avoid having your readers jump into your argument with objections you've overlooked—"Sure, the government creating jobs for people on welfare sounds like a good idea, but what about the cost? And what about personal responsibility? Doesn't this just make people dependent in a different way?"—or rushing to the defense of objections you have characterized unfairly—"Not all conservative Christians believe women should be barefoot and pregnant."

Refuting Differing Views

For views that differ from yours, summarize them briefly, fairly, and accurately. Then explain what's wrong with them. Your best chance of persuading readers that your position is preferable to others is to clarify the differences that divide you and explain what you see as the weaknesses in other lines of reasoning.

To return to the student evaluations, the first student could strengthen his or her argument about what good teaching is by anticipating, summarizing, and refuting elements in the second student's argument. He or she might argue, for example, that while peer response to the written work of others may sound like a good idea, in fact it doesn't really help students improve their writing; he or she would then explain why. It would enhance the persuasiveness of the argument, of course, if the explanation consisted of more than personal anecdotes ("why peer review didn't help me")—for example, references to research studies on the effects of peer review.

Note: The author of this book does not endorse the view that peer review doesn't work, but does recognize it as an arguable claim.

Conceding Differing Views

When differing views have merit, don't avoid them. Remember that your readers will likely think of these objections, so you're better off taking them head-on. Summarize the view and explain what you concede. Such concessions are often signaled by words and phrases such as *admittedly, granted, while it may be true, despite the fact,* and *of course she is right to say.*

The purpose of concession is not to give up on your argument but to explain how it relates to differing views. In this sense, it's another means of clarifying differences and explaining your position in the fullest possible way. To concede effectively, follow it up right away with an explanation of how your position relates to the point you have conceded. Otherwise, you may give readers the impression that you endorse the point.

In the case of the student evaluations, the first student could make good use of concession. For example, he or she might concede the second student's point that an important goal of education is developing independent judgment.

The student then could go on to show that in practice the teacher's methods don't really lead to independent judgment but instead leave students to flounder on their own. In fact, conceding the point offers the student a line of reasoning he or she could pursue to strengthen the argument by explaining how the development of independent judgment depends on constant interaction with and regular evaluation from a more experienced and knowledgeable person.

Finding Viable Alternatives

Finding viable alternatives means identifying possible points of agreement in differing views. Once again, your purpose is not to abandon your views but to see if you can find any common ground with those who hold differing positions. Think of it as combining elements in reasonable differences in order to come up with new solutions and perspectives. Sometimes this is possible, but not always. Still, it's worth trying, because negotiated differences can strengthen your argument by broadening its appeal and demonstrating your desire to take into account as many views as possible.

Back to the student evaluations. The first student might concede that the teacher's portfolio system of evaluation has some merit because it bases grades on student improvement. But from this student's perspective, it still has the problem of not providing enough evaluation and information on the teacher's expectations. To negotiate these differences, the student might propose that the teacher grade but not count the first writing assignment so that students can see the teacher's evaluative standards in practice. The student might also suggest that the teacher give students a midterm progress report on where they stand in the class, and again grade but not count one paper between midterm and the end of class.

Such a solution may not satisfy everyone, but it is likely to enhance the reader's impression of the student as someone who doesn't just criticize but tries to deal with differences constructively.

QUALIFIERS

Qualifiers modify or limit the claim in an argument by making it less sweeping, global, and categorical. For most claims, after all, there are exceptions that don't necessarily disprove the claim but need to be noted. Otherwise, you will needlessly open your claim to attack and disbelief. In many instances, a qualifier is as simple as saying "Many students at Ellroy State drink to excess" instead of "The students at my school get drunk all the time." Qualifiers admit exceptions without undermining your point, and they make statements harder to refute with a counterexample—"I know students who never drink" or "Some students drink only occasionally" or "My friends drink moderately."

You can qualify your claim with words and phrases such as *in many cases, often, frequently, probably, perhaps, may* or *might, maybe, likely,* or *usually.* In some instances, you will want to use a qualifying clause that begins with *unless* to limit the conditions in which the claim will hold true: "Unless the DNA evidence proves negative, everything points to the accused as the murderer."

PUTTING THE PARTS TOGETHER

To see how the various parts of argument we've just discussed can help you make an argument, let's look at the notes a student wrote to plan an argument opposing a recent proposal to the local school committee that would require students to wear uniforms at Middlebrook High School. No one contests that there are real problems at Middlebrook—declining test scores, drug use, racial tensions, lack of school spirit, a growing sense of student alienation. But, as you will see, the student doesn't think school uniforms can really address these problems.

Claim

Middlebrook High School should not require students to wear uniforms.

Evidence

School uniforms don't have the intended effects. I could use examples from schools that require uniforms to show they don't increase discipline, improve self-esteem, or alleviate social tensions.

Teachers oppose requiring uniforms because it would make them into cops. I could get some good quotes from teachers.

Even if they are required to wear uniforms, students will figure out other ways to show what group they are in. Jewelry, hairstyles, shoes, jackets, body piercing, tattoos, and so on will just become all the more important.

Uniforms violate students' right to self-expression. I could call the American Civil Liberties Union to see if they have any information I could use.

Requiring uniforms will make students hate school. I could get more on this by talking to students.

Enabling Assumption

A uniform requirement doesn't really address the problems at Middlebrook. Instead, it would make things worse.

Backing

The uniform proposal is based on a faulty view of what influences student behavior. More rules will just lead to more alienation from school.

To address Middlebrook's problems, students must be given more responsibility, instead of given regulations from above. They need to be brought into the decision-making process so they can develop a stake in what happens at school.

The proposal to require uniforms is based on the desire to return to some mythic age in Middlebrook's past when students were orderly, disciplined, filled with school spirit—namely, all the same kind of white, middle-class students. Middlebrook has changed, and the proposal doesn't deal with these changes.

Differing Views

Some uniform supporters claim that the success of Catholic and private schools is based on the fact students are required to wear uniforms. I need to show the causes of success are not uniforms but other factors.

I'll concede that there are real problems at Middlebrook but maintain my position that uniforms aren't the way to deal with them.

I could also concede that what students wear sometimes gets out of hand but argue that the best way to deal with this is to get students involved, along with teachers and parents, in writing a new dress code. In fact, I could extend this argument to say that the way to deal with some of the problems is for the school to get the different groups—whites, Latinos, blacks, and Cambodians— together to look at the problems and propose some solutions.

Qualifiers

My position is set. I'm against uniforms, period. But maybe I should state my claim in a way that takes uniform supporters' views into account. For example, I could say, "Admittedly there are a number of problems at Middlebrook that need attention, but requiring uniforms will not solve these problems."

As you can see, using the parts of argument has given this student a lot of material to work with and some leads about where to get more. Just as important, using the parts of argument offers a way to see the connections among the available material and how they might fit together in developing the writer's line of reasoning. Not all of this material will necessarily turn up in the final version of the student's argument, of course. This can be determined only through the process of drafting and revising. In fact, she might turn up new material and new arguments as she composes.

NEGOTIATING DIFFERENCES

Knowing how to argue persuasively and responsibly for your side is an important skill. Without it, people would be powerless in many situations. Unless you can make an effective argument, there may well be occasions when your perspective will go unheard and your views unrepresented. Moreover, if you do not argue for what you and others with shared values hold in common, someone else is likely to do your talking for you.

There is little question, then, that arguing for your side is a crucial means of participating in public life and influencing public opinion. Still, as noted earlier in the chapter, one of the limits of pro/con arguments is that they put people in an adversarial stance toward those with whom they disagree. Instead of clarifying the issues and reaching mutual understandings, the goal of the argument may turn into defeating your opponent.

Further, by polarizing issues along adversarial lines, pro-and-con arguments frequently limit the perspectives available in public debate to two—and only two—sides: those for and those against. This may well restrict who is entitled to be heard to the members of rival camps and thereby limit the alternatives considered in making decisions.

Finally, the pro/con, winner-take-all style of adversarial argument makes it nearly impossible for participants to identify the points of agreement and common ground they might share with others. The search for common ground does not assume that everyone is going to drop their differences and harmonize their interests. Instead, trying to find common ground can establish areas of agreement, large or small, that people can use as a basis to talk about their differences.

■ EXERCISE

Looking at Polarized Arguments

Write an account or prepare an oral presentation of an argument you witnessed or took part in that polarized into opposing sides. Describe what happened, and explain why the polarization took place. The point of this exercise is not to condemn the people involved but to understand what happened and why. Remember, polarization is not necessarily a bad thing. It may be unavoidable as people begin to identify their differences or invoke a matter of principle, where a person finds no alternative but to make a counterargument and take a stand. Your task here is to analyze what took place and to consider whether the polarization was inevitable or could have been avoided.

BEYOND PRO AND CON

A number of strategies offer writers approaches to reasonable differences that divide people. In sections that follow, we examine three:

1. Dialogue with others.
2. Recognizing ambiguities and contradictions.
3. Locating common ground.

These strategies enable writers to remain committed to their own goals and values but at the same time avoid some of the limitations of simply arguing for or against, pro and con, in an adversarial relation to others. They will help you to engage people with whom you may differ—to enter into a dialogue that seeks not a victory in debate but a clarification of the issues that may ultimately make it easier for you and others to live together and perhaps to locate common ground.

As you will see, these strategies do not deny differences in the name of having everyone get along for the common good. Nor do they assume that people can easily reconcile their differences or harmonize conflicting interests. Too often, some members of society—women, minorities, working people, seniors, teenagers, and children—have been asked to keep quiet and sacrifice their interests to create what is in fact a false unity. Instead of setting aside differences, these strategies seek to use them constructively in order to take more interests and perspectives into account.

The strategies that follow seek to bring differences out into the open—but not in an adversarial way. Instead of imagining issues in terms of warring camps, you can use these strategies to negotiate—to understand how others feel about the issues, why people might be divided in their views, and what is thereby at stake for all involved. Negotiating differences does not mean abandoning the goal of influencing others, but it does recognize that we need to be open to influence from others—if not to change our minds, at least to deepen our understanding of other views and ways of thinking.

Dialogue with Others

It is difficult to think of people negotiating their differences unless they recognize one another as reasonable beings in the first place. To recognize another person does not mean to see him or her as an opponent to be defeated in debate or as someone to overwhelm with convincing arguments or manipulate with emotional appeals. It means to start by listening to what that person has to say—to put yourself in his or her shoes and imagine how the world looks from his or her perspective. It is presumptuous, of course, to think that you can be totally successful in understanding those with whom you differ. (Just assuming you can understand them, after all, may well imply a sense of your own superiority.) But it is the engagement with others that counts—the willingness to keep talking and trying to understand.

The reading selection that follows illustrates how recognizing others can lead people into dialogue and open the possibility of mutual understanding. As you read, notice that the strategy of recognizing others differs in important respects from the standard moves of adversarial argument—refuting opposing views or making concessions to them.

AN ELECTRONIC EXCHANGE OF VIEWS

The following correspondence brings together two people who are strangers—a gay teacher and a Vietnam vet—joined in conversation on an electronic bulletin board by the technology of the Internet. While the two correspondents do not know each other personally, they are nonetheless engaged, as you will see, in a deeply personal dialogue.

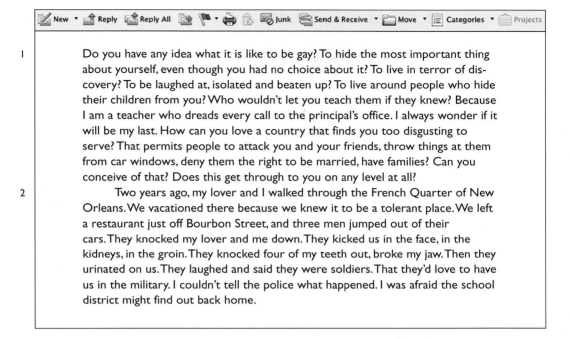

1   Do you have any idea what it is like to be gay? To hide the most important thing about yourself, even though you had no choice about it? To live in terror of discovery? To be laughed at, isolated and beaten up? To live around people who hide their children from you? Who wouldn't let you teach them if they knew? Because I am a teacher who dreads every call to the principal's office. I always wonder if it will be my last. How can you love a country that finds you too disgusting to serve? That permits people to attack you and your friends, throw things at them from car windows, deny them the right to be married, have families? Can you conceive of that? Does this get through to you on any level at all?

2   Two years ago, my lover and I walked through the French Quarter of New Orleans. We vacationed there because we knew it to be a tolerant place. We left a restaurant just off Bourbon Street, and three men jumped out of their cars. They knocked my lover and me down. They kicked us in the face, in the kidneys, in the groin. They knocked four of my teeth out, broke my jaw. Then they urinated on us. They laughed and said they were soldiers. That they'd love to have us in the military. I couldn't tell the police what happened. I was afraid the school district might find out back home.

And a reply:

1   I was very touched by your message, buddy. What happened to you was horrible, unsupportable. That's not what I lost three toes for in Vietnam, for scum to beat up on people like you and your friend. I fought so you could do whatever you wanted so long as you didn't hurt anybody or break the law. You and I have no quarrel. But we do have these problems, and I'll be straight with you about it, just like you were with me. Do you have any idea what it's like to be in a field or jungle or valley with bullets and shells blowing up all around you? With your friends being cut down, ripped apart, bleeding, dying right next to you screaming for their moms or kids or wives? Do you know how much trust and communication it takes to get through that? Do you have any idea what it's like to go through that if there's tension among you?

2   I'm not saying this can't be worked out. I'm saying, go slow. Don't come in here with executive orders and try to change things in a day that should take longer. Don't make me into a bigot because I know it takes an unbelievable amount of feeling to crawl down there into a valley of death. It takes love of your buddy. And that's something both of us can understand, right? But if you hate him, or fear him or don't understand him—how can you do it?

■ FOR CRITICAL INQUIRY

1. Describe the gay teacher's posting. What does his purpose seem to be? What kind of relationship is he trying to establish with his readers? How can you tell? What cues does he give readers about how he would like them to respond?

2. Consider the Vietnam vet's reply. What does he see as at stake in the gay teacher's posting? To what extent is he able to see things from the teacher's perspective? What is he getting at when he says, "You and I have no quarrel. But we do have these problems"? What, if anything, does the writer offer to work these problems out? To what extent does the Vietnam vet seem committed to a dialogue with the teacher?

3. Imagine that the gay teacher had replied to the Vietnam vet. What kind of response would help keep the dialogue open? What kind of response would tend to close it or turn it into a polarized argument?

4. The teacher and the vet are strangers. They do not know each other personally. What is the effect of such anonymity on this exchange of views?

5. Find someone who holds a position or represents a point of view that you don't share. Arrange an interview with the person. The point of the interview is to engage in a dialogue that can help you understand where the person is coming from and why. You will need to explain your own position or point of view, but your goal is not to argue with the other person. Instead, try to reach some understanding of how and why you differ. If you can, tape and transcribe the interview. Follow a presentation of the interview with your own account of what you learned about the differences that divide you and the other person. Indicate how or whether you changed your mind in any respect.

RECOGNIZING AMBIGUITIES AND CONTRADICTIONS

To negotiate differences is to recognize ambiguities and contradictions. Recognizing ambiguities and contradictions goes beyond acknowledging that there are differing sides, perspectives, and interests that divide people over particular issues. It further suggests that the positions people hold may themselves contain internal differences—that things may not be as simple as they seem at first glance, with views neatly arranged for and against.

Recognizing the ambiguities or contradictions in your position does not mean that you are abandoning what you believe in. It means that you maintain your views but are willing to talk about gray areas, troubling aspects, and conflicting loyalties.

ABORTION IS TOO COMPLEX TO FEEL ALL ONE WAY ABOUT

ANNA QUINDLEN

Anna Quindlen is a newspaper columnist and fiction writer. The following essay was first published in her column for the New York Times. *As you read, notice how Quindlen writes about the abortion debate by expressing a range of contradictory feelings.*

Abortion Is Too Complex to Feel All One Way About

It was always the look on their faces that told me first. I was the freshman dormitory counselor and they were the freshmen at a women's college where everyone was smart. One of them could come into my room, a golden girl, a valedictorian, an 800 verbal score on the SATs, and her eyes would be empty, seeing only a busted future, the devastation of her life as she knew it. She had failed biology, messed up the math; she was pregnant.

That was when I became pro-choice.

It was the look in his eyes that I will always remember, too. They were as black as the bottom of a well, and in them for a few minutes I thought I saw myself the way I had always wished to be—clear, simple, elemental, at peace. My child looked at me and I looked back at him in the delivery room, and I realized that out of a sea of infinite possibilities it had come down to this: a specific person born on the hottest day of the year, conceived on a Christmas Eve, made by his father and me miraculously from scratch.

Once I believed that there was a little blob of formless protoplasm in there and a gynecologist went after it with a surgical instrument, and that was that. Then I got pregnant myself—eagerly, intentionally, by the right man, at the right time—and I began to doubt. My abdomen still flat, my stomach roiling with morning sickness, I felt not that I had protoplasm inside but instead a complete human being in miniature to whom I could talk, sing, make promises. Neither of these views was accurate; instead, I think, the reality is something in the middle. And there is where I find myself now, in the middle, hating the idea of abortions, hating the idea of having them outlawed.

For I know it is the right thing in some times and places. I remember sitting in a shabby clinic far uptown with one of those freshmen, only three months after the Supreme Court had made what we were doing possible, and watching with wonder as the lovely first love she had had with a nice boy unraveled over the space of an hour as they waited for her to be called, degenerated into snipping and silences. I remember a year or two later seeing them pass on campus and not even acknowledge one another because their conjoining had caused them so much pain, and I shuddered to think of them married, with a small psyche in their unready and unwilling hands.

I've met 14-year-olds who were pregnant and said they could not have abortions because of their religion, and I see in their eyes the shadows of 22-year-olds I've talked to who lost their kids to foster care because they hit them or used drugs or simply had no money for food and shelter. I read not long ago about a teenager who said she meant to have an abortion but she spent the money on clothes instead; now she has a baby who turns out to be a lot more trouble than a toy. The people who hand out those execrable little pictures of dismembered fetuses at abortion clinics seem to forget the extraordinary pain children may endure after they are born.

I believe that in a contest between the living and the almost living, the latter must, if necessary, give way to the will of the former. That is what the fetus is to me, the almost living. Yet these questions began to plague me—and, I've discovered, a good many other women—after I became pregnant. But they became even more acute after I had my second child, mainly because he is so different from his brother. On two random nights 18 months apart the same two people managed to conceive, and on one occasion the tumult within turned itself into a curly-haired brunet with merry black eyes who walked and talked late and loved the whole world, and on another it became a blond with hazel Asian eyes and a pug nose who tried to conquer the world almost as soon as he entered it.

If we were to have an abortion next time for some reason or another, which infinite possibility becomes, not a reality, but a nullity? The girl with the blue eyes? The improbable redhead? The natural athlete? The thinker? My husband, ever at the heart of the matter, put it another way. Knowing that he is finding two children somewhat more overwhelming than he expected, I asked if he would want me to have an abortion if I accidentally became pregnant again right away. "And waste a perfectly good human being?" he said.

Coming to this quandary has been difficult for me. In fact, I believe the issue of abortion is difficult for all thoughtful people. I don't know anyone who has had an abortion who has not been haunted by it. If there is one thing I find intolerable about

most of the so-called right-to-lifers, it is that they try to portray abortion rights as something that feminists thought up on a slow Saturday over a light lunch. That is nonsense. I also know that some people who support abortion rights are most comfortable with a monolithic position because it seems the strongest front against the smug and sometimes violent opposition.

But I don't feel all one way about abortion anymore, and I don't think it serves a just cause to pretend that many of us do. For years I believed that a woman's right to choose was absolute, but now I wonder. Do I, with a stable home and marriage and sufficient stamina and money, have the right to choose abortion because a pregnancy is inconvenient right now? Legally I do have that right; legally I want always to have that right. It is the morality of exercising it under those circumstances that makes me wonder.

Technology has foiled us. The second trimester has become a time of resurrection; a fetus at six months can be one woman's late abortion, another's premature, viable child. Photographers now have film of embryos the size of a grape, oddly human, flexing their fingers, sucking their thumbs. Women have amniocentesis to find out whether they are carrying a child with birth defects that they may choose to abort. Before the procedure, they must have a sonogram, one of those fuzzy black-and-white photos like a love song heard through static on the radio, which shows someone is in there.

I have taped on my VCR a public-television program in which somehow, inexplicably, a film is shown of a fetus in utero scratching its face, seemingly putting up a tiny hand to shield itself from the camera's eye. It would make a potent weapon in the arsenal of the antiabortionists. I grow sentimental about it as it floats in the salt water, part fish, part human being. It is almost living, but not quite. It has almost turned my heart around, but not quite turned my head.

■ FOR CRITICAL INQUIRY

1. Although Quindlen characterizes the abortion debate as a "quandary," she nonetheless takes a position. What is it? What evidence does she use to support her position?

2. How does Quindlen describe the two sides in the debate? What does her attitude toward them seem to be? How does Quindlen locate her own position in relation to the two sides? How can you tell?

3. What do you think Quindlen is trying to accomplish by exploring the "quandary" of the abortion debate? How are readers likely to respond?

4. Think of an issue about which you have ambiguous or contradictory feelings. How could you plan an essay that explains your thinking?

LOCATING COMMON GROUND: CALL FOR A MORATORIUM ON EXECUTIONS

Locating common ground is built on the strategies we have just looked at but seeks to go one step further by identifying how people can join together, in spite of their differences, to address an issue of mutual concern. Locating common ground is a strategy for looking for ways out of the impasse of polarized debate. Instead of focusing on the arguments that divide people, it tries to establish basic points of agreement in order to get people talking to each other about what can be done. In this sense, locating common ground amounts to consensus building—forming alliances and coalitions with others.

As you can see, the "*New York Times* Ad Campaign" letter and the "Call for a Moratorium on Executions" advertisement seek to unite individuals and organizations, whether they support or oppose the death penalty.

No one would doubt that capital punishment has been one of the most divisive and volatile issues in American political life. Recently, however, there has been a growing dialogue among people who are worried that the death penalty is not being applied fairly, whether they support executions on principle or not. The "*New York Times* Ad Campaign" letter seeking support for the "Call for a Moratorium on Executions" ad shows how people who differ in fundamental beliefs about capital punishment can nonetheless find common ground and identify issues of shared concern.

The "*New York Times* Ad Campaign" and "Call for a Moratorium on Executions" are shown on the next two pages.

New York Times Ad Campaign

September 1999

Dear Friend,

Later this fall, the United Nations General Assembly is expected to vote on a resolution calling for a moratorium on executions worldwide. This vote will prove pivotal to the international community's vision of human rights as we enter the next millennium.

The reasons for a moratorium on executions *here in the US* are particularly compelling:

▶ Legal representation for most capital defendants – the vast majority of whom are indigent – is grossly inadequate. Poor people are most likely to be sentenced to death, and innocent people are inevitably going to be executed.

▶ Race continues to play a primary role in determining who lives and who dies.

▶ Juvenile offenders and the mentally disabled continue to be subject to executions despite international condemnation.

This reality led the American Bar Association, which has never taken a position for or against the death penalty, to call for an immediate halt on executions in 1997. The ABA has concluded that inequities in our system are so pervasive that they undermine confidence in the outcome of capital trials *and* appeals.

In 1998, the United Nations Commission on Human Rights issued a condemnatory report on the US death penalty, urging the US government to halt all executions while it brings the states into compliance with international standards and law.

Yet our nation's use of the death penalty is increasing. Already, 66 people have been executed this year. At this pace, the number of executions in 1999 could top 100, approaching rates last seen during the Great Depression.

The UN vote presents an international moment for citizens of the US to raise our voices for a moratorium.

We urge you to join us in signing an ad urging a moratorium to run in *The New York Times* in the weeks preceding the General Assembly's vote.

The ad statement is on the reverse side. Your name can be added for a gift $35. Organizational signatures are $50. Consider becoming a endorser for $100 or a co-sponsor for $1,000. We will send a copy of the final ad to all signers, and it will be published on our website, www.quixote.org/ej. *The deadline for signatures is November 4.*

Whether you support or oppose the death penalty, please stand with us publicly in this call for simple justice. We need to hear from you soon!

Sincerely,

Bianca Jagger
Human Rights Activist

Bud Welch
father of Oklahoma City
bombing victim, Julie Welch

Noam Chomsky
Professor of Linguistics, M.I.T.

Arthur Schlesinger, Jr.
Historian

Bishop Thomas J. Gumbleton
(Roman Catholic)

Susan Sarandon
Actress

The Very Rev. James Parks Morton
The Interfaith Center of New York

QUIXOTE CENTER
PURSUING JUSTICE, PEACE & EQUALITY
P.O. BOX 5206, HYATTSVILLE, MD 20782
301-699-0042 / [FAX] 301-864-2182 / WWW.QUIXOTE.ORG / EJUSA@QUIXOTE.ORG

(Ad Statement)

Call for a Moratorium on Executions

Signature Deadline: November 4

A Story from Death Row

  Anthony Porter was to be executed by the State of Illinois on September 23, 1998. Just 48 hours before his scheduled death, the Illinois Supreme Court granted a stay to consider last-minute questions about whether Porter, whose IQ is 51, should be legally barred from execution because he could not understand what was happening to him.

  The delay gave four Northwestern University journalism students time to conduct an independent investigation of the case. No physical evidence tied Porter to the 1982 double murder in Chicago. His conviction was based solely on eyewitness testimony. After visiting the crime scene, the students found that this testimony did not add up. With the aid of a private investigator, they began questioning witnesses. Thanks to the students' efforts, another man confessed to the murders for which Porter was almost executed. Porter was freed in February 1999 after 17 years on death row.

W e, the undersigned, are US citizens and organizations. Some of us support the death penalty and some oppose it. Yet we *all* join together today to call for an immediate moratorium on executions because of the way capital punishment is applied in our country.

  We support a moratorium because of the increasing risk of executing innocent people like Anthony Porter. Nationwide, 82* innocent death row prisoners have been released since 1973 – six in 1999 alone. Some were saved only days before their scheduled execution. The average time these prisoners spent on death row was seven years.[1] Efforts by courts and legislatures to speed up the time between conviction and execution mean that other prisoners likely have been and will be executed before their innocence is discovered. Porter's story is a painful reminder that all too often, a prisoner's innocence is discovered only because of the extraordinary and fortuitous efforts of people *outside* the system.

  We support a moratorium because – as the American Bar Association (ABA) has concluded – "fundamental due process is now systematically lacking in capital cases."[2] Porter's case is symptomatic of this crisis in death penalty jurisprudence. Like *90 percent* of those facing capital charges, Porter was too poor to hire his own attorney.

  Most indigent defendants suffer from grossly inadequate legal representation.[3] Furthermore, the US General Accounting Office has found "a pattern of evidence indicating racial disparities in charging, sentencing and imposition of the death penalty."[4] Many states continue to execute people who are mentally retarded or who were under age 18 at the time of their crimes or both – even in the face of nearly unanimous international condemnation.

  Unfairness and mistakes in the application of the death penalty are undermining public confidence in the criminal justice system and fueling the call for a moratorium. **More than 600* groups and tens of thousands of people across the US are now calling for an immediate halt to executions.** Among them is the ABA, which led the way in early 1997. Opinion polls show that many people in the US embrace alternatives to a death sentence if other means are taken to ensure that the guilty do not further endanger the innocent.[5]

I n the coming weeks, the United Nations General Assembly will vote on a resolution urging an international moratorium on executions. We note that many governments of the world are already observing a moratorium, while 105 countries have abandoned capital punishment in law or practice. We urge our government to join in the proposed UN resolution.

  We also urge President Clinton, all members of the US Congress, our respective governors and state legislators and members of our state and federal judiciary to enact an immediate moratorium on executions.

*Numbers will be updated at publication of ad as necessary.

[1] *Innocence and the Death Penalty: The Increasing Danger of Executing the Innocent*, Death Penalty Information Center, 1320 18th St. NW, 5th Floor, Washington, DC 20036, 202-293-6970, July 1997. See also www.essential.org/dpic.

[2] Report accompanying ABA Death Penalty Moratorium Resolution (107) adopted by the ABA House of Delegates in February 1997.

[3] Same as note 2. To date, no state has met *all* of the American Bar Association (ABA) policies for administration of the death penalty, including standards for representation for indigent defendants.

[4] *Death Penalty Sentencing: Research Indicates a Pattern of Racial Disparities,* General Accounting Office report, February 1990.

[5] See Death Penalty Information Center website at www.essential.org/dpic/po.html.

■ FOR CRITICAL INQUIRY

1. Analyze the argument presented in the "*New York Times* Ad Campaign" letter and the "Call for a Moratorium on Executions" ad. What is the main claim? What evidence is offered to support it? What enabling assumptions link the claim and evidence?

2. Explain what you see as the common ground the letter seeks to establish. What line of reasoning might lead someone who supports the death penalty to support the call for a moratorium on executions?

3. How do you think people who oppose the death penalty would respond to the letter and the ad?

4. Take up an issue that has divided your campus, your community, or the nation. Imagine ways to offer common ground on which people with polarized views might nonetheless join together in a shared undertaking such as the call for a moratorium on executions. What arguments would be needed to establish such a common ground?

RHETORICAL ANALYSIS OF AN ARGUMENT

The annotations on the sample analysis of the argument in "Call for a Moratorium on Executions" point out some of the things you can do in your own analysis of an argument.

SAMPLE ANALYSIS OF THE ARGUMENT IN "CALL FOR A MORATORIUM ON EXECUTIONS"

Shah 1

Vikram Shah
English 17
Prof. Sole
18 March 2003

Identifies the timing and purpose of the call

The "Call for a Moratorium on Executions," along with an accompanying letter, was sent out in September 1999 to solicit signatures and contributions for an ad in the *New York Times,* just before the United Nations General Assembly voted on a resolution calling for a moratorium on the death penalty. The Call focuses on the issue of capital punishment in the United States.

Shah 2

Summarizes the argument

It does not argue against the death penalty in principle. Instead, the Call argues that "[u]nfairness and mistakes in the application of the death penalty" are "undermining public confidence in the criminal justice system." In particular, the Call notes the lack of due process in capital cases, the inadequate legal representation of poor people charged with capital crimes, the racial disparities in the use of the death penalty, and the fact that juveniles and the mentally retarded are executed in the U.S. Since 1973, 82 innocent death row prisoners were released, due largely to efforts of people outside the criminal justice system, such as the Northwestern University journalism students who succeeded in freeing Anthony Porter in 1999, after another man confessed to the crime for which Porter was to be executed.

Describes the context of issues

The debate over the death penalty, of course, has long divided the American people. As the Call says the number of executions has been increasing in recent years. In general the American public supports capital punishment, although support has dropped from 80% in 1997 to 66% today. The Call, however, includes both supporters and opponents of the death penalty as its intended readers. By focusing on whether the death penalty is being applied fairly, the Call reaches out to both sides in the death penalty debate on the basis of people's shared beliefs in due process and justice.

Analyzes the rhetorical stance

Ethos

Pathos

The Call establishes its rhetorical stance by saying that some of us "support the death penalty and some oppose it." The ethos it projects is that of reasonable, concerned citizens and groups who are troubled by the current flaws in capital punishment. The tone is serious, and the Call seeks to enhance its authority and credibility by drawing on the conclusions of such reputable organizations as the American Bar Association and the General Accounting Office of the federal government. In terms of pathos, the Call appeals to readers who will be worried by unfairness in the current system and do not want to see innocent people executed. The inclusion of the Story from Death Row personalizes the policy issue of capital punishment and

Shah 3

Logos

gives it a sense of urgency and immediacy for readers. The logos of the Call sends the message that readers do not have to be against the death penalty to recognize that the system is not working the way it is supposed to.

Analyzes the parts of the argument

Claim

Evidence

The argument in the Call begins with the claim that executions should be suspended because of the unfairness of the system. The evidence includes the story about Anthony Porter, the number of innocent death row prisoners released since 1973, the American Bar Association's report that poor defendants lack adequate legal representation, and the General Accounting Office's finding of racial disparities in charging and sentencing in capital cases.

Enabling Assumptions

The enabling assumptions that link this evidence to the Call's claim are beliefs in due process and the right to competent legal counsel. These assumptions are backed up by the U.S. Constitution and the American legal tradition that everyone (rich or poor, black or white) is equal in the eyes of the law. The Call does not include either differing views or qualifiers in regard to its argument for a moratorium on executions.

Examines strategy for negotiating differences

Identifies type of issue

The major purpose of the Call is to provide a common ground on which both opponents and supporters of the death penalty can join together to deal with inequities in the present system. This emphasis on an issue of policy helps both to clarify the current situation of the death penalty and to allow the broadest group of readers to join the call for a moratorium. Some supporters of the death penalty might argue that a moratorium would permit guilty death row prisoners to evade capital punishment. Nonetheless, one of the enabling assumptions in the Call is that the concern for fairness and the public good is worth the risk. It is always difficult to know whether individual readers will be persuaded, but the Call's overall strategy of reaching out on the basis of fairness is certainly a reasonable one in the circumstances.

Evaluation of overall effectiveness

WRITING ASSIGNMENT

Analyzing an Argument

Your task is to write an essay that analyzes a short argument. Use the sample rhetorical analysis of an argument as a guideline, but be flexible in the way you approach the argument you're analyzing. What you emphasize will depend in large part on the nature of the argument you're analyzing.

Directions

1. Select a short argument (five to ten paragraphs is a good length). You can use one of the readings in this chapter or elsewhere in this book, a newspaper editorial or op-ed piece, a featured column in a newspaper or magazine, magazine commentary, political ads, or ads for advocacy groups as sources for your analysis.

2. Analyze the argument. Here are some guidelines for your analysis:

   ■ Summarize the argument. What is the main claim?

   ■ Identify the type of issue—substantiation, evaluation, policy.

   ■ Describe the context of issues. Is the argument part of an ongoing debate, discussion, or controversy? What positions have people taken in the past?

   ■ Describe the intended readers and explain how the argument seeks to influence them (to take action, support or oppose a policy, reconsider an established fact or belief, make a value judgment).

   ■ Analyze the rhetorical stance. How does the writer integrate ethos, pathos, and logos?

   ■ Analyze the parts of the argument—claim, evidence, enabling assumptions, differing views, qualifiers—and how the writer puts them together.

   ■ Examine any strategies used to negotiate differences.

   ■ Evaluate the overall effectiveness of the argument. Keep in mind that the goal of argument is to clarify reasonable differences as well as to convince others.

3. Use your analysis to write your essay. Begin by summarizing the argument. Then provide an analysis in the order that best suits your material. End with your evaluation of the argument's effectiveness. ■

writing projects

© Dan Jaeger/stock.xchng. Image altered for design purposes.

2

INTRODUCTION: GENRES OF WRITING

The term "genre" refers to different types of writing and the actions they enable writers to perform. We recognize genres in part by recurring textual features, such as the opening line "Once upon a time . . . " in fairy tales, the predictable parts of a laboratory report (Introduction, Methods, Results, Discussion), or a Facebook page. But we also recognize genres according to the characteristic way they respond to a rhetorical situation, when, for example, a music critic reviews the latest Coldplay or Beyoncé CD or Amnesty International circulates a petition to free a political prisoner. Based on their past experience with written texts, people fit what they read into patterns that provide them with information about how to understand and respond to the various genres that circulate in contemporary society.

Writing and Genre Knowledge

Similarly, writers draw on genre knowledge to make sense of the situations that call on them to write. As writers identify a call to write, they typically review past experience to help them determine the genre best suited to the current occasion. To do this, they look for recurring patterns:

- How is this writing situation similar to ones I've encountered in the past?

- How well do genres of writing I've used in the past match the demands of the present?

- Are there genres I haven't used before that fit this situation?

- What genre best fits my purposes, given the situation and the intended readers?

In the following chapters, you'll see how writers use various genres to respond to recurring writing situations. You'll see how writers' choice of genre takes into account the occasion that calls for writing, the writer's purposes, and the relationship the writer seeks to establish with readers.

While writing teachers do not always agree on how best to classify genres of writing, the eight chapters in Part Two offer practical examples of how writers use some of the most familiar genres. These chapters are by no means a comprehensive account of all genres of writing. Nor are the genres of writing fixed once and for all. New genres are always emerging in response to new conditions, as you can see in the proliferation of email, instant messaging, message boards, blogs, and Web sites. In the following chapters, some of the most common genres illustrate how writers respond to the call to write. You will find these genres helpful when you are called on to write in college, in the workplace, and in public life.

chapter 4

letters
thinking about
the genre

Letters are easy to recognize. They have a predictable format that usually includes the date of writing, a salutation ("Dear Jim"), a message, a closing (such as "Sincerely" or "Yours truly"), and a signature. There are many occasions for letter writing, and the genre of letters can be divided into a number of subgenres, such as personal letters, thank-you notes, email, text messages, business letters, letters to the editor, and letters of appeal. Nonetheless, letters are easy to identify because of the way they appear on the page, computer screen, or cell phone.

But it's not only the visual form that makes letters a distinct genre. Just as important is the way letters—along with their digital extension as email and instant messaging—address readers and establish a relationship between the writer and the reader. In a sense, the letter is the genre that comes closest to conversation between people. When you read a letter, you can almost hear the voice of the person writing to you. Letters are also like conversation in that letter writers typically seek to engage the reader in an ongoing interaction, often calling for a response—whether it's to RSVP a party invitation, attend a meeting, donate to a worthy cause, pay an overdue bill, or just write back.

One way that letters differ from conversation is that the person you're writing to can't talk back, at least not immediately. (Instant messaging is an interesting exception.) As a writer, you therefore have certain advantages. In a letter, you can talk directly to someone without being interrupted. And you know that the reader can return several times to your letter and reflect on its message before responding to you.

Thus, permanence is also a difference between letters and conversation. Once you've sent a letter, you can't take your words back as easily as you can in conversation. By expressing thoughts and feelings in a letter and sending it to someone, the letter writer may be taking a greater risk than by talking face to face or on the phone.

G. K. Chesterton once described the mailbox as "a sanctuary of the human heart" and the letter as "one of the few things left entirely romantic, for to be entirely romantic, a thing must be irrevocable." Many people save the letters they receive from relatives, friends, lovers, and other correspondents as a personal record of what their life was like at a particular time. There is a long tradition of letters in which writers reveal their deepest, most intimate thoughts to readers in a language that would be unimaginable in conversation—love letters, letters of advice, letters of friendship, letters of condolence, letters of despair, and letters written on the eve of death.

Other kinds of letters play just as important a role as personal letters in maintaining the social networks that link people together. In this chapter, we explore some familiar types of public letters—open letters, letters to the editor, and letters of appeal—as well as newer digital variations on the letter such as text messaging.

■ WRITING FROM EXPERIENCE

List the kinds of letters you write and receive, including email correspondence. Classify the letters according to the relationship they are based on—letters to and from family, letters to and from friends, love letters, letters to you as a consumer or a potential donor, letters from your college, and so on. Are there particular letters you wrote or received that are especially important to you? What makes these letters important? Do you save letters? If so, what kinds of letters, and why? Compare your answers with those of your classmates.

READINGS

OPEN LETTER

METH SCIENCE NOT STIGMA: OPEN LETTER TO THE MEDIA

As the following letter indicates, the media has been filled in recent years with sensationalistic accounts of "meth" or "ice" babies left in the wake of a nationwide methamphetamine epidemic. Circulated widely on the Internet by David C. Lewis and Donald G. Millar of Brown University, this open letter of July 25, 2005, was signed by ninety-two researchers and clinicians who study the effects of prenatal exposure to drugs.

July 25, 2005

Contact: David C. Lewis, M.D.
Professor of Community Health and Medicine
Donald G. Millar Distinguished Professor of Alcohol & Addiction
Studies
Brown University
Phone: 401-444-1818
E-Mail: David_Lewis@brown.edu

To Whom It May Concern:

1 Opening establishes credentials of open-letter signers and purpose of letter

As medical and psychological researchers, with many years of experience studying prenatal exposure to psychoactive substances, and as medical researchers, treatment providers and specialists with many years of experience studying addictions and addiction treatment, we are writing to request that policies addressing prenatal exposure to methamphetamines and media coverage of this issue be based on science, not presumption or prejudice.

2 Explains problem of stigmatizing labels

The use of stigmatizing terms, such as "ice babies" and "meth babies," lacks scientific validity and should not be used. Experience with similar labels applied to children exposed prenatally to cocaine demonstrates that such labels harm the children to which they are applied, lowering expectations for their academic and life achievements, discouraging investigation into other causes for physical and social problems the child might encounter, and leading to policies that ignore factors, including poverty, that may play a much more significant role in their lives.

Uses comparison as evidence

The suggestion that treatment will not work for people dependent upon methamphetamines, particularly mothers, also lacks any scientific basis.

3

Despite the lack of a medical or scientific basis for the use of such terms as "ice" and "meth" babies, these pejorative and stigmatizing labels are increasingly being used in the popular media, in a wide variety of contexts across the country. Even when articles themselves acknowledge that the effects of prenatal exposure to methamphetamine are still unknown, headlines across the country are using alarmist and unjustified labels such as "meth babies."

4

Just a few examples come from both local and national media:

Gives examples of stigmatizing labels

- CBS NATIONAL NEWS, "Generation of Meth Babies" (April 28, 2005) at CBSNews.com
- ARKANSAS NEWS BUREAU, Doug Thompson, "Meth Baby Bill Survives Amendment Vote" (Mar. 5, 2005)
- CHICAGO TRIBUNE, Judith Graham, "Only Future Will Tell Full Damage Speed Wreaks on Kids" ("At birth, meth babies are like 'dishrags'") (Mar. 7, 2004)

- THE LOS ANGELES TIMES, Lance Pugmire, "Meth Baby Murder Trial Winds Up" (Sept. 5, 2003 at B3)
- THE SUNDAY OKLAHOMAN, "Meth Babies" (Oklahoma City, OK; May 23, 2004 at 8A)
- APBNEWS.COM, "Meth Infants Called the New 'Crack Babies' (June 23, 2000).

5   Other examples include an article about methamphetamine use in the MINNEAPOLIS STAR TRIBUNE that lists a litany of medical problems allegedly caused by methamphetamine use during pregnancy, using sensationalized language that appears intended to shock and appall rather than inform, ". . . babies can be born with missing and misplaced body parts. She heard of a meth baby born with an arm growing out of the neck and another who was missing a femur." Sarah McCann, "Meth ravages lives in northern counties" (Nov. 17, 2004, at N1). In May, one Fox News station warned that "meth babies" "could make the crack baby look like a walk in the nursery." Cited in "The Damage Done: Crack Babies Talk Back," Mariah Blake, COLUMBIA JOURNALISM REVIEW Oct/Nov 2004.

6   *Concession*

Appeal to experience and expertise

Although research on the medical and developmental effects of prenatal methamphetamine exposure is still in its early stages, our experience with almost 20 years of research on the chemically related drug, cocaine, has not identified a recognizable condition, syndrome or disorder that should be termed "crack baby" nor found the degree of harm reported in the media and then used to justify numerous punitive legislative proposals.

7   *Gives definition of "addiction"*

The term "meth addicted baby" is no less defensible. Addiction is a technical term that refers to compulsive behavior that continues in spite of adverse consequences. By definition, babies cannot be "addicted" to methamphetamines or anything else. The news media continues to ignore this fact.

Further examples

- A CNN report was aired repeatedly over the span of a month, showing a picture of a baby who had allegedly been exposed to methamphetamines prenatally and stating: "This is what a meth baby looks like, premature, hooked on meth and suffering the pangs of withdrawal. They don't want to eat or sleep and the simplest things cause great pain." CNN, "The Methamphetamine Epidemic in the United States," Randi Kaye. (Aired Feb. 3, 2005–Mar. 10, 2005).
- One local National Public Radio station claims that "In one Minnesota County, there is a baby born addicted to meth each week." (Found at news.minnesota.publicradio.org from June 14, 2004).

8

Provides research findings

In utero physiologic dependence on opiates (not addiction), known as Neonatal Narcotic Abstinence Syndrome, is readily diagnosable and treatable, but no such symptoms have been found to occur following prenatal cocaine or methamphetamine exposure.

9

Similarly, claims that methamphetamine users are virtually untreatable with small recovery rates lack foundation in medical research. Analysis of dropout, retention in treatment and re-incarceration rates and other measures of outcome, in several recent studies indicate that methamphetamine users respond in an equivalent manner as individuals admitted for other drug abuse problems. Research also suggests the need to improve and expand treatment offered to methamphetamine users.

10

Questions media sources

Too often, media and policymakers rely on people who lack any scientific experience or expertise for their information about the effects of prenatal exposure to methamphetamine and about the efficacy of treatment. For example, a NEW YORK TIMES story about methamphetamine labs and children relies on a law enforcement official rather than a medical expert to describe the effects of methamphetamine exposure on children. A police captain is quoted stating: "Meth makes crack look like child's play, both in terms of what it does to the body and how hard it is to get off." (Fox Butterfield, Home Drug-Making Laboratories Expose Children to Toxic Fallout, Feb. 23, 2004 A1)

11

Points out policy implications

How to access signers of open letter

We are deeply disappointed that American and international media as well as some policymakers continue to use stigmatizing terms and unfounded assumptions that not only lack any scientific basis but also endanger and disenfranchise the children to whom these labels and claims are applied. Similarly, we are concerned that policies based on false assumptions will result in punitive civil and child welfare interventions that are harmful to women, children and families rather than in the ongoing research and improvement and provision of treatment services that are so clearly needed.

12

Please click here for a pdf version of the open letter with the complete list of signatures.

13

Offers further assistance

We would be happy to furnish additional information if requested or to send representatives to meet with policy advisors, staff or editorial boards to provide more detailed technical information. Please feel free to contact David C. Lewis, M.D., 401-444-1818, David_Lewis@brown.edu, Professor of Community Health and Medicine, Brown University, who has agreed to coordinate such requests on our behalf.

Analysis: Responding to the Call to Write

"Meth Science Not Stigma: Open Letter to the Media" offers a good example of how open letters respond to a shared sense of urgency on the part of a group of people, in this case leading medical and psychological researchers. Notice how the letter first establishes the credentials of the signers and next identifies the occasion for writing, namely the media coverage of "meth" babies. To establish the reality of the problem, the letter provides examples and then examines two particular fallacies in the media accounts—the idea that newborns can be addicted and the claim that methamphetamine users cannot be treated. Throughout, the letter uses scientific evidence to correct what the signers argue is flawed and misleading coverage in the media.

■ FOR CRITICAL INQUIRY

1. Describe the ethos of the letter. How does it establish the signers' credibility? What role does it give the authority of science?

2. Examine the argument in the letter. How does it support the claim that media coverage of "meth" babies is stigmatizing? How does the letter connect such a claim to wider policy consequences in the last paragraph? What assumptions enable this connection?

3. Notice the open letter is addressed to "To Whom It May Concern." Why do you think the writers used this convention? What does it reveal about who they imagine their audience to be?

LETTERS TO THE EDITOR

The newspaper column and letters to the editor presented in this section follow a cycle of writing that is common in newspapers—a pattern of call and response where the writers respond to the views of those who wrote before them. First, newspaper columnist Mark Patinkin of the *Providence Journal-Bulletin* wrote a column on an item in the news: the authorities in Singapore had sentenced Michael Fay, an American teenager who lived there, to be caned as a punishment for spray-painting cars. Patinkin's column led to a round of letters, including those from Kristin Tardiff and John N. Taylor.

Reprinted by permission of Mark Patinkin, Providence Journal

THE COLUMN

Commit a crime, suffer the consequences

Mark Patinkin

At their best, columnists are supposed to leave people thinking, "That's just how I feel and didn't know it until reading that." Well, it took reading a column by an 18-year-old student to crystallize my own feelings about an issue I've been perusing day to day.

The Singapore caning case: The American teenager who's about to be flogged because he spray-painted several cars. From the start, I'd viewed it as a barbaric punishment for a poor kid who just did a little mischief. Then I read a column by an 18-year-old telling Michael Fay, the convicted American, to take it like a man, and learn from it.

Something in me instantly said, "She's right."

Yes, I know caning is harsh, but am I the only one who's tired of Michael Fay's whining? Am I the only one who feels President Clinton has better things to do than to write letters appealing for leniency?

Singaporeans get caned all the time for vandalism. Are we Americans supposed to be exempt when we break their laws? What are we — princes?

I'll tell you what else I'm tired of: Michael Fay's father — his biological father here in America — traveling the country insisting his precious boy didn't do it.

It's a setup, the father says. Supposedly, he says, Michael only pleaded guilty as a bargain with the police — after the local cops leaned on him — with the promise of little punishment.

But suddenly the judge sentenced him to six strikes with a cane.

Not once have I read Michael's parents saying their child was out of line. They just make excuses. Gee, I wonder if a life of such excuse-making is part of why he's so troubled.

See, that's the other line here. First, the father says he didn't do it. Then he says, well, Michael also has personal problems, like Attention Deficit Disorder. I happen to think that's a legitimate syndrome, but not for excusing crimes like vandalizing cars.

All this is just part of the new American game of always saying, "It's not my fault." No one, when caught, seems ready to admit having done wrong anymore. They just whine and appeal. As in: "Your honor, the stabbing was not my client's fault. He had a bad childhood. And was caught up in a riot at the time. In fact, he's not a criminal at all, he's one of society's victims."

That's Michael Fay. All those cars he spray-painted? Not his fault. He's had a hard life.

I might have had sympathy for him if he'd only said, "I admit it. I did a dumb thing. I was with the wrong crowd and crossed the line into criminality. I deserve to pay. And I'm truly sorry for the victims."

But we're not hearing that.

There's another thing. Many articles on this — including a paragraph in a column I wrote — have referred to what Michael Fay did as "mischief."

Well, it's not. It's hardcore vandalism. He spray-painted a bunch of cars.

Michael Fay might want to think about what it feels like to the car owners. Anyone whose car has been vandalized knows. Personally, I've had about four car stereos stolen. I still remember the shock — each time — of seeing the broken window and the damage. I remember having to take a good half day out of work to deal with it. And during the times I had little money, I remember how badly it pinched to have to pay the deductible on the insurance.

Finally, I remember how creepy and unnerving it was. It took weeks before I could approach my car again without feeling nervous. It erodes your trust in the world. And it's worse for women, I think, who feel a heightened vulnerability to crime in the first place.

In short, it's beyond mischief, beyond obnoxious — it's vandalism. A violation. And it's downright mean-spirited.

But after he was caught, Michael Fay and his family have been telling the world that he — not the car owners but HE — is the victim.

Sorry, Michael, you're not the victim. You're the criminal. Caning may well be rough.

But if you do the crime, you've got to pay the price.

Mark Patinkin is a Journal-Bulletin columnist. His column appears in Lifebeat each Tuesday and Thursday, and in the Metro section each Sunday.

KRISTIN TARDIFF, LETTER TO THE EDITOR

To the Editor,

I wonder why I continue to read Mark Patinkin's columns. At best they bore me, at worst they anger me. I've thought before of responding to his maudlin whining or self-righteous hypocrisy, but this time I really had to put pen to paper.

Mr. Patinkin has chosen this time to attack Michael Fay, the 18-year-old boy who has been accused of spray-painting some cars in Singapore. Mark, jury of one, has decided that Fay is unequivocally guilty, and that his sentence of jail term, fine, and caning is fitting punishment. "Stop whining, take it like a man," he says.

I find it interesting that Mr. Patinkin has completely ignored the statements of those who may have a little more experience with the Singaporean police than he does. What about the Navy officer who said that our military police were under order to immediately take into custody any American soldier who was going to be arrested by the Singaporean police to protect them? Did he make that up? What about those who have had the experience of being detained in Singapore and tell of torture and forced confessions? Are they just wimpy bleeding hearts in Mark's eyes?

Perhaps as a teenager Mr. Patinkin never made a mistake, never did anything considered wrong in the eyes of the law. Hard to believe, but I'll give him the benefit of the doubt. Had he, however, ever been caught and punished for some infraction, that punishment certainly would not have involved being tied up with his pants around his ankles while someone split his cheeks the opposite way with a water-soaked cane. Nor do I think he would have considered that just. The punishment should fit the crime.

Michael Fay is willing to serve his time in jail and make restitution. He has already suffered physically and psychologically, and has, I'm sure, seen the error of his ways. Is this not enough punishment? Have we become so warped by the violence of our society that we now see justice as incomplete without the imposition of physical pain? Do we really want to see the young graffiti artist in our neighborhood caned? (I hear some saying yes, but what if it turns out to be your child? Think about it.) Is this really the way we want society to turn? What comes next? Amputation for thieves and maybe prolonged torture and death for drug dealers? Should we just kill all the "bad" people? Why can't we for once work on the causes instead of lashing out blindly at the symptoms?

Just one more thing. Regarding Mr. Patinkin's criticism of Fay's parents' pleas for leniency for their son, as a parent he should have more empathy. What else can parents do when they truly feel that their child is being unjustly treated?

I hope Mark's children all turn out as perfect as their dad. Maybe he should send to Singapore for a cane. Just in case.

Kristin Tardiff
Providence

JOHN N. TAYLOR, LETTER TO THE EDITOR

To the Editor,

1   The letters . . . denouncing Mark Patinkin's support for caning Michael Fay ("Patinkin should know better than to advocate caning," 5/3) are no different from any of the other whiny, moralizing claptrap we hear from those mawkish people who fear more for Mr. Fay's buttocks than for those who are victimized everyday by the crimes of young punks like Fay. The arguments . . . are laden with the rancid, canting self-righteousness common to all opposing Fay's caning, and evince concern only for the criminal while telling crime victims to go eat cake.

2   From Ms. Tardiff, we get a lot of sarcasm, a lot of questions, and no answers. If she can't propose any semblance of an idea for controlling crime, then neither she (nor anyone else) has the moral authority to condemn a nation which has come up with its own means of dealing with criminals. . . .

3   Singapore has in recent years carried out canings of 14 of its own citizens who were convicted of offenses similar in nature to those of Mr. Fay. Why should Fay be treated any differently from these people? Just because Fay is an affluent white American with many powerful supporters in America (like President Clinton) doesn't mean he should be above the law of the nation where he resides. To let Fay out of the caning simply because he has the support of powerful leaders is an affront to the people of Singapore, who have abided by the law or taken their lumps for violating same. Clemency for Fay would effectively divide Americans and Singaporeans into separate, unequal classes, whereby the former avoid punishment because of America's political and economic clout while the latter, who do not enjoy such powerful connections, suffer the consequences.

4   The caning of Fay is simply an affirmation of the principle that all people, whether they are wealthy white Americans or poor Chinese Singaporeans, are equal in the eyes of the law. . . . It has much to do with upholding Singaporean mores and nothing to do with Fay being American or U.S. political traditions; these sanctions, as applied to crimes like vandalism and other non-political offenses, are designed to discourage repetition of criminal behavior. And they succeed in this goal. How many drive-by shootings go down in Singapore?

5   Like American authorities, the Singaporeans perceive crimes to be the individual act and choice of the perpetrator.

6   There is no doubt Singapore is a non-democratic nation which punishes even peaceable political dissent, and there is no doubt that Singapore's criminal laws are harsh. But Michael Fay knew what the laws were like and freely assumed the risks of getting punished when he engaged in his spree of vandalism. It is the height of arrogance and folly for Americans living or traveling abroad to expect to be protected by the Bill of Rights when they break other nations' laws.

7   Americans have no right demanding a blanket exemption from foreign laws they violate, or that foreign governments give them easier treatment than they would give their own people under similar circumstances.

8   And if caning is immoral, is not the American criminal justice system itself laden with unfairness? Where is the morality in releasing quadruple murderer Craig Price into the community after only four years? Is it right that in the U.S., a murderer draws an average sentence of only about six years? Is it right that dangerous criminals are dumped onto communities simply because the prisons don't meet the standards of some soft-headed judge? We in America sacrifice the lives of innocent people in the name of criminals' civil rights, and then have the gall to denounce Singapore as harsh and oppressive! If anyone's justice is extremist, it is America's.

9   America's approach to crime is to do nothing and let the community be damned, while Singapore has opted to let the offender be damned. What the Michael Fay fan club here in America conveniently forgets while moaning about Singaporean tyranny is the everyday tyranny of violence and fear imposed on millions of Americans by violent criminals in our inner cities and suburbs. These people are oppressed by a dictatorship of criminals and their rights are violated on a massive scale every day. Yet I see more concern for Michael Fay's rear end than I do for people who bear the scars of bullets and knives of criminals.

10   My heart will not bleed if Fay's rear end does. Given the carnage on America's streets, and in Rwanda, Bosnia and Haiti, the supporters of Michael Fay will just have to excuse me if I fail to shed a tear.

John N. Taylor Jr.
North Providence

Analysis: A Public Forum

Like a lot of newspaper columnists, Mark Patinkin uses short paragraphs, an informal, conversational tone, and a commonsense man-in-the-street approach to his readers. Notice that he speaks to his readers as an equal, not as someone who is more knowledgeable or somehow above them. This approach in effect positions the column as something that readers can and should respond to. The controversial nature of the topic—and of some of Patinkin's comments about the topic—make it all the more likely that readers will respond.

In the letters to the editor, the writers argue a position in response to what they've read. The letters to the editor reveal an intensity of feeling, and at times they resort to logical fallacies and other questionable tactics. These tactics include name-calling: Kristin Tardiff refers to Patinkin's "maudlin whining" and "self-righteous hypocrisy." By the same token, John N. Taylor says Tardiff's letter contains the "whiny, moralizing claptrap" of "mawkish people." The writers use exaggeration: "What comes next? Amputation for thieves and maybe prolonged torture and death for drug dealers?" (Tardiff). They are not always completely accurate: "in the U.S., a murderer draws an average sentence of only about six years" (Taylor). At times, they beg the question instead of explaining the point: "What else can parents do?" (Tardiff) and make questionable comparisons: "If caning is immoral, is not the American justice system laden with unfairness?" (Taylor). The letters are definitely opinionated, and finally that is the point: letters to the editor give people the chance to talk back, to take strong positions, to have their say in a public forum.

■ FOR CRITICAL INQUIRY

1. Reread Tardiff's letter to the editor. What is it about Patinkin's column that seems to call on her to respond? How does she define her own position in relation to what Patinkin has written? To what extent does her letter respond directly to Patinkin's column? To what extent does it introduce other issues?

2. Reread the letter from Taylor. How would you describe his response to the call to write? How does he define his own position in relation to Patinkin and Tardiff?

3. What is this exchange of letters really about? Although the letters are ostensibly about Michael Fay, his punishment doesn't exactly seem to be the main issue. Try to distill the main issues that emerge and explain how the letters relate to these issues and to each other. What is at stake for these writers?

TEXT MESSAGES

THE PLEASURES OF THE TEXT

CHARLES McGRATH

Charles McGrath is a writer at large for the New York Times, *where this brief article appeared in "The Way We Live Now" section of the* New York Times Magazine *January 22, 2006.*

There used to be an ad on subway cars, next to the ones for bail bondsmen and hemorrhoid creams, that said: "if u cn rd ths u cn gt a gd job & mo pa." The ad was promoting a kind of stenography training that is now extinct, presumably. Who uses stenographers anymore? But the notion that there might be value in easily understood shorthand has proved to be prescient. If u cn rd these days, and, just as important, if your thumbs are nimble enough so that u cn als snd, you can conduct your entire emotional life just by transmitting and receiving messages on the screen of your cellphone. You can flirt there, arrange a date, break up and—in Malaysia at least—even get a divorce.

A WORLD OF TEXT

Text messages sent, by country, in the third quarter of 2005.
- China   76.4 billion
- Philippines   21.4 billion
- United States[*]   19.4 billion
- United Kingdom   8.1 billion

[*] The figure for the United States is based on the four major carriers (Cingular, Verizon, Sprint Nextel and T-Mobile).

Source: Informa Telecoms & Media

Lauren Greenfield/INSTITUTE

Shorthand contractions, along with letter-number homophones ("gr8" and "2moro," for example), emoticons (like the tiresome colon-and-parenthesis smiley face) and acronyms (like the ubiquitous "lol," for "laughing out loud"), constitute the language of text-messaging—or txt msg, to use the term that txt msgrs prefer. Text-messaging is a refinement of computer instant-messaging, which came into vogue five or six years ago. But because the typical cellphone screen can accommodate no more than 160 characters, and because the phone touchpad is far less versatile than the computer keyboard, text-messaging puts an even greater premium on concision. Here, for example, is a text-message version of "Paradise Lost" disseminated by some scholars in England: "Devl kikd outa hevn coz jelus of jesus&strts war. pd'off wiv god so corupts man (md by god) wiv apel. devl stays serpnt 4hole life&man ruind. Woe un2mnkind."

As such messages go, that one is fairly straightforward and unadorned. There is also an entire code book of acronyms and abbreviations, ranging from CWOT (complete waste of time) to DLTBBB (don't let the bedbugs bite). And emoticonography has progressed way beyond the smiley-face stage, and now includes hieroglyphics to indicate drooling, for example (:-) . . .), as well as secrecy (:X), Hitler (/.#() and the rose (@};–). Keep these in mind; we'll need them later.

As with any language, efficiency isn't everything. There's also the issue of style. Among inventive users, and younger ones especially, text-messaging has taken on many of the characteristics of hip-hop, with so much of which it conveniently overlaps—in the substitution of "z" for "s," for example, "a," for "er" and "d" for "th." Like hip-hop, text-messaging is what the scholars call "performative"; it's writing that aspires to the condition of speech. And sometimes when it makes abundant use of emoticons, it strives not for clarity so much as a kind of rebus-like cleverness, in which showing off is part of the point. A text-message version of "Paradise Lost"—or of the prologue, anyway—that tries for a little more shnizzle might go like this: "Sing hvnly mewz dat on d :X mtntp inspyrd dat shephrd hu 1st tot d chozn seed in d begnin hw d hvn n erth @};– outa chaos."

Not that there is much call for Miltonic messaging these days. To use the scholarly jargon again, text-messaging is "lateral" rather than "penetrative," and the medium encourages blandness and even mindlessness. On the Internet there are several Web sites that function as virtual Hallmark stores and offer ready-made text messages of breathtaking banality. There are even ready-made Dear John letters, enabling you to dump someone without actually speaking to him or her. Far from being considered rude, in Britain this has proved to be a particularly popular way of ending a relationship—a little more thoughtful than leaving an e-mail message but not nearly as messy as

breaking up in person—and it's also catching on over here.

Compared with the rest of the world, Americans are actually laggards when it comes to text-messaging. This is partly for technical reasons. Because we don't have a single, national phone company, there are several competing and incompatible wireless technologies in use, and at the same time actual voice calls are far cheaper here than in most places, so there is less incentive for texting. But in many developing countries, mobile-phone technology has so far out-stripped land-line availability that cellphones are the preferred, and sometimes the only, means of communication, and text messages are cheaper than voice ones. The most avid text-messagers are clustered in Southeast Asia, particularly in Singapore and the Philippines.

There are also cultural reasons for the spread of text-messaging elsewhere. The Chinese language is particularly well-suited to the telephone keypad, because in Mandarin the names of the numbers are also close to the sounds of certain words: to say "I love you," for example, all you have to do is press 520. (For "drop dead," it's 748.) In China, moreover, many people believe that to leave voice mail is rude, and it's a loss of face to make a call to someone important and have it answered by an underling. Text messages preserve everyone's dignity by eliminating the human voice.

This may be the universal attraction of text-messaging, in fact: it's a kind of avoidance mechanism that preserves the feeling of communication—the immediacy—without, for the most part, the burden of actual intimacy or substance. The great majority of text messages are of the "Hey, how are you, whassup?" variety, and they're sent sometimes when the messenger and the recipient are within speaking distance of each other—across classrooms, say, or from one row of a stadium to another. They're little electronic waves and nods that, just like real waves and nods, aren't meant to do much more than establish a connection—or a disconnection, as the case may be—without getting into specifics.

"We're all wired together" is the collective message, and we'll signal again in a couple of minutes, not to say anything, probably, but just to make sure the lines are still working. The most depressing thing about the communications revolution is that when at last we have succeeded in making it possible for anyone to reach anyone else anywhere and at any time, it turns out that we really don't have much we want to say.

Analysis: txt msg

Many commentators have noted that instant messages and text messages are examples of how new communication media have blurred the line between speaking and writing that seemed so set in print culture. Writing takes on some of the aspects of speech. Instant messaging, for example, enables the immediacy of spoken conversation, while text messages are a form of writing that goes through the telephone—and in many parts of the world provides a cheaper alternative to the phone call.

Though these forms of communication resemble speech in some ways, they have also developed new visual codes for writing that are maximally compact, inventive, and playful. What may be most significant about text messages is how they have reconfigured the available modes of communication—speaking, writing, and visual communication.

■ FOR CRITICAL INQUIRY

1. Consider the relations among speaking, writing, and visual communication in instant messages and text messages. How are the new forms like or unlike older ways of communicating? How do they resemble letters? How are they different? How do they put the modes of communication together in new ways?

2. If you have access to instant messaging sessions, analyze an exchange or two. What questions would you use to examine the language and the interactions that take place?

3. The visual display "A World of Text" reports by country the number of text messages sent in the third quarter. Do some research to update these figures. What do you see as the significance of the comparative data?

4. Charles McGrath ends his article on a rather dismissive note, saying that the attraction of text messaging is that it's an "avoidance mechanism." For him, the "most depressing thing about the communication revolution" is that people have very little to say. What enabling assumptions might lead to such claims? Are there other ways you can think of to evaluate the use of text messaging?

LETTERS OF APPEAL

DOCTORS WITHOUT BORDERS/MEDECINS SANS FRONTIERES (MSF)

Doctors Without Borders/Médecins Sans Frontières (MSF) delivers emergency medical care to people in crisis in nearly eighty countries worldwide. An independent, international humanitarian organization, MSF was awarded the Nobel Peace Prize in 1999.

Analysis: The Visual Design of Letters of Appeal

This letter from Doctors Without Borders (next page), along with an enclosed report on the medical costs of war in the Democratic Republic of Congo, is typical of the letters of appeal that humanitarian and advocacy groups rely on to bring their work to public attention. The letter includes such standard features as the organization name and logo on the letterhead, a salutation (the familiar "Dear Friend"), a signature, and a P.S. Notice also how selective underlining adds a sense of urgency to the letter. The accompanying report describes how Doctors Without Borders provides medical care to victims of the war.

■ FOR CRITICAL INQUIRY

1. Logos are symbols that identify organizations. Think, for example, of the Nike swoosh or the CBS eye. What does the Doctors Without Borders logo seem to represent? What does it suggest about the organization? Consider, too, how the logo is used.

2. Notice that the actual appeal for contributions appears at the bottom of the letter. Why do you think it is located there? Explain how the writing that precedes it sets up the appeal.

3. What sort of relationship does this letter want to establish with readers? What assumptions about intended readers does the letter seem to make?

4. How does the enclosed report support the letter's appeal?

MÉDECINS SANS FRONTIÈRES
DOCTORS WITHOUT BORDERS

Awarded the 1999
Nobel Peace Prize

333 Seventh Avenue, 2nd Floor
New York, NY 10001

Tel: (212) 679-6800
Fax: (212) 679-7016

Web: www.doctorswithoutborders.org

Dear Friend,

In September 2008, I was checking on a clinic in the town of Sake in North Kivu province in the eastern Democratic Republic of Congo. Violent fighting had recently broken out close to the town—and it was getting worse. As head of logistics for Doctors Without Borders/Médecins Sans Frontières (MSF), I was there to see if the roads around the town were still passable and to see if the clinic needed help caring for the war-wounded.

I will never forget that day. Entire families stood anxiously in the doorways of their homes, listening to the rumble of artillery explosions in the hills to the west of town and hoping they wouldn't have to run and leave everything behind. Suddenly, something changed–and thousands of women, children, and men were flooding the streets in panic. With straw mats, blankets, and water jugs in hand, they fled for their lives.

With no choice but to flee with them, we made room in our car for as many people as we could–including three pregnant women and their young children. For just that brief moment, I experienced what daily life is like for literally hundreds of thousands of people who have known nothing but violence, displacement, and terror for the past 15 years.

Thanks to your support, Doctors Without Borders has been a consistent provider of urgently needed medical care throughout the war. And as the fighting continues to escalate, we need your continued support more than ever.

We have treated thousands of children and women who have been wounded, beaten, or raped in a war that has trapped the most vulnerable in a chaos of lawlessness and violence. We work in overstretched hospitals and clinics and send teams by car, motorcycle, bicycle, and even on foot to bring medical care to families in remote villages and to those uprooted from their homes who have found shelter with generous local families or in overcrowded camps.

In June, four children came down with measles in a huge camp of recently displaced people on the outskirts of Kitchanga in North Kivu province. We immediately ordered more than 100,000 doses of the vaccine and all the supplies and equipment needed to mount a mass vaccination campaign. We hired local community members to tell people when and where to bring their children. Meanwhile, the disease was spreading–80 cases on day two, 140 on day three. By day four, were vaccinating children: 7,000 one day, 10,000 the next.

With your support, our medical teams vaccinated 80,000 children against measles–the vast majority in just six weeks. In doing so, we averted what could have been a devastating measles epidemic.

Meanwhile, the war goes on. Year after year everyone waits, and waits, to see if the latest round of violence will bring a period of calm. Year after year people are disappointed. I stayed long enough to live through two of these cycles. The already displaced are displaced again, and then again. Another agricultural season is missed. Another school year is missed. Another relative is lost to violence or preventable illness.

As the front lines move, so the people move, and so must Doctors Without Borders move to find them. In Masisi province, we discovered 10,000 people who had fled to a region so insecure that they were completely cut off from any kind of assistance, trapped between different front lines of fighting. After intense negotiations with militia leaders on all sides of the conflict, our mobile clinic team of five nurses, a doctor, and two logisticians finally made it. And we went back every week, as security allowed, to make sure they had access to primary medical care.

Each time we went back, hundreds of people were there to greet us. They were so appreciative that we had made the effort to find them–and to know that they had not been forgotten. That someone was there to listen to their stories.

Doctors Without Borders is the only international organization delivering medical care to some of the most insecure parts of North Kivu. Our neutrality, our medical work, and our reputation allow us to work on all sides of the front lines–thanks to your generosity. It is your financial support that gives us the independence to provide humanitarian assistance that is neutral and impartial, that is based on need alone.

I originally signed up to work in the Congo for three months. But I was so moved by the constant fighting, displacement, and human suffering that are as much a part of the landscape as the volcanoes in this beautiful terrain that I stayed 14 months. And despite the distance, a part of me is still out there with those who are not lucky enough to be able to make the decision to leave.

As I write, I know from colleagues in the region that the situation has worsened even further. Please give generously so that we can continue to deliver medical care to those who need it the most.

Sincerely,

Andre Heller

Andre Heller
Logistics Coordinator
North Kivu, Democratic Republic of Congo

P.S. The day after 35,000 people fled Sake, I returned to find a ghost town where once a bustling market town stood. The nurse in charge of the clinic was locking its doors, on his way to join those who had fled to camps. This is what war does. What we do at Doctors Without Borders is to make sure that as many children, women, and men as possible survive–thanks to the support of people like you.

DRC:

TREATING VICTIMS OF WAR

In August 2008, after 10 years of simmering conflict, tensions in the North Kivu province of the Democratic Republic of Congo (DRC) exploded into outright war.

Fighting between government forces and rebel groups has displaced some 250,000 people since August. The violence has turned an already disastrous situation into a humanitarian catastrophe as people weakened by years of fighting are forced to flee again and again. Cholera, measles, and other deadly diseases are rampant.

Doctors Without Borders/Médecins Sans Frontières (MSF) is in the midst of this volatile situation that changes from hour to hour. Currently 778 staff are delivering critical medial care throughout North Kivu.

Read this report to see how our teams near the embattled eastern towns of Kitchanga, Rushuru, and the provincial capital, Goma, are treating war-wounded victims, battling contagious outbreaks, and providing essential medial aid to internally displaced people (IDP) who are desperate and exhausted from constantly running for their lives.

MÉDECINS SANS FRONTIERES
DOCTORS WITHOUT BORDERS

Dominic Nahr/Oeil Public

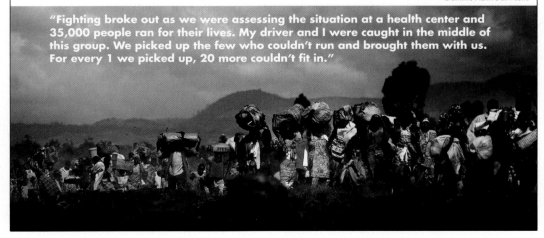

"Fighting broke out as we were assessing the situation at a health center and 35,000 people ran for their lives. My driver and I were caught in the middle of this group. We picked up the few who couldn't run and brought them with us. For every 1 we picked up, 20 more couldn't fit in."

"People are literally fleeing into the wild..."

Dominic Nahr/Oeil Public

After years of displacement, people are struggling with fragile health. Doctors Without Borders runs medical clinics at two camps for internally displaced people (IDP) in Kitchanga which have about 42,000 people, where our teams treat respiratory infections, cholera, and measles.

"Conditions are desperate," said Annie Desilets, Doctors Without Borders project coordinator. "Kitchanga is at a high altitude, so it rains and it's cold. A lot of people don't have blankets or plastic sheeting to get away from the rain. They get food when they can, but it's not enough to sustain a family of seven or eight people. **We're providing water and health care but basic survival is difficult.**

"A lot of families are fleeing into the bush. They are vulnerable to the elements and the fighting. In the Kitchanga and Mweso areas, we have set up mobile clinics to reach people who cannot reach us.

"**It's not always easy to find displaced people. We go to an area one week where there is a village and we go back the next week and it's empty.** Are they in a camp where we can provide health care? Or are they hiding in the bush where we cannot access them? We don't know."

Together, we can save more lives.

Civilians Caught in the Crossfire

In early November, intense fighting erupted around Rushuru. Doctors Without Borders teams were trapped inside the hospital, treating war-wounded patients while listening to the sound of heavy shelling outside. **In one two-day period, our surgical teams worked around the clock treating 80 severely injured victims, including children.**

Sixteen-year-old J. was critically injured during fighting in the nearby Nyanzale area. **"We were caught between two groups shooting at each other,"** he said. "Suddenly there was a heavy blast next to me. I fell and lost consciousness. When I woke up, my younger brother was screaming. I felt a heavy pain in my left arm and looked down. It was totally destroyed."

"When J. arrived at the hospital, he was in really bad shape," said François, Doctors Without Borders' head of surgery in Rutshuru, where J. was brought by our field team for help. "He had lost a lot of blood, was unconscious, and needed an operation right away. **The surgeons tried to save his arm or part of it, but it wasn't possible. The bone was too damaged to be saved."**

Sven Torfinn/Panos Pictures

"When there are explosions or gunfire, you don't have time to take your belongings. If you're working in your field, you leave everything and flee."

DISPLACED MAN IN KIBATI

Espen Rasmussen/Panos Pictures

Alarming Spike in Cholera

Massive population displacement led to multiple outbreaks of cholera in November, especially in the area around Goma. Cholera, which causes uncontrollable vomiting and diarrhea, is highly contagious. It can spread like wildfire in crowded IDP camps where there is poor sanitation and lack of clean water. **If untreated, the disease can kill with devastating speed, often within hours of the onset of symptoms.**

In Goma, Doctors Without Borders treated 190 cholera patients in the first three weeks of the month. At the same time, our teams treated an average of 60 patients a week in the nearby town of Minova. And in Kibati camp, just north of the city, **Doctors Without Borders treated 188 patients in our cholera treatment center, 48 of them in just three days.** Our teams are continuing to truck clean water into the camp to control the spread of the disease.

Although the number of new cases began to decrease toward the end of the month, Doctors Without Borders teams remain vigilant against further outbreaks of this lethal illness.

Sven Torfinn/Panos Pictures

MEDECINS SANS FRONTIERES
DOCTORS WITHOUT BORDERS

Thanks to your support, we can save more lives.

$35   Purchases one kit of basic reusable instruments for dressing wounds.

$75   Purchases enough vaccine to inoculate 37 people against measles, which kills half a million children each year, according to the World Health Organization.

$100   Purchases equipment to chlorinate enough water to provide 1,773 people with 20 gallons of clean water per day for 7 days.

$500   Purchases 1,250 doses of antibiotics to fight bacterial infections.

Please won't you help today?

AWARDED THE 1999 NOBEL PEACE PRIZE **WWW.DOCTORSWITHOUTBORDERS.ORG** • 333 SEVENTH AVENUE, 2ND FLOOR, NEW YORK, NY 10001 • 888-392-0392

LETTER AS ESSAY

MY DUNGEON SHOOK: LETTER TO MY NEPHEW
JAMES BALDWIN

James Baldwin (1924–1987) was a novelist, playwright, and essayist, whose works include the essays Notes of a Native Son *(1955), the novels* Go Tell It on the Mountain *(1953) and* Another County *(1962), and the play* Blues for Mister Charlie *(1964). This letter from Baldwin to his nephew was published in* The Fire Next Time *(1962).*

Dear James:

1   I have begun this letter five times and torn it up five times. I keep seeing your face, which is also the face of your father and my brother. Like him, you are tough, dark, vulnerable, moody—with a very definite tendency to sound truculent because you want no one to think you are soft. You may be like your grandfather in this, I don't know, but certainly both you and your father resemble him very much physically. Well, he is dead, he never saw you, and he had a terrible life; he was defeated long before he died because, at the bottom of his heart, he really believed what white people said about him. This is one of the reasons that he became so holy. I am sure that your father has told you something about all that. Neither you nor your father exhibit any tendency towards holiness: you really are of another era, part of what happened when the Negro left the land and came into what the late E. Franklin Frazier called "the cities of destruction." You can only be destroyed by believing that you really are what the white world calls a *nigger*. I tell you this because I love you, and please don't you forget it.

2   I have known both of you all your lives, have carried your Daddy in my arms and on my shoulders, kissed and spanked him and watched him learn to walk. I don't know if you've known anybody from that far back; if you've loved anybody that long, first as an infant, then as a child, then as a man, you gain a strange perspective on time and human pain and effort. Other people cannot see what I see whenever I look into your father's face, for behind your father's face as it is today are all those other faces which were his. Let him laugh and I see a cellar your father does not remember and a house he does not remember and I hear in his present laughter his laughter as a child. Let him curse and I remember him falling down the cellar steps, and howling, and I remember, with pain, his tears, which my hand or your grandmother's so easily wiped away. But no one's hand can wipe away those tears he sheds invisibly today, which one hears in his laughter and in his speech and in his songs. I know what the world has done to my brother

and how narrowly he has survived it. And I know, which is much worse, and this is the crime of which I accuse my country and my countrymen, and for which neither I nor time nor history will ever forgive them, that they have destroyed and are destroying hundreds of thousands of lives and do not know it and do not want to know it. One can be, indeed one must strive to become, tough and philosophical concerning destruction and death, for this is what most of mankind has been best at since we have heard of man. (But remember: most of mankind is not all of mankind.) But it is not permissible that the authors of devastation should also be innocent. It is the innocence which constitutes the crime.

3   Now, my dear namesake, these innocent and well-meaning people, your countrymen, have caused you to be born under conditions not very far removed from those described for us by Charles Dickens in the London of more than a hundred years ago. (I hear the chorus of the innocents screaming, "No! This is not true! How *bitter* you are!"—but I am writing this letter to *you,* to try to tell you something about how to handle *them,* for most of them do not really know that you exist. I *know* the conditions under which you were born, for I was there. Your countrymen were *not* there, and haven't made it yet. Your grandmother was also there, and no one has ever accused her of being bitter. I suggest that the innocents check with her. She isn't hard to find. Your countrymen don't know that *she* exists, either, though she has been working for them all their lives.)

4   Well, you were born, here you came, something like fourteen years ago; and though your father and mother and grandmother, looking about the streets through which they were carrying you, staring at the walls into which they brought you, had every reason to be heavy-hearted, yet they were not. For here you were, Big James, named for me—you were a big baby. I was not—here you were: to be loved. To be loved, baby, hard, at once, and forever, to strengthen you against the loveless world. Remember that: I know how black it looks today, for you. It looked bad that day, too, yes, we were trembling. We have not stopped trembling yet, but if we had not loved each other none of us would have survived. And now you must survive because we love you, and for the sake of your children and your children's children.

5   This innocent country set you down in a ghetto in which, in fact, it intended that you should perish. Let me spell out precisely what I mean by that, for the heart of the matter is here, and the root of my dispute with my country. You were born where you were born and faced the future that you faced because you were black and *for no other reason.* The limits of your ambition were, thus, expected to be set forever. You were born into a society which spelled out with brutal clarity, and in as many ways as possible,

that you were a worthless human being. You were not expected to aspire to excellence: you were expected to make peace with mediocrity. Wherever you have turned, James, in your short time on this earth, you have been told where you could go and what you could do (and *how* you could do it) and where you could live and whom you could marry. I know your countrymen do not agree with me about this, and I hear them saying, "You exaggerate." They do not know Harlem, and I do. So do you. Take no one's word for anything, including mine—but trust your experience. Know whence you came. If you know whence you came, there is really no limit to where you can go. The details and symbols of your life have been deliberately constructed to make you believe what white people say about you. Please try to remember that what they believe, as well as what they do and cause you to endure, does not testify to your inferiority but to their inhumanity and fear. Please try to be clear, dear James, through the storm which rages about your youthful head today, about the reality which lies behind the words *acceptance* and *integration*. There is no reason for you to try to become like white people and there is no basis whatever for their impertinent assumption that *they* must accept *you*. The really terrible thing, old buddy, is that *you* must accept *them*. And I mean that very seriously. You must accept them and accept them with love. For these innocent people have no other hope. They are, in effect, still trapped in a history which they do not understand; and until they understand it, they cannot be released from it. They have had to believe for many years, and for innumerable reasons, that black men are inferior to white men. Many of them, indeed, know better, but, as you will discover, people find it very difficult to act on what they know. To act is to be committed, and to be committed is to be in danger. In this case, the danger, in the minds of most white Americans, is the loss of their identity. Try to imagine how you would feel if you woke up one morning to find the sun shining and all the stars aflame. You would be frightened because it is out of the order of nature. Any upheaval in the universe is terrifying because it so profoundly attacks one's sense of one's own reality. Well, the black man has functioned in the white man's world as a fixed star, as an immovable pillar: and as he moves out of his place, heaven and earth are shaken to their foundations. You, don't be afraid. I said that it was intended that you should perish in the ghetto, perish by never being allowed to go behind the white man's definitions, by never being allowed to spell your proper name. You have, and many of us have, defeated this intention; and, by a terrible law, a terrible paradox, those innocents who believed that your imprisonment made them safe are losing their grasp of reality. But these men are your brothers—your lost, younger brothers. And if the word *integration* means anything, that is what it means: that we, with love, shall force our brothers to see themselves as they are, to cease fleeing from reality and begin to change it. For this is your home, my friend, do not be driven from it, great men have done great things here, and will again, and we can make America what America must become. It will be hard, James, but you come from sturdy, peasant stock, men who picked cotton and dammed rivers and built railroads, and, in the teeth of the most terrifying odds, achieved an unassailable and monumental dignity. You come from a long line of great poets, some of the greatest poets since Homer. One of them said, *The very time I thought I was lost, My dungeon shook and my chains fell off.*

6   You know, and I know, that the country is celebrating one hundred years of freedom one hundred years too soon. We cannot be free until they are free. God bless you, James, and Godspeed.

Your Uncle,
James

Analysis: Private and Public Audiences

Of all the genres of writing gathered in this book, letter writing may appear to be the most personal and the most intimate. As James Baldwin writes to his nephew, "I keep seeing your face."

But as the opening lines of Baldwin's letter indicate—"I have begun this letter five times and torn it up five times"—writing on such intimate terms can bring with it certain complications, especially in this case, because Baldwin actually has two audiences, his nephew and a public audience of readers.

On the one hand, Baldwin represents himself as a concerned and loving uncle writing a letter of advice to his namesake nephew, thereby invoking the sacred institution of the family as the ground to speak. On the other hand, the advice he offers his nephew—to accept white people without accepting their definitions of him—is meant to be overheard by Baldwin's other audience.

When Baldwin explains to his nephew that white people are trapped in a history of race relations they don't understand and can't escape, he is also explaining to his white readers how their own identities have been based on a belief in the inferiority of African Americans. By using the form of a letter of advice from one family member to another, Baldwin is simultaneously offering his white readers a way to reposition themselves in relation to their own history and identities.

■ FOR CRITICAL INQUIRY

1. Where in the letter does Baldwin first indicate his main point and reason for writing to his nephew? Mark this passage and explain why you think he locates his main point here. How does this passage connect what comes before and what follows?

2. A good deal of the long fifth paragraph involves Baldwin's admonition to his nephew "to be clear . . . about the reality that lies behind the words *acceptance* and *integration*." What is the reality Baldwin alludes to here? What does he see as the relation between "acceptance" and "integration"? What assumptions have led him to this view?

3. Baldwin wrote a number of essays concerning race relations in the United States. In this instance, however, he has chosen the more personal form of a family letter addressed directly to his nephew but published for all to read. How does this traditional letter of advice from an older family member to a younger one influence the way you read the letter? What advantages do you see in Baldwin's strategy of addressing his nephew instead of the more anonymous audience of people who read *The Fire Next Time,* in which "My Dungeon Shook: Letter to My Nephew" appeared? Are there things Baldwin can say to his nephew that he can't say directly to this audience?

ETHICS OF WRITING

USING THE INTERNET

One of the most exciting aspects of the Internet is its capacity to open up new public forums for the exchange of ideas. A posting from an individual to a mailing list or message board can connect him or her to people all over the world with an immediacy that promotes rapid feedback and response. But precisely because email offers such exciting possibilities for transmitting information and ideas, it is important to use it properly—to understand what can be sent to whom under what conditions.

❏ **Author's permission:** Communicating on the Internet requires the same attention to copyright and intellectual property as print communication. In other words, you need to cite your sources, and if you want to forward a message written by someone else, you need to secure permission first.

❏ **Reader's permission:** Don't just assume that people will want to be added to a regular mailing list or newsgroup. You need to secure people's permission before adding their names. Readers are likely to resent unsolicited email and feel imposed upon. Be careful not to flood cyberspace with junk email. ■

FURTHER EXPLORATION: LETTERS

■ RHETORICAL ANALYSIS

Analyze the writer's argument in one of the letters included in this chapter. Pay particular attention to how the writer establishes a rhetorical stance that combines the persuasive appeals of ethos, pathos, and logos. See guidelines and a sample rhetorical analysis of an argument in Chapter 3.

■ GENRE CHOICES

Like letters, email, chat rooms, newsgroups, and listservs are forms of correspondence that enable writers to stay in touch and exchange views. Despite this similarity, there are also significant differences between letters and these new electronic genres. Draw on your own experience to examine the similarities and differences between print letters and electronic correspondence. Take into account the occasions when it makes sense to use one or the other. When, for example, is it better to write a letter than email? Or, given something urgent to say, when would you write a letter to the editor, to a politician, or to an organization, and when would you post your views online?

WRITING ASSIGNMENT

Letters

Here are some possibilities:

■ An open letter to a public official, organization, or company arguing for policy change.

■ A letter to your parents or to a friend explaining the impact of a public event on you personally, how you make sense of it, and, if appropriate, what you have done or plan to do.

■ A letter to the editor of a newspaper or magazine responding to a news story, feature article, editorial, or column that particularly moved you. Or you might raise an issue that's important to you but hasn't yet appeared in the press.

■ A letter to a younger relative or student. You might use James Baldwin's letter to his nephew as a model here. That is, speak directly to the younger person but include a public audience as your intended readers. You might explain what it takes to survive in college or how to handle particular kinds of peer-group pressures such as drinking, drugs, and sex. Or you might explain what it's like to be a scholarship athlete, a woman, an African American, a gay or lesbian, a Latino, or a working-class student in a middle-class college.

- A letter of appeal, calling on readers to support a cause, take an action, or make a contribution. You can identify an organization or cause that you believe deserves support, and design a letter that presents the aims and activities of the organization and that calls on readers to do something—to become a member, to send a donation, to write a letter. You may want to design this letter of appeal for the Internet.

- A posting to an electronic discussion group.

Invention

Identifying the Call to Write

Identify something that moves you to write.

- Has a particular subject been making you curious or angry?
- Are you learning something in one of your courses that you want to tell someone about?
- Have you recently read something in a newspaper or magazine that you'd like to respond to?
- Is there a public issue in your community, on campus, at home, or on the national or international scene that has captured your interest?

■ EXERCISE

Writing a Statement of Purpose

Write a statement of purpose, using these questions to guide you:

1. What calls on you to write?
2. What do you want to accomplish in your letter? What are you going to say?
3. To whom are you writing? How do you want your reader to respond?

Understanding Your Readers

How successful you will be in eliciting the response you want from your readers depends in part on how well you understand them and your relationship to them. To gather ideas about how you can most effectively address your reader, respond to these questions:

1. On what terms do you know your reader: family, personal, institutional? Describe your relationship to the person. Is it formal or informal? How does this relationship affect what you can and cannot say in your letter? If you are writing online, how does the electronic forum of the Internet affect your relationship to your reader?

2. What is an effective way to present yourself to your reader? What will it take to establish the credibility and authority of what you have

to say? What kind of personality or attitude is your reader likely to respond to?

3. What attitude is your reader likely to have toward your letter? What is your reader's interest in what you have to say? Will your reader care personally or read your letter as part of work?

4. What is your reader likely to know about the message you are sending? How much shared information is involved? How much do you need to explain?

5. What values and beliefs do you think your reader might hold about the subject of your letter? What common ground can you establish? What shared values can you appeal to?

Background Research: Finding Models

To determine how to communicate with your readers, find some models of the type of letter you want to write.

1. What is the occasion that calls on people to write the letters?

2. How do writers define the rhetorical situation? How do they develop a rhetorical stance? Consider here especially the ethos of the letter—the attitude and personality that it projects.

3. Consider the formal features of the letter. Do paragraphs tend to be short or long or vary? What is the tone of voice—how formal or informal? Are there any notable ways the letter uses language?

Planning

Establishing the Occasion

Letters often begin by establishing their timeliness: why they're written at that moment, in response to what call to write, to what person or people, on the basis of what relationship. Notice the ways in which writers establish the occasion in the reading selections:

- Explaining the writers' professional credentials ("Meth Science Not Stigma")

- Establishing authority to speak and familiarity with the topic (Kristin Tardiff, regular reader of Mark Patinkin's column)

- Characterizing an opponent's position, expressing sense of outrage (John N. Taylor, "whiny, moralizing claptrap")

- Locating the writer in a scene (Doctors Without Borders, "In September 2008, I was checking on a clinic in the town of Sake")

- Invoking family ties as the right to speak (James Baldwin)

In your letter, you need to design an opening that treats the occasion of the letter and your relationship to the reader. How explicitly you do this will depend on what your reader needs to hear. Politicians, businesspeople, government officials, and newspaper editors all appreciate letters that get right to the point. In letters home and other personal letters, staying in touch (as much as or more than the letter's content) may be the main point of writing.

Arranging Your Material

List the points you want to make and the information you want to include in your letter. Arrange the material in an outline that consists of three sections:

1. **Opening:** To establish occasion, relationship, and the point of the letter.
2. **Main body:** To explain and develop the point of the letter, whether that means concentrating on one main topic or including a number of separate topics.
3. **Closing:** To reiterate the main point of the letter, whether that involves calling for action, firing a final salvo, reaffirming your relationship to the reader, sending regards, or thanking the reader for his or her time.

Working Draft

Once you have a list of the main points, write a working draft. As you write, new ideas may occur to you. Don't censor them by trying rigidly to follow your list of points. Instead, try to incorporate new points by connecting them to the ones you have already listed. If you can connect them, the new points probably belong in the letter. If you can't, then you'll need to think carefully about whether they really fit your letter. As you write your working draft, keep in mind the overall movement you want in your letter—from an opening that sets the occasion, to a main body that explains your key points, to a closing that wraps things up for the reader.

Beginnings and Endings: Using an Echo Effect

One effective way to begin and end your letter may be to use an echo effect by looping back in the ending to issues raised in your opening. This echo effect can provide a satisfying sense of closure because it reminds readers of the major themes you introduced earlier.

Andre Heller uses an echo effect in his letter on behalf of Doctors Without Borders. In the opening paragraph, he describes the situation in the town where he was working, "Sake in North Kivu province in the eastern Democratic Republic of Congo":

> Violent fighting had recently broken out close to the town—and it was getting worse. As head of logistics for Doctors Without Borders/Médecins Sans Frontière (MSF), I was there to see if the roads around the town were still passable and to see if the clinic needed help caring for the war-wounded.

Then, after detailing the work of Doctors Without Borders in North Kivu province, Heller returns to his own situation: "I originally signed up to work in the Congo for three months. But I was so moved by the constant fighting, displacement, and human suffering that are as much a part of the landscape as the volcanoes in this beautiful terrain, that I stayed 14 months." Using this testimony of personal commitment to close the letter, Heller creates a heightened sense of urgency about donating to MSF by noting "that the situation has worsened even further."

You may want to try this echo effect in your own writing. Take a look at your opening and see if you find a theme that you would like to have recur in your closing. Or think about adding a theme to your introduction that you will return to at the end of your letter.

Using Topic Sentences

Topic sentences help to guide readers by establishing a paragraph's focus and by explaining how the paragraph is linked to earlier ones. The most common type of topic sentence appears at the beginning of a paragraph and thereby enables readers to anticipate what is to come in the rest of the paragraph. When writers stick to the topic they've announced in the opening topic sentence, paragraphs are easier to follow. They unify the letter, since they don't digress or run off the point. Notice how Mark Patinkin uses a topic sentence in the following paragraph from his column about the Michael Fay caning. The first sentence (which we have italicized in the example) establishes the focus of the paragraph; then the rest of the sentences explain it more fully:

> *All of this is just part of the new American game of always saying, "It's not my fault."* No one, when caught, seems ready to admit having done anything wrong anymore. They just whine and appeal. As in: "Your honor, the stabbing was not my client's fault. He had a bad childhood. And was caught up in a riot at the time. In fact, he's not a criminal at all, he's one of society's victims."

Topic sentences also link paragraphs together. To keep readers oriented to the train of thought as it moves from paragraph to paragraph, writers often show how a particular paragraph's focus is linked to the paragraphs that precede and follow.

Sometimes topic sentences appear at the end of a paragraph instead of the beginning. Building toward the topic sentence can give a paragraph a powerful dramatic structure. James Baldwin uses this type of dramatic structure in the second paragraph of his letter by moving from the personal toward a general point about the "crime of which I accuse my country and my countrymen":

> I have known both of you all your lives, . . . I know what the world has done to my brother and how narrowly he has survived it. And . . . this is the crime of which I accuse my country and my countrymen, and for which neither I nor time nor history will ever forgive them, that they have destroyed and are destroying hundreds of thousands of lives and do not know it and do not want to know it.

> One can be, indeed one must strive to become, tough and philosophical concerning destruction and death, for this is what most of mankind has been best at since we have heard about man. (But remember: most of mankind is not all of mankind.) But it is not permissible that the authors of devastation should also be innocent. *It is the innocence which constitutes the crime.*

By the end of this paragraph, Baldwin has worked his way from a loving tribute about his brother to a painful critique of society's destruction. The topic sentence at the end of the paragraph (which we have italicized here for emphasis) sets Baldwin up to make a transition that links his "countrymen's" crime of innocence to the next paragraph:

> Now, my dear namesake, these innocent and well-meaning people, your countrymen, have caused you to be born under conditions not very far removed from those described for us by Charles Dickens in the London of more than a hundred years ago.

Peer Commentary

Exchange working drafts with a classmate. Depending on your teacher's direction, you can do this peer commentary electronically via email or a class listserv. In classes without computer access, you will probably want to write your comments either on your classmate's paper itself or on a separate sheet of paper. Comment on your partner's draft by responding to these questions:

1. What is the occasion of the letter? Where in the letter did you become aware of the writer's purpose? Be specific—is there a particular phrase, sentence, or passage that alerted you to the writer's purpose? If not, where would you like this information to be?

2. What kind of relationship does the writer seem to want to establish with the reader? How does the writer seem to want the reader to respond? How can you tell? Are there places where you think the writer should make the relationship or the desired response more explicit?

3. Does the writer address the reader in a way that makes a positive response likely or possible? Explain your answer. What could the writer do to improve the chances of making the impression he or she wants?

4. Describe the tone of the letter. What kind of personality seems to come through in the letter? What identity does the writer take on in the letter? Do you think the intended reader will respond well to it? If not, what might the writer change?

Revising

Review the peer commentary you received about your letter. Based on the response to your working draft, consider the following points to plan a revision:

1. Have you clearly defined the occasion and your purpose?

2. Does the letter establish the kind of relationship with your reader that you want?

3. Do you think your reader will respond well to the way you present yourself?

4. Do you think you accomplished your purpose with your letter?

Once you are satisfied with the overall appeal of your letter, you can fine-tune your writing. You might look, for example, at your topic sentences to see if they establish focus and help the reader see how ideas are linked in your letter.

Strengthening Topic Sentences for Focus and Transition

The following two paragraph excerpts show how one student, Michael Brody, worked on his letter to the editor (the final version appears below in Writers' Workshop). Notice how he clarifies the focus of the third paragraph by rewriting the topic sentence so that it emphasizes what "readers need to understand" about the Singapore government's use of the Michael Fay case. Clarifying the focus in paragraph 3's topic sentence also strengthens the transition between paragraphs and makes it easier for readers to see how the ideas in the two paragraphs are linked.

---

2   . . . As readers point out, the crime rate in Singapore is low, the streets are

safe, and there are no drive-by shootings. While this picture of Singapore may

appear to be reassuring to some readers, it hides the fact that beneath a

polished, secure, and business-like facade Singapore is ruled by a brutal

dictatorship that keeps its people in fear by punishing not only vandalism and

spraypainting but chewing gum as antisocial crimes.

  Readers need to understand how the

3   . . . ~~Michael Fay's actions were~~ [admittedly immature and illegal], ~~calling for~~

  Michael Fay case is being used by the Singapore government as

~~some official response. But this should not blind us to the problems in~~

  a lesson to its own people about the decadence of American ways

~~Singapore and how the government is using the Michael Fay case.~~ The leaders

of Singapore are portraying Michael Fay as a living illustration of all that's

flawed about American values of freedom and individual rights., *and his admittedly*

  immature and illegal actions are held up as a

  direct consequences of the American way of life.

Mark Patinkin and his supporters have failed to see . . .

W WRITERS' WORKSHOP

Michael Brody wrote the following letter to the editor in a first-year writing class after he read Mark Patinkin's column "Commit a Crime, Suffer the Consequences," which appeared in the *Providence Journal-Bulletin* on April 19, 1994 (he then followed with two more letters to the editor on May 3 and May 9, 1994). As you will see, entering the caning debate at this point enables Brody to summarize positions people have already taken as a way to set up his own main point. The letter to the editor is followed by a commentary Brody wrote to explain his approach to the issue.

MICHAEL BRODY, LETTER TO THE EDITOR

To the Editor:

Mark Patinkin's column "Commit a crime, suffer the consequences" (4/19) has generated heated responses from readers and understandably so. For some, the sentence of six strokes of the cane, at least by American standards, does indeed seem to be "cruel and unusual punishment," no matter what Patinkin writes about Michael Fay's "whining." On the other hand, Patinkin and those readers who side with him are right that Michael Fay is the criminal in this case, not the victim, and that he deserves to suffer the consequences of his actions.

I happen to agree with readers who argue for leniency. Let Michael Fay pay for his crime by fines and a jail sentence. It worries me that some readers are willing to tolerate or even endorse caning. Obviously, these sentiments show how fed up Americans are with the problem of crime in our society. But there is a tendency in some of the pro-Patinkin letters to idealize Singapore's strong measures as a successful get-tough solution to crime. As readers point out, the crime rate in Singapore is low, the streets are safe, and there are no drive-by shootings. While this picture of Singapore may appear to be reassuring to some readers, it hides the fact that beneath a polished, secure, and business-like facade Singapore is ruled by a brutal dictatorship that keeps its people in fear by punishing not only vandalism and spraypainting but chewing gum as antisocial crimes.

Readers need to understand how the Michael Fay case is being used by the Singapore government as a lesson to its own people about the decadence of American ways. The leaders of Singapore are portraying Michael Fay as a living illustration of all that's flawed about American values of freedom and individual rights, and his admittedly immature and illegal actions are held up as direct consequences of the American way of life. Mark Patinkin and his supporters have failed to see how the Michael Fay incident is more than a matter of whether America, unlike Singapore, is soft on crime, coddles law breakers, and ignores the true victims. For the Singapore government, the caning of Michael Fay is a stern warning to the people of Singapore against the dangers of American democracy.

What is ironic about this attempt to use Michael Fay for anti-American purposes is the fact that caning is itself not a traditional Singapore means of punishment. It's tempting to think of caning as the barbaric practice of cruel Asian despots, but in reality Singapore learned about caning from the British colonial powers who once ruled the country. The British Empire, as I'm sure Mark Patinkin is well aware, took a tough stand on law and order in the colonies and routinely crushed native movements for freedom and independence. I wish Mark Patinkin and others who are properly concerned about crime would consider the lessons Singapore leaders learned from their former masters about how to control and intimidate those they rule. Caning is not a matter of different national customs, as some people make it out to be. Nor is it an extreme but understandable response to crime in the streets. In Singapore, caning is part of both a repressive judicial system and a calculated propaganda campaign to discredit democratic countries and silence dissent.

Michael Brody
Worcester, MA

When I read Mark Patinkin's column, I got angry and wanted to denounce him as a fascist. Then I read the letters readers had written opposing or supporting Patinkin's point of view, and they made me realize that I didn't want to follow them because they all seemed to be too emotional, just gut responses. I wanted to find a different approach to the whole caning incident so that I could raise an issue that was different or had been overlooked.

Now I must admit that when I first heard about the sentence of caning, I thought it was barbaric, probably something typical of Asian dictatorships. I thought of the massacre at Tiananmen Square, and I dimly recalled what I had heard when I was young about how the Chinese Communists tortured Catholic missionaries, stuff like bamboo slivers under the fingernails. Then I read somewhere that caning was brought to Singapore by the British in colonial days, and I started to think along new lines. It occurred to me that maybe the caning wasn't just about crime but had something to do with how governments ruled their people.

As I read more in the newspapers, *Time,* and *Newsweek* about the incident, I was shocked to discover how Michael Fay was being used by Singapore leaders to build up anti-American sentiment, to paint America as a permissive society that coddled its criminals. I decided that I'd try to write something that looked at how the case was being used by Singapore's rulers. The more I thought about it, this seemed to give me an angle to go beyond agreeing or disagreeing with Patinkin's column and still have something interesting to say.

When I was getting ready to write, I made a quick outline of my points. I wanted to sound reasonable so I decided to concede that both sides, for or against caning, had some valid points. I decided to show this in my opening and wait until the second paragraph to indicate where I was coming from. I wanted to create the effect that there's this debate going on, which I figured readers would know about and already have their own opinions about, but that I had an angle people maybe hadn't thought about. So I tried to get this point to emerge in the second paragraph and then drive it home at the beginning of the third paragraph with the sentence that starts "Readers need to understand . . . "

That sentence set me up to give my own analysis of the incident and of how Patinkin and the pro-caning people failed to see the full political picture. I decided to leave the idea that caning came from British colonial powers until the end as my clincher. I figured this would do two things. First, it would surprise people, who like me thought caning was a barbaric Asian punishment. Second, it would have an emotional charge because I assumed most people would be against colonialism, especially British colonialism, given that America had to fight England for our independence. Besides I'm Irish, and I know a lot of people where I live are against the British in Ireland, and I knew they'd be against anything associated with the British empire.

I'm not totally sure the irony I talk about in the opening line of the last paragraph works. I remember learning about irony in English class in high school, and how funny or odd it is when things don't turn out the way you expected. So I wanted to throw that in, to make readers feel, well I thought it was one way but when you look at it again, it's another way. I thought this might work in the very end to show that caning is not just this (a barbaric national custom) or that (an extreme form of punishment) but also a form of political intimidation.

■ WORKSHOP QUESTIONS

1. When you first read Michael Brody's letter to the editor, at what point did you become aware of his perspective on the caning debate? Is it just a matter of being for or against caning? Note the sentence or passage that enabled you to see where Brody is coming from.

2. Brody devotes considerable space in the first two paragraphs to presenting positions people have already taken on the caning debate.

What kind of relationship does he seem to want to establish with his readers by doing so?

3. Describe the tone Brody uses in the letter. How does it compare to the tone in Mark Patinkin's column and in the letters to the editor from Kristin Tardiff and John N. Taylor? Do you think Brody's tone works well? Explain your response.

4. Reread Brody's commentary. If you could talk to him, how would you respond to what he says about composing his letter?   ■

REFLECTING ON YOUR WRITING

Use the commentary Michael Brody wrote as a model for writing your own account of how you planned and composed the letter you wrote. Explain how you defined the call to write and how you positioned yourself in relation to your readers, your topic, and what others had already said about your topic (if that applies to your letter). Notice that Brody explains how he developed his own position by considering what others had said and reading newspapers and magazines on the Michael Fay incident. Explain, as Brody does, in a step-by-step way how you composed your letter, what effects you were trying to achieve, and what problems or issues emerged for you along the way. Indicate any aspects of the letter that you're not certain about. Add anything else you'd like to say.

chapter 5

memoirs

THINKING ABOUT THE GENRE

Writing a *memoir,* as the word itself suggests, involves memory work. Memoirists draw on their pasts, looking back at events, people, and places that are important to them, in order to re-create, in written language, moments or episodes of lived experience. This re-creation of particular experiences distinguishes memoir from the genre of autobiography, which seeks to encompass an entire life. But memoirists don't just re-create moments of experience—they seek to imbue them with a significance readers will understand.

The call to write memoirs comes in part from the desire people have to keep track of the past and to see how their lives have intersected with public events. This impulse to remember is what leads people to take photographs, compile scrapbooks, and save letters and keepsakes of all sorts. Long after a particular experience is over, these objects help remind us of how things were at that moment. They also help remind us of how we were.

This sense of connection between present and past is at the center of memoir writing. By re-creating experiences from the past and exploring their significance, memoirists identify the continuities and discontinuities in their own lives. Writing memoirs is at least in part an act of self-discovery, of clarifying where the writer has come from and what he or she has become. The memoir writer is both participant and observer. On the one hand, the writer often appears as a character in the memoir, a participant in the events that unfold. On the other hand, the writer is also an observer who comments on and interprets these unfolding events, giving them a shape and meaning for the present.

Memoir writers typically focus on details that reveal deeper meanings to themselves and to readers. Memoirist Patricia Hampl records details such as a "black boxy Ford" in a photograph, a "hat worn in 1952," an aunt polishing her toenails, and the "booths of the Gopher Grill" at the University of Minnesota. Such details can move writers to recover and convey to readers what might otherwise be overlooked in their pasts—the "intimate fragments . . . that bind even obscure lives to history."

As Hampl notes, memorists often put their experiences into a historical or cultural context. They present their pasts in part as exemplifying and shedding light on something larger—what it meant, say, to grow up during the 1960s or to experience the attacks on September 11, 2001. The point here is that as detailed, specific, and filled with sensory impressions as successful memoirs typically are, it is the larger context that gives these details their significance.

Ultimately, people are called on to write memoirs not only to establish a connection to the past and to inform and entertain readers about the past but also from a sense of responsibility to the past, from a desire to bear witness to things that might otherwise be overlooked or forgotten. In many respects, memoirs derive their unique power to move readers from the way writers position themselves in the present in order to bear witness to the past, thus revealing the secrets and unsuspected meanings of ordinary lives that turn out to be not so ordinary after all.

■ WRITING FROM EXPERIENCE

Consider Patricia Hampl's point that memories are stored in the details of photos, a particular hat, and the booths at a campus hangout. Write a list of things that somehow capture an important moment or period in your life—such as photos, popular songs, hairstyles, articles of clothing, movies, posters, stuffed animals, toys, letters, cards, newspaper clippings, school or team uniforms, art objects, or souvenirs. Compare your list with your classmates' lists. What generalizations can you make about the capacity of things to hold and evoke memories?

READINGS

FROM *AN AMERICAN CHILDHOOD*

ANNIE DILLARD

Annie Dillard is a poet, novelist, essayist, and memoirist. She won the Pulitzer Prize in 1975 for Pilgrim at Tinker Creek, *an account of the year she spent observing nature in the Roanoke Valley of Virginia. The following selection is a chapter from* An American Childhood, *her memoir of growing up in Pittsburgh.*

1

Opening:
* estab-
lishes
focus on
playing
with boys

Some boys taught me to play football. This was fine sport. You thought up a new strategy for every play and whispered it to the others. You went out for a pass, fooling everyone. Best, you got to throw yourself mightily at someone's running legs. Either you brought him down or you hit the ground flat out on your chin, with your arms empty before you. It was all or nothing. If you hesitated in fear, you would miss and get hurt; you would take a hard fall while the kid got away, or you would get kicked in the face while the kid got away. But if you flung yourself wholeheartedly at the back of his knees—if you gathered and joined body and soul and pointed them diving fearlessly—then you likely wouldn't get hurt, and you'd stop the ball. Your fate, and your team's score, depended on your concentration and courage. Nothing girls did could compare with it.

2

* states
main
theme

Boys welcomed me at baseball, too, for I had, through enthusiastic practice, what was weirdly known as a boy's arm. In winter, in the snow, there was neither baseball not football, so the boys and I threw snowballs at passing cars. I got in trouble throwing snowballs, and have seldom been happier since.

3

Main
Body:
* shifts to
a specific
day

On one weekday morning after Christmas, six inches of new snow had just fallen. We were standing up to our boot tops in snow on a front yard on trafficked Reynolds Street, waiting for cars. The cars traveled Reynolds Street slowly and evenly; they were targets all but wrapped in red ribbons, cream puffs. We couldn't miss.

4

* intro-
duces
characters

I was seven; the boys were eight, nine, and ten. The oldest two Fahey boys were there—Mikey and Peter—polite blond boys who lived near me on Lloyd Street, and who already had four brothers and sisters. My parents approved of Mikey and Peter Fahey. Chuckie McBride was there, a rough kid, and Billy Paul and Mackie Kean too, from across Reynolds, where the boys grew up dark and furious, grew up skinny, knowing, and skilled. We had all drifted from our houses that morning looking for action, and had found it here on Reynolds Street.

5

* leads up
to decisive
event

It was cloudy but cold. The cars' tires laid behind them on the snowy street a complex trail of beige chunks like crenellated castle walls. I had stepped on some earlier; they squeaked. We could have wished for more traffic. When a car came, we all popped it one. In the intervals between cars we reverted to the natural solitude of children.

6

I started making an iceball—a perfect iceball, from perfectly white snow, perfectly spherical, and squeezed perfectly translucent so no snow remained all the way through. (The Fahey boys and I considered it unfair actually to throw an iceball at somebody, but it had been known to happen.)

7

I had just embarked on the iceball project when we heard tire chains come clanking from afar. A black Buick was moving toward us down the street. We all spread out, banged together some regular snowballs, took aim, and, when the Buick drew nigh, fired.

8   A soft snowball hit the driver's windshield right before the driver's face. It made a smashed star with a hump in the middle.

9   Often, of course, we hit our target, but this time, the only time in all of life, the car pulled over and stopped. Its wide black door opened; a man got out of it, running. He didn't even close the car door.

¶s 9–14:
* describes the chase

10   He ran after us, and we ran away from him, up the snowy Reynolds sidewalk. At the corner, I looked back; incredibly, he was still after us. He was in city clothes: a suit and tie, street shoes. Any normal adult would have quit, having sprung us into flight and made his point. This man was gaining on us. He was a thin man, all action. All of a sudden, we were running for our lives.

* notice the chrono-logical order

11   Wordless, we split up. We were on our turf; we could lose ourselves in the neighborhood backyards, everyone for himself. I paused and considered. Everyone had vanished except Mikey Fahey, who was just rounding the corner of a yellow brick house. Poor Mikey, I trailed him. The driver of the Buick sensibly picked the two of us to follow. The man apparently had all day.

12   He chased Mikey and me around the yellow house and up a backyard path we knew by heart: under a low tree, up a bank, through a hedge, down some snowy steps, and across the grocery store's delivery driveway. We smashed through a gap in another hedge, entered a scruffy backyard and ran around its back porch and tight between houses to Edgerton Avenue; we ran across Edgerton to an alley and up our own sliding woodpile to the Hall's front yard; he kept coming. We ran up Lloyd Street and wound through mazy backyards toward the steep hilltop at Willard and Lang.

13   He chased us silently, block after block. He chased us silently over picket fences, through thorny hedges, between houses, around garbage cans, and across streets. Every time I glanced back, choking for breath, I expected he would have quit. He must have been as breathless as we were. His jacket strained over his body. It was an immense discovery, pounding into my hot head with every sliding, joyous step, that this ordinary adult evidently knew what I thought only children who trained at football knew: that you have to fling yourself at what you're doing, you have to point yourself, forget yourself, aim, dive.

* notice descriptive detail

14   Mikey and I had nowhere to go, in our own neighborhood or out of it, but away from this man who was chasing us. He impelled us forward; we compelled him to follow our route. The air was cold; every breath tore my throat. We kept running, block after block; we kept improvising, backyard after backyard, running a frantic course and choosing it simultaneously, failing always to find small places or hard places to slow him down, and

* notice action verbs

discovering always, exhilarated, dismayed, that only bare speed could save us—for he would never give up, this man—and we were losing speed.

15
¶s 15–19:

He chased us through the backyard labyrinths of ten blocks before he caught us by our jackets. He caught us and we all stopped.

16

* climax
of the
story

We three stood staggering, half blinded, coughing, in an obscure hilltop backyard: a man in his twenties, a boy, a girl. He had released our jackets, our pursuer, our captor, our hero: he knew we weren't going anywhere. We all played by the rules. Mikey and I unzipped our jackets. I pulled off my sopping mittens. Our tracks multiplied in the backyard's new snow. We had been breaking new snow all morning. We didn't look at each other. I was cherishing my excitement. The man's lower pants legs were wet; his cuffs were full of snow and there was a prow of snow beneath them on his shoes and socks. Some trees bordered the little flat backyard, some messy winter trees. There was no one around: a clearing in a grove, and we the only players.

17

It was a long time before he could speak. I had some difficulty at first recalling why we were there. My lips felt swollen; I couldn't see out of the sides of my eyes; I kept coughing.

18

"You stupid kids," he began perfunctorily.

19

* moment
of revela-
tion

We listened perfunctorily indeed, if we listened at all, for the chewing out was redundant, a mere formality, and beside the point. The point was that he had chased us passionately without giving up, and so he had caught us. Now he came down to earth. I wanted the glory to last forever.

20

But how could the glory have lasted forever? We could have run through every backyard in North America until we got to Panama. But when he trapped us at the lip of the Panama Canal, what precisely could he have done to prolong the drama of the chase and cap its glory? I brooded about this for the next few years. He could only have fried Mikey Fahey and me in boiling oil, say, or dismembered us piecemeal, or staked us to anthills. None of which I really wanted, and none of which any adult was likely to do, even in the spirit of fun. He could only chew us out there in the Panamanian jungle, after months or years of exalting pursuit. He could only begin, "You stupid kids," and continue in his ordinary Pittsburgh accent with his normal righteous anger and the usual common sense.

Ending:
* reflects
on mean-
ing of the
chase

21

* echoes
last
sentence
of ¶2

If in that snowy backyard the driver of the black Buick had cut off our heads, Mikey's and mine, I would have died happy, for nothing has required so much of me since as being chased all over Pittsburgh in the middle of winter—running terrified, exhausted—by this sainted, skinny, furious redheaded man who wished to have a word with us. I don't know how he found his way back to his car.

Analysis: Re-creating Experience

At their best, memoirs re-create experience so that readers can actually feel what it was like to be alive at that moment in the writer's life. In this chapter from *An American Childhood*, Annie Dillard isn't just recalling the time she and some friends were out throwing snowballs and this guy stopped and chased them around the neighborhood. Instead she takes us with her as she flees from the man pursuing her. To make the chase come alive, Dillard has re-created the young girl she was at the age of seven. Accordingly, as readers, we experience what takes place from the young girl's perspective and share her sense of excitement and exhilaration. In many respects, this memoir hinges on Dillard's ability to shape the person she once was into a believable character.

■ FOR CRITICAL INQUIRY

1. In the opening paragraphs, Dillard talks about playing football and baseball. What does this reveal about the character of Dillard as a seven-year-old? How does this information prepare readers for what's to come?

2. Dillard doesn't just tell a story about something that happened. She invests the experience with meaning: "I got in trouble throwing snowballs, and have seldom been happier since." What made her so happy? Point to particular words, sentences, and passages where she develops the meaning of the experience.

3. In the final paragraph, Dillard describes the man who chased her as "this sainted, skinny, furious redheaded man who wished to have a word with us." How do the adjectives *sainted, skinny, furious,* and *redheaded* go together in her description? Why does she use the word *sainted*?

4. One could argue that throwing snowballs is dangerous and irresponsible behavior. In fact, that is probably what the man who chased Dillard and her friends was thinking. Dillard avoids the issue, however, and puts the emphasis instead on her "immense discovery." What assumptions about readers' reactions does she seem to count on in doing so?

FORTUNATE SON

DAVE MARSH

Dave Marsh is one of today's leading and rock-and-roll critics, Sirius radio show host on "Kick Out the Jams," and author of books on Bruce Springsteen, Elvis Presley, George Clinton and P-Funkadelic, and the Beatles, among others. This memoir appeared as the introduction to a collection of Marsh's shorter critical essays and reviews titled Fortunate Son *(1983).*

Introduction

I

This old town is where I learned about lovin'
This old town is where I learned to hate
This town, buddy, has done its share of shoveling
This town taught me that it's never too late
—*Michael Stanley, "My Town"*

1   When I was a boy, my family lived on East Beverly Street in Pontiac, Michigan, in a two-bedroom house with blue-white asphalt shingles that cracked at the edges when a ball was thrown against them and left a powder like talc on fingers rubbed across their shallow grooves. East Beverly ascended a slowly rising hill. At the very top, a block and a half from our place, Pontiac Motors Assembly Line 16 sprawled for a mile or so behind a fenced-in parking lot.

2   Rust-red dust collected on our windowsills. It piled up no matter how often the place was dusted or cleaned. Fifteen minutes after my mother was through with a room, that dust seemed thick enough for a finger to trace pointless, ashy patterns in it.

3   The dust came from the foundry on the other side of the assembly line, the foundry that spat angry cinders into the sky all night long. When people talked about hell, I imagined driving past the foundry at night. From the street below, you could see the fires, red-hot flames shaping glowing metal.

4   Pontiac was a company town, nothing less. General Motors owned most of the land, and in one way or another held mortgages on the rest. Its holdings included not only the assembly line and the foundry but also a Fisher Body plant and on the outskirts, General Motors Truck and Coach. For a while, some pieces of frigidaires may even have been put together in our town, but that might just be a trick of my memory, which often confuses the tentacles of institutions that monstrous.

5   In any case, of the hundred thousand or so who lived in Pontiac, fully half must have been employed either by GM or one of the tool-and-die shops and steel warehouses and the like that supplied it. And anybody who earned his living locally in some less directly auto-related fashion was only fooling himself if he thought of independence.

From "Introduction" by Dave Marsh, 1985, *Fortunate Son*. Reprinted by permission of the author.

6   My father worked without illusions, as a railroad brakeman on freight trains that shunted boxcars through the innards of the plants, hauled grain from up north, transported the finished Pontiacs on the first leg of the route to almost anywhere Bonnevilles, Catalinas, and GTOs were sold.

7   Our baseball and football ground lay in the shadow of another General Motors building. That building was of uncertain purpose, at least to me. What I can recall of it now is a seemingly reckless height—five or six stories is a lot in the flatlands around the Great Lakes—and endless walls of dark greenish glass that must have run from floor to ceiling in the rooms inside. Perhaps this building was an engineering facility. We didn't know anyone who worked there, at any rate.

8   Like most other GM facilities, the green glass building was surrounded by a chain link fence with barbed wire. If a ball happened to land on the other side of it, this fence was insurmountable. But only very strong boys could hit a ball that high, that far, anyhow.

9   Or maybe it just wasn't worth climbing that particular fence. Each August, a few weeks before the new models were officially presented in the press, the finished Pontiacs were set out in the assembly-line parking lot at the top of our street. They were covered by tarpaulins to keep their design changes secret—these were the years when the appearance of American cars changed radically each year. Climbing *that* fence was a neighborhood sport because that was how you discovered what the new cars looked like, whether fins were shrinking or growing, if the new hoods were pointed or flat, how much thinner the strips of whitewall on the tires had grown. A weird game, since everyone knew people who could have told us, given us exact descriptions, having built those cars with their own hands. But climbing that fence added a hint of danger, made us feel we shared a secret, turned gossip into information.

10   The main drag in our part of town was Joslyn Road. It was where the stoplight and crossing guard were stationed, where the gas station with the condom machine stood alongside a short-order restaurant, drugstore, dairy store, small groceries and a bakery. A few blocks down, past the green glass building, was a low brick building set back behind a wide, lush lawn. This building, identified by a discreet roadside sign, occupied a long block or two. It was the Administration Building for all of Pontiac Motors—a building for executives, clerks, white-collar types. This building couldn't have been more than three-quarters of a mile from my house, yet even though I lived on East Beverly Street from the time I was two until I was past fourteen, I knew only one person who worked there.

11   In the spring of 1964, when I was fourteen and finishing eighth grade, rumors started going around at Madison Junior High. All the buildings on our side of Joslyn Road (possibly east or west of Joslyn, but I didn't know directions then—there was only "our" side and everywhere else) were about to be bought up and torn down by GM. This was worrisome, but it seemed to me that our parents would never allow that perfectly functioning neighborhood to be broken up for no good purpose.

12   One sunny weekday afternoon a man came to our door. He wore a coat and tie and a white shirt, which meant something serious in our part of town. My father greeted him at the door, but I don't know whether the businessman had an appointment. Dad was working the extra board in those years, which meant he was called to work erratically— four or five times a week, when business was good—each time his nameplate came to the top of the big duty-roster board down at the yard office. (My father didn't get a regular train of his own to work until 1966; he spent almost twenty years on that extra board, which meant guessing whether it was safe to answer the phone every time he actually wanted a day off—refuse a call and your name went back to the bottom of the list.)

13   At any rate, the stranger was shown to the couch in our front room. He perched on that old gray davenport with its wiry fabric that bristled and stung against my cheek, and spoke quite earnestly to my parents. I recall nothing of his features or of the precise words he used or even of the tone of his speech. But the dust motes that hung in the air that day are still in my memory, and I can remember his folded hands between his spread knees as he leaned forward in a gesture of complicity. He didn't seem to be selling anything; he was simply stating facts.

14   He told my father that Pontiac Motors was buying up all the houses in our community form Tennyson Street, across from the green glass building, to Baldwin Avenue— exactly the boundaries of what I'd have described as our neighborhood. GM's price was more than fair; it doubled what little money my father had paid in the early fifties. The number was a little over ten thousand dollars. All the other houses were going, too; some had already been sold. The entire process of tearing our neighborhood down would take about six months, once all the details were settled.

15   The stranger put down his coffee cup, shook hands with my parents and left. As far as I know, he never darkened our doorstep again. In the back of my mind, I can still see him through the front window cutting across the grass to go next door.

16   "Well, *we're* not gonna move, right, Dad?" I said. Cheeky as I was, it didn't occur to me this wasn't really a matter for adult decision-making—or rather, that the real adults,

over at the Administration Building, had already made the only decision that counted. Nor did it occur to me that GM's offer might seem to my father an opportunity to sell at a nice profit, enabling us to move some place "better."

17   My father did not say much. No surprise. In a good mood, he was the least taciturn man alive, but on the farm where he was raised, not many words were needed to get a serious job done. What he did say that evening indicated that we might stall awhile—perhaps there would be a slightly better offer if we did. But he exhibited no doubt that we would sell. And move.

18   I was shocked. There was no room in my plans for this . . . rupture. Was the demolition of our home and neighborhood—that is, my life—truly inevitable? Was there really no way we could avert it, cancel it, *delay* it? What if we just plain *refused to sell*?

19   Twenty years later, my mother told me that she could still remember my face on that day. It must have reflected extraordinary distress and confusion, for my folks were patient. If anyone refused to sell, they told me, GM would simply build its parking lot—for that was what would replace my world—around him. If we didn't sell, we'd have access privileges, enough space to get into our driveway and that was it. No room to play, and no one there to play with if there had been. And if you got caught in such a situation and didn't like it, then you'd really be in a fix, for the company wouldn't keep its double-your-money offer open forever. If we held out too long, who knew if the house would be worth anything at all. (I don't imagine that my parents attempted to explain to me the political process of condemnation, but if they had, I would have been outraged, for in a way, I still am.)

20   My dreams always pictured us as holdouts, living in a little house surrounded by asphalt and automobiles. I always imagined nighttime with the high, white-light towers that illuminated all the other GM parking lots shining down upon our house—and the little guardhouse that the company would have to build and man next door to prevent me from escaping our lot to run playfully among the parked cars of the multitudinous employees. Anyone reading this must find it absurd, or the details heavily derivative of bad concentration-camp literature or maybe too influenced by the Berlin Wall, which had been up only a short time. But it would be a mistake to dismiss its romanticism, which was for many months more real to me than the ridiculous reality—moving to accommodate a *parking lot*—which confronted my family and all my friends' families.

21   If this story were set in the Bronx or in the late sixties, or if it were fiction, the next scenes would be of pickets and protests, meaningful victories and defeats. But this isn't

fiction—everything set out here is as unexaggerated as I know how to make it—and the time and the place were wrong for any serious uproar. In this docile Midwestern company town, where Walter Reuther's trip to Russia was as inexplicable as the parting of the Red Sea (or as forgotten as the Ark of the Covenant), the idea that a neighborhood might have rights that superseded those of General Motors' Pontiac division would have been regarded as extraordinary, bizarre and subversive. Presuming anyone had had such an idea, which they didn't—none of my friends seemed particularly disturbed about moving, it was just what they would *do*.

22   So we moved, and what was worse, to the suburbs. This was catastrophic to me. I loved the city, its pavement and the mobility it offered even to kids too young to drive. (Some attitude for a Motor City kid, I know.) In Pontiac, feet or a bicycle could get you anywhere. Everyone had cars, but you weren't immobilized without them, as everyone under sixteen was in the suburbs. In the suburb to which we adjourned, cars were *the* fundamental of life—many of the streets in our new subdivision (not really a neighborhood) didn't even have sidewalks.

23   Even though I'd never been certain of fitting in, in the city I'd felt close to figuring out how to. Not that I was that weird. But I was no jock and certainly neither suave nor graceful. Still, toward the end of eighth grade, I'd managed to talk to a few girls, no small feat. The last thing I needed was new goals to fathom, new rules to learn, new friends to make.

24   So that summer was spent in dread. When school opened in the autumn, I was already in a sort of cocoon, confused by the Beatles with their paltry imitations of soul music and the bizarre emotions they stirred in girls.

25   Meeting my classmates was easy enough, but then it always is. Making new friends was another matter. For one thing, the kids in my new locale weren't the same as the kids in my classes. I was an exceptionally good student (quite by accident—I just read a lot) and my neighbors were classic underachievers. The kids in my classes were hardly creeps, but they weren't as interesting or as accessible as the people I'd known in my old neighborhood or the ones I met at the school bus stop. So I kept to myself.

26   In our new house, I shared a room with my brother at first. We had bunk beds, and late that August I was lying sweatily in the upper one, listening to the radio (WPON-AM, 1460) while my mother and my aunt droned away in the kitchen.

27   Suddenly my attention was riveted by a record. I listened for two or three minutes more intently than I have ever listened and learned something that remains all but indescribable.

It wasn't a new awareness of music. I liked rock and roll already, had since I first saw Elvis when I was six, and I'd been reasonably passionate about the Ronettes, Gary Bonds, Del Shannon, the Crystals, Jackie Wilson, Sam Cooke, the Beach Boys and those first rough but sweet notes from Motown: the Miracles, the Temptations, Eddie Holland's "Jamie." I can remember a rainy night when I tuned in a faraway station and first heard the end of the Philadelphia Warriors' game in which Wilt Chamberlain scored a hundred points and then found "Let's Twist Again" on another part of the dial. And I can remember not knowing which experience was more splendid.

28   But the song I heard that night wasn't a new one. "You Really Got a Hold on Me" had been a hit in 1963, and I already loved Smokey Robinson's voice, the way it twined around impossibly sugary lines and made rhymes within the rhythms, of ordinary conversation, within the limits of everyday vocabulary.

29   But if I'd heard those tricks before, I'd never understood them. And if I'd enjoyed rock and roll music previously, certainly it had never grabbed me in quite this way: as a lifeline that suggested—no, insisted—that these singers spoke *for* me as well as to me, and that what they felt and were able to cope with, the deep sorrow, remorse, anger, lust and compassion that bubbled beneath the music, I would also be able to feel and contain. This intimate revelation was what I gleaned form those three minutes of music, and when they were finished and I climbed out of that bunk and walked out the door, the world looked different. No longer did I feel quite so powerless, and if I still felt cheated, I felt capable of getting my own back, some day, some way.

Trapped

II

It seems I've been playing your game way too long
And it seems the game I've played has made you strong
—Jimmy Cliff, "Trapped"

30   That last year in Pontiac, we listened to the radio a lot. My parents always had. One of my most shattering early memories is of the radio blasting when they got up—my mother around four-thirty, my father at five. All of my life I've hated early rising, and for years I couldn't listen to country music without being reminded almost painfully of those days.

31   But in 1963 and 1964, we also listened to WPON in the evening for its live coverage of city council meetings. Pontiac was beginning a decade of racial crisis, of integration pressure and white resistance, the typical scenario. From what was left of our old neighborhood came the outspokenly racist militant anti-school busing movement.

32   The town had a hard time keeping the shabby secret of its bigotry even in 1964. Pontiac had mushroomed as a result of massive migration during and after World War II. Some of the new residents, including my father, came from nearby rural areas where blacks were all but unknown and even the local Polish Catholics were looked upon as aliens potentially subversive to the community's Methodist piety.

33   Many more of the new residents of Pontiac came from the South, out of the dead ends of Appalachia and the border states. As many must have been black as white, though it was hard for me to tell that as a kid. There were lines one didn't cross in Michigan, and if I was shocked, when visiting Florida, to see separate facilities labeled "White" and "Colored," as children we never paid much mind to the segregated schools, the lily-white suburbs, the way that jobs in the plants were divided up along race lines. The ignorance and superstition about blacks in my neighborhood were as desperate and crazed in their own way as the feelings in any kudzu-covered parish of Louisiana.

34   As blacks began to assert their rights, the animosity was not less, either. The polarization was fueled and fanned by the fact that so many displaced Southerners, all with the poor white's investment in racism, were living in our community. But it would be foolish to pretend that the situation would have been any more civilized if only the natives had been around. In fact the Southerners were often regarded with nearly as much condescension and antipathy as blacks—race may have been one of the few areas in which my parents found themselves completely in sympathy with the "hillbillies."

35   Racism was the great trap of such men's lives, for almost everything could be explained by it, from unemployment to the deterioration of community itself. Casting racial blame did much more than poison these people's entire concept of humanity, which would have been plenty bad enough. It immobilized the racist, preventing folks like my father from ever realizing the real forces that kept their lives tawdry and painful and forced them to fight every day to find any meaning at all in their existence. It did this to Michigan factory workers as effectively as it ever did it to dirt farmers in Dixie.

36   The great psychological syndrome of American males is said to be passive aggression, and racism perfectly fit this mold. To the racist, hatred of blacks gave a great feeling of

power and superiority. At the same time, it allowed him the luxury of wallowing in self-pity at the great conspiracy of rich bastards and vile niggers that enforced workaday misery and let the rest of the world go to hell. In short, racism explained everything. There was no need to look any further than the cant of redneck populism, exploited as effectively in the orange clay of the Great Lakes as in the red dirt of Georgia, to find an answer to why it was always the *next* generation that was going to get up and out.

37   Some time around 1963, a local attorney named Milton Henry, a black man, was elected to Pontiac's city council. Henry was smart and bold—he would later become an ally of Martin Luther King, Jr., of Malcolm X, a principal in the doomed Republic of New Africa. The goals for which Henry was campaigning seem extremely tame now, until you realize the extent to which they *haven't* been realized in twenty years: desegregated schools, integrated housing, a chance at decent jobs.

38   Remember that Martin Luther King would not take his movement for equality into the North for nearly five more years, and that when he did, Dr. King there faced the most strident and violent opposition he'd ever met, and you will understand how inflammatory the mere presence of Milton Henry on the city council was. Those council sessions, broadcast live on WPON, invested the radio with a vibrancy and vitality that television could never have had. Those hours of imprecations, shouts and clamor are unforgettable. I can't recall specific words or phrases, though, just Henry's eloquence and the pandemonium that greeted each of his speeches.

39   So our whole neighborhood gathered round its radios in the evenings, family by family, as if during wartime. Which in a way I guess it was—surely that's how the situation was presented to the children, and not only in the city. My Pontiac junior high school was lightly integrated, and kids in my new suburban town had the same reaction as my Floridian cousins: shocked that I'd "gone to school with niggers," they vowed they would die—or kill—before letting the same thing happen to them.

40   This cycle of hatred didn't immediately elude me. Thirteen-year-olds are built to buck the system only up to a point. So even though I didn't dislike any of the blacks I met (it could hardly be said that I was given the opportunity to *know* any), it was taken for granted that the epithets were essentially correct. After all, anyone could see the grave poverty in which most blacks existed, and the only reason ever given for it was that they liked living that way.

41   But listening to the radio gave free play to one's imagination. Listening to music, that most abstract of human creations, unleashed it all the more. And not in a vacuum. Semiotics, the New Criticism, and other formalist approaches have never had much appeal to me, not because I don't recognize their validity in describing certain creative structures but because they emphasize those structural questions without much consideration of content: And that simply doesn't jibe with my experience of culture, especially popular culture.

42   The best example is the radio of the early 1960s. As I've noted, there was no absence of rock and roll in those years betwixt the outbreaks of Presley and Beatles. Rock and roll was a constant for me, the best music around, and I had loved it ever since I first heard it, which was about as soon as I could remember hearing anything.

43   In part, I just loved the sound—the great mystery one could hear welling up from "Duke of Earl," "Up on the Roof," "Party Lights"; that pit of loneliness and despair that lay barely concealed beneath the superficial bright spirits of a record like Bruce Channel's "Hey Baby"; the nonspecific terror hidden away in Del Shannon's "Runaway." But if that was all there was to it, then rock and roll records would have been as much an end in themselves—that is, as much a dead end—as TV shows like *Leave It to Beaver* (also mysterious, also—thanks to Eddie Haskell—a bit terrifying).

44   To me, however, TV was clearly an alien device, controlled by the men with shirts and ties. Nobody on television dressed or talked as the people in my neighborhood did. In rock and roll, however, the language spoken was recognizably my own. And since one of the givens of life in the outlands was that we were barbarians, who produced no culture and basically consumed only garbage and trash, the thrill of discovering depths within rock and roll, the very part that was most often and explicitly degraded by teachers and pundits, was not only marvelously refreshing and exhilarating but also in essence liberating— once you'd made the necessary connections.

45   It was just at this time that pop music was being revolutionized—not by the Beatles, arriving from England, a locale of certifiable cultural superiority, but by Motown, arriving from Detroit, a place without even a hint of cultural respectability. Produced by Berry Gordy, not only a young man but a *black* man. And in that spirit of solidarity with which hometown boys (however unalike) have always identified with one another, Motown was mine in a way that no other music up to that point had been. Surely no one spoke my language as effectively as Smokey Robinson, able to string together the most humdrum phrases and effortlessly make them sing.

46   That's the context in which "You Really Got a Hold on Me" created my epiphany. You can look at this coldly—structurally—and see nothing more than a naked marketing mechanism, a clear-cut case of a teenager swaddled in and swindled by pop culture. Smokey Robinson wrote and sang the song as much to make a buck as to express himself; there was nothing of the purity of the mythical artist about his endeavor. In any case, the emotion he expressed was unfashionably sentimental. In releasing the record, Berry Gordy was mercenary in both instinct and motivation. The radio station certainly hoped for nothing more from playing it than that its listeners would hang in through the succeeding block of commercials. None of these people and institutions had any intention of elevating their audience, in the way that Leonard Bernstein hoped to do in his *Young People's Concerts* on television. Cultural indoctrination was far from their minds. Indeed, it's unlikely that anyone involved in the process thought much about the kids on the other end of the line except as an amorphous mass of ears and wallets. The pride Gordy and Robinson had in the quality of their work was private pleasure, not public.

47   Smokey Robinson was not singing of the perils of being a black man in this world (though there were other rock and soul songs that spoke in guarded metaphors about such matters). Robinson was not expressing an experience as alien to my own as a country blues singer's would have been. Instead, he was putting his finger firmly upon a crucial feeling of vulnerability and longing. It's hard to think of two emotions that a fourteen-year-old might feel more deeply (well, there's lust. . .), and yet in my hometown expressing them was all but absolutely forbidden to men. This doubled the shock of Smokey Robinson's voice, which for years I've thought of as falsetto, even though it really isn't exceptionally high-pitched compared to the spectacular male sopranos of rock and gospel lore.

48   "You Really Got a Hold on Me" is not by any means the greatest song Smokey Robinson ever wrote or sang, not even the best he had done up to that point. The singing on "Who's Loving You," the lyrics of "I'll Try Something New," the yearning of "What's So Good About Goodbye" are all at least as worthy. Nor is there anything especially newfangled about the song. Its trembling blues guitar, sturdy drum pattern, walking bass and call-and-response voice arrangement are not very different from many of the other Miracles records of that period. If there is a single instant in the record which is unforgettable by itself, it's probably the opening lines: "I don't like you/But I love you . . ."

49   The contingency and ambiguity expressed in those two lines and Robinson's singing of them was also forbidden in the neighborhood of my youth, and forbidden as part and

parcel of the same philosophy that propounded racism. Merely calling the bigot's certainty into question was revolutionary—not merely rebellious. The depth of feeling in that Miracles record, which could have been purchased for 69¢ at any K-Mart, overthrew the premise of racism, which was that blacks were not as human as we, that they could not feel—much less express their feelings—as deeply as we did.

50   When the veil of racism was torn from my eyes, everything else that I knew or had been told was true for fourteen years was necessarily called into question. For if racism explained everything, then without racism, not a single commonplace explanation made any sense. *Nothing* else could be taken at face value. And that meant asking every question once again, including the banal and obvious ones.

51   For those who've never been raised under the weight of such addled philosophy, the power inherent in having the burden lifted is barely imaginable. Understanding that blacks weren't worthless meant that maybe the rest of the culture in which I was raised was also valuable. If you've never been told that you and your community are worthless—that a parking lot takes precedence over your needs—perhaps that moment of insight seems trivial or rather easily won. For anyone who was never led to expect a life any more difficult than one spent behind a typewriter, maybe the whole incident verges on being something too banal for repetition (though in that case, I'd like to know where the other expressions of this story can be read). But looking over my shoulder, seeing the consequences to my life had I not begun questioning not just racism but all of the other presumptions that ruled our lives, I know for certain how and how much I got over.

52   That doesn't make me better than those on the other side of the line. On the other hand, I won't trivialize the tale by insisting upon how fortunate I was. What was left for me was a raging passion to explain things in the hope that others would not be trapped and to keep the way clear so that others from the trashy outskirts of barbarous America still had a place to stand—if not in the culture at large, at least in rock and roll.

53   Of course it's not so difficult to dismiss this entire account. Great revelations and insights aren't supposed to emerge from listening to rock and roll records. They're meant to emerge only from encounters with art. (My encounters with Western art music were unavailing, of course, because every one of them was prefaced by a lecture on the insipid and worthless nature of the music that I preferred to hear). Left with the fact that what happened to me did take place, and that it was something that was supposed to come only out of art, I reached the obvious conclusion. You are welcome to your own.

Analysis: Setting Up a Moment of Revelation

Instead of using straight chronology, as Annie Dillard does in the previous memoir, Dave Marsh divides this piece of writing into two parts. Part I tells the story of why Marsh's family moved from Pontiac to the suburbs, but Part II returns to Pontiac before the move took place, to dwell there a little longer so that Marsh can draw out the meaning of the place in the fateful years 1963 and 1964. Notice how Marsh's return to Pontiac amounts to a reframing of his experience growing up in Pontiac that depends on what we've learned in Part I but that sets the stage for the memoir's moment of revelation—"the context," as Marsh says, "in which 'You Really Got a Hold on Me' created my epiphany."

■ FOR CRITICAL INQUIRY

1. Dave Marsh uses the Smokey Robinson and the Miracles' song "You Really Got a Hold on Me" to anchor his memoir and to provide the grounds for the "intimate revelation" or "epiphany" that Marsh sets up in Part I and then explains more fully in Part II. What exactly is this revelation and how does it emerge from Marsh's experience of listening to rock and roll?

2. Consider the shift in perspective that takes place as the memoir moves from Part I to Part II. How does Marsh position himself in relation to his experience growing up in Pontiac in each of the sections? How would you describe the relationship between these two perspectives?

3. At the end of the memoir, Marsh says "I reached the obvious conclusion. You are welcome to your own." What is Marsh's conclusion? How does telling readers they are welcome to their own indicate the kind of relationship he is seeking to establish with his audience? Is he really suggesting that any conclusion is valid?

4. Marsh uses lines from two songs as the epigraphs to the sections. What meanings do the quotes invest in each section and in the memoir as a whole?

TEENAGE ANGST IN TEXAS

GAIL CALDWELL

Gail Caldwell is the chief book critic at the Boston Globe. *Caldwell adapted this short piece of writing from her memoir* A Strong West Wind *(2006). "Teenage Angst in Texas" appeared in the* New York Times Magazine *on January 29, 2006.*

In the mid-1960's, the wind-swept plains of the Texas Panhandle could be a languid prison for an adolescent girl with a wild spirit and no place to go. I buried myself in Philip Roth novels and little acts of outrage, and on lonesome afternoons, I would drive my mother's Chevrolet out onto the freeway and take it up to 90 m.p.h., smoking endless cigarettes and aching with ennui. I was bored by the idea of mainstream success and alienated from what the world seemed to offer—one of my poems from those days weighs heavily on the themes of coffins, societal hypocrisy and godlessness. And yet I cannot locate the precise source of my anger. For years I thought all teenagers were fueled by a high-octane mix of intensity and rage; I only know that what sent me onto the highways and into my own corridors of gloom was inexplicable to others and confusing to me.

Around this time my father began what I dismally thought of as our Sunday drives. As kids, my sister and I were bored but tolerant when we had to tag along on his treks, which were always aimless. But now his itinerary was to chart the path of my dereliction, and that meant getting me alone in the car so that we could "talk": about my imminent doom, about my mother's high blood pressure. Thus incarcerated, slouched in the shotgun seat with my arms folded against my chest, I responded to his every effort by either staring out the window or yelling back. I don't remember a word I said. What I still feel is the boulder on my heart—the amorphous gray of the world outside the car window, signaling how trapped I felt, by him and by the hopeless unawareness of my age.

My father, far more than I, seemed to sense that the country was raging, that it was a bad time to surrender your daughters to strange lands. But these things—a war somewhere far away, a civil rights movement over in the Deep South—belonged to the evening news, not to the more intimate treacheries of car rides and deceits and disappointments, and so were rarely addressed on any personal level, not yet. Instead we fought about curfews or bad boyfriends; we fought about straightening up and flying right. We fought about everything but the truth, which was that I would be leaving soon.

I had already seen two casualties claimed by history, men who were lighting out for the territory to avoid the 1-A draft notices they had just received. The first was a boy who stopped by the house to say goodbye a few days before leaving for Toronto. When the other young man disappeared, the federal authorities came sniffing around my high school, and I covered for him without a shred of hesitation. I told them I thought he went east, to his mother's in Missouri, when I knew it was the one place he would never go.

These losses and the lies they demanded frightened me, in vague and then inarticulable ways, about just who was in charge—about the dangers posed by the institutions that were supposed to keep you safe. It was difficult in those days to care much about the College Boards, or to think that the path in front of me would hold the traditional landscapes of marriage and family. In some ways the tempests of my adolescence had set me against myself; I'd found that introspection couldn't buy you love, that poetry helped only momentarily, that straight A's and spelling bees were no guarantee of knowing where to turn. Worse and more pervasive, I was maturing under the assumption that you should never let men know how smart you were, or how mouthy—a girl's intelligence, brazenly displayed, was seen as impolite, unfeminine and even threatening.

So I kept quiet; when I dated a boy who liked George Wallace, I rolled my eyes and looked out the window. The smarter you were, the more subversive you had to be. Girls could excel in English, say, or languages, as long as they didn't flaunt it or pretend to be superior to males. But God forbid, they should try to carve a life out of such achievements. God forbid they display a pitcher's arm, or an affinity for chemistry or analytic prowess in an argument with a man.

In the end, my own revisionism was unconscious but thorough. I neglected anymore to mention the mysterious test, taken at age 7, that resulted in my skipping second grade. Toward the end of high school, I began lying to my peers about my high scores on placement exams, and I blew admission, with half-intention and private relief, into the National Honor Society. The summer before college, in 1968, I had to declare a major; I took a deep breath and wrote "mathematics" on my admission forms. And when friends asked me what I'd chosen, I lied about that too.

Analysis: Using Episodes

Instead of telling a story from her past in chronological order, from start to finish, Gail Caldwell brings together a series of episodes to re-create a sense of what her life was like as a teenager in the Texas Panhandle during the mid-1960s. Notice how she moves from one episode to another—driving ninety miles an hour, the rides with her father, the two young men fleeing the military draft, how she lied about the major she wrote on her college admissions forms. Notice also how the episodes are arranged to work together, creating a moment in time that enables readers to see an individual life in the midst of historical events (the Vietnam War, the civil rights movement, the presidential campaign in 1968 of the segregationist George Wallace) and the cultural realities of the day (parent-child relations, pressures on young women).

■ FOR CRITICAL INQUIRY

1. How does Gail Caldwell establish her situation in the opening paragraph? Notice she says it was "inexplicable to others and confusing to me." By the time you get to the end of this brief memoir, what light has been shed on this confusion? How would you describe the arc of the memoir, from where it begins to where it ends?

2. How do the various episodes contribute to the memoir? How does Caldwell put them together? Examine the order she uses and the amount of explanation.

3. How does your experience of reading Caldwell's episodes compare to the chronological order in Annie Dillard and Gary Soto?

4. As is typical of memoirs, the writer is very much in the present looking at the past. What does Caldwell's attitude toward her past seem to be? How does this attitude compare to her state of mind in the past? How do these past and present perspectives shape the reader's experience of Caldwell's memoir?

AUDIO MEMOIRS
STORY CORPS

This photo was provided courtesy of StoryCorps, a national nonprofit dedicated to recording and collecting stories from every day people. www.storycorps.org

StoryBooth in Grand Central Station, New York City, where StoryCorps began in 2003.

This photo was provided courtesy of StoryCorps, a national nonprofit dedicated to recording and collecting stories from every day people. www.storycorps.org

MobileBooths have recorded stories in more than one hundred cities in forty-eight states.

StoryCorps is a nonprofit public service project to record the stories of ordinary people. Since it began in 2003, over ten thousand people have recorded interviews of family and friends through StoryCorps. Those interviewed get a free CD, and their stories also appear regularly on National Public Radio and are archived at the Library of Congress, creating what has become a vast oral history of everyday Americans recalling important moments in their lives. In this sense, StoryCorps is a kind of audio memoir project, to encourage people to record their memories as part of a collective portrait. Visit the StoryCorps Web site www.storycorps.org and listen to some of the stories. Consider to what extent they resemble written memoirs in terms of looking at the past from the perspective of the present. Is there a sense that those interviewed invent a first-person narrator, as memoirists typically do? Is there a moment of revelation?

GRAPHIC MEMOIRS

PERSEPOLIS

MARJANE SATRAPI

IN THE SHADOW OF NO TOWERS

ART SPIEGELMAN

Marjane Satrapi and Art Spiegelman are two of the leading writer/illustrators who have developed the visual conventions of the comic book into the graphic novel or, more accurately in the case of the work here, the graphic memoir. These brief excepts come from the opening chapter of Satrapi's Persepolis: The Story of a Childhood *(2003) and the beginning of Spiegelman's* In the Shadow of No Towers *(2004).*

From *Persepolis: The Story of a Childhood* by Marjane Satrapi, translated by Mattias Ripa and Blake Ferris, Translation copyright 2003 by L'Association, Paris, France. Used by permission of Pantheon Books, a division of Random House, Inc.

From Persepolis: The Story of a Childhood by Marjane Satrapi, translated by Mattias Ripa & Blake Ferris, Translation copyright © 2003 by L'Association, Paris, France. Used by permission of Pantheon Books, a division of Random House, Inc.

From *In the Shadow of No Towers* by Art Spiegelman, copyright © 2004 by Art Spiegelman. Used by permission of Pantheon Books, a division of Random House, Inc. and Penguin Group UK.

OF NO TOWERS

From *In the Shadow of No Towers* by Art Spiegelman, copyright © 2004 by Art Spiegelman. Used by permission of Pantheon Books, a division of Random House, Inc. and Penguin Group UK.

■ **FOR CRITICAL ANALYSIS**

The contrast between the visual and verbal styles of Marjane Satrapi and Art Spiegelman brings out interesting differences in how they represent themselves, as both the first-person narrator and a character. How would you describe these differences in rhetorical stance? How do visual elements—such as their use of panels (and, in Spiegelman's case, at times abandoning panels momentarily), color versus black and white, and the differences in their drawing styles—contribute to the rhetorical effect? Consider the differences and similarities between these graphic memoirs and print memoir.

THE NINTH LETTER OF THE ALPHABET: FIRST-PERSON STRATEGIES IN NONFICTION
RICHARD HOFFMAN

Richard Hoffman is writer-in-residence at Emerson College and the author of Half the House: A Memoir *(2005) and the poetry collections* Without Paradise *(2002) and* Gold Star Road *(2007).*

Even setting aside the naïve reader who believes that the process of writing a memoir is 1. having an interesting life, and 2. writing it down (that's what they always say to me after a reading or a panel: "One day I'm going to write it down"), there are many otherwise sophisticated readers who choose to believe that the memoir is a species of journalism, albeit gussied up with some techniques borrowed from fiction writers. It seems to me more accurate to see the memoir, as it has evolved, as a subgenre of the novel, a kind of first-person historical novel, a dramatic work that agrees to be bound by fact. What is being explored is not only what happened, but how one has remembered what happened, including the gaps in the story and one's lapses of memory. The contract with the reader one makes, by calling a work a memoir, i.e. nonfiction, is that you honor what actually took place and write about it, and about the process of remembering it, with honesty.

Although readers want the same pleasures (what Aristotle called delight and instruction) from a memoir as from a work of fiction, they approach the two very differently. I am more than willing to suspend my disbelief in order to be entranced by a work of fiction, but I approach a memoir, because it claims to be nonfiction, with a certain skepticism. A novel need only be consistent with its own imagined world. A memoir needs to be consistent with the world of facts and events that we share.

One more thing remains to be said before we begin a consideration of who or what is represented by the ninth letter of the alphabet. Here I want to issue a disclaimer, cautioning you to hold what I say here in a kind of suspension. The terms I'll be using, terms like "the engaged I," "the reconstructed I," "the reminiscent I," are provisional terms of my own. There may be better names and, more to the point, other *kinds* of "I"s. We're not trying to create a filing system for ourselves as readers; rather we're trying, as readers, to look at the full potential of this most important and basic component of first-person narrative. It's better to think of these terms as refractions through a prism; besides, these various "I"s shade off into one another as we move from one part of a text to another. In most authors you'll find a tendency to shift through these different first-person strategies like moving through so many gears as the story's changing terrain makes different demands. Many authors primarily toggle back and forth between a couple of the possibilities while others use the full array. Let's have a look.

The engaged I: I want to start with a use of the first-person pronoun I call the "engaged I" because so many memoirists also start with it, and not because it is a primary kind of narration. It does have certain virtues, as we'll see in a moment, that are especially suitable for beginnings.

The engaged I makes overt editorial or political statements on behalf of a worldview, belief system, or social/political agenda. We see what the author is engaging in the work: injustice, ignorance, heresy, misunderstanding, life-threatening illness. It is often a bold statement of the reason for the work. Here, for example, is Maxim Gorky expressing his moral indignation and engagement with the issue of childhood poverty and cruelty:

> Sometimes when I recall the abominations of that barbarous Russian life I ask myself whether it is worthwhile to speak of them. And, with renewed conviction, I answer—yes, it is; for they are the vicious, tenacious truth, which has not been exterminated to this very day. They represent the truth which must be exposed to its roots and torn out of our grim and shameful life—torn out of the very soul and memory of man.
>
> Maxim Gorky, *Childhood*

Another kind of engagement is that of the writer with his material, with the labor to translate the vision to the page:

> Not long after our arrival, we went to a bookshop; she asked for an English-German grammar, bought the first book they showed her, took me home immediately, and began instruction. How can I depict that instruction believably? I know how it went—how could I forget?—but still I can't believe it myself.
>
> Elias Canetti, *The Tongue Set Free*

What's more, because every memoir, on one level, is also about the act of remembering, this engaged I sometimes struggles with memory itself:

> I am sorry to be so vague, especially because I am proud of my good memory, and many have remarked upon it, but all I can remember is sitting on my one suitcase (I travel light) and waiting for hours to get going. Anywhere.
> Neither can I remember how I got to the pier, although obviously it was on the boat from Paris.
>
> Mary Cantwell, *Speaking with Strangers*

So, what I'm calling "the engaged I" appears most often early in the story, in the first chapter or even the prologue to a memoir, and then gives up its place to "the reminiscent I," "the reconstructed I," and others we'll talk about in a moment. Because "the engaged I" is often didactic, a little of its use goes a long way. Too much or too often and you're haranguing your reader who, even if he or she agrees with your view, is no longer in the thrall of your storytelling.

The reminiscent I invites us to accompany the narrator in her remembering. The simplest form of this is a sentence that begins, "I remember . . .," or, "I recall . . . ." Here the narrator views the past at least mostly from the vantage of the present. In any case, this "reminiscent I" straddles two time frames—one foot in the present, one in the past. It is the most usual, probably because it is the most natural, form of the first-person that memoirists use.

> When I first sat down in that great sea of tedium I thought somebody at the *Times* was trying to make me feel humble about working for the paper that printed all the news that was fit to print. Everything seemed aimed at making me feel like the smallest fish in the biggest pond on earth.
>
> Russell Baker, *The Good Times*

The reconstructed I is often introduced by "the reminiscent I," as a way of establishing the time, place, and particulars needed in order to enter into the reconstructed consciousness of the narrator in an earlier time.

Almost all of Frank McCourt's *Angela's Ashes* is written from the reconstructed vantage of a young boy. Nothing young Frankie could not know is recorded, whether because he couldn't have seen it or because he couldn't have understood it; though, as we'll see, much that the boy could not know is nonetheless communicated. When we narrate in the reconstructed voice and consciousness of a child, accepting those bounds, we rely on the reader to interpret and or interpolate things in a way the child cannot. This gap between what the child experiences but cannot understand, or misunderstands, and what the reader, once a child himself, *now* understands can be, in skillful hands, an irresistable invitation to empathy, whether with joy or suffering.

Even when "the reconstructed I" is not the remembered/imagined voice of a child, but the representation of the self in an earlier period, it gives the writer the opportunity to play a scene from the past against some knowledge of what has happened since then, thus involving the reader by engaging her own historical experience. Take, for example, the holocaust memoir of Primo Levi, which derives at least some of its power from the fact that both "the reminiscent I" and the reader know full well the horrors to come that "the reconstructed I," the younger first-person narrator, speaking from within an earlier time frame, cannot.

> Now another German comes and tells us to put the shoes in a certain corner, and we put them there, because now it is all over and we feel outside the world and the only thing is to obey. Someone comes with a broom and sweeps away all the shoes, outside the door in a heap. He is crazy, he is mixing them all together, ninety-six pairs, they will all be unmatchable.
>
> Primo Levi, *Survival in Auschwitz*

The self-regarding I is the I interrogating and exploring itself within a specific time frame. A memoir that doesn't catch the first-person narrator, at whatever age, being self-conscious, hesitant, unsure, is not being honest about the complexity of the self. In another words, if I am to trust the narrator in the present, I need to see him [or her] being honest about his or her motives and mistakes and confusions and shortcomings perhaps even at some cost to our estimation of him.

> I hate to say it, but hearing Frank's stories, I became grateful my father died when I was still young before my own hopes got in his way. I say it in part because I'm glad I never had to fight with him, never got stepped on in the way my brothers did. I also say it because I know the range of my own anger and determination, and my own awful, unswerving stubbornness.
>
> Mikal Gilmore, *Shot in the Heart*

The imagining I is fairly straightforward in announcing itself; usually it's heralded by the simple phrase "I imagine," or "I imagined," although sometimes, for effect, the writer may prefer to let this realization sneak up on the reader.

This is a simple and useful tool for filling in gaps in the story. You either remember what you imagined to be the case when you were a certain age, or you announce "I imagine . . . " now, meaning that acknowledge the limits of your knowledge as a writer, and that you're going to give us the following scene courtesy of your imagination.

In the hospital room as my father told it all to me I could see the journey through his eyes: Mrs. Macek moving before him, her shoulders resolute, and before her the tall figure of Dr. Macek and more distantly, the moving shadow of Pisa. The forest floor and the mountain fields were a combination of snow, puddles and mud, and it was cold and raw. Sometimes at the edge of the snowy meadows, they could see footprints where the border patrol had just been.

Joseph Hurka, *Fields of Light*

The documentary I is an EYE, really, and not much else. This may be the eye, view, or vantage of a "reconstructed I" but it is different in the intensity of its connection to what is going on. This is a narrator who is at one remove from the scene, watching, and not filtering what's seen through any feelings or interpretations. It is as if the camera is on the shoulder of the narrator, merely recording what is visible as she walks on the street, stands in a room, watches and listens. What the reader gets is the place, the events, the other people. The "documentary I" gets its power from the complete lack of commentary, and from a tight focus and careful selection of what's being shown to us.

Afghan rugs. In the 1980s, Afghan rugs, which had drawn their designs from age-old tradition, developed new patterns: helicopters and tanks.

Adam Zagajewski, *Another Beauty*

The men are drinking stout from bottles again the women are sipping sherry from jam jars. Uncle Pat Sheehan tells everyone, This is my stout, this is my stout, and Grandma says, Tis all right, Pat No one will take your stout. Then he says he wants to sing "The Road to Rasheen" till Pa Keating says, No, Pat, you can't sing on the day of the funeral. You can sing the night before. But Uncle Pat keeps saying, This is my stout and I want to sing "The Road to Rasheen," and everyone knows he talks like that because he was dropped on his head. He starts to sing his song but stops when Grandma takes the lid off the coffin and Mam sobs, Oh Jesus, oh, Jesus, will it ever stop? Will I be left with one child?

Frank McCourt, *Angela's Ashes*

Any first-person narrative, but particularly memoir with its insistence on at least the subjective veracity (i.e. *honesty*) of the tale it tells, must engage the reader on several levels to be successful. The memoirist, like the novelist, must take pains to create a multifaceted, emotionally three-dimensional chararacter whose name is I. He or she must be continually aware of the gap between what the narrator knows, what the reader knows, and what the character—I—knows, and how to make use of those understandings to create trust and empathy in the reader. Making use of a number of first-person strategies gives a story complexity, texture, and authenticity, and results in a dramatic work that will satisfy even the most sophisticated reader.

Analysis: First-Person Strategies

Richard Hoffman's catalog of first-person strategies in memoir writing offers insight into the variety of ways memoirists present their own experience through acts of remembering. These are not simply tricks of the trade but figure more consequentially, as Hoffman notes, in determining the relationship between the memoirist and readers, in eliciting empathy, trust, and identification. In this sense, Hoffman's "provisional" categories enable us to see how the "contract with the reader one makes" takes shape in memoirs.

■ FOR CRITICAL INQUIRY

1. Consider the memoirs that appear in this chapter in terms of the first-person strategies employed. You may not find examples of all the categories Hoffman presents, but see if you can identify a number of them. What functions do they perform in the context of specific memoirs?

2. Hoffman makes the point that memoirs depend, at least in part, on gaining the trust of readers. Pick one or two memoirs in this chapter and explain how the memoirist seeks to gain the reader's trust and the extent to which you think he or she is successful.

3. Consider Hoffman's idea that there are actually three kinds of knowledge in memoirs—"what the narrator knows, what the reader knows, and what the character—I—knows." Pick one of the memoirs that illustrates the three types of knowledge and explain why and how there is a "gap" between them.

ETHICS OF WRITING

BEARING WITNESS

Part of a memoirist's authority derives from the fact of his or her having been an eyewitness to the events recounted. Memoirists are participants as well as observers. For these reasons, memoirists face some important ethical issues concerning their responsibility as witnesses to the past. How does the memoirist represent the other people involved? What are the memoirist's responsibilities to these people? What is the memoirist entitled to divulge about his or her private life? What are the memoirist's loyalties to those he or she writes about? Might such loyalties conflict with obligations to readers? What impact will the memoir have on the writer's relationship with others in the present, and does this potential impact affect the retelling? In cases where the memoirist feels hurt, angry, or offended by what took place, can he or she nonetheless be fair?

These are questions that memoirists invariably struggle with, and there are no easy answers, especially when a memoir treats situations that are difficult or painful. The memoir, don't forget, is an act of self-discovery, and yet memoirs are written for the public to read. As witnesses to the past, memoirists can handle their responsibility to others in an ethical way by seeking to understand the motives and character of those involved, including themselves. ■

FURTHER EXPLORATION: MEMOIRS

■ RHETORICAL ANALYSIS

Consider the writers' ethos in the memoirs you've just read. See the section below "First-Person Strategies" (pp. 159) for ideas about the various "I" speakers that appear in memoir. You can focus on one memoir or compare two or more. How do the writers construct themselves as characters and as first-person narrators? Does the writer set up the relationship between herself as the memoir's narrator in the present and herself as a character in recollected experience from the past? How have the writers handled their ethical responsibility to others involved in the memoir? What kind of relationship do they want to establish with their readers?

■ GENRE AWARENESS

Imagine you are going to turn one of the print memoirs in this chapter into a graphic memoir. Turn the opening three paragraphs into panels. How many would you need? What drawings and words would you put in them? How would you set up the transition from one panel to the next? Consider what this exercise reveals about the two types of memoir. What does the reliance on written text in the print memoir make possible? What does the combination of words and images in the graphic memoir make possible? What can each do that the other can't?

WRITING ASSIGNMENT

Memoir

Your task is to write a memoir, to bring to life a moment in the past to explore the meanings it has for the present. Since memoirs enable both writers and their readers to understand the past, this assignment can be a good time for you to probe significant times in your life, revisiting them now that you have some distance from them.

- Consider the tensions or conflicts you experienced in high school, as Gail Caldwell does.

- Use a pop song, as Dave Marsh does, to write a memoir about a time and place. Or use a TV show, film, video game, dance craze, clothes, or hairstyle, or other aspect of the media or popular culture to focus your memoir in a time and place.

- Pick a photograph that holds memories and emotional associations. Focus on a particular detail that recalls a particular moment in the past to explore how your family's history intersects larger social and historical forces.

- Recall a particular family ritual, such as visits to grandparents, Sunday dinners, summer vacations, holiday celebrations, weddings, and so on, as a way to focus on an event or a person that is especially significant to you.

- Consider some aspect of your own cultural ancestry—whether it is the language your ancestors spoke, a kind of food or music, a family tradition, an heirloom that has been passed down from generation to generation—to explain how the past has entered your life and what it reveals about your relationship to the culture of your ancestors.

- Focus on a childhood incident, as Annie Dillard does, to re-create the event and your own perspective as a younger person.

- Look through an old diary or journal, if you have kept one. Look for moments when you faced an occasion that challenged your values or where you had a difficult decision to make, experienced a situation that turned out unexpectedly, or were keenly disappointed.

Invention

Past and Present Perspectives

To clarify the purpose of your memoir and what you want it to mean to readers, consider what your feelings were at the moment things were taking place in the past and what they are now as you look back from the perspective of the present.

Considering the memory you're writing about from past and present perspectives can help you to clarify the double role of the memoir writer—as a participant and as an observer—and to decide what relative emphasis each of the two perspectives will take on in your memoir.

■ EXERCISE

Exploring Past and Present Perspectives

Past perspective: Recall in as much detail as possible what your feelings were at the time you are writing about in your memoir. Spend five minutes or so responding to these questions in writing:

1. What was your initial reaction to the moment in the past you're writing about? What did you think at the time? How did you feel? What did other people seem to think and feel?

2. Did your initial reaction persist or did it change? If it changed, what set of feelings replaced it? What caused the change? Were other people involved in this change?

Present perspective: Now think about your present perspective. Write for another five minutes or so in response to these questions:

1. Looking back on the moment in the past, how do the feelings you experienced at the time appear to you today? Do they seem reasonable? Why or why not?

2. Have your feelings changed? Do things look different from the perspective of the present? If so, how would you explain the change?

3. As you compare your feelings from the past and your feelings in the present, what conclusions can you draw about the significance the memory has for you? Are your feelings resolved, or do they seem unsettled and changing? In either case, what do you think has shaped your current perspective?

Review the two writings: Use them to write a third statement that defines what you see as the significance of the memory you're writing about and what your purpose is in recreating it for your readers. What does the memory reveal about the past? How do you want to present yourself in relation to what happened in the past? If there is conflict or crisis, what are your loyalties toward the people and the events?

Background Research: Putting Events in Context

As the by memoirs Dave Marsh and Gail Caldwell show, placing your memories and experiences in a larger cultural and historical context can add layers of meaning to the event or events you are telling. In this way, you can link your life with social trends and political events happening around you at the time.

You may want (or need) to look in the library and on the Internet for more help in responding to these questions. Check, for example, *The New York Times Index* for that particular year, or the *Facts on File Yearbook.* Weekly periodicals such as *Time, Newsweek,* and *U.S. News & World Report* have an end-of-year issue that can help provide both cultural and historical perspectives.

Isolate the year in which your chosen event happened. If you are examining a ritual that occurred many times, pick one such instance and focus only on that. In answering the following questions, you might need to ask family members or friends for their impressions, insights, and suggestions.

- Was there anything remarkable about that year in the context of national and world events? Is that year "famous" for anything?

- What was the "news story" of the year? What was the "success story" of the year? Who were the "heroes" that year?

- What were the major social conflicts that year? Were there important political demonstrations or social movements in any part of the country? If so, what were they about? Were there any natural disasters that captured national attention that year?

- Is there a generation associated with that year (World War II veterans, baby boomers, Generation X, millennials)?

- What kind of music was most popular? What TV shows and movies?

Review your responses. What links, if any, can connect your own experience and the experiences of others at the historical moment you are considering? What cultural and historical contexts might be illuminating in your memoir?

Planning

Arranging Your Material

Memoir writers sometimes tell a story in chronological order, from beginning to end, as Annie Dillard does. Notice how Dillard begins paragraphs in the early part of her memoir to keep track of the events as they unfold over time:

¶3: "On one weekday morning after Christmas . . . "

¶6: "I started making an iceball . . . "

¶7: "I had just embarked on the iceball project when we heard tire chains come clanking from afar."

¶9: "Often, of course, we hit our target, but this time, the only time in all of life, the car pulled over and stopped."

On the other hand, instead of chronological order, Dave Marsh uses a two-part structure to arrange his memoir so that he can treat his experience growing up in Pontiac from more than one angle, looping back in Part II to return to the song that ends Part I. Likewise, Gail Caldwell chooses not to use chronology but to present a sequence of episodes that work together, like a mosaic, to create a dominant impression of her teenage years in Texas:

¶1: Driving mother's car ninety miles an hour.

¶2–3: Rides with her father and "talks."

¶4: Two young men Caldwell knows flee to Canada to avoid the military draft.

¶6: Caldwell keeps quiet about George Wallace.

¶7: Caldwell blows admission to National Honor Society and lies about her major.

Here are some questions to help you design a working draft:

- **How will you begin?** Do you want to ease into the moment from the past or state it outright? How can you capture your readers' interest? Do you need to establish background information? How will you present yourself—as a participant in the past or as an observer from the perspective of the present? Consider the first-person strategies Richard Hoffman describes in "The Ninth Letter of the Alphabet."

- **What arrangement best suits your material?** If you are telling a single story, how can you keep the narrative crisp and moving? Do you need to interrupt the chronology with commentary, description, interpretation, asides? If you are using selected incidents, what order best conveys the point you want them to make? Do the separate incidents create a dominant impression?

- **How will you set up the moment of revelation** that gives your memoir its meaning and significance? Do you want to anticipate this moment by foreshadowing, which gives readers a hint of the revelation that is to come? Or do you want it to appear suddenly?

- **How will you end your memoir?** Do you want to surprise readers with an unsuspected meaning? Or do you want to step back from what has taken place to reflect on its significance? Is there a way in which you can echo the opening of the memoir to make your readers feel they have come full circle?

Based on your answers to these questions, make a working outline of your memoir. If you're planning to tell a story from start to finish, indicate the key incidents in the event you're remembering. If you're planning to use a sequence of memories, block out the separate events. Then you can consider the best order in which to present them.

Selecting Detail

Memoirists often use techniques you can find in fiction: scene setting, description of people, action, and dialogue. These techniques enable memoirists (like fiction writers) to re-create the past in vivid and convincing detail. Designing a memoir (like fiction writing) involves decisions about the type and amount of detail you need to make your re-creation of the past memorable to readers.

- **Scene setting:** Use vivid and specific description to set the scene; name particular objects; give details about places and things; use description and detail to establish mood.

- **Description of people:** Use descriptions of people's appearances to highlight their personalities in your memoir; describe the clothes they are wearing; give details about a person's physical presence, gestures, facial features, and hairstyle; notice personal habits; use description and detail to establish character.

- **Dialogue:** Put words in your characters' mouths that reveal their personalities; invent dialogue that is faithful to people's ways of speaking (even if you don't use their exact words); use dialogue to establish relationships between characters.

- **Action:** Put the characters in your memoir in motion; use narrative to tell about something that happened; use narrative to develop characters and reveal the theme of your memoir.

Working Draft

Review the writing you have done so far. Draw on the sketching you have done, the writing that compares past and present perspectives, and your analysis of cultural and historical contexts. Consider the tentative decisions you've made about how to arrange your material—in chronological order or as a related sequence of events. As you begin composing a working draft of your memoir, you'll need to think about how you can best bring out the significance of your memories.

Beginnings and Endings: Framing Your Memoir

Notice how the writers frame their memoirs to highlight the revelations that make these writings meaningful. For example, in his opening paragraph Gary Soto introduces the idea that there are "two kinds of work," and then, after telling about his experience at the tire factory, he returns in the last six paragraphs to explore what he found out about work that "uses muscle."

Annie Dillard also uses this strategy to frame her essay. In the opening passage she anticipates the larger significance of the event she is about to re-create: "I got in trouble throwing snowballs, and have seldom been happier since." Then she tells the story of the man who chased her and of her "immense discovery." At the end of the memoir, Dillard extends the meaning of the opening lines: "If in that snowy backyard the driver of the black Buick had cut off our heads, Mikey's and mine, I would have died happy, for nothing has required so much of me since as being chased all over Pittsburgh in the middle of winter—running terrified, exhausted."

Peer Commentary

Once you've written a working draft, you are ready to get feedback from others. Before exchanging papers, work through the following exercise. Then, you can guide your partner or group members in how to best help you.

■ EXERCISE

Analyzing Your Draft

1. Write an account of your working draft.
   a. What made you want to write this memoir? Describe in as much detail as you can what you experienced as the call to write.
   b. What is your purpose in the working draft? What are you trying to reveal about the moment in the past? What significance does this moment hold for you?
   c. What problems or uncertainties do you see in your working draft? Ask your readers about particular passages in the draft so that you can get specific feedback.
2. Your readers can offer you feedback, either oral or written, based on your working draft and the commentary you have written. Here are questions for your readers to take into account.
   a. Does the writer's purpose come across clearly? Are you able to see and understand the significance of the moment in the writer's past? If the significance of the moment is not revealed clearly enough, what suggestions can you offer?

   b. Is the memoir organized effectively? Does the moment of revelation appear in the best place? Does the essay begin with sufficient background information and scene setting? Comment on the ending of the memoir. Does the writer pull things together in a way that is satisfying to the reader?

   c. Is the writing vivid and concrete in re-creating particular scenes and moments from the past? Point to passages that are particularly vivid. Are there passages that are too vague, obscure, or abstract? Do the narrative passages move along crisply or do they seem to drag?

Revising

Use the commentary you have received to plan a revision.

1. Do you re-create the experience you're remembering, as opposed to just telling your readers what happened?

2. Can readers easily follow what you're remembering? Are there first person strategies that you could use to revise?

3. Will readers be able to see clearly how you experienced the events in the past and how you think about them now? Is there a moment of revelation that gives the memoir significance?

4. Are the events and people in the memoir vivid? Do you need more detail?

5. What, if anything, should you cut? What do you need to add?

From Telling to Showing

Jennifer Plante revised the opening paragraphs of her memoir (a complete draft of the memoir is included in the Writers' Workshop below) to move from a summary of Sunday afternoons at her grandparents' house to a much fuller scene setting. Her revision is a good example of the difference between telling and showing. Plante said she wanted to begin by just telling about these family gatherings. Telling about them helped her to bring her memories to consciousness. At the same time, however, she wasn't satisfied that the first version really captured the feeling of those afternoons. There's more she wanted to show about what those afternoons were really like. Notice how the memories in one paragraph of the early draft generate two paragraphs.

Early Draft

When I was ten years old, my family used to go to my grandparents' house every Sunday for dinner. It was a kind of ritual. My grandmother would cook a pot roast—I should say she overcooked it—and at the dinner table, my grandfather would carry forth on his political views. He was an intimidating, opinionated man. Nonetheless, this was a special time for me. As a ten-year-old, I didn't really understand the politics but I did know I was a special granddaughter.

After dinner, my grandfather and I would watch the New England Patriots if they were on TV that week. He was the kind of hardcore fan who shouted at the Patriots players as if he were the coach, and I imitated him.

Revised Version

The smell of over-cooked pot roast still magically carries me back to Sunday afternoons at my grandparents' house. I was all of ten years old; a tom-boyish, pig-tailed girl who worshiped the ground that her elders walked on. Back then, my grandfather seemed like an enormous man, every bit as intimidating as he was loving. He knew what he wanted, what he believed in, he thought that President Reagan was a demigod, and he thought that his only granddaughter was one of the biggest joys of his life. I remember that every time my family went over to my grandparents' humble home, I would run into my grandfather's warm arms and get swallowed up in a loving hug. Then, he'd sweep me off of my feet and twirl me around in the air until I was giggling so hard that I could no longer breathe.

After we ate the charcoaled roast, I would follow my grandfather into the living room. Light always seemed to radiate from the huge picture window spreading warmth into the living room; it never seemed to rain while I was at my grandparents' house. I would proceed to sit on my grandfather's lap while he stretched out in his La-Z Boy and flipped through the T.V. channels to find the New England Patriots' football game. He would often shout at the players as if he was their coach, and trying to emulate him, I would shout equally as loud not knowing what the hell I was talking about (face-masking means nothing to a ten-year-old girl). This is how every Sunday afternoon of my childhood was spent; the sequence of events was very ritualistic, and the only thing distinguishing one Sunday from another was which meal my grandmother would decide to burn. ■

W WRITERS' WORKSHOP

Jennifer Plante wrote the following two pieces in response to an assignment in her composition class that called on students to write a memoir. The first piece is Plante's commentary on an early working draft of a short memoir based on her recollections of Sunday afternoon visits to her grandparents' house. In this commentary, she describes the call to write that got her started on the piece in the first place and her own sense of both the potential and the problems of her work in progress. You'll notice that she wrote her commentary as a kind of interim report—to explain what she was trying to do and to request feedback, constructive criticism, and suggestions from her readers.

The second piece of writing is the working draft itself, before Jennifer went on to revise it. As you read, remember that Jennifer's memoir is a work in progress. Try to read it through her commentary, to see what advice or suggestions you would give her concerning revision.

JENNIFER PLANTE'S COMMENTARY

What got me started on this piece of writing is exactly what I begin with—the smell of over-cooked pot roast. For some reason, when I was thinking about a memoir I might write, this smell suddenly seemed to leap out at me and bring me back to the Sunday afternoons we spent at my grandparents. In one way, I wanted to remember these days because I loved them so much. I felt so safe and secure and loved, with not only my parents but my grandparents surrounding me. I tried to find images of warmth, light, and enclosure to re-create this feeling. I wanted the opening to have a Norman Rockwell-like, almost sentimental feel to it—of the "typical" American family living out the American dream of family gatherings. A ritualistic feel.

But I also wanted the paragraphs to serve as a set-up for what was to come, which is really the point of the memoir. It was on a typical Sunday when I was ten that my father and grandfather argued, and my grandfather made these incredibly racist and homophobic comments. I didn't understand at the time exactly what my grandfather meant but I did understand the look on my father's face—and that something had happened that was going to change things.

I think I've done a decent job of setting this scene up, but I don't think it fully conveys what I want it to. So I had to add the final section reflecting back on it and how I now feel betrayed by my grandfather. I think this last part is probably too obvious and maybe even a little bit preachy or self-righteous, though I try to explain how my grandfather is a product of his upbringing. I want readers to understand how my feelings toward my grandfather went from completely adoring to totally mixed and contradictory ones. I don't think this is coming out clearly enough and I would appreciate any suggestions about how to do it or to improve any other parts of the essay.

JENNIFER PLANTE, SUNDAY AFTERNOONS

The smell of over-cooked pot roast still magically carries me back to Sunday afternoons at my grandparents' house. I was all of ten years old; a tom-boyish, pig-tailed girl who worshiped the ground that her elders walked on. Back then, my grandfather seemed like an enormous man, every bit as intimidating as he was loving. He knew what he wanted, what he believed in, he thought that President Reagan was a demigod, and he thought that his only granddaughter was one of the biggest joys of his life. I remember that every time my family went over to my grandparents' humble home, I would run into my grandfather's warm arms and get swallowed up in a loving hug. Then, he'd sweep me off of my feet and twirl me around in the air until I was giggling so hard that I could no longer breathe.

After we ate the charcoaled roast, I would follow my grandfather into the living room. Light always seemed to radiate from the huge picture window spreading warmth into the living room; it never seemed to rain while I was at my grandparents' house. I would proceed to sit on my grandfather's lap while he stretched out in his La-Z Boy and flipped through the T.V. channels to find the New England Patriots' football game. He would often shout at the players as if he was their coach, and trying to emulate him, I would shout equally as loud not knowing what the hell I was talking about (face-masking means nothing to a ten-year-old girl). This is how every Sunday afternoon of my childhood was spent; the sequence of events was very ritualistic, and the only thing distinguishing one Sunday from another was which meal my grandmother would decide to burn.

One Sunday afternoon, my grandfather and I had assumed our normal positions on the brown, beat-up chair and found our Patriots losing to some random team. I'm not exactly sure how the subject came up, but my grandfather and my dad began discussing politics and our society. My grandfather and my dad held different opinions about both topics, so as usual, the debate had gotten pretty heated. I began feeling a bit uncomfortable as the discussion wore on; they talked for what seemed like hours and they must have discussed every issue that was of importance to our society. To numb my discomfort, I became focused on the T.V. screen—Steve Grogan had just completed a 30-yard touchdown pass, but the referee had called that "face-masking" thing on the offense, sending Patriot fans into a frenzy. Then, just as quickly as it had started, the debate ended in dead silence. My father sat, open-mouthed, in disbelief at what he'd just heard; my grandfather had finally spoken his mind.

"What is this interracial marriage garbage? Decent white people shouldn't be marrying those blacks. And what is this perverted gay business? All the gays should go back into the closet where they belong!"

I didn't understand what my grandfather had said at the time, but I did notice the look on my father's face. It was as if my grandfather had just slapped him, only I somehow knew that what he'd said had hurt my father much more than any slap ever could have. And I did notice that, for the first time ever, a hard rain began to fall outside.

I look back on that day now and I understand why my father looked so hurt. I also understand now what my grandfather had said, and can't help but feel betrayed that a man that I admired so much had managed to insult over half of the population in one breath. I do feel bitter towards my grandfather, but I can't really blame him for his ignorance; he is a product of his time, and they were taught to hate difference. But ever since that day, I have vowed that, when my grandchildren come to visit me on Sunday afternoons, they will never see a hard rain falling outside of my picture window.

■ WORKSHOP QUESTIONS

1. Do you agree with Jennifer Plante that she has done a "decent" job of scene-setting in the opening sections of her memoir? Does the memoir's opening effectively re-create the "ritualistic feel" of family gatherings? Does it become too sentimental? Explain your responses to these questions and make any suggestions you might have for strengthening the opening.

2. Plante's memoir relies on a moment of revelation—when her grandfather makes racist and homophobic remarks and these remarks have an effect on her father. Does this moment have the dramatic value and emotional force it needs as the pivotal point in the memoir—the moment that "changed things"? What suggestions, if any, would you offer to strengthen this crucial point in the memoir?

3. Plante seems dissatisfied with the final section of the memoir, in which she writes from the perspective of the present, reflecting back on a moment in the past. She worries about seeming "obvious," "preachy," and "self-righteous" in describing her sense of betrayal. Do you think this is a problem in the draft? What advice would you offer to strengthen this section of the memoir? ■

REFLECTING ON YOUR WRITING

Write an account that explains how you handled the dual role of the memoir writer as a participant and as an observer. How did you re-create yourself as a character in your memoir? What is the relationship between your self in the past and the perspective of your present self? If memoirs are in part acts of writing that bear witness to and thereby take responsibility for the past, how do the selves you have created and re-created express loyalties and social allegiances?

public documents

THINKING ABOUT THE GENRE

People in contemporary society rely on public documents to organize and carry out a wide range of social activities. Public documents serve to codify the beliefs and practices of a culture, a community, an organization—any group of people who share a mutual concern. Unlike many of the genres of writing in this textbook, public documents derive their authority from collective sources instead of from the individual who wrote them. Public documents speak on behalf of a group of people to articulate the principles and procedures that organize their purposes and guide their way of life.

Some public documents, such as the Ten Commandments or the Declaration of Independence, have taken on a sacred or nearly sacred character because they codify principles of morality and political liberty that are considered fundamental to a whole way of life. Their power resides in the authority people have invested over time in these documents as basic accounts of what they believe and hold most dear.

Other public documents serve to codify customary behavior and legal arrangements. Marriage vows, contracts, wills, and other agreements commit parties to binding relationships that are publicly and legally recognized. Government documents of all types—from laws and passports to driver's license applications and tax forms—establish relationships between the state and citizens.

Still other documents charter the mission and activities of voluntary associations people have formed to respond to particular needs—organizations such as student clubs, neighborhood associations, trade unions, and non-profits. Writing a constitution for such a group literally constitutes it as a public entity by giving the group a name and a statement of purpose. Not only does this establish an identity for members of the group, but it also enables them to be heard on the public record and to shape public opinion. Civic organizations, advocacy groups, and professional associations routinely issue petitions calling for change and policy statements addressing public concerns.

Public documents can tell us a lot about the culture we're living in. The encounters people have with public documents reveal how writing links individuals to social institutions. Just as important, you can write and use documents on your own behalf to accomplish your ends—to establish new voluntary associations and their purposes, to define policies and procedures you're willing to live by, to recruit sympathizers to a cause you believe in, to articulate new social identities, and to define new directions for the future.

■ WRITING FROM EXPERIENCE

List as many documents from your college or university as you can that involve students. Pick one that in your view reveals something interesting about students' relationship to others. It could be your college's honor code or its policy on sexual harassment, a student loan form, or a job description. Analyze the relationship the document seeks to establish between the individual student and others. Describe what the document covers. What rights and responsibilities does it assign to the individual student? What rights and responsibilities does it assign to others? What beliefs does the document attempt to put into practice?

READINGS

MANIFESTOS

DECLARATION OF INDEPENDENCE

By July 4, 1776, when the Continental Congress approved the Declaration of Independence written by Thomas Jefferson, fighting had already broken out between American patriots and the British military. The Declaration of Independence is a manifesto that marks the decisive moment when severing ties to England and establishing a new nation become the goals of the struggle.

Establishes the occasion

Gives a reason why declaration was written and identifies audience

IN CONGRESS, July 4, 1776

The unanimous Declaration of the thirteen United States of America,

When in the Course of human Events, it becomes necessary for one People to dissolve the Political Bands which have connected them with another, and to assume among the Powers of the Earth, the separate and equal Station to which the Laws of Nature and of Nature's God entitle them, a decent Respect to the Opinions of Mankind requires that they should declare the causes which impel them to the Separation.

We hold these truths to be self-evident, that all Men are created equal, that they are endowed by their Creator with certain unalienable Rights, that among these are Life,

Liberty and the pursuit of Happiness.—That to secure these Rights, Governments are instituted among Men, deriving their just Powers from the Consent of the Governed, That whenever any Form of Government becomes destructive of these ends, it is the <u>Right of the People to alter or to abolish it</u>, and to institute new Government, laying its Foundation on such Principles and organizing its Powers in such Form, as to them shall seem most likely to effect their Safety and Happiness. Prudence, indeed, will dictate that Governments long established <u>should not be changed for light and transient Causes</u>; and accordingly all Experience hath shewn, that Mankind are more disposed to suffer, while Evils are sufferable, than to right themselves by abolishing the Forms to which they are accustomed. But <u>when a long Train of Abuses and Usurpations</u>, pursuing invariably the same Object evinces a Design to reduce them under absolute Despotism, it is Right, it is their Duty, to throw off such Government, and to provide new Guards for their future security. Such has been the patient Sufferance of these Colonies; and such is now the Necessity which constrains them to alter their former Systems of Government. The history of the present King of Great-Britain is a history of repeated Injuries and Usurpations, all having in direct Object the Establishment of an absolute Tyranny over these States. To <u>prove this, let Facts be submitted</u> to a candid World.

He has refused his Assent to Laws, the most wholesome and necessary for the public Good.

He has forbidden his Governors to pass Laws of immediate and pressing importance, unless suspended in their Operation till his Assent should be obtained; and when so suspended, he has utterly neglected to attend to them.

He has refused to pass other Laws for the Accommodation of large Districts of People, unless those People would relinquish the Right of Representation in the Legislature, a Right inestimable to them and formidable to Tyrants only.

He has called together Legislative Bodies at Places unusual, uncomfortable, and distant from the Depository of their public Records, for the sole Purpose of fatiguing them into Compliance with his Measures.

He has dissolved Representative Houses repeatedly, for opposing with manly Firmness his invasions on the Rights of the People.

He has refused for a long Time, after such Dissolutions, to cause others to be elected; whereby the Legislature Powers, incapable of Annihilation, have returned to the People at large for their exercise; the State remaining in the mean time exposed to all the Dangers of Invasion from without, and Convulsions within.

Margin annotations:

Sets out fundamental premises

Claims a right based on premises

Qualifies right

Establishes grounds for independence

Presents evidence of tyranny

Lists king's oppressive acts

He has endeavoured to prevent the Population of these States; for that Purpose obstructing the Laws for Naturalization of Foreigners; refusing to pass others to encourage their Migrations hither, and raising the Conditions of new Appropriations of Lands.

He has obstructed the Administration of Justice, by refusing his Assent to Laws for establishing Judiciary Powers.

He has made Judges dependent on his Will alone, for the Tenure of their Offices, and the Amount and Payment of their Salaries.

He has erected a Multitude of New Offices, and sent hither Swarms of Officers to harass our People, and eat out their Substance.

He has kept among us, in Times of Peace, Standing Armies without the Consent of our Legislatures.

He has affected to render the Military independent of and superior to the Civil Power.

He has combined with others to subject us to a Jurisdiction foreign to our Constitution, and unacknowledged by our Laws; giving his Assent to their Acts of pretended Legislation:

For quartering Large Bodies of Armed Troops among us:

For protecting them, by a mock Trial, from Punishment for any Murders which they should commit on the Inhabitants of these States:

For cutting off our Trade with all Parts of the World:

For imposing Taxes on us without our Consent:

For depriving us in many Cases, of the Benefits of Trial by Jury:

For transporting us beyond Seas to be tried for pretended Offences:

Lists oppressive acts of colonial government

For abolishing the free System of English Laws in a neighbouring Province, establishing therein an arbitrary Government, and enlarging its Boundaries so as to render it at once an Example and fit Instrument for introducing the same absolute Rule into these Colonies:

For taking away our Charters, abolishing our most valuable Laws, and altering fundamentally the Forms of our Governments:

For suspending our own Legislatures, and declaring themselves invested with Power to legislate for us in all Cases whatsoever.

He has abdicated Government here, by declaring us out of his Protection and waging War against us.

He has plundered our Seas, ravaged our Coasts, burnt our Towns, and destroyed the Lives of our People.

Lists
further
actions by
king

He is, at this Time, transporting large Armies of foreign Mercenaries to compleat the Works of Death, Desolation and Tyranny, already begun with circumstances of Cruelty & perfidy scarcely paralleled in the most barbarous Ages, and totally unworthy the Head of a civilized Nation.

He has constrained our fellow Citizens taken Captive on the high Seas to bear Arms against their Country, to become the Executioners of their Friends and Brethren, or to fall themselves by their Hands.

He has excited domestic Insurrections amongst us, and has endeavoured to bring on the Inhabitants of our Frontiers, the merciless Indian Savages, whose known Rule of Warfare, is an undistinguished destruction of all Ages, Sexes and Conditions.

In every stage of these Oppressions <u>We have Petitioned</u> for Redress in the most humble Terms: Our repeated Petitions have been answered only by repeated Injury. A Prince, whose character is thus marked by every act which may define a Tyrant, is unfit to be the Ruler of a free People.

Explains
efforts to
remedy
situation

<u>Nor have We been wanting in Attentions</u> to our British Brethren. <u>We have warned</u> them from Time to Time of Attempts by their Legislature to extend an unwarrantable Jurisdiction over us. We have reminded them of the Circumstances of our Emigration and Settlement here. <u>We have appealed</u> to their native Justice and Magnanimity, and <u>we have conjured</u> them by the Ties of our common Kindred to disavow these Usurpations, which, would inevitably interrupt our Connections and Correspondence. They too have been deaf to the Voice of Justice and of Consanguinity. We must, therefore, acquiesce in the Necessity, which denounces our Separation, and hold them, as we hold the rest of Mankind, Enemies in War, in Peace Friends.

We, therefore, the Representatives of the united States of America, in General Congress, Assembled, appealing to the Supreme Judge of the World for the Rectitude of our Intentions, do, in the Name, and by Authority of the good People of these Colonies, solemnly Publish and Declare, That these United Colonies are, and of Right ought to be Free and Independent States; that they are Absolved from all Allegiance to the British Crown, and that all political Connection between them and the State of Great Britain, is and ought to be totally dissolved; and that as Free and Independent States, they have full Power to levy War, conclude Peace, contract Alliances, establish Commerce, and to do all other Acts and Things which Independent States may of right do.—And for the support of this Declaration, with a firm reliance on the Protection of divine Providence, we mutually pledge to each other our Lives, our Fortunes, and our sacred Honor.

Declares
independ-
ence as
only logi-
cal con-
clusion

Lists
Signers

Declaration of Independence (Stone engraving of original document)

Image copyright Mark R., 2009. Used under license from Shutterstock.com

Analysis: Self-evident Truths

One of the key tasks Thomas Jefferson faced in writing the Declaration of Independence was presenting persuasive grounds for dissolving the political ties between the American colonies and the British Empire. It was not enough, for example, to say that the rights of Englishmen had been violated (as American colonists had been arguing), for that could be corrected within the framework of the empire. Instead, Jefferson appeals to "the Laws of Nature and of Nature's God" to justify rebellion and independence. These natural rights to life, liberty, and the pursuit of happiness, as Jefferson puts it, are held to be "self-evident," something that all reasonable people will recognize. In turn, these "self-evident" truths become the enabling assumptions of independence. By shifting political authority from the king or the empire to the consent of the governed, the Declaration of Independence argues that when the people's natural rights have been abridged, they are empowered to overthrow their ruler and establish new forms of government.

FIRST THINGS FIRST 2000 MANIFESTO

The First Things First 2000 manifesto was initiated by Adbusters *magazine, signed by thirty-three high-profile graphic designers, and published simultaneously in* Adbusters, Émigré, AIGA Journal of Design, *and a number of other design magazines. Its call to reexamine the role of the graphic designer in commercial culture is an update of the original First Things First manifesto published in 1964.*

We, the undersigned, are graphic designers, art directors and visual communicators who have been raised in a world in which the techniques and apparatus of advertising have persistently been presented to us as the most lucrative, effective and desirable use of our talents. Many design teachers and mentors promote this belief; the market rewards it; a tide of books and publications reinforces it.

Encouraged in this direction, designers then apply their skill and imagination to sell dog biscuits, designer coffee, diamonds, detergents, hair gel, cigarettes, credit cards, sneakers, butt toners, light beer and heavy-duty recreational vehicles. Commercial work has always paid the bills, but many graphic designers have now let it become, in large measure, what graphic designers do. This, in turn, is how the world perceives design. The profession's time and energy is used up manufacturing demand for things that are inessential at best.

Many of us have grown increasingly uncomfortable with this view of design. Designers who devote their efforts primarily to advertising, marketing and brand development are supporting, and implicitly endorsing, a mental environment so saturated with commercial messages that it is changing the very way citizen-consumers speak, think, feel, respond and interact. To some extent we are all helping draft a reductive and immeasurably harmful code of public discourse.

There are pursuits more worthy of our problem-solving skills. Unprecedented environmental, social and cultural crises demand our attention. Many cultural interventions, social marketing campaigns, books, magazines, exhibitions, educational tools, television programs, films, charitable causes and other information design projects urgently require our expertise and help.

We propose a reversal of priorities in favor of more useful, lasting and democratic forms of communication—a mindshift away from product marketing and toward the exploration and production of a new kind of meaning. The scope of debate is shrinking; it must expand. Consumerism is running uncontested; it must be challenged by other perspectives expressed, in part, through the visual languages and resources of design.

In 1964, 22 visual communicators signed the original call for our skills to be put to worthwhile use. With the explosive growth of global commercial culture, their message has only grown more urgent. Today, we renew their manifesto in expectation that no more decades will pass before it is taken to heart.

signed:

Jonathan Barnbrook	Simon Esterson	Armand Mevis
Nick Bell	Vince Frost	J. Abbott Miller
Andrew Blauvelt	Ken Garland	Rick Poynor
Hans Bockting	Milton Glaser	Lucienne Roberts
Irma Boom	Jessica Helfand	Erik Spiekermann
Sheila Levrant de Bretteville	Steven Heller	Jan van Toorn
Max Bruinsma	Andrew Howard	Teal Triggs
Siân Cook	Tibor Kalman	Rudy VanderLans
Linda van Deursen	Jeffery Keedy	Bob Wilkinson
Chris Dixon	Zuzana Licko	
William Drenttel	Ellen Lupton	and many more
Gert Dumbar	Katherine McCoy	

Analysis: Declaring New Identities

One of the key rhetorical actions that manifestos perform is to declare new identities. You can find examples in the political sphere (the Declaration of Independence [1776], *The Communist Manifesto* [1848], the South African National Congress's Freedom Charter [1955]); the avant-garde art world (the Futurist Manifesto [1909], the Surrealist Manifesto [1924]); and cyberspace (the Hacker's Manifesto [1986], the Hacktivismo Declaration [2001]). In the case of

First Things First 2000, notice that it contains, as manifestos typically do, a critique of the current situation, how the signers have become "increasingly uncomfortable" with the "mental environment" they have helped to design. Then First Things First 2000 proposes a "reversal of priorities" away from "manufacturing demand for things that are inessential at best" toward "more useful, lasting, and democratic forms of communication"—and new social roles for graphic designers to challenge consumerist culture.

■ FOR CRITICAL INQUIRY

1. Describe the overall organization and movement of the Declaration of Independence. Consider how the enabling assumptions connect the main claim of the document to the evidence it brings forward.

2. First Things First 2000 is meant to renew the original First Thing First manifesto of 1964. Find the 1964 First Things First online. Compare it to the 2000 manifesto. What differences and similarities do you see? How would you account for them?

3. Compare how the opening paragraph in the Declaration of Independence and in First Things First 2000 establish the occasion for the two manifestos. What is the call to write in each case?

4. Both manifestos are calling to establish new identities. Explain how they do this.

ENCOUNTERS WITH PUBLIC DOCUMENTS

The following two reading selections offer accounts of how ordinary people encounter public documents and glimpses of what is at stake in these encounters. The first reading is taken from Abraham Verghese's book *My Own Country,* an account of his experience as a doctor working with HIV-positive and AIDS patients in Johnson City, Tennessee. This selection recounts a medical emergency where Verghese had to determine whether to put a patient on life support machines. As you will see, legal documents concerning both the patient's wishes and who will make the decision play prominent roles in shaping the outcome.

The second reading is from Ellen Cushman's *The Struggle and the Tools,* a study of how African Americans in an inner-city neighborhood negotiate with various public institutions. This selection focuses on how a particular individual, Lucy Cadens, makes sense of the forms to apply for the Home Emergency Assistance Program (HEAP) that provides help to offset high utility costs.

FROM *MY OWN COUNTRY*

ABRAHAM VERGHESE

1   Bobby Keller called me in the office as I was about to leave for home. He sounded shrill and alarmed.

2   "Doc? Ed is very sick! He is very, very short of breath and running a fever. A hundred and three. Dr. Verghese, he's turning blue on me."

3   "Bobby, call the emergency ambulance service—tell them to bring you to the Johnson City Medical Center."

4   Ed Maupin, the diesel mechanic, had had a CD4 count of 30 the previous week when I had seen him in clinic; Bobby Keller's was 500. At that visit, Ed's oral thrush had cleared up but he was still feeling tired and had been missing work. When I had examined Ed, the lymph nodes in his neck, which had been as big as goose eggs, had suddenly shrunk: I had thought to myself that this was either a good sign or a very bad sign; his immune system had either given up the fight or successfully neutralized the virus. The latter was unlikely.

5   Bobby, at that visit, had looked well and continued to work in the fashion store. I hoped now that Bobby's description of the gravity of the situation was just histrionics.

6   I was at the Miracle Center well ahead of the ambulance. Soon it came roaring in, all its lights flashing. When the back door opened, I peeked in: Ed's eyes were rolled back in his head, and he was covered with a fine sheen of sweat. Despite the oxygen mask that the ambulance crew had on, his skin was the color of lead. His chest was making vigorous but ineffective excursions.

7   Bobby, who had ridden in the front, was scarcely able to stand up. His face was tremulous; he was on the verge of fainting.

8   "Don't put him on no machines, whatever you do," Bobby begged me. "Please, no machines."

9   "Why?"

10   "Because that's what he told me. He doesn't want it."

11   "When did he tell you? Just now?"

12   "No. A long time ago."

13   "Did he put it in writing? Does he have a living will?"

14   "No . . ."

15   In the emergency room, I stabilized Ed as best I could without intubating him. I took his oxygen mask off momentarily and looked at his mouth. His mucous membranes were loaded with yeast again—it had blossomed in just a week. But I was examining his

mouth to try to decide how difficult it would be to intubate him. His short, receding lower jaw, which the beard concealed well, could make this a tricky intubation. I asked him to say "aaah." He tried to comply; his uvula and tonsils just barely came into view, another sign that he would be a tough intubation.

16   Ideally, an anesthetist would have been the best person to perform intubation. But I didn't want to call an anesthetist who, given the patient, might or might not be willing to do this procedure. Time was running out.

17   Ed was moaning and muttering incomprehensibly; his brain was clearly not getting enough oxygen. His blood pressure was 70 millimeters of mercury systolic over 50 diastolic. This was extremely low for him, because he had baseline hypertension. His cold, clammy extremities told me that the circulation to his arms and legs had shut down in an effort to shunt blood to the brain; even so, what blood got to the brain was not carrying enough oxygen. Ed's chest sounded dull in the bases when I percussed it; on listening with my stethoscope, he was wet and gurgly. The reason he was not oxygenating his blood was clear: his lungs were filled with inflammatory fluid. I ordered a stat chest x-ray and arterial blood gases. I had only a few minutes before I had to either breathe for him, or let him go. I needed more guidance from Bobby as to Ed's wishes.

18   I had an excellent nurse assisting me; she had already started an IV and brought the "crash cart." The respiratory therapist was administering oxygen and had an Ambu bag ready. I asked them to get goggles and masks in addition to their gloves, and to get a gown, mask and gloves ready for me. They were to put theirs on and wait for me. The curtains were pulled and Ed's presence was largely unnoticed in the bustle of the ER. An orthopedist was putting a cast on an individual in the next room, and patients were waiting in the other cubicles.

19   I came out to the waiting room, but Bobby was not there!

20   I hurried outside.

21   Bobby and three other men and one woman were near the ambulance entrance, smoking. The men bore a striking resemblance to Ed Maupin—the same sharp features, the slightly receding chin. One of them, the oldest, wore a green work uniform. I recognized his face as a familiar one, someone who worked in an auto parts store where I had ordered a replacement bumper for the rusted one that had fallen off my Z. Bobby Keller, still trembling, introduced me to Ed's brothers, all younger than Ed. The woman was the wife of one of the brothers.

22   "Bobby," I asked, "can I tell them what's going on?"

23   "Tell them everything," Bobby said, the tears pouring down uncontrollably, his body shaking with sobs.

24   I addressed the brothers: "Ed is very sick. A few months ago we found out he has AIDS." (There was no point in trying to make the distinction between HIV infection and AIDS. If Ed had not had AIDS when I saw him in the clinic, he most certainly did now.) "Now he has a bad pneumonia from the AIDS. I need to put him on a breathing machine in the next few minutes or he will die. I have a feeling that the pneumonia he has can be treated. If we put him on the breathing machine, it won't be forever. We have a good chance of getting him off. But Bobby tells me that Ed has expressed a desire not to be put on the machine."

25   The assembled family turned to Bobby who nodded vigorously: "He did! Said he never wanted to be on no machines."

26   The family was clear-eyed, trying to stay calm. They pulled hard at their cigarettes. The smoke rose quietly around their weathered faces. They looked like a Norman Rockwell portrait—small-town America's citizens in their work clothes in a hospital parking lot, facing a family crisis. But this situation was one that Norman Rockwell hadn't attempted, one he had never dreamed of. I felt they were fond of their oldest brother, though perhaps disapproving of his relationship with Bobby. Yet judging by how they had all been standing around Bobby when I walked out, I didn't think they had any strong dislike for Bobby—it was almost impossible to dislike him. They had had many years to get used to the idea of Bobby and Ed, the couple, and it was only the idea, I sensed, that they had somehow not accepted.

27   "We need to discuss this," the older brother said.

28   "We have no time, I need to go right back in," I said.

29   They moved a few feet away from Bobby and me. I asked Bobby, "Do you have power-of-attorney or anything like that to make decisions for Ed?" Bobby shook his head.

30   We looked over to where the family was caucusing. The oldest brother was doing all the talking. They came back.

31   "We want for you to do everything you can. Put him on the breathing machine, if you have to."

32   At this a little wail came out of Bobby Keller and then degenerated into sobs. I put my hand on Bobby's shoulder. He shook his head back and forth, back and forth. He wanted to say something but could not find a voice.

33   The oldest brother spoke again. His tone was matter-of-fact and determined:

34   "We are his family. We are legally responsible for him. We want you to do everything for him."

35   We are his family. I watched Bobby's face crumble as he suddenly became a mere observer with no legal right to determine the fate of the man he had loved since he was seven years old. He was finally, despite the years that had passed and whatever acceptance he and Ed found together, an outsider.

36   I took him aside and said, "Bobby, I have to go on. There is no way for me not to at this point. There's a really good chance that I can rescue Ed from the pneumonia. If I thought it would only make Ed suffer, I wouldn't do it. If this is Pneumocystis, it should respond to treatment."

37   Bobby kept sobbing, shaking his head as I talked, fat tears rolling off his eyes onto the ground, onto his chest. He felt he was betraying Ed. He could not deliver on his promise.

38   I had no time to pacify Bobby or try to convince him. I rushed back in. Ed looked worse. As I went through the ritual of gowning and masking (it was reassuring to have rituals to fall back on, a ritual for every crisis), it struck me that the entire situation had been in my power to dictate. All I had to do was to come out and say that the pneumonia did not look good, that it looked like the end. I mentioned the respirator, I offered it as an option. I could have just kept quiet. I had, when it came down to the final moment, given Ed's brothers the power of family. Not Bobby.

39   But there was no time to look back now.

FROM *THE STRUGGLE AND THE TOOLS*
ELLEN CUSHMAN

1   Community members often interpreted the demeaning attitudes of institutional agents by assessing the oral and literate language used in day-to-day proceedings of public service organizations. The first example shows typical forms required to access programmatic services. Whether a DSS, Medicaid, or HUD application, they all came with a list of documents required in order to validate the completed form, an information sheet describing the program, and the actual application. Applicants completed the Home Emergency Assistance Program (HEAP) forms when they needed to offset their high utility costs. In

January of 1996, Lucy Cadens picked up a HEAP application when she received a notice of termination of service from her utility company. Although she paid $45 or more a month on her bill, the high costs of gas and electric heat for a poorly insulated three-bedroom apartment continued to add up over the cold months. Her bill for January alone was close to $400, bringing her total owed to just over $960 for the winter of 1996. Lucy had heard about HEAP from a neighbor. Working on a limited budget of state funds, the HEAP office was opened only through January and mid-February before its funding ran out. Lucy and I looked over the ten pages of the application materials in my car.

2   "Jesus, these things are long," I flipped through my copies before I started the car. We were headed to our favorite buffet.

3   "They try to scare you out of applying. Try to discourage you. And it do for some folks. They see all these forms and all the shit you got to bring with you and they think, 'Hell, it gonna take me four or five hours just to pull this shit together.' And they don't do it. You spend all that time and what do you get in return?" We reached the buffet, parked in the slushy snow and buttoned our coats against the wind and flurries. I brought the application with me hoping she would talk more about it. We got our first round of food, chicken and rice soup, salads, and rolls, and we sat in a booth. Lucy took the "documentation requirements" sheet off the top of the stack and shook her head.

4   "Look at the hoops they make us jump through. Like we got nothing better to do than give them 'One or more of the following'" she read from the sheet. "Why would they need more than my Social Security card anyways?" She shook her head, poked at her pasta salad, and checked off the listed items she already had. She decided she needed to make more photocopies of everyone's birth certificates, but resented the assumptions behind the application: "They think we give up easy. Or that if we really need it, then we better be willing to work for it. That's why they need two verifications of my address. They think all poor people be tryin' to get a free ride. Or, we poor so we got to be watched, you know? They be doublechecking us all the time." She sucked on her teeth in disgust and pushed her soup and salad dishes away. Turning to the application, she glanced over the first page. "I can go through this whole thing and tear it up. Every bit of it bullshit."

5   Lucy interprets the class-based prejudices permeating the language of this application. She understands that this public service organization views her as an unethical, shifty person by virtue of her having to complete the application in the first place. While many bureaucracies have long and involved forms to complete, community members attached significance to this length. The number of documents indicates to Lucy that the institution has hidden agendas. With the length of the form alone, the institution daunts the applicants ("They try to scare you out of applying. Try to discourage you."). The application as a whole places high demands on those seeking services.

LDSS-3421 (Rev. 7/99)   PAGE 3
SECTION 4: HOUSEHOLD INCOME

CHECK (✓) YES OR NO FOR EVERY QUESTION. REPORT ANY INCOME FOR ALL HOUSEHOLD MEMBERS. ATTACH ADDITIONAL SHEETS IF NECESSARY.
INDICATE IF YOU OR ANYONE WHO LIVES WITH YOU GETS MONEY FROM:

	TYPE OF INCOME	CHECK ONE (✓)	WHO RECEIVES?	SOURCE OF INCOME	IF YES, GIVE AMOUNT
1.	SOCIAL SECURITY/SOCIAL SECURITY DISABILITY including direct deposit	☐ NO ☐ YES			MONTHLY AMT. $
2.	SUPPLEM				
3.	PENSION				
4.	VETERAN				
5.	DISABILIT				
6.	CONTRIB				
7.	CHILD SU				
8.	ALIMONY				
9.	RENTAL I				
10.	ROOM/BC				
11.	WORKER				
12.	UNEMPLC				
13.	TAP, PELI				
14.	INTEREST etc.				
15.	DIVIDEND				
16.	Does anyc				

PAGE 4   LDSS-3421 (Rev. 7/99)

PERSONAL PRIVACY LAW - NOTIFICATION TO CLIENTS

The State's Personal Privacy Protection Law, which took effect September 1, 1984, states that we must tell you what the State will do with the inform PAGE 2

LDSS-3421 (Rev. 7/99)

IS THERE ANYONE LIVING IN YOUR HOME/APARTMENT, INCLUDING YOURSELF, WHO IS:

BLIND OR DISABLED	☐ NO	☐ YES	IF YES, WHO? _____
60 YEARS OR OLDER	☐ NO	☐ YES	IF YES, WHO? _____
UNDER 8 YEARS OLD	☐ NO	☐ YES	IF YES, WHO? _____

LDSS-3421 (Rev. 7/99)

HOME ENERGY ASSISTANCE PROGRAM APPLICATION

(HEAP)
Home Energy Assistance Program

IMPORTANT NOTICE

YOU SHOULD BE AWARE THAT THERE IS LIMITED MONEY AVAILABLE FOR HEAP BENEFIT PAYMENTS. ONCE AVAILABLE MONEY IS USED UP, NO BENEFITS WILL BE ISSUED AND THE PROGRAM WILL CLOSE. THEREFORE, IT IS STRONGLY RECOMMENDED THAT YOU COMPLETE AND RETURN YOUR APPLICATION AS SOON AS POSSIBLE. BE AWARE THAT IN PAST YEARS THE PROGRAM HAS CLOSED DOWN AS EARLY AS MARCH 12.

DSS-3431 (Rev. 6/93) FACE

APPLICANT NAME	DATE

(HEAP)
Home Energy Assistance Program

HOME ENERGY ASSISTANCE PROGRAM (HEAP)

DOCUMENTATION REQUIREMENTS

☐ WHEN YOU APPLY FOR HEAP ASSISTANCE IN PERSON, YOU MUST PROVIDE PROOF FOR ALL ITEMS LISTED BELOW.

☐ IF YOU HAVE ALREADY APPLIED FOR HEAP ASSISTANCE, YOU MUST PROVIDE PROOF OF THE ITEMS CIRCLED. BRING THESE STATEMENTS NO LATER THAN _____ OR YOUR APPLICATION MAY BE DENIED.

ADDRESS (Where you now live)

You must provide one or more of the following:

- Current rent receipt with name and address
- Copy of lease with address
- Water, sewage, or tax bill
- Mortgage payment books/receipts with address
- Homeowners insurance policy
- Deed

ALL PEOPLE IN YOUR HOUSEHOLD

You must provide one or more of the following for each person in your household:

- Birth certificate
- Baptismal certificate
- School records
- Social Security card
- Driver's license
- Marriage certificate

FUEL/UTILITY BILLS

- If you pay a fuel or utility bill, bring a copy of your most recent fuel/utility bill.
- If you pay for neither heat nor utilities, bring a statement from your landlord that indicates heat and utilities are included in your rent.
- If you have a utility emergency, bring your utility termination notice.

INCOME

You must provide proof of income for all household members who receive any type of income, earned or unearned, including but not limited to:

- Pay stubs for the most recent four weeks
- If self-employed or have rental income, business records for the most recent three months
- Child support or alimony checks
- Bankbook/dividend or interest statement
- Statement from roomer/boarder
- Other _____

COPY OF MOST RECENT CHECK OR AWARD LETTER:

- Social Security/Supplemental Security Income (SSI)
- Veteran's Benefits
- Pensions
- Worker's Compensation/Disability
- Verification of Unemployment Insurance Benefit amount
- Educational Grants/Loans

RESOURCES (For emergency applications only)

- Statement claiming zero resources
- Bank Statement showing current balance for checking, savings, and credit union accounts, IRA's, etc.
- Stocks, bonds, dividends

Depending on your circumstances, additional documentation may be required.

If you have any questions, please call _____

First, the demand is on time and energy and can be seen in the number of hours it takes to complete these forms ("it gonna take me four or five hours just to pull this shit together"). Second, the demands are on literate skills. To make this application successful, individuals selected only information they could convincingly support. Without certain verifications, such as one or more forms of identification, community members' applications would not present a compelling display of need. Residents understood that these demands were shaped from the belief that poor people need to "work" (read: appease gatekeepers) for their public assistance. "Look at the hoops they make us jump through," Lucy says. In order to receive their "awards," residents had to fill numerous institutional requirements.

6   Lucy also perceives the ways the institutions mistrust those they serve. Public service agencies view community members as often trying to manipulate the system of benefits in order to receive more ("they think all poor people be tryin' to get a free ride"). Because poor people are presumably unscrupulous, they will resort to illegal means more quickly, and therefore need to be policed ("We poor so we got to be watched, you know? They be doublechecking us all the time"). These forms often asked for the same information to be presented in different ways. So verifications must accompany what the applicant lists, and when applicants handed in these forms, they often were asked verbally to recount what appears on the application. The caseworker would ask the applicant to recall specific lines of information (i.e., "so do you receive disability payments?") and doublecheck the verbal answers against the written. While one could argue that caseworkers are merely checking the internal consistency of the application, their verifications and questions indicated to residents that the institution perceives applicants as typically unethical and needing to be kept under surveillance.

7   My point here isn't so much that this literacy artifact represents the insidious values it does, but that Lucy critically reads this artifact, locates these insidious assumptions, and analyzes the politics imbued in this form. As she says, "I can go through this whole thing and tear it up. Every bit of it bullshit." She understands how public service institutions degrade those they seek to serve. She knows how institutional representatives view her using their own classist presumptions. She understands too that despite how much she balks at the institutions present throughout this application, she will still apply because she needs to keep her apartment warm. She did apply for this program, and did receive the aid she sought—four months after she submitted the application.

Analysis: Encountering Public Documents as Literacy Events

We can analyze these two reading selections as describing literacy events in which public documents—or their absence—play a key role in how people interact with each other and make sense of things.

In the excerpt from *My Own Country,* the absence of two crucial public documents shapes the outcome of this event. There is no "living will" to express Ed's wishes about medical treatment. Nor is there a marriage license or power of attorney, entitling Bobby legally to make decisions on Ed's behalf. Instead, as Ed's oldest brother tells Abraham Verghese, "We are his family. We are legally responsible for him." It is precisely because the brothers' relationship to Ed can be documented in the public record that they have the legal right to make decisions. Family ties can be verified, while Bobby and Ed's relationship remains private and unofficial, neither legally recognized nor culturally sanctioned.

The selection from *The Struggle and the Tools* explores a case where a public document—the six-page HEAP application—is a source of mutual suspicion between public assistance workers and poor people seeking help. As Lucy Cadens points out, the sheer length of the application can discourage people from applying. Just as telling, Cadens reads the application as one that expresses mistrust of the applicants—that, in effect, assumes the worst about them.

■ FOR CRITICAL INQUIRY

1. Describe how the decision to put Ed on the respirator was made. Why is Abraham Verghese conflicted by the decision? Do you think he could or should have acted differently given the circumstances?

2. Here is the main text of a sample "living will," which Ed Maupin did not have on record. What protections does it offer a patient?

   Declaration

   If I should have an incurable and irreversible condition that has been diagnosed by two physicians and that will result in my death within a relatively short time without the administration of life-sustaining treatment or has produced an irreversible coma or persistent vegetative state, and I am no longer able to make decisions regarding my medical treatment, I direct my attending physician, pursuant to the Natural Death Act of California, to withhold or withdraw treatment, including artificially administered nutrition and hydration, that only prolongs the process of dying or the irreversible coma or persistent vegetative state and is not necessary for my comfort or to alleviate pain.

   If Ed had had a signed living will, do you think Verghese's decision about putting him on a respirator would have been different? Why or why not?

3. Notice how Lucy Cadens identifies assumptions that public assistance agencies make about poor people and how these assumptions are reflected in their application forms. What are these assumptions? What must Cadens assume in order to identify the attitudes expressed in forms such as the HEAP application?

4. What experience, if any, have you had filling out application forms? How does it compare to Cadens's experience? How would you explain differences and similarities?

5. Explain how the two readings could be analyzed as literacy events. In Chapter 1, literacy events are defined as "ways to think about how reading and writing enter people's lives and shape their interactions with others." Apply the definition to the two readings. How does the presence and absence of public documents influence how the literacy event takes place?

PETITIONS

Petitions are an indispensable part of a democratic society, offering citizens the means to express their views and call for changes in public policy. This gallery of petitions provides three examples of how individuals and advocacy groups call on people to support their aims. The first petition comes from Amnesty International, while the second two were circulated online by individuals. Analyze the tone of voice in each of the petitions. How do they differ? Assess the appropriateness of the tone, given the occasion and the person addressed.

9 June 2009

CALL ON KENYA TO EASE THE SUFFERING OF NAIROBI'S 2 MILLION SLUM DWELLERS

1   More than half of Nairobi's population—some two million people—live in slums and informal settlements. Crammed into makeshift shacks on just one per cent of the city's usable land, people live without adequate access to water, hospitals, schools and other essential public services.

2   Up to a million people live in Kiberia, Nairobi's largest slum, crowded onto just 550 acres of sodden land that straddles the main railway line. Most earn barely enough to rent a mud-floored, tin-roofed wooden shack with no toilet or running water.

3   Slum Dwellers are under the constant threat of forced evictions, which are illegal under international human rights law. These evictions are often carried out with brutality and victims are not compensated despite losing their homes, businesses and possessions.

4   Sometimes private developers are behind forced evictions and sometimes it's the government. Residents of the Deep Sea settlement have suffered waves of forced eviction by government authorities. Other forced evictions have been carried out in preparation for government infrastructure projects such as the construction of roads.

5   The Kenyan government's slum upgrading programme, while a positive step, is doing little or nothing to address the immediate and desperate needs of slum dwellers in Nairobi.

6   Despite government promises to provide affordable housing outside the slums, its housing policies have not prioritized people living in slums and settlements, or others who may face the greatest difficulties in accessing their right to adequate housing.

7   During her June visit to Nairobi, Amnesty International's Secretary General, Irene Khan, urged the Kenyan authorities to immediately stop all forced evictions and to ensure that Kenya fulfils its obligations in relation to the right to adequate housing for the most vulnerable.

8   Write to Kenyan President Mwai Kibaki urging the authorities to address the immediate and desperate needs of slum dwellers in Nairobi.

Write a Letter to President Mwai Kibaki

Dear President Mwai Kibaki,

9   I am writing to express my deep concern for the 2 million slum dwellers in Nairobi. These people live in squalor and under the constant threat of forced evictions.

I call on you to:

- Immediately stop all forced evictions and to adopt guidelines for essential evictions that comply with international human rights law.
- Ensure genuine consultation with the affected communities about the planned mass evictions related to the Nairobi River Basin Programme and proposed infrastructure projects to identify all feasible alternatives to eviction and to develop a comprehensive relocation and compensation plan.
- Ensure that implementation of the slum upgrading programme complies with Kenya's obligations in relation to the right to adequate housing, including to consult adequately affected communities and to ensure the affordability and accessibility of housing for all.
- Ensure that the slum upgrading programme and policies address immediate needs in relation to security of tenure and access to essential services.

Yours sincerely,

STIMULATE THE ECONOMY—FORGIVE STUDENT LOANS
TARGET: PRESIDENT OBAMA

SPONSORED BY: KEVIN M. BARTOY

1   We the Undersigned are writing to you to ask for a real economic stimulus plan for America.

2   Hundreds of billions of our tax dollars have been given to Wall Street and other corporations in hopes of "jump starting" the economy. We want to see our tax dollars going directly to Main Street rather than routed through Wall Street.

3   Americans are increasingly saddled with debt. Chief among this debt is student loan debt. We provide the best education in the world in our colleges and universities, but we leave our graduates at a severe disadvantage as they leave our institutions with a degree and a mountain of debt. This debt inhibits many of these young people from achieving their dreams and making productive contributions to America and the American economy.

4   We ask you to consider a relief package for student loan debtors. By forgiving student loan debt, we can invest in our future and save our economy. Families pay upwards of a third to half of their monthly incomes trying to pay down student loan debt. If this real wealth was freed, our educated masses could spend that money by creating new businesses, which would in turn create new jobs. Freed from debt, these families could also begin to invest in themselves by purchasing homes and land. This would infuse our economy with real wealth that would benefit all sectors not just the wealthy few on Wall Street.

5   We ask you to make a real investment in America. We ask you to truly stimulate this economy. We ask you to use our tax dollars to relieve the burden of student debt and allow our graduates to truly use their education to give back to this great country.

6   Thank you for bringing hope to America. Now, let us help you turn that hope into a brighter future.

7   Please join our Facebook Group for more information and discussion of this important issue:

http://www.new.facebook.com/home.php?ref=home#/
group.php?gid=58440324477&ref=mf

**TIGER WOODS—STAND UP FOR
EQUALITY—AUGUSTA NATIONAL GOLF CLUB**

JASON PIERCE

Dear Tiger Woods,

1   We, the undersigned, request that you stand up for Equal Rights by boycotting the Masters golf tournament this coming April [2003] unless the all-male Augusta National Club admits women members.

2   As the world's most famous golfer, like it or not, you have unique power and the responsibility that goes with it. You are well aware, particularly given the tremendous public outcry against the all-male club, that your decision to participate in the Augusta tournament will effectively be an endorsement of that club's policies.

3   You've been a wonderful inspiration for young golfers, your dedication and hard work are admirable, but please, do not now send the message that you support sexism.

4   William W. "Hootie" Johnson, chairman of the Augusta National Golf Club, would like us to believe the issue is about the rights of a private club. And while the club does have a legal "right" to discriminate (its first black member was only admitted in 1990, and the 300 CEOs and other wealthy men who belong are invited to join by invitation only)—why would you want to support that?

5   Your decision to play or not to play at Augusta will be a strong statement. That is a given, and it is one of the prices of fame. Please make the right decision.

MISSON STATEMENTS

Mission statements are brief written statements, usually just one or two paragraphs, that articulate the vision of a business or organization—its reason for being, its main aims, its primary stakeholders, and the products or services it provides. The three examples here are all nonprofits, and their mission statements range from one to three paragraphs. Consider the information included in each mission statement. How would you account for the differences in their length? Taken together, what generalizations can you draw about the genre of mission statements?

PEN CENTER USA

Mission

PEN USA's mission is to stimulate and maintain interest in the written word, to foster a vital literary culture, and to defend freedom of expression domestically and internationally.

- PEN USA defends and promotes freedom of expression throughout the world by advocating for the release of imprisoned writers, and for the protection of writers who suffer political prosecution, persecution, and censorship.
- Through programming and services, PEN USA cultivates a diverse, dynamic and engaged literary community that includes emerging and existing writers, translators, editors, agents, publishers, booksellers, teachers, librarians, readers: everyone who loves and supports language and literature.

THE HIPHOP ARCHIVE @ THE W.E.B. DU BOIS INSTITUTE, HARVARD UNIVERSITY

The Hiphop Archive at Harvard University was officially established in 2002. It found its permanent home in the Du Bois Institute January 2008. The Hiphop Archive's mission is to facilitate and encourage the pursuit of knowledge, art, culture and responsible leadership through Hiphop. We are uncompromising in our commitment to build and support intellectually challenging and innovative scholarship that both reflects the rigor and achievement of performance in Hiphop and transforms our thinking and our lives. These objectives are met through our Website: http://hiphoparchive.org/ which provides information about all activities and projects and serves as a resource for those interested in knowing, developing, building, maintaining and representing Hiphop. The Hiphop Archive works with other groups and individuals who support hiphop culture. We also sponsor and facilitate projects, events and numerous other activities at the Hiphop Archive @ The Du Bois Institute, Harvard University.

Hiphop's incursion into higher education took place within the same tradition as Black Studies, Chicano Studies, Asian American Studies, Women's Studies, etc. In those cases, students used non-violent protest as well as arguments of standards and inclusion to achieve representation within the academic curriculum. The students who introduced Hiphop to colleges and universities bum-rushed their campuses by introducing hiphop classes themselves. They were seldom from the same communities as Hiphop artists.

Yet, as they listened and participated in hiphop culture, they also recognized the emergence of theories, ideas and critiques that reinvigorated intellectual debates and challenged societies and nations to address issues of justice, freedom and equality. Researchers are also interested in how Hiphop incorporates and critiques culture and society and especially issues of representation and power. Hiphop is concerned with the major questions of philosophy, identity, ideology, art and existence. It is also interested in how oppressed people and voices move into dominant culture and often create a space for themselves. Whether one calls this space the counterpublic or underground, it threatens dominant discourse about black and urban youth and forces recognition from society and its educational system. This system regularly ridicules serious questions and ideas that emerge from popular culture—especially when they originate from youth, people of color and poor people. Students of hiphop are well aware of the society's unwillingness to hear the analysis, critique and story within Hiphop and agitate for its inclusion.

Scholarship on Hiphop now exists in education, psychology, anthropology, sociology, political science, philosophy, theater, art, business, physics, religion, English, linguistics, American Studies, history, communications, African American Studies, music and more. It is a celebration of the level of support and commitment throughout the world for Hiphop to be incorporated into higher education without losing and compromising what Hiphop is and means to those who introduced it and to those who continue to develop and sustain Hiphop culture.

ADVOCACY CAMPAIGN

STOP GLOBAL WARMING
GREENPEACE

Greenpeace is an international environmental activist organization that, in the words of its mission statement, uses "non-violent confrontation to raise the level and quality of public debate" by "exposing threats to the environment and finding solutions." We include some items from Greenpeace's ongoing campaign to stop global warming found on the group's Web site—two press releases, Greenpeace Response to President Obama's Award of the Nobel Peace Prize and Greenpeace Statement on Apple Leaving the Chamber of Commerce; pages from the Greenpeace Climate Rescue Toolkit; and a petition to President Obama. As rhetorical situations change, Greenpeace updates its campaign material accordingly. Visit www.greenpeace.org for the most current publicity and other materials.

GREENPEACE | USA

You Are Here: Media Center > News Releases

Greenpeace Response to President Obama's Award of the Nobel Peace Prize

October 09, 2009

▸ Print   ▸ Tell a friend

"We hope that the award of the Nobel Peace prize to President Barack Obama will give him the courage of his convictions on climate change. That it will spur him to take personal leadership on climate change to avert climate catastrophe. If allowed to go unchecked, climate change will wreak havoc on our societies - spurring mass migration, mass starvation and mass extinction. It will spark conflicts worldwide.

"If President Obama is to be a true Nobel Peace Laureate he must reverse the United States current blocking role in the climate negotiations to secure a fair, ambitious and binding deal for the climate this December. He must use his power to avert future climate conflicts and chaos.

"In accepting the award in Oslo on December 10th, President Obama has an incredible opportunity, and responsibility, to then travel to the UN Copenhagen Climate Summit, which is happening at the same time, and help avert climate chaos and conflict." said Gerd Leipold, Greenpeace International Executive Director.

The announcement from the Nobel Committee comes as two weeks of UN climate talks in Bangkok limped to a close this week. All eyes are on President Obama's administration to make the shift to the deep emissions cuts that the world has been wanting for decades.

"The US is trying to impose its own domestic limitations on the international community - limitations driven largely by the fossil fuel lobby. It is climate science and the needs of the most vulnerable that should determine the Copenhagen outcome, not oil and coal companies and their allies in Congress," said Damon Moglen, Greenpeace USA Global Warming Director.

"The Nobel Prize speaks to the desire, the hope of people around the world who want our President to lead with vision and fairness. In the next two months, President Obama must commit to ambitious action if he is to be the climate leader the world is waiting for."

Contact information

Joe Smyth, Greenpeace USA Media Officer, 831-566-5647
Damon Moglen, Greenpeace USA Global Warming Campaign Director, 202-352-4223

▸ Print   ▸ Tell a friend

- DONATE
- TAKE ACTION
- GREENPEACE
- MEDIA CENTER
  - ▸ Press Contacts
  - ▸ Picture Desk
  - ▸ News Releases
  - ▸ Reports
  - ▸ Bloggers' Center
  - ▸ Experts

TWITTER UPDATES

I'm on the ground in Sumatra at Greenpeace's Climate Defenders Camp. http://ow.ly/xDxO about 2 hours ago

@OsVerdesdeTapes thanks for letting me know, you should also get in touch w/ @greenpeacebr about 19 hours ago

sure is!!! RT @jessica_trzyna -Nice to see some good news from the Amazon: http://tinyurl.com/yk6xk5q about 20 hours ago

if you haven't, check out @350's amazing vid from the oct 24th global day of action... right now! http://bit.ly/CfxmR #350ppm about 21 hours ago

Thx @350 - !! RT: Our friends @greenpeaceusa put 2gether a gr8 vid too! -- http://bit.ly/EfH4z #350ppm about 21 hours ago

▸ follow us on Twitter

PRESS CONTACTS

The following contacts are for press inquiries only. If you are not a member of the press and you have a question about Greenpeace's work, please call: 800-326-0959.

Michael Crocker
Washington, D.C.
202-319-2471
E-mail

Molly Dorozenski
New York
646-862-1509
E-mail

Daniel Kessler
San Francisco
510-501-1779
E-mail
twitter: dkess

Jane Kochersperger
Washington, D.C.
202-319-2493
E-mail

Joe Smyth
Washington, D.C.
831-566-5647
E-mail

For weekend and holiday media requests, please call: 202-415-5414.

For photo requests:
Bob Meyers
E-mail
202-319-2453

For video requests:
Tim Aubry
E-mail
202-319-2429

RELATED CAMPAIGNS

▸ Global Warming and Energy

Greenpeace

GREENPEACE | USA .

You Are Here: Media Center > News Releases

- ⩔ DONATE
- ⩔ TAKE ACTION
- ⩔ GREENPEACE
- ⩔ MEDIA CENTER
- ▸ Press Contacts
- ▸ Picture Desk
- ▸ News Releases
- ▸ Reports
- ▸ Bloggers' Center
- ▸ Experts

TWITTER UPDATES

I'm on the ground in Sumatra at Greenpeace's Climate Defenders Camp. http://ow.ly/xDxO about 2 hours ago

@OsVerdesdeTapes thanks for letting me know, you should also get in touch w/ @greenpeacebr about 19 hours ago

sure is!!! RT @jessica_trzyna -Nice to see some good news from the Amazon: http://tinyurl.com /vk6xk5q about 20 hours ago

if you haven't, check out @350's amazing vid from the oct 24th global day of action... right now! http://bit.ly /CfxmR #350ppm about 21 hours ago

Thx @350 - !! RT: Our friends @greenpeaceusa put 2gether a gr8 vid too! -- http://bit.ly/EfH4z #350ppm about 21 hours ago

▸ follow us on Twitter

Greenpeace Statement on Apple Leaving The Chamber of Commerce

October 08, 2009

▸ Print   ▸ Tell a friend

International — In response to Apple's decision to leave the U.S. Chamber of Commerce, Greenpeace Toxics Campaigner Casey Harrell issued the following statement:

Greenpeace applauds Apple's decision to be the first technology company to leavethe United States Chamber of Commerce over the organization'sopposition to mandatory limits on greenhouse gases. Many companies inthe Chamber have progressive and responsible policy positions onclimate change that are diametrically opposed to that being advocated in their name by the largest lobby group in the United States (1)

Greenpeace's work in the sector has highlighted where IT companies have a tremendousbusiness opportunity to provide the 21st century energy efficient andhigh tech solutions to reduce greenhouse gases economy wide. Greenpeacespecifically calls upon IBM and Microsoft, who sit on the Chamber's Executive Board, as well as all other IT firms who claim to be leaderson climate change, to publicly and emphatically renounce the Chamber'sposition on limiting greenhouse gases and demand a change in itsdirectorship, or follow Apple's leadership and leave the body in protest.

Notes to Editor

(1) $488 Million from 1998-2009, more than twice that of the second biggest spender. www.opensecrets.org

Vision, video, photos, report information

Contacts: Daniel Kessler, Greenpeace USA Press Officer, 510.501.1779; Casey Harrell, Greenpeace International Toxics Campaigner, 510.808.4330

▸ Print   ▸ Tell a friend

PRESS CONTACTS

The following contacts are for press inquiries only. If you are not a member of the press and you have a question about Greenpeace's work, please call: 800-326-0959.

Michael Crocker Washington, D.C. 202-319-2471 E-mail

Molly Dorozenski New York 646-862-1509 E-mail

Daniel Kessler San Francisco 510-501-1779 E-mail twitter: dkess

Jane Kochersperger Washington, D.C. 202-319-2493 E-mail

Joe Smyth Washington, D.C. 831-566-5647 E-mail

For weekend and holiday media requests, please call: 202-415-5414.

For photo requests: Bob Meyers E-mail 202-319-2453

For video requests: Tim Aubry E-mail 202-319-2429

Greenpeace

Global Warming Toolkit

GREENPEACE

We Need Leaders, Not Politicians

While we struggle to recover from the worst economic recession in decades, it's become clear that we can't afford to return to the policies of the past— letting industry do as it pleases, with no regard for the impact on people or the planet. The days of coal and oil barons writing our country's energy policy are over.

In order to implement climate solutions successfully, we need our elected officials in Washington D.C. to act like leaders and not politicians. Join us in continuing to build a movement that demands President Obama and Congress do the following:

• Respond to climate science and not to polluters. Enact science based emissions reductions targets in order to prevent a 2-degree Centigrade global temperature increase.

• Negotiate at the United Nations Climate Conference in December on the basis of the science-based UN Intergovernmental Panel on Climate Change emission reduction targets.

• Invest in renewable and clean energy and away from coal, oil and gas (the prime sources of global warming emissions).

Greenpeace

Global Warming Toolkit   GREENPEACE

Student power

Students have always been at the forefront of social movements. To defend our future against unparalleled environmental challenges we must get organized. Elected officials need to hear loud and clear that we will not stand for anything less than science based solutions to climate change.

Take Action on campus and in your community:

1. Turn Politicians into Leaders
President Obama promised us to work with Congress to implement science based climate solutions, yet he has not lived up to what he said on the campaign trail. Let's hold our politicians accountable. Grab their attention by lobbying, organizing creative actions and telling the media. Check out the tipsheet* for more ideas on how to turn politicians into leaders.

2. Make Your School a Coal Free Campus
Fifty Percent of the United States' electricity is provided by coal, the leading global warming polluter. Right now, the coal barons are hard at work protecting their business by weakening US climate legislation. Tell the coal industry to get off your campus—whether there is a coal plant on your campus, an administrator is on the board of a coal company, or there is a coal plant in the nearby community. See the tipsheet* to learn more about how you can join the coal fight.

3. Use the Media to Insert the Youth Voice into the Climate Debate
Leading up to the UN Climate Conference in December, it will be vitally important to make sure that the general public and politicians hear from youth. Afterall, it is our future that politicians are deciding. See the tipsheet* for more ideas and best practices on how to generate media around your work.

4. Join the Climate Connections Project
The USA and China (the two largest producers of global warming pollution) have stood in the way of all nations coming to the table and agreeing to a global treaty. Therefore, we have teamed up with Greenpeace China to launch "Climate Connections." Join this project and you will be paired with a Chinese youth to share stories about why you care and how you are acting to fight climate change. These stories will be used to send a united, global message to American and Chinese leaders that they must act and stop fooling around with our future. Sign up to be a part of the project by September 1st at
www.greenpeace.org/climateconnections.

Greenpeace

Global Warming Toolkit

GREENPEACE

Student power

5. Host an "Age of Stupid" moving screening and "Stupid Action"

Recruit new activists and raise funds for your group by hosting an "Age of Stupid" movie screening. It's a film about a man "living alone in the devastated world of 2055, looking at old footage from 2009 and asking: why didn't we stop climate change when we had the chance?" Think about it as "Inconvenient Truth," but with more of an edge. Its got an activist bent too, so it will encourage folks to go out after the film and stage events to highlight things that are "stupid" and contribute to climate change. Screenings are in early October. Contact students@ sfo.greenpeace.org if you would like to host a screening on your campus.

6. Attend a Regional Power Shift

It is important to come together as a community, share ideas, learn, strategize, and mobilize to show the overwhelming support for climate solutions. This October, the Energy Action Coalition (which we are a part of) will be hosting dozens of regional summits across the country. Contact us at students@ sfo.greenpeace.org for a list of locations and for more information about how you can get involved.

7. Participate in the October 24th Global Day of Climate Action

On October 24, activists around the world will be mobilizing to demand that world governments act to put a cap on global warming pollution. This day of climate action is going global: events are already planned from Bangladesh to the Barrier Reef. Mark the day by organizing an attention-grabbing event in your community. Contact us at students@sfo.greenpeace.org for support pulling of your event.

Greenpeace

Petition to President Obama: Be a leader on Global Warming!

Global warming is an environmental crisis the likes of which we've never faced before. And given the powerful forces who are actively working to delay action on global warming as long as possible, addressing it adequately will require bold leadership, not political dealing.

While President Obama and the G8 may have accepted an upper limit on warming of 2 degrees Celsius as a goal — a mark already endorsed by 109 nations — the critical question is whether they will take the action needed to keep warming below this threshold. To do so, scientists say the United States and other industrialized countries must cut their emissions by 25-40 percent below 1990 levels by 2020. Yet the Obama Administration, like Congress, continues to promote emission reductions that fall far short of this target, focusing instead on longer-term reductions.

We cannot put off for tomorrow what science tells us we need to do today. While the 2 degree commitment appears to recognize the severity of the crisis we face, the G8 has failed to provide any plan for staying below this critical threshold."

In President Obama's inaugural address, he vowed to "restore science to its rightful place" and make America a real global leader again. It's time for him to live up to that promise. Sign our petition now to call on President Obama to honor his commitment to restoring science by being a true leader, not a politician.

Sign the Petition

YOUR INFORMATION

- Required fields
- Title:
- First Name:
- Last Name:
- Your Email:
- Address 1:

Address 2:

- City:
- State / Province:

  Choose a State

- ZIP / Postal Code:

PETITION

Be a Leader on Global Warming

Dear President Obama,

When it comes to stopping global warming, we need you to be a leader, not a politician. Show Congress and the world that America is ready to take strong and immediate action to avert a climate catastrophe.

Sincerely,
[Your Name]
[Your Address]
[City, State ZIP]

Greenpeace

Analysis: Multigenre Campaigns

The variety of documents presented here, along with more recent ones you can find at the Greenpeace Web site www.greenpeace.org, provides a good opportunity to consider the role different genres play in an advocacy campaign and how the genres work together to create the campaign as a whole. Notice, for example, how audience and purpose differ with each genre. The press releases are clearly aimed at getting Greenpeace perspectives into the news. In the case of the response to Obama's Nobel Peace Prize, the press release offers reporters quotable material from both Gerd Leipold, Greenpeace International Executive Director, and Damon Moglen, Greenpeace USA Global Warming Director. On the other hand, the Climate Rescue Toolkit contains resources for activists and the petition is addressed to President Obama.

■ FOR CRITICAL INQUIRY

1. Compare the two Greenpeace press releases. Consider how each takes an event in the news and turns it into a rhetorical situation, to define Greenpeace's orientation and to get its point of view before the public. How does each develop a rhetorical stance? How do the stances differ?

2. Consider the three pages from the Climate Rescue Toolkit. What information and resources does the toolkit provide for Greenpeace activists?

3. Notice how the petition to President Obama echos the campaign slogan "We Need Leaders, Not Politicians" that appears in the Climate Rescue Toolkit. What is the rhetorical appeal of the slogan? How is it worked into the petition? How is the petition related to the press releases and toolkit in terms of Greenpeace's campaign to stop global warming

4. Visit the Greenpeace Web site. Identify other genres of writing that appear there. What roles do they play in Greenpeace campaigns? Notice also how Greenpeace uses online communication such as YouTube, Twitter, Facebook, and blogs. What role do these media play in Greenpeace campaigns?

FURTHER EXPLORATION: PUBLIC DOCUMENTS

■ GENRE AWARENESS

Consider how a set of written documents define your classroom in institutional terms. How do genres of writing like course descriptions, syllabi, textbooks, WebCT, writing assignments, student essays, peer reviews, teacher comments, course evaluations, and so forth work together to bring into being a writing classroom and the activities that take place there? Think of the various genres as a network of texts that exist only in relation to each other. How does this network of texts compare to the networks of texts that bring other social sites and organizations (for example, advocacy campaigns, companies, nonprofits, government agencies, medical care facilities, sports teams) into being?

WRITING ASSIGNMENT

The writing assignments in this chapter are divided into those that call for analysis of public documents and those that call for the design and production of one or more documents.

Analysis

- **Analysis of encounters with public documents as literacy events:** Analyze an encounter you have had with a public document. Explain how the document shaped roles, relationships, and outcomes. Consider how your encounter can be understood as a literacy event (as explained in the Chapter 1 "Writing Assignment: Analyzing a Literacy Event").

- **Rhetorical analysis:** Analyze one (or more) of the documents in this chapter or a public document of your choice, such as *The Communist Manifesto*, the Freedom Charter of the African National Congress in South Africa, the Hacker's Manifesto, or the Hacktivismo Declaration. Consider how the document constructs and responds to a rhetorical situation and how it creates a rhetorical stance to make an argument.

Design and production

- **Manifesto:** Write a manifesto that explains what calls on you to publicly proclaim a new identity, mission, and purpose. Consider the persona you are inventing in the manifesto and on whose behalf the manifesto is speaking. Explain why the current situation needs to be changed and what you are calling on like-minded people to do.

- **Petition:** Write a petition that calls on a public official or figure to do something. Explain an existing problem and what should be done about it. Consider the tone of voice you want to use and how you will need to persuade readers to sign the petition and the recipient to take action.

- **Mission statement:** Write a mission statement for your writing class, for an organization that you make up, or for yourself.

- **Advocacy campaign.** Write a plan for an advocacy campaign by an existing organization or one that you make up. Create a name and a logo for the campaign; include the goals and strategy of the campaign, its audience, and the types of written and visual material needed to carry out the campaign.

- **Class charter:** Work together as a class to design and produce a charter for your writing course. You can break into working groups to draft sections. The charter might include (1) a preamble or mission statement; (2) statement of teacher's role, rights, and responsibilities to students; (3) statement of students' role, rights, and responsibilities to the teacher and to each other; and (4) bylaws governing classroom life (list of numbered points concerning attendance, timely completion of work, how to ensure that everyone is heard in class discussion, how to handle differences of opinion, how to make group work productive, and so forth).

- **Policy statement:** Write a statement of policy that takes a position on a public concern or sets standards of practice. (See the Warehouse State Honor Code in this chapter.)

Invention

Chapters 1, 2, and 3 provide guidelines to analyze an encounter with a public document as a literacy event and to analyze the rhetorical situation and the rhetorical stance of the argument, so we'll focus in this section on designing and producing documents such as manifestos, petitions, mission statements, policy statements, and advocacy campaigns.

Clarifying Purpose, Audience, and Genre

Consider what you want to accomplish in your document. The following questions can help get you started.

1. What calls on you to write? Do you want to articulate the identity of a group you belong to (for example, Goths, geeks, alternative, straight-edge, jocks, preps, or whatever) or a group you want to create? Or are you seeking to persuade others to join you in petitioning for change? Are you creating an organization that responds to an unmet need or setting policy?

2. Consider the problems and issues that concern you personally—whether global warming, the occupation of Iraq, domestic violence, or the dorm rules on your campus. Has a new law or public policy been proposed that you're concerned about? Is there something specific that you think should be changed? Or something that the people in charge could be doing that they're not? In these cases, you may have an idea to write a petition to a particular public official or figure, calling for some new course of action.

3. Are you addressing an already-existing audience or are you trying to bring a new audience into being?

4. What genre makes sense to embody your purposes and address your readers?

Background Research: Understanding the Rhetorical Situation

You may need to do some background research to clarify the rhetorical situation that is calling on you to write. Consider who is involved in the situation you're addressing and what interests are at stake. You can do background reading and talk to people who know about the situation. For petitions, you'll need to determine the appropriate person to whom you'll send the petition.

Planning

Public documents often follow a set pattern, making them easily recognizable to readers and easily reproducible by writers to account for new situations. Different genres—whether a manifesto, petition, mission statement, policy statement, or charter—have their own typical design. If you are designing a document, a good way to begin is to find one or more examples of a document like it to identify its typical features. If you are analyzing an existing document, you will also want to pay attention to its design features.

As you can see from the examples in this chapter, manifestos tend to have an open form, while petitions typically state the problem or issue and then present their demand or demands. Charters almost always have a preamble that explains an organization's mission and goals, followed by clearly defined sections and often a list of bylaws.

Readability and the Visual Design of Public Documents

Here are some considerations to take into account, whether you're designing or analyzing a public document. These visual design features enhance the readability of a document by helping readers mentally organize the material presented.

See Chapter 19, "Visual Design," for more on white space, page layout, headings, and fonts.

- **Title and logo:** How is the document titled? Does it use a logo or other identifying graphic feature?

- **Preamble or background section:** Does the document have a preamble or a background section that explains the occasion that called for it and its general principles? If not, how does it begin?

- **White space:** Does the document use white space to separate sections in the document and to emphasize key points?

- **Headings and subheadings:** Does the document use headings and subheadings to denote separate sections? How do such divisions make the document easier to read?

- **Bullets:** Does the document use bullets to emphasize key points? Notice, for example, how Amnesty International's "Call for Human Rights in Russia" uses a list of bulleted points to present its demands.

- **Fonts:** Does the document use capital letters, italics, boldface, underlinings, or designer fonts to emphasize key words or phrases?

- **Parallelism:** Does the document use parallel grammatical structures? Here are some of the most commonly used structures:

  Infinitives: Notice how the Preamble to the United Nations charter uses infinitive phrases, such as "to save" and "to reaffirm":

  We the People of the United Nations Determined

  to save succeeding generations from the scourge of war, which twice in our lifetime has brought untold sorrow to mankind, and to reaffirm faith in fundamental human rights, in the dignity and worth of the human person, in the equal rights of men and women and of nations large and small, and

to establish conditions under which justice and respect for the obligations arising from treaties and other sources of international law can be maintained, and

to promote social progress and better standards of living in larger freedom,

Repeated phrases: In listing the king's oppressive acts, the Declaration of Independence repeats the phrases "He has refused," "He has dissolved," "He has obstructed."

Imperatives: Greenpeace's Climate Rescue Toolkit lists a series of imperatives on the Student Power pages, "Turn politicians into leaders," "Make your school," "Use the media," and so on.

- **Signature:** Is the document signed? If so, by whom? What does signing commit people to?

Working Draft

Whether you are analyzing a document or designing one of your own, you will want to consider the tone of the writing—the voice readers hear in the written text.

Tone and Rhetorical Distance

A writer's tone of voice is one key way of establishing his or her relationship to readers. Notice how the following examples of informal, standard, and official tone put the writers into quite different relationships with readers:

- **Informal:** Writing that speaks in the first-person singular, addresses readers as "you," uses colloquialisms and contractions, poses rhetorical questions, and generally strives to sound like spoken language creates an informal tone that reduces the distance between the writer and readers. Notice how the petition to Tiger Woods uses a personal tone:

    As the world's most famous golfer, like it or not, you have unique power. . . .

    You've been a wonderful inspiration for young golfers. . . .

- **Standard:** The tone of voice readers hear in many instances of professional communication, journalism, textbooks, and other forms of nonfiction prose can be characterized as "standard" because it relies on a plain, relatively formal (but not elevated or pretentious) style. This tone does not usually call attention to the writer's personality, as is often the case with an informal tone, or address readers intimately as "you." Instead, it seeks to establish a relationship with readers based on shared interests and the mutual respect of reasonable persons exchanging views. The first three paragraphs of Amnesty International's Call on Kenya to Ease the Suffering of Nairobi's 2 Million Slum Dwellers is a good example:

> More than half of Nairobi's population—some two million people—live in slums and informal settlements. Crammed into makeshift shacks on just one per cent of the city's usable land, people live without adequate access to water, hospitals, schools and other essential public services.
>
> Up to a million people live in Kiberia, Nairobi's largest slum, crowded onto just 550 acres of sodden land that straddles the main railway line. Most earn barely enough to rent a mud-floored, tin-roofed wooden shack with no toilet or running water.
>
> Slum dwellers are under the constant threat of forced evictions, which are illegal under international human rights law. These evictions are often carried out with brutality and victims are not compensated despite losing their homes, businesses and possessions.

- **Official:** An official tone creates the most distance between the written document and readers. The voice that readers hear is not that of an individual writer but of an institution or collective body speaking. The style of writing tends to have a certain bureaucratic or legalistic tone. The controversial Proposition 215 to legalize medical uses of marijuana that appeared on the California state ballot—and passed—in 1996 is a typical example:

> The people of the State of California hereby find and declare that the purposes of the Compassionate Use Act of 1996 are as follows:
>
> To ensure that seriously ill Californians have the right to obtain and use marijuana for medical purposes where that medical use is deemed appropriate and has been recommended by a physician. . . .
>
> This measure amends state law to allow persons to grow or possess marijuana for medical use when recommended by a physician.

Peer Commentary

Exchange drafts with a classmate. Depending on whether you have analyzed or designed a public document, use the appropriate guidelines.

For Analysis of a Document

1. Explain what you see as the writer's purposes—analyzing a personal encounter with a public document, doing a rhetorical analysis, or something else? Is the main point of the analysis clearly stated and easy to find?

2. Describe how the writer develops an analysis. Does the analysis fulfill the writer's purposes or some other purposes? What suggestions can you offer to extend or deepen the analysis?

3. Do you agree with the analysis? If so, explain why.

For the Design and Production of a Document

1. Is the purpose of the document clear and easy to find? Explain where you became aware of its purpose. Will readers understand what, if anything, it calls on them to do?

2. What suggestions can you offer to improve or strengthen the format of the document? Consider its layout, organization, use of numbered or bulleted items, and other design features.

3. Is the language of the document precise and easy for readers to understand? Underline words, phrases, or passages that might be written more clearly. Explain why you marked them. Is the tone appropriate for the type of document your partner has designed? Why or why not? Circle words, phrases, or passages where you think the tone does not work well. Explain.

Revising

Review the peer commentary you have received and then consider these questions, depending on whether you've designed or analyzed a document:

For Analysis of a Document

Is the purpose your reader identified what you intended? What suggestions about your analysis does your reader offer? Why do you think your reader made these suggestions? What assumptions about your analysis does your reader seem to be making in agreeing or disagreeing with it? How do these assumptions compare to assumptions you make in the draft?

For Design and Production of a Document

Is the purpose of your document easy for the reader to identify? Have you ordered your points in a way that is easy to follow? Check at this point to make sure similar points are parallel in structure. Is each point clearly separate from other points? Consider the feedback you have received on the tone of the document.

Locating Common Ground

Public documents such as laws, contracts, and codes are agreements about the way we will conduct ourselves and our relations with others. Because of this, documents rely on consent—through advocacy, voting in elections, and other forms of participation in decision making. When individuals and groups believe their views have not been represented in shaping the policies outlined in public documents, they are less likely to invest authority in or abide by these documents.

An interesting case in point occurred at Warehouse State College recently. The Ad Hoc Committee on Academic Honesty, consisting of students, faculty, and administrators, issued a draft version of an academic honor code which, if approved, all members of the Warehouse State community would be expected to sign and to follow. (The complete draft appears below in Writers' Workshop.) The following section caused a particular controversy among students:

> As a member of the Warehouse State community, I shall not intentionally or knowingly violate the bonds of academic trust among us, nor shall I tolerate violations of this trust.

A later section in the draft specified students' responsibilities:

Upon witnessing any act of academic dishonesty, a student must:

a. Communicate either verbally or in writing, either directly or anonymously, with the student or students who have committed the act of academic dishonesty, informing this or these students that an act of academic dishonesty has been observed. A student must also:
b. Give prompt notification to the Academic Honor Council that a violation has occurred. The student reporting the violation must identify him or herself and the name(s) of the violator(s).

These provisions in the honor code draft quickly became known as the "rat rule," sparking a heated discussion. Some students argued that they went to Warehouse State to be educated, not to "spy" on other students. Some worried that if they observed cheating during an exam, the responsibility to report violations would interfere with their own academic performance. Others supported the proposed code. Seeking to preserve the spirit of the honor code and, at the same time, to satisfy objections and establish a common ground, the committee revised the two sections. Changes are in italics.

> As a member of the Warehouse State community, I shall not intentionally or knowingly violate the bonds of academic trust among us. *I recognize that protecting academic integrity is the collective responsibility of students, faculty, and staff at Warehouse State.*
>
> Upon witnessing any act of academic dishonesty, *a student will be guided by conscience whether to report the act or to take other appropriate action.*

Whether removing the "rat rule" waters down the original intention or provides a common ground all can agree to is an open question. ■

W WRITERS' WORKSHOP

Here is the complete draft, before the revision you've just seen, of the proposed academic honor code for Warehouse State College.

THE WAREHOUSE STATE HONOR CODE

Ad Hoc Committee on Academic Honesty

Proposal for an Academic Honor Code

February 21, 2009

Preamble

At Warehouse State, the bonds of academic trust among all members of the academic community are paramount. Establishing and maintaining these bonds require a unified commitment to the principles of academic integrity and honesty in all educational interactions. To this end, Warehouse State students, faculty, and administrators affirm the following pledge.

I. **Honor pledge**

As a member of the Warehouse State community, I shall not intentionally or knowingly violate the bonds of academic trust among us, nor shall I tolerate violations of this trust.

II. **Definition of Academic Trust**

Academic trust is the assurance that teacher and student will faithfully abide by the rules of intellectual engagement established between them. This trust can exist only when students adhere to the standards of academic honesty and when faculty test and evaluate students in a manner that presumes that students are acting with academic integrity.

III. **Definition of Academic Dishonesty**

Any willful act that either interferes with the process of evaluation or misrepresents the relation between the work evaluated and the student's actual state of knowledge is an act of academic dishonesty and a violation of academic trust. The following are some examples of dishonesty:

a. *Cheating.* Misrepresentation of the work of another as one's own; use of purchased term papers; copying on exams; submission of homework, programs, projects, and take-home exams with portions done by another; use of unauthorized materials or sources of information, such as "crib sheets" or unauthorized storing of information in calculators; assistance of another person in cases where prohibited.

b. *Fabrication.* Alteration of grades or official records; changing of exam answers after the fact; falsifying or inventing laboratory data.

c. *Facilitating Academic Dishonesty.* Assisting or facilitating any act of academic dishonesty.

d. *Academic Sabotage.* Sabotage of another student's work or academic record.

e. *Plagiarism.* Representing the work or ideas of another as one's own without giving proper credit.

IV. **Responsibilities**

A. Student Responsibilities

1. Know and uphold the Honor Pledge.

2. Do not commit any acts of academic dishonesty.

3. Upon witnessing any act of academic dishonesty, a student must:

a. Communicate either verbally or in writing, either directly or anonymously, with the student or students who have committed the act of academic dishonesty, informing this or these students that an act of academic dishonesty has been observed. A student must also:

b. Give prompt notification to the Academic Honor Council that a violation has occurred. The student reporting the violation must identify him or herself and the name(s) of the violator(s).

4. When in doubt about classroom or project rules, ask the professor.

B. Faculty Responsibilities

1. Know and uphold the Honor Pledge.

2. Foster an educational environment that is consistent with the definition of academic trust.

3. Communicate to students individual policies concerning evaluation procedures and expectations pertaining to academic integrity and trust.

4. Report any act of academic dishonesty to the Academic Honor Council.

5. Recognize that judgments about academic dishonesty are the sole responsibility of the Academic Honor Council. If a student is found not guilty on a charge of academic dishonesty, the instructor will not penalize the student in any way.

C. Institutional Responsibilities

1. Disseminate annually the Academic Honor Code to all students, faculty, and staff.

2. Through Faculty and New Student Orientation, promote discussion of the Academic Honor Code and the value Warehouse State places on integrity.

3. Have new students sign the Academic Honor Pledge upon joining the institution.

4. Give administrative support to the Academic Honor Council to ensure ongoing implementation of the Academic Honor Code.

5. Maintain appropriate confidential mechanisms for reporting honor code violations.

V. **Acceptance of the Academic Honor Pledge**

Students sign a pledge they will uphold the principles of academic trust and that they will fulfill their responsibilities concerning the Academic Honor Code as part of their admission to the institution. A student's placing his or her name on an exam, paper, or project shall be understood as a reaffirmation of the student's pledge to abide by the Academic Honor Code. Faculty are expected to conduct classes according to the spirit of academic trust and to follow academic honor code procedures concerning violations.

■ **WORKSHOP QUESTIONS**

1. Imagine that the Ad Hoc Committee on Academic Honesty at Warehouse State College has asked you to review its draft of the Academic Honor Code. How would you respond? Does the Preamble clearly articulate the purpose of the document? Are the definitions of terms and of student, faculty, and institutional responsibilities clearly stated? Are there things not included that you think the document should contain?

2. Evaluate the revision of the two sections of the honor code that appear in the preceding section. Consider student objections to the "rat rule." Do you think they are valid? Do you think an academic honor code should require students to report violations?

3. Does your college or university have an honor code? If so, what does it commit students, faculty, and administrators to do? How is it similar to or different from the Warehouse State draft? What revisions, if any, do you think it needs? If your school does not have an honor code, do you think there should be one? What should it cover?   ■

REFLECTING ON YOUR WRITING

Write a short account of your experience analyzing or composing a public document. Take into account the authority you drew on to write the document or the source of authority the document you analyzed drew on. On whose behalf did you write the document or was the document written? What problems or issues did you encounter in your writing? Explain how you dealt with them.

profiles

THINKING ABOUT THE GENRE

Talking about people and places amounts to a sizeable component of conversation—whether you're telling your parents what your new roommate or a campus organization you've just joined is like or describing to friends the neighborhood where you grew up. This impulse to describe, to analyze, and to understand seems to grow out of a genuine need to come to terms with our social experience, the places we live, the groups we take part in, and our relationships with others.

It's not surprising, then, that a genre of writing—the profile—is devoted to describing and analyzing people and places. Profiles are a regular feature in magazines such as *Rolling Stone, Sports Illustrated, Ebony,* and the *New Yorker,* as well as in newspapers. Many profiles are of well-known people, and the allure of such profiles is that they promise a behind-the-scenes look at celebrities.

But profiles also focus on ordinary people. When an issue moves to the forefront of the public's attention, ordinary people often become the subject of profiles that describe, say, the lives of undocumented workers or the plight of a corporate executive laid off in an economic downturn. Such profiles of ordinary people supplement statistical and analytical treatments of issues, making concrete and personal what would otherwise remain abstract and remote. These profiles can take readers beyond their preconceptions to explore the remarkable variety of people, backgrounds, lifestyles, and experiences that are frequently reduced to a single category such as "the elderly" or "blue-collar workers."

Likewise, there are profiles of places and organizations. A profile might look, for example, at the fate of the Ninth Ward in New Orleans four years after Katrina or focus on a community group that is trying to decrease gang violence in the west end of Providence, Rhode Island.

Sometimes, profiles seem to take place in real time. They may tell what a person does over the course of a day, what a place is like at a moment in time, or what a group's characteristic activities are. Such profiles create a sense of immediacy and intimacy, as though the reader were there on the spot, watching and listening to what's going on. Readers of profiles have come to expect that they will be able to visualize people and places, to hear what people sound like, and to witness revealing incidents.

To convey this sense of immediacy and intimacy, writers of profiles often rely on interviewing and observation. This doesn't mean that library research isn't involved. On the contrary, consulting written sources can supplement interviewing and observation and make them much more effective.

In any case, one point to keep in mind is that no matter how immediate a profile seems to be, we are not seeing a person or a place or an organization directly but rather through the eyes of the writer. A profile—and the impact it has on readers—depends as much on the writer as on the subject profiled. Profiles express, explicitly or implicitly, the author's point of view. No profile will really work for its readers unless it creates a dominant impression—a particular and coherent sense of its subject.

■ WRITING FROM EXPERIENCE

We talk about other people all the time. Think about the conversations you have with others—friends, relatives, coworkers, neighbors, acquaintances, or strangers. In these conversations, what kinds of stories and comments about people come up? List four or five occasions when you or someone else told a story or made a comment about another person. What was the purpose?

Compare your list with the lists of your classmates and see whether any patterns emerge. Are there, for example, any differences between men's and women's stories and comments? Can you classify these examples—by purpose or by who is speaking or whom the stories or comments are about?

READINGS

INSURGENT IMAGES: MIKE ALEWITZ, MURALIST

PAUL BUHLE

Paul Buhle is a historian of labor and popular arts at Brown University. His books include The New Left Revisited *(2003),* Tender Comrades: A Backstory of the Hollywood Blacklist *(1999), and* C.L.R. James's Caribbean *(1992). The following profile is of Mike Alewitz, one of the most prominent American muralists in the last twenty years, an art teacher at Central Connecticut State, and a noted social activist. Buhle and Alewitz collaborated on the book* Insurgent Images: The Agitprop Murals of Mike Alewitz *(2002), which features examples of Alewitz's murals, including those that appear here.*

Mike Alewitz

Si Se Puede, Oxnard, California, 1993

Opening
* describes an Alewitz mural
* puts Alewitz and murals in historical context

1   A large outside wall of Cesar Chavez High School in Oxnard, California, carries the portrait of the famed Latino labor leader and social visionary, "the Chicano Martin Luther King, Jr.," against a background of grape fields and a foreground of the message "Si se puede! Yes! It can be done!" Chavez is seen holding up a book, open to facing pages in English and Spanish, with the text: "We need a meaningful education, not just about the union, but about the whole idea of the cause. The whole idea of sacrificing for other people . . . " Not himself Chicano, not even a Californian, muralist Mike Alewitz was (as actor Martin Sheen pronounced at the 1993 dedication ceremony) the natural choice of artists.

2   Alewitz is happiest in a small crowd of amateur painters and community members who meet to discuss with him what kind of mural would best suit the purposes of the community and the building. Artistic choices are important, but this is public art, its role in some ways better understood in the past than today: art that becomes part of the daily life of ordinary people by picturing their aspirations and struggles in cartoons, murals, posters, and banners. Beginning with the tumultuous labor conflicts in the decades after the Civil War, a public art grew out of union-organizing, agitation against war, and the radical dreams of the American left for women's liberation, racial equality, and social

Mike Alewitz

Monument to the Workers of Chernobyl, right panel, 1996

justice. Like many of his artistic predecessors, Alewitz was a factory or office worker for most of his working life, until he became a full-time painter.

3

* gives
biographi-
cal details

Born in 1951 and growing up in Wilmington, Delaware and Cleveland, Alewitz was barely aware that his Cleveland neighborhood had produced the creators of Superman, and was about to bring forth such noted popular artist-creators as Harvey Pekar (subject of an award-winning 2003 film, *American Splendor*) and Peter Kuper (current artist of *Mad* magazine's feature, "Spy Versus Spy"). These artists all shared a sense for the vernacular: the art that almost never reaches gallery walls, but captures the attention of young people in particular. He almost didn't make it to college, and dropped out after a year. That college was Kent State.

4

By an accident of fate, he had landed on the most explosive campus in North America. At President Richard Nixon's announcement of the US invasion of Cambodia in May 1970, enlarging the Vietnam War dramatically, peace demonstrators took over the grounds of universities and colleges for days, and police and National Guardsmen moved in to halt the demonstrations. At Kent State, guardsmen shot into the crowd, killing students and prompting the most provocative rock music hit of the season, "Four Dead in Ohio" by Crosby, Stills, Nash and Young. Alewitz, a central leader of the Kent antiwar movement, dropped out of school to coordinate the Committee of Kent State Eyewitnesses and to help explain the events and their importance to the national student strike then in progress.

5

Mike Alewitz found a second home in the college town and state capital, Austin, Texas, where he ran for local office as a peace candidate. He began painting signs again, for the growing antiwar activity among GIs in basic training at nearby Fort Killeen. He was locally famous (or notorious) for his visual sense of humor, aimed at the clichés of activists, politicians and the military alike.

Mike Alewitz

Monument to the Workers of Chernobyl, left panel, 1996

* describes some of Alewitz's murals

6   For most of the next twenty years, he worked on railroad lines, at printshops, and most happily as a billboard and sign painter. He painted his first murals in Central America, during the regional conflicts of the 1980s, but received his first major commission almost accidentally in 1984 while visiting a historic packinghouse not far from the twin cities of St.Paul/Minneapolis, in Austin, Minnesota. There, a committee of strikers in local P-9, United Food and Commercial Workers (UFCW) asked him to paint a large wall on the side of their union hall. With the help of strikers and local sympathizers, Alewitz created a panorama of labor dignity, assaulted by corporate mismanagement. The mural was dedicated to Nelson Mandela, then-imprisoned leader of the African National Congress and destined to be the black president of a future South Africa. Widely recognized as one of labor's most important artistic statements in decades, it was destroyed at the orders of national union officials who had decided to end the strike and take control of the union local.

7   Many similar adventures followed in strikes, Labor Day parades, demonstrations for the rights of working people, women, immigrants and minorities. Alewitz became a widely-recognized artist for unions like the Oil, Chemical and Atomic Workers and the United Brotherhood of Carpenters, the movement for a Labor Party (for which he served as Chair of the Cultural Workers and Artists Caucus), but also for many local causes in his adopted New Jersey, and for school buildings. He also traveled abroad, painting for the endangered atomic-plant workers in Chernobyl, Ukraine, site of the world's worst nuclear energy disaster, to the Middle East and to Mexico.

8   The last was very much like coming home in an artistic sense. The foremost muralists of the Americas in the twentieth century, along with the Works Progress Administration public artists during the 1930s, were the giants of Mexican muralism, especially

* explains how Alewitz's style emerged

Diego Rivera, David Alfaro Siqueiros, Jose Clemente Orozco. These artists, with some of their outstanding 1930s work painted in the U.S., more than anyone else restored painting to its public role in conjunction with social movements whose participants best understood what art might become once again. From them, Alewitz learned purpose. But he had to develop his own style.

9   Everything under the sun is suitable for reworking as an Alewitz image. From comic strips to earth-shaking events like revolutions and wars, labor leaders and ordinary workers, social heroes and martyrs, nature scenes, factories and neighborhoods, funny and tragic lessons alike. Perhaps most continuous and vividly expressed, though, is the reality of working for a living in hundreds of different ways, old style factories to new style computer terminals—and the overwhelming importance of education.

10   All this goes into the making of the mural. Painters and assorted volunteers help to procure materials, erect scaffolding, repair and prime walls for painting, and often block in large areas of color as well. He has also developed methods of providing space for casual or symbolic contributions to the painting by a larger group of supporters. Artists, poets, musicians and activists of all sorts are invited to create work around the project, at concerts, dedication ceremonies and other public events.

* explains how Alewitz works

11   Alewitz himself meanwhile takes strong and direct control of the imagery. He does not believe that his role is to attempt to paint "as if" someone else might, but rather to express those events, struggles and personalities through his own experiences as worker, artist and activist. He has learned that art by committee usually fails because art cannot be negotiated without being homogenized. That said, he works out a final design after thorough discussion. He prefers, for the most part, to work with young assistants who will go through the experience and learn skills that will help them create mural art of their own.

12   One of Alewitz's most revealing murals stands on the Highlander Center in New Market, Tennessee, a historic center of civil rights activity and craft training. On one side, leading to a loaf of bread and sumptuous tomatoes (because Highlander is famous for its own produce), is Dr. Martin Luther King, Jr., and on the other side, Highlander's founder, the late Myles Horton, with multiracial working people marching underneath, and the banner-message, "Sin accion, no hay conocimiento/Without action, there is no knowledge."

Ending
* uses a particular mural to make closing point

13   Democracy, Alewitz's paintings boldly insist, demands active citizens, proud of themselves for what they produce, educated to take responsibility for their history and the better future that America may hold.

Analysis: Using Cultural and Historical Background

Rather than focusing on a particular time and place, Paul Buhle's profile of Mike Alewitz looks at his work in a number of locations, from Cesar Chavez High School, where the profile opens, to Austin, Minnesota, where Alewitz painted one of his most important murals, to Alewitz's travels to Chernobyl, the Middle East, and Mexico, to the closing scene at the Highlander Center in Tennessee. To create a dominant impression that conveys the signficance of Alewitz's wide-ranging work, Buhle provides crucial cultural and historical background.

Notice how Buhle skillfully integrates information and commentary into his profile at a number of key points: by defining the function of public art in the second paragraph; by describing in the third paragraph Alewitz's Cleveland neighborhood as the home of Superman's creators and other popular artists; by recounting the events of May 1970 at Kent State in the fourth paragraph; and by explaining in the eighth paragraph the muralist traditions of Mexican painters and public artists of the Works Progress Administration in the 1930s.

■ FOR CRITICAL INQUIRY

1. In the last sentence of the opening paragraph, Paul Buhle says that Mike Alewitz was the "natural choice of artists" to paint the mural at Cesar Chavez High School, but he doesn't explain why this is so. Consider whether a satisfactory answer emerges for readers by the end of the profile. What is the effect of letting the question of why Alewitz was the "natural choice" float throughout the profile? Do you think it's a good opening strategy?

2. Use the annotations to consider how (or whether) the profile creates a dominant impression of Mike Alewitz. Trace how this impression develops from the opening scene to the end of the profile. List some of the words, phrases, and sentences that are central to conveying a dominant impression.

3. The single-sentence final paragraph is an eloquent commentary on what "Alewitz's paintings boldly insist." What exactly is Buhle's evaluation of Alewitz's work? Do you think the profile has prepared readers to understand and perhaps to share the sentiments of the last sentence? Why or why not?

PROFILES AND PUBLICITY

Single-page profiles that combine text and image are a staple of advertising, public relations, and advocacy campaigns. The profile of Flora Gonzalez's book recommendations is part of a campaign by Iwasaki Library at Emerson College to encourage reading for pleasure, while the profile of the hedge fund manager was designed by Phonak, in what it has called "the edgiest campaign in the company's (and probably the industry's) history," to overcome the stigma of using hearing aids on the part of "younger baby-boomers." Consider, in each case, how the profile personalizes the publicity campaign.

Flora Gonzalez profile

Phonak ad

Emerson College

Jerzyworks/Masterfile

PROFILE OF A COMMUNITY ORGANIZATION

AN EMPIRE FOR POOR WORKING WOMEN, GUIDED BY A GANDHIAN APPROACH

SOMINI SENGUPTA

Somini Sengupta was the New York Times *bureau chief in Delhi, India, from 2004 to 2008. Her profile of Ela Bhatt and the Self-Employed Women's Association appeared in the* New York Times *on March 6, 2009.*

RUTH FREMSON/The New York Times/Redux

"Why should there be a difference between worker and worker, whether they are working in a factory, or at home or on the footpath?" ELA BHATT AHMADABAD, India

Thirty-five years ago in this once thriving textile town, Ela Bhatt fought for higher wages for women who ferried bolts of cloth on their heads. Next, she created India's first women's bank.

Since then, her Self-Employed Women's Association, or SEWA, has offered retirement accounts and health insurance to women who never had a safety net, lent working capital to entrepreneurs to open beauty salons in the slums, helped artisans sell their handiwork to new urban department stores and boldly trained its members to become gas station attendants—an unusual job for women on the bottom of India's social ladder.

Small, slight and usually dressed in a hand-spun cotton sari, Mrs. Bhatt is a Gandhian pragmatist for the New India.

At 76, she is a critic of some of India's embrace of market reforms, but nevertheless keen to see the poorest of Indian workers get a stake in the country's swelling and swiftly globalizing economy. She has built a formidable empire of women-run, Gandhian-style cooperatives—100 at last count—some providing child care for working mothers, others selling sesame seeds to Indian food-processing firms—all modeled after the Gandhian ideal of self-sufficiency but also advancing modern ambitions.

She calls it the quest for economic freedom in a democratic India.

Her own quest offers a glimpse into the changing desires of Indian mothers and daughters, along with their vulnerabilities. Tinsmiths or pickle makers, embroiderers or vendors of onions, SEWA's members are mostly employed in the informal sector. They get no regular paychecks, sick leave or holidays. Calamities are always just around the corner, whether traffic accidents or crippling droughts. Without SEWA, they would be hard pressed to have health benefits or access to credit.

SEWA's innovations bear lessons for the majority of workers in the new Indian economy. Since economic reforms kicked off in 1991, the share of Indians employed in the informal sector—where they are not covered by stringent, socialist-era labor laws from the time of the cold war—has grown steadily to more than 90 percent, according to a recent government-commissioned report.

Among them, the report found, nearly three-fourths lived on less than 20 cents a day and had virtually no safety net. "Why should there be a difference between worker and worker," Mrs. Bhatt wondered aloud, "whether they are working in a factory, or at home or on the footpath?"

WITH 500,000 members in western Gujarat State alone, the SEWA empire also includes two profit-making firms that stitch and embroider women's clothing. More than 100,000 women are enrolled in the organization's health and life insurance plans. Its bank has 350,000 depositors and, like most microfinance organizations, a repayment rate as high as 97 percent. Loans range from around $100 to $1,100, with a steep interest rate of 15 percent. "We don't have a liquidity problem," its manager, Jayshree Vyas, pointed out merrily. "Women save."

A SEWA loan of roughly $250 allowed Namrata Rajhari to start a beauty salon 15 years ago from her one-room shack in a working-class enclave called Behrampura. At first, the neighborhood women knew little about beauty treatments. They only wanted their hair trimmed.

Then Mrs. Rajhari began threading their eyebrows to resemble perfect half-moons, waxing the hair off their forearms and offering facials. During the wedding season, business blossomed. Mrs. Rajhari, who only has a 10th-grade education, expanded to a small room in the next lane.

With money from her business, Mrs. Rajhari installed a toilet at home, added a loft and bought a washing machine. "Before, I felt blank. I didn't know anything about the world," she said the other day. "Now, with my earnings, my children are studying."

Mrs. Rajhari then motioned to an object of pride in the living room. "The computer is also from my parlor money," she beamed. A daughter, Srishti, is now enrolled in a private English school. She wants to be an astronomer.

Behrampura buzzed with work and hustle on this morning. Men disassembled old television sets and put together new sofas. A woman pushed a cart loaded with used suitcases. Another herded a half-dozen donkeys loaded with construction debris.

Nearby, in another slum, shortly after dawn, Naina Chauhan rode a motorized rickshaw across town to start her shift as a gas station attendant. Her mother, Hira, now 65, had spent a lifetime ferrying coal, cleaning hospitals and going house to house to collect old newspapers. Naina said she resolved never to slog as her mother had.

Today, she contributes about $1 a month to her own SEWA-run pension plan. A SEWA loan has allowed her to clear a debt from relatives. She easily makes three times what her mother made collecting newspapers and as she shyly admitted this afternoon, almost as much as her husband, a hospital cleaner. She just recently married, and plans to move into her husband's family home soon. She said she hoped he would let her manage at least some of her own money.

Mrs. Bhatt's Gandhian approach is most evident in the way she lives. Her two-bedroom bungalow is small and spare. The one bit of whimsy is a white swing that hangs from the ceiling in the center of the living room. She uses her bed as a desk chair. Her grandson has painted a child's pastoral mural on the bedroom wall. She is known for having no indulgences.

"Above all you should emphasize her simplicity," said Anil Gupta, a professor at the Indian Institute of Management here who has followed SEWA's work for over a decade, sometimes critically. "In her personal life, there is not the slightest tinge of hypocrisy."

Mrs. Bhatt is not without detractors. The chief minister of Gujarat, Narendra Modi, accused her group of financial irregularities three years ago in the management of a rehabilitation program for earthquake victims. SEWA denied the charges and pulled out of the government-run program. Mrs. Bhatt accused Mr. Modi of trying to discredit the organization. Their war of words has since cooled down.

BORN to a privileged Brahmin family, Mrs. Bhatt charted an unusual path for a woman of her time. She earned a law degree and chose the man she would marry. She began her career as a lawyer for the city's main union for textile workers, the vast majority of them men, and broke away in 1981 to create a new kind of union for women.

Early on, she won higher rates for women porters, then a landmark legal victory that allowed women to sell fruits and vegetables on the street without harassment from the police. The fishmongers and quilt-makers who were SEWA Bank's earliest customers sometimes stashed their checkbooks in the bank's steel cabinets, she recalled, lest their husbands discover they had money of their own.

At first, the women's ambitions were limited, she said. They wanted toilets, hair shears or sewing machines for work and money to pay for their children's school fees. Slowly, she noticed, they began to dream big. Mothers now want their daughters to learn to ride a scooter and work on a computer.

"They didn't see the future at that time," she said. "Expectations have gone very high."

Not long ago, Mrs. Bhatt recalled, she asked SEWA members what "freedom" meant to them. Some said it was the ability to step out of the house. Others said it was having a door to the bathroom. Some said it meant having their own money, a cellphone, or "fresh clothes every day."

Then she told of her favorite. Freedom, one woman said, was "looking a policeman in the eye."

Analysis: Portrait of an Organization and Its Founder

Somini Sengupta offers readers a profile of both the organization Self-Employed Women's Association (SEWA) and its founder Ela Bhatt. Notice how the profile opens by introducing Ela Bhatt, next shifts to a long middle section that describes SEWA's work, and then closes by returning to Bhatt. As the founder of SEWA, Bhatt is clearly a key figure in this profile, but Sengupta doesn't intend it to focus on Bhatt alone. Rather, the profile includes other women involved in SEWA and their stories as well. In this way, Sengupta balances the important role of Bhatt, as the founder of SEWA, with vivid sketches of two women, Namrata Rajhari and Naina Chauhan, and what their participation in SEWA has meant to them.

■ FOR CRITICAL INQUIRY

1. Somini Sengupta knows her readers are not likely to know about SEWA and, accordingly, that she needs to provide them with enough background information to understand the significance of the organization's work. Where does she do that? How do you think she made decisions about the amount and type of information to include?

2. What is the dominant impression of this profile? How would you describe it in a sentence? What are some of the key rhetorical strategies Sengupta uses to create this impression?

3. Ela Bhatt gets the last words in this profile, but they are her recollection of what SEWA members told her when she asked what "freedom" meant to them. How do Bhatt's accounts of what the women told her provide a sense of closure to the profile?

VISUAL DESIGN

Photo Essay

CANCER ALLEY: THE POISONING OF THE AMERICAN SOUTH

RICHARD MISRACH, PHOTOGRAPHS, AND JASON BERRY, ESSAY

Richard Misrach is a photographer whose work has often focused on the American desert, including studies of former nuclear testing sites and bombing ranges. Jason Berry is a writer and documentarian who lives in New Orleans. His novel *Last of the Red Hot Poppas* explores the politics of pollution. His investigative books include *Lead Us Not Into Temptation* and *Vows of Silence: The Abuse of Power in the Papacy of John Paul II*. This is an excerpt from a photo essay that originally appeared in *Aperture* (Winter 2001). It includes the full text of Jason Berry's essay and three of the twelve photographs by Richard Misrach.

Richard Misrach, Courtesy Fraenkel Gallery, SF, Marc Selwyn Fine Art, LA and Pace/MacGill Gallery, NY

Analysis: How Photographs and Texts Go Together

Photo essays consist of a series of photographs that work together by telling a story, describing a place, portraying individuals or groups of people, or otherwise evoking emotions in order to create a dominant impression. Some photo essays rely on photographs alone. Others, like "Cancer Alley," combine photographs and texts. In this excerpt, you can see two common features of the photo essay—the two-page spread and the use of captions—that join words and images together. Notice in "Cancer Alley" that the photographs do not simply illustrate ideas in the written text, nor does the written text simply explain what the photographs are showing. Instead, the relationship between photographs and text is dynamic and reciprocal.

Richard Misrach, Courtesy Fraenkel Gallery, SF, Marc Selwyn Fine Art, LA and Pace/MacGill Gallery, NY

WITNESS

CANCER ALLEY
THE POISONING OF THE AMERICAN SOUTH

PHOTOGRAPHS / RICHARD MISRACH
ESSAY / JASON BERRY

"Baton Rouge was clothed in flowers, like a bride—no, much more so; like a greenhouse. For we were in the absolute South now," wrote Mark Twain of the vistas from a riverboat in his 1883 classic *Life on the Mississippi*. "From Baton Rouge to New Orleans," he continued, "the great sugar-plantations border both sides of the river all the way, and stretch their league-wide levels back to the dim forest of bearded cypress in the rear. The broad river lying between the two rows becomes a sort of spacious street."

Twain caught the ninety-mile river corridor between the old Capitol and New Orleans at a poignant moment. Plantations still harvested profits in cotton and sugarcane; the black field workers, no longer slaves, were sharecroppers or virtual serfs. The river flowed through a land riddled with injustice. Yet there was beauty in the waterway and surrounding landscape, and beauty—although burdened with an unsavory history—in those old houses of "the absolute South," with their porticoes and pillared balconies.

By the 1940s, when Clarence John Laughlin trained his lens upon the area, some of the mansions had been torn down and others lay in ruins. The wrecked buildings riveted his eye as much as the several dozen that were still preserved (then starting to shift from farming to tourist sites, which most remain today). A haunting sense of loss suffuses the black-and-white surrealism in Laughlin's remarkable book *Ghosts Along the Mississippi*.

Between the time of Twain's reportage and Laughlin's elegiac photographs from the mid-twentieth century, oil and petrochemical

ABANDONED TRAILER HOME

West Bank Mississippi River, near Dow Chemical plant, Plaquemine, Louisiana, 1998

no. 162 Aperture / 31

producers bought up vast pieces of land along the river and began grafting an industrial economy over the old agricultural estates. The refineries and plants—like the derricks that dot the Cajun prairie and the oil-production platforms in Louisiana coastal waters off the Gulf of Mexico—boosted the economies of communities once mired in poverty. The downside has been a political mentality blind to the ravages of pollution.

ORIGINS OF CANCER ALLEY

Standard Oil opened a refinery in 1909 on the fringes of Baton Rouge. In 1929 Governor Huey P. Long erected the new Capitol, a thirty-four-story Art Deco tower near the Standard plant. Today that political temple stands out in high relief from the expanded grid of pumping stacks and smoke clouds where Exxon (Standard's successor) functions like a city-within-the-city. The Capitol and the massive oil complex issuing pungent clouds have melded into an awesome symbol of Louisiana politics: pollution as the price of power.

Providence Plantation, which dated to the 1720s, was in the river town of Des Allemands, and on its grounds was a massive tree known as the Locke Breaux Live Oak, which was 36 feet around and 101 feet high, with a limb span of 172 feet. That majestic tree, estimated to be over three hundred years old, died from exposure to pollution in 1968: the new owner of its site, Hooker Chemical, had it cut up and removed.

The human toll has been even more harsh.

By the 1980s, according to the Louisiana Office of Conservation, thousands of oil-waste pits, many leaching toxic chemicals, were scattered across Louisiana; hundreds of them were seeping into areas of the fertile rice belt in Cajun country. As awareness spread about groundwater contamination and diseases in communities along the river's industrial corridor, activists began calling the area "Cancer Alley."

Although Louisiana ranks in the top 10 percent of states in terms of its cancer mortality rate, petrochemical interests dismiss the term "Cancer Alley" as factually unsupported, a provocation. Black irony coats their charge.

The Louisiana Chemical Association provided base funding for the state Tumor Registry, which assembles the data on cancers. The registry is undertaken by a division of the Louisiana State University Medical Center, which is a beneficiary of donations from polluting industries. Louisiana's Tumor Registry, unlike those in most other states, offers no reliable data on incidences of childhood cancer, or incidences by parish (county), or incidences on a yearly basis. It reports trends only in larger geographic groupings; as a result, disease clusters cannot be pinpointed. Rare forms of cancer can't be tracked geographically. Much information gathered by physicians who treat cancer patients is anecdotal.

And that, in the opinion of Dr. Patricia Williams, is just the way business and petrochemical lobbyists want it. "Without reliable data, no one can link disease patterns to pollution," says Williams, who is herself a professor at the LSU Medical School, and is at the forefront of attempts to change the system.

"We're being denied the raw data and it's unconscionable," says Williams. "Embryonic tumors are not being reported as they are diagnosed. Raw data, by parish, would allow prevention programs. If you see a particular trend of brain cancers, you could begin to sort out what's going on. . . . The same [holds true] with cancer clusters."

Despite the state's history of being at or near the top of statistical lists in categories of toxic emissions, plaintiff attorneys have a great deal of trouble getting medical data to prove the impact of pollution in a given community.

Like Clarence John Laughlin before him, Richard Misrach captures the tones of a culture in spiritual twilight—clinging to a past beauty in the old mansions and icons of Catholicism—now facing a darkness brought about by big oil. Misrach's use of color sets him apart from Laughlin stylistically, as does his striking sense of juxtapositions: the petrochemical specters shadowing fields, ponds, buildings, cemeteries, and basketball courts. Misrach's commitment to discovering the ravaged landscape, while conceptually similar to Laughlin's, is rooted in the land itself. His longterm exploration of the American West and its defilement, the epic "Desert Cantos," are relentlessly straightforward. The "Bravo 20" series of the late 1980s—photographs of Nevada's disturbingly stunning bombing ranges—allow the terrain to create its own dark metaphors. Misrach's work reveals the primary emblems and moods of these frightening landscapes; the Louisiana images are thus as mysterious as they are horrific.

CITIZENS TAKE A STAND

Clarence Laughlin was a romantic who saw industry in symbolic terms—machine against man. In 1980, he took a firm stand at a news conference in New Orleans, lashing out against a plan to put the world's largest toxic-waste incinerator next to the historic Houmas House plantation, in Ascension Parish, midway along the river corridor south of Baton Rouge. A California-based company called Industrial Tank (I.T.) had begun with a $350,000 grant from the state government in Baton Rouge for a site feasibility study. I.T. recommended the construction of a massive disposal complex on a piece of land that was a proven flood plain, below sea level, in an already congested industrial road fronting the Mississippi River. In a move that reeked of corrupt politics, state officials then awarded I.T. the necessary permits to build the complex—whose feasibility I.T. had just been paid to assess. (In fact, the company had put money down on the land before it even got the permits.)

Reports soon surfaced that I.T. had pollution problems at its California sites, and was utterly inexperienced in managing a project of the scope envisioned in Louisiana. A citizens' group filed suit against I.T. and the state. In 1984, the state Supreme Court threw out the permits, killing the project. By then, activists were challenging industry over other conflicts.

DYNAMICS OF CHANGE

Amos Favorite, a seventy-eight-year-old black man, is now retired after many years in the union at Ormet Aluminum. Favorite grew up speaking the Creole French patois in the town of Vacherie, where Fats Domino was born. He remembers when ponds were blue. As a teenager he moved to nearby Geismar, where he has lived ever since.

"This was a good place to live at one time," says Favorite. "All the meat was wild game. I was raised on rabbits, squirrels, and deer." He hated work in the fields, however, and when he came home from infantry in World War II, Favorite bought a dozen acres of Geismar plantation, which was being sold off at thirty-five dollars an acre. The town is named for the family that owned the estate. Favorite's nine children grew up on his acreage; one of his sons was building a handsome two-story house next door to Amos Favorite's this past August.

One of his daughters, artist Malika Favorite, was the first black child to desegregate the local white school. Because of that, two KKK members tried to dynamite the family home. Before they could set the charge, Amos Favorite took his shotgun and started blasting. "I gave 'em the red ass, yes I did," he laughs. "They went runnin' to the sheriff, but that sheriff didn't do nothin' to me."

That was in 1968. A few years later, Favorite began to realize that people were getting sick from wells that drew water from the local aquifer, and he started speaking out against Ascension Parish's sacred cow: industry. BASF, the largest chemical company in the world, and Vulcan, which produces perchloroethylene (the chemical that goes into dry cleaning fluid) have plants in the area.

Despite opposition from management at thirteen major plants in Geismar, including BASF and Vulcan, Favorite won support from union members in those industries for his attempt to establish a public water system and separate district for Geismar. Favorite found a valuable ally in Willie Fontenot, the environmental investigator in the state attorney general's office. Fontenot has made a career of helping communities organize and gather research against polluters and unresponsive state agencies.

"The local government in Ascension had failed to provide adequate water," says Fontenot. "Amos Favorite and the Labor Neighbor project [a cross section of activists from various walks of life] broke the impasse and got the Baton Rouge water company to extend piping and set up a distribution system in Ascension to supplant the old private wells. . . . It was a pretty big victory for a ragtag citizens' group."

The most recent "ragtag" victory came in the town of Convent, where a company called Shintech wanted to build a huge chemical plant in an area of low-income black residents. Tulane University's Environmental Law Clinic helped the citizens challenge the state's operating permits, citing new EPA standards to guard against environmental racism. Shintech pulled out, and found another site, rather than risk being the first major test case of EPA's guidelines. The law clinic took a pounding from Governor Mike Foster and the State Supreme Court, which issued a ruling that severely restricts law students from working with community groups on environmental cases.

The people who live and work in this region of the Mississippi take a long view of their struggle. "The pendulum is going to swing," says Dr. Williams, who lives in LaPlace, twenty miles upriver from New Orleans. "Pollution is such a problem that people are becoming aware of cancers in their friends. They're becoming suspicious. Ten or fifteen years from now, what has happened to big tobacco companies is going to happen to industries that are polluting here." A surge of civil-damage suits against industry is inevitable, she predicts, "because there has been such a concerted effort to conceal what's happened."

Richard Misrach, Courtesy Fraenkel Gallery, SF, Marc Selwyn Fine Art, LA and Pace/MacGill Gallery, NY

HOLY ROSARY CEMETERY AND UNION CARBIDE COMPLEX

Taft, Louisiana, 1998. The Union Carbide Corporation purchased the property of the Holy Rosary Church, built circa 1866. A replacement church was constructed in the 1960s in nearby Hahnville, but the cemetery was left behind.

Richard Misrach, Courtesy Fraenkel Gallery, SF; Marc Selwyn Fine Art, LA and Pace/MacGill Gallery, NY

Richard Misrach, Courtesy Fraenkel Gallery, SF, Marc Selwyn Fine Art, LA and Pace/MacGill Gallery, NY

REVETMENT SIGN AND HALE-BOGGS BRIDGE, WEST BANK, MISSISSIPPI RIVER

Luling, Louisiana, 1998. The Mississippi is the dominant river basin in North America and drains more than 1.2 million square miles, or about 40 percent of the continental United States. It provides 18 million people with drinking water, 1.5 million in Louisiana alone. In a recent study of pollutants discovered in the drinking water of a single Louisiana parish, over 75 toxins were found, including the carcinogens carbon tetrachroride, chloroform, O-chloronitrobenzene, p-chloronitrobenzene, 1,4-dichlorobenzene, DDT, DDE, and DDD, dichloromethane, alachlor, atrazine, dieldrin, heptachlor epoxide, hexachlorobenzene, and pentachlorobenzene. The thirteen Louisiana parishes that depend on the Mississippi as a source of drinking water have some of the highest mortality rates in the United States from several forms of cancer.

NORCO CUMULUS CLOUD, SHELL OIL REFINERY

Norco, Louisiana, 1998. Norco, twenty-five miles upriver from New Orleans, is the site of a massive Shell Oil Refinery. Throughout the day, natural-looking clouds, nicknamed "Norco cumulus," hover over the site, created by the comingling of moisture and volatile hydrocarbons originating in the refinery process of gasoline, jet fuel, cooking oil, and other products. Louisiana ranks second in the nation, behind Texas, in the amount of toxic substances released into the air and water: 183 million tons of toxic chemicals were emitted in 1997.

no. 162 Aperture / 41

■ FOR CRITICAL INQUIRY

1. Consider how the two-page spread opens the photo essay. How does Richard Misrach's photograph of the abandoned trailer establish the mood of the photo essay? What terms would you use to describe the dominant impression the photo essay makes?

2. How do the captions and the photographs work together? What would it be like if just text or just photographs appeared without the other?

3. As you can see, Misrach's photographs of pollution and environmental devastation are quite beautiful. What is the relationship between this beauty and the damage the photos document?

SOUNDMAP

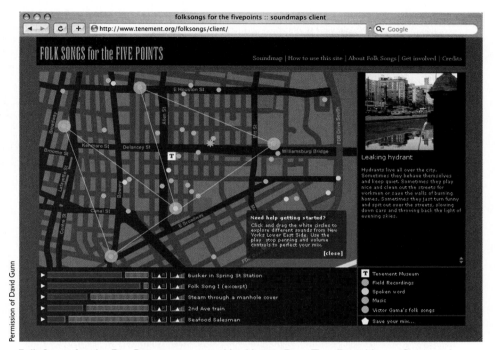

Permission of David Gunn

Folk Songs for the Five Points was created by Alastair Dant, Tom Davis, Victor Gama, and David Gunn for the Lower East Side Tenement Museum's Digital Artists in Residence Program in response to an invitation for "works that explore contemporary immigrant experience in New York City." You can visit Folk Songs for the Five Points at www.tenement.org/folksongs/client. Compare this soundmap of the Lower East Side to the photo essay "Cancer Alley." What does each bring to light about the place it is profiling?

A CONVERSATION WITH PAULINE WIESSNER
WHERE GIFTS AND STORIES ARE CRUCIAL TO SURVIVAL

CLAUDIA DREIFUS

Claudia Dreifus writes the "Conversation with . . ." feature in the science section of the New York Times. *A collection of these interviews appears in* Scientific Conversations: Interviews on Science from the New York Times *(2002). This conversation was published on May 26, 2009.*

The anthropologist Pauline Wiessner, at the University of Utah, studies the value of social networks among hunter-gatherers like the !Kung of South Africa (the exclamation point represents a click sound characteristic of their language). I spoke with Dr. Wiessner, who is 61 and goes by the name Polly, during a break at last month's "Origins" symposium at Arizona State University and later in an interview in New York City. An edited version of the conversations follows.

Nicholas Wiessner

Pauline Wiessner eating a lizard in the Australian desert.

One of the groups you study, the !Kung people of Southern Africa's Kalahari Desert, are native to one of the most unforgiving corners of the planet. How do they survive in a place of frequent droughts, floods, and famine?

They have an intricate system of banking their social relationships and calling on them when times get rough. The system is maintained through gift-giving, storytelling and visiting. It works like insurance does in our culture.

I first arrived in the Kalahari in the early 1970s, when the !Kung were still primarily hunter-gatherers. My question then was: how do people without meat on the hoof, grain in the larder and money in the bank survive hard times?

When I was there for about a year, some answers came. There was a heavy rain. The desert plants died and the wild game dispersed. As people grew hungrier, they began telling vivid stories about loved ones who lived as far as 200 kilometers away. They spoke about how they much missed them. Soon people were busily crafting beautiful objects—gifts. Finally, when push came to shove, 150 !Kung began trekking to the encampments of the people they'd been remembering. There they stayed until conditions in their home area improved.

What I'd witnessed was a structured system at play. The Bushmen used the storytelling to keep feelings for distant persons alive. The gifts are their way of telling the receiver, "I've held you in my heart." Over the years, I saw this repeated many, many times. It would turn out that the !Kung spent as much as three months a year visiting "exchange partners," and this was the key to their survival.

Were there any special messages in the gifts?

That the relationship was alive and well, and to remind the exchange partner that they had a kind of contract to call on each other in times of need.

Actually, in the Kalahari, people send gifts to their exchange partners even when there isn't a crisis. Like Christmas cards and presents, these objects are information on the status of the relationship. We may not particularly want Aunt Sally's holiday fruit cake, but we'd be troubled if it didn't arrive every year. In the Kalahari, if gifts aren't sent, it means the relationship is in poor repair. People know their networks are crucial to how they get past the hard times, and they tend them with loving care.

Why are these networks worth studying?

I think they are a clue to how modern humans moved out of Africa around 45,000 years ago. Unless these migrants had support systems in a founding group and could maintain ties with them, it probably wouldn't have been possible to keep pushing into unknown territory.

It only took modern humans some 5,000 years to move out of Africa, cross Eurasia and end up in Australia. I think that the invention of social networks—the storing of relationships for a time when you will need them—is what facilitated this expansion.

It may also have played a role in the development of culture. People who made exquisite gifts and told enthralling stories would have been more successful in maintaining relationships. They might have been the ones who would have had better opportunities for survival and to pass their genes on to the next generation.

Do you see any contemporary examples of this behavior?

Facebook. People who use it say it keeps memories of distant friends alive and it sometimes brings long-lost relationships back home.

We all know of people who've been "friended" by old pals from college and former neighbors they've lost touch with. When they see pictures of them and read "sharings" from their Facebook partners, they are reminded of their presence in their lives.

One constantly hears stories of people finding jobs and business opportunities through these sites. Hey, and what does a blogger do? Tell stories! The videos and snapshots that people post echo the exchange gifts of the !Kung. They are a kind of token that says, "I've kept you in my heart."

Do your Bushmen friends keep you in their networks when you're back in Utah?

There are signs they do. About five years ago, my phone in Salt Lake City rang in the middle of the night. Some of my friends managed to gain access to a satellite telephone left untended by a safari tour operator. They'd even found someone who knew how to work the thing. They said they'd just rung up a well-known American who'd been to the Kalahari a few years earlier making a documentary. He had, according to the !Kung, promised to send their soccer team some athletic shoes. Would I, they asked, purchase them in Utah and then send him the bill? He'd agreed to this, they claimed. I could bring the shoes next time I traveled to Namibia.

Were you annoyed?

No. I frequently worried about how the !Kung could survive the modern world. Just that day I had worked with data showing that in the 30 years since they'd moved to permanent settlements, their caloric intake had declined from what it had been when they were hunting and gathering.

This call showed that the !Kung could combine new technologies with age-old strategies to get things they needed.

These Bushmen had survived for millennia by maintaining ties of mutual support with people outside their immediate group. By accessing this satellite phone and devising this complex strategy to get the shoes, they'd extended the range of their support network from 200 to 15,000 kilometers.

Analysis: Doing an Interview

Interviews are a type of profile in which we come to know the subject in his or her own words. Interviews can be wide ranging and cover many topics, as in the long interviews of Bob Dylan, John Lennon, Donald Trump, Michael Jordan, and other celebrities that have appeared in *Rolling Stone* and *Playboy*. Or they can be relatively short and highly focused, as in "A Conversation with Pauline Wiessner." As part of the weekly Science Times section in the *New York Times,*

Claudia Dreifus's questions tend to concentrate on Wiessner's research. We get some sense of Wiessner's personal side, to be sure, but the main emphasis is on her scholarly work.

To get the thousand words or so that make up this interview, Dreifus spoke to Wiessner (and no doubt taped the conversation) on two occasions. The result is an edited version that gives a selective profile of some main themes in Wiessner's research. Part of the work on Dreifus's part was doing this editing, to make Wiessner's specialized research accessible to readers. Just as important was Dreifus's preparation for the interview, to become familiar with the research and to develop a series of questions that would guide Wiessner in explaining her work for readers who may be interested but are unlikely to know a good deal about the !Kung. In this sense, we can see the task of the interviewer as a go-between who can bridge the gap between specialized researchers and the reading public.

■ **FOR CRITICAL INQUIRY**

1. Consider the sequence of questions that Claudia Driefus asks of Pauline Wiessner. How do they progress in terms of describing and explaining the significance of Wiessner's research? How does the sequence expand the reader's understanding of her research?

2. Compare this interview to the previous profiles in this chapter. How are interviews alike or different from the profiles?

3. Interviews appear on television and radio as well as in print. Find a few TV or radio interviews and compare them to this print interview. What do you see as the main differences and similarities? What can print do that video or sound can't do? By the same token, what does video or sound do that print interviews can't do?

ETHICS OF WRITING

RESPONSIBILITY TO THE WRITER'S SUBJECT

What is a writer's responsibility to his or her subject? How does this responsibility interact with the writer's responsibility to readers? What potential conflicts are there between the two responsibilities? These are questions profile writers invariably grapple with.

Profiles, after all, are meant to inform readers and offer them the writer's honest perspective—not to serve as publicity or public relations for the person or place profiled. If profile writers are to have an independent voice and fulfill their responsibilities to readers, they must be able to make their own judgments about what is fit to print. But an important basis for these judgments is a sense of responsibility toward the subject. ■

FURTHER EXPLORATION: PROFILES

■ RHETORICAL ANALYSIS

Profiles and biographies are both genres of writing that inform readers about people, but they do so in different ways. To understand what distinguishes profiles and biographies, read one or two short biographies in a standard reference source, such as an encyclopedia, the *Dictionary of American Biography,* or *Current Biography,* to compare to one of the profiles that appears in this chapter. How do the profile and the biographical entry differ in terms of the type and arrangement of information? What differences do you see in the writers' relationship to the subject of the profile or biography and to their readers? What do the differences in rhetorical stance tell you about the two genres?

■ GENRE AWARENESS

Profiles and interviews appear on radio (for example, National Public Radio's *Democracy Now, Fresh Air, On Point,* and *World Café*), on television (for example, the *Larry King Show, Nightline, Charlie Rose,* and *60 Minutes*), and in films (for example, *Crumb,* about the comic artist; *Tupac: The Resurrection,* about the rapper Tupac Shakur; and *Fog of War,* about Robert McNamara, Secretary of Defense during the Vietnam War). There are also documentary profiles of ordinary people (including Amish youth in *The Devil's Playground,* Seattle street kids in *Streetwise,* and young basketball players in *Hoop Dreams*) and places (such as the POV features on asbestos contamination in *Libby, Montana,* and on sweatshop factories in *Made in L.A.*). Working in a group of three or four, identify a radio or television program or a film that profiles an individual, a group, or a place. Develop an oral presentation that analyzes the profile or interview. Use audio or video clips to illustrate the attitude of the profile and how it wants the audience to see the subject being profiled. Consider what audio or video makes possible that differs from print profiles. What can print profiles do that audio or video ones can't?

WRITING ASSIGNMENT

Profile

Choose a person, a group, or a place to write a profile about. The point of this assignment is to bring your subject to life in writing so that you can help your readers see and understand what makes your subject worth reading about.

Here are some possibilities to help you think about whom you might profile:

■ Pick an individual, like Mike Alewitz, whose work will interest readers, whether the person is an artist, a worker, or a professional.

■ Pick a place to profile. It could be somewhere you hang out, a neighborhood, a park, or as in "Cancer Alley," an industrial site. You could do this as a photo essay.

- Pick an organization that deserves recognition. Consider the community organizations in your town or city, as well as national organizations.
- Do an interview with a scholar, an administrator, or a distinguished teacher at your college or university.
- Do a soundmap or radio interview or video profile.

Invention

Finding a Subject

Take some time to decide on the person, place, or organization you want to profile. Don't limit yourself to just those that are familiar to you.

■ EXERCISE
Developing Your Topic

1. **Make a list:** Make a list of people or places that, for one reason or another, interest you. Try to come up with at least ten. This will give you some choices.
2. **Talk to others:** Meet with two or three other students in your class and share the lists each of you has developed for feedback and advice about the most promising subjects. Ask the other students to tell you which people or places are most interesting to them, why, and what they would like to know about them.
3. **Decide tentatively on a subject:** Use the feedback you have received to help you make a tentative decision about which subject you will profile. Take into account your partners' reasons for being interested in a person or place.
4. **Contact your subject:** If you are planning an interview, you will need to contact your subject. Explain that you're a student working on an assignment in a writing course. You'll be amazed—and reassured—by how helpful and gracious most people will be. If they don't have time, they'll tell you so, and then you can go back to your list and try your second choice. Most likely, however, you'll be able to schedule a time to meet and talk with the person. Ask if he or she can suggest anything you might read or research as background information before the interview to help you prepare for it.

At this point it may also be helpful for you to sketch out a schedule for yourself. To write this profile, you will need to allow time for the several stages of both research and writing.

Clarifying Your Purpose

Write a brief statement of purpose. This can be helpful preparation for an interview or as exploratory writing for a profile from memory or based on research.

■ **EXERCISE**

Developing a Statement of Purpose

Take fifteen minutes to answer the following questions:

■ Why are you interested in the particular person or place you're profiling? What is your attitude toward the subject?

■ What do you already know about the person and his or her job, hobby, political or community activity, or social role? If you are profiling a place, what do you know about its history, culture, and current issues?

■ What do other people think about the person or place you're writing about? Do you share these views? What makes your perspective unique?

■ What do you expect to find out by interviewing a person or observing a place?

■ What is your purpose in profiling this particular person or place?

Background Research: Deciding What Information You Need

Whether you're planning an interview, writing from memory, or profiling a place, you'll need to determine the type of information called for by your profile. The nature of this research, of course, will vary depending on whom you're profiling and what your purpose is. Here are some questions to help you make appropriate decisions:

1. How much information do you need? Are there key moments or periods that you should focus on? How is this information pertinent to your profile? Is this information readily available or do you need to find ways to get it?

2. If you are profiling a person, how much do you need to know about the person's field of work? How much do you already know? How can you find out more, if needed? If you're doing an interview, can your subject suggest things you could read before you meet?

3. Are there relevant social, cultural, or political issues you need to know about for the profile? Do you need to understand the historical context? If so, what's important to understand?

4. What, if anything, has already been written about the person or the place? What would be useful to read?

For more information about how to conduct interviews, see the "interviewing" section in *Chapter 15*.

Planning

Deciding on the Dominant Impression

As you have seen from the reading selections in this chapter, the purpose of a profile is to capture your subject at a particular moment in time and to take your readers into your subject's world. In these ways, profiles offer readers a dominant impression of the person (or persons) being profiled. In a profile, you need to inform your readers about the person in question, but you also need to provide your readers with a point of view—a way of seeing and understanding the significance of the person being profiled.

Here are some questions to help you determine the dominant impression you want to create:

- What is the most interesting, unusual, or important thing you have discovered about your subject?
- What are your own feelings about your subject?
- What do others say about your subject? Are these responses to your subject consistent, or do people differ?
- Can you think of two or more dominant impressions you could create to give readers a way of understanding your subject?

Use your answers to these questions to refine your sense of purpose. It may help at this point to talk to a friend or classmate. Explain the different ways in which you might portray your subject. Ask how the dominant impressions you are considering affect the way your classmate or friend understands your subject.

Arranging Your Material

Inventory the material you have to work with. Look over your notes and notice how many separate items about your subject you have. These are the building blocks of your profile, the raw material that you will put together to construct it. Label each item according to the kind of information it contains—such as physical description, biographical background, observed actions and procedures, revealing incidents or anecdotes, direct quotes, things you have read, and things other people have told you.

Once you have inventoried your material, your task is to sketch a tentative plan for your profile. Consider two options illustrated by the readings in this chapter—open form and claims and evidence.

Notice that Paul Buhle's profile of Mike Alewitz is organized in clusters of information that create a web of meaning with a dominant impression. The point or main claim of the profile is implied rather than stated explicitly. The form is open and works through the connections readers make between the information clusters. Buhle's profile can be represented by this chart:

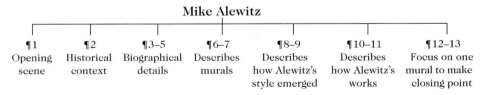

Mike Alewitz

¶1	¶2	¶3–5	¶6–7	¶8–9	¶10–11	¶12–13
Opening scene	Historical context	Biographical details	Describes murals	Describes how Alewitz's style emerged	Describes how Alewitz's works	Focus on one mural to make closing point

Somini Sengupta's profile of Ela Bhatt and SEWA is arranged in more of a top-down fashion, with an explicit statement of the dominant impression ("She calls it the quest for economic freedom in democratic India") that works as the claim of the profile, with the following paragraphs providing evidence. A chart of Sengupta's profile might look like this:

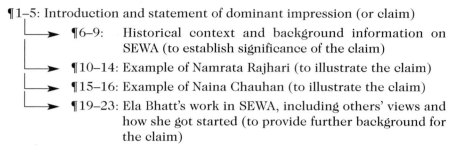

¶1–5: Introduction and statement of dominant impression (or claim)

¶6–9:   Historical context and background information on SEWA (to establish significance of the claim)

¶10–14: Example of Namrata Rajhari (to illustrate the claim)

¶15–16: Example of Naina Chauhan (to illustrate the claim)

¶19–23: Ela Bhatt's work in SEWA, including others' views and how she got started (to provide further background for the claim)

¶24–25: Ending returns to the theme of freedom in the claim.

Experiment with the clusters of information you have. Consider whether open form or a claims and evidence arrangement is better suited. Try a couple of different arrangements of the order of information to determine what's most effective for your purposes and the dominant impression you want to create.

Working Draft

By this time you have organized a lot of material from your research. In fact, you are likely to have more material than you can use, so don't worry if you can't fit everything in as you write a working draft. Consider drafting by clusters of information, with the idea that you might change the order of arrangement when you revise.

Beginnings and Endings: Letting Your Subject Have the Last Word

A standard way to end profiles of people is to give them the final word. This is what happens in Somini Sengupta's profile of Ela Bhatt and SEWA, although, in this case, it's Bhatt relaying answers that SEWA members gave her to the question what does freedom mean to them. In this regard, the ending is particularly appropriate because Bhatt serves as a go-between so readers can hear SEWA members's voices and what they have to say, just as she has enabled the women in SEWA to gain a measure of economic freedom.

Paul Buhle does a variation on giving the subject the final word. However, this time it's not the subject of the profile, Mike Alewitz, who speaks but rather, in a metaphorical way, his paintings. Buhle gives them voice by writing that "Alewitz's paintings boldly insist" that democracy "demands active citizens, proud of themselves for what they produce, educated to take responsibility for their history and the better future that America may hold."

Peer Commentary

Exchange drafts with a partner. Respond in writing to these questions about your partner's draft:

1. Describe what you see as the writer's purposes. Does the working draft create a dominant impression? Does it imply or state a main point? Explain how and where the draft develops a dominant impression (and main point, if pertinent).

2. Describe the arrangement of the working draft. Divide the draft into sections by grouping related paragraphs together. Explain how each section contributes to the overall impression the profile creates. Do you find the arrangement easy to follow? Does the arrangement seem to suit the writer's purposes? If there are rough spots or abrupt shifts, indicate where they are and how they affected your reading.

3. How effective are the beginning and ending of the draft? What suggestions would you make to strengthen the impact, increase the drama, or otherwise improve these two sections of the draft? Should the writer have used a different strategy?

4. Do you have other suggestions about how the writer could enhance the profile? Are there details, reported speech, descriptions, or incidents that the writer could emphasize? Are there elements the writer should cut?

Revising

Use the peer commentary to do a critical reading of your draft.

1. Consider first how your reader has analyzed the arrangement of your profile. Notice in particular how the commentary has divided the draft into sections. Do these sections correspond to the way you wanted to arrange the profile? Are there ways to rearrange material to improve its overall effect?

2. If you are using open form, are the clusters of information clear to your reader? Are there ways to enhance the presentation?

3. If you are presenting a claim and evidence, was this pattern of organization clear to your reader? Are there ways to enhance its presentation?

4. Does the draft create the kind of dominant impression you intended?

5. What did your writing partner suggest? Evaluate specific suggestions.

Establishing Perspective from the Beginning

The beginning of your profile is a particularly important place to establish a perspective on the person, place, or group you're writing about. The strategy you use to design an opening will depend both on your material and on the attitude you want your readers to have toward your subject. Notice how Richard Quitadamo revised the opening paragraph of his profile. (The full draft is included in Writers' Workshop, below.) The early draft reads more like a paragraph from a biography of Edward Sweda, while the revised version takes us into Sweda's world.

Early Draft of "A Lawyer's Crusade Against Tobacco"

Edward Sweda began his career as an anti-smoking activist over twenty years ago, when he became involved as a volunteer in a campaign to provide non-smoking sections in restaurants. He is currently the senior staff attorney for the Tobacco Product Liability Project (TPLP) at Northeastern University. Since 1984, when TPLP was established, Sweda and his associates have battled the powerful tobacco interests.

Revised Version of "A Lawyer's Crusade Against Tobacco"

The office of the Tobacco Product Liability Project (TPLP) at Northeastern University in Boston is decorated with anti-smoking propaganda. One poster shows the damage that smoking has done to someone's lungs. The office secretary sat at her desk and typed busily, while Edward Sweda, senior attorney of the TPLP, conversed on the phone with Stanton Glantz, author of the well-known exposé of the tobacco industry *Cigarette Papers*.

Here is a list of techniques for establishing perspective at the beginning of a profile:

1. **Set the scene:** Describe the place where you encounter your subject; give details about the physical space; describe other people who are there; explain what the people are doing; set the stage for your subject's entrance.

2. **Tell an anecdote:** Narrate an incident that involves your subject; describe how your subject acts in a revealing situation.

3. **Use a quotation:** Begin with your subject's own words; use a particularly revealing, provocative, or characteristic statement.

4. **Describe your subject:** Use description and detail about your subject's appearance as an opening clue to the person's character.

5. **Describe a procedure:** Follow your subject through a characteristic routine or procedure at work; explain the purpose and technical details; use them to establish your subject's expertise.

6. **State your controlling theme:** Establish perspective by stating in your own words a key theme that will be developed in the profile. ■

W WRITERS' WORKSHOP

Richard Quitadamo wrote the following profile, "A Lawyer's Crusade Against To-bacco," for a course that focused on the politics of public health. Quitadamo plans on becoming a lawyer, and he wanted to find out more about the kind of work lawyers do in the public interest, particularly in the area of product liability. What appears here is Quitadamo's working draft, followed by his questions for a peer commentary. Read the draft, keeping in mind that it is a work in progress. Then consider how you would respond to the questions Quitadamo raises in his note.

RICHARD QUITADAMO, A LAWYER'S CRUSADE AGAINST TOBACCO [WORKING DRAFT]

The office of the Tobacco Product Liability Project (TPLP) at Northeastern University in Boston is decorated with anti-smoking propaganda. One poster shows the damage that smoking has done to someone's lungs. The office secretary sat at her desk and typed busily, while Edward Sweda, senior attorney of the TPLP, conversed on the phone with Stanton Glantz, author of the well-known exposé of the tobacco industry *Cigarette Papers*.

Sweda seemed fixated on one subject, the recent banning of RJ Reynolds' "Joe Camel" cartoon character from Camel cigarette advertisements. He felt it was a small victory in the ongoing war against smoking. "Look, Stanton, Joe is gone and that's great, but that really doesn't affect the foreign market. It seems the percentage of people outside the US who smoke has risen dramatically. There's got to be something we can do." They talked for a few more moments, and then Sweda hung up the phone.

Edward Sweda, a tall, slender man, with graying hair, turned in his office chair. A button on his sweater read "No Smoking." He began to discuss the history of the war on tobacco and the part he has played in it.

Sweda began his career in 1979 as a local volunteer against cigarette smoking in Massachusetts. "I hated smoking from day one. It was disgusting, and besides it can kill you." In the late 1970s, the dangers of smoking were a novel concept, and industry leaders were quick to cover up the ill effects of smoking.

It was also at this time that medical professionals, political activists, and health care advocates began pushing for stronger regulation of tobacco products.

In 1980, Sweda worked in Newton, MA, for regulations that would require restaurants to provide at least 15% of its seating to non-smokers. "People have to breathe, and if other people are smoking in close proximity to you, then they are infringing on your right to breathe fresh air. That's a crime. I as a non-smoker really feel strongly about this issue."

Sweda has also worked to stop free samples of cigarettes from being dispersed. "It reminded me of drugs. The first time was free, but after that, you had to pay. I figured I could stop this vicious cycle before it got a chance to start. That's why we eventually formed the TPLP, to use litigation as a tool to make the tobacco industry take responsibility for its actions."

TPLP was established in 1984, and since then Sweda and his associates have battled the tobacco industry. "Tobacco industry knew smoking was bad long before TPLP ever showed up. The first report of the Surgeon General on smoking in 1964 proved that cigarette smoking could have harmful effects on human health." But, Sweda continued, the only thing that the anti-smoking campaign got out of the Surgeon General's report was the Fanning Doctrine, which stated that there must be a comparable number of anti-smoking public service announcements (PSAs) to the number of cigarette advertisements. This doctrine, Sweda said, may or may not have led to the drop off of cigarette sales noticeable between 1966 and 1970.

However, on January 1, 1971, cigarette advertising was banned from TV, and along with them, the antismoking PSAs. "At first, I was overjoyed," Sweda said, smiling. "What a fool I was. The tobacco industry used other methods to lure potential smokers to their products, the PSAs were gone, and the levels of smoking increased nationwide. It seemed they could sidestep every regulation we imposed."

As Sweda spoke, his secretary called attention to the flashing computer screen. Sweda rose from his chair and observed the screen. "You see this? This is something I'm working on right now." Sweda was looking at the next date scheduled for hearings of the Massachusetts State Public Health Council on new proposed legislation to force the tobacco industry to disclose their secret ingredients. "What we want to do at this hearing is to make the industry sweat. They failed to block the hearing and were forced to appear. They didn't even testify on their own behalf, and I just kept talking about the list of secret ingredients and the falsified tests. You should have seen their faces."

Yet, Sweda is cautious with his optimism about the future of anti-smoking initiatives. He has seen things go wrong before. The tobacco industry has many influential lobbyists on their side, along with the political backing of tobacco state politicians. They are able to hide information and falsify reports to government officials. This makes the industry virtually untouchable at the federal level. Nonetheless, Sweda said he was more confident this time around. "Things are different in this day and age. People are more educated about the dangers of smoking. With the banning of Joe Camel and the Liggett case of 1996, we seem to be gaining ground on them. The Liggett case is probably the biggest breakthrough in our struggle because it's the first time a tobacco manufacturer cracked and admitted what we've known all along about the health hazards of smoking. And it actually resulted in a settlement."

Sweda paused, then sighed. "But there is still the problem of youth. They seem more susceptible to smoking. Maybe it's the age, maybe it's a rebellion thing, or maybe it's the advertisements. The ads seem to target youth. That's why I'm glad Joe Camel is gone."

The TPLP has been working with the Federal Drug Administration on a game plan that focuses specifically on the youth smoking problem. The plan centers on keeping youth from smoking through education and other programs. "I hate to admit it, but it seems our best bet for beating smoking and the industry is to forget adult smokers. They've made their decisions, and it's their choice to continue smoking. Cessation programs and medical help groups exist for those who want to quit. But by focusing on youth, we are taking away the customers of the future. This is important because as the older generation of smokers fades away, the tobacco industry will be looking to recruit new smokers."

As Sweda stepped away from the computer, he said, "We'll get them, the industry, that is," and stepped to his desk, picked up the phone, and began to dial a number. This is all in a day's work for Edward Sweda and his TPLP group. They exist to promote public health and stop the growth of the tobacco industry, or as Sweda refers to them, "the merchants of death."

RICHARD QUITADAMO'S COMMENTARY

I think I do a pretty good job in this draft of setting the scene and showing Sweda at work. The guy was a great interview, and I got a lot of good quotes to use. Do these seem effective? Are they easy to understand? Do you need more information at points? Is it clear, for example, what happened in the Liggett case and why anti-smoking people consider it such a huge victory? Any suggestions in this regard would be greatly appreciated.

Another thing I'm not certain about is whether I should give more information about Sweda himself. I don't provide much background information on him or talk about his personal life. I wanted to focus on him mainly as an anti-smoking activist and felt too much biographical detail would distract from this. What do you think?

My last question involves the notorious "dominant impression" we've been talking about in class so much. Do you feel that this draft gives you a strong perspective on the person? I wasn't sure whether I should provide more commentary on my own. I want readers to see Sweda as an embattled crusader but not a fanatic. Does this come across?

■ **WORKSHOP QUESTIONS**

1. Consider Richard Quitadamo's first set of questions concerning the information in the draft. Are there places where you needed more information to understand the issues? If so, indicate the passage or passages in question and explain what's not clear to you.

2. Quitadamo's second question focuses on whether he should give more background on Sweda. What is your opinion? To answer this question, take into account what Quitadamo's purpose seems to be in this profile. Would more biographical detail further his purpose or, as he worries, distract from it? Explain your response.

3. One mark of a successful profile is that it creates a dominant impression of the subject. Explain in your own words the impression of Sweda this draft created for you. Given what you've read here, what kind of person does he seem to be? How well does the impression you've formed match Quitadamo's goals in portraying Sweda? How could Quitadamo strengthen or enhance his portrayal? ■

REFLECTING ON YOUR WRITING

Write an account of how you put your profile together. Explain why you selected your subject. Then describe the interview, if you did one. Explain whether your final version confirmed or modified your initial preconceptions about your subject. Finally, explain how writing a profile differs from other kinds of writing you have done. What demands and satisfactions are there to writing profiles?

reports

THINKING ABOUT THE GENRE

Reports are a genre of writing that presents the results of research. Reports can be as simple as the morning weather report or as complex as an in-depth explanation of climate change, its causes and consequences. Sometimes the writer's task is to organize information in a useful and accessible way. Other times, report writers analyze the research and draw conclusions.

The forms that report writing takes vary tremendously, depending on the writer's setting and purposes. News reports and feature articles in newspapers and magazines, scholarly articles in academic journals, briefings and fact sheets, brochures, informational Web sites, studies from government agencies and advocacy groups, community newsletters, corporations' annual reports—all these are instances of report writing that informs and explains.

Report writers typically begin by identifying a need to know on the part of the public at large or a specific group of readers about events, trends, and ideas. Accordingly, the focus in a report tends to be placed on the research the writer has done—the questions raised and the results—rather than on the writer's experience and perceptions. Unlike, say, a memoir, where the reader is asked to share an important moment of revelation with the writer, a report writer's relationship to readers is normally less personal and more concerned with the topic at hand.

By the same token, reports differ from genres such as commentary, proposals, and reviews, where the writer's argument dominates as the central feature of the writing and the research results that appear are meant as evidence to bolster the writer's claim. In reports, on the other hand, the analysis, interpretations, and conclusions often seem to emerge logically from the data, as claims that have been suggested by the nature of the research itself.

While a report writer's rhetorical stance tends to be that of an impartial observer, persuasion nonetheless plays a powerful role in informative writing. Writers are not simply transferring information to readers. Importantly, report writers seek to persuade their readers that the questions they ask and the information they have sifted through and selected are pertinent and meaningful.

From this perspective, persuasion in report writing has to do with the credibility readers invest in the writer as a reliable, honest, and responsible source of information and analysis. Even in such apparently straightforward accounts as a weather report or a simple news story, readers believe the facts speak for themselves precisely because they have already been persuaded that the source of information is authoritative. If, however, the writer's own views figure prominently, then readers will sense they are encountering a commentary and not a report. But if the writer successfully maintains a focus on the relevance of the research and the significance of the findings, readers are likely to take the data and conclusions seriously, even as they realize that the writer may have taken a strong role in shaping the presentation of the material and interpreting the results.

■ WRITING FROM EXPERIENCE

When you need to know something, where do you turn? What are your main sources of information, both in and out of school, and what are your purposes in using them? Make a list of information sources to compare to those of your classmates. Next, pick three or four information sources to analyze in some detail, choosing sources that differ from each other. Analyze the way each source makes information available. What is the purpose of the information source? How does the source select information to include? How does the source organize the information? What uses do people make of the information?

READINGS

NEWS REPORTS

The following two news reports on a study of the relationship of mental illness and violence appeared on the same day in 1995. The first comes from the Associated Press and was published in many local newspapers. The second was written for the *New York Times* by Fox Butterfield, one of its staff reporters at the time. Both provide accurate reports of the findings published in *The Archives of General Psychiatry* by a team of researchers. The question remains, though, what kind of impression the two reports created in the minds of their readers.

Providence Journal   May 14, 1995

Headline:

Mentally Ill People Aren't More Violent, Study Finds

*Lead:
main
event
findings
of study*

*¶2:
Consequen-
ces of main
event*

*¶s 3–5:
Details of
main
event*

*¶5: Detail
of how
study was
conducted*

*¶6:
Comment
from
author of
study*

CHICAGO (AP)—*Mentally ill people who do not abuse alcohol or drugs are no more violent than their neighbors, a study has found.*

Mental-health advocates and former patients say the finding could help chip away at the stereotypes that have provoked unnecessary fear and driven misguided public policy for years.

Discharged mental patients with substance-abuse problems are five times as likely to commit acts of violence as people without drug problems, according to the study, published in this month's edition of the *Archives of General Psychiatry.*

Non-patients with substance abuse problems had three times the violence rate of the general population. But the violence rate was about the same for patients and non-patients who were drug-free.

The study followed 951 acute psychiatric patients in the year after their discharge in 1994 from hospitals in Pittsburgh, Kansas City and Worcester, Mass. Researchers compared the findings with a sample of 519 non-patients who lived in the same neighborhoods as the patients discharged in Pittsburgh.

John Monahan, one of the study's authors, says several recent surveys, including some conducted at Columbia University, have shown that most Americans believe mentally ill people are prone to violence.

"I think the public's fears are greatly exaggerated," said Monahan, a psychologist at the University of Virginia School of Law.

Analysis: Organization of Information in a Newspaper Report: The Inverted Pyramid

Newspaper stories report the information with the highest value first. The assumption is that busy readers, skimming the newspaper, may not read the entire news report. Accordingly, a condensed version of the most important information needs to be frontloaded, with other information following.

- **Headline:** this tells in a very brief way what the main event is (in the case of this news report, what the "study finds").

- **Lead:** the opening paragraph or two present in capsule form the most important information about the main event ("mentally ill people . . . are no more violent").

- **Details of the main event:** this provides further information on what happened, who was involved, where, how, and why.

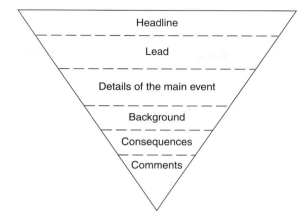

- **Background:** sometimes reporters will fill in background information about the main event.

- **Consequences:** this explains the larger significance of the main event (in this case, "the finding could help chip away at stereotypes").

- **Comments:** this provides insights and opinions ("'I think the public's fears are greatly exaggerated,' said Monahan").

The headline and lead always appear first. After that, the order may vary. Consider in the next news report—on the same study of violence and mental illness—how the order of information is organized.

New York Times   May 14, 1995

Studies of Mental Illness Show Links to Violence
New Finding Cites Role of Subtance Abuse

Fox Butterfield

BOSTON, May 14—After a generation of believing that the mentally ill are no more violent than other people, psychiatrists and advocates for the emotionally disturbed are wrestling with studies that show that the mentally ill may indeed be more violent in some circumstances.

Their difficulty was underscored today in a report of the latest of these studies in *The Archives of General Psychiatry,* a publication of the American Medical Association. The studies found that mental patients discharged from a hospital stay are no more violent than other members of their community, unless they have been abusing alcohol or drugs. Substance abuse increased the rates of violence by mental patients by up to five times, the study concluded, while it tripled the rate of violence by other people.

The finding about substance abuse is particularly important because the mentally ill are almost twice as likely as other people to be alcoholics or on drugs, the report said.

The study, paid for by the MacArthur Foundation, is part of a broad effort by researchers to find out why recent reports have found higher levels of violence among the mentally ill than in the general population, contradicting previous research dating from the 1950's and 1960's.

The relationship between mental illness and violence is an extremely sensitive subject because the public has long believed that the emotionally disturbed are more dangerous, despite the experts' views, and this popular perception has helped stigmatize the mentally ill.

To complicate the situation, with the closure of most state hospitals in recent years an increasing number of the mentally ill have been sent to jail or prison, where they receive little treatment, then are released only to be arrested again.

"We wanted to find some factors that distinguished which patients were at higher risk of violence, and substance abuse turned out to be a key distinction," said John Monahan, an author of the report who is a psychologist and a law professor at the University of Virginia. "We hope this will lead people not to tar everybody who is discharged from the hospital with the same brush."

The study also found that the types of violence committed by the mentally ill were largely the same that other people committed and that more than 85 percent of the violence committed by the mentally ill was directed at family members or friends, with only 14 percent of the attacks involving strangers.

"These findings clearly indicate that public fears of violence on the street by discharged patients who are strangers to them are misdirected," Professor Monahan said.

The study was conducted on 1,000 patients discharged from hospitals in Pittsburgh, Kansas City, Mo., and Worcester, Mass.

Another recent study, by Bruce Link, a professor at the Columbia University School of Public Health, found that the mentally ill are more violent if they are suffering from paranoia or from certain delusions and hallucinations.

Still another new study, by Jeffrey Swanson, an assistant professor of psychiatry at Duke University Medical Center, showed an increased risk of violence for mentally ill patients who are substance abusers and who stop taking their antipsychotic drugs a frequent problem.

As an indication of how sensitive the issue of mental illness and violence is, the authors of the MacArthur Foundation study conducted focus groups before writing their report. "Language is important, and we wanted to cast things in the least inflammatory way," Professor Monahan said.

As a further indication of this sensitivity, the report immediately produced different reactions from the two major advocacy groups.

Mike Faenza, president of the National Mental Health Association, the nation's oldest and largest mental health organization, said: "This study's findings counter the fictional and highly stigmatizing images propagated by Hollywood movie studios and New York ad men. It is time we kill our cultural fantasy of deranged psychotic killers on the loose. The public's fear is out of time with reality."

Mr. Faenza said the report also underscored the need to "bring mental health and substance abuse treatment services together." He maintained that because of the ingrained habits of mental health professionals and the way government money is allocated, people now tend to be treated for either mental illness or for substance abuse but not jointly for both. This practice, he said, lets many patients fall through the cracks.

But Dr. E. Fuller Torrey, a psychiatrist affiliated with the National Alliance for the Mentally Ill, an advocacy group made up of family members of the emotionally disturbed, said the authors of the report had failed to draw the most important conclusion from their own data. These were data showing that mentally ill people who underwent hospitalization had a 50 percent reduction rate in violent acts in the year after their release, and people who were both mentally ill and abused drugs or alcohol had a 54 percent reduction rate in violent behavior.

"This is the first time that anyone has shown what we have long suspected, that if you treat mental illness, you can reduce the violence," said Dr. Torrey, who is executive director of the Stanley Foundation research programs in Washington.

Dr. Torrey's point was echoed in an editorial in *The Archives of General Psychiatry* by Professor Link of Columbia, who said that the most important finding in the MacArthur study is that the mentally ill tend to be violent when they are "symptomatic" in the period before hospitalization, and that after treatment, when their symptoms wane, "the risk for violence declines to the point where it is no different from the base level in the community."

Dr. Torrey is an outspoken critic of the restrictive laws against involuntary hospitalization of the mentally ill, believing that many disturbed people do not understand their disease and therefore resist attempts to treat them. This can sometimes result in untreated mentally ill people harming themselves or others.

Laurie Flynn, executive director of the National Alliance, said, "This violence is preventable." But she added that the lack of access to treatment "is a direct contributor to the criminalization problem," the growing number of mentally ill people who are sent to jail or prison rather than a clinic or hospital.

Trying not to tar every discharged mental patient with the same brush.

The situation is especially hard on family members who care for the mentally ill, Ms. Flynn said, since, as the new study found, it is relatives and friends who are most likely to be the victims of violence.

"People end up telling us it is easier to get your relative arrested than to get them treatment," she said "It is a kind of family secret."

Dr. Torrey said he believes the amount of violence by the mentally ill has been increasing because of the closing of state hospitals and with financial pressures resulting in shorter stays for those patients who are hospitalized. Dr. Torrey estimates that the mentally ill are responsible for about 1,000 homicides a year in the United States.

But Professor Swanson said that in an earlier study he conducted in five cities, he found that the mentally ill were responsible for only about 4 percent of overall violence. Mental illness, he found, is a much smaller risk factor for violence than is being young, male, poor or addicted to alcohol or drugs.

Analysis: Framing the Story

News reports seem to be among the most straightforward forms of writing beause they appear simply to inform readers about something that happened. In this case, an important study was published in *The Archives of General Psychiatry* on a question of great public interest, namely the relationship between mental illness and violence, and accordingly both the Associated Press and the *New York Times* decided to cover the story. As you can see, the two reporters' accounts of the study's findings are very similar—and yet, if you were to read just the two headlines, you might think otherwise.

It's not only the headlines that seem to create two different and perhaps divergent accounts. News reporting is never simply a matter of telling what happened. The news has to be produced—put into intelligible shape by the reporter's writing. One of the key devices reporters use to produce the news is the technique of *framing*. Notice how the headlines contribute to two quite different ways of framing the story. For the Associated Press news report, the study, as mental health advocates and former patients say, may "chip away" at "stereotypes," "unnecessary fear," and "misguided public policy." For Fox Butterfield, on the other hand, his longer news report enables him to frame the story by putting it in the context of an ongoing debate over the "extremely sensitive subject" of the relationhip between mental illness and violence and what to do about it.

■ FOR CRITICAL INQUIRY

1. What was your immediate reaction when you read the two headlines? Was this reaction modified or changed as you read the two news reports?

2. Notice who is quoted in each of the news reports. How do these quotes shape the way readers are likely to understand the study? What differences, if any, do you see in the use of quotes?

3. Describe what you see as the two news reporters' purposes. To what extent are they similar? How do they differ? How would you account for these differences?

4. Work in a group with two other students. Choose a recent event that all know something about and that interests you. By yourself, write a headline and one or two opening paragraphs, just enough to frame the event. Now compare your versions. How do they differ? How is each likely to influence readers' understanding of the event?

Fact Sheets

The Sentencing Project is a nonprofit research and advocacy organization that promotes reduced reliance on incarceration and increased use of alternatives to deal with crime. It is a nationally recognized source on criminal justice, providing data, policy analysis, and program information. Sentencing Project fact sheets, such as the one that appears here, organize a lot of information in a highly accessible format. Notice how the bulleted points give each item of information a separate focus but, at the same time, an accumulative picture begins to emerge from the data and suggest certain conclusions. How does the order of information frame your understanding of the current situation of prisons and prisoners? In what sense is the design of the Sentencing Project fact sheet persuasive as well as informative?

THE
SENTENCING
PROJECT
RESEARCH AND
ADVOCACY FOR REFORM

FACTS ABOUT PRISONS AND PRISONERS

The Growing Corrections System

- The number of inmates in state and federal prisons has increased nearly seven-fold from less than 200,000 in 1970 to 1,540,805 by midyear 2003. An additional 785,556 are held in local jails, for a total of 2.3 million.

- Between 2000 and 2007, the state prison population increased by an average annual rate of 1.6%, the federal population by 5.0%, and jail population by 3.3%

- As of 2008,1 of every 131 Americans was incarcerated in prison or jail.

- The number of persons on probation and parole has heen growing dramatically along with institutional populations. There are now more than 7.3 million Americans incarcerated or on probation or parole, an increase of more than 290 percent since 1980.

- One in ten. (10.4%) black males aged 25–29 was in prison or jail in 2008 as were I in 26 (3.8%) Hispanic males and 1 in 63 (1.6%) white males in the same age group.

- Nationally, 69 females per 100,000 women are serving a sentence in prison; 957 males per 100,000 men are in prison.

- The 2008 United States' rate of incarceration of 762 inmates per 100,000 population is the highest in the world.

Who is in our Prisons and Jails?

- 93% of prison inmates are male, 7% female.

- As of 2008, there were 207,700 women in state and federal prison or local jail.

- 40% of persons in prison or jail in 2008 were black and 20% were Hispanic.

- 63% of jail inmates in 2008 were unconvicted and awaiting trial, compared to 51% in 1990.

- 82% of those sentenced to state prisons in 2004 were convicted of non-violent crimes, including 34% for drug offenses, and 29% for property offenses.

- 1 in 4 jail inmates in 2002 was in jail for a drug offense, compared to 1 in 10 in 1983; drug offenders constituted 20% of state prison inmates and 55% of federal prison inmates in 2001.

- Black males have a 32% chance of serving time in prison at some point in their lives; Hispanic males have a 17% chance; while males have a 6% chance.

Source: Bureau of Justice Statistics.   04/09

514 Tenth St. N.W., Suite 1000, Washington, DC 20004 • Tel. 202.628.0871 • Fax 202.628.1091 •
www.sentencingproject.org

NATIONAL REPORTS

EXECUTIVE SUMMARY

A PORTRAIT OF UNAUTHORIZED IMMIGRANTS IN THE UNITED STATES

JEFFREY S. PASSEL AND D'VERA COHN

PEW HISPANIC CENTER

The Pew Hispanic Center is a project of the Pew Research Center, a nonprofit and nonpartisan think tank that conducts public opinion polling and social science research on a broad range of issues, including the Internet and American life, religion and public life, global attitudes, and the press. A Portrait of Unauthorized Immigrants in the United States was published on April 14, 2009. This is the Executive Summary. You can find the complete report at/pewhispanic.org/.

Analysis: Keeping Track of Change

Unlike the Sentencing Project, the Pew Hispanic Center is a nonadvocacy organization that does not take positions on public policy. Its mission rather, as the Center suggests, is "to improve public understanding of the diverse Hispanic population in the United States and to chronicle Latinos' growing impact on the nation." Like other think tanks, research institutes, foundations, academic centers, and government agencies, it is involved with keeping track of changing attitudes and trends, to provide data for public deliberation and policy making. Still, though it would certainly be out of step with its mission for the Center to take a position on what should be done about undocumented immigrants, the very questions its researchers ask and the results of its studies play a shaping role in determining how the wider public discussion takes place, what the main issues are, and how trends in the Latino population acquire significance. By striving to improve public understanding through its research, the Pew Hispanic Center also provides the themes to understand the changing realities of Latinos in the United States.

■ FOR CRITICAL INQUIRY

1. Imagine you are a reporter assigned to do a news report on *A Portrait of Unauthorized Immigrants*. Write a headline and two-sentence lead paragraph. Compare your headline and lead paragraph to what your classmates have written. What do you see as the main differences and similarities? Consider how the headlines and lead paragraphs frame the information presented in the Pew report.

2. In the opening section of the Executive Summary, the authors highlight a few of the "key findings" in the report. Consider their selection here. Why do you think they emphasized the data they did? What effect does it have in terms of framing recent trends in the experience of undocumented immigrants? Given the data that appears in the Executive Summary, can you imagine other openings, with other key findings, that might produce a different framing?

4.14.2009

A Portrait of Unauthorized Immigrants in the United States

by Jeffrey S. Passel, Senior Demographer, Pew Hispanic Center, and D'Vera Cohn, Senior Writer, Pew Research Center

Unauthorized immigrants living in the United States are more geographically dispersed than in the past and are more likely than either U.S. born residents or legal immigrants to live in a household with a spouse and children. In addition, a growing share of the children of unauthorized immigrant parents—73%—were born in this country and are U.S. citizens.

These are among the key findings of a new analysis by the Pew Hispanic Center, a project of the Pew Research Center, which builds on previous work estimating the size and growth of the U.S. unauthorized immigrant population. A 2008 report by the Center estimated that 11.9 million unauthorized immigrants lived in the United States; it concluded that the undocumented immigrant population grew rapidly from 1990 to 2006 but has since stabilized. In this new analysis, the Center estimates that the rapid growth of unauthorized immigrant workers also has halted; it finds that there were 8.3 million undocumented immigrants in the U.S. labor force in March 2008.

Based on March 2008 data collected by the Census Bureau, the Center estimates that unauthorized immigrants are 4% of the nation's population and account for 5.4% of its workforce. Their children, both those who are unauthorized immigrants themselves and those who are U.S. citizens, make up 6.8% of the students enrolled in the nation's elementary and secondary schools.

Nearly Half of Unauthorized-Immigrant Households are Couples with Children
(% of households that are couples with children for each status group)

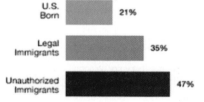

Source: Pew Hispanic Center

About three-quarters (76%) of the nation's unauthorized immigrants are Hispanic. The majority of undocumented immigrants (59%) are from Mexico. Significant regional sources of unauthorized immigrants include Asia (11%), Central America (11%), South America (7%), the Caribbean (4%) and the Middle East (less than 2%).

These estimates are based mainly on data from March Current Population Surveys, conducted by the Census Bureau, through 2008, augmented with legal status assignments and adjusted to compensate for undercount; some estimates are from the 1990 and 2000 Censuses. For more details, see the report's Methodology appendix.

3. Consider the role that the figures and tables play in presenting the research results. What do they add to the written text? Can you identify other findings in the Executive Summary that might be represented by a figure or table? How would you design the visual display of information?

IDEAS & TRENDS

Warmer, Fuzzier: The Refreshed Logo

By BILL MARSH

THE WORLD ECONOMY is in mid-swan dive. Wallets are in lockdown. So how does a company get people to feel just a little bit better about buying more stuff? (And perhaps burnish a brand that has taken some public relations lumps?)

Behold the new breed of corporate logo — non-threatening, reassuring, playful, even child-like. Not emblems of distant behemoths, but faces of friends.

"A logo is to a company what a face is to a person," said Michel Tuan Pham, a professor of marketing at the Columbia Business School. "It's hard to memorize facts about a person when you only know their name but you haven't seen their face." So logos remind consumers about companies' traits and pluck at emotions, "the glue that ties all the information about the brand name together," Mr. Pham said.

The economy, environment, image repair — new logos may address all of these. They are also meant to stand out in a crowd, but there are striking similarities among recent redesigns.

TONED-DOWN TYPE   Bold, block capital letters are out. Their replacements are mostly or entirely lower case, softening the stern voice of corporate authority to something more like an informal chat.

"Logos have become less official-looking and more conversational," said Patti Williams, a professor of marketing at the University of Pennsylvania's Wharton School. "They're not yelling. They're inviting. They're more neighborly."

Blogs and e-mail, Ms. Williams said, may be encouraging a quieter, calmer, lower-case branding vernacular. Who isn't tired of screeds that assault the reader via THE CAPS LOCK KEY?

Here are two remakes:

Wal-Mart before  and after

Kraft before  and after

Letterforms are lighter and rounder — an extended family of homogenized fonts that would be comfortable on a local newsletter or generic Web page.

FRIENDLY FLOURISHES Kraft Foods has joined Amazon.com and Hasbro, all represented by logos that smile. And to further lighten the corporate mood, whimsy in the form of sprigs and bursts has been appended to several big brands.

Wal-Mart's old mark was navy blue, but it felt Red State. The company has been under heavy attack for its labor and environmental practices, bruising its brand in bluer quarters.

A major image overhaul is under way, and a new logo is starting to appear across the country. The military-style Wal-Mart star has given way to a yellow twinkle that punctuates a new message: this is a company that cares, with fast and friendly service and a fresh, innovative outlook, according to Linda Blakley, a Wal-Mart spokeswoman.

HAPPIER COLORS   "The economy is the No. 1 influence this year," said John H. Bredenfoerder, a color expert and design director at Landor Associates, the brand-consulting company that produced the new Cheer detergent emblem. Amid all the gloom, he said, "people need a little joy in their lives." Cue the new logos: electric blue type with accents in school bus yellow, red, purple, orange and green.

Last year's top influence, green for sustainability, remains; leaves still sprout across the corporate landscape.

Mr. Bredenfoerder said that blue was also gaining as a stand-in for the environment (think of earth's blue orb as seen from space, or clear blue waters) as well as for fresh optimism. But please, make it a joyful sky blue — not dark, corporate-titan navy.

Signs of Change

THEN	now	
WAL★MART	**Walmart** ✳	With little fanfare, **Wal-Mart** began replacing its commanding all-capitals logo with lighter blue text in September, punctuated by what the company calls a "spark."
KRAFT	**kraft** foods ✳ Make today delicious	The food giant **Kraft** unveiled a new corporate identity, with a smile and "flavor burst," in February. Its old racetrack-shaped, block-capitals emblem remains on packaging.
cheer	**cheer** brightCLEAN	The compressed black letters on the old **Cheer** detergent logo appeared to squint. Bouncy new blue "ee" twins seem to laugh under a colorful spray.

Analysis: Explanatory Report

Bill Marsh is the graphics editor of the Week in Review section of the Sunday New York Times, where "Warmer, Fuzzier: The Refreshed Logo" appeared on May 31, 2009. Marsh is reporting here on recent redesigns of corporate logos and explaining what he notices they have in common. To do that, he identifies three recurring features—"toned down type," "friendly flourishes," and "happier colors"—and explains how they are embodied in the redesigns and the effects they have. Using these features to organize his brief report into three sections helps make it easy to follow, but it also adds to the credibility of the report. Readers are likely to feel confident that Marsh has done his research, sifted through the data, and come up with useful labels for the three logo changes. There is the sense that he knows what he's talking about and is entitled to draw generalizations about a range of redesigns. The fact that Marsh's categories are followed by a series of examples that illustrate the three changes lends further credibility.

■ FOR CRITICAL INQUIRY

1. Consider how Marsh sets up the context of the logo redesigns. He doesn't use the term but we could think about these corporations facing a particular rhetorical situation and responding by redesigning their logos. What is the rhetorical situation in this case, what we might refer to as the call to redesign?

2. Marsh quotes three experts, along with a Wal-Mart spokesperson. How does Marsh use these quotes strategically to develop his explanation of the logo redesigns? What do they add to the report that making the same point in Marsh's own words wouldn't do?

3. This report appeared simultaneously in print and digital versions of the *New York Times*. The information content is the same, but the format differs. Visit the digital version www.nytimes.com/2009/05/31/weekinreview/31marsh.html?_r=1. Consider how the interactive features present the information compared to the print version. How does the experience of processing the information differ?

AN INFORMATIONAL WEB SITE

The Triangle Factory Fire, www.ilr.cornell.edu/trianglefire, is an informational Web site, designed by the Kheel Center for Labor-Management Documentation and Archives at Cornell University, about one of the worst industrial disasters of the twentieth century, the fire of 1911 that killed 146 immigrant workers in a clothing factory in New York City.

Notice how the Web site uses horizontal organization in its six main pages to tell "The Story of the Fire" as a chronological sequence, with the "Introduction" page giving a brief overview, the "Sweatshops and Strikes before 1911" page providing historical background, and then the four pages—"Fire!" "Mourning and Protest," "Relief Work," and "Investigation, Trial, and Reform"—recounting the cause of the fire and its consequences in roughly the order in which things happened. Notice next how the information on the six main pages is organized vertically to display types of information that enable visitors to go into greater depth on various aspects of the fire.

Cornell University ILR school

Compare "The Triangle Factory Fire" with other informational Web sites you have visited in the past. What do you see as the main differences and similarities? What generalizations might you draw about the features of information design that make Web sites effective?

SCHOLARLY AND POPULAR ARTICLES

UNCERTAINTY AND THE USE OF MAGIC
RICHARD B. FELSON AND GEORGE GMELCH

CAN A LUCKY CHARM GET YOU THROUGH ORGANIC CHEMISTRY?
GEORGE GMELCH AND RICHARD FELSON

George Gmelch and Richard B. Felson wrote these two articles based on their research to test Bronislaw Malinowski's theory that people use magic to relieve anxiety in situations of uncertainty. The first appeared in a leading academic journal, Current Anthropology, *while the second appeared in the popular magazine* Psychology Today. *Taken together, these two articles offer a good case study of how writers translate scholarly research for a broad readership.*

Vol. 20 • No. 3 • September 1979 **CURRENT ANTHROPOLOGY**

Uncertainty and the Use of Magic[1]

by RICHARD B. FELSON AND GEORGE GMELCH
Department of Sociology/Departement of Anthropology, State University of New York at Albany, Albany, N.Y. 12222, U.S.A. 18 I 79

Probably the most widely cited theory of magic is that of Malinowski (1948). Malinowski postulated that people resort to magic in situations of chance and uncertainty, where circumstances are not fully under human control. In what has become one of the most frequently cited examples of magic in primitive societies, he described the Trobriand Islanders' use of magic in fishing. On the open sea, where catches were uncertain and there was considerable danger, the islanders used a variety of magical practices. When fishing within the safety and plenty of the inner lagoon, they used none.

A number of other qualitative studies support the relationship between uncertainty and magic within modern, more scientifically oriented societies (e.g., Stouffer et al. 1949, Vogt 1952, MacNiece 1964, Gmelch 1978). The only previous quantitative test of this proposition, however, does not support Malinowski. Lewis (1963) found that the use of magic by American mothers with sick children depended on the mothers' knowledge of medicine and not on the uncertainty or danger of a particular illness. However, Lewis's use of length of illness as the measure of uncertainty is questionable.

According to Malinowski, people use magic to alleviate or reduce the anxiety created by conditions of uncertainty. Through the performance of the appropriate rituals, people "work off" the tensions aroused by fear. An alternative explanation would be that magic results from purely cognitive processes and represents an effort to produce favorable results. In other words, people believe that unknown forces—"good luck" and "bad luck"—play a role in the outcome of events and that these forces can be manipulated by magic.

This study examines these relationships using a sample of American and Irish college students. It considers the use of magic in six activities—gambling, athletics, exam-taking, illness, face-to-face interaction, and dangerous activities—in relation to the degree of uncertainty of each. It investigates the relationship between the use of magic and anxiety within each activity. Finally, it examines students' beliefs about the ability of magic to alleviate anxiety and produce favorable outcomes.

Questionnaires were administered to students in sociology classes in the United States (State University of New York at Albany; N = 270) and in the Republic of Ireland (University College, Dublin; N = 180). The students in the American sample were primarily urban and from middle-class and either

[1]We wish to thank Marcus Felson, Sharon Gmelch, and Walter P. Zenner for their comments on an earlier draft and Don Bennett, Des McCluskey, Kevin Buckley, Debbie O'Brien, and Ruth Pasquirello for their assistance in collecting the data.

Catholic or Jewish background. The students in the Irish sample were predominantly Catholic, of mainly middle-class background, with as many from small towns and villages as from the city. A list of concepts and the items used to measure them is presented in table 1.

Following Malinowski, we wished to compare activities known to vary in degree of uncertainty. Since it is extremely difficult to construct objective measures of uncertainty, we used independent judges—another group of sociology students ($N = 40$)—to rank the activities according to the degree of uncertainty.

The percentage of students who use magic for each activity and at each level of anxiety is presented in table 2. For the American sample, the correlation between mean uncertainty and mean use of magic over these six activities is quite strong, whether anxiety level is controlled or not. Respondents use more magic for uncertain activities like danger and gambling than they do for more certain activities like illness and exam-taking. For the Irish sample, the overall relationship between mean uncertainty and mean use of magic is slight. However, when anxiety level is controlled, the relationship between uncertainty and magic increases substantially.

For each activity, students who experience more anxiety are more likely to use magic. Contrary to Malinowski's hypothesis, however, the uncertainty of an activity does not have a positive relationship to the amount of anxiety experienced. In fact, this relationship is negative for both samples.

TABLE 1

Concepts and Questionnaire Items Used To Measure Them

CONCEPT	QUESTIONS ASKED	CODING AND RESPONSES
Use of Magic	Do you do anything special before or during the following activities in order to give yourself luck? *(a)* when you're gambling; *(b)* when you play in a sports contest; *(c)* when taking an exam; *(d)* before an important meeting, date, or interview; *(e)* in regard to something dangerous	1. Yes 0. No Missing Data: I can't answer since I don't engage in this activity
Confidence in efficacy of magic	How certain are you that such things can bring luck?	1. Certain that they do not affect luck 2. Not at all certain 3. Somewhat certain 4. Very certain
Anxiety about activity	How much do you worry about the following? *(a)* gambling; *(b)* sports contests; *(c)* exams; *(d)* important meetings, dates, or interviews; *(e)* illness; *(f)* accidents	1. Not at all 2. A little 3. Very much Missing Data: I haven't engaged in this activity

TABLE 1

Concepts and Questionnaire Items Used To Measure Them (*continued*)

CONCEPT	QUESTIONS ASKED	CODING AND RESPONSES
Belief that magic reduces do anxiety	Does it every make you feel better when you do things to give yourself luck?	1. Yes 0. No Missing Data: I don't things to give myself luck.
Uncertainty	For some things it is very certain before you start how well you'll do. For other things it is pretty upredictable and uncertain. Rank the following in terms of certainty about the outcome you would feel before gambling; when you're ill; when you have an important meeting, date, or interview; when you play in a sports contest; when you're taking an exam	

TABLE 2

Percentage of Respondents Who Report Using Magic in Activities Varying in Uncertainty, Controlling for Anxiety

	ANXIETY							
	U.S.A.				IRELAND			
Activity	High	Medium	Low	Total	High	Medium	Low	Total
Gambling (4.8)[a]	63	57	39	48	_[b]	65	23	33
Dangerous activities (4.4)	59	40	21	41	61	47	42	49
Exams (3.3)	45	24	_[b]	39	65	48	29	57
Sports (3.1)	67	34	19	40	36	34	19	26
Face-to-face interaction (2.9)	42	27	33	35	51	50	13	48
Illness (2.5)	40	18	16	21	39	26	10	23
Correlation with uncertainty	.64	.92	.53	.82	.64	.78	.69	.21
Probability level	.08	.01	.18	.02	.12	.03	.06	.34

[a]Mean uncertainty rank; a high rank indicates high uncertainty.
[b]Only three American students had low anxiety about exam-taking, and only one Irish student had high anxiety about gambling.

Irish students use more magic than American students in four of the six activities: exam-taking, face-to-face interactions, illness, and dangerous activities. There is also a slight tendency for Americans to use more magic in gambling and sports, although the differences between the two groups are not statistically significant. Frequency distributions for degree of confidence in the efficacy of magic for the total sample and for users and nonusers of magic are presented in table 3. The table indicates very little confidence about the efficacy of magic, even among persons who use it. On the other hand, most students who use magic indicate that it often relieves their anxiety. When asked if it ever made them feel better to use magic, 76% of the Americans and 71% of the Irish who do so answered yes.

This study supports Malinowski's basic notion that people use magic in situations of uncertainty. Students reported using more magic in activities that are relatively uncertain (e.g., gambling) and less in activities that are relatively more certain (e.g., illness). It also supports Malinowski's contention that magic is used to reduce anxiety. For a given activity, the greater the anxiety the students experience, the more magic they use. Furthermore, the students indicated that using magic reduces their anxiety. The evidence, however, does not support the notion that uncertainty results in use of magic because of the anxiety it produces. It appears instead that magic is used under conditions of uncertainty because of a belief in its ability to alter the forces of luck rather than its ability to reduce anxiety.

The fact that a significant amount of magic is used among the college students in our sample suggests that magic is not simply superstitious, irrational behavior confined to primitive peoples. Rather, magic appears to be used in various activities to produce favorable outcomes where other techniques are limited in their effectiveness. Magic is irrational, of course, if one accepts the scientific position that luck is unalterable.

Irish students reported using more magic than Americans in four of the six activities. This is not surprising, given that Ireland is a more traditional society than the United States. However, in two activities, gambling and sports, the Americans appeared to be slightly more

TABLE 3

PERCENTAGE OF USERS AND NONUSERS OF MAGIC REPORTING VARIOUS DEGREES OF CONFIDENCE IN THE EFFICACY OF MAGIC

DEGREE OF CONFIDENCE	AMERICANS			IRISH		
	USERS ($N = 183$)	NON-USERS ($N = 81$)	TOTAL	USERS ($N = 183$)	NON-USERS ($N = 81$)	TOTAL
Very certain	1	1	2	11	2	9
Somewhat certain	27	12	23	31	12	26
Not at all certain	54	46	51	33	28	31
Certain it does not bring luck	18	41	25	25	58	34

likely to use magic than the Irish. This may be due to the fact that gambling and sports are more important and anxiety-producing for Americans.

While most students feel that magic reduces their anxiety, they do not feel as confident that it will produce favorable results. This suggests that many students are merely playing it safe. They are not sure that magic works, but they use it just in case. The cost of performing magic is small, and there is always the possibility that it may help. The lack of strong belief in the efficacy of magic may be one of the major differences between industrialized and primitive societies in the use of magic. Put simply, tribal man has faith that his magic works; modern man lacks faith but is not taking any chances.

References Cited

GMELCH, G. 1978. Baseball magic. *Human Nature* 1(8):32–39.

LEWIS, L. S. 1963. Knowledge, change, certainty, and the theory of magic. *American Journal of Sociology* 69:7–12.

MACNIECE, L. 1964. *Astrology.* London: Aldus Books.

MALINOWSKI, B. 1954. *Magic, science, and religion and other essays.* New York: Anchor Books.

STOUFFER, S., et al. 1949. *The American soldier.* Princeton, Princeton University Press.

VOGT, E. 1952. Water witching: An interpretation of a ritual pattern in a rural American community. *Scientific Monthly* 75:175–86.

Analysis: Testing a Theory

"Uncertainty and the Use of Magic" follows the scholarly conventions of the research article. Although Felson and Gmelch do not mark the sections of their article, as research reports often do, their report nonetheless conforms to the standard format (and may remind you of laboratory reports in science classes):

- **¶s 1–4: Introduction.** Defines the problem to be investigated by reviewing prior research on Malinowksi's theory of magic and uncertainty. Establishes the purpose of the research as testing the theory. Explains the main research questions.

- **¶5–6: Methods.** Explains how researchers investigated the questions—the administration of questionnaires, the sample size, characteristics of subjects, and use of judges.

- **¶7–9: Results.** Presents the results or refers to tables, without comment on the meaning or significance.

- **¶10–12: Discussion.** Explains how the data relate to the central problem posed in the introduction. Often begins with the principal finding or strongest claim (for example, "This study supports Malinowski's basic notion . . . ").

- **¶13: Conclusion.** Summarizes main findings and points out wider significance.

CAN A LUCKY CHARM GET YOU THROUGH ORGANIC CHEMISTRY?

BY GEORGE GMELCH AND RICHARD FELSON

A large majority of college students employ rituals or charms to try to influence the fates, a study on two campuses now suggests. Why do they do it—and are they convinced of its efficacy as were the Trobriand Islanders?

During his stay in the South Seas in World War I, Bronislaw Malinowski observed that the Trobriand Islanders used magic in situations of danger and uncertainty, when circumstances were not fully under human control. In a classic illustration of this principle, the anthropologist compared two forms of Trobriand fishing—fishing in the inner lagoon and fishing in the open sea. In the safety of the lagoon, fish were plentiful and there was little danger; the men could rely on their knowledge and skill. On the open sea, however, fishing was dangerous and yields varied widely; to ensure safety and increase their catch, the men turned to rituals and fetishes for help. Malinowski wrote that the fishermen's magic was performed "over the canoe during its construction, carried out at the beginning and in the course of expeditions, and resorted to in moments of real danger."

Even in our technologically advanced society, we are often at the mercy of powerful, unknown forces. How do we handle this uncertainty and unpredictability in our personal lives? Some people are fatalistic— What will be will be. Others try to manipulate unknown forces. When they request a deity to intercede in their behalf, we call it prayer; when they attempt to influence unknown forces through ritual or the use of charms, we call it magic.

For example, when Gloria, a university secretary, has an outdoor activity planned for the day and the sun is shining, she is careful not to comment on the weather. "I think it's bad luck," she explains. "If I said it was a gorgeous day, the sky would fill up with clouds and it'd rain. I know, it's happened to me. So now I am careful not to pass any comment on the weather when I've got something planned." Gloria has a lucky number—7—and would never work for a company located on the 13th floor. She reads her horoscope in the newspaper every morning and sometimes makes a wish on the first star she sees at night. An amber glass piggy bank sits atop her dresser containing the 20 lucky pennies she has found over the years.

Mary Sue is a B+ student at the State University of New York at Albany. Each time she prepares for an exam, she travels 12 miles to the library of another university and sits in the same carrel to study. She once got an exceptionally high mark on a physics test after studying in that library, and ever since, she has returned.

It is perhaps surprising to some that enlightened people in an advanced society can be serious when they behave in such ways. Not long ago, we decided to investigate the use of magic among supposedly sophisticated college students. We wanted to understand why they seemed to use magic—whether their motives were similar to those of the Trobrianders and other preliterate peoples. Magic, as defined by anthropologists, refers to rituals that are meant to influence events and people but have not been proved empirically to have the desired effect. We wanted to know whether the student practitioners of magic really believed in its efficacy or were simply trying to alleviate the anxiety created by uncertain conditions by making a ritual gesture of some kind.

We distributed questionnaires on the subject to 270 students in sociology classes at the State University of New York at Albany and to 180 students at University College Dublin, in Ireland. (The choice of Irish students was a matter of convenience; one of us, Gmelch, often works in Ireland.) The students in the American sample were primarily urban and from middle-class Catholic or Jewish backgrounds. In the Irish sample, as many students came from small towns and villages as from cities; the group was predominantly Catholic and mainly middle class.

Students were asked if they did anything special to give themselves luck in each of six circumstances: when they were gambling; in a dangerous situation; taking exams; playing in a sports contest; before an important meeting, date, or interview;

when they were ill. We also asked students how much they worried about each of those circumstances. In addition, we asked them how much they cared about the outcome; if using magic made them feel less anxious; and if they really believed that magic worked. We had independent judges—40 sociology students who were not included in our sample—rank the six circumstances according to how difficult it was to predict the outcome (for instance, a grade on an exam). The raters put gambling at the top of the list as entailing most uncertainty, followed by dangerous situations, exams, sports, face-to-face encounters, and, lastly, illness.

Of the 450 subjects, about 70 percent used magic. The percentage of users was about the same in the two countries: 69 percent of the Americans, 75 percent of the Irish. But larger between-nation differences were found in the circumstances under which magic was used. As the following table shows, a significantly higher proportion of the Irish employed magic in exams and face-to-face encounters, while a significantly higher percentage of Americans used it in gambling and sports.

Situation	Americans	Irish
Gambling	48%	33%
Dangerous situations	41%	49%
Exams	39%	57%
Sports	40%	26%
Face-to-face encounters	35%	48%
Illness	21%	23%

Students used both productive magic (for example, carrying a good-luck charm to an exam), to improve achievement, and protective magic (such as crossing one's fingers), to ward off danger. Several rituals were shared by subjects of both nationalities. Asked if they had a lucky number, 43 percent of the Americans and 32 percent of the Irish said yes. Other shared practices were crossing fingers (38 percent of the Americans, 44 percent of the Irish), knocking on wood (41 percent of the Americans, 47 percent of the Irish), carrying good-luck charms (19 percent of the Americans, 13 percent of the Irish),

---

Magic rituals gave students a sense of control and boosted confidence—which may have improved their performance.

---

and wearing particular clothing for luck (25 percent of the Americans, 14 percent of the Irish). Not all rituals were shared. Only the Americans—23 percent—said they walked around ladders.

Overall, the difference between the Irish and American students was not large, possibly because the uncertainties of student life are similar in the two countries. Particular kinds of rituals, such as knocking on wood, had large numbers of adherents in both countries. (It has been suggested that knocking on wood originated when men lived in huts. Supposedly, if a man was prosperous, it was important for him not to let evil gods or spirits

know about it. If he knocked on the wooden walls while he spoke of his good fortune, he would cover the sound of his voice, and the gods would not hear him.)

Much student magic was associated with particular activities, for instance, exams. One young woman who was never confident that her preparation for tests was adequate believed that using a particular pen could boost her performance. "I took an economics test and afterward thought I had failed," she said. "But I got a B on the test. I knew it couldn't be me who had done that well; it must have been the pen."

In card playing, the favorite gambling activity among students, the most frequently mentioned good-luck practice was not looking at one's cards until all the cards were dealt. One student reported that he waited to look at his cards until all the other players had looked at their hands.

Athletes were among the most ardent practitioners of magic. Wearing a piece of clothing associated with a previous good performance was mentioned by both males and females. Also cited was the use of crucifixes, neck chains, and coins as good-luck charms. Some of the most elaborate personal rituals were those of male students on intercollegiate teams. Unable to attribute an exceptional performance to skill alone but hoping to repeat it in future contests, players superstitiously singled out something they had done in addition to their actual play as partially responsible for their success. That "something" might be the food they had eaten before the game, the new pair of socks or sneakers they had worn, or just about anything they had done that was out of the ordinary. Mike, a linebacker on a varsity football team, vomited and was the last player to come on the field before a game in which he made many tackles. Before each game during the remainder of the season, he forced himself to vomit and made certain he was the last to leave the locker room.

The fact that students could easily repeat the behavior they had decided was crucial to success gave them the illusion that they could influence their performance simply through repetition of that behavior. That sense of control, however groundless in reality, increased their confidence, which may have improved their performance.

To learn more about the kinds of students who practiced magic, we asked subjects whether or not, and to what degree, they believed in God,

---

As societies become more technologically advanced, use of magic in some activities may increase, not decrease.

---

science, astrology, ESP, and the supernatural. The Irish were more likely than the Americans to believe in the supernatural (66 percent versus 50 percent), but otherwise the two student groups were similar in their beliefs.

In general, students had more doubt about God than about science. Approximately 90 percent claimed a belief, either strong or weak, in science, while about 80 percent said they had either a strong or a weak belief in God. Prayer was more frequent than the use of magic; for example, 39 percent of the Americans said they often prayed that things would turn out well for them, 51 percent said they occasionally prayed for favorable outcomes, and only 10 percent said they never did so. Students who used prayer tended also to use magic, suggesting that the two are related and that both may be responses to uncertainty.

Students who used magic were likely to believe in God, astrology, ESP, and the supernatural, although the relationships were not strong. Strong believers in science were just as likely as weak believers to use magic. Generally, the use of magic accompanied more practical, scientifically approved, actions. Exam magic, for instance, did not replace studying hard but supplemented it.

Despite their rational acceptance of the need to study, many students nevertheless do not accept the scientific fact that luck is random, that an outcome dependent on chance is independent of previous outcomes. Fully 27 percent of the Americans and 35 percent of the Irish agreed with the following statement: "If one has some good luck, one can expect some bad luck in the future." This implies a belief in what Piaget called "imminent justice," meaning that unknown forces will act in a just and equitable way to even things up, balancing a run of good fortune with some hard going.

Our findings confirm Malinowski's observation that people practice magic chiefly in uncertain situations. There was a statistically significant correlation between the uncertainty of an activity and the amount of magic the students used. (For the Irish, this relationship was apparent only when we controlled for anxiety, that is, when we held anxiety constant by comparing students with similar levels of anxiety.) The more uncertain the outcome, the more likely the student was to use magic. Thus, as the table on page 76 shows, more American students used magic in gambling, the activity rated most uncertain, than in exams and sports, activities with medium uncertainty. Magic was least common during illness, which had the lowest uncertainty rating. There were small to moderate correlations between the anxiety students experienced in various activities and the amount of magic they used. And, when we asked students if using magic ever made them feel better, more than 70 percent said it did. In short, magic *did* reduce anxiety.

This anxiety appeared to stem from the importance students attached to particular activities. As one might expect, responses to our questionnaire suggest that those students who care most about the outcome of exams, sports, or gambling feel most anxious about them and use more magic as a result.

In general, the more people care about the outcome of an activity, the more they'll use magic to "ensure" that the outcome is favorable. This leads to an interesting anomaly. As societies become more technologically advanced, people become more highly educated and, as a result, presumably less inclined to use magic. However, emphasis on achievement and success also increases with modernization. Since people seem to use more magic when they care most about the outcome of a performance, the use of magic in some activities may *increase* with modernization, not decrease.

We have left to last our most paradoxical finding. Although many of our subjects practiced magic, they didn't believe in it very strongly—at least not consciously. When we asked, "How certain are you that such things [magic rituals] can bring luck?" only 1 percent of the American users were "very certain." Another 27 percent answered "a little certain"; 54 percent answered "not at all certain"; and 18 percent said that they were "certain that they did not bring much luck." The comments of a 20-year-old senior illustrate the attitudes of many students. "I usually wear a certain ring and earrings every day, but I make doubly sure I wear them on the day of a test," she said. "It's not that I believe I will do poorly if I don't wear them; it's just that they were given to me by someone special, so I like to make sure I have them with me in tough situations. You could say they give me confidence."

In short, most students seem to be at least intellectually aware of the fact that magic does more to reduce their anxiety than it does to bring about favorable results. The psychoanalyst might say that belief in magic probably persists beneath the level of awareness. We prefer to say that students are just playing it safe when they practice magic. They are not sure it works, but they are not sure it doesn't, either. Since the cost of performing magic is small, they use it—just in case. This lack of strong belief in the efficacy of magic may

be the major factor distinguishing practitioners of magic in industrialized societies from those in preliterate cultures. Put simply, the Trobriand fisherman had faith that his magic worked. The student with her "magic" pen lacked faith but wasn't taking any chances.

George Gmelch is an assistant professor of anthropology at the State University of New York at Albany.

Gmelch, who was educated at Stanford University and the University of California at Santa Barbara, has done extensive research on tinkers and migrants in Ireland. He is the author and editor of four books and numerous scholarly articles and is studying the impact of return migration on small communities in Newfoundland.

Richard Felson, who earned his Ph.D. at Indiana University, is an assistant professor of sociology at the State University of New York at Albany. He has written articles on the self, social perception, and situational factors in aggression.

Analysis: Translating Scholarly Research

"Can a Lucky Charm Get You Through Organic Chemistry?" presents the same research question, methods, and results that appear in "Uncertainty and the Use of Magic" but in a way that is geared to a wider audience of readers. One of the key differences is how George Gmelch and Richard Felson provide an entry point for readers in the two articles. In the case of the scholarly article, which will be read mainly by other anthropologists, the entry point needs to be a problem that will be recognized by academic specialists as important to their field of study, and accordingly Gmelch and Felson frame the problem in terms of Malinowski's theory of magic as a response to uncertainty and whether subsequent researchers have confirmed his ideas. For nonspecialist readers, however, the authors reframe the problem in more general and personal terms—as "How do we handle this uncertainty and unpredictably in our personal lives?"—thereby providing readers with a way to identify the relevance of the research to their own lives.

■ FOR CRITICAL INQUIRY

1. Consider how Felson and Gmelch set up the theory they plan to test in the introduction of "Uncertainty and the Use of Magic." How do they integrate and evaluate previous research? How does this create a space for their own research? Identify a sentence or sentences that presents their purpose.

2. Consider the strategies Gmelch and Felson use in "Can a Lucky Charm Get You Through Organic Chemistry?" to translate their scholarly research for a broader audience. How do they make the presentation for specialists accessible to nonspecialists?

3. Compare your experience reading the two articles. How did you go about making sense of "Uncertainty and the Use of Magic"? What particular challenges, if any, did the scholarly article pose? What reading strategies did you use to deal with these challenges? How did your reading of "Can a Lucky Charm Get You Through Organic Chemistry?" differ from the way you read the scholarly article? What reading strategies did you use in this case?

FURTHER EXPLORATION: REPORTS

■ RHETORICAL ANALYSIS

Compare the Pew Hispanic Center's study *A Portrait of Unauthorized Immigrants* to *Jennifer* Gordon's "Workers Without Borders" in Chapter 10, pages 315–317. Both treat the question of undocumented workers living and working in the United States, but while the Pew report is concerned with presenting research findings in an impartial way, Gordon's proposal makes an explicit argument. Analyze the rhetorical stance developed in each piece of writing. What strategies do they use to promote their credibility to readers? What do these strategies reveal about the differences between reports and proposals?

■ GENRE AWARENESS

Pick a current topic. It could be the bank bailout program, obesity, video games, social-networking Web sites, recent trends in eyeglass design, bhangra music, charter schools, or something else. Consider how you could present the information on the topic in at least two different modes of communication—writing (print or online), visual display of information (page, poster, brochure, and so forth), audio, video, museum exhibit, PowerPoint presentation, multimedia. What purpose would the information serve? Who would intended readers be? What would you imagine them doing with the information? How would things vary depending on the mode of communication? Under what circumstances might one mode of communication be more appropriate than another?

WRITING ASSIGNMENT

Reports

For this assignment, design the presentation of information on a subject that interests you and that you think your intended readers have a need to know about. How much research you do will depend on time and your teacher's instructions. Here are some preliminary ideas about how to approach this assignment.

■ **News report** on a recent event—whether on campus, in your local community, or on the national or international scene. Or you could take a recent report by a research institute like the Pew Research Center or a recent scholarly article and translate it into a news story.

- **Fact sheets** are particularly suitable if you want to introduce readers to a subject or issue they may not know much about. You could, for example, design a fact sheet such as the "Facts about Prisons and Prisoners" on a current issue to give readers a quick understanding of what is at stake concerning, say, the use of medical marijuana, U.S. military support of the Colombian government, same-sex marriage, or swine flu.

- **Explanatory report:** Short explanatory reports, like Bill Marsh's "Warmer, Fuzzier: The Refreshed Logo," inform readers about things such as the significance of a work, the meaning of a concept, or the importance of an event. You might, for example, explain a concept you've learned in one of your classes or elucidate the importance of a musician, writer, or artist.

- **Popular article:** Articles such as "Can a Lucky Charm Get You Through Organic Chemistry?" report on scholarly research for nonspecialist readers. You could find a recent scholarly article that interests you and translate it for a wider audience.

- **Web site:** You could design a Web site to inform readers about a particular topic or issue that concerns you. You don't have to have the technical ability to put up a Web site online to design one on paper. See the directions in Chapter 20, "Web Design."

Invention

Identify situations that call for the kind of informative and explanatory writing featured in this chapter. Make a list of topics that interest you. Think about the information people could use and the issues that involve you and others.

Subjects	Needed Information	Issues
Torture	What constitutes torture? Does it differ from "enhanced interrogation"?	Did the United States torture detainees?
Resident assistants	What is their role?	Should RAs be required to turn in students for drinking?
The problem of commercial overfishing	What is the scope of the problem?	What are the effects? What alternatives have been proposed?
Women in science	How many women go into scientific careers?	What limits or enables the participation of women? What programs work?

Clarifying Your Purpose and Your Readers' Need to Know

Listing information people could use and issues facing you and others helps show what gives these topics an urgency or importance that would make them worth writing about.

■ EXERCISE

Getting Started

Pick one (or more) of the subjects of interest on your chart. Then write on each subject for five minutes or so:

1. What interests you about this subject? Why is it important to you?

2. Who are your intended readers? Why do they need information about your subject? What are they likely to know already about it? What information do you think they need? What should they be able to do with this information?

3. Read over what you have just written. What do you now see as the purpose of informing your readers about the subject? Do you want to help them understand something, show them how to do something, persuade them about an issue, identify something of interest, or do you have some other purpose? Assess whether this purpose is consistent with what you see as your readers' need to know. What genre appears most suitable? Why?

Background Research: Surveying the Information at Hand

Once you have determined your purpose and what your readers need to know, the next step is to assess your current state of knowledge—to determine whether the information you already have available is adequate to your purposes or whether you need to do more research.

1. Write a list of questions that cover what you think your readers need to know. Here, for example, is a list concerning the status of public bike paths that you can use as a model:

   a. What is the current status of the bike path system?

   b. What actions or land acquisitions are pending?

   c. How do such acquisitions generally take place?

   d. What local action is needed to support additional acquisitions?

   e. How have other communities responded?

   f. What has been done in this community in the past?

   g. What are the greatest obstacles to getting more land for this project?

2. Use your list of questions to survey the information you have. Can you answer the questions with the information at hand? Is your information up-to-date, reliable, and authoritative? Is it relevant to your readers' needs? If you need more information, where can you get it?

3. Take into account the information you have at hand, the information you need to get, and the amount of time you have to complete this

assignment. Will you be able to find what you need in the time available? If not, consider whether the scope of your project is too broad. How can you set priorities based on your sense of purpose and of what your readers need to know?

Planning: Organizing the Information

Whether you're designing a Web site or writing a fact sheet, an explanatory report, or an article, the organization of information you provide readers is crucial to the way they navigate your work. News reports have a distinctive inverted pyramid structure that presents the key information in the first paragraph or two, as you can see in "Mentally ill People Aren't More Violent, Study Shows" and "Studies of Mental Illness Show Links to Violence." The academic article "Uncertainty and the Use of Magic" uses a standard format: Introduction, Methods, Results, and Discussion, while the Web site "The Triangle Factory Fire" has six main pages that lead vertically to further pages of information for readers who want to go into more depth. Notice in Bill Marsh's report "Warmer, Fuzzier: The Refreshed Logo" how the opening four paragraphs set up readers to follow easily three trends in logo redesign:

¶1–4:   there are striking similarities between recent redesigns
¶5–9:   toned down type (trend 1)
¶10–12:   friendly flourishes (trend 2)
¶13–15:   happier colors (trend 3)

■ EXERCISE

Organizing Your Report

To help determine how you'll organize your report, respond to the following directions:

1. Write a list of all the information you have about your topic. Make it as complete as possible.

2. What items of information can be combined? Revise your list by grouping closely related topics into clusters.

3. If there are items that don't seem to fit, put them aside for the moment.

4. Number the revised list according to the order in which the items might appear in your report. Then label the function of each cluster of information. What will they do in the report you're planning?

5. Does any of the information you've set aside now seem to fit into your planning? What purpose will it serve?

Drafting: Introducing the Topic

Readers justifiably expect that the kind of reports featured in this chapter will cue them right away to the topic at hand. There are various ways to create this focus. Here are some options.

You can be direct and focus right away on the information you are reporting and its significance, as in "Mentally Ill People Aren't More Violent, Study Finds."

Or you can use a question, as Bill Marsh does in his report on logo redesign:

> The world economy is in mid-swan dive. Wallets are in lockdown. So how does a company get people to feel just a little better about buying more stuff?

Or you could put things in historical and geographical perspective, as Daniel Pauly and Reg Watson do in "Counting the Last Fish":

> Georges Bank—the patch of relatively shallow ocean just off the coast of Nova Scotia, Canada—used to teem with fish. Writings from the 17th century record that boats were often surrounded by huge schools of cod, salmon, striped bass and sturgeon. Today it is a very different story. Trawlers trailing dredges the size of football fields have literally scraped the bottom clean—including supporting substrates such as sponges—along with the catch of the day. Farther up the water column, longlines and drift nets are snagging the last sharks, swordfish and tuna. The hauls of these commercially desirable species are dwindling, and sizes of individual fish being taken are getting smaller; a large number are even captured before they have time to mature. The phenomenon is not restricted to the North Atlantic but is occurring across the globe.

Peer Commentary

Exchange your working draft with a classmate and then answer these questions in writing:

1. Explain to the writer what you knew about the subject before you read the working draft, what you learned from reading it, and what (if anything) surprised you.

2. Explain to the writer whether you found the working draft easy to understand. Point to sections that are especially clear or interesting. Also point to any parts you found confusing.

3. What questions, if any, does the draft raise in your mind that you believe are not adequately answered? Are there points in the draft where you wanted more information from the writer? If so, explain.

4. Comment on the design. Is the purpose clear at the outset? Does the draft break the information into manageable chunks? Is the order of information easy to follow?

5. What suggestions do you have for revision?

Revising

Use the peer commentary to do a careful critical reading of your working draft.

1. Did your reader find the purpose clear?

2. Are the amount and type of information adequate? Is the information easy to understand?

3. Is the information presented in the best possible order?

4. Does the design enable your reader to move easily from point to point?

Getting the Right Order

Thinking about the order in which you present information can help you see whether one item leads to the next, what you have left out, and what you can combine.

Here are the questions on a student's working draft of a fact sheet about the herpes simplex virus:

Is there a cure for herpes?

How contagious is the virus?

Besides the unappealing sores, does the virus pose any other health risk?

What can be done to prevent it?

How does herpes really spread?

What about the possibility of herpes being spread by a toilet seat?

How often do the symptoms recur?

How is herpes treated?

What can I do to prevent herpes?

After getting a peer commentary, the student revised the order by combining information, adding further information, and developing a new set of questions:

What is herpes?

What are the symptoms?

How does it spread?

What are the health risks?

How is herpes treated?

How can I prevent herpes? ■

W WRITERS' WORKSHOP

Michael E. Crouch's draft-in-progress of the article "Lost in a Smog" is modeled on the kind of writing that appears in *Scientific American*. Crouch emulates the page layout of *Scientific American* by including a headline, photos, sidebars, and information boxes.

Bettman/Corbis

Lost in a SMOG

By Michael E. Crouch

TRAFALGAR SQUARE [above] thickly shrouded in the Great Smog of 1952. Similarly, the Canary Wharf skyline [right] obscured by a blue cloud of ozone during the heat wave of summer 2003. Even 50 years after the environmental disaster, London's skies are susceptible to choking smogs that pose serious health threats to its citizens.

The nights come on fast during a London December, but when the sun was not visible by midday on December 6, 1952, something was obviously wrong. This was no solar eclipse; the combination of a harsh cold front and a cityís dependency on coal produced the greatest peace-time disaster in London's long history: a cloud of thick, impenetrable pollution that covered the city and everything within a 20-mile radius for three days.

Provoked by a particularly harsh winter, a large portion of London's 8.3 million citizens fired up their coal stoves and hid away in the warmth of their homes to avoid the bitter cold. Their reaction to the chilly weather was intuitive; the unfortunate outcome was not. Millions of chimneys unleashed sooty, sulphurous smoke, a by-product of coal-burning, into the atmosphere. A weak winter sun, the cold front, and low winds gave the smoke nowhere to go. A well-intentioned population had no idea about the disaster they were in the process of unleashing.

When the Londoners emerged, the sight was – well, there was no sight. Visibility had dropped to near zero, and the air was thick with acrid coal smoke. The sun could scarcely penetrate the massive cloud of haze, a condition with which Londoners were all too familiar. So frequent were the hazes that in 1905, Dr. HA Des Vouex created the term 'smog,' a word combined of 'smoke' and 'fog,' two of London's most common wintertime occurrences. Most smogs proved only an inconvenience, and a scant few even approached the death tolls seen in 1952. The Great Smog, however, was suffocating, and for a few harrowing days, London found itself completely enveloped in its pollutants.

When the smog had cleared on December 9, the people of London saw more than they were ready to. The death toll was disturbingly high: nearly 4,000 Londoners had succumbed to the elements of the deadly poison and its after-effects from December 5 until Christmas. In one week alone, 4,703 people met their ends, though in truth, not all of those who died that week expired because of the smog. In 1951, the number of Londoners who had died in the same time span equaled 1,852 people, mean-

Rex USA

ing that the death toll was up by more than 150% in 1952. The smog-related deaths did not cease with the exit of the cloud. Two recent publications in *Environmental Health Perspectives*, one by Michelle L. Bell and Devra Lee Davis and the other from Andrew Hunt and a team of researchers, suggest that lingering effects of the smog killed more than 8,000 Londoners within the next year. In all, they contend the Great Smog claimed approximately 12,000 lives.

What bearing does this have on the lives of 8 million Londoners today? A trio of Clean Air Acts, the first of which the British government passed in 1956 as a response to the Great Smog of 1952, has insured that London's skies are free from the excess sulfur dioxide (SO_2) and particulate matter that accompanied coal burning. The three laws instituted smokeless zones around London – effectively stopping the use of coal domestically – and forced industries to utilize large smoke stacks so that pollution would be released higher in the air and more easily dispersed by the wind. Furthermore, coal itself – replaced by cleaner burning fuels – is no longer such a popular source of heat and energy in the famed city. Knowing all this, one might be tempted to write off disasters like the

Great Smog and insist that they cannot happen today. Doing so, however, would be a grave mistake.

Today coal-burning chimneys pollute the skies above London much less frequently, but motor-vehicle emissions pump out air toxins that are just as harmful, if not worse. Millions of cars and buses add to a wealth of air pollution, much of which is nearly invisible. Coal smoke contributed mainly sulfur dioxide (SO_2) and particulate matter (PM) to the atmosphere; motor vehicles pump out carbon monoxide (CO), nitrogen dioxide (NO_2), and PM. This deadly mix, a poisonous cocktail that can lead to the creation of harmful ground-level ozone (O_3), kills thousands of Londoners prematurely every year. To say that skies above London are in the clear just because they are seldom overcast with a sickening mixture of smoke and fog is to ignore the fact that the city, and much of the rest of the world, has a lot to learn about air pollution.

Microscopic Killers

THESE DAYS, it is widely understood that inhaling smog or smoke is a health risk, yet few actually understand why this is. Still fewer even know what smog is, whether it is the smog that enveloped London in 1952 or the smog that we are more familiar with in the 21st century. Understanding these facts is an important step in learning that modern air pollution, too, presents a serious threat.

Smogs that killed prior to 1952 were not without precedence in London, but most posed smaller health risks

The days of oppressive killer smogs are gone, but pollution lingers on in a new form

than the Great Smog. Londoners died with great frequency during the smogs of December 1813, January 1880, February 1882, December 1891, December 1892 (1,000 dead), and November 1948 (700-800 dead). Smogs continued to plague London even after 1952 and the passage of the first Clean Air Act, which created for the first time in London smokeless zones where only clean fuels could be burned. The last large-scale smog occurred in 1962 and claimed 750 lives. Inferring from these disasters, it seems simple to think polluted air could kill, but how does it do so?

Let us look to 1952 for an example. Precipitating the disaster, fog formed. On December 5, the air near the ground was thick with moisture, and the ground itself was cool. The two conditions together caused condensation, and all the water vapor that formed settled onto unseen dust particles that always inhabit the air, thus creating the relatively harmless condition of fog. The naturally occurring fog trapped in its midst all the coal smoke released from countless London chimneys. Aided by the winter sun, which could neither warm the air enough to get it moving nor penetrate the smog to shed light on the dismal situation, the pollution became even thicker between December 6 and December 8. Visibility was at times only a few meters; at others, pedestrians could not even see their feet. The air, thick and humid, was an irritant to both the eyes and respiratory systems of Londoners.

Coal smoke fills the air with acids containing free ions of hydrogen. These ions can create acid rain that is

strong enough to kill plants. Today one can still see the remnants of the acidic smogs of London on the city's older buildings, a shade darker than they were when the architects of the past built them.

The unpleasant smog reeked havoc on the throats and lungs of Londoners. In humans, the acid irritates the throat and bronchial tubes, causing them to become inflamed and produce excess mucus. Thusly, smog adversely affects those with existing lung and heart conditions. Cases of asthma, pneumonia, bronchitis, and tuberculosis all flare up under these conditions. As one would imagine, the dead in London were comprised mostly of the people afflicted with these conditions, the elderly, and the very young. The smog also hit hard those with heart disease. Inhaling mostly coal smoke limited the amount of oxygen they took into their systems, and many died because of low levels of the compound in their blood.

Several new studies suggest that the Great Smog also affected the long-term health of those who lived through it. Along with releasing sulfur dioxide, coal smoke burns off small, sooty particles covered in moisture, called PM. Michelle L. Bell of Johns Hopkins Bloomberg School of Public Heath and Devra Lee Davis, acclaimed author and a researcher at Carnegie Mellon University, suggest that "the true scope and scale of the health effects linked with London's lethal smog extended over a longer period than originally estimated." The team, which waded through and analyzed piles of 50-year-old data to come to its conclusions, contends that illnesses in January and February of 1953 had a strong correlation to both the sulfur dioxide and PM levels during the Great Smog. Bell and Davis believe this correlation means that the excess deaths were due to a lagged effect of exposure to PM.

Picking up where Bell and Davis' research left off, Andrew Hunt and a team of researchers from the State University of New York Upstate Medical University and the Royal London Hospital studied archived lung tissues from 16 Londoners who perished in the Great Smog in order to determine how PM affected their deaths. The team found high concentrations of PM in the tissue samples. Particu-

Overview/Troubling Pollutants

- Recent reviews of London's Great of Smog of 1952 indicate that particulate matter (PM) can have both severe short and long-term effects on the human cardiac and respiratory systems.
- Coal smoke is no longer the most dangerous toxin that occupies London's air. Motor vehicles are the main source of pollution in the modern day capital. Their toxins do as much, if not more, harm to humans as coal smoke does.
- Although PM and sulfur dioxide levels in London are lower than they were 50 years ago, carbon monoxide, nitrogen dioxide, and ground-level ozone levels are now much higher. It is estimated that, along with PM, these three chemical compounds cause 1,600 to 2,000 Londoners to die prematurely every year.

CHANGE OF SEASONS

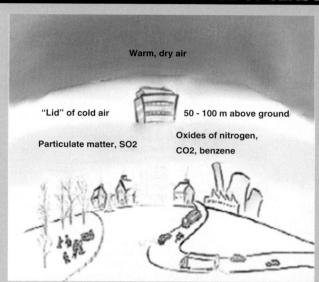

Warm, dry air

"Lid" of cold air   50 - 100 m above ground

Particulate matter, SO2   Oxides of nitrogen,
CO2, benzene

Summer Smog (Below)

While London must now endure summer smogs, or photochemical smogs, they are not alone in such an experience. Virtually every urban area in the world has to deal with this sort of pollution thanks to the advent and proliferation of the automobile.

Summer smogs, unlike their winter counterparts, contain very little smoke, so the term smog is somewhat misleading. However, the mixture of pollutants in summer smogs varies greatly; seven ingredients make up a summer smog: ozone, carbon monoxide, nitrogen dioxide, hydrocarbons, lead, PM and sulfur dioxide. Hydrocarbons – of which VOC are a subgroup – react with the sun's solar energy and nitrogen dioxide to produce ozone. As is the case in the winter, the formation of smog is aided by low winds. When the sun is not visible, summer smog is not a problem.

Winter Smog (Above)

London particulars, another phrase for the cityís frequently occurring smogs, are a part of the mystique of London, but they are by no means particular to the capital city. Donora, Pennsylvania, saw 20 of its residents die and nearly half of its population of 14,000 became ill when a smog settled overhead in October 1948. In December 1930, over 60 residents of the Meuse Valley in Belgium succumbed to a five-day smog.

How did all these disasters occur? They begin with the arrival of an anticyclone, a weather system marked by low wind speeds and moist air near ground level. Colder air remains further up in the atmosphere while warmer air stays near the ground, allowing the cooler earth to cause condensation-forming fog. Any pollutants released into the air mingle with the fog, trapped in place by the anticyclone's high pressure. Thick smog then slowly poisons anyone unfortunate enough to be lost amidst its cloudy form.

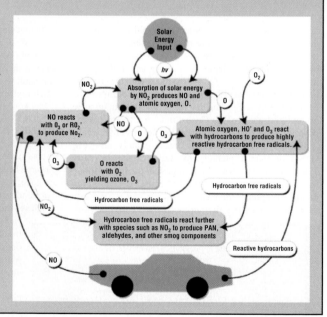

Solar Energy Input

hv

NO_2

Absorption of solar energy by NO_2 produces NO and atomic oxygen, O.

O_2

O

NO reacts with O_3 or RO_2' to produce No_2.

NO

O

O_3

Atomic oxygen, HO' and O_3 react with hydrocarbons to produce highly reactive hydrocarbon free radicals.

O_3

O reacts with O_2 yielding ozone, O_3

Hydrocarbon free radicals

NO_2

Hydrocarbon free radicals

Hydrocarbon free radicals react further with species such as NO_2 to produce PAN, aldehydes, and other smog components

Reactive hydrocarbons

NO

COVER-UPS AND BLUNDERS

ONLY AFTER A GREAT push from the public and the media did the British government decide to take action to curb more smog disasters. Even then, the official reaction was lukewarm at best. "Today everybody

A PROPOSAL for an air cannon that would blast away London's pollution woes.

Guildhall Library, London

expects the government to solve every problem. It is a symptom of the welfare state. For some reason or another 'smog' has captured the imagination of the press and people…. Ridiculous as it appears, I suggest we form a committee. We cannot do very much, but we can be seen to be very busy, and that's half the battle nowadays," wrote Harold Macmillan, then Minister of Housing, in a secret memo shortly after the Great Smog of 1952. Unfortunately, his attitude was typical of most government officials of the time.

England had mounted a war debt of over £31 billion, and the government was hesitant to add new expenditures to its budget. Britain took drastic measures, such as the selling of horsemeat for food, to overcome its deficit. Most shocking, however, is that the country sold all its cleaner-burning coal to foreign industries in order to make a larger profit. Those inside the country received the leftovers: sooty coal whose smoke filled the London sky for five days in 1952.

Actions originally taken by the government to battle the fog were wholly ineffective. The National Health Service distributed over three

late matter inhabited two different areas of the lung tissues: those associated with short-term storage (lung airways) and those associated with long-term storage (situated around the vessels and bronchioles of the lung and in the lymph nodes). Carbonaceous PM, synonymous with the combustion of coal and diesel fuel, was found in both retention compartments, suggesting that the people of London were not only hit hard by the Great Smog, but they were exposed to these kinds of PM over long periods of time.

Neither group purports to know exactly how PM causes deaths. A plethora of studies since the early 1990s, however, have tried to establish the link. Among the many possibilities are that PM causes decreased red blood-cell counts, increased blood viscosity, heart rate changes, increased arrhythmias, and increased defibril-

lator discharges. None of these hypotheses have been established. All that is known is that in smog incidents, elevated PM concentration is highly correlated with increased death rates. Understanding of the PM problem is crucial to populated cities where pollution levels are much higher than those found here in America.

A New Danger

THANKS TO the first Clean Air Act, homes in London can no longer burn coal as a means to generate heat. Londoners instead turned to the cleaner systems of electric and gas-powered heating. Thus, the days of oppressive killer smogs are gone, but pollution lingers in a new form. The vehicles that Londoners rely on are slowly poisoning the city's air.

Diesel fuel, when burned, gives off nearly the same carbonaceous PM that coal burning does. The trucks, buses, and taxis that rely on this fuel spit out cancer-causing chemicals, such as benzo-a-pyrenes, while they transport citizens and goods about the city.

These vehicles and others also subject the city to carbon monoxide. Carbon monoxide is undetectable by humans, being both colorless

THE AUTHOR

MICHAEL E. CROUCH is in his final year of study at Worcester Polytechnic Institute in Massachusetts, where he majors in Technical, Scientific, and Professional Communication. This article is a portion of his MQP, the WPI senior project, which he is completing abroad in the city of London. Crouch has written about health communication on the Internet and researched ancient Near Eastern artifacts for the Higgins Armory Museum of Worcester, MA.

million face masks made of gauze to the people of London. The masks did nothing to prevent the harmful effects of the smog, something Health Minister Iain Macleod knew even before the NHS gave them out. One American tobacco company offered to donate to the British government 100,000 masks that employed a filtering technique designed for cigarettes. The ministers refused the offer in order to curb advertising.

London had a history of eccentric fixes to its smog problem. A plan from 1925 proposed that several giant air cannons be placed around the city. When smog rolled in, the cannons would fire several blasts of powerful winds until the acrid haze was dispersed. Nothing like this was ever constructed. London post-1952 had no shortage of these unique "solutions." Anti-fog lozenges gave the consumer a false sense of security against the poisonous air. Fog flares, designed to guide buses through the premature darkness that smogs brought during the day, proved that the government had no hope – or perhaps no intention – of preventing more deadly clouds of pollution.

When none of these solutions proved helpful, government officials, eager to take the onus off themselves, explained that 5,655 of the deaths which occurred in the months following the Great Smog were due to a bout of influenza. This explanation was widely accepted until 2001, when Michelle Bell and Devra L. Davis published their study of the fatalities. In order for the number of reported influenza deaths to fit the average number of people who succumb to the disease (0.2%), almost one in every three Londoners would have to have contracted the illness. There is simply no evidence that such a widespread epidemic occurred.

There is no telling whether the British government could have saved lives if they had taken action against London's pollution problems sooner than it did. Four major smog events took place between 1956 and 1962, killing another 2,700 people. Not until 1956 did the Clean Air Act put an end to coal burning in homes and some industrial settings. Perhaps legislation in 1952 could have prevented some of these later disasters; perhaps not. What is clear is that a government must tackle the issue of pollution and environmental health in order to better the lives of its citizens.

and odorless. When inhaled, the gas attaches itself to human red blood cells, preventing the distribution of carbon monoxide and oxygen to and from the lungs. A large amount of carbon monoxide can lead to asphyxiation, the consequence of sitting in an idling car without proper ventilation for too long.

Another byproduct of fuel combustion, nitrogen dioxide is visible as reddish-brown gas and has a pungent and irritating acrid odor. Nitrogen dioxide, like coal smoke, is associated with acid rain. In humans, it can aggravate cases of asthma and other lung conditions.

Though it is directly attributed to automobiles, ground-level ozone is not emitted from any vehicle. Instead, nitrogen dioxide reacts with Volatile Organic Compounds (VOC) – organic chemicals commonly found in household cleaners and some fuels – and sunlight to form the gas, which in its pure form is bluish and has a penetrating odor. Studies have shown ozone at ground level to be harmful to those with lung ailments, and it has the ability to damage crops and forests. Some believe it also causes asthma.

The combination of these three gases and PM makes air hazardous to breath and prematurely kills between 1,600 to 2,000 Londoners every year. Surges in the levels of these pollutants send people to hospitals with respiratory ailments in great numbers. This is no surprise as England's relaxed standards on motor vehicle emissions means that the country has higher concentrations of carbon monoxide, nitrogen dioxide, and ground-level ozone than the US and many countries in Europe.

London has begun to experience more smog in the summertime. Increased global warming and automobile emissions are combining to make summers unbearable on the historically cold island. The summer of 2003 saw the first ever temperatures above 100° F in England. The season's harsh sun not only caused heat exhaustion, but also increased ozone levels in the air, creating a deadly trio of extreme heat, humidity, and smog. An estimated 2,045 people died from exposure to all three. Clearly, problems with pollution are not over for England, and much still needs addressing.

A Grim Future

IF LONDONERS have anything to look forward to in the next century, it is that their winters will likely become warmer, and the feared smogs that accompany the season will be a thing of the past. That may be where the hope ends, though. Projections suggest that global warming will increase summertime temperatures, too. High temperatures could consistently reach 100° F and above. Summer smogs, the air full of ozone, would be the new concern for Londoners.

Other predictions foretell a future much less desirable. A group of scientists who make up the Intergovernmental Panel on Climate Change (IPCC) have predicted that the combination of global warming and pollution will prove so overwhelming by the year 2100 that the entire northern hemisphere will be enveloped in an impenetrable smog. Summon up what it would be like to live the title to Devra Davis' acclaimed book, *When Smoke Ran Like Water*. Much of the population would have to escape to the southern hemisphere, as the north would no longer be hospitable to animals or plants.

This horrible scenario is, of course, only a prediction. Whether or not it will come to pass remains to be seen. The world has nearly ten decades to prevent or prepare for this outcome. In the meantime, most countries are moving forward with stricter air pollution regulations.

The search for a new fuel source to power automobiles is surging forward. London already has three hydrogen-powered buses in its fleet. With no carbon in their fuel source,

the buses produce much less pollution. Other buses in the city are being retrofitted with pollution filtering devices to bring down PM and nitrogen dioxide emissions.

Instead of pushing expensive cars with alternative fuel systems onto its citizens, London is trying to promote a better public transportation system. City officials also encourage Londoners to use their vehicles only when necessary, such as when going to work. The campaign has been successful; the last year has seen a 30 percent increase in the number of cyclists in the city.

Despite the many attempts to clean up London's historically polluted air, both the government and the public have much to do in order to prevent more smog disasters. If no one takes action on this issue, Londoners may want to start hoping that their government plans to join the US in occupying the moon within the next century because instead of premature darkness, their city could be experiencing perpetual darkness. SA

MORE TO EXPLORE

The Big Smoke: A History of Air Pollution in London since Medieval Times. Peter Brimblecombe. Methuen, 1987.

Toxicologic and Epidemiologic Clues from the Characterization of the 1952 London Smog Fine Particulate Matter in Archival Autopsy Lung Tissues. Andrew Hunt, Jerrold L. Abraham, Bret Judson, and Colin L. Berry in *Environmental Health Perspectives*, Vol. 111, No. 9, pages 1209-1214; July 2003.

When Smoke Ran Like Water: Tales of Environmental Deception and the Battle Against Pollution. Devra Lee Davis. Basic Books, 2002.

London Air Quality Network Homepage: **www.erg.kcl.ac.uk/london/asp/home.asp**

■ **WORKSHOP QUESTIONS**

1. How do the photos on the first page of Michael E. Crouch's "Lost in a Smog" help you visualize the topic he's writing about?

2. Crouch's article is divided into four sections. Describe the function each section seems intended to perform. Do you think the order of information works well?

3. What do the diagram "Change of Season," the sidebar "Cover-Ups and Blunders," and the "Overview" information box add to Crouch's presentation of information?

4. What advice would you give Crouch to revise this work?   ■

REFLECTING ON YOUR WRITING

Think about how you wrote and revised the informative writing you did as this chapter's work. What did you discover along the way about informative writing that you didn't know before?

chapter 9

commentary

Commentary is a genre of writing that uses analysis and interpretation to find patterns of meaning in events, trends, and ideas. The purpose of commentary is not simply to report on things but to give readers a way to make sense of them.

This purpose should be clear if you think about the commentaries you've heard on radio and television and read in newspapers and magazines. For example, when television news commentators such as Keith Olbermann or Bill O'Reilly present their remarks, you don't see news footage on the television screen—just the commentator speaking directly to you. Thus, the focus has shifted away from the news itself to the commentator's analysis and interpretation of the news.

In contemporary society, in which new ideas emerge and trends and events occur at a dizzying pace, commentators perform several crucial functions. For one thing, they perform a *labeling* function, identifying current trends and giving readers names for these trends (for example, "metrosexuals," "outsourcing," "gentrification," "the network society"). For another, by seeking to find patterns of meaning in events, trends, and ideas, commentators call on readers to think about the *causes and consequences* of what is happening in the world today (for example, "The economic downturn has alerted average Americans to the need to cut down on spending and save more" or "The drop in reading scores results from the neglect of phonics instruction"). Finally, in the process of explaining, commentators often apportion *praise and blame*—whether of solidarity, indignant reaction, or ironic distance (for example, "No Child Left Behind has been a disastrous failure" or "It's amusing to watch the baby boomers of the psychedelic sixties tell their children not to use drugs").

Commentary is also an important genre in academic writing, where books and articles seek to provide persuasive explanations of issues in a particular field—whether it is the meaning of Hamlet's melancholia, the causes of slavery in the New World, the nature of human–computer interactions, the role of trade in Paleolithic economies, or the results of new AIDS therapies. In academic commentaries, the issues are often more technical and specialized than the issues commentators treat in the popular media. But in many respects, it is the same desire to go beyond the given facts—to find patterns of meaning, identify underlying causes, explain consequences, and make judgments—that drives academic inquiry.

287

Whatever the context may be, the call to write commentary grows in part out of this desire to analyze and explain what happens around us—to have satisfying accounts of our experience and to find patterns of meaning that can make the world cohere. In conversation, we routinely offer commentary on events, trends, and other people. We want to get a handle on the local scene at work, in school, in our neighborhood, and so we talk about what is going on, analyzing the motives for actions and the reasons for events. A good deal of everyday talk, in fact, serves as a kind of social analysis that shapes how we negotiate our relationships with others.

■ WRITING FROM EXPERIENCE

Think of a place where you routinely talk with others. It could be your workplace, the family dinner table, your dormitory, or any place you hang out. What topics come up in conversations—events, trends, ideas, people? What makes these topics of interest to the people involved? Characterize the kinds of comments people make. What role does such talk play in the particular setting? Use your findings to see if you can form any tentative generalizations about how people use conversation to find patterns of meaning and manage their lives.

READINGS

REMEMBER WHEN PUBLIC SPACES DIDN'T CARRY BRAND NAMES?

ERIC LIU

Eric Liu is a regular commentator on MSNBC. A second-generation Chinese American, Liu has written a memoir, The Accidental Asian: Notes on a Native Speaker *(1998), that raises questions about assimilation, ethnicity, and race. His commentary on "branding" appeared in* USA Today.

Opening:
* uses example to identify issue
* reveals his perspective

* generalizes from example to wider trend

In a few weeks, when the world champion New York Yankees open their home season, will they take the field at Trump Stadium? Time Warner Park? Maybe AT&T Arena?

Chances are the park will still be called Yankee Stadium. But it won't be that way for long. Quietly, and with strikingly little protest, the Yankees have announced that they are planning to sell the "naming rights" to their Bronx homestead. By the time the 2000 season arrives, some lucky corporation may well have bought the sign outside the House that Ruth Built. And frankly, that turns my stomach.

It's not just that Yankee Stadium is a national treasure. It's not just that allowing the highest bidder to rename this 76-year-old icon feels like an insult—to New Yorkers, to tradition and to the memory of Yankees past, such as Joe DiMaggio. It's also that what is about to happen to Yankee Stadium is part of a deeper, accelerating trend in our society, the relentless branding of public spaces.

¶s 3–7:
* Provides examples as evidence of trend

The sports world gives us piles of examples. San Francisco's fabled Candlestick Park is now 3Com Park. The selling of bowl names has reached sublimely ridiculous levels. (Remember the Poulan/Weed Eater Independence Bowl?) And the trend is hardly confined to sports. Branding—the conspicuous marking of places and things with corporate names and logos—is now everywhere in the civic square.

Consider the public schools, some of which are flooded with advertising for merchandise and fast food. Districts around the country are raising money by making exclusive deals with Pepsi or Coke or with credit card companies or banks. In one Texas district, Dr. Pepper recently paid $3.45 million in part to plaster its logo on a high school roof to attract the attention of passengers flying in and out of Dallas.

Other efforts to turn public spaces into commercial vessels are no less corrosive. Rollerblade now hawks its wares in Central Park under the banner "The Official Skate of New York City Parks." Buses in Boston and other cities don't just carry ad placards anymore; some of them have been turned into rolling billboards.

¶s 8–9:
* Makes qualification and explains his promise about public space

How far can this go? Over in England, the legendary white cliffs of Dover now serve as the backdrop for a laser-projected Adidas ad. Here in America, we haven't draped Mount Rushmore with a Nike "swoosh." But things are heading in that general direction.

You might say at this point, "What's the big deal? America is commercialized—get over it!" And I admit my views may sound a bit old-fashioned. But this isn't a matter of priggishness or personal nostalgia.

¶s 10–14:
*Explains consequences of branding

Public spaces matter. They matter because they are emblems, the physical embodiments, of a community's spirit and soul. A public space belongs to all who share in the life of a community. And it belongs to them in common, regardless of their differences in social station or political clout. Indeed, its very purpose is to preserve a realm where a person's worth or dignity doesn't depend on market valuations.

So when a shared public space, such as a park or a schoolhouse, becomes just another marketing opportunity for just another sponsor, something precious is undermined: the idea that we are equal as citizens even though we may be unequal as consumers.

What the commercialization of public spaces also does, gradually and subtly, is convert all forms of identity into brand identity.

We come to believe that without our brands, or without the right brands, we are literally and figuratively no-names. We question whether we belong in public, whether we are truly members.

We forget that there are other means, besides badges of corporate affiliation, to communicate with one another.

It could, of course, be said, with a place like Times Square in mind, that brands, logos, and slogans are now our most widely understood public language. It could be said that in this age of cultural fragmentation, the closest thing we have in common is commerce.

But is this the best vision of American life we can muster?

In the military, they worry about "mission creep." In civilian life, the problem is "market creep." And the question now is how to stem this creeping sickness. We

Ending:
* uses rhetorical question to shift to closing section
* projects possible counter tendercies
* ends on note of caution

know that there is some limit to what people will accept: a 1996 April Fools announcement that the Liberty Bell had been purchased and rechristened the "Taco Liberty Bell" provoked a storm of angry calls. Drawing the line there, though, isn't protecting an awful lot.

Maybe the renaming of Yankee Stadium will shame some legislators or zoning czars into action. Maybe the "corporatization" of our classrooms will spark some popular protest. Maybe the licensing away of Central Park will awaken us to the disappearance of public space—and to the erosion of the public idea.

Then again, maybe not. In which case, we'd better keep a close eye on Mount Rushmore.

Analysis: Conversing with Readers

Eric Liu's commentary is typical in many respects of the kind of commentary you'll find in newspapers and on television. The tone is informal and the paragraphs are short; though the topic is serious, Liu treats it with a good deal of humor. As readers, we feel Liu is a person of goodwill who wants to engage us in a conversation about something he's noticed (not unlike the way we talk about things with friends).

Liu's breezy presentation, however, does not just make his commentary inviting to readers and easy to read. Notice at two key points how he incorporates what readers might be thinking. In the eighth paragraph, after he has substantiated the reality of the "branding" by giving a series of examples, Liu addresses readers directly and says, "You might say at this point, 'What's the big deal?'" Next, after acknowledging that he "may sound old-fashioned," Liu pinpoints the main issue of his commentary, namely that public spaces belong to everyone and that branding threatens to "convert all forms of identity into brand identity." Then, in the fourteenth paragraph, Liu anticipates his readers again, this time by imagining that people might say that brands "are now our most widely understood public language" and the "closest thing we have in common is commerce." By conversing with his readers at two pivotal points in his commentary, Liu establishes the groundwork for readers to join him in asking the question "Is this the best vision of American life we can muster?"

■ FOR CRITICAL INQUIRY

1. Almost half of Liu's commentary—the first seven paragraphs—is devoted to establishing the reality of the branding phenomenon. As you read, when did you become aware of Liu's perspective on this trend? What cued you to Liu's point of view?

2. What exactly is Liu's argument against branding? Is there a sentence or sentences anywhere that express his main claim? What evidence does Liu offer to

support his claim? What enabling assumptions connect the evidence to the claim? Are these assumptions stated explicitly or implied?

3. As noted, Liu anticipates what readers might be thinking at two key points in the commentary—at the beginnings of paragraphs 8 and 14. How does Liu handle these possible differing views? How successful do you think he is in countering or negotiating such differences?

HOW TO FIGHT THE NEW EPIDEMICS

LUNDY BRAUN

Lundy Braun teaches pathology to medical students and courses on the biological and social origins of disease to undergraduates at Brown University. Braun wrote this commentary in response to public fascination with media accounts of "killer viruses" and other epidemic diseases.

One of the hottest topics in the news these days seems to be "killer" viruses. With the outbreak of bird flu and the popular accounts of epidemics of virus infection in feature films, made-for-television movies and best-selling nonfiction, the public has been captivated by the apparent power of microorganisms to sweep through towns and villages unfettered.

But hidden behind our fascination with these real and fictional epidemics is a profound feeling of betrayal, stemming from the widely held view that science had won the war against microbial infections.

The recent outbreaks have taken us by surprise, threatening our carefully nurtured sense of health and well-being. We diet, consume vitamins and exercise vigorously to ward off heart disease and cancer. But infectious diseases strike in a seemingly unpredictable pattern, leaving us feeling unprotected and vulnerable. With the re-emergence of tuberculosis as a significant public health problem in the United States, cholera in Latin America, the plague epidemic in India last year and the Ebola virus infection in Zaire, HIV infection, formerly considered an isolated occurrence confined to marginalized populations, now seems a harbinger of ever more terrifying microbial agents.

Yet, the reasons for the re-emergence of infectious diseases are not particularly mysterious. In reality, infectious diseases never were conquered, and the recent epidemics are quite predictable. For centuries, infectious diseases have been the major cause of death in the developing world. Moreover, even in the developed world, successful management relies on active disease surveillance and public health policies.

In 1966, the eminent Australian immunologist Sir MacFarlane Burnet declared, "In many ways one can think of the middle of the 20th Century as the end of one of the most important social revolutions in history, the virtual elimination of infectious disease as a significant factor in social life." Shared by most of the scientific community, this view is rooted in the rise of the germ theory in the late

19th and early 20th centuries that associated specific microbial agents with particular diseases.

The germ theory took hold not only because of the spectacular technical achievements represented by the isolation of the microorganisms, but also because infectious disease, once seen as divine retribution for past sins, now appeared potentially controllable. The discovery of antibiotics and the development of vaccines lent further support to this notion of control. Thus, the germ theory effectively replaced disease prevention policies based on sanitary reforms, including improvement in sewage systems and better housing conditions, which were primarily responsible for the dramatic decline in the death rates from infectious disease.

The possibility of control over these great afflictions of humankind became even more appealing in the post–World War II period when a sense of endless optimism about the future was fueled by economic expansion in industrialized countries. Unfortunately, during this period, we also began to rely exclusively on science to solve the problems of disease. Throughout this century the role of the natural and social environment in the development of disease has been largely ignored by the scientific and medical communities and policy-makers.

Yet, the obstacles to management of many infectious diseases are social as well as scientific, and disease prevention policies based exclusively on science leave us ill-prepared to respond effectively to the current epidemics.

In the case of tuberculosis, we know how the bacterium is transmitted, how it causes disease and until recently, we had drugs that were relatively effective in reducing transmission and the development of disease. Despite this wealth of medical knowledge, tuberculosis continues to thrive, primarily in marginalized groups with minimal or no access to medical care. Without a concerted effort to improve access to the health care system, tuberculosis will remain a formidable challenge irrespective of the development of new drug treatments or more effective vaccines.

In the case of AIDS, basic scientific research coupled with education, public health measures and the political will to address difficult social issues are essential to managing this epidemic.

There are many other examples of microbial diseases where the failure to integrate scientific knowledge with social programs has hampered the development of sound disease prevention policies. Cervical cancer, for example, is the second most common cause of cancer-related mortality in women worldwide. Over a decade ago, sexually transmitted human papillomaviruses were linked to this cancer. Yet years later, we still know relatively little about the mechanisms by which human papillomaviruses contribute to the development of cervical cancer. To reduce the morbidity and mortality associated with this infection we need to develop more precise ways of identifying women at increased risk of progression to cancer.

An investment in basic microbiological research will be required to answer these questions. Meantime, however, we have more than sufficient scientific information to begin to educate the population most at risk of contracting the disease, namely adolescents. Again, the failure to implement such programs is fundamentally a political issue, reflecting our reluctance as a society to deal with adolescent sexuality.

Effective management of infectious diseases is achievable. Many of the agents associated with recent outbreaks are not new microbes but rather newly recognized ones that have appeared in human populations as a consequence of social disorganization and ecological disruption. To be successful, disease-prevention policies must be based on more than technical solutions. They must be firmly rooted in an ecological perspective of disease that does not separate scientific knowledge from an understanding of the influence of the natural environment on disease and a commitment to social justice.

There are no magic bullets. We will have little impact on infectious diseases without addressing the living conditions of large segments of our society and rebuilding our public health infrastructure. In the absence of such a policy, however, future outbreaks will continue to be viewed with the mixture of fascination, fear, helplessness and misdirected social policy that has characterized our response to the recent epidemics.

Analysis: Explaining Causes and Effects

"How to Fight the New Epidemics" opens by noting the public's "fascination" when new and mysterious "killer diseases" became hot topics in the news. As you can see, Lundy Braun felt called on to address the fascination with these epidemics and the "profound feeling of betrayal" that science had not won the war against infectious diseases. For Braun, the purpose of characterizing this public mood goes beyond simply labeling a trend in the popular mind. As her commentary unfolds, readers quickly become aware that this public mood is only an occasion for her to explain the limits of the germ theory of disease and the failure of scientific and medical policy making to take social conditions into account in preventing and controlling disease. Accordingly, Braun is asking her readers to reconsider the dominant theory of disease causation and to see that disease prevention and control relies on integrating scientific knowledge with social programs.

■ FOR CRITICAL INQUIRY

1. How does Braun use the hot news topic of "killer viruses" to frame her commentary?

2. Braun is addressing general readers, but she is also positioning her commentary in relation to the scientific community's understanding of modern medicine. What are the main issues involved? What are the main points of agreement and disagreement?

3. Consider how Braun uses examples of diseases such as tuberculosis and cervical cancer as evidence. How does she link these examples to specific claims? What do her enabling assumptions seem to be?

4. Do you find Braun's argument about disease causation, prevention, and control persuasive? Explain your reasoning.

SPOOF ADS

ADBUSTERS

Adbusters Media Foundation is a nonprofit network of artists, writers, educators, and activists dedicated to promoting a critical awareness of the impact of commercial forces on the environment and cultural life. The organization www.adbusters.org sponsors events like Buy Nothing Day and Turn Off TV Week and publishes Adbusters magazine. It is perhaps best known for its Spoof Ads—visual commentaries that rework familiar advertising campaigns to uncover the logic of consumer culture. Consider how the two Spoof Ads use parody to bring unstated meanings to light.

Courtesy www.adbusters.org

Courtesy www.adbusters.org

BLOGS

PORTRAITS OF THINKING: AN ACCOUNT OF A COMMON LABORER
MIKE ROSE

*Mike Rose is an award-winning writer and professor of education at UCLA.
The following commentary is drawn from Rose's book* The Mind at Work *(2004)
and appeared on Mike Rose's Blog for the first time on May 29, 2009. In the
opening three paragraphs, Rose explains the purpose of the series of "portraits
of thinking" featured on the blog.*

FRIDAY, MAY 29, 2009

PORTRAITS OF THINKING: AN ACCOUNT OF A COMMON LABORER

For the sixth story about cognition in action, I want to go back into history and
reflect on the infamous description of a man named Schmidt, a common
laborer in Frederick Winslow Taylor's 1911 *The Principles of Scientific
Management.* Taylor's portrayal of Schmidt reveals an undemocratic and
contradictory American attitude toward physical work, one that carries with it
strong biases about intelligence. For those of you who missed the previous
entries where I discuss the purpose of these portraits of thinking, I'll repeat two
introductory paragraphs now. If you did read the earlier entries, you can skip
right to the reflection on Schmidt, which is drawn from *The Mind at Work.*

As I've been arguing during the year of this blog's existence—and for some
time before—we tend to think too narrowly about intelligence, and that
narrow thinking has affected the way we judge each other, organize work,
and define ability and achievement in school. We miss so much.

I hope that the portraits I offer over the next few months illustrate the majesty
and surprise of intelligence, its varied manifestations, its subtlety and nuance.
The play of mind around us.

Following is one of the most reproduced depictions of a laborer in Western
occupational literature, drawn from Taylor's *The Principles of Scientific
Management.* It captures American industry's traditional separation of
managerial intelligence from worker production.

Taylor was a fierce systematizer and a tireless promoter of time study and
industrial efficiency. He uses an immigrant laborer named Schmidt to illustrate
how even the most basic of tasks—in this case, the loading of pig iron—could

be analytically broken down by the scientific manager into a series of maximally effective movements, with a resulting bonus in wages and a boom in productivity. Schmidt, Taylor claimed, jumped his rate from twelve-and-a-half tons of pig iron per day—each "pig" an oblong casting of iron weighing close to one-hundred pounds—to an astonishing tonnage of forty-seven.

Before he introduces Schmidt, Taylor sets the scene with a dispassionate analysis of the loading of pig iron at Bethlehem Steel, Schmidt's place of employment. Enter Schmidt, "a little Pennsylvania Dutchman," seemingly inexhaustible (he "trots" to and from work), frugal, in the process of building "a little house for himself." Then comes this interaction between Taylor and Schmidt:

'Schmidt, are you a high-priced man?'

Vell, I don't know vat you mean.'

'Oh, yes, you do. What I want to know is whether you are a high-priced man or not.'

'Vell, I don't know vat you mean.'

'Oh, come now, you answer my questions. What I want to find out is whether you are a high-priced man or one of these cheap fellows here.

What I want to find out is whether you want to earn $1.85 a day or whether you are satisfied with $1.15, just the same as all those cheap fellows are getting.'

'Did I vant $1.85 a day? Vas dot a high-priced man? Vell, yes, I vas a high-priced man.'

'Oh, you're aggravating me. Of course you want $1.85 a day—every one wants it! . . . For goodness' sake answer my questions, and don't waste any more of my time. Now come over here. You see that pile of pig iron?' . . .

Taylor badgers Schmidt for a little while longer—one wonders what Schmidt thinks of all this—and then introduces him to the supervisor who will direct his scientifically calibrated labor:

Well, if you are a high-priced man, you will do exactly as this man tells you to-morrow, from morning till night. When he tells you to pick up a pig and walk, you pick it up and you walk, and when he tells you to sit down and rest, you sit down. You do that right straight through the day. And what's more, no back talk. Now a high-priced man does just what he's told to do, and no back talk. Do you understand that? When this man tells you to walk, you walk; when he tells you to sit down, you sit down, and you don't talk back at him.

"This seems to be rather rough talk," Taylor admits, but "[w]ith a man of the mentally sluggish type of Schmidt it is appropriate and not unkind." Later, Taylor observes that Schmidt "happened to be a man of the type of an ox . . . a man so stupid that he was unfitted to do most kinds of laboring work, even."

There's much to say about this depiction, and a number of critics, beginning with Upton Sinclair, have collectively said it: the insidious mix of scientific pretension, class and ethnic bias, and paternalism; the antagonistic management stance, the kind of authoritarian control that would lead to industrial inflexibility; the absolute gulf between managerial brains and worker brawn; the ruthlessness of full-blown industrial capitalism. All true.

In addition, though, I keep thinking of Schmidt himself, rereading Taylor's rendering, trying to imagine him beyond the borders of Taylor's page. Let us follow him through the plant, out into his world, down the road home. Though Taylor claims that a man like Schmidt "is so stupid that the word 'percentage' has no meaning to him," Taylor also tells us that Schmidt is building a house from his meager earnings. So, Schmidt had to calculate and budget, and even if he could not do formal arithmetic—we don't know if he could or couldn't—he would have to be competent in the mathematics necessary for carpentry. And for him to plan and execute even a simple structure, use hand tools effectively, solicit and coordinate aid—all this requires way more intelligence than Taylor grants him.

Taylor does not tell us if Schmidt is literate, but does note that many of the laborers "were foreigners and unable to read and write." If Schmidt were illiterate, did he develop informal literate networks to take care of personal and civic needs? We know that ethnic communities were rich in fraternal organizations that served as places of entertainment, but also as sites of political discussion and the exchange of news about the old country. Literate members would write letters, read newspapers aloud, both in their native language and English, and act as linguistic and culture brokers with mainstream institutions. The parish church or synagogue was another source of exposure to literate practices and social exchange, and, for some, a place of reflection.

Though Bethlehem Steel was not yet a site of significant union activity, labor unrest had already erupted in some sectors of steel, and discussions about safety, work conditions, and the length of the work day were in the air. Schmidt might well have heard the early rumblings about these issues and might have talked about them to others in the yard, the saloon, the neighborhood.

The point is that one cannot assume—as so many have—that the men looking back at us impassively from those photographs of the open ditch or the pouring of fiery steel, faded, blurring to silver, had no mental life, were sluggish, dull, like oxen.

Analysis: Commentary as Critical Reading

Mike Rose's intention in this blog is to rescue Schmidt from his portrayal in Frederick Winslow Taylor's *The Principles of Scientific Management*—to make his life and work intelligible from a more generous angle. To do this, Rose first briefly reviews what previous critics of Taylor, starting with Upton Sinclair, have said, thereby establishing in broad strokes the grounds for a critical reading of Taylor's treatment of Schmidt. Then, he uses clues in Taylor's portrait to imagine an alternative way of making sense of Schmidt, noting the significance of details, such as Schmidt's building his own house, that Taylor passes over. By linking these details to what we know about the richness of the social and cultural life of ethnic working-class communities in the early twentieth century, Rose locates Schmidt in his historical times. We cannot know with certainty what Schmidt was like, but Rose has fashioned a portrait of Schmidt that ascribes to him a lively mental life that is both plausible and a critical rejection of Taylor's notion of workers as dull and sluggish.

■ FOR CRITICAL INQUIRY

1. To get more background, look up "Frederick Winslow Taylor" and "scientific management" on Wikipedia. Use this information to consider what Taylor's enabling assumptions about the nature of work and workers seem to be—and how this influences his interaction with Schmidt.

2. What alternative assumptions does Rose seem to be making in his critical reading of the encounter between Taylor and Schmidt? Where are these assumptions manifest? How do they provide the framework for an alternative understanding of Schmidt?

3. Go to Mike Rose's Blog www.mikerosebooks.blogspot.com and click on the "Comments" at the end of this blog entry. Describe the range of responses. What are people saying? How do they connect to this particular blog entry? What does this add to your reading of Rose's blog?

4. Find another blog on a topic that interests you. Follow the comments posted to a couple of blog entries. What differences, if any, do you see between what people say in these comments and those posted on Mike Rose's Blog? What similarities? How do you account for these differences and similarities? Compare your findings to what classmates have come up with on the blogs they visited. How do you make sense of the variety of blogs and the range of commentaries bloggers put up and readers post to?

ART AS SOCIAL COMMENTARY

ASMA AHMED SHIKOH

Asma Ahmed Shikoh is a Pakistani artist who moved to the United States in 2002. Her art in Pakistan included paintings on the country's colonization by fast-food restaurants, such as The Invasion, *where Ronald McDonalds overrun the streets of Karachi. (You can find this painting at Ahmed Shikoh's Web site www.asmashikoh.com.) Her more recent paintings have taken a different turn that explores the immigrant experience and her identity as a Muslim woman in the United States who has decided to wear a hijab (or head scarf). "Self Portrait—1" pictures the Statue of Liberty in a Pakistani wedding dress, while* Vanwyck Blvd. *rewrites the New York City subway map in calligraphic script as an Urdu manuscript. The other two works come from a series of pictures Ahmed Shikoh made daily, using the head scarf as the central image—one hijab with a built-in iPod and the other made of Play-Doh, with Dora the Explorer figures. These four artworks are not as direct in their social commentary as* The Invasion, *but they do nonetheless seek to make sense of Ahmed Shikoh's experience by rewriting existing images. Consider what the meaning of this visual commentary might be. Compare Ahmed Shikoh's works to the Adbusters' Spoof Ads, which also use rewriting.*

Self Portrait—I

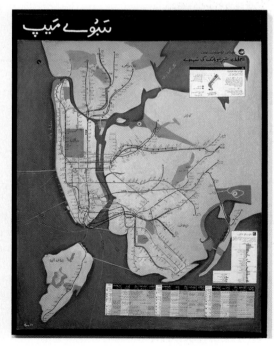

VanWyck Blvd

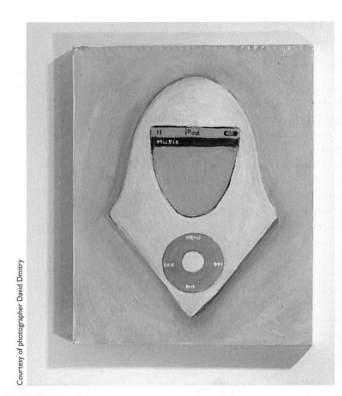

Courtesy of photographer David Dmitry

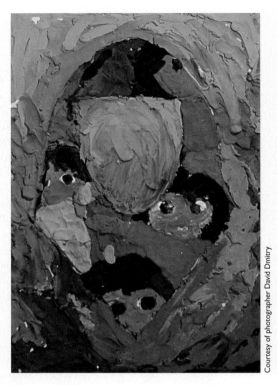

Courtesy of photographer David Dmitry

ETHICS OF WRITING

IN WHOSE INTEREST?

Commentators often seek to persuade an audience that their commentaries represent the best interests of the public and the common good. By speaking on behalf of the public, commentators play a vital role in a democracy, holding accountable those in positions of power and explaining what the public's stake is in events, trends, and ideas.

Speaking in the name of the public, however, is rarely a simple matter, and it brings with it ethical responsibilities that writers need to take into account. Since commentary offers explanations, it presumes, for example, to represent other people's motives. Commentators therefore need to avoid falling into stereotyped representations of groups of people

("Gay men are promiscuous," "Young people today don't have a social conscience"). Such stereotypes not only characterize groups unfairly but also turn these groups into "them" who are different from "us," and often present the interests of these groups as incompatible with the public interest.

Writers need to be aware that speaking in the name of the public may in fact amount to speaking on behalf of some people or groups and distancing themselves from others. Writers need to examine their own assumptions about who is included in the public and try to understand how the people they write about perceive themselves and their experience. ■

FURTHER EXPLORATION: COMMENTARY

■ RHETORICAL ANALYSIS

Write a rhetorical analysis of a blog and its comments, paying particular attention to how bloggers and the people who post comments on blogs construct their rhetorical stances. Consider whether they are writing as their "real name" selves or as invented online identities or as some combination. What voice do they use? How do they respond to others' comments? What differences, if any, do you see between print commentary that appears on the op-ed page of a newspaper or in a magazine and digital commentary that appears online? What significance do you see in the differences and similarities?

GENRE AWARENESS

Compare the kind of written commentary that appears on the op-ed page of a newspaper with another genre of writing or mode of communication. You can use any of the written commentaries in this chapter (by Liu, Braun, and Rose) or you can find a commentary on another topic. For purposes of comparison you could use a visual commentary (like those by Adbusters and Ahmed Shikoh), satire such as *The Daily Show* or *The Colbert Report,* or genres of writing and visual design in advocacy campaigns or informational presentations concerned with the same issues the commentary treats. What do you see as the main similarities and differences? Consider how the written commentary and the other document or communication are related to the place of publication or presentation where readers encounter them. How does the context (newspapers in the case of written commentaries) shape how writers design the texts and how readers use them? What do you see as the significance of the differences?

WRITING ASSIGNMENT

For this assignment, write a commentary that addresses a topic of interest to you. To help you get ideas for this assignment, consider what has called on the writers in this chapter to write commentary.

- **Trends:** Labeling trends gives readers a handle on what is taking place around them. Trends rely on the interpretive powers of commentators to name what's happening, thereby giving a series of events a distinct identity. The idea of "branding" in Eric Liu's commentary is a good example of how identifying and labeling trends can bring an issue into focus. There are plenty of other trends as well— body piercing, tattooing, nostalgia for the 1980s, the growth of microbreweries, and corporate downsizing are just a few. You might write about the significance of a particular trend that is already well known, or you can invent a new label to characterize a trend that has not been noticed before.

- **Policy issues:** Commentators often address issues of public policy. For example, Lundy Braun's commentary, "How to Fight the New Epidemics," analyzes the causes of infectious disease and the adequacy of the "germ theory" to control disease. You might write a commentary that focuses on the causes of an issue that interests you and the implications for public policy. Accounting for why things happen is often the first step in explaining what should be done—to endorse, alter, or control the situation.

- **Current events:** Stories that break in the news seem to call for a swift response by commentators to shape the public's mood and its sense of issues. You might draw on a recent event to serve as the springboard for your commentary, something current that your readers are likely to know about but where the meaning is still up for grabs.

- **Rereading historical events:** You could comment on a historical event, as Mike Rose does when he rereads the notorious encounter between Frederick Winslow Taylor and the workman Schmidt to find new meanings. Commentators often analyze past events and point out implications that would otherwise go unnoticed. You could write a commentary about the significance of a historic event, an invention, a social movement, or an everyday occurrence.

- **Visual commentary:** Visual commentaries like Adbusters' Spoof Ads use parody to bring out the unstated logic of an event or situation. Satire and humor can be used effectively to question conventional ideas. You might write a satirical commentary that uses humor to rework existing ways of thinking. Or, if your instructor is agreeable, you might design and produce a poster, a cartoon, or a comic strip to comment on a current event, issue, or idea. Or write and perform a comic skit either as a monologue or with others.

- **Casebook:** A casebook brings together writings on a topic. You may have used casebooks in other courses—on the causes of World War I, say, or on interpretations of *The Scarlet Letter.* A casebook typically organizes a range of perspectives on a topic so that readers can reconstruct for themselves the context of issues surrounding the topic. This is a good project to do in groups of two or three. Pick an issue that has generated debate. It could be affirmative action, immigration, eligibility standards for college athletes, Allen Ginsberg's poetry, or any other issue that has provoked a good deal of commentary. Assemble a casebook on the issue for high school students.

First you'll need to do some library research, to search newspapers and magazines for commentaries written from different positions. (Don't assume that there are just two sides—most controversies have many sides.) Select five or six commentaries that are representative of the various positions you find.

After rereading the commentaries you've selected, design your casebook in the following way:

- Write a brief introduction that gives readers an overview of the issue—what it is, how it began, why it is controversial—and mentions the articles you have selected.

- Include the readings. Before each reading, give a headnote that tells who the writer is and briefly introduces the reading. After each reading, provide discussion questions to promote thinking about it. (You can use the headnotes and discussion questions in this book as models.)

- At the end of the casebook, include several questions that pull together the various readings to make sure the students have understood the overall issue.

Invention

As you have seen, the reading selections in this chapter offer perspectives after the fact—after events have taken place, personalities have emerged in the media, or ideas, styles, fads, and moods have started floating around in the public consciousness. The point of commentary is to name a topic, identify an important issue, and explain its significance. Commentators, in effect, are asking their readers to consider one possible way of making sense of what has happened in the past and what is going on in the present.

Naming the Topic

Corporate branding, the new epidemics, and the life of working-class communities are topics because they refer to things your readers are likely to have read about or observed in their personal experience.

Topics have names—whether those of individuals (Barack Obama, LeBron James), historical and political events (slavery, the Vietnam War), social and cultural trends (increase in two-career families, animal rights advocacy), or concepts (natural selection, Einstein's theory of relativity, the germ theory of disease). You can look up a topic and find information on it in the library. Your topic is the source of your commentary, the information whose significance you want to explore.

Background Research: Assessing Your Knowledge of the Topic

To write an effective commentary, writers often begin by assessing their knowledge of the topic they're writing about in order to make decisions about further research they might need to do. Here are some steps to help you assess your knowledge. State your topic in the form of a noun phrase (the Protestant Reformation, conversation patterns between men and women, global warming). Then, to identify what you already know and what you need to find out about the topic, respond to the following questions in writing:

1. What do you know about the topic? What is the source of your knowledge? List as many sources as you can. Which might it be helpful to reread?

2. What do you think other people know about the topic? Is it widely known, or is it likely to be of interest to a more limited readership?

3. Are there conflicting views or a range of opinions on the topic? If you're not aware of opposing views, consider whether they exist and how you could find them. If you do know, how would you describe the conflict or difference of opinion? Are there readily distinguishable sides involved? If so, do you tend to have allegiances to one side rather than the other? Explain how you align yourself to the topic and to what others have said about it.

4. Based on your answers to these questions, what further research might you do to explore your topic?

Identifying the Issue

An *issue* refers to how the writer focuses attention on what he or she thinks is important about the topic. This is where the function of commentary comes in. Commentators identify issues to explain some meaningful aspect of the topic according to their own perspective.

Let's say, for example, that you want to write a commentary about video games. There are a number of issues you could use to focus your commentary.

- What role do video games play in identity formation?
- How have video games changed over time?
- Do video games neglect the interests of girls and women?
- What is public opinion about video games?

To identify an issue is also to begin explaining what it holds at stake for you and others. Why should your readers be concerned and interested? Why is the issue being raised in the first place? If you're writing about an issue that has not received attention, why has the issue been ignored and why do you want to raise it?

■ EXERCISE

Finding an Issue

1. Locate three readings (from newspapers, magazines, journals, or books) on the topic you are planning to write about. List as many issues as you can. You don't have to agree with the sense of the issue or be interested in writing about it just yet. The point at this stage is to get as wide a picture as possible of available issues.

2. Circle the three or four issues that interest you most. Consider what, if anything, they have in common with one another. How do they differ? Does one bring to light something that the others don't? If you notice a connection between the issues you've circled, that connection may well be worth writing about in your commentary.

3. Decide tentatively on one issue to write about. What would you say about the issue in a commentary? How does this perspective align you with some people and positions? What common ground do you share?

4. Consider the positions of people who differ with you. What are the key points of difference? What objections might people have to your commentary? Are any valid? How can you use these in your commentary? What differences need to be addressed in your statement?

5. Think about the implications of your commentary. If people were persuaded by your position, what would happen? How would this be an improvement over the present condition of things? If your readers take your commentary seriously, what would you hope to achieve? Is there something you would like them to do?

Planning

Framing the Issue

Framing does two things. First, it focuses readers' attention by identifying significant features of a topic they are likely to already know something about. Framing the issue often begins with the familiar and then seeks to add a new or different angle or way of analyzing and explaining what is known.

Second, framing the issue sets up the writer to present the main point of his or her commentary. Depending on how the writer frames the issue, he or she will enter into one or another relationship to the topic and what other people have said about it.

Planning the Introduction

Commentary writers use various techniques in their introductions to name the topic and frame the issue. Here are a few:

- **Describe an event or an existing situation:** The point is to establish what is known in order to set yourself up to explain what new perspective you are going to bring to the issue. The amount of detail will depend on how familiar you think your readers will be with your topic.

- **Describe the sides of a controversy, conflict, or debate:** On issues where people differ, commentary writers often briefly sketch the opposing views to explain what they believe is at stake and to set up to their own perspective.

- **Explain the causes or origins of an issue:** Explaining the causes or origins of an issue can show readers how something came to have the importance it does, who's responsible for it, who it affects, how it's changed over time, and so forth.

- **Explain how you became aware of the issue:** Writers sometimes describe how reading, observation, or experience brought a particular issue to their attention—how something hit home for them.

- **Explain points and principles you have in common with readers:** Affirming shared values and attitudes early on in a commentary can gain consideration for your views and help set you up to introduce ideas that may diverge from the common thinking.
- **Use examples or personal anecdotes:** Beginning with an example or anecdote is a way to draw explicit connections to the larger issue by way of a specific and concrete illustration.

Planning the Ending

Endings apply the final frame to the writer's position. They give the writer the chance to have the last word, to leave readers with a closing sense of the issue and the writer's stand. Here are some ways writers design endings:

- **Point out the consequences of your position:** What would happen if your position were taken up? How would that improve the current situation?
- **Reaffirm shared values and beliefs:** What common values and beliefs does your commentary draw on? How does your position express these values and beliefs?
- **Make recommendations:** What would your commentary look like if it were carried through in practice? What concrete proposals does it lead to?
- **Call on readers to take action:** What steps can readers take, assuming they agree with you? What changes in thinking, personal habits, or public policy follow from your commentary?

Working Draft

Write a page or two as quickly as you can. Write as if you were warming up to write the "real" first draft. Begin by identifying the topic and the issue you're writing about. Explain your perspective on the issue, and quickly sketch an ending. Now you can use this writing as a discovery draft to clarify your own perspective on the issue you are writing about, to explore your own sympathies, and to understand on whose behalf you want to speak and with whom you differ. Use this draft to produce a working draft of your commentary.

Emphasizing Your Main Point and Distinguishing Your Perspective

Readers of commentary expect a writer to give them something to think about. They assume that the point of reading a commentary is not just—or even primarily—to be informed about an issue but to consider what the writer has to say about it. For this reason, it is important that the writer's main point be easy to find.

One way to make sure readers can readily see your perspective is to distinguish it from another perspective. This is a widely used technique in commentary, as we can see in Lundy Braun's "How to Fight the New Epidemics":

To be successful, disease-prevention policies must be based on more than technical solutions. They must be firmly rooted in an ecological perspective of disease.

It's easy enough to see in this passage where Braun is coming from, in part because she shows how her perspective differs from the germ theory as a way of managing disease.

Peer Commentary

Exchange working drafts and respond in writing to these questions about your partner's draft:

1. Identify the topic of the draft. How does the writer frame the main issue? Point to a phrase or sentence. Where did you become aware of the writer's perspective? If you can't identify particular phrases or sentences, explain what you think the writer's perspective is.

2. Who is likely to agree with the writer's commentary? What beliefs and values does the commentary appeal to? Does the commentary seem to choose sides? If so, who else is on the writer's side? Who is excluded?

3. Do you share the writer's perspective on the issue? If so, does the writer make the most effective case in presenting that perspective? Can you offer suggestions about ways to improve it? If you don't share the writer's perspective, explain why. Describe your own perspective.

Revising

Read the peer remarks on your working draft. Use them to take the following questions into account:

1. Does the introduction frame the issues and forecast the main point and the direction of your commentary?

2. Is the main point located at an effective place in the commentary? How much background or context is necessary for your main point to take on significance? When it does appear, is the main point stated as clearly as possible?

3. Are details, facts, and other information about the topic clearly related to your main point? If you use examples, is it clear what point or points they are intended to illustrate?

4. Do your explanations develop the main point of the commentary, or do they raise other issues? If they do, is this intended on your part, or are you starting to jump from issue to issue? Can you point out the connection between issues so that readers will be able to follow your line of thought?

5. Does the ending offer a satisfying sense of closure? Will readers find it easy to see how you arrived at your final point? Does the ending help to emphasize the main point or lesson of the commentary?

Maintaining a Reasonable Tone

Commentary offers writers the opportunity to stake out a position on issues they are passionate about. Commentators often want to make sense of things because they are invested and believe there is really something that matters. For this reason, commentators pay attention to the tone of their writing so that their readers, whether they share the writer's perspective or not, will at least take the commentary seriously as a reasonable effort to explain and analyze.

To see how a student worked on the tone of her commentary, go to the next section, Writers' Workshop. ■

W WRITERS' WORKSHOP

Below you will find the first draft of a commentary "Socially Acceptable Discrimination" that Rachel Smith wrote for her first-year writing course, the revised version of the essay, and an interview with the writer.

FIRST DRAFT

I am so sick of the way born-again Christians are portrayed in the media. What's wrong with people? Do they think all born-agains are narrow-minded, Bible-waving bigots?

Is the desire for sensationalism so strong that the media have to make every born-again a Bible-waving fanatic who chains herself to abortion-clinic doors and supports the madmen who shoot the doctors that perform abortions? It is so unfair to focus on the extremist fringe and ignore all the normal people who are born-again Christians.

This movie is only one example of the way that born-again Christians are portrayed in the media. America's most popular image of a born-again Christian is a narrow-minded, Bible-waving bigot who doesn't know how to have fun.

Now, don't get me wrong; I'm not saying that we don't sometimes wave our Bibles around. There are people who call themselves born-again Christians who find it absolutely imperative that they shove their beliefs down everyone's throat, "waving their Bible" all the while. They chain themselves to abortion-clinic doors and support the madmen who shoot the doctors that perform abortions.

In this draft, as a peer reviewer suggested to Rachel, her anger, though arguably justified, was getting in the way of her analysis of how born-again Christians are portrayed in the media. The peer reviewer thought Rachel was calling too much attention to her own feelings ("I am so sick" and "It is so unfair") and blaming others ("What's wrong with these people?") when she should have been explaining the issue and its significance. The peer reviewer also mentioned that the rhetorical questions at the end of the opening paragraph and beginning of the second made her feel that Rachel was trying to strong-arm her readers instead of persuading them. Notice in the revised version how Rachel turns the sequence of questions into analytical statements that explore the issue at hand instead of assuming agreement on the reader's part. Rachel also enhances the reasonable tone of the commentary by making the rhetorical question in the second paragraph into a concession on her part that it's true some born-agains are extremists.

REVISED VERSION

Smith 1

Rachel Smith
Writing 1
Prof. Thesen
1 October 2009

Socially Acceptable Discrimination?

I looked up at the billboard as we drove home from church one Sunday and saw the advertisement for the newest Steve Martin movie, *Leap of Faith*. Martin stood in the center of the board, arms raised above him, his suitcoat gaudy and sparkling. His face was tilted upwards. A slight smile on his lips, his eyes were squinted. His stance suggested religious worship. Lights shone down from behind him, and the words *Leap of Faith* were pasted on the board over his head. At first glance, the picture looked sincere; here was a man worshipping God. However, when I noticed the overdone clothes and the pious look on his face, I knew that this was not a picture of a man praising his God. This was an advertisement for a movie whose sole purpose was to make a "hilarious" comedy out of the life of a television evangelist. Later, when I saw the preview trailers for *Leap of Faith* on television, I saw Steve Martin pushing fat, sweating women to the floor in a cheap imitation of what sometimes happens at real evangelical tent meetings. He had this look of intense pleasure on his face, his body language wide and over-the-top, almost as if he was getting a sexual kick out of what he was doing. The character was described as being "a born-again, Spirit-filled, holy-rollin' Christian," and often spouted "Well, Peraaaise God!" This movie is only one example of the way that born-again Christians are portrayed in the media. America's most popular image of a born-again Christian is a narrow-minded, Bible-waving bigot who doesn't know how to have fun.

Now, don't get me wrong; I'm not saying that we don't sometimes wave our Bibles around. There are people who call themselves born-again Christians who find it absolutely imperative that they shove their beliefs down everyone's throat, "waving their Bible" all the while. They chain themselves to abortion-clinic doors and support the madmen who shoot the doctors that perform abortions. There are people in every group, whether it is feminists, African Americans, those of Middle Eastern descent, or teenagers, who are the "black sheep," so to speak, of the group. They are the radicals and therefore are sensational. They get the publicity and portray their group as being as radical and unbalanced as they are. Not all African Americans harbour deep, hateful grudges against whites. Actually, a large majority of them don't. Often, in movies, they are portrayed in the stereotype that they all hate whites, as in *Malcolm X*. This portrayal is the most sensational, and therefore the most newsworthy. Why hasn't anyone made a major, widely released movie about the life of Martin Luther King Jr.? Because he didn't have a checkered past, his life wasn't filled with violence and anger (on his part, at least), and he preached a message of forgiveness. Those things aren't sensational. They aren't as newsworthy as the radical, insane things that the media prefer to focus on.

Because of the media's attraction to the sensational, often groups are represented erroneously. What's sensational about the rest of the born-again Christians? They don't attack doctors and plant explosives in office buildings.

They don't all go around condemning everyone they meet to hell. They live just like everyone else. Granted, they don't frequent too many bars and brothels, they tend to spend more time in church than most Americans, and they live, very strictly, by the Bible. Because of this last point, many believe that Christians don't have any fun. That is one of the main reasons movies like *Leap of Faith* were made. The media say that underneath that "good" image, Christians are probably really warped human beings, following some long-dead cult that says the world will come to an end pretty soon, so all the rest of us had better join up or we'll be in lots of trouble. *Leap of Faith* just gives people a laugh and helps relieve them of the little suspicion that those crazy, born-again Christians just might have something. When a prominent televangelist is exposed, the media jump into the fray and triumphantly hold up the tattered pieces, flaunting the fall of someone supposed to be "good." This concentration on the negative side of Christianity lends itself to making the public see born-again Christians as completely unbalanced, non-rational, bigoted people. We are portrayed in only the worst ways.

My intent in writing on this subject is not to whine about injustice and the liberal media, but to bring out the other side of the issue. To put it plainly, every special interest group in America has gained a lot of publicity for fighting discrimination, except for the born-again Christians. Politically correct speech is the newest fad; everyone is careful about what they say. More movies are being released that center on the lives of homosexuals, there is a rise in the frequency of African American sitcoms, Greenpeace gets news coverage every time they try to sue a lumber company, and whenever there is a story on abortion, a majority of the personal interviews come from the pro-choice side. In all this "political correctness," born-again Christians are invariably left out by the media because the beliefs that we hold do not embrace all the personal preferences that people have. We live by a definite standard of right and wrong, and because people do not want to be told that something they are doing is wrong, they invent their own morality: situation ethics. Born-again

Smith 4

Christians do not fit into that jelly-mold of American society. When a movie like *Leap of Faith* came out, the only protests against such discrimination were in Christian magazines and books. We fight the currents, and yes, we do make people uncomfortable sometimes, but why is discrimination against us more culturally acceptable?

Interview with Rachel Smith

Q: *What prompted you to write "Socially Acceptable Discrimination"?*

A: I have felt for a long time that people unfairly judge born-again Christians like myself. If you go by the newspapers, born-agains are narrow-minded bigots, madmen who kill abortion doctors, or hypocrites like Jim Bakker. I know this isn't the real story, but it seemed that these stereotypes of born-agains are just something I had to live with—that I couldn't really do anything about it. Then I saw the Steve Martin movie, *Leap of Faith*, and I began to think that this might give me an occasion to try to correct perceptions.

Q: *How did you decide to focus on the particular issues you explore in "Socially Acceptable Discrimination"?*

A: I knew I wanted to change the way people perceive born-again Christians but I also knew I couldn't just say, "Hey, you've got it all wrong. That's not the way we really are." I'd be asking people to accept my personal experience, and I was pretty sure this wasn't going to work. So I thought that if I focused on how the media portrayed born-again Christians, and tied this to the idea that the media love to sensationalize things, I might get a different response from readers. I figured most people think the media are sensationalistic and that by using this as a kind of common ground with readers, I could introduce my own point of view in a way that might get a hearing.

Q: *What conflicts, if any, did you experience writing this commentary?*

A: It's hard because movies like *Leap of Faith* and all the media coverage of crazed evangelicals really gets me angry. I know it's a false picture and totally unfair to me and other born-agains, who are just normal people who happen to believe in God and want to follow the Bible. I wanted to make this point, but I also knew that if I let my anger come out too strongly, I was going to lose readers—or maybe even confirm their impression that we're all nuts. So I definitely experienced this conflict of wanting to be loyal to other believers and to get their real story out and, at the same time, knowing that I had to write in a reasonable tone. That's where the Steve Martin movie and the idea of media sensationalism were so helpful to me. By analyzing them (instead of screaming at people, which is what I felt like doing), I think I got some critical distance and could still be true to what I wanted to say.

■ WORKSHOP QUESTIONS

1. As Rachel Smith notes in the interview, her main purpose is to "correct perceptions" of born-again Christians. What was your attitude toward born-again Christians before you read "Socially Acceptable Discrimination"? Did reading her commentary confirm, modify, change, or otherwise affect the attitude you began with? Given your experience reading the essay, what suggestions would you offer Smith to help achieve her purpose?

2. Smith says that she realized she couldn't persuade people solely on the basis of her personal experience as a born-again Christian. Instead, she focuses on how the media portray born-agains. Evaluate this strategy. To what extent does it offer the common ground with readers that she hopes to find? Are there ways she could strengthen this appeal?

3. Smith notes a conflict between her loyalty to other believers and her desire to reach out to her readers. One way this conflict manifests itself is in the tension between the anger she feels about being portrayed unfairly and the need she acknowledges to maintain a reasonable tone in her writing. How well do you think she handles this tension? What suggestion would you offer about how to manage this conflict?   ■

REFLECTING ON YOUR WRITING

Use the following questions from the interview with Rachel Smith to interview someone who has recently written a commentary. It could be a classmate, but also consider interviewing columnists of your student or local newspaper.

1. What prompted you to write the commentary?

2. How did you decide to establish the focus of the piece?

3. What conflicts, if any, did you experience when you wrote it?

Compare the writer's experience writing the commentary with your own.

chapter 10

proposals

THINKING ABOUT THE GENRE

Proposals put forth plans of action and seek to persuade readers that those plans should be implemented. Like commentary, proposals involve analyzing issues, taking a position, and making an argument. However, proposals go beyond commentaries by defining problems that need attention and proposing a solution.

This difference between commentaries and proposals is not an absolute one but a matter of emphasis. After all, the positions writers take in commentaries have consequences. Whether writers of commentaries make it explicit or not, their positions imply certain policies, courses of action, and ways of living. But proposals emphasize this dimension. The focus of attention shifts from the statement and explanation of the writer's position to what we ought to do about it.

Let's look at a situation that might call for a proposal. A local community group thinks that a vacant lot the city owns could be converted into a neighborhood park. The group knows there's strong support for local parks among city residents and municipal officials. But it also knows that the city's resources are limited, so any proposal involving spending would need ample justification—to show that the proposed park would solve a problem of some urgency. So the group might show that, compared to other areas of the city, the neighborhood lacks recreational facilities. Or, if the lot has given rise to other problems—for example, as a site for drug dealing—the group might argue that a park could simultaneously solve that problem.

In its proposal, the group would need to show that the proposed solution will have the intended effects. If the group claims drug dealing is part of the problem, then its proposal needs to explain exactly how turning the lot into a park can get rid of the dealers. But this isn't enough. The group would also need to show that the solution deals with the problem in the best, most appropriate way, given the alternatives available and the needs and values of the people affected (perhaps drug dealing could be dealt with more cheaply and effectively through increased police surveillance; perhaps the lot is too small

314

to serve all age groups, and the neighborhood and city would be better off expanding a park in an adjoining neighborhood). A proposal that is both capable
of solving the problem and suitable for doing so is said to be *feasible*. To have
a chance of being implemented, a proposal needs to establish that it passes
the *feasibility test*—that its solution will have the intended effects and that it
fits the situation.

Proposals typically require research. The community group proposing the
park could strengthen its case by showing that the proposed park fits the
needs of the neighborhood, given the age and interests of its residents. This
information could be obtained by surveying households, as could specifics
about the kinds of recreational facilities to include in the park.

Proposals need to convince readers—to fund a project, to implement a solution, to change a policy. Proposals are a form of persuasive writing, and clear
statements of problems and solutions, demonstrations of feasibility, documentation through research, and careful organization can all help make a proposal
persuasive to readers.

■ WRITING FROM EXPERIENCE

In our daily lives, we are constantly making proposals. Analyze one such proposal by
describing an instance in which you encountered a situation, defined it as a problem,
and proposed a solution. Explain the steps you followed to define the problem, consider
alternatives, anticipate objections, and formulate a feasible solution—even though you
probably did not experience the problem solving you engaged in as a series of steps.
Looking back on this experience, what made your solution successful or unsuccessful?
Were there any unforeseen consequences?

READINGS

WORKERS WITHOUT BORDERS

JENNIFER GORDON

*Jennifer Gordon is professor of labor and immigration law at Fordham Law
School. This proposal appeared in the* New York Times *on March 10, 2009.*

*States
problem*

AMERICANS are hardly in the mood to welcome new immigrants. The last thing we
need, the reasoning goes, is more competition for increasingly scarce jobs. But the
need for immigration reform is more urgent than ever. The current system hurts wages and
working conditions—for everyone.

Today, millions of undocumented immigrants accept whatever wage is offered. They
don't protest out of fear of being fired or deported. A few hundred thousand guest workers,

brought in for seasonal and agricultural jobs, know that asserting their rights could result in a swift flight home. This system traps migrants in bad jobs and ends up lowering wages all around.

Presents solution

The solution lies in greater mobility for migrants and a new emphasis on workers' rights. If migrants could move between jobs, they would be free to expose abusive employers. They would flow to regions with a shortage of workers, and would also be able to return to their home countries when the outlook there brightened, or if jobs dried up here.

Imagine if the United States began admitting migrants on the condition that they join a network of workers' organizations here and in their home countries—a sort of transnational union. Migrants could work here legally. They could take jobs anywhere in the country and stay as long as they liked. But they would have to promise to report employers that violated labor laws. They could lose their visas by breaking that promise.

This plan, which I call Transnational Labor Citizenship, would give employers access to many more workers on fair terms. It would give people from countries like Mexico greater opportunities to earn the remittances upon which their families and economies rely. It would address the inconsistency and inhumanity of policies that support free trade in goods and jobs but bar the free movement of people.

Describes implementation

How could we make this happen? Congress could certainly mandate the change. If that seems unlikely, we could start with a bilateral labor migration agreement with a country like Mexico, making membership in a transnational workers' organization and a commitment to uphold workplace laws a requirement for Mexicans to obtain work here.

We might try a smaller pilot project involving a single union in an industry like residential construction or agriculture. One model would be the Farm Labor Organizing Committee's guest worker union, which protects migrant agricultural workers on some North Carolina farms. The union provides representation and benefits wherever the workers are. It has organizers near North Carolina's tobacco and cucumber fields, and an office in Mexico, where the laborers return home for the winter.

Examines a precedent

Migrant mobility has been tried with success in the European Union. When the Union expanded in 2004 to include eight Eastern European countries, workers in Western Europe feared a flood of job seekers who would drive down wages. In Britain, for example, the volume of newcomers from countries like Poland was staggering. Instead of the prediction of roughly 50,000 migrants in four years, more than a million arrived.

Yet, as far as economists can tell, the influx did not take a serious toll on native workers' wages or employment. (Of course, what happens in the global downturn remains to be seen.) Migrants who were not trapped in exploitative jobs flocked to areas that needed workers and shunned the intense competition of big cities. And when job opportunities grew in Poland or shrank in Britain, fully half went home again.

Concedes a problem

To be sure, Europe's approach has its problems. Some migrants were cheated on their wages and worked in unsafe conditions. This illustrates that mobility alone is not enough. We also need good workplace protections, and effective support to realize them.

Refines proposal

Unions could play a key role in rights enforcement if they embraced migrants as potential members, becoming for the first time truly transnational institutions. And government could partner with workers' organizations. Recently, the New York Department of Labor announced that it had begun to work with immigrant centers and unions to catch violators. This is a promising example of a new alliance to protect the rights of both immigrants and native-born workers.

Describes what will happen without change

Like it or not, until we address the vast inequalities across the globe, those who want to migrate will find a way. Despite stepped-up enforcement at the borders, hundreds of thousands of immigrants still come illegally to the United States every year. Raids terrorize immigrants but do not make them go home. Instead, rigid quotas, harsh immigration laws and heavy-handed enforcement lock people in. As the recession deepens, undocumented immigrants will hunker down more. They may work less, for worse pay, but they will be terrified to go home out of fear they can never return.

Reiterates solution

The United States needs an open and fair system, not a holding pen. The best way forward is to create an immigration system with protection for all workers at its core.

Analysis: Developing a Solution

Jennifer Gordon's proposal for a transnational organization of workers without borders starts with a problem that many Americans will recognize immediately—namely that undocumented workers are providing the labor for employers in United States in agriculture, construction, gardening, hotels, restaurants, meatpacking, manufacturing, and other industries. She doesn't spend much time laying out the problem, aside from noting that it "traps migrants in bad jobs and ends up lowering wages all around." Her focus rather is on the solution and how to implement it. To make her case for migrant mobility, she cites the experience of the European Union. This is meant to be reassuring in that the influx of migrant workers did not lower native workers' wages or limit their employment. But in a key rhetorical move, she also concedes problems, in that some workers "were cheated on their wages and worked in unsafe conditions." Notice how this sets her up to make a refinement in her proposal by saying that workplace protection, as well as mobility, is a crucial part of her proposal.

■ FOR CRITICAL INQUIRY

1. Anyone making a proposal has to consider the ratio between defining the problem (and its urgency for action) and the proposed solution. Consider how Jennifer Gordon does this. What does she assume about her readers in doing so?

2. Identify the reasons Gordon offers for her proposal. What unstated enabling assumptions is she making?

3. What objections might one make to Gordon's proposal? How do you think she would respond?

Visualizing the Debate about Undocumented Immigrants

Jennifer Gordon's proposal for Transnational Labor Citizenship enters into an ongoing policy debate about undocumented immigrants in the United States. Here are two visual representations from differing sides. The first is the cover of a report, *The Costs of Illegal Immigration to Virginians,* from the Federation for American Immigration Reform (FAIR), a nonprofit advocacy group that seeks to halt undocumented immigration by enhancing border control and to limit the number of legal immigrants. The second is a graphic from the National Immigrant Solidarity Network, a coalition of community, labor, religious, and civic organizations that seeks to stop raids by Immigration and Customs Enforcement, end deportations, and support immigrant workers' rights. Their solutions to the problem of undocumented immigrants could not be more different—and so are the visual styles of their publicity. Consider how the visual styles fit with the proposals they are making in the debate about undocumented immigrants.

Courtesy of Fairus.org

Federation of American Immigration Reform

National Immigrant Solidarity Network/www.immigrantsolidarity.org

National Immigrant Solidarity Network

PROPOSAL FROM A COMMUNITY ORGANIZATION

Proposals by neighborhood associations and community organizations are familiar means of participating in public policy by making known the needs and interests of ordinary people. Often such proposals, as in the case here, involve allocation of resources—for a child care center, an after-school youth program, a literacy program for recent immigrants, or a street tree program. As you can see, the following proposal uses four main headings—Problem, Solution, Benefits, and Conclusion—to make visible its underlying argument.

THE BE GREEN NEIGHBORHOOD ASSOCIATION
"Creating a Sustainable, Healthy Community For All"

Proposal for a Neighborhood Street Tree Program

1   The Be Green Neighborhood Association proposes a street tree program to enhance the environmental, aesthetic, and social aspects of our community.

Problem

2   Our neighborhood suffers from a lack of green space. Environmentally, large areas of concrete and pavement exacerbate already high temperatures in summer months. A lack of trees and shaded spaces on our streets means higher pollution levels, higher home cooling costs, and greater strain on electric utility already over-taxed in the summer. Aesthetically, long stretches of road, concrete sidewalks, paved driveways and parking lots create an eyesore and depress property values.

Solution

3   Neighborhood associations in cities such as Berkeley, Chicago, Sacramento, Seattle, Charlotte, Los Angeles, and Providence have implemented street tree programs to address, at the local level, the effects of climate change, pressures on city electricity grids, and high pollution levels as well as to beautify their neighborhoods. The US Forest Service estimates "for a planting cost of $250–6000 one street tree returns over $90,000 of direct benefits in the lifetime of the tree" (Burden). In addition, street trees can be planted in all climates.

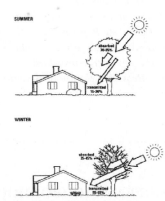

Figure 1   Street trees cool in
summer and heat in winter.

4   The Be Green Neighborhood Association proposes the creation of a tree-planting
program in our community. The city's already-existing Urban Forest will provide
the trees to the neighborhood association free of charge, and the citizens of our
association agree to be involved in the planting of the trees and to water and
maintain them (weeding and mulching). The president of the neighborhood
association will submit a request, in writing, for each tree to the director of the
Urban Forest by November 1 of each year. If the request is approved, street trees
will be delivered and planted on a Saturday in the spring of the following year.

5   Street trees in our community will be planted 4 to 8 feet from the curb so as not
to obscure traffic lights, signposts, streetlamps, or driveways. We will adopt trees
of an uneven age distribution, as a combination of young and mature trees is
essential for a successful street tree program. Where possible, we will promote
species diversity, which is also important for the long-term health of the trees.

Benefits

6   The planning, planting, and maintenance of street trees promote environmental,
social, and financial wellbeing of communities.

Environmental

7   Trees catch air pollution particles on their leaves and help remove pollutants
such as nitrogen oxides, sulphur, ammonia, and dust particles (Benefits of
Trees). Street trees also absorb and store carbon, the main ingredient of smog,
removing it from the atmosphere. The US Forest Service explains that "trees in

Center for Environmental Studies at Brown University

Figure 2   Street trees provide environmental, social, financial, and aesthetic benefits.

street proximity absorb 9 times more pollutants than more distant trees, converting harmful gasses back into oxygen and other useful and natural gasses" (Burden). According to the Street Tree program in Los Angeles, one tree can produce enough oxygen for a family of four in one year (Bureau of Street Services). Street trees also absorb storm water, which decreases runoff and soil erosion. Street trees lower indoor air temperatures by shading houses and residential buildings. One urban forest program estimates that energy savings can be up to 25% per year. In addition, street trees block UV rays harmful to the eyes and skin, and provide protection from rain and sun that extends pavement life (City of St. Louis).

Social

8 Studies have shown that people drive at lower and more reasonable speeds because "urban street trees create vertical walls framing streets and a defined edge, helping motorists guide their movement and assess their speed." Street trees also make walking areas safer "by forming and framing visual walls and providing distinct edges to sidewalks so that motorists better distinguish between their environment and one shared with people" (Burden). Street trees can reduce noise pollution, which reduces stress, lowers blood pressure, dissipates road rage, and provides a connection to the natural world.

Financial and Aesthetic

9   Studies show that businesses surrounded by street trees bring in 20% more revenue than businesses in areas without street trees (Burden). Street trees increase residential property values by up to 20% (Bureau of Street Services). Aesthetically, street trees beautify streets and parking and walking areas.

Conclusion

10   The Be Green Neighborhood Association believes that a street tree program in our community would greatly improve life in an environmentally sustainable manner. In partnership with the city's Urban Forest department, we can plant and maintain a number of trees that will add important environmental, social, aesthetic, and financial value to our neighborhood for a modest start-up cost.

Works Cited

Benefits of Trees. www.streettree.org/BenefitsofTrees/tabid/258/Default.aspx.

Burden, Dan. "22 Benefits of Urban Street Trees."
    http://www.ufei.org/files/pubs/22BenefitsofUrbanStreetTrees.pdf.

Bureau of Street Services, Street Tree Division, City of LA.
    http://www.cityofla.org/BOSS/streettree/UrbanForest.htm

City of St. Louis.
    http://stlouis.missouri.org/citygov/parks/forestry_div/TreeProgram.pdf.

Analysis: Making Purposes Visible

Some proposals take the form of an essay, as is the case with the pieces of writing in this chapter by Ross Gelbspan and Leon Botstein, which appeared originally on op-ed pages in newspapers. In other cases, however, such as Lucia Trimbur's fieldwork proposal or proposals like this one from the Be Green Neighborhood Association, proposal writers rely on conventions of visual design to make the purposes of their proposal visible to readers. The Be Green Neighborhood Association uses a familiar pattern of organizing proposals:

¶1: Introduction: goal of the proposal

¶2: Problem

¶3–5: Solution

¶6–9: Benefits

- Environmental
- Social
- Financial and aesthetic

¶10: Conclusion

The Proposal for a Neighborhood Street Tree Program is meant to be read as a plan of action that responds to a felt need. By identifying the structure of its argument through familiar headings and subheadings, the proposal enables readers to easily follow its line of reasoning.

■ FOR CRITICAL INQUIRY

1. Notice how the four main sections of the "Proposal for a Neighborhood Street Tree Program" display the steps in the proposal's reasoning. Consider what each section contributes to the development of the argument to start a street tree program. What is the persuasive effect of the order in which the sections appear?

2. In terms of the proportion of space devoted to it, the section "Problem" is by far the shortest in the proposal. Consider the neighborhood association's rhetorical decision to keep this section brief. What is the overall effect of emphasizing the "Solution" and "Benefit" sections? What assumptions do the proposal writers seem to be making about their intended audiences and those audiences' need to know? Take into account here the various audiences who might read this proposal and their various perspectives that make them stakeholders in the proposed program.

3. Notice how the proposal writers draw on authorities, including two municipalities and the U.S. Forestry Service, to make their case for a street tree program. What gives these authorities their persuasive force in this proposal? What, in turn, does this reveal about the beliefs of readers in the reliability of sources?

A RESEARCH PROPOSAL

Lucia Trimbur was a graduate student in sociology and African American studies at Yale when she wrote this proposal for funding for a fieldwork project.

Training Fighters, Making Men: A Study of Amateur Boxers
and Their Trainers at Gleason's Gym

Lucia Trimbur

Background

Significant research has been devoted to the sport of boxing, the majority of which has concerned itself with the economic achievements and careers of professional fighters (Dudley, 2002; Wacquant, 1998, 1995a, 1995b, 1992; Early, 1996; Sugden, 1987; Gorn, 1987; Evans, 1985; Hare, 1971;

Weinberg & Arond, 1957). Yet the sport of boxing is pursued not only by professional pugilists but also by amateur and recreational boxers, for whom economic success and fame are not necessarily the primary motivation. Rather, for a substantial number of athletes, boxing affords a set of possibilities that may not be available elsewhere. In a time of deindustrialization, changing social circumstances, and transformation of urban space (Davis, 1999), pugilism may enable the formation of identity accessible in few other social spaces. With declining employment opportunities, especially for inner-city men of color, the workplace is not always available as a site for young men to construct masculine selves. Thus, the boxing gym may offer one of the last social realms for the construction of identity, the expression of masculinity, and the negotiation of violence and aggression.

Objectives

Mention the terms "manly art" and "sweet science of bruising," or merely the word boxing, and gender is implicit. Yet in order to understand the forms of masculinity implicit in the sport, gender must be analyzed explicitly. The research I propose examines the formation of identity in a boxing gym to understand how competitive amateur fighters use the culture of training and bodily discipline to create forms of masculinity. Michel Foucault suggests that discipline is a form of power that takes the body as its object; in institutions such as prisons, schools, the military, and, as I would contend, the gym, bodies are manipulated, trained, and thus transformed (Foucault, 1977). I would like to understand how the discipline demanded in the gym facilitates the production and transformation of masculinities and attendant forms of incorporated identity[1] (Connerton, 1989).

---

[1]In his work *How Societies Remember,* Paul Connerton makes the distinction between "assigned" and "incorporated" identities. Whereas assigned identities are largely non-negotiable, incorporated identities, such as forms of masculinity, are those individuals seek to produce or attempt to transform (Connerton, 1989).

Understanding the formation of identity requires apprehending the social relations cultivated in the boxing gym. For this reason, my research examines the relationships developed between trainers and their boxers. Coaches and fighters characterize their relationships as those of life mentoring and deep social trust rather than as merely athletic. As coaches consider it their responsibility to provide both athletic and life guidance, I would like to understand the experiences that inform and shape the advice they impart and how they disseminate such information. Many trainers have, in their pasts, participated in criminal activity, been incarcerated, and engaged in a process of rehabilitation. I would like to discern how trainers simultaneously coach their athletes and discourage them from partaking in similar criminal activity. Thus my project seeks to examine the effect trainer-knowledge has on their athletes in relation to crime and life choices.

Finally, I want to understand the connections between the identities constructed in the gym and those produced in other social institutions, such as the workplace, family, and prison. For instance, many amateur athletes have been incarcerated, and the gym is frequently sought out by boxers recently released from prison, a phenomenon that might suggest boxing offers a way to re-enter society after prison. I would like to analyze the practices and techniques of training and discipline that allow athletes to regroup after the trauma of prison life.

Focusing on trainers and amateur athletes, my specific research questions are: (1) what identities are created and performed in the boxing gym? What are the practices and techniques of the sport's training and regimen that facilitate this identity formation? (2) how is violence managed in the gym? For example, violence is inherent to the sport yet its management is crucial; what are the practices that control violence? How does this management relate to identity? And what does engaging in boxing enable and/or preclude that other sports may not? and (3) how do trainers influence life choices? How do trainers train their boxers in extra-athletic ways?

Research Plan and Methodological Approaches

My research will be conducted at Gleason's Gym in New York City. I have chosen this gym because, founded in the lower Bronx in 1937, it is the oldest and one of the most famous gyms in the United States. Pugilists such as Jake LaMotta, Mike Belloise, Jimmy Carter, and Muhammad Ali, trained at Gleason's Gym, cultivating the gym's reputation as a producer of highly-ranked contenders and unbeatable world champions. Today the gym, which relocated to Brooklyn in 1984, boasts 78 trainers, who work with 850 athletes. Because of its reputation, Gleason's draws some of the most talented amateur and professional boxers in the world, all of whom have a deep investment in their participation in the sport. This investment amplifies the intensity of the gym and creates a rigorous sporting climate.

To examine the process by which identity is constructed and social relations between trainers and their athletes forged, I will employ two methods: participant observation and interviewing. Participant observation will allow me to document the patterns of social interaction in Gleason's Gym and to examine the multiple ways identity is formed and trainer guidance delivered (Emerson, Fretz, & Shaw, 1995). Interviewing will allow me to investigate the dynamics of the relationships among boxing, identity formation, masculine selfhood, and life choices.

Participant Observation

Over the course of one year, I will follow a group of 25–30 amateur athletes, who train for the Golden Gloves of New York City, the most prestigious annual amateur event in boxing, and their trainers. I will recruit my sample based upon 5 trainers with whom I have established a close working relationship and who have agreed to collaborate with me. I plan to observe these athletes and their mentors beginning in September 2003, when training typically commences, and through the course of the tournament, which runs January through May. I also plan to observe the group after the tournament has finished—over the summer months—to study how the fighters use the gym and interact with their trainers when competition is not imminent. Over this year, I will examine the mundane daily activities and regimens of boxers and their trainers in the gym five days a week. I will also accompany them to the tournament in order to observe their extraordinary experiences of competition, talking with them before and after the fights. As they prepare for the Golden Gloves, I plan to analyze the social relations between the amateurs and their trainers, examining how homosocial bonding develops and shapes the process of training. I plan to study how the athlete-coach relationship emerges and influences the decisions boxers make about labor, leisure, and crime.

Interviewing

In addition to participant observation, I will also conduct 25–30 extensive, open-ended interviews with the amateur boxers and their trainers. One goal of the interviews is to identify the range of recurring themes associated with identity, mentoring, violence, and life choices. These interviews will focus on the meanings that informants attach to their participation in the sport, the range of experiences they have had with boxing, and the alternatives boxing may offer to street crime. In structuring and conducting these interviews, I am particularly interested in fighters' own expectations of training and competition: why they became involved and how they assess their progress. Of crucial importance is how they conceptualize violence and corporeal harm in the sport and how they envision their participation in this dynamic of physical conflict. I will also examine the connections between their activities in the gym and other aspects of their lives, such as labor, leisure, education, and family.

Based upon these open-ended interviews, I will then re-interview the group of boxers and trainers with a structured battery of questions about the factors involved in their senses of identity, their connection with boxing and with the mentor-mentee relationship. I will standardize my list of questions in order to facilitate a comparison of my respondents' answers. Together, these methods will enable an understanding of how identity and masculinity are formed, contested, or perhaps exposed as unstable. They will also provide an elucidation of how trainers intervene, inform and shape this process.

References

Connerton, P. (1989). *How societies remember*. New York: Cambridge University Press.

Davis, A., & Gordon, A. (1999). Globalization and the prison industrial complex: An interview with Angela Davis. *Race and Class, 2–3,* 145–157.

Dudley, J. (2002). Inside and outside the ring: Manhood, race, and art in the literary imagination. *College Literature, 29,* 53–82.

Early, G. (1996). Mike's brilliant career. *Transition, 71,* 46–59.

Emerson, R. M., Fretz, R. I., & Shaw, L. L. (1995). *Writing Ethnographic Fieldnotes*. Chicago: University of Chicago Press.

Evans, A. (1995). Joe Louis as key functionary: White reactions toward a black champion. *Journal of Black Studies, 16,* 95–111.

Foucault, M. (1977). *Discipline and punish: The birth of the prison*. New York: Pantheon Books.

Gorn, E. (1987). *The manly art: Bare-knuckle prizefighting in America*. Ithaca, NY: Cornell University Press.

Hare, N. (1971). A study of the black fighter. *Black Scholar, 3,* 2–8. *Slavery to Freedom*. New York: Oxford University Press.

Sugden, J. (1987). The exploitation of disadvantage: The occupational sub-culture of the boxer. *Sociological Review Monograph, 33,* 187–209.

Wacquant, L. (1992). The social logic of boxing in black Chicago: Toward a sociology of pugilism. *Sociology of Sport Journal 9,* 221–254.

Wacquant, L. (1995a). The pugilist point of view: How boxers think and feel about their trade. *Theory and Society, 24,* 489–535.

Wacquant, L. (1995b). Pugs at work: Bodily capital and bodily labour among professional boxers. *Body and Society, 1,* 63–93.

Wacquant, L. (1998). A fleshpeddler at work: Power, pain, and profit in the prizefighting economy. *Theory and Society, 27,* 1–42.

Weinberg, S. K., & Arond, H. (1952). The occupational culture of the boxer. *American Journal of Sociology, 57,* 460–469.

Analysis: Research Proposals

Research proposals are similar in many respects to other types of proposals, whether to change a policy or improve a service. The same task of defining a problem and then proposing a satisfactory solution is common to all. What distinguishes a research proposal is that the problem is one of understanding something—the structure of DNA, the effects of asbestos on the health of South African miners, or the legacy of slavery in the United States—and the solution is to design a workable research plan to investigate the subject and produce new insights. Most research proposals seek to persuade the reader about the merit of the research and the researcher's ability to carry it out. In the case of these two fieldwork proposals, the goal is that the graduate students will secure funding to carry out their research.

The research question or questions in a proposal are crucial. As you can see in these two proposals, the research plan follows from the questions the two graduate students want to answer. Explaining the central research questions accomplishes two things in the proposal. First, it tells readers why the research is meaningful. Second, it enables them to judge whether the proposed plan of action is in fact well-suited to answer the questions.

■ FOR CRITICAL INQUIRY

1. Consider the first two sections of "Training Fighters, Making Men." How does the Background section identify a neglected area of study? How does the Objectives section raise specific questions about amateur boxers?

2. Evaluate the match between the research questions and the research plan in the proposal. Does the research plan seem capable of providing answers to the questions each of the fieldwork proposals raises? Why or why not?

3. What do you see as the strengths and weaknesses of each of the fieldwork proposals? Would you approve them? What suggestions would you offer to modify or refine the proposed research?

BEWARE THE MANIPULATION OF THE FUNK

TRICIA ROSE

Tricia Rose is professor of Africana Studies at Brown University and the author of Black Noise *(1994), one of the earliest studies of hip-hop, and* Longing to Tell: Black Women Talk about Sexuality and Intimacy *(2003). This reading comes from her recent book* The Hip Hop Wars *(2008).*

On countless occasions over the past decade or so, I have found myself listening, driving, or dancing to a song, yet only later really heard the lyrics. One such song was Dr. Dre and Snoop Dogg's 1992 classic and unbelievably funky "Gin and Juice"; another was 50 Cent's 2003 hit, "In da Club." In some cases I was unaware of the words because I couldn't actually make out the lyrics or translate the slang; but then there were the times I heard the "clean version" and then got depressed when I learned what the artist really wanted to say. At still other times, I was mostly listening to the music or merely letting the music, the style, and the swagger move me so completely that only the most oft-repeated phrases really sunk in. Once I really listened to the words and thought about the story being told, it was hard to know what to do: Respond to the funk and ignore the words, or reject the story and give up the funk that goes with it. The moment I realized that I was being asked to give myself over to the power of the funk—which in turn was being used as a soundtrack for a story that was really against me—was very sad for me. I thought my feelings must be very much like those of *Washington Post* writer Lonnae O'Neal Parker when she reached a turning point with this music, saying that she could no longer sacrifice her self-esteem or that of her two daughters on the "alter of dope beats and rhymes."

Some people swear that they can "ignore" the words and just enjoy the music. No matter what gets said, they are not affected; the words don't matter. I've asked my students if there was any limit at all for them—any lyric that would upset or anger them enough to make them reject the song outright. The hip hop fans among my students would bravely say "No, the words don't matter" to show that they would always be down with hip hop. So, then I'd ask them if a pro–Ku Klux Klan performer came up with an incredible, infectious, undeniable beat and rhyme, but the words celebrated the domination of black people, would they just "block out the words" and still claim that "the words don't matter"? Of course, few would still say "yes." My point in drawing this volatile analogy is not to imply that hip hop lyrics are in any way comparable to white supremacist rhetoric. But I want to point out that we all have a line to draw. It's not a "free for all," "anything goes as long as it's funky" situation but, rather, a matter of recognizing that before we reach our limit, we are saying "yes" to what we shake our hips to. My analogy also reveals that once we have pledged allegiance to something, we will submit to excesses and a negative influence that, if expressed by others, would be grounds for self-defense.

Were this about one bitty song that uses the word "bitch," or only one or two rhymes that use violence, metaphorically or otherwise, to settle "beef"; or if only an occasional song relied on insults such as calling neighborhood enemies "bitch ass niggas," well, maybe we wouldn't need to raise our defenses so high. But unfortunately, this kind of spirit has become too common in commercial hip hop. Yes, we can ignore some lyrics on occasion; but when the music that gets played over and over at the clubs and on hip hop-oriented commercial radio, BET, and MTV is saturated with hustlers, gangstas, bitches, hoes, tricks, pimps, playas, and the stories that glamorize domination, exploitation, violence, and hustlers—when this becomes the primary vocabulary for hip hop itself—then the power of the funk has been manipulated. The life force of the funk has been wedded to a death imperative.

Black music has played an extraordinary role in the history of black people and in the world. It has helped black people to protect, nourish, and empower themselves, and to resist forces operating against their freedoms. This music has not always been explicitly political or dubbed as "protest music." Indeed, its political significance has gone far beyond the confines of a direct protest standard, registering in the positive spirit of sounds tied to stories that exhibit a fundamental love of black people.

There is no doubt that this tradition lives today. But it *is* under duress, and we need to pay attention, to be aware of the manipulation of the funk. It is being pressed into a spirit-crushing repetition of unreflective, instant gratification. As Cornel West said during BET's October 2007 *Hip Hop vs. America* forum: "Dominant forms of hip hop are about what? A repetition of the present; over and over again—the next orgasm, the next pleasure; no history, no future. No different future can emerge in a present that's just repeating itself over and over again without a difference." It is not just about saying "no" to manipulative uses of the funk; it is about saying "yes" to music that doesn't force us to block out the words as a form of self-protection. For those who don't melt at the power of an amazing rhythm, drum, or bass line, this may be hard to understand. The funk is the Achilles' heel for lovers of black music. The love of a great funky beat is like kryptonite for Superman. Our places of weakness make us vulnerable but also open us up to our greatest places of connection. This is why the music must be revered, not discarded. But, like any other powerful and compelling force, beats can be distorted, used as a baseline for stories that undermine the spirit. Music comes from but also makes community, so the question becomes: What kind of community do we want to make?

Analysis: Proposal as Awareness

"Beware the Manipulation of the Funk" is one of "Six Guiding Principles for Progressive Creativity, Consumption, and Community in Hip Hop and Beyond," the final chapter of *The Hip Hop Wars,* an analysis of claims by critics and defenders of the current state of commercial hip-hop and its "keep it real" marketing of gangstas, pimps, and hos to a predominantly white audience. In the final chapter's call for a revitalization of hip-hop's "conscious" mission, Rose shows how proposals aren't limited to programs and policies but can include the way we understand contemporary culture and how we position ourselves in its controversies. Here Rose poses the problem of how to deal with the undeniable funkiness of the beats and rhymes in songs whose lyrics glorify sexism and violence.

■ FOR CRITICAL INQUIRY

1. In the opening paragraph, Tricia Rose poses the problem in terms of her own experience listening to hip-hop. What exactly is the problem she's bringing to light? How does drawing on her own experience add to the credibility of the problem statement?

2. Paragraphs 2 focuses on how hip-hop fans have attempted to deal with the problem by evading or denying it. Consider how this deepens our understanding of the reality of the problem.

3. What are the implications of Rose's assertion that the "life force of the funk has been wedded to a death imperative"?

4. What solution is Rose proposing? Where does it appear? What reasons does she give in support of the solution?

ETHICS OF WRITING

PROBLEMS AND CONFLICTS

Understanding the situations that confront us in everyday life and in public affairs as problems that can be solved is a powerful way of making reality more manageable. Once you have defined a problem, it then becomes possible to think in terms of a solution.

However, problems take shape according to the way people define them. Depending on how the problem is defined, particular solutions seem more—or less—logical than others. Yet, underlying many definitions of problems are real conflicts about values and beliefs. And genuine differences in beliefs lead to very different statements of the problem and thus to different proposed solutions.

Formulating a problem invariably means taking a position in relation to what others think and believe—aligning yourself with particular values and beliefs and distancing yourself from others. If you assume that you can simply define a problem objectively, you might well wind up ignoring the underlying conflicts in the situation and interpretations and in the needs of others. Such ethical issues arise with other genres, but they become especially important with proposals because proposals are focused on action and in many cases influence decisions about the use of limited resources. ■

▪ FURTHER EXPLORATION: PROPOSALS

▪ RHETORICAL ANALYSIS

Analyze the argument in one (or more) of the proposals in this chapter. Pay particular attention to the enabling assumptions that connect the claim (the writer's proposal) and the evidence. Consider how the shape of the writer's argument is likely to influence readers' evaluations of whether the proposal is feasible or not.

▪ GENRE AWARENESS

Think of a current problem—campuswide, local, national, or international. Imagine a feasible solution to the problem. You could write a formal proposal to solve the problem, as the students who proposed a campus coffeehouse did—see the Writers' Workshop section, later in this chapter. Let's assume you're really serious about getting your proposal implemented. What other genres of writing might you use to publicize your proposal?

WRITING ASSIGNMENT

For this assignment, write a proposal that formulates a problem and offers a solution. Think of an existing situation that calls for attention, whether it is on campus or at the local, national, or international level. Something may be wrong that needs to be changed. Something may be lacking that needs to be added. Something worthwhile may not be working properly and therefore needs to be improved. Or it may be that a situation needs to be redefined in order to find new approaches and solutions.

Proposals can be group projects or done individually.

Here are some possibilities:

- **Public policy proposals:** These range from op-ed pieces in newspapers, like Jennifer Gordon's "Workers Without Borders," to actual legislation that proposes to do things such as change immigration laws, recognize gay and lesbian relationships, require a balanced budget, or devise a national health care plan.
- **Proposals for new or improved services:** Proposals call on government agencies, professional associations, educational institutions, and private foundations to provide new or improved services—for example, in health care, education, and recreation. The Be Green Neighborhood Association's proposal and the student "Proposal for a Campus Coffee House" (see Writers' Workshop) are good examples of this type of proposal. You might write a proposal based on a situation you see on campus—to improve residential life, food service, social climate, advising, or academic

programs. Or you may want to write a proposal for new or improved services in your local community or at the state or federal level.

- **Research proposals:** Lucia Trimbur's "Training Fighters, Making Men" offers an example of a research proposal. You might draw on one of the classes you're taking right now to write a research proposal. What is an interesting and important problem or issue that has emerged in readings, lectures, and discussions? How would you go about researching it?

- **Proposals for new awareness:** Tricia Rose's "Beware the Manipulation of the Funk" illustrates how proposals work to expand our awareness of a problem and to clarify or revise our understanding of what's at stake. The call to action involves changing, modifying, or consolidating attitudes and values, and the underlying problem, as Rose puts it, is often "What kind of community do we want to make?"

- **Advocacy campaign:** Write a proposal for an advocacy campaign by an existing organization or one that you make up. Create a name and a logo for the campaign; include the goals and strategy of the campaign, its audience, and the types of written and visual material needed to carry out the campaign. See the Greenpeace Stop Global Warming campaign in Chapter 6.

Invention

To think about proposals you might write, work through the following exercises. Your proposal may well grow out of a situation you are currently in, or it may stem from an experience you have had in the recent past.

1. Start by taking an inventory of the issues around you that might call for a solution. Begin by thinking small and local. What groups, clubs, teams, or other organizations do you belong to? What issues face these groups? What issues face students at your college or university?

2. Now broaden your thinking to national and international issues. What do you see as real problems? Which problems do you care enough about to spend time researching and proposing a solution to? Who might listen to you? What is the best forum for getting people to hear your proposal?

3. Once you have created your list of possibilities, narrow it down to the three most promising options, beginning with the ones you care most about or that have the potential to make your life (or that of others) markedly better.

4. Decide tentatively on the audience. Who can realistically make changes happen? To whom do you have realistic access? With whom do you have credibility? Create a list of possible audiences and consider the implications each audience holds for the successful implementation of your proposal. Your definition of the problem may change depending on your audience. Do these shifts in definition hold any consequences for you or for those you are trying to help?

Background Research: Formulating the Problem

By formulating problems, writers take situations that already exist and point out what aspects call for urgent attention and action. In this sense, problem formulation is always in part an interpretation—a way of establishing the relevance of a problem to readers.

Illegal drugs are a good example of how problems can be defined in a number of ways. Some would say, for example, the problem is that illegal drug trade results in police corruption and powerful underworld drug cartels. Others would argue that drugs are causing social decay and destroying the moral fiber of a generation of American young people. Still others would hold that Americans and drug laws haven't distinguished adequately between recreational drugs like marijuana and addictive drugs like heroin and cocaine. In the following chart, notice how different problem formulation leads to different proposals.

Issue	Illegal drug use		
Problem	Underworld drug trade	Social decay	Need for redefinition
Proposed Solution	Step up war against major drug dealers	Education, jobs programs	Decriminalize marijuana
	Cut off drugs at point of distribution	Eliminate conditions of drug use, such as poverty and hopelessness	Make legal distinctions that recognize differences between kinds of drugs (recreational versus addictive)

Use the chart as a guide to analyze an existing situation by breaking it down into a number of problems and solutions. You will probably not be able to address in one proposal all the aspects of the situation that you identify as problems. In fact, you may find that the proposed solutions suggested by the various problems are contradictory or mutually exclusive.

Assessing Alternatives

Once you have identified a number of possible solutions to the problems you've defined, you can then assess the relative strengths and weaknesses of proposals. One way to do this is to test the feasibility of proposed solutions—their capability and suitability to solve problems. Again, this can be done by using a chart:

Problem	What policy on international drug trade should the government follow?	
Proposed Solution	Legalize drug trade under state control.	Step up the war against international drug trade.
Capability	Unknown. Costs and benefits uncertain. Would require considerable administration. What about possible black market?	Could reduce amount of illegal drugs to enter the United States. However, very costly to have widespread effect. What about domestic trade?
Suitability	Politically unpopular. Voters would interpret as a state endorsement of drug use.	Foreign policy implications need to be carefully considered.

Planning

Relative Emphasis on the Problem and the Solution

In proposals, the amount of space devoted to formulating the problem and to explaining the solution may vary considerably, depending on the writer's situation and purposes. Look, for example, at the relative emphasis on the problem and on the solution in Lucia Trimbur's research proposal "Training Fighters, Making Men" and in Jennifer Gordon's "Workers Without Borders."

"Training Fighters, Making Men"

¶1: Gives background

¶2–5: States objectives of study and research questions (the problem)

¶6–10: Presents research plan and methods (the solution)

¶9: Indicates significance of research

Notice in this case that 50 percent of the proposal (¶¶1–5) is concerned with formulating the problem in the Background and Objectives sections, while the second half of the proposal (¶¶6–10) consists of explaining the solution in the Research Plan. This makes sense, for a research proposal needs to indicate how a researcher plans to answer her research question. On the other hand, Jennifer Gordon devotes only the first two paragraphs (out of thirteen total) to formulating the problem and the rest to presenting a solution (in ¶¶3–11).

Developing a Working Outline

Review the writing and thinking you've done so far. Use the following guidelines to sketch a working outline of your proposal. The guidelines indicate the main issues that writers typically address to design persuasive proposals.

1. **State the problem:** Decide how readily readers will recognize the problem and how much agreement already exists about how to solve it. Your first task is to establish the relevance of the problem to your intended audience. Who does the problem affect? What makes it urgent? What will happen if the problem is not addressed?

2. **Describe the solution:** Since effective proposals present both general goals that appeal to shared values and attitudes and the specific solution to be accomplished, you need to state the goals you have identified and then state clearly how and why your proposed solution will work. Describe the solution and the steps needed to implement it. Decide on the level of detail required to give readers the necessary information to evaluate your proposal.

3. **Explain reasons:** Identify the best reasons in support of your proposal. Consider the available alternatives and to what length you need to address them. Finally, think about what counterarguments are likely to arise and to what length you need to deal with them.

4. **Ending:** Some proposals have short endings that reinforce the main point. Others, such as the advertisements commonly found in magazines and newspapers, end by calling on readers to do something.

Working Draft

Use the working outline you have developed to write a draft of your proposal.

Matching Problems and Solutions

Perhaps the most important feature of a persuasive proposal is the match between the problem as the writer defines it and the solution as the writer describes and explains it. Unless the two fit together in a logical and compelling way, readers are unlikely to have confidence in the proposal.

Proposal writers often link solutions to problems in two ways—in terms of long-term goals and specific objectives. Long-term goals project a vision of what the proposed solution can do over time, while specific objectives tell who is going to do what, when they are going to do it, what the projected results will be, and (in some instances) how the results will be measured.

As you design your proposal, consider how you can effectively present your goals and objectives. Your goals will give readers a sense of your values and offer common ground as the basis for readers' support, while your objectives will help convince readers you have a concrete plan of action that can succeed.

Peer Commentary

Once you have written a draft proposal, exchange drafts with a classmate. If you are working in a group, exchange drafts between groups. Write a commentary to the draft, using the following guidelines.

1. How does the proposal establish the need for something to be done—by defining a problem, describing a situation, using an example, providing facts and background information? Is the need for action convincing? Who is likely to recognize and want to address the main issue of the proposal? Who might feel excluded? Is there any way to include more potential supporters?

2. Where does the proposal first appear? Is it clear and easy to find? Put the proposal in your own words. If you cannot readily paraphrase it, explain why. What are the long-term goals? What are the specific objectives of the proposal? Is it clear who is going to do what, when, how much, and (if appropriate) how the results will be evaluated? Do you think the proposal will have the results intended? Why or why not? What other results might occur?

3. What reasons are offered on behalf of the proposal? Do you find these reasons persuasive? Why or why not? Are these the best reasons available? What other reasons might the writer use?

4. Does the solution appear to be feasible? Why or why not? Does the writer need to include more information to make the proposal seem more feasible? What would it take to convince you that this proposal would work?

5. Is the proposal addressed to an appropriate audience? Can the audience do anything to support the actions suggested in the proposal? If not, can you suggest a more appropriate audience? If so, does the way the proposal is written seem suitable for that audience? Point to specific places in the text that need revision. What kinds of changes would make the proposal work better for the audience?

Revising

Now that you have received feedback on your proposal, you can make the revisions you think are necessary—to make sure that the solution you propose follows logically and persuasively from the problem as you have defined it. To help you assess the relationship between your problem formulation and the solution you propose, consider this early draft of the problem and solution sections of the "Proposal for a Campus Coffee House."

Notice two things. First, this proposal devotes approximately equal space to the problem and to the solution. Second, the early draft does not clearly separate the problem statement from the solution statement. In fact, as you can see, the problem is initially defined as the lack of a solution—a logical confusion that will make readers conclude that the reasoning is circular (the reason we need X is because we don't have it), which is not likely to be

very persuasive. To see how the writer straightened out the relationship between problems and solutions, compare this early draft to the revised version
that appears in Writers' Workshop.

Early Draft

The Problem: Drinking on Campus

The absence of an alcohol-free social life has become a major problem
at Warehouse State. Because there are no alternatives, campus social life is
dominated by the fraternities, whose parties make alcohol easily available to
minors. Off campus, local bars that feature live bands are popular with students,
and underage students have little difficulty obtaining and using fake IDs.

The Student Counseling Center currently counsels students with drinking
problems and has recently instituted a peer counselor program to educate
students about the risks of drinking. Such programs, however, will be limited and
largely reactive unless there are alcohol-free alternatives to social life on campus.

The Solution: Campus Coffee House

The Student Management Club proposes to operate a campus coffee house with
live entertainment on Friday and Saturday nights in order to provide an alcohol-
free social environment on campus for 200 students (capacity of auxiliary dining
room in Morgan Commons when set up cabaret-style).

Such a campus coffee house would have a number of benefits. It would help
stop the high levels of drinking on campus by both legal and underage students
(Martinez & Johnson, 1998), as well as the "binge drinking" that has increased
the number of students admitted to the student infirmary for excessive drinking
by almost 50% in the last four years. It would serve as a public endorsement of
alcohol-free social life, enhance student culture by providing low-cost alcohol-
free entertainment on campus, and support current ongoing alcohol abuse
treatment and prevention programs. ■

W WRITERS' WORKSHOP

A group of three students wrote the following "Proposal for a Campus Coffee
House" in response to an assignment in a business writing class that called on
students to produce a collaboratively written proposal to deal with a campus
problem. Their commentary on the decisions they made formulating problems
and solutions and designing the format appears after the proposal.

PROPOSAL

Proposal for a Campus Coffee House

To meet the problem of excessive drinking on campus, we propose that a coffee house, open on Friday and Saturday nights with live entertainment, be established in the auxiliary dining room in Morgan Commons and operated by the Student Management Club to provide an alcohol-free alternative to undergraduate social life.

The Problem: Drinking on Campus

A recent study by the Student Health Center indicates high levels of drinking by undergraduates on campus (Martinez & Johnson, 1998). Both legal and underage students drink frequently (Fig. 1). They also increasingly engage in unhealthy "binge drinking" to the point of unconsciousness. The number of students admitted to the student infirmary for excessive drinking has increased almost 50% in the past four years (Fig. 2). These patterns of drinking conform to those observed in a recent national study (Dollenmayer, 1998). Like many

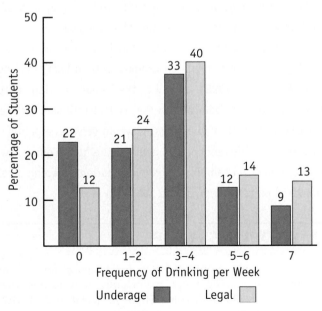

Fig. 1   Frequency of Drinking Per Week, Underage and Legal

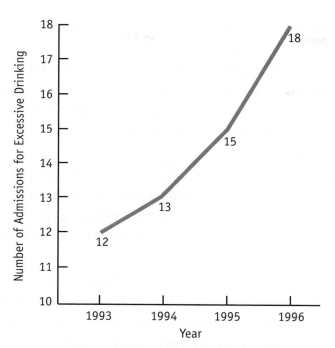

Fig. 2   Admissions to Student Infirmary for Excessive Drinking

other colleges and universities, Warehouse State is faced with a serious student drinking problem (Weiss, 1997).

Currently there are few alternatives for students seeking an alcohol-free social life. Campus social life is dominated by the fraternities, whose parties make alcohol easily available to minors. Off campus, local bars that feature live bands are popular with students, and underage students have little difficulty obtaining and using fake IDs.

The Solution: Campus Coffee House

The Student Management Club proposes to operate a campus coffee house with live entertainment on Friday and Saturday nights in order to provide an alcohol-free social environment on campus for 200 students (capacity of auxiliary dining room in Morgan Commons when set up cabaret-style).

Such a campus coffee house would have a number of benefits. It would serve as a public endorsement of alcohol-free social life, enhance student culture by providing low-cost alcohol-free entertainment on campus, and support current ongoing alcohol abuse treatment and prevention programs. The Student Counseling Center currently counsels students with drinking problems and has recently instituted a promising peer counselor program to educate students about the risks of drinking. Such programs, however, will be limited and largely reactive unless there are alcohol-free alternatives to social life on campus.

Organizational Capability

The Student Management Club has the experience and expertise needed to run the proposed coffee house. Since 1991, it has successfully run a coffee counter in Adams Union, open five days a week from 8 to 3:30. Management majors are interested in expanding their work into the areas of arts programming and publicity.

Budget

The proposed campus coffee house will require initial funding of $1,250 to begin operations. See cost breakdown in Table 1, Initial Expenditure. We believe, however, that such expenditures are one-time only and that the campus coffee house should become self-supporting. See projected budget in Table 2.

Table 1   Initial Expenditures

Supplies (mugs, plates, spoons, forks, paper products, etc.)	$ 750
Coffee, tea, milk, pastries	250
Publicity	250
Total	$1,250

Table 2   Projected Budget

Per evening of operation

Income		Expenses	
(estimated)	$400	Entertainment (band or singer)	$100.00
		Staff (2 persons, 5 hrs each @$5.35)	53.50
		Supplies	75.00
		Food	100.00
		Publicity	25.00
		Total	$353.50

References

Dollenmayer, L. C. (1998). Patterns of alcohol use among American college students. *Journal of the American Medical Association, 275*(16), 223–229.

Martinez, M., & Johnson, R. (1998). Alcohol use and campus social life. Livingston, NM: Student Health Center, Warehouse State University.

Weiss, I. (1997, December 2). Drinking deaths prompt concern on campus. *New York Times,* pp. 1, 7.

WRITERS' COMMENTARY

Following are excerpts from a group meeting, which the participants taped. Here are some passages from the transcript where the three group members, Kathy, Andrea, and Bruce, talk about why they got involved in the coffee house project and how they went about writing the proposal.

KATHY: One of the things that has been interesting about working in this group is that the members come to it from different perspectives. Andrea and I see the coffeehouse more as a crusade against drinking, which we've watched do a lot of damage to some people we know. So that's a pretty big motivation to get involved, to provide alternatives. Bruce, I think, is into it more out of his interest in folk music and running coffeehouses.

BRUCE: Yeah, I mean I do support the idea of having alcohol-free alternative places for students to go. That makes sense to me. But, I agree, definitely. My main thing is arts programming and administration, that whole business. If I can, that's what I want to do when I graduate.

BRUCE: Some of that came up when we were trying to think of reasons for the coffeehouse, and I was into how it would help promote the arts on campus. We ended up not using that stuff.

ANDREA: Right, but I think Kathy and I became more aware of how we had to make sure the proposal didn't sound moralistic. Remember at first we defined the problem as "drinking on campus" and only later changed it to "excessive drinking." We wanted the proposal to sound positive—that a coffeehouse would enhance student life.

BRUCE: Exactly. We didn't want it to sound like punishment. And you're right, the proposal doesn't really come out against drinking as the problem but against excessive drinking, binge drinking. I mean alcohol is legal for people over 21. Besides it's unrealistic to think a campus coffeehouse or anything else for that matter is going to end drinking on campus.

ANDREA: Another thing I felt we tried to do in the proposal was link the coffeehouse concept to other campus anti-drinking programs. I thought we did a pretty good job of listing benefits in the solution section.

■ WORKSHOP QUESTIONS

1. Consider how well the proposed solution matches the problem defined in this proposal. Is the problem well-defined and substantiated by adequate evidence? Does the proposed solution seem to offer a feasible approach to excessive drinking on campus? Are there other important factors the writers have not taken into account?

2. The writers, as you may have noticed, are reasonably concerned that their proposal doesn't sound moralistic, even though Kathy and Andrea were initially interested in the idea because of their strong feelings about drinking. Do you think they have been successful in presenting their proposal as a "positive" step to "enhance student life"? If so, what is it about the proposal that creates this impression? If not, why?

3. Imagine that you are on a campus committee that reviews proposals and decides which ones to support. There are more worthy proposals than there are funds available, so you will have to make some hard decisions. The proposal for a campus coffeehouse is one of the finalists, and the committee plans to meet each group of proposers before making its decision. Draw up a list of questions you would ask Kathy, Andrea, and Bruce to help you make a decision. ■

REFLECTING ON YOUR WRITING

If you did a group proposal, when you have finished, hold a meeting to look back and evaluate the experience of working together.

1. Explore the reasons each member was drawn to the problem the proposal addresses. To what extent do these reasons overlap? How are they distinct from each other? How did they combine in the group? What influence did this have on writing the proposal?

2. Describe how the group went about writing the proposal. What parts went smoothly? What problems, if any, did the group have? How did individual members and the group deal with problems in the writing?

If you wrote an individual proposal, ask similar questions: What called you to the problem you address? What made it important or urgent? How did you go about writing the proposal? What was easy about it? What problems, if any, did you have? How did you deal with these problems?

reviews

THINKING ABOUT THE GENRE

Reviews are a genre of writing people turn to when they are called on to make evaluations. Of course, reviewers normally describe and analyze whatever they are reviewing—whether it is a movie, a CD, an employee's performance, or a government program. Still, as readers are aware, reviewers provide this background information and analysis as evidence for the evaluation they are making.

Reviews take place informally all the time in everyday life. Part of daily conversation is talking about what people need, what they have seen and done, and what kinds of judgments they make about their experience: What kind of lawn mower should I buy? Is the psychology course you're taking any good? Is the latest Spike Lee movie worth seeing? Do you like your new car? Where's a good place to get a cheap meal?

Perhaps the most familiar written reviews are newspaper and magazine reviews of the arts—reviews of books, music, film, art, architecture, television, and dance. But newspapers and magazines also feature other kinds of reviews. In addition, Web sites of various sorts feature reviews of music, films, television shows, books, and consumer products. As these examples suggest, readers use reviews in a variety of ways: to get information, to get advice from experts, and to compare their judgments to the reviewer's.

You've probably written book reviews in school. Sometimes students think the point of book reviews is to prove to teachers they've read the book, but it's important to understand the role that reviewing plays in academic work. Like newspapers and magazines, scholarly journals feature reviews that assess the contribution of new books to a field of study. Just as key, though, is the way scholars and researchers are persistently reviewing the literature in their field to frame their own intellectual projects and explain the significance of their work. One of the standard features of an academic article is a literature review that locates the work being presented in relation to previous work, whether by applying an established concept to a new case, tackling a neglected topic, or offering a counterinterpretation.

At the center of all these reviews are the criteria used to make evaluations. The criteria reviewers use may be explicit or implicit. *Consumer Reports,* for example, uses explicit criteria based on quantitative data. Readers can find them listed and explained on the page. Often, however, the criteria are far less explicit. In movie reviews, for example, readers must frequently figure out the criteria from the critic's discussion and analysis of the film.

Whether readers find a review persuasive will depend to a large extent on whether they believe the criteria used are justifiable. At times readers may accept the criteria used and yet not agree with how the criteria are applied. In other cases of evaluation, people disagree not because they apply shared criteria in different ways but because their criteria of evaluation differ altogether. In a heterogeneous society such as our own, it is virtually inevitable that people's evaluations—whether in politics, academic work, the arts, or other areas—and the criteria and assumptions that underlie them will differ considerably.

■ WRITING FROM EXPERIENCE

How do you and the people you know find out about movies, CDs, television shows, live music, books and magazines, restaurants, plays, dance performances, concerts, and Web sites? Do you read reviews that appear in newspapers, magazines, or online? How often do you hear and make use of informal, word-of-mouth reviews from family, friends, or coworkers? Think of a discussion you had in which people's evaluations differed. What was being reviewed? What did people say? Why did their evaluations differ? Did they seem to be using the same criteria but applying them differently, or were they using different criteria? How did the discussion end? Did anyone modify his or her views?

READINGS

REVIEW ESSAY

THE QUEEN: BEYONCÉ, AT LAST
SASHA FRERE-JONES

Sasha Frere-Jones is the pop music critic at the New Yorker, *where this review appeared in the February 9, 2009, issue.*

Poses question

Bruce Springsteen is the de-facto governor of New Jersey, and if America were Europe Aretha Franklin would have a duchy, so both obviously belonged at the joyous Obamathon. But what about Beyoncé Knowles, the twenty-seven-year-old who was chosen to sing for Obama at two inaugural events?

Back-ground

The world met Beyoncé in 1998 as the leader of Destiny's Child, a girl group conceived in part and managed by Matthew Knowles, her father. Destiny's Child was high-tech declarations of autonomy and flair: "No, No, No," "Bills,

Vince Bucci/Getty Images for AMA

Bills, Bills," "Independent Women, Pt. 1," and "Survivor." To underestimate Knowles and her rotating cast of backup singers is to find yourself on the business end of a No. 1 song. (Destiny's Child is the most successful female R. & B. group in history.) Yet none of this involved Beyoncé cursing, committing infidelity, or breaking any laws, even in character. The Knowles empire is delicately balanced on one of the thinnest-known edges in pop feminism: as unbiddable as Beyoncé gets, she never risks arrant aggression; and as much of hip-hop's confidence and sound as she borrows, she never drifts to the back of the classroom. She is pop's A student, and it has done her a world of commercial good.

Makes an evaluation

She is also a strange and brilliant musician. Young black female singers rarely get past the red rope and into the Genius Lounge—the moody, the male, and the dead crowd that room. But with or without co-writers, Knowles does remarkable things with tone and harmony. The one time I met her, backstage at a Destiny's Child concert in Peoria in 2000, she talked about listening to Miles Davis and Fela Kuti—affinities I didn't know how to process until I heard "Apple Pie à la Mode," from the following year's Destiny's Child album, "Survivor." It's a slinky song, something of a throwaway, except that Prince or D'Angelo could easily have done the throwing away. Who else in the stratosphere of R. & B. pop plays around with the conversational voice like Beyoncé? Who feels comfortable with adding so much unexpected, generous harmony to a trifle about a delicious crush? Anyone else with "Apple Pie à la Mode" in the bag would flip over backward, buy a retro-glam outfit, and construct an entire side project around it. Knowles simply kept moving.

Poses a more specific question

Where she was heading, as she and her father must have always known, was toward a gigantic solo career. That meant that she would have to choose among unity of purpose (the way Céline Dion chose the power ballad as her sidearm of choice), full-on idiosyncrasy (as Björk did, after leaving the Sugarcubes for a life of dedicated unpredictability), or some compromise between the two that could retain old fans while convincing tourists that she was worth following. Executed successfully, this move is called the Sting (who never matched the songwriting quality of his old band the Police but has provided himself with a robust living and a large, loyal following). Done wrong, it's called—well, many names, all of which involve repeated pleas for the old band to regroup.

Question remains unanswered

Beyoncé has yet to come to a decision, though her success as a solo artist seems to be entirely secure. (She has made three solo albums, all of them yielding No. 1 songs.) This is a testament to something deeply appealing about Beyoncé, because her first album, "Dangerously in Love" (2003), has three good songs, at best; her second, "B'Day" (2006), is completely enjoyable; and her new one, "I Am . . . Sasha Fierce" (featuring a supposedly new, wilder alter ego), is something of a mess. Apparently, Knowles felt that it was high time to offer a different definition of Beyoncéness. But why?

Reviews current CD

"I Am . . . Sasha Fierce" stretches an hour's worth of material over two compact disks, the first supposedly by our old friend Beyoncé, the second by Ms. Fierce. The album began arriving on the Internet in November with "Single Ladies (Put a Ring on It)," whose video has eclipsed the song itself. (The choreography for Beyoncé and her two dancers is borrowed from some old Bob Fosse routines and has inspired dozens of imitations, including one by an almost-naked man dancing in the Alaskan snow and one with Justin Timberlake, doing his best drag routine for "Saturday Night Live.") The song, produced by The-Dream and Tricky Stewart, is reminiscent of the best moments on "B'Day." The rhythms are provided in part by handclaps, and the chanting vocal line is underscored by a swell of weird, dark synthesizers that don't seem to know about the party going on in the rest of the song. But, then, the whole thing is a bit off. The singer is out on the town, engaging her single lady friends and enjoying the attention of a new man. Why is she out on the town? Because her man didn't "put a ring on it." But this is Sasha Fierce we're talking about here. And what does Sasha want? Matrimony! When does she want it? Before "three good years" are up. "Single Ladies" is an infectious, crackling song and would be without fault if it weren't the bearer of such dull advice. The wild R. & B. vampire Sasha is advocating marriage? What's next, a sultry, R-rated defense of low-sodium soy sauce?

Puts new CD in context of redfini-tion

"I Am . . . Sasha Fierce" trips on this idea of redefinition, largely because Beyoncé has been relatively fierce since she started. The first disk's initial single, "If I Were a Boy," is a slow, almost rocklike ballad that ponders the gender differential. Boys get to wear what they want, chase girls, and enjoy normative privilege. Y'know—the patriarchy. But Destiny's Child handled all this on "Independent Women, Pt. 1," and with a lot more verve.

Puts Beyoncé in another context

For all that, liking Beyoncé is still a wise bet. What Knowles fails to convey with Sasha Fierce she accomplishes in the movie "Cadillac Records," with her portrayal of someone who headlines in the Genius Lounge—Etta James. When Beyoncé rolls her body and her voice into James's music, the results are not safe. Her version of James is a worthy tribute to the sexuality and craft of the woman we know from her Chess recordings. Why Knowles could not make her own record as spontaneous and magnetic probably has something to do with the Knowles vision of Beyoncé's fans and how much actual fierceness they can take.

Final evaluation

When Beyoncé sang for the Obamas at the Neighborhood Ball on January 20th, the whole shebang revealed itself in a synergistic flash. The song of choice was Etta James's "At Last." Team Knowles was not going to waste one of the year's biggest broadcast events. As the exuberant First Couple slow-danced, Knowles did her part to turn basic romantic folderol into historic prophecy: our lonely nights are gone, the skies are blue, we've all found a dream. One slightly artless twirl-about was all that the crowd needed to cheer the President on. Knowles gave the song the right blend of smoothness and grit, watching the couple, and holding back what looked like bona-fide tears. It was pitch-perfect and seemed genuine. And maybe this is why Beyoncé's audience isn't much bothered by her need to futz about with unconvincing role-playing. She's really good at being good.

Analysis: Beyoncé in the Context of a Career

Sasha Frere-Jones's review was occasioned by the release of Beyoncé's *I Am . . . Sasha Fierce* in 2008. From the title of the review ("The Queen") and the opening paragraph, however, we sense that there's something more at stake than just how good her latest CD is. Frere-Jones is asking how the recent album fits into Beyoncé's career as a whole and how it defines her identity. This question is in part a recognition that the twenty-seven-year-old Beyoncé has become a major force in pop music, a performer who sang at the Obama inauguration, along with such legendary figures as Bruce Springsteen and Aretha Franklin, and put on a stunning portrayal of Etta James in the film *Cadillac Records*. In this sense, Frere-Jones is inviting his readers to think not just about the music on the recent album but about what it reveals about Beyoncé's unfolding career.

■ **FOR CRITICAL INQUIRY**

1. In the third paragraph, Frere-Jones locates Beyoncé at a kind of crossroads, where "she would have to choose among unity of purpose." What, from Frere-Jones's perspective, is involved in this decision? What role does this idea of Beyoncé having to make a decision play in the review?
2. Consider the two paragraphs Frere-Jones devotes to *I Am . . . Sasha Fierce*. What is his evaluation of the CD? What do his criteria of judgment seem to be?
3. Reread the final two paragraphs. What function do they perform in the review? What does Frere-Jones mean when he says that "liking Beyoncé is still a wise bet"?
4. Overall, how does Frere-Jones want readers to come to terms with Beyoncé?

NOTICE REVIEWS

Notice reviews, like this one from *Rolling Stone,* are brief assessments of new CDs, films, video games, art exhibits, and so on. Notice reviews often use rating systems that award stars (or some other symbol). Consider how the notice review differs from Sasha Frere-Jones's longer review-essay. How do they treat the CD under consideration? What does each bring into view for readers?

BEYONCÉ, *I AM . . . SASHA FIERCE*

Beyoncé
I Am . . . Sasha Fierce
★★★ 1/2

Having transitioned into a more grown-up sound, Beyoncé has gotten conceptual on us: Her third album offers two discs, a collection of heartfelt ballads credited to Beyoncé and a danceable set credited to "Sasha Fierce," the pop diva's more brash, lady-empowering alter ego. Though some of the slow songs have thoroughly memorable tunes, the lyrics are full of bland self-affirmation and saggy lines like "You're everything I thought you never were." But the "Sasha" disc boasts Beyoncé's most adventurous music yet: She rides frothy techno on "Radio," turns out modal-sounding hooks over 808 bass on "Diva" and juices the eerie, Nine Inch Nails-style beats of "Video Phone" with lines like "Press 'record' and I'll let you film me." Another plus: The girl who blew up going all melismatic has never sung with more restraint than she does on Sasha.

—Christian Hoard

ORPHAN'S LIFELINE OUT OF HELL COULD BE A GAME SHOW IN MUMBAI

MANOHLA DARGIS

Manohla Dargis is one of the film reviewers at the New York Times. *Her review of the Academy Award winner for best picture in 2008,* Slumdog Millionaire, *appeared on November 12, 2008, when the film opened.*

A gaudy, gorgeous rush of color, sound and motion, "Slumdog Millionaire," the latest from the British shape-shifter Danny Boyle, doesn't travel through the lower depths, it giddily bounces from one horror to the next. A modern fairy tale about a pauper angling to become a prince, this sensory blowout largely takes place amid the squalor of Mumbai, India, where lost children and dogs sift through trash so fetid you swear you can smell the discarded mango as well as its peel, or could if the film weren't already hurtling through another picturesque gutter.

Mr. Boyle, who first stormed the British movie scene in the mid-1990s with flashy entertainments like "Shallow Grave" and "Trainspotting," has a flair for the outré. Few other directors could turn a heroin addict rummaging inside a rank toilet bowl into a surrealistic underwater reverie, as he does in "Trainspotting," and fewer still could do so while holding onto the character's basic humanity. The addict, played by Ewan McGregor, emerges from his repulsive splish-splashing with a near-beatific smile (having successfully retrieved some pills), a terrible if darkly funny image that turns out to have been representative not just of Mr. Boyle's bent

humor but also of his worldview: better to swim than to sink.

Swimming comes naturally to Jamal (the British actor Dev Patel in his feature-film debut), who earns a living as a chai-wallah serving fragrant tea to call-center workers in Mumbai and who, after a series of alternating exhilarating and unnerving adventures, has landed in the hot seat on the television game show "Who Wants to Be a Millionaire." Yet while the story opens with Jamal on the verge of grabbing the big prize, Simon Beaufoy's cleverly kinked screenplay, adapted from a novel by Vikas Swarup, embraces a fluid view of time and space, effortlessly shuttling between the young contestant's past and his present, his childhood spaces and grown-up times. Here, narrative doesn't begin and end: it flows and eddies—just like life.

By all rights the texture of Jamal's life should have been brutally coarsened by tragedy and poverty by the time he makes a grab for the television jackpot. But because "Slumdog Millionaire" is self-consciously (perhaps commercially) framed as a contemporary fairy tale cum love story, or because Mr. Boyle leans toward the sanguine, this proves to be one of the most upbeat stories about living in hell imaginable. It's a life that begins in a vast, vibrant, sun-soaked, jampacked ghetto, a kaleidoscopic city of flimsy shacks and struggling humanity and takes an abrupt, cruel turn when Jamal (Ayush Mahesh Khedekar), then an exuberant 7, and his cagier brother, Salim (Azharuddin Mohammed Ismail), witness the murder of their mother (Sanchita Choudhary) by marauding fanatics armed with anti-Muslim epithets and clubs.

Cast into the larger, uncaring world along with another new orphan, a shy beauty named Latika (Rubina Ali plays the child, Freida Pinto the teenager), the three children make their way from one refuge to another before falling prey to a villain whose exploitation pushes the story to the edge of the unspeakable. Although there's something undeniably fascinating, or at least watchable, about this ghastly interlude—the young actors are very appealing and sympathetic, and the images are invariably pleasing even when they shouldn't be—it's unsettling to watch these young characters and, by extension, the young nonprofessionals playing them, enact such a pantomime. It doesn't help even if you remember that Jamal makes it out alive long enough to have his 15 televised minutes.

It's hard to hold onto any reservations in the face of Mr. Boyle's resolutely upbeat pitch and seductive visual style. Beautifully shot with great sensitivity to color by the cinematographer Anthony Dod Mantle, in both film and digital video, "Slumdog Millionaire" makes for a better viewing experience than it does for a reflective one. It's an undeniably attractive package, a seamless mixture of thrills and tears, armchair tourism (the Taj Mahal makes a guest appearance during a sprightly interlude) and crackerjack professionalism. Both the reliably great Irfan Khan ("A Mighty Heart"), as a sadistic detective, and the Bollywood star Anil Kapoor, as the preening game-show host, run circles around the young Mr. Patel, an agreeable enough if vague centerpiece to all this coordinated, insistently happy chaos.

In the end, what gives me reluctant pause about this bright, cheery, hard-to-resist movie is that its joyfulness feels more like a filmmaker's calculation than an honest cry from the heart about the human spirit (or, better yet, a moral tale). In the past Mr. Boyle has managed to wring giggles out of murder ("Shallow Grave") and addiction ("Trainspotting"), and invest even the apocalypse with a certain joie de vivre (the excellent zombie flick "28 Days Later"). He's a blithely glib entertainer who can dazzle you with technique and, on occasion, blindside you with emotion, as he does in his underrated children's movie, "Millions." He plucked my heartstrings in "Slumdog Millionaire" with well-practiced dexterity, coaxing laughter and sobs out of each sweet, sour and false note.

Analysis: A "Reluctant Pause"

Slumdog Millionaire was a blockbuster that received widespread critical acclaim, including the Academy Awards for best picture, directing (to Danny Boyle), cinematography, film editing, sound mixing, and musical score and song. As Manohla Dargis notes, "It's hard to hold any reservations in the face of Mr. Boyle's resolutely upbeat pitch and seductive visual style." Nonetheless, Dargis says the film "makes for a better viewing experience than it does for a reflective one." By drawing a line between viewing pleasure and reflection, Dargis sets up criteria of judgment that give her "reluctant pause" about the film. Her review can hardly be considered a negative one, for there is clearly much about the film she admires. Still, she identifies a flaw in the film that qualifies her praise, giving her review a "yes, but . . . " character.

■ FOR CRITICAL INQUIRY

1. Consider the opposition Dargis sets up between a "viewing experience" and a "reflective one." What do you think she means by these terms? What assumptions enable her to draw this distinction in the first place?

2. Dargis's reservations about the film come only in the last two paragraphs. Consider what she is doing in the first five paragraphs. How does she combine description and evaluation?

3. Notice how Dargis refers to the director Danny Boyle's earlier films. What function do these references perform in the review?

FIELD GUIDES

Stray Shopping Cart Project

The Stray Shopping Cart Project uses the features of a familiar genre—the field guide of birds, plants, animals, and so on—to classify two main types of stray shopping carts, "false strays" and "true strays." What started as a Web site has turned into a book *The Stray Shopping Carts of Eastern North America: A Guide to Field Identifications.* Certainly this is a parody of the genre of field guides, but it also uses and exposes the systems of identification and classification that the genre of field guide relies upon. Go to www.strayshoppingcart.com, and visit the page "Understanding the System" for the project's explanation of its classification scheme and terminology.

Gather a number of field guides to examine in class. Consider how they classify and organize information, who their intended readers are, and what purposes they serve. How do the field guides integrate text and visuals? Based on this examination, develop a working difinition of field guides as a genre of writing. You could do the same exercise for travel guides. In either case, consider how these guides are similar to and different from the reviews in this chapter or other reviews you have read.

The work of the Stray Shopping Shopping Cart Project is an invitation to imagine how you might identify and classify other previously neglected things in a field guide.

↘ CONCEPTS / TERMINOLOGY

SOURCE

Any business that uses shopping carts in a conventional manner.

CLOSED SOURCE: A SOURCE that has gone out of business.

SOURCE AGENTS: Employees or subcontractors of the SOURCE who collect and return stray carts.

CLASS A: FALSE STRAYS

1) A shopping cart that while on the SOURCE lot is diverted from its primary function, damaged, or otherwise rendered useless.

2) A shopping cart that appears to be a stray cart but that is ultimately returned to service in the SOURCE from which it originated.

CLASS B: TRUE STRAYS

1) A cart that will not be returned to the SOURCE from which it originated.

2) CLASS B: TRUE STRAY TYPES may be used as secondary designations for CLASS A: FALSE STRAY specimens.

TYPES

The subdivisions of CLASSES A and B.
(There are currently 11 CLASS A TYPES and 22 CLASS B TYPES included in the System.)

SPECIMEN

A cart that has been photographically documented and assigned a single or multiple TYPE designations.

ICONS

The subdivisions of CLASSES A and B, abbreviated by using the CLASS letter alone with the TYPE number.

A green CLASS B TYPE icon with a brown border represents a secondary CLASS B TYPE designation.

SU

SOURCE UNKNOWN

DESIGNATION RETAINED

When an image contains multiple carts and there is no notation indicating otherwise, the TYPE designations should be assumed to refer to all carts in the image.

GAP SPACES

Vacant lots, ditches, spaces between buildings, behind buildings, under bridges and overpasses, and all manner of vacant GAPS between properties, public or private.

8 / INTRODUCTION

CLASS A TYPE 1

CLOSE FALSE

→ A cart found at the edge of the SOURCE parking lot or within a two-block radius.

→ Often found in ditches, on median strips, and on grassy areas adjacent to the SOURCE parking lot.

→ A/1 carts are often subject to acts of B/12 SIMPLE VANDALISM.

↑ A/1 This specimen was found just beyond the edge of its native SOURCE lot.

©2009 Julian Montague

16 / CLASS A: FALSE STRAYS

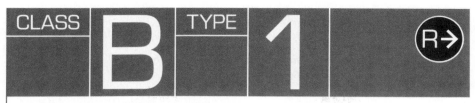

CLASS **B** TYPE **1**   R→

OPEN TRUE

→ A cart situated on a street or sidewalk, or in a park or parking lot, outside of a two-block SOURCE radius.

→ Impossible to differentiate from A/9 REMOTE FALSE.

→ All TRUE STRAY carts theoretically transition through and retain the B/1 designation, thus all CLASS B TYPES are B/1 OPEN TRUE.

↑ B/1   This specimen was found four miles from its SOURCE of origin.

30 / CLASS B: TRUE STRAYS

©2009 Julian Montague

SLUM VISITS: TOURISM OR VOYEURISM?

ERIC WEINER

Eric Weiner's review of "slum tours" appeared in the Travel section of the New York Times *on March 9, 2009.*

JOHN MAIER /The New York Times/Redux

Marcelo Armstrong, pointing, founder of Favela Tour, takes visitors through Rio's Vila Canoas slum. His company has spawned several imitators.

Michael Cronin's job as a college admissions officer took him to India two or three times a year, so he had already seen the usual sites—temples, monuments, markets—when one day he happened across a flier advertising "slum tours."

"It just resonated with me immediately," said Mr. Cronin, who was staying at a posh Taj Hotel in Mumbai where, he noted, a bottle of Champagne cost the equivalent of two years' salary for many Indians. "But I didn't know what to expect."

Soon, Mr. Cronin, 41, found himself skirting open sewers and ducking to avoid exposed electrical wires as he toured the sprawling Dharavi slum, home to more than a million. He joined a cricket game and saw the small-scale industry, from embroidery to tannery, that quietly thrives in the slum. "Nothing is considered garbage there," he said. "Everything is used again."

Mr. Cronin was briefly shaken when a man, "obviously drunk," rifled through his pockets, but the two-and-a-half-hour tour changed his image of India. "Everybody in the slum wants to work, and everybody wants to make themselves better," he said.

Slum tourism, or "poorism," as some call it, is catching on. From the favelas of Rio de Janeiro to the townships of Johannesburg to the garbage dumps of Mexico, tourists are forsaking, at least for a while, beaches and museums for crowded, dirty— and in many ways surprising—slums. When a British man named Chris Way founded Reality Tours and Travel in Mumbai two years ago, he could barely muster enough customers for one tour a day. Now, he's running two or three a day and recently expanded to rural areas.

Slum tourism isn't for everyone. Critics charge that ogling the poorest of the poor isn't tourism at all. It's voyeurism. The tours are exploitative, these critics say, and have no place on an ethical traveler's itinerary.

"Would you want people stopping outside of your front door every day, or maybe twice a day, snapping a few pictures of you and making some observations about your lifestyle?" asked David Fennell, a professor of tourism and environment at Brock University in Ontario. Slum tourism, he says, is just another example of tourism's finding a new niche to exploit. The real purpose, he believes, is to make Westerners feel better about their station in life. "It affirms in my mind how lucky I am—or how unlucky they are," he said.

Not so fast, proponents of slum tourism say. Ignoring poverty won't make it go away. "Tourism is one of the few ways that you or I are ever going to understand what poverty means," said Harold Goodwin, director of the International Center for Responsible Tourism in Leeds, England. "To just kind of turn a blind eye and pretend the poverty doesn't exist seems to me a very denial of our humanity."

The crucial question, Mr. Goodwin and other experts say, is not whether slum tours should exist but how they are conducted. Do they limit the excursions to small groups, interacting respectfully with residents? Or do they travel in buses, snapping photos from the windows as if on safari?

Many tour organizers are sensitive to charges of exploitation. Some encourage —and in at least one case require— participants to play an active role in helping residents. A church group in Mazatlán, Mexico, runs tours of the local garbage dump, where scavengers earn a living picking through trash, some of it from nearby luxury resorts. The group doesn't charge anything but asks participants to help make sandwiches and fill bottles with filtered water. The tours have proven so popular that during high season the church group has to turn people away. "We see ourselves as a bridge to connect the tourists to the real world," said Fred Collom, the minister who runs the tours.

By most accounts, slum tourism began in Brazil 16 years ago, when a young man named Marcelo Armstrong took a few tourists into Rocinha, Rio de Janeiro's largest favela, or shantytown. His company, Favela Tour, grew and spawned half a dozen imitators. Today, on any given day in Rio, dozens of tourists hop in minivans, then motorcycles and venture into places even Brazil's police dare not tread. Organizers insist the tours are safe, though they routinely check security conditions. Luiz Fantozzi, founder of the Rio-based Be a Local Tours, says that about once a year he cancels a tour for security reasons.

The tours may be safe, but they can be tense. Rajika Bhasin, a lawyer from New York, recalls how, at one point during a favela tour, the guide told everyone to stop taking pictures. A young man approached the group, smiling and holding a cocked gun. Ms. Bhasin said she didn't exactly feel threatened, "just very aware of my surroundings, and aware of the fact that I was on this guy's turf."

Still, she said, the experience, which included visiting galleries featuring the work of local artists, was positive. "Honestly, I would say it was a life-changing experience," Ms. Bhasin said. Saying she understood the objections, she parried, "It has everything to do with who you are and why you're going."

Chuck Geyer, of Reston, Va., arrived for a tour in Mumbai armed with hand sanitizer and the expectation of human misery incarnate. He left with a changed mind. Instead of being solicited by beggars, Mr. Geyer found himself the recipient of gifts: fruit, and dye to smear on his hands and face, as people celebrated the Hindu festival of Holi. "I was shocked at how friendly and gracious these people were," Mr. Geyer said.

Proponents of slum tourism say that's the point: to change the reputation of the slums one tourist at a time. Tour organizers say they provide employment for local guides and a chance to sell souvenirs. Chris Way has vowed to put 80 percent of his profits back into the Dharavi slum.

The catch, though, is that Mr. Way's company has yet to earn a profit on the tours, for which he charges 300 rupees (around $7.50). After receiving flak from the Indian press ("a fair criticism," Mr. Way concedes), he used his own money to open a community center in the slum. It offers English classes, and Mr. Way himself mentors a chess club. Many of those running favela tours in Brazil also channel a portion of their profits into the slums. Luiz Fantozzi contributes to a school and day-care center.

But slum tourism isn't just about charity, its proponents say; it also fosters an entrepreneurial spirit. "At first, the tourists were besieged by beggars, but not anymore," said Kevin Outterson, a law professor from Boston who has taken several favela tours. Mr. Fantozzi has taught people, Mr. Outterson said, "that you're not going to get anything from my people by begging, but if you make something, people are going to buy it."

Even critics of slum tourism concede it allows a few dollars to trickle into the shantytowns, but say that's no substitute for development programs.

Mr. Fennell, the professor of tourism in Ontario, wonders whether the relatively minuscule tourist revenue can make a difference. "If you're so concerned about helping these people, then write a check," he said.

Analysis: Blurred Genre

Eric Weiner's article is one of the "Heads Up" features that appear regularly in the Travel section of the Sunday *New York Times* on topics such as Berlin's "hidden restaurants," the secondhand clothing stores in Antwerp, or the allure of airport hotels. It differs from the other reviews in this chapter because it doesn't really make an evaluation of "slum tours," giving readers, say, a first-person account of the highlights of Be a Local Tours in Rio de Janeiro, as a travel review typically would do. Instead, it reviews a current controversy in tourism by reporting on what critics and proponents have to say. In this sense, it combines elements of the news report, including quotes from tourism experts at universities, with elements of the review, including quotes from tourists about their experiences. By blurring the line between reporting and reviewing, Weiner provides potential "slum tourists" with a sense of the issues involved in taking a tour of a favela or shantytown—and, in this respect, fulfills one of the key functions of a travel review by giving people information to make their own plans about what to see and do.

■ FOR CRITICAL INQUIRY

1. What are the terms of the controversy over "slum tourism"? What divides the critics and proponents? What do their enabling assumptions seem to be?

2. Eric Weiner's rhetorical stance appears to be impartial, just a matter of reviewing the two sides of a controversy. Notice, however, that he gives the first and last words to David Fennell, a critic of "slum tourism." How does this positioning frame the controversy? To what extent do you think it's likely to influence readers' assessment of the debate?

3. One could say that the film *Slumdog Millionaire* is another instance of "slum tourism," brought to the wide screen. What, if anything, do you think the film and the tours have in common? To what extent could you apply the terms of the "slum tourism" debate to the film?

4. It is perhaps fitting that the final reading selection in this part of the book, which has presented a range of writing genres, is an article that arguably could have appeared in the Reports chapter as easily as in the Reviews chapter. Consider the placement of the reading in *Call to Write,* making a case for keeping it here in the Reviews chapter or moving it somewhere else. What are your criteria of judgment? What does the question of where "Slum Visits: Tourism or Voyeurism?" best fits bring to light about the idea of genre?

ETHICS OF WRITING

REVIEWING AS A PARTISAN ACTIVITY Reviewers are by no means neutral observers. On the contrary, they are in the business of being partisan. After all, even the more quantitative and objective reviews, such as the product ratings in *Consumer Reports,* require that criteria for evaluation be chosen and weighted.

Reviewers have a responsibility to their readers because something of consequence is at stake: a consumer wants to spend money on the best available product; an employer wants to know which workers to promote; a business or government agency needs to know what changes in the system are needed.

For precisely this reason, reviewers have a responsibility to those whose products and performances are being reviewed. Even if unfair, negative reviews can kill a play or cost an employee his or her job.

As you begin considering what kind of review you might write, these issues of partisanship and responsibility will inevitably arise. On whose behalf will you be writing? What are the potential consequences of the evaluations you will make? What responsibilities does this bring to you as a reviewer? ■

FURTHER EXPLORATION: REVIEWS

■ RHETORICAL ANALYSIS

Pick one or two of the reviews in this chapter. Identify the main criteria of evaluation. Notice that in each review's argument, the criteria of evaluation play the role of enabling assumptions. Explain how the criteria enable the reviewer to connect the evidence provided to the review's central claim. Consider how widely shared the criteria of evaluation are likely to be on the readers' part. What does the reviewer's assumption seem to be? Does the reviewer appear to assume that the criteria can be taken for granted as something most readers already believe, or do the criteria seem to require explanation and justification?

■ GENRE AWARENESS

To what extent is Sasha Frere-Jones's "The Queen: Beyoncé, At Last" as much a profile of her career as a review of her *I Am . . . Sasha Fierce*? To what extent do you find elements of one genre incorporated into another in the reading selections in this part of the book or elsewhere? Find an example of a piece of writing you could call a blurred genre. What makes it blurred?

WRITING ASSIGNMENT

Write a review. Pick something to review that you know well or that you find interesting and would like to learn more about. You will write this review for a particular group of readers, so you might target a particular publication, such as a student or local newspaper or one of the national magazines. This will help you anticipate what your readers already know, what they value, and what criteria they accept as a basis of evaluation.

The subject of your review can be drawn from many spheres of life. Here are some common types of reviews:

- **Media:** Television programs, radio shows, movies, and musical recordings are all possible subjects for reviews. You could write a review essay of a film or CD and also a notice review—and then reflect on the differences.

- **Live performances:** Attend a musical concert, a play, or a club with live music and write a review of the performance.

- **The Web:** As the Internet grows more crowded, people can use help finding which sites are worth visiting and which are not. Gather an assortment of related Web sites and write a comparative review of them. Or just focus on one site and review it in depth.

- **Exhibits:** Local museums, on and off campus, may be featuring special art, historical, or scientific exhibits that you could review.

- **Books:** You could review a best-seller, a recent book in an academic field that interests you, a controversial book, a book that is particularly popular with college students, or an older book that invites a revisit.

- **Sports:** Write a preview of an upcoming season of a college or professional sport, or make a prediction about an important game.

- **Leisure and entertainment:** Write a restaurant review, a guide to entertainment on campus, or an evaluation of backpacking routes you have taken. Visit historical places, local parks, or parts of a city, and write a review of what they have to offer.

- **Education:** Write a review of a course you have taken, a textbook, or a program you have been involved in (such as an orientation for first-year students or a summer program).

- **Rating systems:** Design a rating system for reviewing consumer products, musical recordings, movies, restaurants, or some other product or service.

- **Greatest or best lists:** You could list the top ten (or twenty-five or one hundred) rap songs, punk bands, teenage movies, game shows, actresses, hockey players, or presidents and explain your criteria of evaluation. Some lists focus on the best of the year, while others identify the all-time greatest.

- **Paired reviews:** Work with a partner to write paired reviews that offer differing judgments about a CD, movie, upcoming sports event, or who is going to win an Academy Award.

- **Course review:** Work together as a class to review your writing course. The review will require planning questions and methods, conducting research, compiling and analyzing the information obtained, and finally, evaluating the course based on that information. Here is a procedure, which you may want to modify, depending on the size of your class and the scope of your review:

  1. Establish criteria for evaluating the course.
  2. Make a list of questions to give you information related to the criteria you're using.
  3. With your questions in mind, decide how you will get answers. You could use surveys, written evaluations, interviews, or discussion groups. Decide which methods would be practical as well as most useful for getting the information you need.
  4. Conduct the research and compile the results. How you compile results will, of course, depend on the method of gathering information you used. For example, survey responses can be tallied, whereas interviews would have to be analyzed.
  5. Interpret the results of your research and prepare a review based on this analysis.

Invention

Exploring Your Topic

To get started thinking about your topic and how you might approach it in a review, assess what you already know and what further information you need.

■ EXERCISE

Assessing What You Know

A common feature of reviews is to explain how a particular book, film, or recording fits into a larger body of work ("*London Calling* is the Clash masterpiece that pulls together the range of musical sources in their earlier work") or a particular genre ("James Ellroy's *LA Confidential* belongs on the same shelf as the great *noir* novels of Dashiell Hammett, Raymond Chandler, and Jim Thompson"). Such explanations help readers see the significance of the work in question and establish the credentials of the reviewer as a knowledgeable person. Here are some questions to identify background information you can use in your review:

- What do you know about the author of the book, the director of the film, the composer or musical leader? What other works do you know by the same person? How is this work like or different from those other works?

- How would you describe the genre of the work? What do you know about the history of the genre? What other examples can you think of?

- What is the critical evaluation of the writer, director, or composer? Do you know of reviews, articles, or books on your subject? Do the critics and reviewers seem to agree, or are there debates, differences, or controversies? If so, what's at stake?

Establishing Criteria of Evaluation

Criteria are the standards critics and reviewers use to justify their evaluations. They can be described as the enabling assumptions by which reviewers link their claim (the movie was good, bad, disappointing, sensationalistic, and so on) to the available evidence (the movie itself). In some circumstances, you will need to justify the criteria explicitly (for example, "the only way to make sense of *Slumdog Millionaire* is to suspend any expectation of a gritty realistic drama about poverty in Mumbai and to see the film instead as a fairy tale"), while, in others, you can assume readers will share your criteria (for example, "though some of the slow songs [on Beyoncé's *I Am . . . Sasha Fierce*] have thoroughly memorable tunes, the lyrics are full of bland self-affirmation").

■ EXERCISE

Identifying Criteria

To identify criteria that may help you in your evaluation, respond to the following questions.

- What is a particularly good example of the type of item you are reviewing? What qualities make it good?

- What makes a particularly bad example? Don't simply write the opposite of the "good" qualities listed above. Instead, think of several bad examples, and identify what made them stand out as inferior.

- Find three or four sample reviews. What criteria do reviewers use in their evaluations? To what extent are these different or similar to the criteria in the good and bad examples you've chosen? What is the significance of these differences and similarities?

Assessing Your Criteria

To assess how you might apply the criteria you have identified, consider these questions:

- Write down a series of assertions you want to make about what you are reviewing. Use this form of sentence: "X is significant because Y" or "What made X a great movie is Y."

- Analyze the assertions. What criteria are you applying in each instance? Do you think readers are likely to accept these criteria as reasonable ones? Why or why not?

- How might people apply the same criteria but come up with a different evaluation? Are there criteria of evaluation people might use that differ from those you use? How would these criteria influence a reviewer's evaluation?

Planning

Considering the Relation Between Description and Evaluation

One issue reviewers face is how much they need to describe what they are reviewing. How much detail should you give? Should you summarize the plot of the movie or book? If so, where and in what detail? How can you best combine such description with your evaluation?

Answers to these questions will depend in part on what your readers are likely to know about the topic. Their level of familiarity will shape how much you are called on to provide as background information and description.

These are very real considerations. At the same time, however, it is important to see description and evaluation not as separate writing strategies that require separate space in a review but as strategies that are related to each other.

Manohla Dargis's review of *Slumdog Millionaire!* offers a good example of how writers integrate description and evaluation. Notice that her opening paragraph *characterizes the genre* of the film, and the second paragraph *puts the film in context* by locating it within the director Danny Boyle's body of work. These are standard review strategies to set up a frame of reference for readers.

In the next three paragraphs, we get plot summary combined with description and commentary. Dargis starts by focusing on the story of the main character Jamal "who earns a living as a chai-wallah" and "who, after a series of exhilirating and unnerving adventures, has landed on the television game show." Then she comments on the screenplay ("it flows and eddies—just like life") and the tone of the film ("one of the most upbeat stories about living in hell imaginable"). Finally, returning to plot details, Dargis describes a flashback to Jamal's life as an orphan as a "ghastly interlude" that is "undeniably fascinating" and "unsettling" at the same time.

The first five paragraphs set up Dargis to present her evaluation of the film in the closing two paragraphs. These final paragraphs also include description and commentary ("Beautifully shot with great sensitivity to color"), but we sense at the opening of the sixth paragraph that the terms of the review have changed when Dargis says, "It's hard to hold any reservations," and then proceeds to explain exactly what her reservations are.

Using Comparison and Contrast

Reviewers use comparison and contrast to put what they are reviewing in perspective, by seeing how it stacks up to something similar—whether it is other work of the same kind or other work by the same artist.

Notice, for example, how Sasha Frere-Jones uses both comparison (they all performed at the Obama inauguration) and contrast (Bruce Springsteen and Aretha Franklin have clearly defined identities but not Beyoncé) to pose the question that gives the review its main focus.

> Bruce Springsteen is the de-facto governor of New Jersey, and if America were Europe Aretha Franklin would have a duchy, so both obviously belonged at the joyous Obamathon. But what about Beyoncé Knowles, the twenty-seven-year-old who was chosen to sing for Obama at two inaugural events?

And Frere-Jones also compares and contrasts Beyoncé's current to past work:

> The first disk's initial single, "If I Were a Boy," is a slow, almost rocklike ballad that ponders the gender differential. Boys get to wear what they want, chase girls, and enjoy normative privilege. Y'know—the patriarchy. But Destiny's Child handled all this on "Independent Women, Pt. 1," and with a lot more verve.

Working Draft

Use the writing you have already done to get started. Consider how your opening can characterize what you're reviewing and make your evaluation clear to readers. Reviewers do not necessarily point out the criteria of judgment they are using. Nonetheless, to engage your readers, you need to make sure the criteria are easy to identify, even if they are only implied. Consider, too, how you can weave description and other background information into your review. Are there comparisons and contrasts worth making?

Distinguishing Your Views

Sometimes, reviewers not only evaluate a work or performance; they also locate the evaluation in relation to evaluations others have made. Doing so enables them to distinguish their views from what others have said or written and thereby clarify exactly where they are coming from and what criteria they are using.

Take, for example, Jon Pareles's review of Coldplay's third album *X&Y* in 2005, "The Case Against Coldplay":

> Clearly Coldplay is beloved: by moony high school girls and their solace-seeking parents, by hip hop producers who sample its rich instrumental sounds and by emo rockers who admire Chris Martin's heart-on-sleeve lyrics. The band emanates good intentions, from Mr. Martin's political statements to lyrics insisting on its own benevolence. Coldplay is admired by everyone—everyone except me.

Pareles's stance is contentious, but it is certainly clear. In other cases, rather than going head-on with others, reviewers will emphasize what others have neglected or downplayed:

> Reviewers have justifiably noted how sinister John Travolta is in *The Taking of Pelham 1 2 3* but missed the sly self-effacing sense of humor he brings to the role.

Peer Commentary

Exchange the working draft of your review with a classmate. Respond to the following questions in writing:

- Is the subject defined clearly? Does the review give the reader enough details and background information to understand the reviewer's evaluation? Are there things you wanted to know that the writer left out? Are there things the writer mentions but that you would like to know more about?

- Does the reviewer's evaluation come across clearly? As you read the draft, where did you become aware of the reviewer's evaluation? Point to the sentence or passage. Do you understand what the reviewer's criteria are? Do they need to be stated more clearly? Are they reasonable criteria? Are there other criteria you think the writer should take into account?

- Does the review seem balanced? How does the reviewer combine description and evaluation? Does the reviewer talk about good and bad points, positive and negative aspects? Is the tone appropriate?

- Does the reviewer use comparisons? If so, where and for what purposes?

- What suggestions would you make to strengthen the review?

Revising

Use the peer responses to revise your working draft. Consider these issues:

- Do you bring the work or performance into focus for your readers by using strategies such as describing it, characterizing what type or genre it is, explaining how it is similar to or differs from others of its kind, and providing adequate background information?

- Is your evaluation clear and easy to understand, or are you hedging in one way or another?

- Does it make sense in your review to engage what others have already written or said about the work or performance? If so, how can you distinguish your own perspective from others'?

- Do you attend to both good and bad points, positive and negative features? Remember, being balanced does not mean being objective or neutral. To make an evaluation you have to commit yourself and explain how, given the good and the bad, you have made a judgment based on criteria.

Options for Meaningful Endings

The ending of your review should do more than just summarize what you have already said. Look at the ending as an opportunity to leave your readers with something further to think about regarding the significance of the work or performance you've reviewed.

Notice, for example, the strategy for ending that Denise Sega uses in her working draft "More Than Just Burnouts," a review of Donna Gaines's book *Teenage Wasteland* (the full text appears in Writers' Workshop, below). In this case, Sega ends her review by indicating who would be interested in the book and why.

Working Draft

In conclusion, I believe this is an important book that should be read by anyone interested in finding out more about the "gritty underside of white teen life in the suburbs" (cover notes). Compared to the sensationalistic stories in the press that blame teenage suicide on drugs or heavy metal, Donna Gaines has taken the time to listen—and to hear what the kids have to say.

The strategy Sega has chosen, of course, is not the only possible way to end her review meaningfully. Here are two other strategies reviewers commonly draw on.

■ Anticipate a possible objection.

Some readers may think that Donna Gaines identifies too much with the "burnouts"—and that her research is thereby "contaminated" by her personal allegiances. Gaines's partisanship, however, gives the book its unique authority. By gaining the trust of Bergenfield's heavy-metal kids, Gaines is able to give their side of things and to show how they make sense of their world. After reading *Teenage Wasteland*, it's hard not to think these kids need an advocate who can speak on their behalf.

■ Connect to a larger context of issues.

Youth bashing has become a popular spectator sport in recent years, and events such as the school shootings in Littleton, Colorado, and elsewhere have fueled adult fears and anxieties about teenagers. Perhaps the most important achievement of *Teenage Wasteland* is that it cuts through the moral panic and the sensationalistic stories in the press and on TV about young people. Instead, Gaines gives us an understanding of how alienated teenagers experience their lives. ■

WRITERS' WORKSHOP

Written for a sociology course on youth culture, the following is a working draft of a review of Donna Gaines's book *Teenage Wasteland*. The assignment was to draft a four-page review that evaluated the book, to exchange it with a classmate for peer commentary, and to revise. The writer, Denise Sega, had a number of concerns she wanted her partner to address in the peer commentary. Here's the note she wrote:

> I'm worried that I spend too much time summarizing the book and not enough explaining my evaluation of it. What do you think? Do I say too much about the author and the book's contents? Is my evaluation clear to you? Do you think I give enough explanation of why I liked the book so much? Any other suggestions are also appreciated. Thanks.

As you read, keep in mind what Denise asked her partner. When you finish reading the working draft, consider how you would respond.

DENISE SEGA, MORE THAN JUST BURNOUTS (WORKING DRAFT)

Youth culture. Teenagers have devised many different ways of growing up. From jocks and preps to neo-Beatnicks and hip-hop kids, most high schools contain a range of distinctive social groupings. In *Teenage Wasteland*, Donna Gaines looks at a group of "burnouts" and heavy metal teens in suburban New Jersey, the "dead end" working-class kids who are alienated from school and community. The opening paragraphs explain the situation that led Gaines to write this book:

> When I heard about the suicide pact it grabbed me in the solar plexus. I looked at the pictures of the kids and their friends. I read what reporters said. I was sitting in my garden apartment looking out on Long Island's Jericho Turnpike thinking maybe this is how the world ends, with the last generation bowing out first.

> In Bergenfield, New Jersey, on the morning of March 11, 1987, the bodies of four teenagers were discovered inside a 1977 Chevrolet Camaro. The car, which belonged to Thomas Olton, was parked in an unused garage in the Foster Village garden apartment complex, behind the Foster Village Shopping Center. Two sisters, Lisa and Cheryl Burress, and their friends, Thomas Rizzo and Thomas Olton, had died of carbon monoxide poisoning. (3)

The remainder of the introduction reveals the rationale and research plan for Gaines's investigation of the suicides. What began as an assignment for the *Village Voice*, for which Gaines writes regularly, her investigation eventually became her doctoral work as well as the book in review.

Besides providing more details about the instigating event, the Bergenfield suicide pact, the introductory pages also provide autobiographical details about the author which are essential to understanding Gaines's devotion to her task, as well as her informed frame of reference. Gaines, too, in many ways, was a "burnout." She describes her growing up years and habits. She explains that "like many of [her] peers, [she] spent a lot of [her] adulthood recovering from a personal history of substance abuse, family trauma, school failure, and arrests" (4). To put this life behind her, Gaines turned to social work, first as a "big sister" with junior high students in Brooklyn and then as a helper on a suicide prevention hotline. After becoming a New York State certified social worker, Gaines worked in the special adoptions and youth services divisions and as a street worker providing services for troubled teens. Eventually she moved into research and program evaluation and finally returned to school to complete her doctorate in sociology.

In the introduction, Gaines also explains the need for the book. Initially, she was reluctant to write about suicidal teens because she felt that "if I couldn't help them, I didn't want to bother them" (6). She did not like the idea of turning vulnerable people like the Bergenfield teens into "research subjects" by getting them to trust her with their secrets. Despite these qualms, however, she did decide to go to Bergenfield and ultimately spent two years hanging out with the "burnouts" and "dropouts" of suburban New Jersey, talking to them about heavy metal music, Satanism, work, school, the future, and many other things. Gaines was angry because these teens had been classified by adults as "losers" and never allowed to tell their side of the story. The press had explained the suicides as the result of the individual problems of troubled teens and failed to see, as Gaines does so clearly in her book, how the suicides "symbolized a tragic defeat for young people" (6) and a wider pattern of alienation.

Teenage Wasteland reveals the sense of sadness among the teens in Bergenfield. "By nineteen," Gaines writes, "you've hit the brick wall and you really need something. Because there is nothing to do here and there is nowhere to go" (78). Young people hanging out seems to annoy and even frighten adults. Nevertheless, for these teens, there does not seem to be anything else to do. According to Gaines, they have been neglected by society for so long, experienced so much lack of care in so many ways, that they see no alternatives. They see no hope for anything better.

The only "ticket out" these teens see is to be like Jon Bon Jovi or Keith Richards. The chances of becoming a rock star, of course, is one in a million. The dream breaks down, the kids realize their limitations, and they feel they have run out of choices for the future. There seem to be no alternatives to their bleak situations:

> At the bottom are kids with poor basic skills, short attention spans, limited emotional investment in the future. Also poor housing, poor nutrition, bad schooling, bad lives. And in their bad jobs they will face careers of unsatisfying part-time work, low pay, no benefits, and no opportunity for advancement.

There are the few possibilities offered by a relative—a coveted place in a union, a chance to join a small family business in a service trade, a spot in a small shop. In my neighborhood, kids dream of making a good score on the cop tests, working up from hostess to waitress. Most hang out in limbo hoping to get called for a job in the sheriff's department, or the parks, or sanitation. They're on all the lists, although they know the odds for getting called are slim. The lists are frozen, the screening process is endless. (155)

According to Gaines, these are "America's invisible classes," the "unseen and unheard . . . legions of young people who now serve the baby boom and others, in fancy eateries, video stores, and supermarkets" (157). Given this situation, it is no surprise that Bergenfield's teens turn to Satanism and heavy metal to give them a sense of power and a refuge in a world over which they feel they have no control. There are no good jobs, and the social programs for these teens only label them as "troubled" or "deviant" or "burnouts" and do not work.

One truly fascinating part of the book involves Gaines's etymology of the term "burnout." Besides providing at least twenty-five synonyms for the term, she also explains its evolution. Furthermore, she differentiates between "burnouts" and "dirtbags"—a subtle yet significant distinction. Her discussion of how these terms reflect teens feeling "powerless, useless, and ineffectual" is, in itself, powerful, useful, and effectual in helping readers understand the deep sense of alienation afflicting the "teenage wasteland."

In conclusion, I believe this is an important book that should be read by anyone interested in finding out more about the "gritty underside of white teen life in the suburbs" (cover notes). Compared to the sensationalistic stories in the press that blame teenage suicide on drugs or heavy metal, Donna Gaines has taken the time to listen—and to hear what the kids have to say.

■ **WORKSHOP QUESTIONS**

1. In her note to her partner, Denise Sega raises a number of issues about her working draft. One of these concerns the amount of description and evaluation that appear in the draft. She seems worried that she spends too much time summarizing the book and talking about the author and not enough on evaluation. How would you respond to this concern? What suggestions would you offer?

2. It is obvious that Sega admires *Teenage Wasteland*, but she raises the question of whether the criteria of evaluation she uses come across clearly enough. Reread the draft and mark those passages that make an evaluation or imply one. What seem to be the criteria Sega uses in each case? If the criteria are not stated explicitly, express in your own words what they seem to be. What advice would you give Sega about presenting her criteria of evaluation more explicitly?

3. In the third paragraph, Sega compares the treatment of the Bergenfield suicide pact by the press to Gaines's treatment in *Teenage Wasteland*. What is the point of this comparison? Do you think Sega could do more with it? If so, how could the comparison be extended and strengthened? Do other comparisons appear in the draft? If so, are they effective, or could they use more work? Are there other comparisons you can think of that Sega might use? ■

REFLECTING ON YOUR WRITING

The assignments throughout the chapter have put you in the role of a reviewer and shown how you might evaluate a performance, a program, or a policy. For your portfolio, shift focus to discuss how you have been reviewed by others— by teachers in school, supervisors at work, judges at performances, and peer commentators in your writing course.

First, give a little background on your experiences of being evaluated in and out of school. What were the circumstances of the evaluations? Why were you being evaluated? What criteria were used? What was your response to the evaluations? Were these experiences helpful to you? Explain why or why not.

Second, use this background to reconstruct your attitude toward evaluation when you entered your writing course. Has your attitude changed? Why or why not? What has been the effect on you as a writer, a student, and a person of receiving reviews from both your teacher and your peers? What differences, if any, do you see between teachers' and peers' evaluations? What suggestions would you offer for improving the process of evaluation in your writing course?

writing and research projects

©Dan Jaeger/stock.xchng. Image altered for design purposes.

3

INTRODUCTION: DOING RESEARCH AND THE NEED TO KNOW

People do research all the time, perhaps without even being aware of it.

- High school students do research to decide which colleges to apply to. People looking for a new car may consult *Consumer Reports* or talk to friends. If you are planning a vacation, you might look at travel guides.

- Researchers in the workplace do marketing surveys, product development, and productivity studies. Professional fields like law and medicine are defined in many respects by the kind of research practitioners in those fields do to deal with clients' legal situations or to diagnose patients' conditions and recommend treatment.

- Public opinion polling has become a common feature of politics and journalism. Advocacy and public interest groups conduct research on questions that matter to them—whether it's the impact of mining on national lands, the effect of outsourcing on American jobs, or drunk driving.

- Research defines the fields of study in academia, as well as the work students do in their various courses—term papers, lab reports, case studies, book reviews, and so on.

One thing these examples have in common is that they are all motivated by the need to know. In each case, something is calling on a person or a group of people to do research—to get the information needed, to investigate a problem, to provide a new way of seeing things.

Researchers in different fields, of course, have different ways of asking questions and different ways of answering them. Take the AIDS epidemic, for example. Biomedical researchers ask questions about the nature of the human immunodeficiency virus (HIV) and about treatment that can alter the course of infection, while psychologists and sociologists have studied the effect of AIDS on the identities of HIV-negative gay men and the benefits and drawbacks of needle-exchange programs. Economists calculate the financial impact of AIDS, while researchers in literary and film studies examine the representations of AIDS in fiction and movies.

The following chapters focus on academic research, the kind of assignments you are likely to get in college courses. Nonetheless, the information is just as pertinent to research in other spheres. Chapter 12 explains how to organize a research project. Chapter 13 discusses how to work with sources, and Chapter 14 provides a guide to print, electronic, and other sources. Chapter 15 discusses field research.

chapter 12

the research process
critical essays and
research projects

In college, the call to do research comes from teachers, in the form of a writing assignment. For this reason, it's worth considering what faculty are looking for when they ask students to do research.

In the first part of this chapter, we'll examine faculty expectations about research projects and two familiar writing assignments that call on students to work with sources: the critical essay and the research paper. In the second part of the chapter, we'll take an overview of the research process and follow one student, Amira Patel, as she designs and carries out a research project in an American history course.

WHAT ARE FACULTY LOOKING FOR?
UNDERSTANDING ACADEMIC WRITING

Faculty assign short critical essays and longer research papers because they want students to act like members of a field of study, whether drama critics, literary scholars, design theorists, or historians. Those writing assignments call on the students to enter into an ongoing discussion and to position themselves in relation to what the experts have already said. Faculty know, of course, that students are novices in the field. But that's why faculty ask students to gain some experience of what it means to engage with the questions and issues in a field of study.

To understand critical essays and research papers as genres of academic writing, it can help to consider these faculty expectations:

- **Faculty expect you to work with your sources**—to create an interplay of perspectives and interpretations instead of just summarizing what the authorities have said. For example, it's not enough to report on the causes of the French Revolution in 1789. The real question is, what

377

have historians *said* about the causes of the French Revolution and how do these interpretations differ and why?

- **Faculty expect you to identify the central discussions, debates, and controversies in a field**—and to use them to locate your own thinking in relation to what the authorities have said. In academic writing, it is rare that problems or issues have been settled once and for all and there's nothing left to say. Usually, there are discussions, debates, and controversies taking place, in which scholars argue for a particular interpretation or way of understanding the matter at hand. Your task as a researcher is to understand these ongoing controversies and figure out where you stand in relation to them.

- **Faculty expect you to create you own research space.** A critical essay or research paper does not simply convey information from reliable sources. It uses these sources to establish a problem or issue that has some significance. Even in cases where an instructor assigns the problem or issue to examine—how, say, does futurism embody modernist design—it's still up to you to explain why and how this question is worth investigating and what makes it meaningful.

SAMPLE STUDENT PAPERS FOR ANALYSIS

In the two examples of student writing that follow, we'll look more closely at how students have responded to these faculty expectations. The first paper is a critical essay, which uses Modern Language Association (MLA) citation form. The second paper uses American Psychological Association (APA) style.

SAMPLE CRITICAL ESSAY IN MLA FORMAT

This critical essay' "Radiohead and the Tip-Jar Model" was written for a mass communication course in media and culture. The assignment called on students to identify and analyze a recent event or trend in the media that illustrates changing patterns of content distribution in the digital era.

Yi 1

Stacy Yi

Professor Watkins

Media & Culture

5 November 2009

Radiohead and the Tip-Jar Model

Late in the afternoon of October 3, 2007 I faced a decision that was much more difficult than I'd anticipated: how much did I want to pay for a digital download of Radiohead's seventh album, *In Rainbows*? It should've been easy; the download was offered by the band itself on its website, not a third party linked to through Napster or The Pirate Bay, and the price was given only by the text "it's up to you." Unlike the music I'd downloaded for free in the past, all without the artist's permission, *In Rainbows* came with no embedded moral problem. The band didn't seem to mind if I opted to pay nothing. Eventually I settled on $6, entered my payment information, received my download, and sat back to enjoy the album, but I wondered about the other thousands, and eventually millions, of fans like me, specifically about how they viewed this sudden influx of responsibility and the decisions it led them to make.

I wasn't the only one with questions. Editorials in newspapers and on websites, blog postings and attendant comment sections, and conversations with friends all asked what this experiment would mean for music retail and digital sales, copyright law, and the stability of the industry's conventions. Everyone who took interest in the situation seems to believe, whether they side with or against the band's decision, that Radiohead changed the conversation about content distribution, one that extends beyond music to other media. Would this be the first wave in a gradual rewriting of the industry's rules, or was the band merely exercising its sizable economic muscles in a one-shot deal?

Many of those commentators compared Radiohead's sales plan for *In Rainbows* to the tip jar on the counter of the local coffee shop. The comparison isn't quite parallel because tips are generally given for quality service that accompanies an already-purchased product. In Radiohead's case, however, the

Uses a personal anecdote to introduce the issue of the essay

Generalizes from personal experience to raise the central question

Introduces model

Qualifies its applicablity

product and service are one and the same (at least until *In Rainbows* was released in the stores, months later, on TBD Records). That fits with Greg Kot's observation, from *Ripped: How the Wired Generation Revolutionized Music*, that the band wanted only "to leak its own album, give fans a taste of the new music, and invite them to buy the sonically superior physical product once it became available in a few months" (1). Using an online tip jar for digital sales, then, is not necessarily the best way to make money, but an effective means of promoting a product to be sold later at a fixed rate.

Explains one thing the model brings to light

Although Radiohead aren't the first to use the tip-jar model of sales, their particular tip jar perhaps did have the widest reach, which may have influenced the success of the experiment. "[Radiohead] seems more interested in getting the new album into as many hands as possible, and doing so legally . . . but [the band] has no trouble selling out venues, and . . . it's still in its prime for CD sales," says the editorial page of the *L.A. Times*. If Radiohead's status as a high-profile, top-selling international act is partly responsible for raising sales figures, then the tip-jar model might only change that small segment of the industry that can command such attention. Ayala Ben-Yehuda of *Billboard* puts it succinctly in her article "Networth": "online fan-funding efforts certainly sound like a grass-roots and democratic way to launch a career, but the few bands that can actually motivate enough fans to make donations to their recording effort probably don't need the help."

Considers a limit of the model

Musician Kim Gordon of the band Sonic Youth agrees, arguing "we're not in that position either. We might not have been able to put out a record for another couple of years if we'd done it ourselves: it's a lot of work. And it takes away from the actual making music" (qtd. in Peschek 5). Gordon's emphasis of production and creation over distribution not only implicitly critiques Radiohead's artistic decisions, it also rebuffs the notion that large-scale change is possible in the music industry. If the tip-jar distribution model is too complicated for a band of limited resources (even a comparatively successful, long-lived band like Sonic Youth), then the changes that will come as

Explains the limits

traditional music retail shifts towards a greater online presence will be cosmetic; the advantages presented by the internet will only reinforce a sales model that relies on record labels and distributors to do the work that might otherwise detract from the quality of music produced.

However, the tip-jar model has been widely adopted on the Internet and factors significantly in various proposals for refiguring online news content to recoup lost profits. Some critics argue that clicking on sponsored ads while visiting a favorite website is the same as tipping, while companies like TipJar, LLC, and TipJoy offer tip-collection services for companies and bloggers eager to earn more direct revenue than that offered by ad sales. The programming is relatively simple to integrate into any content outlet, and though the logistics required to distribute an album's worth of mp3s are likely more complex than those involved in offering a 500-word editorial, it's not difficult to imagine a young band, writer, cartoonist, or activist publishing content and earning enough through donations to at least partially subsidize further work. In fact, this sounds much like the "grassroots and democratic way to launch a career" that Ben-Yehuda describes. Furthermore, the social factors that inform the value of those donations may shift the conversation from launching a career to something much larger.

Economists have long held that opting to pay any amount of money for a good when a "free-ride" is possible is impure altruism, and even though the motives behind such giving may not be enlightened, they are no less valid. "Social pressure, guilt, sympathy, or simply a desire for a 'warm-glow' may play important roles in the decisions of agents," says economist James Andreoni, and those influences impact our understanding of what a donation means (464). The positive feelings that come from doing something generally considered good can be seen in Viviana A. Zelizer's concept of special monies, which recognizes that "extraeconomic factors systematically constrain and shape" the uses, users, allocation, control, and sources of money (351). Unlike the rational, "all-purpose" value of money, which is the same in any context, a tip, as a form of

Examines model in another context

Draws implications of the model

Introduces a concept ("special monies") to analyze how tip-jar model works

Yi 4

"special money," can have a different value, or even a different function, depending on the context. From this perspective, the viability of the tip-jar model is determined by the specific relationship between consumer and producer or provider rather than by general guidelines set by an artist, a company, or even the industry. This seems especially true online, where the fragmentation and specialization of those groups defies blanket solutions and plans.

In other words, a tip given to a freelance blogger or an unsigned local musician is essentially different from one given to the *Boston Globe* or Radiohead in that the stakes behind the former are far greater than those of the latter. The social forces motivating people to tip accessible, independent artists are likely to encourage continued giving, particularly when an online tipper's warm-glow feelings stem from a perceived responsibility to the artist's continued content production. The tip feels more "necessary" because the audience has entered into a more direct relationship with the artist, and the online tip becomes not only an investment in the future output of an artist but also a means for the audience to actually participate in production, to become part of the machinery that's responsible for the eventual album, book, or design. Eduardo Porter, in a *New York Times* editorial published shortly after *In Rainbows'* release, extrapolated that participation to include not just the creation of new content, or even a new means of production, but perhaps of a new economy itself (1).

Established bands like Radiohead and Nine Inch Nails (who offered a variation on the tip-jar model with *Ghosts I-IV* in 2008) rose to prominence on the established economy. For them, "pay what you will" schemes are a useful promotional tool, a means of self-sufficiency in the shadow of large corporations, and an interesting experiment. And while that independence is likely satisfying, it isn't likely to create Porter's new economy. That will be left to the artists, publishers, and others toiling unknown in bedrooms and classrooms, pushing exposure via social-networking profiles to the limit, and whatever audience is willing to follow them into a new system of exchange.

Explains potential consequences

Ends by drawing a distinction between "established" and "unknown" artists to suggest where change based on tip-jar model is likely to occur

Yi 5

The first true tip-jar success story seems likely to describe a community effort, the kind often absent from the myth of the individual artist.

The hesitation noted by several voices in the debate is reasonable, particularly as the question of what value, monetary or otherwise, any given consumer will place on a song, album, or entire catalog remains nebulous and somewhat intimidating. Radiohead's gambit may not have been the call to revolt as some had hoped, but it may still contain the DNA for a change to come some years from now.

Yi

Works Cited

Andreoni, James. "Impure Altruism and Donations to Public Goods: A Theory of Warm-Glow Giving." *The Economic Journal* 100.401 (1990): 464–477. Print.

Ben-Yehuda, Ayala. "The Indies Issue: Networth." *Billboard* 28 June 2008. *LexisNexis*. Web. 18 Oct. 2009.

Kot, Greg. "Radiohead Reinvents Itself—An Except from 'Ripped: How the Wired Generation Revolutionized Music.'" *Chicagotribune.com* The Chicago Tribune, 17 May 2009. Web. 16 Oct. 2009.

"Pay What You Want for Radiohead." Editorial. *Los Angeles Times* 2 Oct. 2007. Web. 30 Oct. 2009.

Peschek, David. "Youth Movement." *The Guardian* 5 June 2009. Web. 16 Oct. 2009.

Porter, Eduardo. "Radiohead's Warm Glow." Editorial. *New York Times* 14 Oct. 2007. Web. 16 Oct. 2009.

Zelizer, Viviana A. "The Social Meaning of Money: 'Special Monies.'" *The American Journal of Sociology* 95.2 (1989): 342–377. Print.

Analysis: Working with a Model

One of the interesting features of Stacy Yi's critical essay is her use of a model—the tip jar model that a number of commentators suggested—to examine Radiohead's "pay what you will scheme" and to draw out its implications not only for the music industry but for online content distribution more generally. Notice that Stacy does not apply the tip jar model rigidly. Rather, she uses it flexibly to bring to light certain aspects of online content distribution and the relationship between artists and audience. It's a matter of testing how useful the tip jar model is in explaining recent trends in the media.

■ FOR CRITICAL INQUIRY

1. Consider how Stacy Yi sets up the context of issues in the opening paragraphs of her essay. How does she move from a personal anecdote to the central question of her essay?

2. Consider how Yi develops the tip jar model in the essay. How does she integrate her sources to examine what the tip jar can and cannot explain? Pick one or two passages where she has effectively created an interplay of her sources and the tip jar model. How does this interplay contribute to the essay overall? Are there other passages where she is less successful in working with her sources? Explain your answer.

3. Consider the ending of the essay. What is the final point Yi is making? Does it seem to flow logically from the discussion in the rest of the essay?

RESEARCH PAPER IN APA FORMAT

Andy Mgwanna wrote this research paper in Introduction to Criminal Justice. As you read, consider how Andy establishes the purpose of the paper and how he uses his research as evidence.

Running head: PRISON PRIVATIZATION DEBATE   1

The Prison Privatization Debate:

The Need for a New Focus

Andy Mgwanna

Sociology 101

November 20, 2009

Abstract

The dramatic increase in the privatization of prisons has sparked controversy about the ethics, economics, and administration of prisons-for-profit. This paper examines the arguments made for and against the privatization of prisons and prison services. Proponents argue that privatization provides low-cost, high-quality prisons, saving taxpayers money and generating profits. Opponents question the costs and quality of privately run prisons and argue that profits and incarceration are not compatible. Others, however, have suggested that the prisons-for-profit debate has reached an impasse and the terms of discussion about prison policy need to include a stronger emphasis on rehabilitation and recidivism.

The Prison Privatization Debate: The Need for a New Focus

In 1976, the state of Florida hired a private company to operate the Weaversville Intensive Treatment Unit for Juvenile Delinquents. In 1982, the state privatized a second facility, the Okeechobee School for Boys (Young, 2006, p. 12).

Several years later, federal, state, and local government began privatizing a range of prison services and entire correctional facilities in order to cut costs and accommodate a rapidly expanding number of inmates. This recent wave of privatization in corrections can mean several things. First, it can mean that private companies contract with local, state, and federal governments to provide such services in public prisons as medical care, counseling, mental health, and drug treatment, education and vocational training, laundry and food services, and staff training. Second, privatization can mean that prison labor is contracted out to private companie such as Chevron, Victoria Secret, and Best Western who hire prisoners to enter data, make products, and take telephone reservations (Davis, 2003, p. 102). Third, privatization can mean that a private company owns and operates a correctional facility as a for-profit enterprise.

Almost as soon as the ink from these new contracts had dried, a heated debate about the ethics, economics, and administration of prisons-for-profit erupted. In this paper, I examine the debate about privatization of prisons and prison services in order to identify the issues it raises for prison policy. First I provide some background on privatization. Second, I investigate the arguments for private prisons and the arguments against private prisons. Finally, I suggest that the debate about privatization has reached an impasse and needs to be broadened to include a stronger emphasis on rehabilitation and recidivism. Background on the Privatization of Prisons and Prison Services

Privatization dates back to the mid-1800s when private companies were given contracts to run Louisiana's first prison, Auburn Prison, Sing Sing in New York, and San Quentin in California. As the use of private companies to run jails and prisons increased, a number of groups protested. Businesses and labor advocates objected to the free labor many private prisons contracted out because it was "'unfair' competition." Reformers cited whippings, malnourishment, overwork, and overcrowding as evidence of prisoner abuses in private facilities. By the end of the nineteenth century, states had largely stopped using private companies and assumed full management of correctional facilities themselves (Young, 2006, p. 8).

By the mid 1980s, however, federal, state, and local governments once again were allowing private companies to run their jails, prisons, and detention centers. Phil Smith (2007) attributes this decision to the intersection of the "ideological imperatives of the free market; the huge increase in the number of prisoners; and the concomitant increase in imprisonment costs" (p. 4). The American Federation of State, County, and Municipal Employees (AFSCME), the largest public service employees union in the country, which counts prison employees among its members, says that the trend of privatization at the end of the twentieth century can be attributed to Thomas Beasley, the Tennessee Republican Party chairman, who founded the Corrections Corporation of America (CCA) in 1983, with help from Jack Massy, who started Kentucky Fried Chicken. Since the CCA's inception and with help from Wall Street firms such as Goldman Sachs and Merrill Lynch, the private prison industry has expanded dramatically in scope (Parenti, 1999, p. 14).

Today private companies operate juvenile detention centers, county jails, work farms, state and federal prisons, and INS holding camps all over the United States. The Corrections Corporation is the largest private prison operator. In 2003, it managed 58,732 beds in 59 jails, detention centers, and prisons in 20 states and the District of Columbia. One third of CCA's revenue comes from the federal government, while the remaining two thirds come from state and local government. The CCA's largest clients are Wisconsin, Georgia, Texas, Tennessee, Florida, and Oklahoma. Although the CCA tried to operate facilities overseas, after a series of setbacks, it now works primarily in the United States. It is the sixth largest prison system in the United States with only Texas, California, the Federal Bureau of Prisons, New York, and Florida managing more prisoners (Smith, 2007, p. 9). The CCA owns 49% of U.S. prison beds under private operation, while Wackenhut Corrections, an offshoot of the Wackenhut Corporation, a private security and investigation firm founded by former FBI agent George Wackenhut, controls 21% (Lyon, 2007).

Arguments for Prison Privatization

Proponents of privatization present two main points when they argue that private companies can maintain low-cost and high-quality prisons and prison services while generating a profit for investors. First, they argue that private prisons offer significant savings over government-run prisons. Geoffrey Segal (2002) of The Reason Foundation reviewed 23 articles by government officials and academics and found that private prisons are, on average, 10 to 15%

PRISON PRIVATIZATION DEBATE   6

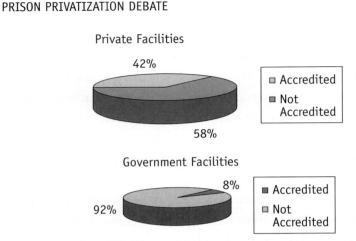

Fig. 1   Facilities with ACA accreditation, from "Prison Privitazation and the Use of Incarceration."

cheaper than government prisons (2). Taxpayers are also saved the expenses and risk of building new facilities ("Prison Privatization a Boon to Taxpayers"). Alexander Tabarrok (2004) says private prisons offer 15 to 25% savings on construction and 10 to 15% on administration. These savings, in turn, pressure public prisons to lower their costs. He notes that between 1999 and 2001 per-prisoner costs increased at a lower rate in states where public prisons competed with private prisons, 8.1 percent, compared to 18.9 percent in states without private prisons (p. 6).

Second, proponents of privatization point to the high quality of private prisons. Segal cites four reasons why quality in private prisons matches or exceeds the quality in public prisons. First, the results of six independent studies, which focused specifically on quality, indicate that private prisons are equal to if not better than government prisons. Second, 44% of private prisons have been accredited by the American Correctional Association, which provides standards for quality, management, and maintenance, while only 10% of government prisons have been accredited (see Fig. 1). Third, almost all contracts with private prisons are renewed. Fourth, no private facilities have been placed under court order for issues of quality.

Others argue that high standards within private prisons are likely to be maintained and even improved upon as more companies enter the market. Frequent rebidding will likely force companies to maintain high quality in order to retain contracts. To preempt the argument that the economic goals of running a prison for profit conflict with the operational objectives, which is providing services, Joel (2004) argues that the state contracting process, which may include termination clauses for poor performance, and scrutiny on the part of courts and the press, serve as safeguards in maintaining adequate standards by the private contractors (p. 5).

Arguments Against Prison Privatization

Those who oppose prison privatizations are a heterogeneous group, and they oppose privatization for several reasons: ethical, financial, and administrative. Those who oppose prison privatization on ethical grounds argue that punishment and profit are not compatible (Smith, 2007, p. 13). Fundamentally the goal of for-profit corporations is to make as much money as possible, and in the case of prisons, profits depend on people being incarcerated. Accordingly, AFSCE objects to privatization on the grounds that it allows private companies to profit from crime. Along similar lines, Mattera, Khan, and Nathan (2003) note that the "existence of an industry based on incarceration for profit creates a commercial incentive in favor of government policies that keep more people behind bars for longer periods of time" (p. 15).

Second, opponents assert that private prisons do not save money. AFSCME asserts that there is no indication that private prisons demonstrate cost savings, while The Sentencing Project writes, "Research to date has concluded that there is little evidence that privatization of prisons results in significant public savings." The General Accounting Office (GAO) conducted a study in 1996, which found that private and public correctional facilities cost the same amount of money (Parenti,

1999, p. 154). In addition, the finances of private prisons are often in disarray. Mattera et al. (2003) point out that CCA nearly went bankrupt in the 1990s after borrowing $1 billion to build speculative prisons and undergoing a troubled corporate restructuring (p. 11). In 2000, the CCA's chief executives lost his job, and the company settled a series of lawsuits from shareholders to the tune of $120 million. CCA today "is weighed down by debt. It also continues to face weak demand for new private prisons at the state and local level" (Mattera et al., p. 21). Wackenhut has not fared much better. The corporation has been charged with squeezing money out of rehabilitation programs, counseling, and literacy courses. In 1995, for example, investigators accused Wackenhut of diverting almost three quarters of a million dollars from a drug treatment program in a Texas facility ("Wackenhut"). Opponents also argue that whatever money may be saved in private prisons is the result of the low wages and substandard benefits staff are given (AFSCME 2000). In discussing the CCA, Mattera, Khan, and Nathan (2003) write that working conditions, low wages, and lack of benefits have led to turnover rates at CCA facilities as high as 60 percent (p. 16).

Third, opponents of private prison facilities charge that CCA and other private companies poorly manage their facilities, allowing prisoner abuse, violence, medical maltreatment, and escapes ("Lock Up Private Prisons"). Mattera et al. (2003) found that CCA routinely failed to give prisoners adequate medical care, create an environment where inmates were safe from harm—both from other prisoners and from correctional staff—and control the drug activities of both prisoners and CCA employees (p. 17). Further, as Christian Parenti (1999) shows, in a 15-month period, the privately-operated Northeast Ohio Correctional Center in Youngstown, Ohio experienced six escapes, 44 assaults, 16 stabbings, and two murders (p. 234). At the same time, prisoners have protested and rioted against substandard conditions. In 1995, North Carolinian prisoners, who were living in overcrowded conditions in a Tennessee prison, burnt their dorms in a several-hour riot (Parenti, 1999, p. 173).

Sexual abuse has been one of the chief allegations against Wackenhut. In 1999, Wackenhut lost a $12 million a year contract with Texas after several correctional officers were indicted for having sexual relations with female prisoners. Wackenhut fired five guards in a work-release facility in Fort Lauderdale, Florida, after learning they were having sex with inmates. After the U.S. Justice Department found Wackenhut subjected inmates to "excessive abuse and neglect," the state of Louisiana reassumed operations of a juvenile prison (The Sentencing Project, 2004).

CCA and other private prison companies have been plagued by escapes and inadvertent releases of violent inmates. Judith Greene (2002) writes that 37 inmates escaped custody from private prisons in 1999 alone (p. 97). Mattera et al. (2003) estimate that at least a dozen inmates have been mistakenly released from custody (p. 25). In some situations, the mistakes are administrative. For example, after one month of operation, an employee at the David L. Moss Criminal Justice Center permitted an inmate to post bond after registering the wrong offense. But in other situations, CCA employees have been fooled by inmates passing as other prisoners, who are eligible for release. Some prisoners are never recaptured. At the same time, important security positions in a facility in Georgia went unfilled for 8-hour shifts 20 times in one month (Lock Up Private Prisons, 1999).

The debate between supporters and opponents of private prisons and the privatization of prison services has reached a stalemate. Supporters argue that well-documented studies of financial savings demonstrate the logic of the market and the superiority of privatization. Opponents argue that privatization amounts to an abdication of government responsibility that has produced systematic abuses. As we have seen, the sides in the debate are deeply divided by their assumptions and beliefs. One of the problems with this impasse, as Thomas O'Brien (2006) of the Horizon Institute for Policy Solutions suggests, is that the key issues of rehabilitation and recidivism, which have significant implications for the cost of the prison industrial complex, have been lost in a polarized debate. O'Brien argues that rather than becoming bogged down in the pros and cons of privatization, we should focus on incentives to both private and public prisons to prevent recidivism:

> If private competition can find the keys to making young offenders become productive citizens rather than career criminals, government will save far more money than the typical 10 to 25 percent savings now found with privatization. Two out of three released convicts are now rearrested. Preventing a young offender from coming back for 20 years can save $400,000 per head (at $20,000 per year in incarceration expenses).

O'Brien helps to redefine the debate about privatization by shifting the measure of success from short-term financial savings to the long-term outcomes of prisoners. This should please opponents of privatization because it makes rehabilitation, instead of profits, the central function of the prison system. At the same time, O'Brien should please supporters of privatization because he does not give up on "private competition" but rather challenges it to develop guidelines and programs that promote rehabilitation and thereby reduce long-term recidivism. In any case, by focusing on outcomes rather than ownership, O'Brien offers at least a starting point to move beyond the current impasse.

References

American Federation of State, County and Municipal Employees (2000). *The evidence is clear, crime shouldn't pay*. Retrieved October 16, 2009, from http://www.afscme.org/private/evidtc.htm

Davis, A. Y. (2003). *Are prisons obsolete?* New York: Seven Stories.

Greene, J. A. (2002). Entrepreneurial corrections: Incarceration as a business. In M. Mauer & M. Chesney-Lind (Eds.), *Invisible punishment: The collateral consequences of mass imprisonment* (pp. 95–113). New York: The New Press.

Huling, T. (2002). Building a prison economy in a rural area. In M. Mauer & M. Chesney-Lind (Eds.), *Invisible punishment: The collateral consequences of mass imprisonment* (pp. 197–213). New York: The New Press.

Joel, D. (2004, May 24). *A guide to prison privatization*. The Heritage Foundation. Retrieved November 1, 2009, from http://www.heritage.org/Research/Crime/BG650.cfm

Lock up private prisons: Chronic problems demonstrate why incarceration should be left to the state. (1999, October 6). *The Atlanta Constitution*. Retrieved October 20, 2009, from http://lexis-nexis.com

Lyon, J. (2007, February 3). Open debate needed over private sector impact on prison system. *The Financial Times*. Retrieved from http://lexis-nexis.com

Mattera, P., Khan, M., & Nathan, S. (2003). *Corrections Corporation of America: A critical look at its first twenty years. A report by Grassroots Leadership, The Corporate Research Project of Good Jobs First, and Prison Privatisation International*. Retrieved October 20, 2009, from www.soros.org/initiatives/justice/articles_publications/cca_20_years_20031201/CCA_Report.pdf

O'Brien, T. (2006, January 26). Letter to the editor. *The Washington Post*. Retrieved November 4, 2009, from http://lexis-nexis.com

Parenti, C. (1999). *Lockdown America: Police and prisons in the age of crisis*. New York: Verso.

PRISON PRIVATIZATION DEBATE   12

Segal, G. (2002). *Corporate corrections? Frequently asked questions about prison privatization*. The Reason Foundation. Retrieved November 7, 2009, from http://www.reason.org/corrections/faq_private_prisons.shtml

Sentencing Project (2004). *Prison privatization and the use of incarceration*. Retrieved October 27, 2009, from http://www.sentencingproject.org/pdfs/1053.pdf

Smith, P. (2007). Private prisons: Profits of crime. *Covert Action Quarterly*. Retrieved October 27, 2009, from http://mediafilter.org/caq/Prison.html

Tabarrok, A. (2004, November 23). PrivatepPrisons have public benefits." *Pasadena Star News*. Retrieved November 3, 2009, from http://lexis-nexis.com

Young, M. T. (2006, January 27). Prison privatization: Possibilities and approaches to the privatization of prisoner security and services. *Criminal Justice Working Papers*. Retrieved October 20, 2009, from http://www.law.stanford.edu/programs/academic/criminaljustice/workingpapers/MTafollaYoung_05.pdf

Analysis: Finding a Place in a Debate

Andy Mgwanna establishes the purpose of his research paper at the end of the second paragraph, when he says that he will (1) give background information on prison privatization, (2) analyze the positions for and against, and (3) explain how the debate has reached an impasse. Notice how the paper builds toward the conclusion it has already anticipated in the introductory section.

¶1–2: Introduction
- Establishes trend toward privatization
- Defines privatization
- Explains purpose of the paper

¶3–7: Background on the Privatization of Prisons and Prison Services
- Provides reasons for the emergence of privatization
- Explains the scope of privatization

¶8–10: Arguments for Prison Privatization
- Economic
- Quality

¶11–16: Arguments Against Prison Privatization
- Ethical
- Economic
- Administrative

¶17–18: Conclusion: A New Focus?
- Concludes debate has reached an impasse
- Suggests a way to refocus

As you can see, one of the important features of this paper is that it does not simply describe the debate about privatization but presents a position on it. Readers may sense that the writer sympathizes with one side in the debate. Opponents of privatization, after all, get twice the space as supporters. However, Mgwanna's main point is that the pro-con debate itself has reached an impasse and that the terms of the debate need to be changed. And, in this way, he goes beyond merely reporting research findings to draw an arguable conclusion about the prison privatization debate.

■ FOR CRITICAL INQUIRY

1. A question readers are entitled to ask about a research paper is whether its conclusions are justified by the evidence presented. Explain the conclusion Andy Mgwanna reaches at the end of the paper. Consider whether the background section and analysis of the privatization debate provide adequate grounds to draw such a conclusion. When you first read the conclusion, did Mgwanna's position seem adequately prepared for?

2. One feature of this paper is that it promises to give a balanced account of the privatization debate. Consider how the writer goes about that in the sections for and against prison privatization. Does the analysis of the debate seem to be a fair and accurate one? Explain your answer by pointing to particular passages in the two sections.

3. How does Mgwanna use his sources? Pick passages in the paper to analyze what the writer is seeking to accomplish by citing sources from his research. Try to identify at least three distinct purposes his sources are meant to serve.

CHECKLIST FOR MLA AND APA STYLE

The two main styles of citation and manuscript preparation in academic research were developed by the Modern Language Association (MLA) and the American Psychological Association (APA). You can find details in Chapter 13, "Working with Sources," about using each style to set up in-text citations and Works Cited or References pages. Here is information about manuscript preparation.

Features Common to Both MLA and APA Style

❑ Manuscript should be double-spaced, including block quotations and Works Cited or References pages. Do not add extra spacing.

❑ Format a one-inch margin all around, top and bottom, left and right.

❑ Indent five spaces to begin a paragraph.

❑ Use ragged right margins.

❑ Don't end the line at the bottom of a page with a hyphen.

❑ Number pages consecutively, including Works Cited or References pages.

Special Features Called for by MLA Style

❑ Unless your teacher tells you to, do not include a separate cover sheet. Type the following information, double-spaced, at the top left corner of the manuscript, in this order: your name, your professor's name, course number, and date. Double-space and center the title of your paper. Follow conventional rules of capitalizing words in a title. Don't use quotation marks, italics, boldface, underlining, all capitals, or showy fonts. Double-space and begin the text.

❑ Insert page numbers in the upper right corner, flush with the right margin, one-half inch from the top of the page. Precede the page number with your last name. Begin the text one inch from the top.

❑ Begin your bibliography on a separate page, titled "Works Cited." Center the title one inch from the top, without any quotation marks, underlining, boldface, or italics. Include in the Works Cited only those works you have cited in

the text of the paper. It is not a comprehensive bibliography (you may have used other works that are not cited).

Special Features Called for by APA Style

❑ Unless your teacher directs otherwise, use a separate cover page. Center your title approximately one-third from the top of the page. Type the title double-spaced if it has more than one line. Follow usual capitalization conventions. Don't use all caps, boldface, quotation marks, underlining, or italics. Double-space and type your name. Double-space again and type the course number, and then, following another double space, type the date.

❑ On the page immediately following the cover sheet, include a one-paragraph "Abstract" of no more than 120 words that summarizes the content of your paper.

❑ Begin the text on the third page. Don't repeat the title. Number all the pages, beginning with the cover sheet as page 1 and the Abstract as page 2. Type a running head (the first two or three words of the title) before the page number.

❑ APA style research papers are much more likely than MLA style papers to use section headings. Some research papers use the conventional headings—"Introduction," "Methods," "Results," and "Discussion"—but others use headings based on the content of the paper. Notice the section headings Jennie Chen uses in her paper.

❑ Begin your References section on a separate page, following the text. Center the word " References" one inch from the top, without any underlining, italics, quotes, boldface, or other special treatment.

THE RESEARCH PROCESS: AN OVERVIEW

In this section, we'll be following Amira Patel as she works on a research paper for her American immigration history course. First, though, we present an overview of the research process—to identify the main steps in responding to the call to write a research paper and some of the key tasks involved at each point.

1. **Defining a research question:** Do preliminary research to get an overview of your topic. Start to focus your reading to develop a research question. Evaluate your research question and revise or modify it, if necessary. Write a proposal to clarify the purpose of your research.

2. **Finding sources:** Use your library's card catalog, indexes, bibliographies, and other databases to identify print and electronic sources. Browse sites on the Internet. Keep a working bibliography.

3. **Evaluating sources:** Take notes. Photocopy sources. Assess the relevance and credibility of the sources. Look for assumptions and biases. Keep an open mind. Be prepared to revise or modify your own thinking in light of what you've read.

4. **Making an argument:** Take into account all you have read. Determine where you stand in debates and controversies. Develop an argument that answers your research question.

5. **Planning and drafting:** Develop a working outline of your paper. Start drafting. Reread sources and find additional information as needed. Revise or modify your outline if necessary.

DEFINING A RESEARCH QUESTION

Research depends in part on knowing what you are looking for. This will depend, of course, on the research assignment. In some cases, the assignment will provide specific directions; in others, it will be open-ended. If you have questions about what the assignment is calling on you to do, make sure you consult with your instructor.

Here is the research assignment Amira Patel was given in her American immigration history course.

The final writing assignment of this course is a term paper, 12 to 15 pages, that researches any topic of your interest in American immigration history, 1880 to present. You should begin by clearly defining your research question and writing a proposal. The paper should establish the importance of the problem you are researching and offer an interpretation. You should not simply report what happened or summarize what you have read. You are expected to read sources from the period you have chosen along with scholarly accounts.

ANALYZING THE ASSIGNMENT

Analyzing the assignment means identifying what it is calling on you to do so that you can clarify your own purposes and determine how you will work with your sources. As we've seen, some assignments provide the purpose for you—for example, to explain why or why not Willie Loman is a tragic hero in *Death of a Salesman*. In other cases, you'll have to figure out what you need to do and what your stance will be in relation to the context of issues, the sources, and your readers.

Here are some common ways that researchers position themselves:

- **To provide an overview of the current thinking of experts:** The purpose in this case is largely an informative one—to report on what experts in the field think about an important issue. You might, for example, explain the current views of experts on the extinction of dinosaurs or report on the latest results of drug treatment of HIV-positive people.

- **To review the arguments in a controversy:** Your purpose is largely informative—to explain to readers the positions people have taken in a current debate. You might, for example, report on the legal controversy prompted by the prosecution of pregnant women for doing harm to their fetuses by drinking or taking drugs.

- **To pose and answer an important question or solve a problem:** In this case, your purpose is not simply to report on what is known but to put forward your own analysis and interpretation. You might, for example, explain the causes of a resurgence of tuberculosis or the consequences of deregulation in the telecommunications industry.

- **To position your own interpretation in relation to what others have said:** In this case, your purpose is similar to that of answering an important question. The key difference is that instead of simply using what others have written as evidence for your interpretation, you also explain how your analysis or interpretation relates to the views of others—how and why it differs, how and why it shares common ground. You might, for example, explain how your analysis of Martin Luther King's "I Have a Dream" speech differs from and is similar to the analyses of others.

- **To take a stand on a controversy:** Here your purpose is not simply to report and analyze but also to persuade. In this case, you have an argument to make. You might claim, for example, that there should (or should not) be mandatory HIV testing. Or you could argue that the United States should (or should not) adopt more stringent limits on commercial fishing in the North Atlantic.

Following a Research Path: Analyzing the Assignment

Amira's First Reaction

This is exactly what I was afraid of. I hate these kind of open-ended writing assignments where the teacher doesn't give you any idea of what you should write about. I have no idea.

Amira's Reaction After Talking to Other Students

OK, I have calmed down a little. I know I've got to get an angle on the assignment. What we were reading about American nativism and negative attitudes toward immigrants between 1880 and 1920 was interesting to me. Maybe I can find something in that. It seems like the important thing is to find a good research question and then explain how to answer it.

PRELIMINARY RESEARCH

Sometimes you know right away what you want to research. In other cases, especially when the topic you're researching is new to you, you'll need to do some preliminary research to develop a research question. The following sources offer good places to start:

- **The Web:** Google can help you identify useful Web sites and other online sources. The quality and reliability of Wikipedia pages varies, but the best ones offer good background information and links.

- **Encyclopedias:** You can find an overview of many topics in general and specialized encyclopedias. See the list of general and specialized encyclopedias in Chapter 14.

- **Recent books:** Skim a recent book on your topic, looking in particular at its introduction to see how the writer describes the issues the book addresses. Check the bibliography for further sources.

- **Recent articles:** Find a recent article in a scholarly journal or a popular magazine on your topic. Read the article, noticing what question or questions the writer poses and (in the case of academic articles) what sources are listed in the references.

- **Classmates, librarians, teaching assistants, faculty members:** Talk to other people who know something about your topic and the current questions people are asking about it. They can help you understand what the issues are and what sources you might look for.

Your preliminary research should give you ideas about the way others have approached the topic you're interested in, the kinds of questions they raise, and the differences of opinion and interpretation that divide them. This research should also help you identify other books and articles on the subject that you may want to consult.

Following a Research Path: Preliminary Research

Amira's Reflections on Getting Started

I thought I'd see what I could find about nativism on the Web and if that would give me any ideas about the paper.

I used "American Nativism" as a key word on Google, and after looking at a couple of sites that didn't seem that helpful, I found the Wikipedia page and a pdf "Cycles of Nativism in U.S. History." I read these and learned that nativism was wider than just 1880 to 1920. Both talked about the English Only movement as a kind of nativism that surfaced in the 1990s. Maybe I should use that as my topic. I think I'd rather do something about recent immigration.

Next, I typed in "English Only" and found a ton of information on English Only at James Crawford's "Language Policy Web Site and Emporium." Crawford seems to be a pretty prominent writer about language issues, and the site has articles and sections of his books. It also gives links to other Web sites so that I could read what supporters of English Only had to say about the issue. [See Fig. 1.]

By this point, I was beginning to feel I had found a good topic in "English Only." I just wasn't sure what my research question should be.

DEVELOPING A RESEARCH QUESTION

Once you've done some preliminary research, answer the following questions to refine your own sense of the research question you want to investigate:

1. What questions, issues, and problems appear repeatedly? Why do people think they are important?

2. Are there arguments, debates, or controversies that appear in what you've read? What positions have others taken? What seems to be at stake in these arguments? Do you find yourself siding with some people and disagreeing with others?

3. Is there some aspect of your topic that people don't seem to pay much attention to? Why do you think this is so? Are they neglecting questions or issues that could provide a good focus for research?

4. Given what you've read so far, what questions, issues, arguments, and controversies do you find most interesting? What, in your view, makes them important?

Following a Research Path: Defining the Research Question

Amira's Further Thoughts about a Research Question

It's interesting that so many Americans in the 1990s started thinking English should be the official language and that bilingual education should be banned. It's almost as though the whole English Only thing just came out of the blue, when organizations like US English started getting together and sponsoring legislation to make English the official language. But that can't be true. There's got to be some reason it happened in the 1990s, when so many new immigrants from Asia and Latin America were coming into the country.

WRITING A PROPOSAL

Some teachers ask students to write a proposal that defines the purpose of their research and indicates their research plan. Even if your teacher does not require a proposal, writing one can be a useful exercise to help you clarify your purpose.

A research proposal typically does three things:

1. Identifies the general topic or problem of the research and explains its significance.

2. Presents the specific issue and the research question you are addressing.

3. Sketches briefly the research plan, indicating how it will answer the research question.

Following a Research Path: Writing a Proposal

Amira's Research Proposal

American nativism goes back as far as the Alien and Sedition Acts of 1798 and anti-Catholic agitation in the 1830s and 1840s, directed toward recent immigrants from Ireland. According to many historians, the period of 1880 to 1920 witnessed virulent outbursts of nativism against the waves of new immigrants arriving in the United States. It seems that every time large numbers of people immigrate to this country, American nativism arises. For my research project, I am interested in American attitudes toward the new immigrants who have been coming to the

United States since the 1990s, from Asia, Central and Latin America, and the Caribbean. I plan to focus specifically on the English Only movement as a response to this immigration. The question I'm researching asks why American nativism emerged in this form in the 1990s. My plan is to do some background research on earlier forms of nativism but to focus mainly on what the English Only movement is and what it believes. I will also research the conditions in the country in the 1990s so I can explain how this movement took root.

FINDING SOURCES

Once you have established a direction for your research project, the next step is in-depth research. You will find detailed information on a wide range of research sources in Chapter 14, "A Guide to Print, Electronic, and Other Sources." In this section, we look first at what the Web and the library have to offer you as a researcher. Then we follow Amira on her research path.

THE WEB AND THE LIBRARY: WHAT THEY OFFER RESEARCH PROJECTS

Part of doing research is understanding what you can expect from the various sources available and which are considered credible for academic research projects. Let's look at what the Web and your college library can offer.

What the Web Is Good For

Web pages such as the Wikipedia entry on American nativism or "Cycles of American Nativism" can offer general background information and useful bibliography, but they are not considered authoritative scholarly sources in their own right. Most teachers would question a research paper that relied very heavily on them.

The Web is very good for getting public documents, reports, studies, and policy statements from government agencies, professional associations, universities, and nonprofits. It is very good at answering specific questions (if, say, you want to know how many people immigrated to the United States between 1965 and 1990 or how many households speak Spanish as the first language). It's also good for finding information about institutions or organizations such as U.S. English, to see how it presents itself and the case for English Only.

You may find sources such as James Crawford's Language Emporium that can be considered credible and authoritative. Crawford is widely recognized as an important writer on language policy, and so the articles and the sections of his books at the Web site are good sources for academic research. You may find such reliable sources at Web sites associated with universities, museums, research institutes, or other organizations. But you can't count on it.

Conclusions: Use the Web for background and specific information. Don't expect to write a research paper based exclusively or primarily on Web sources. The Web can be complementary to library research, but it can't substitute for it.

What the Library Is Good For

College and university libraries provide a number of ways to find appropriate scholarly and popular books and articles, in both print and electronic form.

Searchable library catalogs can be used to make subject searches, which will identify books on a particular topic in the library's holdings. Some books may be available in electronic form.

Searchable online databases and library subscription services such as JSTOR, Project Muse, PubMed, and LexisNexis can identify articles on your topic in scholarly journals, popular magazines, and newspapers, with access to abstracts or the complete text. Note, however, that not all scholarly and popular periodicals are included in these services. For this reason, don't count on finding all the readings you need online. It's quite likely you will need to look up articles in print form in the library stacks.

In fact, it can be rewarding to browse the shelves where books and journals on your topic are kept. Use the call number of a book that looks promising and see what other books are nearby. (You can also do this on many online library catalogs.)

Finally, libraries have knowledgeable librarians who can answer your questions and help guide you in the research process.

Conclusions: Expect that even with the best available online databases and library subscription services, you will not be able to find all the books and articles you need online. Plan to make use of the library in person. Browse the stacks. Consult with librarians.

HOW TO IDENTIFY RELEVANT SOURCES

How you read depends on your purposes and where you are in the research process. Once you have identified a research question, you are probably reading to gather information and to understand what others have said about the question you're investigating. As you're reading a source, ask yourself how relevant it is for your research question:

- Does it provide useful background information?
- Does it review previous research on the question?

- Could it help explain differences of opinion on the question?

- Can you use it as supporting evidence for your analysis and interpretations?

- Does it present evidence or ideas that run counter to your perspective? How should you take these into account?

KEEPING A WORKING BIBLIOGRAPHY

As you identify key research sources, make sure you take down the information you need to find the source as well as the information you'll need for your Works Cited or References section.

- **Books:** Include complete name of the author(s) and any editor or translator; the title and subtitle of the book; the place of publication, name of publisher, and date of publication.

- **Articles:** Include complete name of the author(s): title and subtitle of the article; periodical name, volume and issue numbers, date, and page numbers; name of electronic database and date of access (if applicable).

- **Online sources:** Include author's name (if available); title of the work; title of the overall Web site; publisher or sponsor of the site (if available); date work was published on the site (if available); date of access; URL.

Following a Research Path: Finding Relevant Sources

Let's look at Amira's notes as she looks for useful sources.

Using the Library Catalog

I already had the title of some books from browsing the Web, but I wanted to do a systematic search of the university library.

First, I tried "English Only movement" as a subject heading but only got three books. When I looked up one of them, *Nativism Reborn?*, I noticed the catalog entry listed other subjects: "Language policy—United States," "English language—Political aspects," and "English language—Social aspects—United States." I tried all these, and the best by far was "Language policy—United States." It turned up 33 references. I printed the search and headed for the stacks. [See Fig. 1.]

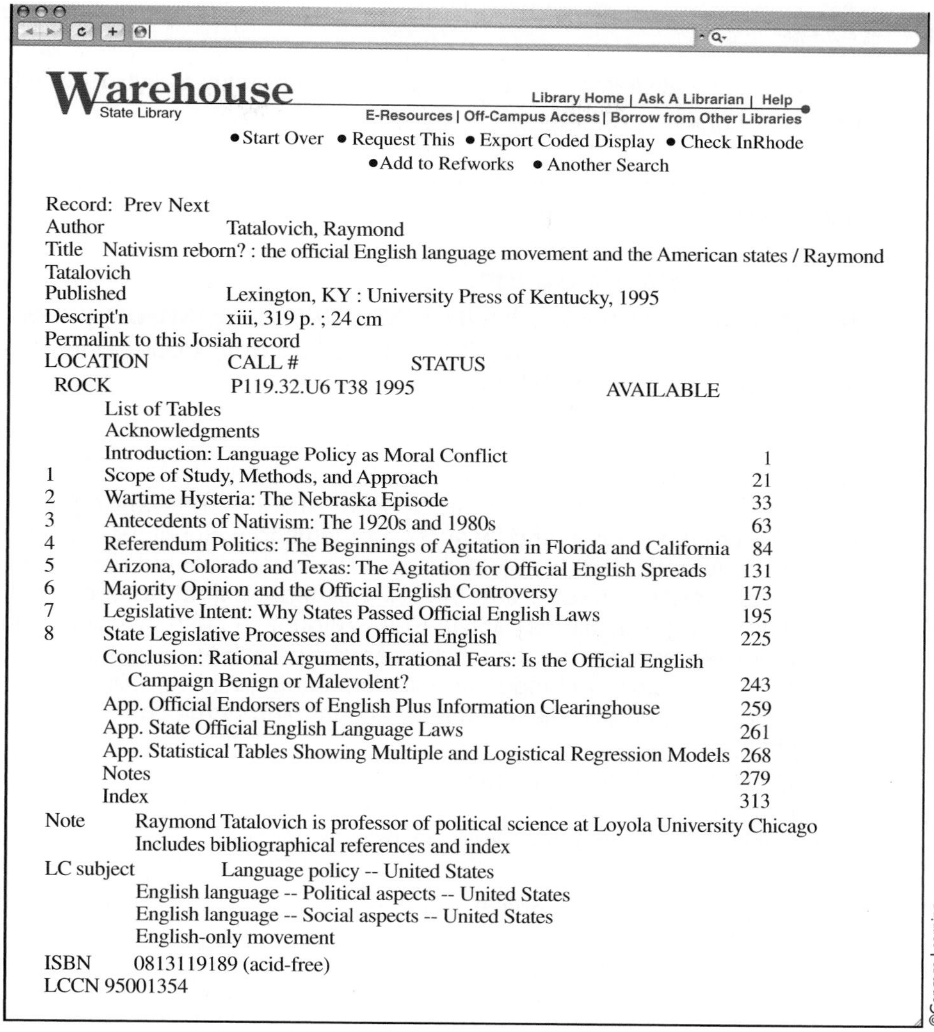
Warehouse
State Library

Library Home | Ask A Librarian | Help
E-Resources | Off-Campus Access | Borrow from Other Libraries

• Start Over • Request This • Export Coded Display • Check InRhode
• Add to Refworks • Another Search

Record: Prev Next
Author Tatalovich, Raymond
Title Nativism reborn? : the official English language movement and the American states / Raymond Tatalovich
Published Lexington, KY : University Press of Kentucky, 1995
Descript'n xiii, 319 p. ; 24 cm
Permalink to this Josiah record

LOCATION	CALL #	STATUS
ROCK	P119.32.U6 T38 1995	AVAILABLE

List of Tables
Acknowledgments
Introduction: Language Policy as Moral Conflict 1
1 Scope of Study, Methods, and Approach 21
2 Wartime Hysteria: The Nebraska Episode 33
3 Antecedents of Nativism: The 1920s and 1980s 63
4 Referendum Politics: The Beginnings of Agitation in Florida and California 84
5 Arizona, Colorado and Texas: The Agitation for Official English Spreads 131
6 Majority Opinion and the Official English Controversy 173
7 Legislative Intent: Why States Passed Official English Laws 195
8 State Legislative Processes and Official English 225
Conclusion: Rational Arguments, Irrational Fears: Is the Official English Campaign Benign or Malevolent? 243
App. Official Endorsers of English Plus Information Clearinghouse 259
App. State Official English Language Laws 261
App. Statistical Tables Showing Multiple and Logistical Regression Models 268
Notes 279
Index 313

Note Raymond Tatalovich is professor of political science at Loyola University Chicago
Includes bibliographical references and index
LC subject Language policy -- United States
English language -- Political aspects -- United States
English language -- Social aspects -- United States
English-only movement
ISBN 0813119189 (acid-free)
LCCN 95001354

©Cengage Learning

Fig. 1 Book entry in online catalog

Using Electronic Databases: Readers' Guide Abstracts

I had used Readers' Guide Abstracts in high school, and I know they list a lot of popular magazines. I wanted to get a sense of what people were saying about English only legislation in the 1990s. I used English-Only as a keyword and set dates from 1990 to 2000. That turned up 26 helpful sources that included abstracts.

Reproduced with the permission of The H.W. Wilson Company ©2009. For additional information on Readers' Guide Abstracts, visit http://www.hwwilson.com/Databases/Readersg.htm#Abstracts

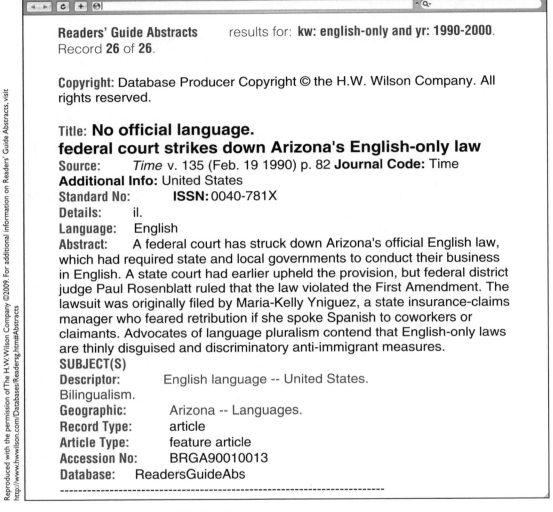

Readers' Guide Abstracts   results for: **kw: english-only and yr: 1990-2000**.
Record **26** of **26**.

Copyright: Database Producer Copyright © the H.W. Wilson Company. All rights reserved.

Title: **No official language.**
federal court strikes down Arizona's English-only law
Source: *Time* v. 135 (Feb. 19 1990) p. 82 **Journal Code:** Time
Additional Info: United States
Standard No: **ISSN:** 0040-781X
Details: il.
Language: English
Abstract: A federal court has struck down Arizona's official English law, which had required state and local governments to conduct their business in English. A state court had earlier upheld the provision, but federal district judge Paul Rosenblatt ruled that the law violated the First Amendment. The lawsuit was originally filed by Maria-Kelly Yniguez, a state insurance-claims manager who feared retribution if she spoke Spanish to coworkers or claimants. Advocates of language pluralism contend that English-only laws are thinly disguised and discriminatory anti-immigrant measures.
SUBJECT(S)
Descriptor: English language -- United States.
Bilingualism.
Geographic: Arizona -- Languages.
Record Type: article
Article Type: feature article
Accession No: BRGA90010013
Database: ReadersGuideAbs

Fig. 2   Results from Readers' Guide Abstracts

Finding Full-Text Articles Through Electronic Databases

I knew the library had full-text subscription services, but I had never used them before. So I asked a librarian where to start, and he suggested Academic Search Premier and JSTOR. Each works a little differently and what you get depends on the keywords you use. Sometimes it's overwhelming, and I had to sort through a lot to find what I was looking for on the English Only movement of the 1990s but I did find a number of really helpful articles.

Finding Immigration Statistics

As I got deeper into my research, I realized that the English Only movement emerged as immigration to the United States increased after the immigration law changed in 1965. I wanted to get some statistics on the patterns of immigration—where people came from, how many there were, where they settled. I remembered looking at the U.S. Citizenship and Immigration Services Web site when I was getting started, so I decided to go back and see what they had. I found the Office of Immigration Statistics that had the information I was looking for. [See Fig. 3.]

Fig. 3   Office of Immigration Statistics

EVALUATING SOURCES

As you continue your research, keep in mind that you can't accept what your sources say at face value. Here are some considerations to keep in mind:

- Is the date the work was published appropriate to your purposes? In many cases, the most recent source is the most authoritative. At the same time, it may be appropriate to read older work that is acknowledged as important. In Amira's case, it makes sense to read sources from the period she is investigating, the 1990s, when the English Only movement emerged.

- What credibility does the writer have? Is he or she acknowledged as an authority?

- What is the writer's point of view? What are his or her political allegiances?

- Is the publication or press in which the source appears of good reputation? What is its editorial slant?

Following a Research Path: Evaluating Sources

Notice how Amira is careful to record information and quotations accurately. She follows with her own notes that evaluate the source and identifies further questions for her research.

Amira's Notes on an Article in the National Review

O'Beirne, Kate. "English as the Official Language of the U.S. and Bilingual Education." *National Review* 1 July 1996: 21.

Cites opinion polls:

- In a 1996 Gallup Poll, 82% favored making English the official language.
- A 1993 poll by the Tarrance Group found 78% registered voters favored official English laws and over 60% favored it strongly.
- A 1993 poll by the *San Francisco Chronicle* found that 90% of Filipinos, 78% of Chinese, and nearly 70% of Latino immigrants in California favored official English.

Gives details on the Republican Party position on official English and bilingual education, ballots, and health care. Argues that given popular support for official English, Republicans should take stronger stand.

Key quote:

"We must stop the practice of multilingual education as a means of instilling ethnic pride or as a therapy for low self-esteem, or out of elitist guilt over a culture built on the tradition of the west." Bob Dole, in a speech to the American Legion.

Notes: Great find. *National Review* is an important conservative magazine, and Kate O'Beirne seems to be a prominent conservative commentator. Helps explain ideas of English Only movement.

Check *San Francisco Chronicle* poll. I may need to explain high support of official English among immigrant groups. May be a sign of desire to assimilate and could be used to argue that official English is unnecessary.

MAKING AN ARGUMENT

Doing research is learning new things and encountering new perspectives. Research involves you in a conversation with other people, who may influence what you think and believe. Stay open to these influences. It's not unusual for researchers to modify their initial ideas in light of what they find in their research.

At the same time, you need to assess what you've been reading so that you can make your own argument about the issues you've been examining. Here are some questions to help you determine the argument you want to make:

- What sources have made the strongest impression on you, whether you agree with them or not?

- How have your sources influenced your thinking? Do you see your research question in the same way as when you started researching? What changes have occurred?

- What new perspectives or questions have you encountered? How do you plan to deal with them?

- Given all this, how can you put an argument together?

Following a Research Path: Making an Argument

Amira's Statement of Purpose

A lot of what I've read about the English Only movement (like James Crawford's *Hold Your Tongue* and Raymond Tatalovich's *Nativism Reborn?*) see it as an anti-immigrant backlash. The articles I've read by supporters of English Only don't come right out and say they are anti-immigrant, but they do talk about how the U.S. is losing its national identity because of immigration and multiculturalism. They use terms like "balkanization" to create the impression that America is fragmenting into separate ethnic groups. They seem to think that the English language can hold everything together.

The feeling I get is that people are afraid that they are going to be overwhelmed by Spanish-speaking immigrants, if not now, then in the near future. Crawford's idea of "Hispanophobia" makes a lot of sense to me as a way to explain the English Only movement. That's what I think I want to say in my paper.

PLANNING AND DRAFTING YOUR PROJECT

There's always more to read, and it may seem that the research process could continue indefinitely. In certain respects, of course, this is true. Individuals have devoted their lives to research and never really reached the end of what they could learn. That's why deadlines are so useful—to remind writers that they need to emerge from the research process and start writing.

An important point here is that you need to make sure you're not using research to procrastinate and avoid writing. As already mentioned, when you're reading and evaluating your sources, you should also be making tentative plans about how to use these materials in your paper. Moreover, you can begin drafting well before you end your research. In fact, many researchers find that drafting helps them refine the focus of their research and directs them to issues they need to investigate further. To put it another way, you don't have to stop your research when you begin writing. But you do have to begin writing.

Following a Research Path: Making an Outline

Amira's First Outline

Set up the issue of English Only

> background information on states with English Only laws

> public opinion polls

emergence of U.S. English and English first in the 1990s

present basic positions and arguments of English Only

State purpose of paper: to explain the emergence of English

Only movement in the 1990s as "hispanophobia" resulting from new

patterns of immigration and cultural anxiety

Historical background

relation of language policy and nativism/Americanization

Anti-Irish literacy requirements for voting (1850s)

American Protective Association's campaign vs. German-language instruction

in parochial schools (1880s)

U.S. Bureau of Americanization (early 1900s)

1965 Immigration Reform Act

ended racial quotas

"new immigration"

demographic shifts increase in Latino population

Analysis of English Only movement

familiar sources of nativism in the 1990s:

economic stagnation (California)

widening gap between rich and poor

distrust of public institutions

breakdown of community

"hispanophobia" in California and the Southwest

historical roots

present manifestations

explain focus on language as symbol of imagined lost community

A CLOSING NOTE

As you can see from Amira Patel's sketch of her outline for her research paper on the English Only movement, she has listed topics and points of analysis that will be central to drafting her paper. Her task now is to begin writing so that she can see how the information and ideas from her research connect to each other.

You'll no doubt reach a similar point in your own research—when it's time to start writing. Remember that you know a lot by this point. You will have information, evidence, and arguments from others that may not be widely available to your readers. Don't assume that just because you know something, everyone else must know it too. You're the authority who is immersed in the topic and issues of your research, and it's your job to explain how it all fits together. Keep in mind what your purpose is in writing your research paper. To what extent do you need to inform, explain, evaluate, or argue about the issues that have come up in your research? What sources are likely to persuade your readers to take your point of view seriously? How can you make the best use of what you've found in the research process?

In the next chapter, we'll look at some of the options for incorporating your sources into critical essays and research papers.

chapter 13

working with sources

As noted already, academic writing does more than simply present the results of research. More importantly, it shows how the writer's research grows out of issues and problems in a particular field of study, and it explains the significance of the research to this ongoing discussion. Integrating and citing sources in a research paper lets your readers know how your work fits into a larger conversation.

Students sometimes think that using sources weakens their writing—that readers will think the important ideas in a paper come from others instead of from them. In college, however, readers expect writers to use and acknowledge sources. Readers want to understand what others have said about the issue you've researched, who has influenced your thinking, and how you stand in relation to the analyses, interpretations, and arguments others have offered. In fact, these expectations define in many respects what it means to work with sources.

In this chapter, we look first at some of the ways academic researchers work with their sources. Next, we present information on what plagiarism is and how to avoid it by properly integrating your sources. Finally, we cover how to document your sources in MLA and APA formats.

WORKING WITH SOURCES TO ANSWER YOUR RESEARCH QUESTION

In academic writing, you want to demonstrate how you are using your sources to create a meaningful answer to your research question. Here are some of the common ways to work with sources in college:

- **To support a position, analysis, or interpretation:** In her discussion of shopping in "I Shop, Ergo, I Am: The Mall as Society's Mirror," Sara Boxer draws on key source to make her point:

  > Shoppers' freedoms are changing. According to Robert Bocock, writing in Consumption, the mall walkers of today do not have the rights

413

that the flaneurs of the 19th century had. "In the United States, 'policing' of who is allowed entry to the malls has become stricter in the last two or three decades of the 20th century."

■ **To assess the uses and limits of an analysis or interpretation:** In "Uncertainty and Uses of Magic, " researchers Richard B. Felson and George Gmelch take as their task testing Bronislaw Malinowki's theory of magic.

> According to Malinowski, people use magic to alleviate or reduce the anxiety created by conditions of uncertainty. Through the perform- ance of the appropriate rituals, people "work off the tensions aroused by fear. An alternative explanation would be that magic results from purely cognitive processes and represents an effort to produce favor- able results. In other words, people believe that unknown forces— "good luck" and "bad luck"—play a role in the outcome of events and that these forces can be manipulated by magic.
>
> This study examines these relationships using a sample of American and Irish college students.

■ **To apply a concept to a new case or situation:** In "Radiohead and the Tip-Jar Model," Stacy Yi uses the notion of the "tip jar" to ana- lyze Radiohead's online release of *In Rainbows?* with the price of "it's up to you":

> Many of those commentators compared Radiohead's sales plan for *In Rainbows* to the tip jar on the counter of the local coffee shop. The comparison isn't quite parallel because tips are generally given for quality service that accompanies an already-purchased product. In Radiohead's case, however, the product and service are one and the same (at least until *In Rainbows* was released in the stores, months later, on TBD Records.) That fits with Greg Kot's observation, from *Ripped: How the Wired Generation Revolutionized Music*, that the band wanted only "to leak its own album, give fans a taste of the new music, and invite them to buy the sonically superior physical prod- uct once it became available in a few months" (1). Using an online tip jar for digital sales, then, is not necessarily the best way to make money, but an effective means of promoting a product to be sold later at a fixed rate.

■ **To change the terms of a debate:** In his research paper, "The Prison Privatization Debate: The Need for a New Focus," Andy Mgwanna shows how the arguments for and against the privatazation of prisons have reached an impasse. Then he explains what has been neglected by the debate and points to a new focus:

> A problem with this impasse, as O'Brien (2006) suggests, is that the key issues of rehabilitation and recidivism, which have significant

implications for the cost of the prison industrial complex, have been lost in a polarized debate. O'Brien (2006) argues that rather than becoming bogged down in the pros and cons of privatization, we should focus on incentives to both private and public prisons to prevent recidivism.

- **To uncover an enabling assumption and its consequences:** In "How to Fight the New Epidemics," Lundy Braun first cites a well-known scientist to establish the dominant view of infectious diseases:

    In 1966, the eminent Australian immunologist Sir MacFarlane Burnet declared, "In many ways one can think of the middle of the 20th Century as the end of one of the most important social revolutions in history, the virtual elimination of infectious disease as a significant factor in social life." Shared by most of the scientific community, this view is rooted in the rise of the germ theory in the late 19th and early 20th centuries that associated specific microbial agents with particular diseases.

    Then she explains the consequences of the germ theory's assumptions about disease causation:

    Thus, the germ theory effectively replaced disease prevention policies based on sanitary reforms, including improvement in sewage systems and better housing conditions, which were primarily responsible for the dramatic decline in the death rates from infectious disease.

WHAT IS PLAGIARISM?

Plagiarism is taking the words or ideas of someone else and presenting them as your own, without properly acknowledging their source in another's work. There are different ways in which plagiarism occurs.

- **Cheating:** Buying a research paper, paying someone else to write a paper for you, or turning in someone's old paper is academic dishonesty, plain and simple, and is obviously intentional.

- **Copying:** Reproducing sentences or passages from a book or article without citation may be intentional or may be due to a lack of understanding how properly to acknowledge sources.

- **Copying patterns:** Plagiarism includes copying sentence structures, even if you change some of the words.

    You can see how copying patterns works in a recent example, where Kaavya Viswanathan says that she "accidentally borrowed" sections from *Sloppy Firsts*, a book by Megan McCafferty, for her novel *How Opal Mehta Got Kissed, Got Wild, and Got a Life*. Because of the plagiarism, her publishers withdrew the novel. Below are the examples of similar passages in the two books.

McCafferty's novel, page 7:

"Bridget is my age and lives across the street. For the first twelve years of my life, these qualifications were all I needed in a best friend. But that was before Bridget's braces came off and her boyfriend Burke got on, before Hope and I met in our seventh grade Honors classes."

Viswanathan's novel, page 14:

"Priscilla was my age and lived two blocks away. For the first fifteen years of my life, those were the only qualifications I needed in a best friend. We had bonded over our mutual fascination with the abacus in a playgroup for gifted kids. But that was before freshman year, when Priscilla's glasses came off, and the first in a long string of boyfriends came on."

McCafferty, page 6:

"Sabrina was the brainy Angel. Yet another example of how every girl had to be one or the other: Pretty or smart."

Viswanathan, page 39:

"Moneypenny was the brainy female character. Yet another example of how every girl had to be one or the other: smart or pretty."

■ **Failure to cite properly:** The most common form of unintentional plagiarism results from not understanding how to use and cite sources properly. For this reason, to avoid plagiarism you need to be aware of the conventions of citation and the various options you have in integrating sources into your writing.

AVOIDING PLAGIARISM: HOW TO CITE PROPERLY

Here is a passage from Alan M. Kraut's chapter "Plagues and Prejudice: Nativism's Construction of Disease in Nineteenth- and Twentieth-Century New York" that appears on page 67 in *Hives of Sickness: Public Health and*

WHAT DO I HAVE TO CITE?

A reliable rule of thumb is that you should cite the source of any information, analysis, interpretation, or argument that is not common knowledge. It is common knowledge, for example, that William Shakespeare was a playwright in Elizabethan England, the Earth travels around the sun, and Darwin formulated the theory of natural selection. This is information so widely known that it doesn't really belong to anyone. On the other hand, a literary critic's interpretation of Hamlet, *an analysis of how Darwin developed his idea of natural selection, or an argument about the consequences of climate change is not considered common knowledge because it belongs to a particular person or group.*

Epidemics in New York City, the type of source you're likely to be working with in academic writing:

> As early as the 1830s, Irish immigrants who lived in rundown shanties and tenements along New York's rivers were being blamed for importing the cholera epidemic (from which they suffered disproportionately). Fear of cholera, especially after the epidemic of 1832, stimulated public demand for inspection of emigrants prior to departure. Soon, those who left from Western European ports began to receive an exam from a physician employed by the country of departure, lest shiploads of emigrants be annihilated by cholera during the voyage.

Problem 1: Copying and Failing to Cite Properly

Notice the following student-written passage plagiarizes (probably unintentionally) by copying sentences and failing to identify the source.

Copied Phrases Are Highlighted

During the 1830s, there was widespread concern about the danger of cholera being brought to the United States by immigrants. Prime suspects were the Irish, who lived in rundown shanties and tenements along New York's rivers and who suffered a high rate of cholera. Following the cholera epidemic of 1832, public pressure mounted to examine emigrants before they left Europe. Physicians hired by the European countries inspected departing passengers, lest shiploads of emigrants be annihilated by cholera during the voyage.

Revised Version

According to Alan M. Kraut, during the 1830s, there was widespread concern about the danger of cholera being brought to the United States by immigrants. Prime suspects were the Irish, "who lived in rundown shanties and tenements along New York's rivers" and who suffered a high rate of cholera. Following the cholera epidemic of 1832, public pressure mounted to examine emigrants before they left Europe. Physicians hired by the European countries inspected departing passengers, "lest shiploads of emigrants be annihilated by cholera during the voyage" (67).

Notice how the revised version (1) turns the source "on" by attributing the ideas to the author ("According to Alan M. Kraut") and then turns it "off" with the page citation (67) at the end of the passage, and (2) carefully puts direct quotes in quotation marks.

Problem 2: Copying Sentence Structure and Failing to Cite Properly

Notice in this example how the student copies sentence structure and does not cite the source of the ideas.

Alan M. Kraut (original source)	Student
Soon, those who left from Western European ports began to receive an exam from a physician employed by the country of departure, lest shiploads of emigrants be annihilated by cholera during the voyage.	Before long, those departing from Western European ports were examined by doctors hired by the country of departure, so that boatloads of emigrants would not die from cholera during the trip.

Revised Version

Following the cholera epidemic of 1832, public pressure mounted to examine emigrants before they left Europe. Physicians in European ports of departure inspected passengers in an effort to prevent the spread of cholera (Kraut 67).

Notice how the revised version (1) integrates ideas into the student's own sentence structure, and (2) includes citation of the author's name and the page number at the end of sentence.

OPTIONS FOR INTEGRATING SOURCES

The three basic methods of integrating sources are *paraphrasing*, *summarizing*, and *quoting*. Whichever you use, be sure to cite properly. Turn your source "on" by citing the author with a phrase like "According to Alan M. Kraut" or "Kraut points out" and "off" by citing the page number in parentheses. When you do not identify the author with one of these phrases, include the author's last name and the page number (Kraut 67).

- **Paraphrasing** means restating in your own words and sentence structure. A paraphrase is typically about the same length as the original and is used when you want to explain the details in the original source:

  > According to Alan M. Kraut, during the 1830s, there was widespread concern about the danger of cholera being brought to the United States by immigrants. Prime suspects were the Irish, who suffered a high rate of cholera. Following the cholera epidemic of 1832, public pressure mounted to examine emigrants before they left Europe. In order to prevent devastating outbreaks of disease onboard the ships, physicians hired by the European countries inspected departing passengers (67).

- **Summarizing** means selecting main ideas from the original and presenting them in your own words and sentence structure. Summaries can range from a sentence to a paragraph or more, depending on the amount of detail you need. Notice in this example, how details are omitted to emphasize a single point:

> During the 1830s the fear that immigrants were bringing cholera with them to the United States led to health inspections of departing passengers in the European ports (Kraut 67).

- **Quoting** means duplicating the exact words as they appear in the original. In general, use direct quotations selectively. Quotations are best suited when you want to capture something in the original you would lose by paraphrasing, or when a direct quotation from an expert will lend authority. Short quotes, even a key word or phrase, are often more effective than longer ones.

Short Quotations

Words

Writers typically quote single words to emphasize important points and represent key concepts in their discussion. Often the quoted word is a term that someone has coined for analytical purposes, as in these two instances:

> The ceremonial suspension of normal identities by World Wrestling Federation stars offers spectators a way to participate in what Victor Turner calls a "liminal" moment, when ordinary time and everyday human affairs come briefly to a halt and the extraordinary takes over.
>
> Stuart Hall's notion of "encoding/decoding" in media communication enables us to see how messages are transformed as they circulate from production to reception.

Notice in these two examples that the key terms "liminal" and "encoding/decoding" appear in quotes and that in each case the author is noted. There are no page numbers, however, because the terms appear throughout the original sources, which are then acknowledged in Works Cited.

Phrases

You can integrate phrases as elements in sentences of your own construction:

> Alan M. Kraut explains how the growing fear that immigrants were bringing cholera to the United States "stimulated public demand for inspection of emigrants prior to departure" from Europe (67).

Sentences

You can use a complete sentence or two from your source:

> According to Alan M. Kraut, "Fear of cholera, especially after the epidemic of 1832, stimulated public demand for inspection of emigrants prior to departure" (67).

LONG QUOTATIONS

Use an indented block for long quotations. MLA identifies long quotations as more than four lines, while APA uses 40 words. Indent one inch (or ten spaces) from the left margin if you are using MLA style, or a half-inch (or five spaces) from the left margin if you are using APA style, and in both cases double-space the passage with no extra space above or below the block. Using this block form tells readers that the material is quoted directly from the original, so you don't need quotation marks. The page citation goes in parentheses after the punctuation at the end of the quote. The example below uses MLA style—indenting ten spaces to form the block. For single paragraphs or portions of a paragraph, do not indent the first line. If you quote two or more paragraphs, indent three additional spaces (one-quarter inch) at the beginning of each successive paragraph.

> Public health historian Alan M. Kraut points out how Americans have long viewed immigrants as carriers of disease:
>
> > As early as the 1830s, Irish immigrants who lived in rundown shanties and tenements along New York's rivers were being blamed for importing the cholera epidemic (from which they suffered disproportionately). Fear of cholera, especially after the epidemic of 1832, stimulated public demand for inspection of emigrants prior to departure. Soon, those who left from western European ports began to receive an exam from a physician employed by the country of departure, lest shiploads of emigrants be annihilated by cholera during the voyage. (67)

FITTING QUOTATIONS TO YOUR SENTENCES

Under certain circumstances, you may modify the material you're quoting. The two basic techniques for modifying the original passage are ellipses and brackets. You use ellipses to omit something in the original and brackets to add or change something. Here are examples of typical uses of each.

Ellipses

Use ellipses when you want to omit part of the original passage. If you are omitting material in the middle of a sentence, use a set of three spaced periods, with a space before and after.

"As early as the 1830s," Alan M. Kraut notes, "Irish immigrants . . . were being blamed for importing the cholera epidemic" (67).

When you quote single words or phrases, you don't need to use ellipses because readers can see you're quoting only part of a passage. If the material you're omitting occurs between sentences, include a fourth period to mark the end of the first sentence.

Alan M. Kraut notes similarities between the official response to cholera, polio, and tuberculosis in the nineteenth and early twentieth centuries and to AIDS in the 1990s:

> In the early 1990s, the federal government continued to pursue institutional means of epidemic control to stop AIDS at the border, a means that stigmatizes immigrants of all nationalities. . . . As in earlier crises, the federal government had sought to use exclusion to control the epidemic; immigrants were subjected to mandatory testing for no clear epidemiological reason other than foreign birth. (83)

Brackets

Brackets are used to make small changes in the original passage so that it fits grammatically into your sentences.

> According to Alan M. Kraut, the federal government's use of mandatory AIDS testing repeats a pattern that can be found in earlier public health crises, "stigmatiz[ing] immigrants of all nationalities" (83).

Brackets can also be used to add clarifying material.

Original

> Wealthy New York City merchants and uptown landowners, who in the early 1850s proposed the creation of Central Park, hoped to create a refined setting for their own socializing. But seeking to establish the public value of their project, they also invoked the language of the English sanitary reformers and claimed the park would improve the health and morals of the city's working people.
>
> *(Alan M. Kraut, "Plagues and Prejudice," p. 57)*

Use of Brackets

> Alan M. Kraut shows how the proposal to create Central Park drew on themes from the public health movement: "seeking to establish the public value of their project, they [wealthy New York City merchants and uptown landowners] also invoked the language of the English sanitary reformers and claimed the park would improve the health and morals of the city's working people" (57).

Quotations Within Quotations

The passage you want to quote may at times contain quoted material. If the passage is long enough to use block form, then keep the quotation marks as they are in the original. If, however, you are going to incorporate a quotation that includes a quotation into your own sentence, then change the double quotation marks in the original into single quotation marks.

Original

Against this backdrop of economic depression, the physician and city inspector John Griscom launched a new phase of sanitary reform in his 1842 report when he singled out "the crowded conditions, with insufficient ventilation" of dwellings as "first among the most serious causes of disordered public health."

(Alan M. Kraut, "Plagues and Prejudice," p. 54)

Quotations Within a Quotation

Alan M. Kraut claims that "John Griscom launched a new phase of sanitary reform in his 1842 report when he singled out 'the crowded conditions, with insufficient ventilation' of dwellings as 'first among the most serious causes of disordered public health'" (54).

CHECKLIST FOR USING QUOTES EFFECTIVELY

The following questions offer further guidelines as you review your work and consider needed revisions.

Do You Need the Quote?

Quoted material should be chosen carefully to advance the line of thinking in a research project. It should emphasize main ideas, not just be used decoratively or as proof that you've read a number of sources.

The plot of *Wuthering Heights* puts the death of the heroine in the middle of the novel. Although she has died in childbirth, Catherine Earnshaw relentlessly haunts Heathcliff until eighteen years later he too finally rests by her side in a grave "on the edge of the churchyard" (Frank 219).

The quoted phrase does not really contain an idea that matters to the discussion. Quotes like this one should be scrutinized closely to see if they are needed.

IS IT CLEAR WHERE SOURCES START AND STOP?

One of the keys to avoiding plagiarism is marking clearly where quoted material starts and stops. In the example below, notice how the first two quotes—the highlighted sentence and phrase—seem to be floating in the paragraph, and how the in-text citation (219) confusingly appears before the writer has finished quoting from the source.

> *Wuthering Heights* uses subtle psychological portrayals of its main characters, Catherine Earnshaw and Heathcliff, to turn them into mythic figures. "They are driven, tormented, violent lovers, and there are no wedding bells for them in the final chapter." In the grip of a titanic passion, their love can only be realized in death. Before his death, Heathcliff arranges to have the sides of his and Catherine's adjoining coffins dismantled "so that in death they might finally achieve the consummation of their love" (219). This is the "perfect and irrevocable union," Katherine Frank says, "which had tormented and eluded them when they were alive."

All the quoted material is from Katherine Frank's book *A Chainless Soul*, but readers will have to guess the source of the first two quotes. This problem can easily be fixed, as you can see by the highlighted revisions:

> *Wuthering Heights* uses subtle psychological portrayals of its main characters, Catherine Earnshaw and Heathcliff, to turn them into mythic figures. "They are driven, tormented, violent lovers," Katherine Frank says, "and there are no wedding bells for them in the final chapter." In the grip of a titanic passion, their love can only be realized in death. Before his death, Heathcliff arranges to have the sides of his and Catherine's adjoining coffins dismantled "so that in death they might finally achieve the consummation of their love." According to Frank, this is the "perfect and irrevocable union—which had tormented and eluded them when they were alive" (219).

ARE SOURCES USED PURPOSEFULLY OR JUST STRUNG TOGETHER?

Make sure your sources are set up so that readers will see how each quoted and paraphrased idea fits into your writing. Sources that are strung together, as in the following example, resemble research notes transcribed directly into a paper. As you can see, the writing seems to ramble from quote to quote without any sense of purposeful direction:

> The musical label "soul" is associated with Motown and Memphis in the 1960s, but the term has been in use much longer. According to gospel singer

Mahalia Jackson, "What some people call the 'blues singing feeling' is expressed by the Church of God in Christ. . . . The basic thing is soul feeling. The same in blues as in spirituals. And also with gospel music. It is soul music" (qtd. in Ricks 139). "Soul assumes a shared experience, a relationship with the listener . . . where the singer confirms and works out the feelings of the audience. In this sense, it remains sacramental" (qtd. in Guralnick 3). "As professions, blues singing and preaching seem to be closely linked in both the rural or small town settings and in the urban ghettos" (Keil 143). Nonetheless, "Ray Charles's transformation of dignified gospel standards into cries of secular ecstasy came in for a good deal of criticism at first, mostly from the pulpit" (Guralnick 2).

A revision of this paragraph would require unpacking each quote by explaining the ideas and connecting them to the main points in the paper. Each quote may need its own paragraph, or the writer might combine two or more quotes in a paragraph. In any case, the quotes need space to breathe.

Do You Provide Commentary Where It Is Needed?

Quotes don't speak for themselves. As you've just seen in the example with the string of quotes, you need to connect your sources to the main points in your paper so that readers can see how and why the sources are significant. Your commentary is crucial to making these connections explicit. In the following example, notice how the quote leaves us hanging because it is not followed up by commentary from the writer:

Wuthering Heights is partially based on the Gothic tradition, a quasi-horror writing that features haunting imagery, desolate landscapes, and supernatural encounters. Bronte draws on the Gothic to turn her main characters, Catherine Earnshaw and Heathcliff, into mythic figures in the grip of a titanic passion. Catherine marries Edgar Linton, and Heathcliff marries Edgar's sister Isabella, but these marriages have no impact on Catherine and Heathcliff's passionate love. Nor does death. Although she dies in childbirth in the middle of the novel, Catherine relentlessly haunts Heathcliff until eighteen years later he too finally rests by her side. As Katherine Frank explains:

> Before he dies, Heathcliff makes a ghoulish arrangement with the sexton to knock out the adjoining sides of his own and Catherine's coffins so that in death they might finally achieve the consummation of their love—a perfect and irrevocable union—which had tormented and eluded them when they were alive. (219)

In earlier Gothic novels, the central narrative is often approached by way of a frame tale that uses diaries, letters, and other documents, which are transcribed or edited by the narrator. Similarly, the reader approaches the narrative of *Wuthering Heights* via an outsider, Lockwood.

A few lines of commentary from the writer would not only consolidate the point in the paragraph but also set up a smoother transition into the next paragraph, as shown in the example that follows.

> . . . the consummation of their love—a perfect and irrevocable union—which had tormented and eluded them when they were alive (219).
> In true Gothic style, Bronte blurs the line between life and death to create an imaginary world of haunted and uncontrollable passions.
> This imaginary world is typically both verified and kept at a mysterious distance in Gothic novels by a frame tale that uses diaries, letters, and other documents, which are transcribed or . . .

DOCUMENTING SOURCES: MLA AND APA STYLE

The two main styles of citation—MLA and APA—use parenthetical citations within the text. Information about the source is included in the text and keyed to a list of sources at the end of the paper—*Works Cited* in MLA style and *References* in APA. The information called for by MLA and APA in the parenthetical citation differs somewhat. MLA uses author and page, while APA uses author, year, and page.

The following pages describe MLA and APA systems for citing sources within the text and for listing sources at the end of the paper. For further information, you can consult *MLA Handbook for Writers of Research Papers* (7th ed., 2009) or the MLA Web site www.mla.org, and *Publication Manual of the American Psychological Association* (5th ed., 2001) or the APA Web site on documenting electronic sources www.apastyle.org/elecref.html.

IN-TEXT CITATIONS

The following list shows how MLA and APA styles set up parenthetical in-text citations for many types of sources.

Sources with One Author

In many instances, you'll be citing the author in the sentence that uses the source material.

MLA

According to Daniel J. Czitrom, following the Civil War, there appeared the "first rush of literature on the pathology of mass communication, with which we are so familiar today" (19).

Note that you do not repeat the author's name when you give the page number at the end of the quotation.

APA

According to Daniel J. Czitrom (1982), following the Civil War, there appeared the "first rush of literature on the pathology of mass communication, with which we are so familiar today" (p. 19).

Note that in APA style, the date of publication appears immediately after the author's name.

If you don't cite the author in the sentence, then use these forms:

MLA

Following the Civil War, there appeared the "first rush of literature on the pathology of mass communication, with which we are so familiar today" (Czitrom 19).

MLA style notes the author and the page number, with no punctuation in between or "p." before the page.

APA

Following the Civil War, there appeared the "first rush of literature on the pathology of mass communication, with which we are so familiar today" (Czitrom, 1982, p. 19).

APA style includes the author's name, the date of publication, and the page number, with commas in between and "p." before the page number.

Notice that for both MLA and APA styles, the final period comes after the citation.

MLA

Following the Civil War, there appeared the "first rush of literature on the pathology of mass communication, with which we are so familiar today" (Czitrom, *Media* 19).

When you have more than one source by an author, MLA style uses the author's name, a shortened version of the title (the full title is *Media and the American Mind: From Morse to McLuhan*), and the page number.

APA

> Following the Civil War, there appeared the "first rush of literature on the pathology of mass communication, with which we are so familiar today" (Czitrom, 1982, p. 19).

APA style remains the same because the work is already noted by the year. However, if you are citing in APA style more than one work published by an author in the same year, arrange the works alphabetically by title, add a letter to the date (1982a, 1982b) and key these to your references at the end of the paper. For example, if you cited a second work Czitrom published in 1982, the first work would be cited as:

> (Czitrom, 1982a, p. 19)

and the second would look like this:

> (Czitrom, 1982b, p. 43)

SOURCES WITH MULTIPLE AUTHORS

MLA and APA use different systems to cite sources having more than one author.

MLA

If the work has two or three authors, cite all:

> Despite the claims made for it, literacy "is not in itself a panacea for social inequity" (Lunsford, Moglen, and Slevin 2).

If the work has more than three authors, use the first author's name followed by "et al."

> What we know of Indian cultures prior to 1700 has mostly been gleaned from the evidence of various artifacts, such as pottery, weapons, and stories passed down from generation to generation (Lauter et al. 5).

APA

If the source you are citing has two authors, include both last names in the reference, separated by an ampersand (&).

> Nigeria home-video movies "are turning out the Nigerian story in a no-holds-barred fashion which leaves no room for anybody to hide" (Ofeiman & Kelani, 2005, p. 245).

For sources with three to five authors, list all of the authors' last names the first time you cite the source, separating each name by a comma and putting an ampersand before the final name.

> Despite the claims made for it, literacy "is not in itself a panacea for social inequity" (Lunsford, Moglen, & Slevin, 1990, p. 2).

For subsequent citations, include simply the last name of the first author followed by "et al." and the year and the page. If a source has six or more authors, use the last name of the first author and "et al." in every citation:

> Despite the claims made for it, literacy "is not in itself a panacea for social inequity" (Lunsford et al., 1990, p. 2).

SOURCES WITH NO AUTHOR LISTED

If no author is listed on the work, both MLA and APA use a shortened version of the title.

MLA

> A 1996 study found that men who frequent prostitutes or have many sexual partners may increase their wives' risk of cervical cancer ("Man's Sex Life").

Note that if your source appears on a single page, MLA does not require you to list the page number.

APA

> A 1996 study found that men who frequent prostitutes or have many sexual partners may increase their wives' risk of cervical cancer ("Man's Sex Life," 1996, p. 15).

The MLA and APA citations use a shortened version of the title of the article, "Man's Sex Life and Cancer in Wife Linked."

ONLINE SOURCES

Sources you have accessed on the Web or through electronic databases are handled in much the same way as print sources.

MLA

> Hurricane Katrina revealed "some of the blank spots and overlooked inequities in race relations that were shocking to many whites but lived realities for most blacks" (Carpenter 2).

If no author is listed, use the title of the document. If the document has numbered paragraphs rather than pages, use the number following a comma and the abbreviation par. (e.g., McKenzie, par. 4). For documents with no numbered pages or paragraphs, no number is listed.

APA

> Hurricane Katrina revealed "some of the blank spots and overlooked inequities in race relations that were shocking to many whites but lived realities for most blacks" (Carpenter, 2006, p. 2).

If no date of publication is given, use "n.d." If no author is listed, use a short-ened version of the title. When there are no page numbers, use paragraph numbers to document quotes:

> The marketing of race-specific drugs such as Bi-Dil has raised "troubling questions about the reinstitution of race as a biological category in medicine" ("Return of Race," n.d., para. 4).

INDIRECT QUOTATIONS

For cases when you want to quote something that appeared as a quote in one of your sources, use "qtd. in" (MLA) or "cited in" (APA). In the following two examples, the writer is quoting the blues musician Son House from an inter-view that appeared originally in Pete Welding's book *The Living Blue* and then was quoted by Greil Marcus's in his book *Mystery Train*.

MLA

> "He sold his soul to the devil to get to play like that," House told blues historian Pete Welding (qtd. in Marcus 32).

APA

> "He sold his soul to the devil to get to play like that," House told blues historian Pete Welding (cited in Marcus, 1975, p. 32).

WORKS CITED (MLA) AND REFERENCES (APA)

Every source that appears in the text should be listed in a separate section at the end of your paper. Don't include works that you read but did not cite. MLA calls the list "Works Cited," while APA uses "References." Both systems alpha-betize by author's last name or the first word in the title of a work with no author.

Books

Here is the basic format for MLA and APA. Notice how they differ.

MLA

> Hedges, Chris. *Empire of Illusion*. New York: Nation Books, 2009. Print.

MLA style uses the complete first name of the author, capitalizes major words in the title, lists the date at the end of the citation, and indents the second line five spaces. The period following the book title is not underlined or italicized. In MLA style, use the abbreviation "UP" for university presses, as in Columbia UP. MLA style gives the publication medium, Print or Web.

APA

> Hedges, C. (2009). *Empire of illusion*. New York: Nation Books.

APA style uses the author's first initial, lists the date right after the author's name, capitalizes only the first word in the title and after a colon (plus any proper nouns), spells out "University Press," and indents the second line five spaces.

Both systems double-space throughout.

Notice in the examples that the place of publication is well known. In these cases, don't add the state. In APA citations where the place of publication is not well known, do add the state: for example, Thousand Oaks, CA: Sage.

Two Listings by One Author

MLA

> Gilroy, Paul. *Postcolonial Melancholia*. New York: Columbia UP, 2005. Print.
> ---. *"There Ain't No Black in the Union Jack": The Cultural Politics of Race and Nation*. Chicago: U of Chicago P, 1987. Print.

When you're listing two or more works by the same author, use alphabetical order according to title. For the second title, type three hyphens and a period in place of the author's name.

APA

> Gilroy, P. (1987). *"There ain't no black in the Union Jack": The cultural politics of race and* nation. Chicago: University of Chicago Press.
> Gilroy, P. (2005). *Postcolonial melancholia*. New York: Columbia University Press. 530–533.

APA style uses chronological order to list works, beginning with the earliest. When an author has more than one work published in the same year, list them in alphabetical order by title and add lowercase letters to the year—for example, 1977a, 1977b:

> Gould, S. J. (1977a). *Ontogeny and phylogeny*. Cambridge, UK: Cambridge University Press.
> Gould, S. J. (1977b). Sociobiology: The art of storytelling. *New Scientist, 80,* 530–533.

Books with Multiple Authors

MLA

For two or three authors, list them in the order in which they appear on the book's title page. Invert only the first author's name.

> Current, Richard Nelson, Marcia Ewing Current, and Loie Fuller. *Goddess of Light*. Boston: Northeastern UP, 1997. Print.

If there are more than three authors, you may list them all or list only the first author followed by "et al."

> Anderson, Daniel, Bret Benjamin, Christopher Busiel, and Bill Parades-Holt. *Teaching On-Line: Internet Research, Conversation, and Composition*. New York: Harper-collins, 1996. Print.

or

> Anderson, Daniel, et al. *Teaching On-Line: Internet Research, Conversation, and Composition*. New York: HarperCollins, 1996. Print.

APA

For works with two to six authors, list the authors in the order in which they appear on the title page, using last name and initials. Use an ampersand before the last author's name.

> Anderson, D., Benjamin, B., Busiel, C., & Parades-Holt, B. (1996). *Teaching on-line: Internet research, conversation, and composition*. New York: HarperCollins.

Books by a Corporate Author or Organization

Give the name of the corporate or organizational author as it appears on the title page.

MLA

> NOW Legal Defense and Educational Fund. *Facts on Reproductive Rights: A Resource Manual*. New York: NOW Legal Defense and Educational Fund, 2004. Print.

APA

> NOW Legal Defense and Educational Fund. (2004). *Facts on reproductive rights: A resource manual*. New York: Author.

Books by an Anonymous Author

In MLA style, if no author is listed or the author is anonymous, begin with the title of the publication.

MLA

> *Primary Colors: A Novel of Politics*. New York: Random, 1996. Print.

APA

> *Primary colors: A novel of politics*. (1996). New York: Random House.

In APA style, begin the entry with the title if no author is listed. If a work's author is designated as "Anonymous," however, use the word "Anonymous" at the beginning of the entry.

An Edition of an Original Work
MLA

> Melville, Herman. *Moby-Dick*. 1851. Ed. Alfred Kazin. Boston: Houghton, 1956. Print.

APA

> Melville, H. (1956). *Moby-Dick* (A. Kazin, Ed.). Boston: Houghton Mifflin. (Original work published 1851.)

An Introduction, Preface, Foreword, or Afterword
MLA

> Kazin, Alfred. Introduction. *Moby-Dick*. By Herman Melville. Ed. Alfred Kazin. Boston: Houghton, 1956. v-xiv. Print.

APA

> Kazin, A. (1956). Introduction. In H. Melville, *Moby-Dick* (A. Kazin, Ed.) (pp. v–xiv). Boston: Houghton Mifflin.

Edited Collections
MLA

> Grumet, Robert S., ed. *Northeastern Indian Lives*. Amherst: U of Massachusetts P, 1996. Print.

APA

> Grumet, R. S. (Ed.). (1996). *Northeastern Indian lives*. Amherst: University of Massachusetts Press.

Works in Collections and Anthologies
MLA

> Fitzgerald, F. Scott. "Bernice Bobs Her Hair." *The Short Stories of F. Scott Fitzgerald: A New Collection*. Ed. Matthew J. Bruccoli. New York: Scribner, 1989. 25–47. Print.
> Ochs, Donovan J. "Cicero's Rhetorical Theory." *A Synoptic History of Classical Rhetoric*. Ed. James J. Murphy. Davis: Hermagoras, 1983. 90–150. Print.

APA

> Fitzgerald, F. (1989). Bernice bobs her hair. In M. J. Bruccoli (Ed.), *The short stories of F. Scott Fitzgerald: A new collection* (pp. 25–47). New York: Scribner.
> Ochs, D. J. (1983). Cicero's rhetorical theory. In J. J. Murphy (Ed.), *A synoptic history of classical rhetoric* (pp. 90–150). Davis, CA: Hermagoras.

Translations
MLA

Sartre, Jean-Paul. *The Age of Reason*. Trans. Eric Sutton. New York: Bantam, 1959. Print.

APA

Sartre, J. P. (1959). *The age of reason* (E. Sutton, Trans.). New York: Bantam Books.

Books in a Later Edition
MLA

Woloch, Nancy. *Women and the American Experience*. 3rd ed. New York: McGraw, 1999. Print.

APA

Woloch, N. (1999). *Women and the American experience* (3rd ed.). New York: McGraw-Hill.

Dictionary Entries and Encyclopedia Articles
MLA

"Australia." *The Concise Columbia Encyclopedia*. 3rd ed. 1995. Print.
"Freeze-etching." *Merriam-Webster's Collegiate Dictionary*. 11th ed. 2003. Print.
Jolliffe, David A. "Genre." *Encyclopedia of Rhetoric and Composition*. Ed. Theresa Enos. New York: Garland, 1996. Print.

In MLA style, for familiar reference works such as *Merriam-Webster's Collegiate Dictionary* and *The Concise Columbia Encyclopedia,* you can omit listing the editors and publication information. For less familiar or more specialized sources, however, you should include all the information. Page numbers are not needed as long as the work is arranged alphabetically.

APA

Australia. (1995). *The concise Columbia encyclopedia* (3rd ed.). New York: Columbia University Press.
Freeze-etching. (2003). *Merriam-Webster's collegiate dictionary* (11th ed.). Springfield, MA: Merriam Webster.
Jolliffe, D. A. (1996). Genre. In Theresa Enos (Ed.), *Encyclopedia of rhetoric and composition*. New York: Garland.

Government Documents
MLA

United States Dept. of Commerce. International Trade Administration. *A Guide to Financing Exports*. Washington: GPO, 2005. Print.

APA

> Department of Commerce, International Trade Administration. (2005). *A guide to financing exports* (Monthly Catalog No. 85024488). Washington, DC: U.S. Government Printing Office.

APA includes the catalog number of the publication.

Unpublished Doctoral Dissertations

MLA

> Barrett, Faith Priscilla. "Letters to the World: Emily Dickinson and the Lyric Address." Diss. U of California, 2000. Print.

APA

> Barrett, F. P. (2000). *Letters to the world: Emily Dickinson and the lyric address.* Unpublished doctoral dissertation, University of California, Berkeley.

ARTICLES IN PRINT PERIODICALS

Here are examples of the basic MLA and APA formats for listing articles that appear in print periodicals such as scholarly journals, magazines, and newspapers. See the next section on Online Sources if you have accessed an article through an online periodical Web site or database.

MLA

> Bangeni, Bongi and Rochelle Kapp. "Identities in Transition: Shifting Conceptions of Home among 'Black' South African University Students." *African Studies Review* 48.3 (2005): 110-31. Print.

MLA style uses the author's full name, marks article titles by using quotation marks and capitalization, and lists both volume (48) and issue (3) numbers for journals, no matter whether there is continuous pagination or not. Notice that MLA separates page numbers with a hyphen and shortens the second number: 110-31.

APA

> Bangeni, B., & Kapp, R. (2005). Identities in transition: Shifting conceptions of home among "black" South African university students. *African Studies Review, 48*(3), 110–131.

APA style uses abbreviations for first and middle names, and the date follows the author's name. APA does not use quotation marks or capitalization for article titles (except for the first word of the title and any subtitle, and any proper nouns and proper adjectives). In APA style, the name of the journal, the volume number (48), and the comma that follows it are all italicized, and the issue number is included in parentheses (3) for journals that page issues separately. Notice that APA uses a dash to separate page numbers and does not shorten the second number.

For journals with continuous pagination, drop the issue number:

Lu, M-Z. (2006). Living-English work. *College English, 68,* 605–618.

Magazine Articles

The first two examples show how to list magazines that appear monthly or bimonthly and weekly or biweekly. The third example is an article without an author listed.

MLA

Kelly, Kevin. "The New Socialism." *Wired* June 2009: 116-21. Print.

"Pleas from Prison." *Newsweek* 24 Nov. 1997: 44. Print.

Grossman, David. "The Age of Genius." *The New Yorker* 8 June 2009: 66-77. Print.

APA

Kelly, K. (2009, June). The new socialism. *Wired,* 116–121.

Pleas from prison. (1997, November 24). *Newsweek,* 44.

Grossman, D. (2009, June 8). The age of genius. *The New Yorker,* 66–77.

Notice that APA style capitalizes "the" in the title of magazines and newspapers such as *The Nation* and *The New York Times*, while MLA style does not use "the" in these cases.

Newspaper Articles
MLA

"AMA Plans Seal of Approval for Physicians." *Providence Journal-Bulletin* 19 Nov. 1997: A5. Print.

Wangsness, Lisa. "Lobbyist at Center of Healthcare Overhaul." *Boston Globe* 30 June 2009: A12. Print.

APA

AMA plans seal of approval for physicians. (1997, November 19). *The Providence Journal-Bulletin,* p. A5.

Wangsness, L. (2009, June 30). Lobbyist at center of healthcare overhaul. *The Boston Globe,* p. A12.

Editorial
MLA

"Lessons from Prudhoe Bay." Editorial. *New York Times* 6 Aug. 2006: A30. Print.

APA

Lessons from Prudhoe Bay [Editorial]. (2006, August 6). *The New York Times,* p. A30.

Review
MLA

> Schwarz, Benjamin. "Land of Hope and Glory." Rev. of *Golden Dreams: California in an Age of Abundance,* 1950–1963, by Kevin Starr. *The Atlantic* July/ August 2009: 113–15. Print.

APA

> Schwarz, B. (2009, July/August). *Land of hope and glory* [Review of the book *Golden dreams: California in an age of abundance*]. *The Atlantic,* 113–115.

If there is no author listed for the review, begin with the title of the review. If there is no title, use "Rev. of *Title*" for MLA format and "[Review of the book *Title*]" for APA. In this case, alphabetize under the title of the book being reviewed.

Letter to the Editor
MLA

> Jenkins, John. Letter. *Dallas Morning News* 18 June 2009: A12. Print.

APA

> Jenkins, J. (2009, June 18). [Letter to the editor]. *Dallas Morning News,* p. A12.

ONLINE SOURCES

For online sources, such as articles accessed through online periodicals or databases and Web sites, MLA and APA guidelines call for much of the same information you use for print sources, such as document title and author's name (if it is available). In addition, both MLA and APA also call for the date of publication or update for online sources, if it is available, and for the date you retrieved the source. MLA style no longer requires listing the URL for online sources, unless the reader would not be able to locate the resource through a Web search for the title or author, or if the publisher requires it. APA does require the inclusion of URLs.

Online Periodicals: Articles in Newspapers and Magazines
MLA

> Robison, Clay. "Word Doesn't Travel Fast on Perry Trips." *Houston Chronicle.* Houston Chronicle, 29 Oct. 2007. Web. 15 May 2008.
> Schiff, Stacy. "Know It All: Can Wikipedia Conquer Expertise?" *New Yorker.* New Yorker, 24 July 2006. Web. 1 July, 2009.

MLA style includes author and title, then both the name of the online periodical in italics and the publisher—followed by date of publication, the medium of publication, and the date of retrieval.

APA

Robinson, C. (2007, October 29). Word doesn't travel fast on Perry trips. *The Houston Chronicle*. Retrieved May 15, 2008, from http://www.chron.com/CDA/archives/

Schiff, S. (2006, 24 July 26). Know it all: Can Wikipedia conquer expertise? *The New Yorker*. Retrieved July 1, 2009, from http://www.newyorker.com/fact/content/articles/060731fa_fact

APA style includes author, date of publication, title, publication, retrieval date, and URL. If the URL continues to a second line, try to break at a backslash.

Online Databases: Articles in Scholarly Journals, Newspapers, and Magazines
MLA

Rodriguez-Alegria, Enrique. "Eating Like an Indian: Negotiating Social Relations in the Spanish Colonies." *Current Anthropology* 46.3 (2005): 253–78. *JSTOR*. Web. 29 Sept. 2009.

Nichols, John. "Sit Down in Chicago." *The Nation* 29 Dec. 2008: 4–6. *Academic Search Premier*. Web. 21 Apr. 2009.

"Lock Up Private Prisons: Chronic Problems Demonstrate Why Incarceration Should Be Left to the State." *Atlanta Constitution* 6 Oct. 1999: 10. *LexisNexis*. Web. 19 Oct. 2008.

MLA style includes information that appears for print articles, with addition of the online database and date of retrieval.

APA

Rodriguez-Alegria, E. (2005). Eating like an Indian: Negotiating social relations in the Spanish colonies. *Current Anthropology, 46*(3), 253–278. Retrieved September 29, 2006, from JSTOR.

Nichols, J. (2008, December 29). Sit down in Chicago. *The Nation,* pp. 4–6. Retrieved April 21, 2009, from Academic Search Premier.

Lock up private prisons: Chronic problems demonstrate why incarceration should be left to the state. (October 6, 1999). *Atlanta Constitution,* p. 10. Retrieved January 18, 2008, from LexisNexis.

APA style includes information that appears for print articles, with the addition of the date of retrieval, followed by the online database.

Online-only Publications and Scholarly Projects
MLA

Foster, George. "Language Policy in Namibia." *Southern African Review* 7.1 (2004): n. pag. Web. 2 July 2009.

Baxter, Bruce, ed. *The Robert Creeley Online Archive.* Warehouse State College, n.d. Web. 2 Dec. 2008.

APA

> Foster, G. (2004). Language policy in Namibia. *Southern African Review, 7*(1). Retrieved July 2, 2009, from http://www.soafricanreview.org
>
> Baxter, B. (Ed.). (n.d.). *The Robert Creeley Online Archive.* Retrieved May 30, 2009, from http://www.wsc.edu/cholsonarchives/html

Notice how n. pag. (no pagination) appears in MLA style for online publications that do not use page numbers and how n.d. (no date) appears in both MLA and APA style, when no date of publication or update is available.

Web Sites

MLA

> Crawford, James. *Language Policy Web Site & Emporium*. n.d. Web. 14 Oct. 2009. <http://ourworld.compuserve.com/homepages/jwcrawford>.
>
> *Kheel Center for Labor-Management Documentation and Archives*. 2009. Cornell University School of Industrial and Labor Relations. Web. 14 July 2009.
>
> *U.S. English Only*. Home page. 19 Jan. 2009. Web. 8 Feb. 2009.

The order of information for MLA: Name of author, creator, or site owner, if available; title of document, if named; title of Web site, if distinct from title of document; date of last posting, if available; name of any institution or organization associated with the date; medium of publication (Web) date of retrieval; URL enclosed in angle brackets <>, if necessary.

In the first example above, no posting date is given, only the date of retrieval. The second example includes both posting and retrieval dates. Notice in the U.S. English Only example, where the Web site is not titled, you add the description "home page" without underlining or putting it in quotes.

APA

> Crawford, J. (n.d.). *Language policy Web site and emporium*. Retrieved October 14, 2009, from http://ourworld.compuserve.com/homepages/ jwcrawford
>
> Kheel Center for labor-management documentation and archives. (2009). Retrieved July 14, 2009, from Cornell University School of Industrial and Labor Relations Web site: http://www.ilr.cornell.edu/library/kheelcenter/default.html?page+home
>
> Upstate Economic Development Council. (2008, March 15). *Prospects for rural revitalization: New crops and new markets*. Retrieved July 7, 2009, from http:www.upecodev.gov/html

The order of information for APA: Name of author, creator, or site owner, if available; date of last posting; title of document, if named; date of retrieval and URL in one sentence, without using angle brackets or a period at the end.

As is true with print sources, APA uses an initial for an author's first and middle names and capitalizes only the first word in a document title and the first word following a colon. Notice in the second example that you use "n.d." (no date) if there is no date of posting available.

Web Sites: Secondary Pages

MLA

de Ferranti, David. "Innovative Financing Options and the Fight against Global Poverty: What's New and What Next?" *Brookings Institution*. July 2006. Web. 29 July 2009.

"The Triangle Factory Fire." *Kheel Center for Labor-Management Documentation and Archives*. 24 Mar. 2007. Cornell University School of Industrial and Labor Relations. Web. 14 Oct 2009. <http://www.ilr.cornell.edu/trianglefire/>.

Notice that the URL links to the Web page cited, not to the home page of the Kheel Center.

APA

de Ferranti, D. (2006, July). *Innovative financing options and the fight against global poverty: What's new and what next?* Retrieved 29 July, 2009, from the Brookings Institution Web site: http://www.brook.edu/index/papersarticles.htm

The Triangle Factory fire. (2005, March 24). Retrieved October 14, 2009, from Cornell University of Industrial and Labor Relations, Kheel Center for Labor-Management Documentation and Archives Web site: http://www.ilr.cornell.edu/trianglefire/

Notice that the Brookings Institution and the Kheel Center Web sites are included in the retrieval statement.

Online Books and Reports

MLA

Wendell, Barrett. *English Composition*. Cambridge, MA: Charles Scribner, 1891. Google Book Search. Web. 14 Sept. 2009.

APA

Harrison Rips Foundation. (2000). *Creating underdevelopment: Capital flight and the case for debt reduction in South Africa.* Retrieved August 5, 2001, from http:// www.ripsfoundation.org/southafrica.report.html

Online Posting to Electronic Forum

MLA

Michael, Toni. "George W. Bush—The Legacy." Online posting. *Table Talk.* 1 Aug. 2008. Web. 15 Nov. 2008.

Marshall, Richard. "The Political Economy of Cancer Research." Online posting. *H-Net List on the History of Science, Medicine, and Technology* 21 Apr. 2003. Web. 28 Sept.

APA

> Michael, T. (2008, August 1). George W. Bush—the legacy. Message posted to Table Talk, archived at http://tabletalk.salon.com/webx?14@@.773d395b/50.

In general, only cite in References those postings that have been archived and thus can be retrieved. See note on APA in next section.

Email

MLA

> Wheeler, Anne C. Message to the author. 25 Feb. 2008. E-mail.
> Dever, Elizabeth. "Re: Eddie Vetter's Conversion." Message to the author. 4 May 2006. E-mail.

For email, list the title (if there is one) from the email's subject heading.

APA

APA style treats email, as well as any nonarchived postings on electronic forums, as a nonretrievable source. Cite emails and other nonretrievable sources in the text as personal communications, but do not list them in the References section. For example:

> Medical historians have challenged Elaine Showalter's view of chronic fatigue syndrome (L. Braun, personal communication, February 25, 2005).

MISCELLANEOUS SOURCES

Films or Video Recordings

MLA

> *Citizen Kane*. Screenplay by Orson Welles. Dir. Orson Welles. RKO, 1941. Film.
> *No Country for Old Men*. Dir. Joel Coen and Ethan Coen. Perf. Josh Brolin, Javier Bardem, Tommy Lee Jones. Paramount, 2008. DVD.

APA

> Nolan, C. (Director). (2008). *The Dark Knight* [DVD]. Hollywood: Warner Bros.
> Welles, O. (Writer-Director). (1941). *Citizen Kane* [Film]. Hollywood: RKO.

The amount of information to include about films and videocassettes depends on how you have used the source. In addition to title and director, you may cite the writer and performers as well.

Television and Radio Programs

MLA

> "Tuskegee Experiment." *Nova*. WGBH, Boston. 4 April 2005. Television.

APA

> Tuskegee experiment. (2005, April 4). *Nova*. Boston: WGBH.

Records, Tapes, and CDs
MLA

Ellington, Duke. *The Far East Suite*. Bluebird, 1995. CD.

Verdi, Giuseppe. *La Traviata*. London Symphony Orchestra. Cond. Carlo Rizzi. Teldec, 1992. CD.

White Stripes. *Get Behind Me Satan*. V2, 2005. CD.

APA

Ellington, D. (Composer). (1995). *The Far East suite* [Record]. New York: Bluebird.

Verdi, G. (Composer). (1992). *La Traviata* [With C. Rizzi conducting the London Symphony Orchestra] [CD]. New York: Teldec.

White Stripes. (2005). *Get behind me Satan* [CD]. New York: V2.

Interviews
MLA

Haraway, Donna. "Writing, Literacy, and Technology: Toward a Cyborg Literature." By Gary A. Olson. *Women Writing Culture*. Ed. Gary A. Olson and Elaine Hirsch. Albany: SUNY, 1995. 45–77. Print.

Press, Karen. Personal interview. 27 Apr 2003.

Sole, Kelwyn. Interview by Anita Amirault. *Cape Town Poetry Newsletter* 20 Mar. 2001: 30–34. Print.

MLA cites interviews by listing the person being interviewed first and then the interviewer. Note that the first two interviews are published and the third is unpublished.

APA

Amirault, A. (2001, March 20). Interview with Kelwyn Sole. *Cape Town Poetry Newsletter,* 30–34.

Olson, G. A. (1995). Writing, literacy, and technology: Toward a cyborg literature [Interview with Donna Haraway]. In G. A. Olson & E. Hirsch (Eds.), *Women writing culture* (pp. 45–77). Albany: State University of New York Press.

APA lists the name of the interviewer first and then puts information on the interview in brackets. APA does not list unpublished interviews in references but cites them only in parenthetical citations in the text: (K. Press, personal interview, April 27, 2003).

Lecture or Speech
MLA

Kern, David. "Recent Trends in Occupational Medicine." Memorial Hospital, Pawtucket, RI. 2 Oct. 2004. Address.

APA

Kern, D. (2004, October 2). *Recent trends in occupational medicine*. Paper presented at Memorial Hospital, Pawtucket, RI.

a guide to print, electronic, and other sources

For most research projects, your college library will be the main source of information, and you can count on spending a good part of your research time reading and analyzing books, articles, and newspapers (although your research question may also lead you to conduct field research—which is treated in the next chapter).

A lot of what you'll need is available online, through electronic databases like JSTOR, Lexis Nexis, and Academic Search Premier. In addition, you can access a world of information and ideas on the Web that ranges from serious scholarly discussion to wildly opinionated debates of questionable value.

In addition, depending on your research project, you may find yourself doing research at live performances and museums or by watching the media. In any case, doing research is a matter of knowing your way around print, electronic, and other sources and understanding how they differ in terms of credibility and authority.

TYPES OF PRINT SOURCES

Books

Books can be sorted into three main types:

- **Scholarly books,** published by university or academic presses and written by faculty and other researchers, are meant to contribute to a field of knowledge. They have gone through a careful review by peer readers who are knowledgeable about the field and editors. At the time they're published, scholarly books should be up-to-date in terms of the issues they engage and the literature in the field they've reviewed. For these reasons, scholarly books have a high degree of credibility, especially among academics, and will likely be seen as respectable sources for any research project. (You still need, of course, to analyze the claims, evidence, and assumptions in a scholarly book and to assess its relevance to your research.)

- **Trade books** are published by commercial presses, such as Penguin or Free Press, and written by journalists, professional writers, and scholars seeking a broader audience. Intended for the general public, trade books can range considerably in quality and credibility. Some are well researched, even though they may be documented in an informal way, and written by highly reputable authors, while others may be rush jobs to capitalize on some event in the news. For these reasons, you will need to assess the authority and credibility of trade books on an individual basis.

- **Other books** from religious and political presses, nonprofits and professional associations, trade unions, and research institutes can be valuable sources, depending on your research process. Some religious and political presses (for example, Maryknoll, Monthly Review, South End) have good reputations and reliable editorial practices. Research institutes (sometimes called "think tanks") like the Brookings Institution often issue books, pamphlets, and reports that are credible. Other presses can be fly-by-night and have much sketchier reputations. Make sure you know the organization behind the press.

Periodicals

Here are five different types of periodicals and a quick look at what they cover.

- **Scholarly journals** (for example, *American Sociological Review, Rhetoric Society Quarterly, New England Journal of Medicine*) contain recent research by scholars in the field written for other scholars. Articles are subjected to a rigorous review process by peer readers and the journal editor, so they have a high degree of credibility and authority.

- **Popular magazines,** such as *Rolling Stone, Glamour, Sports Illustrated,* and *Wired,* focus on a particular market niche—whether music, young women, sports fans, or computer enthusiasts. Others, such as *Discover, Smithsonian,* and *Natural History,* popularize topics in a range of fields for interested readers. Some popular magazines like *People* or *Us* feature mainly lightweight articles about celebrities, while others, such as *Scientific American,* contain serious articles written by reputable writers for the educated public.

- **Public affairs magazines** (for example, *The New Republic, The Nation, Atlantic Monthly*) publish highly reputable and well-researched articles, often by well-known writers, on topics of current interest to their audience of educated readers. Some public affairs magazines have a partisan political perspective (for example, *National Review* is conservative, while *In These Times* is liberal). Others feature a range of perspectives. Public affairs magazines can be helpful in acquiring background information and a sense of the issues about current events.

■ **Newsmagazines** such as *Newsweek, Time,* and *U.S. News and World Report* come out weekly, with news reports and commentaries on current events. Written by experienced journalists, the articles in newsmagazines can help you understand recent and past events in detail—and the editorials and commentaries will give you a sense of the climate of public opinion. They can be a good supplement to your research, but not the main source.

■ **Newspapers** such as the *New York Times, Wall Street Journal,* and *Washington Post* cover the national and international news of the day, along with the latest in science, business, sports, culture, and the arts. These national newspapers have highly credible reputations and are good sources for background, especially if you're researching a historical topic. Local newspapers can provide useful information on local events, past and present.

■ **Trade magazines** (for example, *Advertising Age, PC Computing,* and *Farm Journal*) focus on a particular profession or industry, with articles written by industry experts for others in the field. These magazines can give you a good sense of how a profession or industry sees an issue—and thereby can be a helpful supplement to your research, depending on what your research project is.

THE LIBRARY

Your college library is likely to be your main source for books and periodicals. Many college libraries offer workshops on doing research and how to use the various research sources. Check with your library to see what programs and services it offers students.

THE LIBRARY CATALOG

You can search most online library catalogs by author, title, periodical, subject heading, or keyword. A note on the last two:

■ *Subject headings* are normally based on the Library of Congress Subject Headings (LCSH), a reference source that lists the standard subject headings used in catalogs and indexes. Consult the LCSH to identify subject headings that are relevant to your research. Notice also that book entries in online catalogs include related subject headings. Once you find books that look useful, you can use the subject headings listed.

- *Keywords* include words that appear in the author's name, book title, subject heading, and in some cases a summary or abstract. Keyword searches can be useful because they don't depend on pre-established subject headings (but do include them). Keyword searches also allow you to combine several keywords to give your search more focus.

If you don't find relevant books using subject headings or keywords, consult with a reference librarian. He or she can help you refine your search—and can point you to other resources the library has that you'll find helpful.

REFERENCE BOOKS

Your library is likely to have a range of reference books that can be useful to your research. These may be available in print or electronic form.

- *General and specialized encyclopedias* can help you get started on a research project and provide key information as your research deepens. General encyclopedias, such as *Collier's Encyclopedia* or the *Encyclopedia Brittanica,* can provide overviews on a topic, but specialized encyclopedias, such as the *Encyclopedia of Philosophy* or the *Women's Studies Encyclopedia,* will give more in-depth and scholarly treatments of a subject.

- *Bibliographies* list books and articles published on particular subjects and fields of study. Some are annotated, with brief descriptions and sometimes evaluations of the entries. You can search for bibliographies by adding the term "bibliography" or "annotated bibliography" to a keyword search. Ask a reference librarian what bibliographies your library has that may be relevant to your research.

- *Disciplinary guides and companions*, such as the *Cambridge Companion to Postcolonial Literary Studies* or the *Harvard Guide to American History,* will give you overviews of a field of study by respected scholars. They also include important bibliographical information on important work in a particular discipline.

- *Other reference works* include atlases, almanacs, yearbooks, biographical and historical dictionaries, and handbooks. You can browse the reference section to see what your library has available. Ask a reference librarian to help you identify the reference relevant to your research.

ELECTRONIC RESOURCES

ELECTRONIC DATABASES

There are literally hundreds of searchable electronic databases that provide continually updated lists of newspaper, magazine, and scholarly journal articles, often with the full text available as PDFs. Part of the trick of research is identifying the most relevant electronic resources for your purposes. Most libraries have an index of databases with descriptions of their contents. Reference librarians can help you get started using the most appropriate electronic databases for your research and give you helpful suggestions about how to search them. (Also, see the box "How to Use Keywords" on this page for tips on effective searching techniques.) These electronic databases are library subscription services; availability will vary from library to library.

In addition, as of October 2008 the Google Books Library Project had scanned 7 million books, which can be searched through Google Book Search, to find information and sample chapters for in-copyright books and downloadable full-text versions of public domain and out-of-copyright books.

SEARCH ENGINES

Google is clearly the go-to search engine, handling over half of all searches in 2007. Google also searches for images, maps, video, and online groups. For an academic research project, Google Scholar can be useful. As is true of searches in general, much depends on how you use keywords.

HOW TO USE KEYWORDS

The secret to using search engines or searchable electronic databases is to find the right keyword or combination of keywords. Part of this experimenting is finding the keyword that will give you the hits you want. Here are some techniques in using Boolean operators—AND, OR, NOT, and quotations—to make your searches more efficient.

❑ ***Quotations limit your search.*** For example if you type in the words *death penalty*, you will get over 15,000 hits, most of which have nothing to do with capital punishment. However, if you enter "death penalty", using quote marks, you've created a phrase that will give you a focused search.

❑ ***AND limits your search.*** If you're interested in material on the abolition of capital punishment, enter: "death penalty" AND abolish.

❑ ***NOT limits your search.*** If you are interested in material on the abolition of capital punishment outside the United States, enter: "death penalty" AND abolish NOT U.S.

❑ ***OR expands your search.*** If you are interested in material on the abolition of capital punishment in Russia and want to go back before the Soviet Union fell in 1989, enter: "death penalty" AND abolish AND Russia OR Soviet Union.

GOVERNMENT PUBLICATIONS

The U.S. government publishes massive amounts of information annually, largely through the Government Printing Office (GPO). You can search the catalog of government publications at http://catalog.gpo.gov/F?RN=263462424.

The Library of Congress offers access to an enormous range of government and library resources at www.loc.gov/index.html, including Thomas (after Thomas Jefferson) with legislative information, databases on Congress, current bills, public laws, committee information, the online version of the Congressional Record, and other current and historical documents at thomas.loc.gov.

Many government agencies have their own Web sites, including the Bureau of the Census www.census.gov, which has a vast amount of statistical and demographic data.

OTHER SOURCES

Attending events and performances such as lectures, seminars, readings, plays, and concerts; visiting museums; and watching films, videos, and television or listening to the radio and recorded music can all be important forms of research. Depending on the nature of your research, these activities can provide information and perspectives to supplement your work with print and electronic sources. Or they can be the main focus of your research. This section briefly explains what performances, museums, and the media offer to researchers.

PERFORMANCES AND EVENTS

Your college may sponsor lectures, readings, or seminars that bring noted speakers to campus. Attending such events can provide you with information that you couldn't find elsewhere and give you the opportunity to question the speaker. In addition, college or local theaters and music and dance companies may stage plays and concerts related to your research. Attending such live performances can deepen your understanding, say, of a Shakespeare play, a Verdi opera, or a style of jazz, folk, or popular music—and offer a useful supplement to reading about the topic or listening to recordings. In all these instances, taking notes is probably the most appropriate research strategy.

On the other hand, performances may themselves provide the focus for your research. You might, for example, want to research what takes place at a Metallica concert or a poetry reading in a local bookstore. In cases such as these, you'll likely draw on observation and perhaps interviews, as well as reading pertinent sources or listening to recordings.

MUSEUMS

Visiting art, science, natural history, and history museums can provide you with a wealth of information to enhance your research. Depending on your topic, you can see in person paintings, sculpture, or photographs pertinent to your research; artifacts and displays from a historical period you're investigating; or scientific exhibits. Some museums, as well as historical societies, have special collections and archives that offer research sources unavailable elsewhere. Again, note taking is probably the research strategy you'll use.

Museums can also be the focus of a research project. Museum studies is a relatively new field that covers the subject of who visits museums, why, and what they do. By reading some of the literature in this field, you can frame questions to answer with field research methods—observation, interviews, and questionnaires.

MEDIA

Documentary films, television and radio programs, and music and spoken-word recordings can be good sources of information to add to the print and electronic sources you're using.

At the same time, films, television, radio, or recorded music can also be valuable sources for studying the media and mass communication. For example, if you want to investigate the issue of violence in children's television shows, you may want to watch a variety of children's programs in order to count the incidences of violence and identify the types of violence depicted. Or you could analyze television commercials to see how men and women are depicted and what, if any, gender stereotypes are perpetuated. In this type of research, it can be quite helpful to tape television or radio programs so that you can return to them in the course of your inquiry.

chapter 15

fieldwork and the research report

Not all research is conducted in the library. In fact, the library may be just a starting point, providing you with an overview of your topic and the background information you need in order to undertake field research. Field research includes making observations, conducting interviews, and using questionnaires. In fact, researchers often combine two or more of these methods in a research project.

Researchers turn to these methods of inquiry when they have questions that can't be addressed solely on the basis of print or electronic sources. Here are some examples of research topics and the fieldwork they might lead to:

- To determine whether a shopping mall in the area should enforce a curfew for teenagers, you observe the mall on weekend nights to see what danger or nuisance, if any, teenagers pose.

- To understand the effects of state-mandated testing on classroom teachers, a student in an education course decides to interview ten sixth-grade teachers whose classes will be taking the test.

- To find out how much the undergraduates at their college drink each week, a group of students designs and administers an anonymous questionnaire.

As you can see from these examples, the kind of field research you do and how extensive it will be depend on the questions with which you begin, as well as the amount of time you have. Field research can be time consuming, but it can also give you information and insights that you could not get in any other way.

449

In this chapter, we'll look first at the genre of the research report. Next, we consider how researchers design fieldwork. Finally, we discuss how researchers work in the field and three common methods they use—observation, interviews, and questionnaires.

ETHICS OF RESEARCH

INFORMED CONSENT

Informed consent means that a person who is asked to participate in a research study has adequate information about its purpose and methods to make a voluntary decision about whether he or she will take part. If you are asking people to be interviewed or fill out a questionnaire, you need to explain what your research is about, why you're doing it, and what you plan to do with the results. As a rule, you should guarantee your research subjects' anonymity by not referring to them by name or by using a pseudonym. In some instances, such as oral histories or interviews with public figures, it may be appropriate to use people's real names. Most colleges and universities have Institutional Review Boards that can give you more information about obtaining informed consent. ■

UNDERSTANDING THE GENRE: RESEARCH REPORTS

The research report is the primary means of communication that natural and social scientists, engineers, computer scientists, and other researchers use to present their findings. Academic journals in a range of fields—from biochemistry and astronomy to sociology and psychology—are filled with articles reporting research that employs various methods of investigation. (See "Uncertainty the Use of Magic" by Richard B. Felson and Gmelch in Chapter 8, pages 262–267, for a scholarly research report.)

A research report is really quite simple and fairly standardized in its form. If you have ever done a lab report in a science class, you're already familiar with its parts: Introduction, Literature Review, Methods, Results, Discussion, and Conclusions.

To see how these sections work in an actual research paper, let's look at "Food Sources in South Providence," a research report that Luis Ramirez wrote for a field research assignment in the sociology course "Hunger in America." As you read, notice how each section functions within the report.

Food Sources in South Providence

Luis Ramirez

Introduction

Establishes a general problem

The economic downturn that started in 2008, combined with reductions in state social programs, has made access to food a growing source of concern for low-income individuals and families in Rhode Island. The unemployment rate in Rhode Island increased from 7.1 percent in April 2008 to 11.1 percent in April 2009, the highest in New England and the second highest in the nation (Kaiser Family Foundation, 2009). Moreover, Rhode Island was the only state in New England to experience a decline in median wages between 2000 and 2006; it has the ninth least affordable rents in the country; and social programs for low-income families such as cash assistance through the RI Works Program, housing subsidies, medical care, and child care have been slashed (Brewster, 2008). The convergence of these factors has put a good deal of stress on individual and family budgets. Forty-six percent of Rhode Islanders who seek food assistance through the Rhode Island Community Food Bank network of pantries choose between paying for food and paying for utilities. An additional 32 percent choose between food and medicine or medical care (Rhode Island Community Food Bank, 2009). One of the results is that hunger in Rhode Island has grown from affecting 1 out of 10 households in 1998 to affecting 1 out of 8 households today (Nord and Hopwood, 2008).

Introduces the specific question that the research addresses

Given the state of the economy and a shrinking safety net, it is crucial to understand how low-income individuals and families secure food to meet their household's dietary needs. With the elimination or restriction of public assistance programs, dependence on non-commercial food sources that low-income families use to evade hunger may increase to buffer the cuts and loss of benefits. Non-commercial food sources can be divided into four categories: 1) public assistance programs, 2) home production, 3) emergency relief, and 4) gifts (see Table 1).

Describes prior research

A good deal of research on people's diets has focused on measuring food intake and its nutritional quality by such methods as the "twenty-four-hour recall," the "food frequency" checklist, the "seven day diet record," and direct weighing and measuring of daily meals (Pelto, Jerome, & Kandel, 1980). Other

Creates a research space by indicating a gap in prior research

researchers have attempted to develop indicators to assess hunger (Physicians Task Force on Hunger in America, 1985; Radimer, Olson, & Campbell, 1990). These studies have been useful in providing information about general patterns of food use, diet, nutrition, and the prevalence of hunger. What these studies do not include, however, is information about how people actually acquire their food.

Describes recent research

More recently, researchers have examined how low-income individuals and families use supplemental sources of income beyond public assistance programs and wages to make ends meet (Edin & Lein, 1997; Rank & Hirschl, 1995). These researchers have found that the benefits allocated from food stamps and public assistance are not enough to meet basic needs, despite recipients' attempts to budget and stretch their limited resources. The purpose of this study is to

Proposes to extend recent research

determine whether this is the case with low-income families in South Providence and the extent to which they depend on non-commercial food sources to provide for basic needs.

Table 1

Noncommercial Food Sources

Table 1 gives details of noncommercial food services

1. Public assistance	Food stamps
	AFDC
	Special Supplemental Feeding Program for Women, Infants, and Children (WIC)
	School breakfast and lunch programs
2. Home production	Private and community gardens
	Gathering food (nuts, berries, herbs, greens, etc.) in public parks
	Fishing
3. Emergency food relief	Churches
	Community centers
	Food banks
4. Gifts	Familial networks
	Friends and neighbors

Food Sources 3

Methods

Explains
how
research
was
conducted

A questionnaire on how people acquire their food was administered to thirty low-income individuals who use the services of South Providence Neighborhood Ministries (SPNM). SPNM is a not-for-profit community center which provides a range of services such as emergency food relief, clothing and utility assistance, English as a Second Language classes, tutoring programs, sewing lessons, public health programs, and so on. The questionnaire was administered, with the informed consent of participants, in January and February 2009.

The demographic characteristics of the study population are summarized in Table 2. Of the 30 participants, 28 (93.3%) were women and two (6.6%)

Table 2

Demographic Characteristics of Study Population

Displays
data in
visual
form—
Table 2,
Table 3,
Table 4 and
Table 5

	Number	Percentage
Age		
Younger than 18	1	3.3
18–30	6	20
31–50	18	60
51+	5	16.7
Marital Status		
Married	8	2.7
Not Married	27	73.3
Ethnicity		
Latino/Hispanic	20	66.7
African American	5	16.7
Southeast Asian	3	10
African	2	6.7
Work		
Employed	6	20
Unemployed	24	80

Food Sources 4

were men. Twenty were Latino (66.7%), five (16.7%) African American, three (10%) Southeast Asian, and two (6.7%) African. Six (20%) worked full or part-time, while 24 (80%) were unemployed.

Results

Presents data from research without commenting

This study found that the participants draw on a number of non-commercial food sources to meet their families' dietary needs. As Table 3 illustrates, the majority participated in public assistance programs of one type or another, including RI Works Program (56.7%), food stamps (66.7%), WIC (50%), school lunch programs (84.2%), and school breakfast programs (78.9%).

Table 3

Number and Percentage of Households Using Public Assistance Programs

	Number	Percentage
AFDC		
yes	17	56.7
no	13	43.3
Food Stamps		
yes	20	66.7
no	10	33.3
WIC		
yes	15	50
no	15	50
School Lunch		
yes	16	84.2
no	3	15.8
School Breakfast Program		
yes	15	78.9
no	4	21.1

As shown in Table 4, a number of participants fish for food (26.7%), grow food (30%), and gather food in public parks and other places (20%).

Table 4

*Number and Percentage of Households Engaging in Various Forms of Home
Production (Fishing for Food, Growing Food, Gathering Food)*

	Number	Percentage
Fishing		
yes	8	26.7
no	22	73.3
Growing		
yes	9	30
no	24	70
Gathering		
yes	6	20
no	24	80

Table 5 shows the number of participants who use emergency food relief
and family networks to acquire food. The vast majority of study participants
use food pantries and other emergency food distribution centers (97.6%).
Nineteen (65.5%) say they visit on a regular basis about once a month, and
ten (34.5%) say they go sporadically. Eleven people (44%) eat at a relative's
house at least once a month, and six people (24%) feed relatives at least
once a month.

Discussion

The <u>most significant results</u> of this study are the extent to which
participants use a range of food sources to meet their basic needs. These
results appear to confirm the findings of Rank and Hirschl and of Edin and Lein
that neither public assistance nor low-paying jobs provide people with
sufficient resources to make ends meet. <u>My study found</u> that benefits from RI
Works Program and food stamps are not enough to meet a family's dietary
needs. Therefore, supplemental sources, such as fishing, food production, food
gathering, emergency food relief, and family food sharing are important sources
of food for many low-income people.

*Identifies
most
important
finding*

Food Sources 6

Table 5

Number and Percentage of Households Who Utilize Emergency Relief and Familial Networks

	Number	Percentage
Emergency Relief		
yes	29	97.6
no	1	3.3
Feed Relatives Often		
yes	6	24.0
no	19	76.0
Are Fed by Relatives Often		
yes	11	44.0
no	14	56.0

Explains possible implications of the study results

The study results also suggest that at least some people who are eligible for public assistance do not choose it as a food option. One participant said that he does not like to use government programs and would rather use emergency food relief because the people are "nicer" and "not as condescending." It may be that food pantries are no longer temporary and infrequent means of meeting people's household food needs. Rather, people may be using food pantries as a regular strategy to feed their families, particularly at the end of the month when benefits from RI Works Program and food stamps run out.

Note tentative language ("suggest," "may," "perhaps")

Conclusion

Perhaps the most troubling aspect of this study is that low-income people were already using many means of acquiring food, in addition to public assistance programs, before the economic downturn and the shrinking safety net, and that this reliance, if anything, is likely increase. The number of working poor households served by food pantries has grown from 25 percent in 1997 and 29 percent in 2001 to 32 percent in 2009, at the same time the number of households that use pantries and receive food stamps has decreased from 49 percent in 1997

Food Sources 7

Uses study results to question popular representations of low-income people

and 46 percent in 2001 to 36 percent in 2009 (Rhode Island Community Food Bank, 2009). These figures suggest that emergency food relief sources such as food pantries will continue to be under growing pressure to serve their clients. Familial networks are also vulnerable, as those who are currently feeding other family members lose food support through RI Works Program, food stamps, and SSI.

Food Sources 8

References

Brewster, K. (2008, September). *Rhode Island's shrinking safety net.* Paper presented at the Women Ending Hunger conference, Providence, RI.

Edin, K., & Lein, L. (1997). Work, welfare, and single mothers' economic survival strategies. *American Sociological Review, 61,* 253–266.

Kaiser Family Foundation. Rhode Island unemployment rate (seasonally adjusted), 2008–2009 (2009). Retrieved October 2, 2009, from http://www.statehealthfacts.org/ 23&cat=1&rgn=41

Nord, M., & Hopwood, H. (2009). *A comparison of household food security in Canada and the United States.* (Economic Research Report No. ERR-67). Washington, DC: United States Department of Agriculture.

Pelto, G. H., Jerome, N. W., & Kandel, R. G. (1980). Methodological issues in nutritional anthropology. In N. W. Jerome, R. G. Kandel, & G. H. Pelto (Eds.), *Nutritional anthropology: Approaches to diet and culture* (pp. 27–59). New York: Redgrave.

Physicians Task Force on Hunger in America. (1985). *Hunger in America: The growing epidemic.* Boston: Harvard University School of Public Health.

Radimer, K. L., Olson, C. M., & Campbell, C. C. (1990). Development of indicators to assess hunger. *Journal of Nutrition, 120,* 1544–1548.

Rank, H., & Hirschl, R. (1995). *Eating agendas.* New York: Basic Books.

Rhode Island Community Food Bank. (2009). Statistics. Retrieved October 6, 2009, from www.rifoodbank.org/matriarch/MultiPiecePage.asp_Q_PageID_E_31_A_ PageName_E_StatsThermometerGraphic

Analysis: A Detailed Look at the Genre

If it's easy to identify the sections and the roles they play in this and many other research reports, to understand how the genre works in a fuller sense, we need to take a more detailed look at each section.

■ **Introduction:** Notice how the Introduction establishes the purpose of the research through a series of rhetorical moves:

¶1: *Establishes a general problem* by citing the possible effects of changes in the welfare system on low-income people's access to food.

¶2: *Introduces the specific question* of understanding how low-income people secure food and how much they rely on noncommercial sources.

¶3: *Describes prior research* on people's diets by citing sources from the literature.
Creates a research space by indicating a gap in previous research.

¶4: *Describes more recent research and proposes to extend it* by examining how low-income people meet basic needs.
States the research question of determining how much low-income families in South Providence rely on noncommercial food sources.

As this analysis reveals, the Introduction is a relatively complex passage that works closely with sources first to establish a general problem and then to create a space for the research question by showing how the proposed research fills a gap and how related research can be extended. This Introduction offers a good illustration of how researchers justify their research question by explaining why it is meaningful and how it fits into a body of prior work.

■ **Methods:** The Methods section at first glance may seem straightforward as it describes how the questionnaire was administered and presents the demographics of the study population. The underlying question that the Methods section raises, however, is how well-equipped is the proposed method to answer the research question. We learn that the questionnaire asked thirty low-income people about how they acquired their food. The study population is appropriate, but this section might have included a bit more explanation of how the questions were designed to gather the needed information.

■ **Results:** There are two things to note about the Results section. First, the results of the questionnaire appear without any comment on their meaning or significance. This is one of the key features of research reports: the data are first presented and then interpreted. For students who are used to writing papers with an interpretative claim followed by supporting evidence, the research report may feel backwards. But the logic here is that of displaying the information for all to see before commenting on it. In keeping with this logic is the second feature to note, namely that the complete data are displayed visually in tables and main points summarized in the text.

- **Discussion:** Instead of discussing the results point by point as they appear in the Results section, discussion sections typically begin with the most important finding of the research and explain how it relates to the central research question. That takes place here in the first paragraph. Notice, too, that the interpretations of the results use such tempered terms as "appear to confirm" and "suggest." (No researcher would claim that the results can prove anything definitively. There is always room for further research and new questions.) Finally, notice that the discussion becomes more speculative in the second and third paragraphs, drawing out implications from the results. Accordingly, the writer's tone is appropriately tentative in suggesting what "may" be occurring.

- **Conclusion:** The ending takes a further turn by using the results to refute representations of low-income people by politicians and the media. This is a bold and effective way to summarize the results and relate them to an important context of issues. The final sentence looks ahead with concern to an uncertain future. The conclusion, no doubt, has a bit more of the flair of an essay than is usual in many research reports.

■ WORKING TOGETHER

Analyzing a Research Article

- Work in a group of three or four. Find a short article that reports research in an academic journal such as *Current Anthropology, American Journal of Public Health,* or *American Journal of Sociology.*

- Analyze the introduction (and literature review if it's a separate section). Pay particular attention to how the article establishes the general problem or topic, how it defines the research question, and how it relates that question to prior work.

- Use the rhetorical moves in the analysis of "Food Sources in South Providence" to see how the introduction creates a research space.

DESIGNING A FIELD RESEARCH PROJECT

You can use the discussion of the research report genre as a way to start thinking about how to design a field research project. Many of the key considerations you'll need to take into account have already been raised. Here are some questions to help you use your knowledge of the genre to plan your research:

- What is the general problem or issue that you want to investigate? You might be interested, say, in the experience of Iraq veterans, the Poetry

Slam scene, the problem of cheating, or the role of fraternities and sororities at your college.

- What background information is available on the problem or issue? What specific research has already been done? What questions have guided that research?

- How can you use background information and previous research to help you carve out a research space to develop a significant question? Are there gaps in the research?

- Is there research you could extend? Perhaps there are studies of student attitudes toward cheating and toward fraternities and sororities that could be updated. On the other hand, there may be lots of writing on Poetry Slams but little or no research.

- What research method or combination of methods best fits your research question?

WRITING A PROPOSAL

Once you have answered these questions, write a proposal for the research project. This proposal can serve as the first draft of the Introduction to your research report. A proposal should explain:

- What the general problem or issue is.

- What previous research has been done.

- How the main question you're trying to answer relates to previous work.

- Why the particular method you're planning to use is an appropriate research strategy for answering the question.

- How you plan to conduct the research.

- What you think the significance of the results might be.

OBSERVATION

Observation has an important advantage over other research methods: it gives you direct access to people's behavior. Let's say you've done some background research on how men and women interact in conversations, and you want to test some of the findings in the published literature. You might decide to see whether students at your college follow the pattern described by Deborah Tannen in *You Just Don't Understand*—that men interrupt more during conversations and are less likely than women to use questions to elicit comments from others. Interviewing or surveying wouldn't give you very reliable information, because even if people were willing to be honest about how they behave in conversations, it's not likely that they could be accurate. In contrast, by going to the school dining hall over a period of several days, you could observe what men and women in fact do when they talk and what conversational patterns emerge.

THE PROCESS OF OBSERVATION

Planning

The following questions can help guide your planning. You can use them to write a proposal that explains the role of observation in your research plan (see "Writing a Proposal," above).

- Why does the line of research you're pursuing call for observation? What research question or questions are you addressing?

- How exactly can observations help you answer your research question?

- What kinds of observations would be most useful? Whom and what do you want to observe? What are the best times and places for these observations? How many observations should you do?

- What should your observations focus on? What exactly do you want to record in your field notes? What method or methods will you use to record your observations?

THREE CONSIDERATIONS TO TAKE INTO ACCOUNT WHEN YOU DO OBSERVATIONS

1. Recognize that you'll be observing a limited group and making a limited number of observations. Your findings may confirm or dispute what you've read, or they may suggest new questions and lines of research. Be aware, however, that while your results are valid for the group you observed, the group itself may not be representative of all the students at your college, not to mention all men and women. So when you generalize on the basis of your observations, acknowledge the scope of your research and ensure that the claims you make take these limits into account.

2. Take into account, too, the fact that your presence can have an effect on what you observe. People sometimes behave differently when they know they're being watched. They may clown around, try to make themselves look good, or otherwise act in relation to the observer. The best way to deal with this fact is to conduct multiple observations. In many cases, people being observed will get used to the presence of the observer over time.

3. Finally, be aware of the assumptions you bring to the observations—both when you are conducting the research and when you are analyzing the results. All researchers, of course, operate from a point of view, so there's no reason to think you can be a neutral bystander just recording what happens. For this reason, however, there is a very real danger that you will record in your observations only what you expected to see. Observers' assumptions can cause them to miss, ignore, or suppress important events. Being conscious of your own assumptions can help keep you open to things you had not anticipated.

You may need to request permission to observe, as well as permission to use any recording devices.

Conducting Observations

When you arrive at the place where you'll do your observation, look for a vantage point where you will be able to see what's going on and yet won't be obtrusive. Consider whether you want to move periodically from one spot to another to get a number of different perspectives on the activity or place you're observing. Make sure any equipment you've brought—camera or tape recorder—is ready to use.

Researchers typically develop their own system of taking field notes. Nonetheless, a few suggestions may be helpful. Begin by writing down the basic facts: the date, time, and place. Keep your notes on one side of the page. Depending on your research questions, here are some things to consider:

- **The setting:** Describe the overall size, shape, and layout. You may want to sketch it or draw a diagram. Note details—both what they are and how they are arranged. Pay attention to sounds and smells, as well as to what you can see.

- **The people:** Note the number of people. What are they doing? Describe their activities, movement, and behavior. What are they wearing? Note ages, race, nationality, and gender. How do they relate to one another? Record overheard conversation using quotation marks.

- **Your response:** As you observe, note anything that is surprising, puzzling, or unusual. Note also your own feelings and reactions, as well as any new ideas or questions that arise.

Analyzing Your Notes

After you've finished your observation, read through your notes carefully and, if you want, type them up, adding related points that you remember. Then make sure you analyze your notes from the standpoint of your research questions:

- What patterns emerge from your notes? What are your main findings? What, if anything, surprised you?

- What research questions do your notes address? What issues remain to be addressed?

- Do your observations confirm what you have read? How would you explain any discrepancies?

- What should your next step be? Should you go back to the library? Should you conduct further observations? If further observations are needed, what form should they take?

■ **FIELDWORK PRACTICE**

Observation

After getting their permission, observe the dinnertime conversation and interaction of your family or a group of friends, taking notes of your observations. When you are finished, read through your notes, considering what they reveal about the patterns of interaction you observed. Then answer the following questions:

1. Do you think your presence as an observer had an effect on what people said and did?

2. How difficult is it to observe and keep notes? What, if anything, could you do to make the process easier?

3. What did you expect to happen at dinner? How did these assumptions influence your observations? Were some things you observed unexpected? Do you think your assumptions caused you to miss anything? Were there certain things you chose not to include in your notes? Why?

4. What tentative conclusions do you think are legitimate to draw from your observations?

INTERVIEWS

As noted in Chapter 7, "Profiles," interviews are often an essential part of capturing the personality and opinions of the person being profiled. Interviews, of course, are not limited to profiles; they have a range of uses. Here are three common situations in which researchers can make good use of interviews, either as the main basis of a research project or a component.

■ **Interviews with experts:** Interviewing an expert on anorexia, the 1980s loft jazz scene in New York City, the current status of the cod-fishing industry, or virtually any topic you're researching can provide you with up-to-date information and analysis, as well as a deepened understanding of the issues involved in these topics—and can make a significant contribution to a research project. In such cases, interviewing an expert offers a source of information that supplements print or electronic sources.

■ **Interviews with key participants:** Interviews can do more than just supplement your research. In some cases, interviewing takes on a central role in a research project, especially in research on contemporary issues where it makes sense to talk to the people involved. Suppose you are planning to research the role of public libraries in relation to recent immigrants. You would certainly want to see what's been written about the topic, but you could also interview librarians at neighborhood branches who work with, say, Russian Jews, Southeast Asians, Haitians, or Latinos. In turn, these interviews could lead to further interviews with recent immigrants, as well as community organizations, to get their perspective on what libraries are doing and might do. The research paper you write will quite likely feature prominently the information you've gathered from these interviews as the main source of data, with print and electronic sources providing background and context for your research.

■ **Oral histories:** Interviews with people who participated in significant historical events can provide a useful focus for research. To understand the event from the perspective of a rank-and-file worker, you might interview a trade unionist who participated in a significant strike. Or to understand the origins of the New Right on college campuses in the early 1960s, you might interview someone who was involved in the founding of Young Americans for Freedom. Interviews such as these are often called oral histories because they are the spoken accounts of important historical moments based on people's memories of their lived experience. For this type of research, you need, of course, to look at what historians have said—both to generate questions before the interview and to relate the oral history to professional accounts after the interview as part of the written presentation of your research.

As you can see, the type of interviewing you do depends largely on the kind of research question you're raising and the sources it leads you to.

THE INTERVIEW PROCESS

Planning

The following considerations can help you get started on planning interviews. You can use these considerations to write a proposal that explains how the interviews fit into your research design (see "Writing a Proposal," on page 460).

■ **Background research:** The first step, as in any research, is to get an overview and basic information about your topic. At this point, you are likely to be formulating questions to guide your research. Consider how interviewing can help you answer these questions. What do you hope to find out?

■ **Choosing interview subjects:** The nature of your research question should suggest appropriate subjects to interview. Does it make sense to interview an expert on the topic? Or does your research seem to call for interviews with people involved in the subject you're investigating? Are the people you're considering likely to provide the information you're looking for?

■ **Preparing interview questions:** Use the notes from your background research to prepare interview questions. Interviewers normally use open questions to get their subjects talking—phrasing questions so that the natural answer is a yes or a no generally leads to a dead end. How open, of course, depends on your research question and your subject.

If you are interviewing an expert, your questions should be precise and seek specific information ("Estimates vary on the number of cod in the North Atlantic. Can you give me your view?"). For oral histories, on the other hand, questions often begin at a general level ("Tell me what it was like growing up in Oklahoma") but become more specific ("Do you recall when and why your family decided to migrate to California?"). When you have come up with a list of questions, organize them so that one question leads logically to the next.

■ **Considering the types of interviews**: The in-person, face-to-face interview is probably the best-known type of interview, but there are alternatives you may want or need to consider. The "Four Types of Interviews" box summarizes four possibilities, along with their advantages and disadvantages.

FOUR TYPES OF INTERVIEWS

❏ **In-person interviews:** In-person interviews have some significant advantages over the other types. Often, when answering your question, the person you are interviewing may take the conversation in a new direction. Although at times this means you'll need to guide the conversation politely back to your topic, sometimes the new direction is one that you hadn't thought of and would like to explore. At other times you may realize that your questions aren't working and that to get the information you need, you'll have to revise and supplement them on the spur of the moment.

Some researchers prefer to take handwritten notes during in-person interviews. Doing so, however, poses certain difficulties. Responses to your questions may be long, and you may not be able to write fast enough. And devoting all your attention to note taking makes it harder to think about what the person is saying and harder to guide the interview by choosing the next question or formulating a new one. For these reasons, many researchers use a tape recorder. But be flexible about using one. Most people don't mind, and the tape recorder will simply fade into the background. But some people are bothered by it and might not be as open as they would be if you took

notes. If you feel the disadvantages of tape recording are outweighing the advantages, be prepared to change methods.

❏ **Telephone interviews:** Telephone interviews are similar to in-person interviews. Both enable you to be flexible in your questioning. However, some people may find telephone interviews a bit more difficult to manage because rapport may not emerge as easily as in an in-person interview.

A speakerphone is useful if you've been given permission to record the conversation. Even if you haven't, a speakerphone makes it easier for you to take notes.

❏ **Email interviews:** Sometimes you might prefer or may have to conduct your interview by email. You might, for example, want to interview someone who isn't willing or able to schedule an in-person or telephone interview but who has no objection to answering questions. One advantage of email interviews is that they provide you with a written record. On the other hand, it may be difficult to follow up on interesting ideas or to clarify points. Phrasing and organization of questions are especially crucial in mail or email interviews because you can't adjust your line of questioning as you can in an in-person or telephone interview.

❑ **Online interviews:** Interviews can also be conducted online. Real-time synchronous communication sites, such as IRCs (Internet Relay Chat), MUDs (Multi-User Domains), and MOOs (MUD Object Oriented), allow computer users from around the world to "talk" to each other in writing in real time.

Like email interviews, online interviews help simplify note taking by recording the conversations. Make sure, however, that you are familiar with the technology necessary to record the interview—you don't want to lose all of your hard work.

Setting Up the Interview

Whether the person you plan to interview is a stranger, a friend, or a relative, you'll need to set up the interview. Generally this means writing a letter or making a telephone call, both to ask for permission and to set a time (or a deadline in the case of an interview by mail). Introduce yourself and your purpose. Be honest about what you are doing—many busy people are happy to help students with assignments. However, be prepared to be turned down. Sometimes busy people are just that—busy. If someone seems too busy to meet with you in person, ask whether you could interview him or her by telephone, mail, or email—or whether the person knows someone else you could interview. Above all, be polite. Be sure to schedule the interview far enough in advance of your due date to allow you to follow up with more questions or with further research if the interview leads to areas you had not previously considered. For in-person or telephone interviews that you want to record, ask at this point for permission to record. If it's appropriate, ask the person you're interviewing if there is anything you should read before the interview.

Conducting an In-Person or Telephone Interview

For in-person and telephone interviews, the interview itself is a crucial moment in your research. To get an in-person interview off on the right foot, arrive promptly. Make sure that you dress appropriately and that you bring your questions, tape recorder (if you have permission to record the interview), a pad and pens, and any other materials you might need. For telephone interviews, make sure you call at the time agreed upon.

Because in-person and telephone interviews are really conversations, the results you get will depend in part on your flexibility as a listener and a questioner. The person you're interviewing will be looking to you for guidance, and it is quite likely that you'll be faced with choices during the interview. Let's say you are interviewing someone about why she attends your college. She says, "I came because they've got a really good computer science program, I got a good financial aid package, and I didn't want to go very far from home. You know what I mean?" Then she pauses, looking at you for direction. You've got a choice to make about which thread to follow—the student's academic interests, her financial situation, or her desire to stay near home.

After the Interview

Especially with in-person and telephone interviews, plan time immediately afterward to review the results of the interview and to make further notes. Transcribe your tape, if you recorded the interview, or print out hard copies of email or on-line interviews. Make sure that you've noted direct quotations and that you've written down pertinent information about the interview (such as the time, date, and location).

Analyzing the Transcript

Material from an interview can be used in many different ways in a research project. It can be central to the final report or can provide supplementary quotations and statistics. The ideas you had ahead of time about how you would use the interview might be changed by the interview or by other aspects of your research process. To help you understand what use to make of the interview, write responses to these questions:

- What are the most important things you learned? List what seem to be the main points.

- What, if anything, surprised you? Why?

- What does the interview contribute to your understanding of your research question? How does the information relate to what you've already learned about your topic? If information, opinion, or point of view differ, how do you account for this?

- What questions does the interview raise for further research? What sources does it suggest you use?

A Final Note on Interviews

Be sure to thank the people you interview. (A note or email message is a nice touch.) When you've finished your paper, send them a copy along with a letter or email thanking them again.

■ FIELDWORK PRACTICE

Interviewing

Work with a partner. Interview your partner about why he or she decided to attend your college. Before the interview, think about the questions you want to ask, how you want to conduct the interview—in person, by telephone, online, or via email—and how you want to keep track of what's said. After the interview, write a paragraph or two about the experience. What sorts of questions were most effective? Did any ideas and topics come up that you had not expected? What decisions did you make during the interview about threads to follow in the conversation? What were the advantages and disadvantages of the interview method you chose? What problems did you experience in recording information?

Compare your response to the interview process with those of classmates. What generalizations can you, as a class, draw about interviewing?

QUESTIONNAIRES

Questionnaires are similar to interviews, except that they obtain responses from a number of people by using questionnaires. Questionnaires can target a particular group of people—to find out, for example, why students at your college have chosen to major in biomedical engineering, or why employees at a particular company do or don't participate in community service activities. Or they can examine the beliefs and opinions of the "general public," as is the case with those conducted by political pollsters and market researchers on everything from people's sexual habits to their religious beliefs to their product preferences.

While interview questions are generally open, questionnaires tend to use more "closed" questions, such as true/false, yes/no, checklists, ranking, and preference scales. In this sense, they sacrifice the depth of information to be gotten about one person for the breadth of data about many people.

Deciding whether you should design and distribute a questionnaire depends largely on what you're trying to find out. If, for example, you've read some research on the television-viewing habits of college students and want to find out if students at your school fit the patterns described, it makes sense to ask many students about their habits rather than to interview three or four. The results you get are liable to give you a more accurate picture. At any rate, as a way to start, write a proposal that explains your research project and why a questionnaire is the best method (see "Writing a Proposal," on page 460).

The Process of Designing a Questionnaire

If a questionnaire seems appropriate to your research project, you'll need to decide who your subjects are, prepare the questionnaire, distribute it, and then compile and analyze the results.

Getting Background Information

Designing a questionnaire is similar to designing an interview. Namely, you'll begin by researching your topic to get an overview and background information. Then you'll determine whether a questionnaire is the most appropriate method for addressing your research question: does it make sense to gather information on the opinions and habits of a number of people instead of talking to a few in depth or doing another form of research? At this point, before you expend the time and effort it takes to design and conduct a questionnaire, make sure that a questionnaire is likely to provide you with the information you're seeking.

Selecting Participants

To be sure that they can generalize from the results of their questionnaires, professional researchers try to obtain responses from a representative sample of the population they're investigating. If, for example, you're questioning employees of a company or students who major in bioengineering, it should be easy enough to send questionnaires to all of them. In other cases, however, you may need to choose people within the population at random.

For example, if you're studying the students' opinions of a first-year writing program, you could get a random sample by questioning every tenth person on the class lists. But even in that case, make sure that your responses are representative of the actual population in the classes and reflect their demographic composition. You may need to modify the distribution of your questionnaire to guarantee it reaches a representative sample—men, women, blacks, whites, Latinos, Asians, traditional-age students, returning students.

If your results are to be meaningful, you'll also need to include enough participants in your questionnaire to give it credibility. Keep in mind that regardless of how you conduct your questionnaire, not everyone will participate. In fact, as pollsters are well aware, it's generally necessary to survey many more people than you expect to receive responses from. Often as few as 10 percent of the questionnaires mailed out will be returned. A good rule of thumb is to aim for 40 percent and, if you don't get it the first time, do multiple distributions.

When you write up your findings, any generalizations based on your questionnaire should be limited to the population your questionnaire represents (you should not, for example, generalize about American voters as a whole based on a survey of students at your college). Be sure to discuss any potentially relevant information on questionnaire participants, such as information on age, gender, or occupation.

ETHICS OF RESEARCH

LOADED QUESTIONS

Public opinion polls are a fixture in American politics. Most political candidates, the two major political parties, and many other political organizations and advocacy groups use opinion polls to understand the public's mood and to shape policy. In fact, at times political polls can go beyond simply providing information that will play an active role in the formation of public policy. In political debates, the results of opinion polls are often used to buttress the position of one side or the other. Because opinion polls have become such an important part of political life, there is the temptation to use them in a partisan way.

Take, for example, a poll conducted by advocates of casino gambling in Rhode Island to determine the degree of public support. The main question in the poll— "Would you approve a casino if it would reduce your property taxes and improve education?"—is clearly a loaded one because it stacks the deck with casino proponents' arguments. As political pollster Darrell West noted, the "corollary question from an anti-gambling perspective" might read, "Would you support a casino if you thought it would raise crime rates and increase the level of gambling addiction?"

Not surprisingly, a majority of people polled favored casino gambling when the question was framed in terms of casino revenues reducing taxes and improving education. However, when the question was posed in an unbiased way—"Do you favor or oppose the construction of a gambling casino?"—the results were quite different. Fifty-three percent opposed the casino, 42 percent supported it, and 5 percent had no opinion. ■

Designing the Questionnaire

The results of your questionnaire will depend to a large extent on the questions you ask. Here are some considerations to take into account in designing a questionnaire:

1. Include a short introduction that explains the purpose of the questionnaire and what you will do with the results. Point out that questionnaire participants' opinions are important. Ask them to complete the questionnaire, and give them an estimate of the time it will take to do so.

2. Make sure the questions you ask are focused on the information you need for your research. It's tempting to ask all sorts of things you're curious about. The results can be interesting, to be sure, but asking more questions than you actually need can reduce your response rate. In general, keep the questionnaire brief in order to maximize returns.

3. Design the questionnaire so that it is easy to read. The visual design should suggest that it won't take long to fill out. Don't crowd questions together to save space. And leave plenty of space for open questions, reminding questionnaire respondents that they can write on the back.

4. At the end of the questionnaire, include a thank-you and explain where or to whom it should be returned.

Types of Questions

Questions can take the form of checklists, yes/no questions, categories, ranking scales, and open questions. Each type of question works somewhat differently from the others. Usually you will want to combine several types to give you the particular information you need. You will also need to consider the most effective and logical order to present the questions. Questionnaires typically begin with the least complicated or most general questions and end with open-ended questions.

Here are examples of the most common types of questions designed for a research project investigating whether the political attitudes and involvement of students at the researcher's college support or refute claims in the published literature that students today are generally apathetic when it comes to politics.

Checklist

Which of these political activities have you participated in? Please check all that apply.

_____ voted in national election

_____ voted in state or local election

_____ campaigned for a candidate

_____ worked for a political party

_____ attended a political rally or demonstration

_____ belonged to a political organization or advocacy group

_____ other (specify): _____

Yes/No Questions

Are you a registered voter?

_____ Yes

_____ No

Categories

How would you describe your political views?

_____ left-wing

_____ liberal

_____ moderate

_____ conservative

_____ right-wing

_____ none of the above/don't know

Ranking Scales

Please rank the following items according to their importance as national priorities. (Use 1 for the highest priority, 7 for the lowest.)

_____ strengthening the economy

_____ reducing crime

_____ balancing the budget

_____ improving education

_____ improving the health care system

_____ improving race relations

_____ reducing poverty

Lickert Scale

[Lickert scale questionnaire items gauge the degree of agreement with particular statements of opinion. Researchers typically design a sequence of such items.]

Please indicate the degree to which you agree or disagree with the following statements. Enter the number that best expresses your view on each item.

1—Strongly agree

2—Agree

3—Not Sure

4—Disagree

5—Strongly Disagree

_____ It is important to be well-informed about current political events.

_____ There's no point in getting involved in politics because individuals can have little influence.

_____ Voting in elections is a responsibility, not just a right.

_____ The political system is controlled by politicians and lobbyists.

Open-Ended Questions

[Open-ended questions call for brief responses. Such questions are more time consuming and difficult to tabulate than closed questions, but they can often yield information that other types of questions will not.]

What, if anything, has motivated you to be interested in political affairs?

_____

_____

_____

What, if anything, has posed obstacles to your being interested in political affairs?

_____

_____

_____

After you've prepared your questionnaire, try it out on a few people. Do their answers tell you what you wanted to know? Based on these answers, have you covered all the issues and have you phrased your questions well? If you see any problems, revise your questionnaire. Now is the time to get it right—before you administer it to a lot of people.

Conducting the Questionnaire

Your questionnaire can be distributed in various ways: in person, by mail, by telephone, or online through listservs, newsgroups, or Web sites. Your choice of how to conduct the questionnaire will depend on your choice of a sample population, on your deadline, and on your resources (mail surveys, for example, can be quite expensive because you'll need to provide stamped self-addressed envelopes).

COMPILING, ANALYZING, AND PRESENTING RESULTS

Compiling results amounts to tallying up the answers to each question. This is a fairly straightforward procedure for closed questions such as checklist, yes/no, multiple-choice, and ranking and Lickert-scale items. For open questions, you might write down key words or phrases that emerge in the responses and tally the number of times these (or similar) words or phrases occur. Keep a list of answers that seem of special interest to use in your research report as quotations.

Researchers present the results of closed questions in the form of percentages in the text of their reports. In addition, you may want to design tables or other visual displays of your results to complement the written report.

Remember that your results do not speak for themselves. You need to analyze and explain how they are significant to your research project. The following questions can help you begin such an analysis:

- What patterns emerge from responses to individual questions? What patterns emerge from responses across questions?

- How would you explain these patterns? Try to think of two or more explanations, even if they appear to be contradictory or mutually exclusive.

- What is the significance of these explanations for your research? If the explanations seem contradictory, can you think of ways to reconcile them? If not, on what grounds would you choose one or the other?

- What tentative claims might you make based on your analysis of the results? How would you justify such claims?

■ FIELDWORK PRACTICE

Conducting a Questionnaire

Work in a group of three or four. Your task is to design a pilot questionnaire to determine student opinion about some aspect of the academic program or student services at your college. You could focus on, say, advising, orientation for new students, required first-year courses, tutoring, or anything else that interests you. Begin by listing the kind of information that you want to get. Then write five to ten questions that seem likely to give you this information. Test your questionnaire by administering it to ten to fifteen classmates. Once you've gotten their responses, evaluate your questionnaire:

1. Did you get the information you were looking for?
2. Is each of the questions worded in such a way that it provides the information you anticipated?
3. Should you word any of the questions differently to obtain the information you're seeking? Should you delete any of the questions or add new ones?
4. Explain your answers.
5. Compare your group's experience with that of other groups. What conclusions can you draw about questionnaire design?

writers at work

©Dan Jaeger/stock.xchng. Image altered for design purposes.

4

INTRODUCTION: UNDERSTANDING THE WRITING PROCESS

No two writers compose in the same way, and an individual may work in different ways on different writing tasks. Nonetheless, there are predictable elements in a writing project that can be listed:

- **Invention:** Developing an approach to the topic and to readers, assessing purpose, doing research, choosing the appropriate genre.

- **Planning:** Designing the arrangement of material, finding an appropriate pattern of organization.

- **Drafting:** Creating a working draft, getting ideas down on paper.

- **Peer commentary:** Getting feedback from others, seeing the working draft through the reader's eyes.

- **Revising:** Rereading the working draft, clarifying purpose and organization, connecting the parts.

- **Manuscript preparation:** Designing, editing, and proofreading a document.

Because of the way the elements of writing have been listed, you may think that they constitute a series of steps you can follow. If you look at how writers work, however, you'll see that they may well manage these elements in quite different ways. Some writers like to start drafting before they develop a clear plan, while others would not think of drafting without a carefully developed outline.

Nor are the elements necessarily separate from each other. Some people revise as they draft, working carefully over each section before going on to the next, while others write quickly and then think about needed revisions. Nor do writers spend the same amount of time on each of the elements. Depending on the writing task and their own writing habits, writers learn how to manage the elements in ways that work for them.

Writing can be exhilarating, but it can be aggravating too. You can probably think of times when writing seemed to pour out, leading you to previously unsuspected ideas and precisely the right way of saying things. On the other hand, you may have had moments when you couldn't begin a writing task or got stuck in the middle. The way to get to the source of such difficulties is to think about how you are managing the elements of your writing task. Are you spending your time doing what needs to be done to get the writing task completed? Should you be revising and editing passages that you may eventually discard? Is this keeping you from figuring out how (or whether) the passage connects to other points? If you see your draft diverge from your outline, should you follow it or go back and revise your plan? When you're stuck in the middle of a draft, do you need to turn to invention—to read more or talk to others?

Answers to these questions will vary, of course, depending on the writing task and your own habits as a writer. The point is that experienced writers learn to ask such questions in order to get their bearings, especially when the writing is not going well, to see where they stand in putting a piece of writing together and what they need to do next.

■ REFLECTING ON YOUR WRITING

How You Managed a Writing Task

Think of a writing task you completed recently, in school or out of school. Analyze how you managed the task. To do this, consider the following questions:

1. What called on you to write? Describe how you defined the writing task. How did you establish your purpose? What did your exploration of the topic involve? How did you imagine your readers and the relationship you wanted to establish with them? What genre did you choose? Did you talk to others about your ideas?

2. Explain how you planned the writing. How much planning did you do? When did you plan, and what form did it take?

3. Describe how you drafted. When did you begin? How much invention and planning did you do before you started drafting?

4. Describe what feedback, if any, you received on your draft. What was the effect of this feedback?

5. What kinds of revisions did you make? When did you revise—during drafting, after you had a complete working draft, at various points?

6. What final form did the writing take? Were any considerations of document design involved? Did you edit and proofread the final version?

Now look back over your answers to these questions. What conclusions can you draw about how you managed the elements of the writing process in this instance? What, if anything, would you do differently if you had to do the task again?

the writing process
a case study of a
writing assignment

CASE STUDY OF A WRITING ASSIGNMENT

To see how a student writer manages a writing task and how writers and readers can work together effectively, we'll follow a student, Katie DiMartile, preparing a paper for a popular-culture course.

INVENTION

Understanding the Call to Write

It can be difficult to get started on a writing project if you are uncertain about the call to write and the kind of writing task it presents. You may not be clear, for example, about what an assignment in one of your courses is calling on you to do. If you feel shaky about the purpose of a writing assignment, other students in the class probably do too. Of course, you could talk to the teacher, but you may also want to collaborate with classmates to clarify the purpose of the assignment and develop an approach to it.

Here is the writing assignment Katie DiMartile was given in Introduction to American Popular Culture.

Writing Assignment

INTRODUCTION TO AMERICAN POPULAR CULTURE
Roadside memorials, sometimes in the form of crosses, wreaths, or flowers, line America's roads at the sites of fatal car accidents. Because many of these memorials feature crosses or other religious symbols, many people object to their placement on public land. However, such memorials are also a part of important cultural traditions to many people. The controversy over roadside memorials has resulted in a lively public debate over whether or not such

memorials should be permitted on our nation's roadsides. After reading two short articles on the controversy, write a short (2-page, 500-word) essay in which you take a position on whether or not roadside memorials should be banned. You will need to defend your position by explaining your reasons for supporting or countering a particular perspective in order to persuade your audience to take up your position.

© Jill Nance

■ EXERCISE

Analyzing a Writing Assignment

Work with two or three classmates to analyze the Introduction to American Popular Culture writing assignment and to determine what it is calling on students to do. The following guidelines can be used for virtually any writing assignment. Of course, since you're not a student in the popular-culture class, you won't have all the information available to Katie and her classmates. Nonetheless, you can make some informed guesses by picking up important cues from the assignment.

Guidelines for Analyzing Writing Assignments

■ Look for key words in the assignment—such as *describe, summarize, explain, analyze,* or *evaluate critically.* Discuss what these terms might mean in relation to the material you're being asked to write about and the goals and focus of the course.

- Consider what information you need to do the assignment successfully. Where can you get this information? Does the assignment call for additional research, or is it based on class readings and discussion? Are there things you know or have learned in other classes that might prove useful?

- Look for any special directions the assignment provides about the form of writing. Does it call for a specific genre (such as a report, a proposal, or a review)? Does it call for documentation? Consider the assigned length. What is it possible to do well within these limits?

After your group has answered these questions, compare your response to those of other groups. At this point, what advice would you give Katie as she begins the assignment?

Understanding Readers

Another difficulty in getting started on a writing task may be the writers' uncertainty about what will interest their readers. Sometimes writers believe that if they have thought of something, everyone else must have too. Underestimating the importance of their own ideas, they feel reluctant to express them. One way to test your ideas is to discuss them with other people. That way you can not only reassure yourself that your ideas are valid but also begin to formulate a plan for approaching your readers.

Talking out the ideas you have for a paper is one of the best ways to understand your readers. Here are some guidelines for doing this, followed by a transcript of Katie's discussion with her friend Tyler.

Guidelines for Understanding Your Readers

- Find a willing listener, describe your writing task, and then tell your listener what you are thinking of writing about and what you are thinking of saying about it.

- Ask your listener what she already knows about your subject, what she would like to know about it, and whether she has ideas or information you could use in your writing.

Transcript of Katie's Discussion with Tyler

KATIE: I've got to write this paper for my pop-culture course on roadside memorials. I have to say whether or not I think they should be banned. I never knew there was so much to consider. There is a lot of debate about these memorials.

TYLER: Sounds cool. I've seen those memorials before around my hometown, but I never knew that there was a debate about them. So what are you going to say?

KATIE: Well, that's the problem. A lot of people oppose the memorials because they are shaped like crosses or other religious symbols. Religion is such a touchy subject. I don't feel comfortable writing about it.

I thought I could maybe say something about how the memorials are important because they remind people to be safe on the road. That's definitely what happened when some friends of mine put up a memorial for someone at my school who died in a car accident. Every time I saw it I would slow down or at least think about being more attentive. But I'm worried this is too obvious. What do you think? Does that sound interesting?

TYLER: Oh yeah. I've had the same experience. Even if there are plenty of other signs telling me to slow down or be careful, those memorials really make you think about how important it is to be safe.

KATIE: I kind of also want to say something about how they give the victim's family some closure. I mean, it seems like in all the debates people seem to lose track of the fact we are talking about someone's loved one losing their life.

TYLER: That does seem important. And I think you are right that people seem to get too caught up in the controversy to think about this on an emotional level.

KATIE: You really think so? I mean, do you think I can do something here? My teacher has to like it, you know.

TYLER: That goes without saying. I think you have a couple of solid reasons why these memorials should be allowed on our roadways. Now you just have to get it on paper.

KATIE: I hope so. Thanks, Tyler. I better get to work.

Exploring the Topic

At a certain point, writers need to get some ideas down on paper, even if the writing is of a preliminary sort. One way to start is to do exploratory writing, in which you're tentatively working out the focus and direction of your paper. If you want someone to look at your exploratory writing, you can use the guidelines below. Make sure that the person who reads your writing understands that it is an initial attempt to discover what you want to say.

Guidelines for Responding to Exploratory Writing

- Ask your reader to circle or underline key phrases and interesting ideas, whether or not they seem to be the main point of the writing.

- Ask your reader to tell you if there seem to be, implied or lurking just off the page, ideas that you could develop.

After thinking about her conversation with Tyler, Katie decided to do some exploratory writing. Below is her writing and the response from her friend Kevin.

Katie's Exploratory Writing

I remember during my freshman year of high school, my friend lost his brother in a car accident. My friend maintained a small memorial at the site and I went with him a couple of times to lay down some fresh flowers. I know that the memorial was really important to my friend in coping with the loss of his brother. Also, whenever I drove by the memorial, it really made me think about how driving is such a big responsibility. I could never go past that spot without checking my speed or becoming more alert.

Kevin's Response

I really like how you were able to draw on your own experience a roadside memorial and the impact it had on you and your friend. However, I think you need to be careful with how you write about this experience. As I understand it, your assignment is an analytical and persuasive one, not just a personal essay about your experience. Maybe you could explain more clearly why the memorial was so important to your friend. How can you generalize that to explain why memorials should be allowed in all cases? Maybe you could find a way of connecting how the memorial affected your friend and how it affected you to come up with a main point.

PLANNING

Using discussions with others about their ideas for a writing project, writers need to develop a plan for their writing to highlight the main point and provide supporting evidence.

After Katie talked to Tyler and got a response to her exploratory writing from Kevin, she mulled over the results. She knew it was time to use this information to plan her essay. Tyler and Kevin helped her see that she needed to write an analytical essay that made a central claim and backed it up with evidence. A personal essay that focused on her feelings about her family was not the kind of writing called for by the assignment.

At this point, she worked by herself, developing her main idea and arranging reasons to support it. She sketched the following brief outline so that she could begin drafting.

Katie's Brief Outline

Introduction

Begin with other ways our country memorializes tragedy

Explanation of roadside memorials and the controversy surrounding them

Claim: roadside memorials give a sense of closure to victim's loved ones and
 caution other drivers

Body

Give reasons why this is so

Example of friend's memorial for his brother

Reminds drivers to slow down

Memorials are more difficult to ignore than regular road signs

Ending

Human aspect more important than the controversy

Regulations for what memorials look like?

DRAFTING

Any plan a writer develops needs to be tested by writing a working draft. Outlines, sketches, or other kinds of preliminary planning can tell you only so
much. To see where your ideas are going, you must commit them to paper.

After she sketched a brief outline, Katie wrote a working draft. As you can
see, she used ideas and suggestions from Tyler and Kevin. But, as is the case
in individual writing projects, she worked independently to write the draft.
Here is what she came up with.

Katie's Working Draft

Our culture has always made a point of remembering the dead. For example,
in Washington, D.C., there is the Tomb of the Unknown Soldier, the Vietnam
Memorial, and many others. Additionally, there are memorials at Columbine,
Ground Zero, Oklahoma City, and Virginia Tech honoring those who lost their lives
in those tragedies. With all of these memorials already in place one would think
that remembering victims of car accidents would be acceptable, but there are
people who oppose them. In a country that usually respects and honors the
dead, it is surprising that there could be a controversy over something as simple
as roadside crosses. A roadside memorial to those who died in a car accident gives
the loved ones of the deceased closure and serves as a warning to other drivers.

When someone is killed unexpectedly in a car accident, loved ones are left
with a tragic loss. Coping with such a dramatic loss can be hard and going to the
site and seeing the memorial gives the family closure. By putting a cross, or
another symbol, at the site of a fatal car accident, the victim is being remembered.
One of my friends lost his brother in a car accident during our freshman year of

high school. I went with him several times during that year to put flowers at the site of his brother's accident. Keeping these roadside memorials up helps the families get through the grieving process.

As more people are on the roads, these memorials don't just serve as ways to remember the deceased, they act as warning signs for other drivers. As you're driving down the road and you see a little white cross, you almost always check your speed and become more aware of your surroundings. People can blow off speed limit and other warning signs because they see them all the time. But when you see a small cross, you know someone actually lost their life, they didn't just get a speeding ticket. Roadside memorials make the danger of driving much more real, and therefore make drivers more cautious when they're behind the wheel.

Proposals to ban roadside memorials ignore the important functions they serve. First of all, the memorials provide a place for the loved ones of the victims of car accidents to go to mourn. Being able to commemorate the deceased in this way can help provide closure to such an incomprehensible tragedy. Furthermore, when other drivers see these memorials out on the road, they are reminded to slow down and be more attentive. Roadside memorials can bring something positive to the tragedy by helping others be safer. These functions are too important to be overlooked by those who would see roadside memorials banned. Perhaps the best way to compromise between the different sides of this controversy is to enforce regulations on the form of such memorials.

PEER COMMENTARY

A working draft means just that—a draft to work on by getting feedback and figuring out what kinds of revisions are called for. To get the most useful kind of feedback to a working draft, make sure your readers know they're looking at a work in progress and not a final draft.

There are different kinds of commentary you can get from readers at this point. Your readers can:

- *Describe* the writer's strategy.
- *Analyze* the organization of the essay.
- *Evaluate* the argument.

Each kind of commentary provides different information to help you plan revisions. Sometimes you'll want just one kind of commentary; at other times you'll want more than one.

The following sections describe the different kinds of feedback, explain their purposes, and provide guidelines. After each, you'll find an example of the type of peer commentary in response to Katie's working draft.

Describe the Writer's Strategy

A good first step in getting feedback on a working draft is to ask your reader to suspend judgment for a moment and instead to analyze the function of each paragraph in your working draft—how the paragraphs support the main point and how they are connected to each other. In this way, a reader can give you a blueprint of what you have written. This can help you see how (or whether) the parts fit together. You can use this information to decide how well your paragraphs play the roles you intended for them (or whether they perform some other function). This can also be a good basis for the following two types of commentary, in which readers analyze the organization and evaluate the ideas of a working draft.

Guidelines for Describing the Writer's Strategy

- What is the writer's main point? Identify the sentence or sentences that express the main point. If you don't find such a sentence, write your own version of what you think the main point is.

- Write a statement about each paragraph that explains the function it performs and how it fits into the organization of the working draft. Use words that describe function, such as *describes, explains, gives reasons, proposes,* or *compares.*

Sample Description of Katie's Draft

Main point: Roadside memorials should not be banned.

¶1: Starts with a broad view of the main problem then questions the controversy before introducing reasons for support.

¶2: Further explains one of the reasons introduced in the first paragraph. Generalizes from a personal experience to support the point.

¶3: Elaborates on an idea introduced in the first paragraph. Describes scenario that serves as an example to support the idea.

¶4: Summarizes main points and proposes a solution.

Analyze the Organization

Sometimes, in the struggle to get your ideas down on paper, you may lose perspective on how effectively you've organized them. For this reason, it can be helpful to ask someone to analyze the presentation of your main idea and examine the supporting evidence.

Again, ask readers to put aside their personal responses to your ideas. Explain that you want them to focus instead on the organization of what you have written. If they have already described the function of paragraphs in the draft, they can use that description as the basis of their analysis.

Guidelines for Analyzing the Organization

- What is the main point of the draft? Is it clear and easy to find? Does the introduction help readers anticipate where the draft will be going?

- Do the following paragraphs develop the main point, or do they seem to develop some other point? Is it easy to tell how the paragraphs relate to the main point, or do they need to be connected more explicitly to it?

- Is each of the paragraphs well focused, or do some of them seem to have several ideas contending for the reader's attention? If a paragraph needs more focus, how could this be achieved?

- Within the supporting paragraphs, do some points seem to need more development? Are there points that don't belong at all?

- Is the ending or conclusion effective? Does it provide a sense of closure?

Sample Analysis of the Organization of Katie's Draft

I like the opening because your examples are powerful and make the reader sympathetic. You do a good job of starting general and then focusing in more specifically on the essay question. However, I wasn't totally clear on the main point. You imply that you believe that these memorials should be permitted, but you do not actually state so until the beginning of the last paragraph. I think you could use a clinching statement at the end of the first paragraph that states this main point so that it is really clear.

In paragraph 2, you give an example that illustrates the problem. But the example doesn't help support your claim. You say that your friend's brother was a victim and you describe going to the memorial, but I think you could explain how exactly the memorial helped your friend. Expand on how this personal example connects to the main claim of the paragraph and supports your idea.

Paragraph 3 explains how roadside memorials can serve as warning signs to other drivers. I like the theory you propose, but I think you should emphasize the point that traditional road signs don't have the same impact on drivers as the memorials. This could help clarify what you mean by "memorials make the danger of driving much more real."

Finally, in paragraph 4 you summarize your main points again and begin to develop a possible solution to the problem. I would focus more on the compromise you suggest instead of summing up what you have already said.

Evaluate the Argument

While the first two kinds of commentary ask readers to set aside their evaluation of your ideas, sometimes you'll really want to know what they think. This is especially likely if you're making an argument or dealing with a controversial topic. For this kind of peer commentary in particular, you'll find it helpful to have more than one reader and to discuss with each reader the comments he or she makes. In this way, you'll have the opportunity to see how your ideas relate to other points of view and to understand the enabling assumptions you and others bring to the issue. This can help you make decisions about how to clarify your own position and handle differing views as you revise.

Guidelines for Evaluating the Argument

- Analyze the parts of the argument. What is the claim or main point of the working draft? What supporting evidence is provided? What enabling assumptions connect the evidence to the claim?

- Do you agree with the essay's main point? Do you accept the essay's assumptions? Explain why.

- *If you disagree* with the essay's main point or do not accept one or more of its assumptions, what position would you take on the issue yourself? How would you support your position? What assumptions would you make? How would you refute the main point of the essay? What alternative perspectives does the draft need to take into account?

- *If you agree* with the essay's position, explain why. Do you think the essay makes the best possible argument supporting it? How would you strengthen it? What would you change, add, or omit? Why?

Discuss the responses with your readers. If you disagree, the idea is not to argue about who is right but to keep talking to understand why your positions differ and what assumptions might have led you to take differing positions.

Sample Evaluations of the Argument in Katie's Draft

Commentary 1

Katie, your main claim seems that you support the roadside memorials and think they are important, and you support this idea by talking about how the different ways in which these memorials help people. The reasons you give are that they help families of victims grieve and that they caution other drivers to be safe. You seem to think that the good these memorials do is more important than whatever reasons people have for wanting to see them banned.

I can definitely see what you mean. I think these memorials could be beneficial to both mourners and other drivers. But I don't really see how anyone would disagree with the argument you have crafted without also knowing the reasons people are against them in the first place. I think you could provide more motivation for the essay by explaining the controversy in more depth. Maybe if you clarified why some people are against these memorials in the first place, then your own reasons for supporting them would have more of an impact.

Commentary 2

[Analysis of the parts of the argument is similar to Response 1.]

I don't know if I totally agree with your assumption that the way these memorials help the community is more important than the fact that they could infringe on people's rights. A lot of these memorials are shaped like crosses and I don't think it's right to put religious symbols on public property. I think you have a lot of good points about the potential good these memorials can do, but how would you answer to people who think like me? I think it would be worth at least acknowledging the other side so that you seem well-informed about the issue.

The only other thing is the final paragraph. You seem to mostly repeat the main points that you have already made in the essay. Maybe there's some way you could expand on the solution you propose or point out the larger problems or consequences.

Discuss the commentaries with your readers. You might disagree with them, but the idea is not to argue about who is right but to keep talking to understand why your positions differ and what assumptions might have led you to take differing positions.

REVISING

Writing isn't a precise science with right and wrong answers, and neither is talking about written work in progress. When others comment on your writing, each person will have his or her own responses, insights, and suggestions. At times you'll get differing suggestions about what to do with your working draft, as is the case with the two commentaries on Katie's working draft. This doesn't necessarily mean that one reader has seen the true problem in your writing and the other has missed it altogether. By telling you the effect your writing has on each of them, both readers are giving you information to work with.

It's important to understand why readers have responded to your writing as they did. Try to imagine their point of view and what in your writing might have prompted their response. Peer commentary doesn't provide writers with a set of directions they can carry out mechanically. Rather, they must analyze and interpret their readers' responses.

Here are some guidelines for revising, followed by Katie's commentary about how she made use of the peer commentary she received on her working draft.

Guidelines for Revising

- What do your readers see as the main point of your draft? Is that the main idea you intended? If your readers have identified your main point, do they offer suggestions to make it come across more clearly? If you think they missed your main point, consider why this is so. Do you need to revise the sentence or sentences that express your central point?

- Do your readers see how the evidence you supply supports your main point? If so, do they offer suggestions about strengthening the evidence you're using to back up your main claim? If not, does this mean you need to revise your main point or revise the supporting evidence?

- What do your readers think you assume to connect your evidence to your main claim? Is this what you had in mind? If not, how can you change the relationship between your claim and the evidence you provide?

- If your readers agree with your essay's position, why is this so? Do they think you make the best possible case? If they disagree, consider their positions and the assumptions they are making. Do they offer alternative perspectives you could use?

- Do you provide a meaningful ending that points out an important consequence or implication of your argument?

Katie's Thoughts on Her Peer Commentaries

As I began to write this paper, I wasn't really sure about the topic. I couldn't think of things to say and that frustrated me. All of the suggestions you made will really help me improve the essay. I realized it was a mistake not to state my main point at the end of paragraph 1. In fact, I never really said what my main point was at all. My supporting material needed to be developed. I wasn't really explaining the examples that I gave in paragraphs 2 and 3. I also needed an ending that did more than repeat what I had already written.

Notice in Katie's revisions of her working draft how she uses ideas from the two commentaries to plan a revision. First, we present two paragraphs from the working draft with Katie's annotated plans for revision. This is followed by the final draft.

Katie's Revisions

Our culture has always made a point of remembering the dead. For example, in Washington, D.C., there is the Tomb of the Unknown Soldier, the Vietnam Memorial, and many others. Additionally, there are memorials at Columbine, Ground Zero, Oklahoma City, and Virginia Tech honoring those who lost their lives in those tragedies. With all of these memorials already in place one would think that remembering victims of car accidents would be acceptable, but there are people who oppose them. In a country that usually respects and honors the dead, it is surprising that there could be a controversy over something as simple as roadside crosses. A roadside memorial to those who died in a car accident gives the loved ones of the deceased closure and serves as a warning to other drivers.

- Explain the different sides of the controversy

When someone is killed unexpectedly in a car accident, loved ones are left with a tragic loss. Coping with such a dramatic loss can be hard and going to the site and seeing the memorial gives the family closure. By putting a cross, or another symbol, at the site of a fatal car accident, the victim is being remembered. One of my friends lost his brother in a car accident during our freshman year of high school. I went with him several times during that year to put flowers at the site of his brother's accident. Keeping these roadside memorials up helps the families get through the grieving process.

- Develop this personal example.

- Use as topic sentence to organize the paragraph.

As more people are on the roads, these memorials don't just serve as ways to remember the deceased, they act as warning signs for other drivers. As you're driving down the road and you see a little white cross, you almost always check your speed and become more aware of your surroundings. People can blow off speed limit and other warning signs because they see them all the time. But when you see a small cross, you know someone actually lost their life, they didn't just get a speeding ticket. Roadside memorials make the danger of driving much more real, and therefore make drivers more cautious when they're behind the wheel.

Use as main idea at the beginning.

Proposals to ban roadside memorials ignore the important functions they serve. ~~First of all, the memorials provide a place for the loved ones of the victims of car accidents to go to mourn. Being able to commemorate the deceased in this way can help provide closure to such an incomprehensible tragedy. Furthermore, when other drivers see these memorials out on the road, they are reminded to slow down and be more attentive. Roadside memorials can bring something positive to the tragedy by helping others be safer.~~ These functions are too important to be overlooked by those who would see roadside memorials banned. Perhaps the best way to compromise between the different sides of this controversy is to enforce regulations on the form of such memorials.

–Explain what these regulations would be and why they would work.

Katie DiMartile

American Pop Culture

Prof. Brown

November 14, 2008

Roadside Memorials

Our culture has always made a point of remembering the dead. For
example, in Washington, D.C., there is the Tomb of the Unknown Soldier, the
Vietnam Memorial, and many others. Additionally, there are memorials at
Columbine, Ground Zero, Oklahoma City, and Virginia Tech honoring those who
lost their lives in those tragedies. While all these memorials are accepted by
the public without question, roadside memorials, small monuments marking the
sites of fatal car accidents, are plagued by controversy. Some argue that such
memorials should be banned because they often contain religious symbols that
should not be displayed on public property. Others think that the memorials
could distract drivers and become safety hazards. However, such proposals to
ban roadside memorials ignore the important functions they serve.

One important function that roadside memorials serve is that they can
help the victim's loved ones get through the grieving process. When someone is
killed unexpectedly in a car accident, loved ones are left with a tragic loss.
Coping with such a dramatic loss can be hard and going to the site and seeing
the memorial gives the family closure. By putting a cross, or another symbol, at
the site of a fatal car accident, the victim is being remembered. One of my
friends lost his brother in a car accident during our freshman year of high
school. I went with him several times during that year to put flowers at the
site of his brother's accident. More than visiting his brother's grave or talking
to his family, visiting the memorial seemed to bring my friend peace. I believe
standing where his brother lost his life helped my friend feel closer to him.

Roadside memorials are not just important to families or loved ones, but
they can act as warning signs to other drivers. Roadside memorials make the
danger of driving much more real because they remind drivers of the serious
consequences of reckless behavior on the road. When I drive down the road and
see a memorial, it reminds me to check my speed and become more aware of my
surroundings. It is easy to ignore speed limit and other warning signs because

DiMartile 2

they are so familiar. But when you see a small cross, you know someone actually lost their life, they didn't just get a speeding ticket.

Perhaps the best way to compromise between the different sides of the controversy over roadside memorials is to enforce regulations on the form of these monuments. Memorials could feature pictures of the deceased or meaningful personal items instead of religious symbols. There could be rules for where memorials could be safely erected. Such regulations would still allow roadside memorials to provide important services to loved ones and drivers while also respecting the views of others and maintaining proper safety.

FINAL TOUCHES

Collaboration on a piece of writing includes working on the final touches. Copy editors routinely edit the manuscripts of even the most famous writers, making suggestions about words, phrases, sentences, or passages that might be unclear, awkward, or grammatically incorrect. Then proofreaders carefully review the final draft for any misspellings, missing words, typos, or other flaws.

Directions for Editing

Ask the person editing your manuscript to look for any words, phrases, sentences, or passages that need to be changed. The person can do this in one of two ways: he or she can simply underline or circle problems, write a brief note of explanation in the margin when necessary, and let you make the changes; or he or she can go ahead and make tentative changes for you to consider. Your teacher will let you know which method to follow.

Sample Editing

Notice the editing suggestion here to stay consistent with the personal example in paragraph 3 by using first person instead of "you."

Sentence in Katie's Revised Draft:

As you're driving down the road and you see a little white cross you almost always check your speed and become more aware of your surroundings.

Final Version:

When I drive down the road and see a memorial it reminds me to check my speed and become more aware of my surroundings.

Directions for Proofreading

The person proofreading your final copy can underline or circle grammatical errors, usage problems, typos, and misspellings and let you make the final corrections. Or she or he can supply the corrections. Again, it's up to your teacher which method to follow.

TALKING TO TEACHERS

Much of what has been said here about how writers and readers can collaborate also applies to talking about your writing with teachers. There may be times, for example, when you have trouble figuring out a writing assignment. You may be confused about the suggestions you've received in peer commentaries, or you may not fully understand the teacher's comments. In such situations, you might request a conference with your teacher.

Talking about writing with teachers will be most productive if you prepare ahead of time. If you want to discuss a writing assignment, reread the directions carefully and prepare questions on what isn't clear to you about the assignment. If you want to talk about the feedback you've gotten from peers, reread their commentaries and bring them with you to the conference. If you want to talk about a paper that has already been graded, make sure you read it over carefully, paying particular attention to the teacher's comments.

In any case, have realistic expectations about what can happen at the conference. Don't expect your teacher to change your grade or give you a formula for completing the assignment. The point of the conference is for you to understand what your teacher is looking for in a piece of writing.

GOING TO THE WRITING CENTER

One of the best places to talk about writing is a writing center, where you can meet and discuss your writing with people who are interested in the writing process and in how students develop as writers. Find out if your college has a writing center. It will be listed in the campus directory, and your writing teacher will know about its hours and procedures.

Sometimes students think the writing center is only for those with serious writing problems, but that is not the case. Students of all abilities can benefit from talking to writing tutors. Whether the people who staff the writing center at your college are undergraduates, graduate students, or professional tutors, they are experienced writers who like to talk about writing.

If your campus has a writing center, make an appointment to interview one of the tutors. Ask what kinds of services the center provides and what insights into college writing the tutor can offer. Even better, take a writing assignment you're working on or a paper that's already been graded to serve as the basis for a conversation with the tutor.

chapter 17

the shape of the essay
how form embodies
purpose

The word *essay* is derived from the French word *essai*, which means to try or test out. This derivation captures the spirit of the essay as a genre of writing in which writers invent forms to embody their purposes. Many examples of writing in this book might be described as an essay as well as, say, a memoir, a commentary, or a proposal. The exact meaning of the term *essay* has been debated by scholars in literary studies, rhetoric, and composition. Some want to restrict it to a particular type of literary or journalistic essay that uses a personal voice and other self-revelatory features to fashion experience and observation into writing. Others use it more broadly to refer to writing tasks where the form is open and flexible. In this chapter, we'll use the term *essay* in its broader sense, as a catch-all category that includes a range of other genres. For our purposes, the defining feature of the essay will be the openness and the flexibility it gives writers to shape their thoughts, feelings, and experiences into written forms.

The role of this chapter is to help you understand how this happens—how the essay embodies a writer's purposes and provides the groundwork for readers to engage a writer's ideas. Such an understanding of the formal aspects of writing can help you gain greater control over your own writing projects. We will look in particular at how writers organize their work, write introductions and endings, connect the parts, and design paragraphs.

THINKING ABOUT FORM

Understanding how form works in essays, as well as in other genres of writing, is a matter of understanding how the parts of a piece of writing are related to one another and how that arrangement guides and enables readers to follow the writer's thoughts and purposes.

In some genres of writing, writers and readers alike rely heavily on formal conventions. You can tell, for example, that a piece of writing is a letter simply by looking at it. The same is true for certain kinds of academic writing, such as lab reports and scientific articles, with their fixed sections—introduction, materials and methods, results, discussion. Public documents such as wills, contracts, laws, and resolutions also have highly predictable features that make them immediately recognizable.

However, with the essay, writers cannot turn to a standardized form to shape their material. Instead they often need to devise a form from a repertoire of possibilites that is adequate for their purposes and appropriate to the materials at hand.

In any case, though, whether the form of a piece of writing is standardized or improvised for the occasion, form has two key dimensions—the visual and the psychological.

- **The visual dimension** of form refers to the way written texts are laid out on a page. Writing materializes people's thoughts and purposes in visible form, and written texts take on a particular "look" as they occupy the space of a page. Paragraph breaks, headings and subheadings, the use of bullets and illustrations, the size and style of fonts, the layout of the page—these aspects of writing provide readers with visual cues to follow a piece of writing.

- **The psychological dimension** of form places readers in a particular frame of mind by creating a set of expectations about the writer's purposes and where a piece of writing is going. The form of written texts arouses the reader's anticipation and then goes on to fulfill it in one way or another, whether the resolution is temporary or permanent, expected or surprising.

Looking at how the visual and psychological dimensions of form work together can help you see that organizing a piece of writing is not simply providing a series of containers to pour your thoughts into—at the rate, say, of one main point per essay and one idea per paragraph. This rather mechanical view of form is often the result of learning the five-paragraph theme (thesis, three paragraphs of support, and conclusion) without taking into account how the form of writing serves, both visually and psychologically, to manage the interaction between the writer and readers. Whether the form of writing is fixed in advance or needs to be invented for the occasion, its key function, as you will see, is to produce common expectations and shared understanding between writers and readers.

THREE PATTERNS OF ORGANIZATION

Let's look first at the overall organization of the essay. To see how form works to bring writers and readers together, we will look at three common patterns that writers draw on, depending on their purposes: (1) top-down order; (2) culminating order; and (3) open form.

TOP-DOWN ORDER

This pattern of organization is perhaps the most familiar. Writers tell readers at the outset what their main point is and then go on to develop and support it. This pattern of organization enables readers to hold in mind the writer's central idea and to evaluate its merits based on the evidence that follows. The success of top-down order depends in large part on how well writers deliver on what they have led their readers to anticipate.

I Shop, Ergo I Am: The Mall as Society's Mirror

Sara Boxer

In certain academic circles, "shop till you drop" is considered a civic act. If you follow cultural studies—the academic scrutiny of ordinary activities like eating fast food, buying a house in the suburbs, watching television and taking vacations at Disneyland—you will know that shopping is not just a matter of going to a store and paying for your purchase.

How you shop is who you are. Shopping is a statement about your place in society and your part in world cultural history. There is a close relationship, even an equation, between citizenship and consumption. The store is the modern city-state, the place where people act as free citizens, making choices, rendering opinions and socializing with others.

If this sounds like a stretch, you're way behind the times. The field of cultural studies, which took off in England in the 1970's, has been popular in this country for more than a decade.

The intellectual fascination with stores goes back even further. When the philosopher Walter Benjamin died in 1940, he was working on a long study of the Paris arcades, the covered retail passageways, then almost extinct, which he called the "original temples of commodity capitalism." Six decades later, the study of shopping is well

trampled. Some academics have moved on from early classical work on the birth of the department store and the shopping arcade to the shopping malls of the 1950's and even the new wide aisles of today's factory outlets and superstores—places like Best Buy, Toys "R" Us and Ikea.

Historically, the age of shopping and browsing begins at the very end of the 18th century. In a paper titled "Counter Publics: Shopping and Women's Sociability," delivered at the Modern Language Association's annual meeting, Deidre Lynch, an associate professor of English at the State University of New York in Buffalo, said the word "shopping" started to appear frequently in print around 1780. That was when stores in London started turning into public attractions.

By 1800, Ms. Lynch said, "a policy of obligation-free browsing seems to have been introduced into London emporia." At that point, "the usual morning employment of English ladies," the 18th-century writer Robert Southey said, was to "go-a-shopping." Stores became places to socialize, to see and be seen. Browsing was born.

The pastime of browsing has been fully documented. Benjamin wrote that the Paris arcades, which went up in the early 1800's, created a new kind of person, a professional loiterer, or *flâneur,* who could easily turn into a dangerous political gadfly. The philosopher Jürgen Habermas, some of his interpreters say, has equated consumer capitalism with the feminization of culture. And now some feminists, putting a new spin on this idea, are claiming the store as the place where women first became "public women."

By imagining that they owned the wares, women were "transported into new identities," Ms. Lynch said. By meeting with their friends, they created what feminist critics like Nancy Fraser and Miriam Hansen called "counter publics," groups of disenfranchised people.

Putting Merchants in Their Place

Some feminists point out that as shoppers, women had the power to alter other people's lives. Women who spent "a summer's day cheapening a pair of gloves" without buying anything, as Southey put it, were "fortifying the boundaries of social class," Ms. Lynch said. They were "teaching haberdashers and milliners their place," taunting them with the prospect of a purchase and never delivering. It may not have been nice, but it was a sort of political power.

Women could also use their power for good. In 1815, Ms. Lynch points out, Mary Lamb wrote an essay called "On Needle-work," urging upper-class ladies who liked to do needlework as a hobby to give compensatory pay to women who did it to make a living. Lamb's biographer recently noted that this was how "bourgeois women busily distributed the fruits of their husbands' capitalist gains in the name of female solidarity."

The idea that shopping is a form of civil action naturally has its critics. In one of the essays in a book titled *Buy This Book,* Don Slater, a sociologist at the University of London, criticized the tendency of many academics to celebrate "the productivity, creativity, autonomy, rebelliousness and even . . . the 'authority' of the consumer." The trouble with this kind of post-modern populism is that it mirrors "the logic of the consumer society it seeks to analyze," he said. Such theories, without distinguishing between real needs and false ones, he suggested, assume that shoppers are rational and autonomous creatures who acquire what they want and want what they acquire.

Another critic, Meaghan Morris, author of an essay called "Banality in Cultural Studies," has faulted academics for idealizing the pleasure and power of shopping and underestimating the "anger, frustration, sorrow, irritation, hatred, boredom and fatigue" that go with it.

The field of shopping studies, whatever you think of it, is now at a pivotal point. In the 19th century, emporiums in London and arcades in Paris turned shopping into social occasions; in the 20th century, academics turned shopping into civic action; and in the 21st century, it seems that megastores will bring us into a new, darker era.

Shoppers' freedoms are changing. According to Robert Bocock, writing in *Consumption,* the mall walkers of today do not have the rights that the *flâneurs* of the 19th century had. "In the United States, 'policing' of who is allowed entry to the malls has become stricter in the last two or three decades of the 20th century."

In superstores, the role of shoppers has changed even more radically. Superstores are warehouses that stock an astounding number of goods picked out at a national corporate level, said Marianne Conroy, a scholar of comparative literature at the University of Maryland. Shoppers educate themselves about the goods and serve themselves. Thus, the superstore effectively "strips shopping of its aura of sociality," Ms. Conroy said. There is no meaningful interaction between the salespeople and the shoppers or among the shoppers. The shoppers' relationship is not with other people but with boxes and shelves.

Does the concept of the shopper as citizen still hold? The real test is to see how the citizen-shopper fares at the superstore. In a paper she delivered to the Modern Language Association, titled "You've Gotta Fight for Your Right to Shop: Superstores, Citizenship and the Restructuring of Consumption," Ms. Conroy analyzed one event in the history of a superstore that tested the equation between shopping and citizenship.

In 1996 Ronald Kahlow, a software engineer, decided to do some comparison shopping at a Best Buy outlet store in Reston, Va., by punching the prices and model numbers of some televisions into his laptop computer. When store employees asked him to stop, he refused and was arrested for trespassing. The next day, Mr. Kahlow returned with a pen and paper. Again, he was charged with trespassing and handcuffed.

When he stood trial in Fairfax County Court, he was found not guilty. And, as Ms. Conroy observed, the presiding judge in the case, Donald McDonough, grandly equated Mr. Kahlow's comparison shopping to civil disobedience in the 1960's. Mr. Kahlow then recited Robert F. Kennedy's poem "A Ripple of Hope," and the judge said, "Never has the cause of comparison shopping been so eloquently advanced."

Like Canaries in the Mines

At first, Ms. Conroy suggested they both might have gone overboard in reading "public meaning into private acts," but then she reconsidered. Maybe, she said, it's just time to refine the model.

Ms. Conroy suggested that consumerism should be seen no longer as the way citizens exercise their rights and freedoms but rather as "an activity that makes the impact of economic institutions on everyday life critically intelligible." In other words, shoppers in superstores are like canaries in the mines. Their experience inside tells us something about the dangers lurking in society at large.

What does one man's shopping experience at Best Buy tell us about the dangers of modern life in America? The fact that Mr. Kahlow was arrested when he tried to comparison shop shows that even the minimal rights of citizen-shoppers are endangered, said Ms. Conroy. Not only have they lost a venue for socializing, but they are also beginning to lose their right to move about freely and make reasoned choices.

Without the trappings of sociability, it's easier to see what's what. Stores used to be places that made people want to come out and buy things they didn't know they wanted. And they were so seductive that by the end of the 20th century they became one of the few sites left for public life. But in the superstores, the *flâneurs* and the consumer-citizens are fish out of water. They have nowhere pleasant to wander, no glittering distractions, no socializing to look forward to and no escape from the watchful eyes of the security guards. If this is citizenship, maybe it's time to move to another country.

CULMINATING ORDER

This form reserves or delays the presentation of the writer's central idea until late in the piece of writing. Instead of announcing a claim early on and then using the rest of the writing to support it, here the writing is organized so that it culminates with the payoff for readers. With this pattern of organization, the success of a piece of writing will often depend on how effectively the writer establishes a central issue or set of issues and then organizes the rest of the essay so that when the culminating point arrives it seems inevitable and logical.

Minneapolis Pornography Ordinance

Ellen Goodman

Just a couple of months before the pool-table gang rape in New Bedford, Mass., *Hustler* magazine printed a photo feature that reads like a blueprint for the actual crime. There were just two differences between *Hustler* and real life. In *Hustler,* the woman enjoyed it. In real life, the woman charged rape.

There is no evidence that the four men charged with this crime had actually read the magazine. Nor is there evidence that the spectators who yelled encouragement for two hours had held previous ringside seats at pornographic events. But there is a growing sense that the violent pornography being peddled in this country helps to create an atmosphere in which such events occur.

As recently as last month, a study done by two University of Wisconsin researchers suggested that even "normal" men, pre-screened college students, were changed by their exposure to violent pornography. After just ten hours of viewing, reported researcher Edward Donnerstein, "the men were less likely to convict in a rape trial, less likely to see injury to a victim, more likely to see the victim as responsible." Pornography may not cause rape directly, he said, "but it maintains a lot of very callous attitudes. It justifies aggression. It even says you are doing a favor to the victim."

If we can prove that pornography is harmful, then shouldn't the victims have legal rights? This, in any case, is the theory behind a city ordinance that recently passed the Minneapolis City Council. Vetoed by the mayor last week, it is likely to be back before the Council for an overriding vote, likely to appear in other cities, other towns. What is unique about the Minneapolis approach is that for the first time it attacks pornography, not because of nudity or sexual explicitness, but because it degrades and harms women. It opposes pornography on the basis of sex discrimination.

University of Minnesota Law Professor Catherine MacKinnon, who co-authored the ordinance with feminist writer Andrea Dworkin, says that they chose this tactic because they believe that pornography is central to "creating and maintaining the inequality of the sexes. . . . Just being a woman means you are injured by pornography."

They defined pornography carefully as, "the sexually explicit subordination of women, graphically depicted, whether in pictures or in words." To fit their legal definition it must also include one of nine conditions that show this subordination, like presenting women who "experience sexual pleasure in being raped or . . . mutilated." Under this law, it would be possible for a pool-table rape victim to sue *Hustler*. It would be possible for a woman to sue if she were forced to act in a pornographic movie. Indeed, since the law describes pornography as oppressive to all women, it would be possible for any woman to sue those who traffic in the stuff for violating her civil rights.

In many ways, the Minneapolis ordinance is an appealing attack on an appalling problem. The authors have tried to resolve a long and bubbling conflict among those who have both a deep aversion to pornography and a deep loyalty to the value of free speech. "To date," says Professor MacKinnon, "people have identified the pornographer's freedom with everybody's freedom. But we're saying that the freedom of the pornographer is the subordination of women. It means one has to take a side."

But the sides are not quite as clear as Professor MacKinnon describes them. Nor is the ordinance. Even if we accept the argument that pornography is harmful to women—and I do—then we must also recognize that anti-Semitic literature is harmful to Jews and racist literature is harmful to blacks. For that matter, Marxist literature may be harmful to government policy. It isn't just women versus pornographers. If women win the right to sue publishers and producers, then so could Jews, blacks, and a long list of people who may be able to prove they have been harmed by books, movies, speeches or even records. The Manson murders, you may recall, were reportedly inspired by the Beatles.

We might prefer a library or book store or lecture hall without *Mein Kampf* or the Grand Whoever of the Ku Klux Klan. But a growing list of harmful expressions would inevitably strangle freedom of speech.

This ordinance was carefully written to avoid problems of banning and prior restraint, but the right of any woman to claim damages from pornography is just too broad. It seems destined to lead to censorship.

What the Minneapolis City Council has before it is a very attractive theory. What MacKinnon and Dworkin have written is a very persuasive and useful definition of pornography. But they haven't yet resolved the conflict between the harm of pornography and the value of free speech. In its present form, this is still a shaky piece of law.

OPEN FORM

An open-form pattern of organization gives readers much less guidance than either top-down or culminating order. Instead of explicitly pointing out the connections among the parts, open form often leaves it to the readers to provide these links. If top-down and culminating order operate logically, open form operates associatively, and the parts of the writing take on meaning implicitly by how they are juxtaposed to each other. In this case, the success of a piece of writing largely depends on how skillfully the writer combines apparently disparate materials to create a dominant impression that may never be named outright but that is available to the reader nonetheless.

LOS ANGELES NOTEBOOK

JOAN DIDION

1   There is something uneasy in the Los Angeles air this afternoon, some unnatural stillness, some tension. What it means is that tonight a Santa Ana will begin to blow, a hot wind from the northeast whining down through the Cajon and San Gorgonio Passes, blowing up sandstorms out along Route 66, drying the hills and the nerves to the flash point. For a few days now we will see smoke back in the canyons, and hear sirens in the night. I have neither heard nor read that a Santa Ana is due, but I know it, and almost everyone I have seen today knows it too. We know it because we feel it. The baby frets. The maid sulks. I rekindle a waning argument with the telephone company, then cut my losses and lie down, given over to whatever it is in the air. To live with the Santa Ana is to accept, consciously or unconsciously, a deeply mechanistic view of human behavior.

2   I recall being told, when I first moved to Los Angeles and was living on an isolated beach, that the Indians would throw themselves into the sea when the bad wind blew. I could see why. The Pacific turned ominously glossy during a Santa Ana period, and one woke in the night troubled not only by the peacocks screaming in the olive trees but by the eerie absence of surf. The heat was surreal. The sky had a yellow cast, the kind of light sometimes called "earthquake weather." My only neighbor would not come out of her house for days, and there were no lights at night, and her husband roamed the place with a machete. One day he would tell me that he had heard a trespasser, the next a rattlesnake.

3   "On nights like that," Raymond Chandler once wrote about the Santa Ana, "every booze party ends in a fight. Meek little wives feel the edge of the carving knife and study their husbands' necks. Anything can happen." That was the kind of wind it was. I did not know then that there was any basis for the effect it had on all of us, but it turns out to be another of those cases in which science bears out folk wisdom. The Santa Ana, which is named for one of the canyons it rushes through, is a *foehn* wind, like the *foehn* of Austria and Switzerland and the *hamsin* of Israel. There are a number of persistent malevolent winds, perhaps the best known of which are the mistral of France and the Mediterranean sirocco, but a *foehn* wind has distinct characteristics: it occurs on the leeward slope of a mountain range and, although the air begins as a cold mass, it is warmed as it comes down the

mountain and appears finally as a hot dry wind. Whenever and wherever a *foehn* blows, doctors hear about headaches and nausea and allergies, about "nervousness," about "depression." In Los Angeles some teachers do not attempt to conduct formal classes during a Santa Ana, because the children become unmanageable. In Switzerland the suicide rate goes up during the *foehn*, and in the courts of some Swiss cantons the wind is considered a mitigating circumstance for crime. Surgeons are said to watch the wind, because blood does not clot normally during a *foehn*. A few years ago an Israeli physicist discovered that not only during such winds, but for the ten or twelve hours which precede them, the air carries an unusually high ratio of positive to negative ions. No one seems to know exactly why that should be; some talk about friction and others suggest solar disturbances. In any case the positive ions are there, and what an excess of positive ions does, in the simplest terms, is make people unhappy. One cannot get much more mechanistic than that.

4   Easterners commonly complain that there is no "weather" at all in Southern California, that the days and the seasons slip by relentlessly, numbingly bland. That is quite misleading. In fact the climate is characterized by infrequent but violent extremes: two periods of torrential subtropical rains which continue for weeks and wash out the hills and send subdivisions sliding toward the sea; about twenty scattered days a year of the Santa Ana, which, with its incendiary dryness, invariably means fire. At the first prediction of a Santa Ana, the Forest Service flies men and equipment from northern California into the southern forests, and the Los Angeles Fire Department cancels its ordinary non-firefighting routines. The Santa Ana caused Malibu to burn the way it did in 1956, and Bel Air in 1961, and Santa Barbara in 1964. In the winter of 1966–67 eleven men were killed fighting a Santa Ana fire that spread through the San Gabriel Mountains.

5   Just to watch the front-page news out of Los Angeles during a Santa Ana is to get very close to what it is about the place. The longest single Santa Ana period in recent years was in 1957, and it lasted not the usual three or four days but fourteen days, from November 21 until December 4. On the first day 25,000 acres of the San Gabriel Mountains were burning, with gusts reaching 100 miles an hour. In town, the wind reached Force 12, or hurricane force, on the Beaufort Scale; oil derricks were toppled and people ordered off the downtown streets to avoid injury from flying objects. On November 22 the fire in the San Gabriels was out of control. On November 24 six people were killed in automobile accidents, and by the end of the week the *Los Angeles Times* was keeping a box score of traffic deaths. On November 26 a prominent Pasadena attorney, depressed about money, shot and killed his wife, their two sons, and himself. On November 27 a South Gate divorcee, twenty-two, was

murdered and thrown from a moving car. On November 30 the San Gabriel fire was still out of control, and the wind in town was blowing eighty miles an hour. On the first day of December four people died violently, and on the third the wind began to break.

6   It is hard for people who have not lived in Los Angeles to realize how radically the Santa Ana figures in the local imagination. The city burning is Los Angeles's deepest image of itself: Nathanael West perceived that, in *The Day of the Locust;* and at the time of the 1965 Watts riots what struck the imagination most indelibly were the fires. For days one could drive the Harbor Freeway and see the city on fire, just as we had always known it would be in the end. Los Angeles weather is the weather of catastrophe, of apocalypse, and, just as the reliably long and bitter winters of New England determine the way life is lived there, so the violence and the unpredictability of the Santa Ana affect the entire quality of life in Los Angeles, accentuate its impermanence, its unreliability. The wind shows us how close to the edge we are.

2

7   "Here's why I'm on the beeper, Ron," said the telephone voice on the all-night radio show. "I just want to say that this *Sex for the Secretary* creature—whatever her name is—certainly isn't contributing anything to the morals in this country. It's pathetic. Statistics show."

8   "It's *Sex and the Office,* honey," the disc jockey said. "That's the title. By Helen Gurley Brown. Statistics show what?"

9   "I haven't got them right here at my fingertips, naturally. But they show."

10   "I'd be interested in hearing them. Be constructive, you Night Owls."

11   "All right, let's take one statistic," the voice said, truculent now. "Maybe I haven't read the book, but what's this business she recommends about going out with married men for lunch?"

12   So it went, from midnight until 5 a.m., interrupted by records and by occasional calls debating whether or not a rattlesnake can swim. Misinformation about rattlesnakes is a leitmotiv of the insomniac imagination in Los Angeles. Toward 2 a.m. a man from "out Tarzana way" called to protest. "The Night Owls who called earlier must have been thinking about, uh, *The Man in the Gray Flannel Suit* or some other book," he said, "because Helen's one of the few authors trying to tell us what's really going on. Hefner's another, and he's also controversial, working in, uh, another area."

13   An old man, after testifying that he "personally" had seen a swimming rattlesnake, in the Delta-Mendota Canal, urged "moderation" on the Helen Gurley Brown question. "We shouldn't get on the beeper to call things pornographic before we've read them," he

complained, pronouncing it porn-ee-oh-graphic. "I say, get the book. Give it a chance." The original provocateur called back to agree that she would get the book. "And then I'll burn it," she added.

14   "Book burner, eh?" laughed the disc jockey good-naturedly.

15   "I wish they still burned witches," she hissed.

3

16   It is three o'clock on a Sunday afternoon and 105° and the air so thick with smog that the dusty palm trees loom up with a sudden and rather attractive mystery. I have been playing in the sprinklers with the baby and I get in the car and go to Ralph's Market on the corner of Sunset and Fuller wearing an old bikini bathing suit. That is not a very good thing to wear to the market but neither is it, at Ralph's on the corner of Sunset and Fuller, an unusual costume. Nonetheless a large woman in a cotton muumuu jams her cart into mine at the butcher counter. "What a thing to wear to the market," she says in a loud but strangled voice. Everyone looks the other way and I study a plastic package of rib lamb chops and she repeats it. She follows me all over the store, to the Junior Foods, to the Dairy Products, to the Mexican Delicacies, jamming my cart whenever she can. Her husband plucks at her sleeve. As I leave the check-out counter she raises her voice one last time: "What a thing to wear to the Ralph's," she says.

4

17   A party at someone's house in Beverly Hills: a pink tent, two orchestras, a couple of French Communist directors in Cardin evening jackets, chili and hamburgers from Chasen's. The wife of an English actor sits at a table alone; she visits California rarely although her husband works here a good deal. An American who knows her slightly comes over to the table.

18   "Marvelous to see you here," he says.

19   "Is it," she says.

20   "How long have you been here?"

21   "Too long."

22   She takes a fresh drink from a passing waiter and smiles at her husband, who is dancing.

23   The American tries again. He mentions her husband.

24   "I hear he's marvelous in this picture."

25   She looks at the American for the first time. When she finally speaks she enunciates every word very clearly. "He . . . is . . . also . . . a . . . fag," she says pleasantly.

5

26   The oral history of Los Angeles is written in piano bars. "Moon River," the piano player always plays, and "Mountain Greenery." "There's a Small Hotel" and "This Is Not the First Time." People talk to each other, tell each other about their first wives and last husbands. "Stay funny," they tell each other, and "This is to die over." A construction man talks to an unemployed screenwriter who is celebrating, alone, his tenth wedding anniversary. The construction man is on a job in Montecito: "Up in Montecito," he says, "they got one square mile with 135 millionaires."

27   "Putrescence," the writer says.

28   "That's all you got to say about it?"

29   "Don't read me wrong, I think Santa Barbara's one of the most—Christ, the most— beautiful places in the world, but it's a beautiful place that contains a . . . putrescence. They just live on their putrescent millions."

30   "So give me putrescent."

31   "No, no," the writer says. "I just happen to think millionaires have some sort of lacking in their. . . in their elasticity."

32   A drunk requests "The Sweetheart of Sigma Chi." The piano player says he doesn't know it. "Where'd you learn to play the piano?" the drunk asks. "I got two degrees," the piano player says. "One in musical education." I go to a coin telephone and call a friend in New York. "Where are you?" he says. "In a piano bar in Encino," I say. "Why?" he says. "Why not," I say.

1965–67

■ **FOR CRITICAL INQUIRY**

1. As you read the opening sections of each essay, what did they lead you to anticipate would follow? Were your predictions realized?

2. Explain when you became aware of the writer's main point in each selection. Is it stated explicitly? If so, how did that statement guide your reading? If it was not stated explicitly, how did you identify the writer's purposes?

3. Compare your reading experience in each selection. How did you organize mentally the presentation of material? What patterns of organization in the written text did you rely on? Were there other cues for readers in the text that you used? What do you see as the main differences and similarities in how you read each selection?

SEEING PATTERNS OF ORGANIZATION: HOW FORM EMBODIES PURPOSE

As you can see, the pattern of organization each writer chose embodies a particular purpose and establishes a different relationship with readers.

TOP-DOWN ORDER

In the first selection, "I Shop, Ergo I Am," Sarah Boxer wants to inform *New York Times* readers about a new development in the academic world. For this reason, she makes clear early on how the idea that shopping "is a statement about your place in society" has been taken up by cultural studies scholars.

¶1–3: **Introduction:** presents main idea—"In certain academic circles, 'shop till you drop' is considered a civic act."

> ¶4–8: Background on history of shopping and browsing.

> ¶9–12: Academic debates about consumer power.

> ¶13–18: The role of shoppers and megastores.

¶19–22: **Ending:** Refines the model of shopping as civic action.

Boxer moves from a general statement about shopping and citizenship in the introduction, to particular evidence in the middle section, back to a general level in the ending.

CULMINATING ORDER

In contrast, Ellen Goodman's "Minneapolis Pornography Ordinance" more nearly resembles the rising action of a short story, with an opening exposition of the issues, a mounting conflict, a crisis where two principles seem irreconcilable, and a resolution in the form of Goodman's main claim. By delaying the presentation of her own position, Goodman leads her readers through an explanation of what the Minneapolis ordinance is trying to accomplish and the logic it is based on. A good half of her writing, the first six paragraphs, gives a generous and informative description of the ordinance before Goodman starts to raise questions about its relationship to the values of free speech.

Notice how she slowly raises doubts about the merits of the ordinance, gradually building a case about how it clashes with the values of free speech, up to the final paragraph when she culminates the column by unequivocally stating her position.

> ¶12: Resolves with main claim opposing ordinance.

> ¶8–11: Raises doubts about ordinance.

> ¶4–7: Explains how the ordinance treats the connection.

¶1–3: Raises connection between pornography and rape.

OPEN FORM

In turn, Joan Didion's "Los Angeles Notebook" consists of five sections that at first glance have a kind of freestanding character, as if each were meant to be read by itself. Didion is audacious here in using an open form that operates as a mosaic or collage does by juxtaposing disparate parts to form a whole. The five sections are separate units of attention; yet the fact that they appear under one title sets us to work as readers to see how they resonate with each other and what the unstated connections might be between and among them.

Los Angeles
(implied focus of essay)

| Section 1 | Section 2 | Section 3 | Section 4 | Section 5 |
| Santa Ana wind | Late-night talk show | Wearing bikini to supermarket | Beverly Hills party | Piano bars |

■ EXERCISE

Working with Patterns of Organization

1. Locate a piece of writing that uses a top-down pattern of organization. This could be your own writing or one of the reading selections. Now diagram the pattern of organization in the writing you have chosen by following these steps:
   a. Divide the writing into sections by grouping paragraphs together.
   b. Lay out the sections so that supporting sections are indented in relation to the main point.
   c. Draw arrows to show how the sections are connected.
   d. Write a commentary on your diagram that explains how the sections elicit readers' expectations and then goes on to resolve or fulfill these expectations.

2. Rewrite the opening of Ellen Goodman's "Minneapolis Pornography Ordinance" so that it follows a top-down pattern of organization. What, if anything, do you gain by doing so? What do you lose?

3. Use Joan Didion's "Los Angeles Notebook" as a model to experiment with open form. Write a sequence of sketches that are somehow thematically or attitudinally related. Exchange your writing with a partner in class. Write an analysis of your partner's essay, explaining what you see as the implied focus and what seems to pull the parts together.

A NOTE ON MIXED FORM

The three examples presented here—top-down order, culminating order, and open form—offer relatively pure cases of each pattern of organization. That does not mean, however, that all writing will necessarily fall strictly into one of the patterns. In fact, a good deal of writing combines aspects of the three patterns and therefore might best be described as examples of *mixed form.*

PUTTING THE PARTS TOGETHER

We have looked at the overall form of some short essays. Now we need to look a little more closely at how writers combine the parts of an essay to form a whole. In the following sections, we look first at how writers organize introductions and endings and then at how they connect the parts.

INTRODUCTIONS

The purpose of an introduction is obvious. The opening section needs to let the reader know what the writing is about and how the writer is going to approach the topic.

Sometimes, depending on the situation and the genre, writers just outright tell readers: "This report summarizes the results of the pilot project and makes recommendations for the second stage of implementation" or "This proposal requests funding for a day-care center to serve students, faculty, and staff." In the case of essays, however, introductions need to do more work in establishing a central issue and explaining what is at stake.

Introductions work when they produce a certain meeting of the minds between the writer and reader. This is not to say that they necessarily agree about anything, only that they are mutually engaged in thinking about an issue, problem, or experience. Effective introductions are able to produce this kind of engagement because they identify something that the reader recognizes as interesting, important, controversial, amusing, urgent, whatever—a shareable concern whose relevance is evident.

In other words, writers need to frame their issues in a way that connects to what readers know and care about. Such a framework, then, can become the base from which the writer ventures his or her own views on the matter. The following are some common strategies writers use to establish a common framework and to explain how their own perspective connects to it.

- Describe an existing situation.

- Tell an anecdote.

- Raise a question to answer or problem to solve.

- Use a striking fact, statistic, or other background information.

- Define terms.

- Provide historical background.

- Describe a place, person, or object.

- State a common view and replace it with an alternative perspective.

- Forecast what your writing is designed to do.

■ **EXERCISE**

Analyzing Introductions

Bring to class three pieces of writing (or draw on readings in this book) that use different strategies in their introductions. Work in a group with three or four other students. Take turns explaining the strategies you have found. Consider the differences and similarities among the examples you have found. What generalizations can you draw about how introductions work?

ENDINGS

In terms of the psychological dimensions of form, endings are key moments in writing. Writers know that endings need to provide readers with a sense of closure by resolving their expectations. Without a satisfying sense of an ending, readers are likely to feel let down. Writing that ends abruptly or fails to deliver at the end is going to leave readers up in the air, frustrated, and perhaps annoyed at the writer. In this section, we look at some ways writers typically end short pieces of writing so that they offer readers a satisfying sense of resolution.

Perhaps the most important thing writers can learn about endings is that they perform a function no other part of an essay can perform: they address a question that it doesn't make sense to raise until the writer has developed his or her line of inquiry. This question can be phrased rather bluntly as "so what?"

So what if it is the case, as Sarah Boxer points out, that cultural studies scholars are looking at shopping as civic action? Readers may well have been interested in what Boxer reports about shopping studies. At the same time, it is quite likely that the question "so what?" is lingering at the back of their minds. What's the big picture here, readers will want to know, the consequences and wider implications?

The function of endings is precisely to answer the question "so what?"— to give readers a way to connect the information in Boxer's essay with broader issues. Notice how Boxer has effectively resolved in her ending section the expectations raised in readers' minds when she draws out the connection between shopping and the "dangers of modern life." What might have seemed an esoteric academic topic takes on a wider meaning as Boxer explains how the rise of megastores are changing the character of shopping—and the nature of socializing in contemporary America.

Notice, too, that Boxer is not trying to wrap up everything once and for all in a neat package. Closure doesn't necessarily mean having the final word. In fact, Boxer's ending gives readers something further to think about—to consider what is at stake for them in the whole matter of shopping.

Here are some techniques writers commonly use to write endings that provide a satisfying sense of resolution and closure.

- Point out consequences or the wider significance of the main point.

- Refine the main point in light of the material presented in the piece of writing.

- Offer a recommendation or a solution.
- Consider alternatives.
- Create an echo effect by looping back to something you presented in the introduction.
- Offer a final judgment.

■ EXERCISE

Analyzing Endings

Compare the endings in three pieces of writing in this book or that you have found elsewhere. First identify where the ending begins in each piece. What cues does the writer give? Next, explain the strategy it uses. How does this strategy embody the writer's purposes?

CONNECTING THE PARTS: KEEPING YOUR PURPOSES VISIBLE

If introductions help readers anticipate what is to come and endings explore the consequences or wider implications of the writer's ideas, the middle section (or main body) is where writers unfold their thinking and develop their ideas. The success of the middle section partly depends on readers being able to see how the reasons, evidence, and other supporting materials connect to the main idea presented in the introduction. Writing that is easy to follow, even if the ideas are complex, will use various devices to keep the writer's purposes visible so that readers can stay oriented, identify the relevance of the writer's discussion, and connect it to expectations set up in the introduction.

Here are three standard techniques for connecting the parts.

Use Reasons to Explain

A common way of connecting the parts is to use reasons to explain how the discussion in the middle section develops the main point. In the following sequence of paragraphs, notice how Laurie Ouellette uses reasons to explain why "young women have shunned feminism."

FROM "BUILDING THE THIRD WAVE"
LAURIE OUELLETTE

[W]hat can explain why so many young women have shunned feminism? In her survey of young women, *Feminist Fatale: Voices from the Twentysomething Generation Explore the Future of the Women's Movement*, Paula Kamen found that media-fueled stereotypes of feminists as "man-bashers" and "radical extremists" were behind the fact that many young women don't identify with the women's movement.

But these are not the only reasons. Kamen also points to the lack of young feminist role models as an important factor. The failure of a major feminist organization such as NOW to reach out to a wider spectrum of women, including young women, must be acknowledged as a part of this problem. While individual chapters do have young feminist committees and sometimes officers, they and the national office are led and staffed primarily by older women, and consequently often fail to reflect the interests and needs of a complex generation of young women.

Yet another reason young women have turned away from feminism may lie within its history. If the young women who have gained the most from feminism—that is, white, middle-class women who took advantage of increased accessibility to higher education and professional employment—have been reluctant to associate themselves with feminism, it is hardly surprising that most economically disadvantaged women and women of color, who have seen fewer of those gains, have not been eager to embrace feminism either. The women's movement of the seventies has been called an upper-middle-class white women's movement, and to a large degree I believe that is true. More than a few young feminists—many influenced by feminists of color such as Flo Kennedy, Audre Lorde, and bell hooks—have realized that feminism must also acknowledge issues of race and class to reach out to those women whose concerns have been overlooked by the women's movement of the past. Indeed, numerous statistics, including a poll by the *New York Times*, have noted that young African-American women are more likely than white women to acknowledge many of the concerns conducive to a feminist agenda, including a need for job training and equal earning power outside the professional sector. But for them, feminism has not provided the only answer. Only by making issues of class and race a priority can feminism hope to influence the lives of the millions of women for whom the daily struggle to survive, not feminist activism, is a priority. Will ours be the first generation of feminists to give priority to fighting cuts in Aid to Families with Dependent Children, establishing the right to national health care, day care, and parental leave, and bringing to the forefront other issues pertinent to the daily struggle of many women's lives? If there is to be a third wave of feminism, they must.

We can diagram the pattern of development in the three paragraphs to make visible how it embodies Ouellette's purposes. Notice how the form creates a hierarchy of levels—the main point, the reasons, and the supporting evidence.

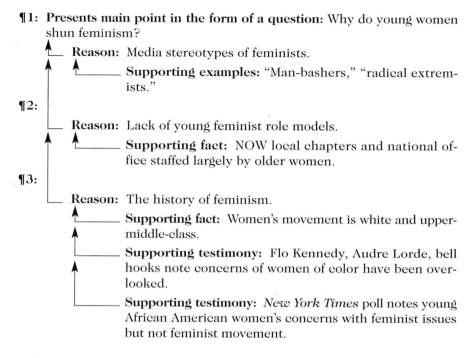

¶1: **Presents main point in the form of a question:** Why do young women shun feminism?

Reason: Media stereotypes of feminists.

Supporting examples: "Man-bashers," "radical extremists."

¶2:

Reason: Lack of young feminist role models.

Supporting fact: NOW local chapters and national office staffed largely by older women.

¶3:

Reason: The history of feminism.

Supporting fact: Women's movement is white and upper-middle-class.

Supporting testimony: Flo Kennedy, Audre Lorde, bell hooks note concerns of women of color have been overlooked.

Supporting testimony: *New York Times* poll notes young African American women's concerns with feminist issues but not feminist movement.

Create Topic Chains

Topic chains help readers establish links between the parts of a piece of writing and allow them to feel that they know where the writer is going. Writers create topic chains by repeating key words, using pronouns and synonyms, and restating main points. Notice the topic chain Sarah Boxer develops by regularly emphasizing the notion of shopping at the beginning of many paragraphs.

¶1–3: In certain academic circles, 'shop till you drop' is considered a civic act.

¶4: The intellectual fascination with stores . . .

¶5: Historically, the age of shopping and browsing begins . . .

¶7: The pastime of browsing . . .

¶9: Some feminists point out that as shoppers . . .

¶11: The idea that shopping is a form of civic action . . .

¶13: The field of shopping studies . . .

¶14: Shoppers' freedoms . . .

¶15: In superstores, the role of shoppers . . .

¶16: Does the concept of the shopper as citizen . . .

¶20: Ms. Conroy suggested that consumerism . . .

¶21: What does one man's shopping experience . . .

Use Transitions

Writers use transitional words, phrases, and sentences to show readers how one statement, paragraph, or section in a piece of writing relates to the next.

Temporal transitions indicate the sequence of events that takes place and the passage of time. In "Black Hair," Gary Soto begins a number of paragraphs with temporal transitions to help readers see the order in his narrative account of work:

¶5: *The next morning,* I arrived early at work.

¶7: I worked carefully *that day.* . . .

¶8: *At five,* the workers scattered. . . .

¶9: From the backyard I walked dully through a residential street, and *as evening came on.* . . .

¶11: When I got up from the lawn *it was late.*

¶13: At work I spent the *morning* at the buffer. . . .

¶15: Iggy worked only *until three in the afternoon.* . . .

Spatial transitions help locate the position of things, people, and events. In her profile of Dr. Susan Love, Molly O'Neill uses spatial transitions so that readers can visualize the scene she is describing.

A radiologist used a pointer to outline the tumor for a group of radiologists, pathologists, and surgeons. Dr. Love stood *in the back* of the conference room, rocking in her bone-colored pumps. Her brown eyes were narrowed *behind* red-frame glasses.

The lab coat she wore was a bulletin board of buttons. "Keep abreast," read one, "Get a second opinion." On another: "T.G.I.F. (Thank God I'm Female)." *Under* the string of fat white pearls *around* her neck was a gold chain with an ankh, an ancient symbol of life. *Above* one of the Chanel-style earrings was a tiny labyrs, the mythical double-bladed ax used by Amazons.

Logical transitions help readers understand how ideas are related to one another. Transitional words and phrases link ideas as the writers move from one paragraph to the next—building on what they have just said as the basis for the paragraph that follows.

Henry Jenkins, in "Lessons from Littleton," uses numbering of points and parallel phrases in the opening sentences of a sequence of paragraphs to help readers follow his explanation of the appeal of violent video games. Then he summarizes the consequences in a paragraph that begins with the phrase "In short":

First, violent entertainment offers teens a fantasy of empowerment. . . .

Second, violent entertainment offers teens a fantasy of transgression. . . .

Third, violent entertainment offers teens an acknowledgement that the world is not all sweetness and light. . . .

Fourth, violent entertainment offers teens an intensification of emotional experience. . . .

In short, teens aren't drawn to *Quake* or *Scream* because they are bloodthirsty. . . .

COMMON TYPES OF TRANSITIONS

To mark sequence and passage of time:	next, later, after, before, earlier, meanwhile, immediately, soon, shortly, often, frequently, again, during, finally, at last
To locate spatially:	near, next to, alongside, facing, adjacent, far beyond, away, off in the distance, between, through, up, down, across, above, below, inside, outside
To give examples:	for example, for instance, namely, specifically, that is
To add further points:	and, in addition, also, furthermore, moreover
To show consequences:	thus, therefore, so, consequently, hence, as a result, for this reason
To compare:	similarly, likewise, also
To contrast:	however, in contrast, but, yet, nevertheless, nonetheless
To compare and contrast:	not only/but also, on the one hand/on the other
To make a concession:	although, even though, granted that

DESIGNING PARAGRAPHS

Paragraphs are the building blocks writers use to assemble larger pieces of writing. That does not mean, of course, that paragraphs come ready-made in standard, prefabricated forms. They need to be designed to perform particular functions depending on the kind of writing and where the paragraph takes place in the larger piece of writing.

SEEING PARAGRAPHS: THE VISUAL DIMENSION

As mentioned earlier, the form of writing has both a visual and a psychological dimension, and this is true as well of paragraphs. Visually, paragraphs are graphic units that mark units of attention for readers by indenting. Paragraph breaks help readers see where a related sequence of ideas begins and ends. In turn, paragraphs provide writers with a means to establish the reader's focus of attention for a period of time.

Experienced writers have learned that the beginning and ending of paragraphs are the points at which readers are most attentive. When a paragraph begins, readers look for cues to tell them what the paragraph is going to be about so that they can concentrate on that particular point and how the writer develops it. When the paragraph ends, readers often pause briefly, to catch their breath and consolidate their sense of what they have just read, before going on to the next paragraph.

In newspaper writing, in part because of the narrow columns in the page layout, paragraphs tend to be short. One of their functions is to make the experience of reading as easy as possible so that readers can get the gist of an article by scanning it quickly. The same thing applies to many kinds of writing in the workplace and the public sphere, where writers and readers alike put a premium on making the information in memos, reports, proposals, news briefings, and brochures concise and easy to process.

In other genres of writing, however, paragraphs have a very different look on the page. Essays, academic writing, and magazine articles often use longer paragraphs, and readers expect that writers will develop their points in greater depth and detail.

The length of a paragraph, in other words, depends on the kind of writing in which it appears and the function it serves.

■ EXERCISE

Analyzing Paragraphs

Following is a passage from Susan Faludi's essay "Shannon Faulkner's Strength in Numbers" without paragraph indentation. You will probably notice right away how dense and forbidding the passage seems. It looks like a lot of extra work to get through it. Your task here is to provide paragraphing to make the passage easier for readers. Follow these steps:

1. On your own, read through the passage and insert paragraph breaks where you think they are most useful.

2. Now work with two or three classmates and compare how each of you has divided the passage into paragraphs. To what extent are the paragraphs alike? To what extent do they differ? In the case of differences, does the effect on readers differ? If so, how? Working together, see if you can come up with one version that everyone in the group can live with. If you can't agree, explain what your differences are and what seems to be at stake.

Out of all the nearly 2,000 cadets who enrolled in an all-male military academy called The Citadel this year [1995], the only one whose name we know was the one the school didn't want: Shannon Faulkner. This distinction seems, on its face, too obvious to mention. Of course she's famous—that she was admitted to the academy at all was a cause célèbre. But the distinction is important, because it goes to the heart of the issue. One reason the other Citadel cadets loathed Shannon Faulkner (aside from her sex) was her individuality, which affronted The Citadel's ethic. The academy purports to educate young men by making them conform. Conformity is enforced through anonymity. From the day the cadets arrive, when they are issued identical uniforms and haircuts, they become so homogeneous that, as an upperclassman explained to me, "mothers can't even tell their sons apart." Through communal living and endless drills and rigid codes of conduct, the cadet's individuality is subordinated to the identity of the group, his strength founded in numbers and teamwork, in esprit de corps and long tradition. Going it alone, as a maverick, isn't done. "Individuals do not make it here," the commandant of cadets warned this year's freshmen on their first day. "If you want to stay an individual, every day will be a tough day." This is what is called a military education, and it was exactly what Shannon Faulkner wanted and could not find elsewhere in her home state of South Carolina. From the start her quest seemed hopeless: by seeking military anonymity in an all-male corps, she had to stand out. But her downfall was hastened by forces beyond The Citadel. The largest obstacle she faced was the popular illusion that history is driven not by the actions and changing beliefs of large numbers of ordinary people, but by a few heroic giants who materialize out of nowhere to transform the landscape.

UNITY AND COHERENCE: THE PSYCHOLOGICAL DIMENSION

Unity and coherence are workshop terms referring to the psychological dimension of writing and to how writing arouses the reader's expectations and then goes on to fulfill them. *Unity* means that a piece of writing has some central point, focus, or center of gravity that readers can readily identify. They don't wonder what the writer is getting at or try to figure out the main point on their own. *Coherence* means that the ideas in the writing seem to come in the right order, leading logically from one point to the next. Readers don't feel that the writing rambles or jumps around from point to point but instead moves along purposefully.

Often, readers are not even aware that well-crafted writing is unified and coherent. They simply experience the writing as easy to read. The writer's ideas seem to be where they belong, and readers can easily follow the writer's thoughts from point to point. The writing just seems to flow, and readers don't feel confused about its direction. Moreover, when this happens, readers believe they are in good hands—and, as a result, are likely to invest a certain amount of confidence and credibility in what the writer is saying. Whether they agree with the ideas or not, they at least think that the writer knows what he or she is doing and is therefore worth considering. In short, unity and coherence are devices for making a meeting of minds possible.

You can see how unity and coherence work at the level of a whole piece of writing by looking back at the writing samples in this chapter. Take, for example, Sarah Boxer's "I Shop, Ergo I Am." Here the unity comes from the opening paragraphs, where Boxer explains how the connection between shopping and civic action has been taken up as a topic by cultural studies scholars. Readers at this point will justifiably expect the essay to tell them more about such shopping studies. And that is exactly what Boxer does. She develops the idea in a coherent order, starting with studies of eighteenth-century shopping and then moving to contemporary instances. In other words, she enables readers to see how the article's parts are relevant to the main idea.

To see how paragraphs use unity and coherence to enhance readability, look at the following paragraph:

Public toilets . . . have become the real frontline of the city's war on the homeless. Los Angeles, as a matter of deliberate policy, has fewer public toilets than any other major North American city. On the advice of the Los Angeles police, who now sit on the "design board of at least one major Downtown project, the redevelopment agency bulldozed the few remaining public toilets on Skid Row." Agency planners then considered whether to include a "free-standing public toilet" in their design for the upscale South Park residential development; agency chairman Jim Wood later admitted that the decision not to build the toilet was a "policy decision and not a design decision." The agency preferred the alternative of "quasi-public restrooms"—toilets in restaurants, art galleries, and office buildings—which can be made available selectively to tourists and white-collar workers while being denied to vagrants and other unsuitables. The same logic has inspired the city's transportation planners to exclude toilets from their designs for Los Angeles's new subway system.

Mike Davis, from City of Quartz

Topic Sentences and Unity

Notice how Davis begins with a topic sentence ("Public toilets . . . have become the real frontline on the city's war on the homeless"). Topic sentences typically focus on a single idea or on a sequence of related ideas that will be developed in the paragraph. At this point, readers can reasonably expect Davis to devote the rest of the paragraph to explaining how public toilets figure into Los Angeles's "war on the homeless."

Discussion and Unity and Coherence

As you can see, the rest of the paragraph, or the discussion, is indeed devoted to explaining how planners eliminated the availability of public toilets; it thereby contributes to the unity of the paragraph and to fulfilling readers' expectations. Notice, furthermore, how the order of sentences seems coherent. Each sentence not only follows from the topic sentence but also picks up on the sentence that precedes it. The way one sentence leads to the next can be analyzed by imagining that each sentence answers a question in the reader's mind raised by the preceding sentence or sentences:

Topic Sentence

Public toilets . . . have become the real frontline in the city's war on the homeless.
(Question: What is this "war"?)

Discussion

Los Angeles, as a matter of deliberate policy, has fewer public toilets than any other major North American city.
(Answers question and raises another about how "policy" was made)

On the advice of the Los Angeles police, who now sit on the design board of at least one major Downtown project, the redevelopment agency bulldozed the few remaining public toilets on Skid Row.
(Answers question about how "policy" was made)

Agency planners then considered whether to include a "free-standing public toilet" in their design for the upscale South Park residential development; agency chairman Jim Wood later admitted that the decision not to build the toilet was a "policy decision and not a design decision."
(Amplifies answer about how "policy" was made by giving another example)

The agency preferred the alternative of "quasi-public restrooms"—toilets in restaurants, art galleries, and office buildings—which can be made available selectively to tourists and white-collar workers while being denied to vagrants and other unsuitables.
(Answers question about how "policy" amounts to "war on the homeless")

The same logic has inspired the city's transportation planners to exclude toilets from their designs for Los Angeles's new subway system.
(Gives a final example of how "policy" makes "war on the homeless")

■ **EXERCISE**

Analyzing Paragraph Units and Coherence

Work together in a group of four or five. Read the following passage aloud. Then answer the questions.

> I have always wanted to be a high school American history teacher. Many teachers are now feeling the pressure to teach the test rather than educate their students in historical understanding. There are certainly skills and knowledge that high school students should acquire in their American history classes. Historical understanding gives students a way to see how the past shapes the present. In American history courses, students have too often memorized facts and dates rather than learning to understand why historical events took place and how they affect the present. I realize that many students are not interested in the past, but my desire is to help students think about American history and the unresolved questions it raises about the legacy of slavery, the American belief in individualism and free enterprise, and the Vietnam War. The current trend to make high schools more accountable emphasizes testing at the expense of genuine learning. Historical understanding is crucial if we want to have an informed citizenry who can make decisions about the complex issues that face us as a nation.

1. What question does the first sentence raise?
2. How is this question answered?
3. Are there other questions that the paragraph seems to raise?
4. How are these questions answered?
5. How would you revise this paragraph for unity and coherence?

working together
collaborative writing
projects

COLLABORATIVE WRITING

Working on collaborative writing projects differs in important respects from working with others on individual writing projects. In the case of individual writing projects, the final result belongs to you; you are accountable for it and you get the bulk of the credit, even though the writing reflects the input of others. Collaborative writing, on the other hand, aims for a collective outcome produced jointly by a team of people with shared responsibility for the results.

Consider, for example, how a group of three students worked together on a research project in an environmental studies course. Their task is to create a map of the sidewalk shade trees the city has planted and maintained in the downtown area over the years and to make recommendations about where new trees should be planted. After they have surveyed the downtown area, sketched a preliminary map, and made tentative decisions about where new trees should go, they give each member a section of the report to draft. One writes the background. One reports their findings. The third student writes the recommendation section. Once the drafts are finished, the group meets to consider what revisions are needed to produce a final report. One student makes these changes while the other two members create the maps.

When individuals work together on collaborative writing projects, they will manage the writing task in various ways, depending on the nature of the task and the decisions the group makes. Sometimes, as in the example above, individuals will each write separate sections, which are then compiled into a single document and edited for uniformity of style. Or, they may work together so closely in planning, drafting, and revising a document that it becomes impossible to distinguish one person's work from another's. In still other cases, the group will work together planning and doing research, one individual will do the drafting, and then the group will work together again to plan revisions.

There is no single best way to work on collaborative writing projects. Experienced writers learn when it makes sense to produce a collaboratively written document and which writing strategy the situation seems to call for.

While collaborative writing projects can differ, each of them reveals one of the most important benefits of working together—namely that the final written product is based on the collective judgment of a group of people. When a group works well together, the resulting energy and involvement can lead to writing that goes beyond what anyone in the group could have produced alone.

Successful collaborative writing depends on organization, meetings, and constant communication. This chapter looks at how groups can produce effective collaborative writing. The first section offers some general guidelines about working in groups. The second section considers how groups can manage a collaborative writing project from start to finish. The final section presents further writing suggestions for groups.

■ WORKING TOGETHER

Exploring Experience

Form a group with three or four other students. Have each student describe an experience in which he or she worked together with other people. The experience can be positive or negative, and it need not involve writing. After everyone has described an experience, try to reach a consensus, even if you agree to disagree, about what makes group work successful or unsuccessful.

GUIDELINES FOR COLLABORATING IN GROUPS

Any group of people working together on a project will face certain issues, and a group collaborating on a writing project is no exception. The following guidelines are meant to keep a group running smoothly and to forestall some common problems.

Recognize That Group Members Need to Get Acquainted and That Groups Take Time to Form

People entering new groups sometimes make snap judgments without getting to know the other people or giving the group time to form and develop. Initial impressions are rarely reliable indicators of how a group will be. Like individuals, groups have life histories, and one of the most awkward and difficult moments is getting started. Group members may be nervous, defensive, or overly assertive. It takes some time for people to get to know one another and to develop a sense of connectedness to the group.

Clarify Group Purposes and Individual Roles

Much of the initial discomfort and anxiety has to do with uncertainty about what the purpose of the group is and what people's roles in the group will be. Group members need to define their collective task and develop a plan to carry it out. That way, members will understand what to expect and how the group will operate.

Recognize That Members Bring Different Styles to the Group

As you have seen, individual styles of composing can vary considerably. The same is true of individuals' styles of working in groups. For example, individuals differ in the way they approach problems. Some like to spend a lot of time formulating problems, exploring the complexities, contradictions, and nuances of a situation. Others want to define problems quickly and then spend their time figuring out how to solve them. By the same token, people have different styles of interacting in groups. Some like to develop their ideas by talking, while others prefer to decide what they think before speaking. Successful groups learn to incorporate the strengths of all these styles, making sure that even the most reticent members participate.

Recognize That You May Not Play the Same Role in Every Group

In some instances you may be the group leader, but in other instances you'll need to play the role of mediator, helping members negotiate their differences; or critic, questioning the others' ideas; or timekeeper, prompting the group to stick to deadlines. You may play different roles in the same group from meeting to meeting or even within a meeting. For a group to be successful, members must be willing and able to respond flexibly to the work at hand.

Monitor Group Progress and Reassess Goals and Procedures

It's helpful to step back periodically to take stock of what has been accomplished and what remains to be done. Groups also need to look at their own internal workings to see if the procedures they have set up are effective and if everyone is participating.

Quickly Address Problems in Group Dynamics

Problems will arise in group work. Some members may dominate and talk too much. Others may withdraw and not contribute. Still others may fail to carry out assigned tasks. If a group avoids confronting these problems, the problems will only get worse. Remember, the point of raising a problem is not to blame individuals but to promote an understanding about what's expected of each person and what the group can do to encourage everyone's participation.

Encourage Differences of Opinion

One of the things that makes groups productive is the different perspectives individual members bring to group work. In fact, groups of like-minded people who share basic assumptions are often not as creative as groups where there are differences among members. At the same time, group members may think that they can't bring up ideas or feelings because to do so would threaten group harmony. Sometimes it's difficult to take a position that diverges from what other members of the group think and believe. But groups are not forms of social organization to enforce conformity; they are working bodies that need to consider all the available options and points of view. For this reason, groups need to encourage the discussion of differences and to look at conflicting viewpoints.

HOW TO WORK TOGETHER ON COLLABORATIVE WRITING PROJECTS

Because collaborative writing differs from individual writing, it is worth looking at each step involved in working on a joint project.

ORGANIZING THE GROUP

One of the keys to collaborative writing is to get off to a good start. You'll need to decide on the size of the group, its composition, what to do at your first meeting, and how to share the labor.

Group Size

For many collaborative writing projects in college classes, a group of three or four is often the best size. A smaller size—only two students—doesn't offer the group as many resources, and anything larger than four can create problems in managing the work with so many involved.

Of course, there can be exceptions. For example, your teacher may decide to do a collaborative project involving the entire class—developing a Web home page for the class or a Web site devoted to a particular topic with everyone's participation.

Group Composition

Some teachers like to put groups together themselves. Others like to give students input into the group they will be in. If the teacher puts the groups together, it's a good idea to ask each student if there is someone in class he or she particularly wants to work with or particularly wants to avoid working with. It can help, too, to take schedules into account and match students who have free time in common when they can meet.

The First Meeting

The first meeting should focus on the basics:

1. Exchange phone numbers, email addresses, campus box numbers, and the best times to reach group members.
2. If possible, establish a listserv of group members on the campus network.

3. Identify the best times for meetings.

4. Agree on some basic procedures for running meetings. For example, do you want a group coordinator to lead meetings? If so, will one person serve throughout the project, or will you rotate that position? How do you plan to keep records of meetings? Will you have a recorder for the project, or rotate? How long will each meeting last? Who is responsible for developing the agenda?

Division of Labor, or Integrated Team?

Some groups approach collaborative projects by developing a division of labor that assigns particular tasks to group members who complete them individually and then bring the results back to the group. This has been the traditional model for collaborative work in business, industry, and government. It is an efficient method of work, especially when groups are composed of highly skilled members. Its limitations are that weak group members can affect the quality of the overall work and that some group members may lose sight of the overall project because they are so caught up in their own specialized work.

More recently, groups have begun to explore an integrated approach in which the members all work together through each stage of the project. An integrated-team approach involves members more fully in the work and helps them maintain an overall view of the project's goals and progress. But it also takes more time—that must be devoted to meetings and, often, to developing good working relationships among members.

These two models of group work are not mutually exclusive. In fact many groups function along integrated-team lines when they are planning and reviewing work, but also farm out particular tasks to individuals or subgroups. So you need to discuss and develop some basic guidelines on group functioning.

ORGANIZING THE PROJECT

The Proposal

The first task is to decide what the project is and what its goals are. One of the best ways to do this is to write a proposal. Your teacher is the logical audience for your proposal. If you are doing a project with an on- or off-campus group, members of that group should also receive your proposal.

Proposals should include:

- **A statement of purpose:** Define the topic or issue you are working on. Explain why it is important or significant. What have others said about it? State what you plan to do and explain why.

- **A description of methods:** Explain how you plan to go about the project. What research will you need to do? How will you do it?

- **A plan for managing the work:** Explain what roles group members will play and what skills they will bring to the task.

- **A task breakdown chart:** A task breakdown (or Gantt) chart shows the tasks involved and their scheduling. Such a chart is especially useful for planning collaborative projects because it shows how tasks relate to each other.

Once the group is up and running, it will need to figure out how to stay on track—how to keep the work moving ahead and how to deal effectively with problems as they arise.

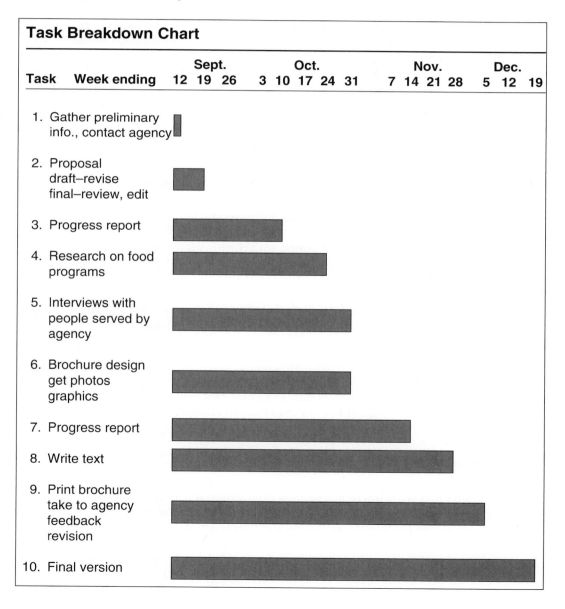

Task Breakdown Chart

Task	Week ending	Sept. 12 19 26	Oct. 3 10 17 24 31	Nov. 7 14 21 28	Dec. 5 12 19
1. Gather preliminary info., contact agency					
2. Proposal draft–revise final–review, edit					
3. Progress report					
4. Research on food programs					
5. Interviews with people served by agency					
6. Brochure design get photos graphics					
7. Progress report					
8. Write text					
9. Print brochure take to agency feedback revision					
10. Final version					

Incorporating a calendar into your task breakdown chart is one way to stay oriented. Two other ways are to run productive meetings and to write interim progress reports.

Productive Meetings

Group meetings are productive when they get work done, address issues and conflicts, and keep group members accountable. Although failing to meet can cause group members to feel disconnected, meeting for no reason can be just as demoralizing. For meetings to be productive, there must be a real agenda and work that needs to be done. One way to set an agenda is to agree at the end of each meeting what will be accomplished before the next meeting, and by whom. That way the agenda grows out of the progress of the project and group members are kept accountable. If problems in group functioning come up, they need to be addressed immediately at the next meeting.

Progress Reports

Progress reports are another way to enhance group members' accountability—both to one another and to their teacher. They serve to chart the development of a project at regular intervals. On your task breakdown chart you will want to include one or two progress reports that follow the completion of major parts of the project. Include in your reports the following:

- **Tasks completed:** Describe with details what you have done.

- **Tasks in progress:** Be specific about what you are doing and give completion dates.

- **Tasks scheduled:** Describe briefly tasks you haven't yet started, including any not originally entered on the task breakdown chart.

- **Issues, problems, obstacles:** Explain how these emerged and how your group is dealing with them.

In some cases, teachers may ask groups for oral as well as written progress reports. This is a good way for everyone in class to see what the other groups are doing.

Confidential Self-Evaluation

In addition to requiring group progress reports, some teachers also like to ask individual students to assess how their group has been functioning and what their role in it has been. These self-evaluations are confidential and directed only to the teacher. They can be useful in helping the teacher anticipate when groups are having difficulties or personality problems. They are also useful to individual students because they offer an occasion to reflect on the experience of group work and what it means to them as writers, learners, and persons.

Drafting, Revising, and Editing

One thing that often surprises students working in groups for the first time is finding out that they have already started to draft their document from the moment they began to put their proposal together.

For many writing tasks, the final document will draw and expand on what is in the proposal—explaining why the issue or problem is important, what others have said about it, what the group has learned about it, and what recommendations the group has to make.

But whatever the writing task happens to be, groups need to make decisions about how to handle drafting, revising, and editing collaboratively written documents. Here are some possible approaches. Your group will need to decide which one best suits your purposes.

- Members draft individual sections. The group compiles the sections and revises together.

- One person writes a draft. The group revises together.

- Members draft individual sections. One person compiles the sections and revises the document.

With any of these approaches, a final editing needs to be done by an individual or by the group.

However you decide to organize drafting, revising, and editing, make sure everyone contributes to the final document. The draft does not become final until everyone has signed off on it.

Collaborative drafting and revising can raise sensitive issues about individual writing styles and abilities. Some people can be protective of their writing and defensive when it is criticized or revised. Be aware of this. If you think other group members either are trying to impose their own style or are feeling discouraged, bring these matters to everyone's attention and try to sort them out before you continue on the writing task.

GIVING CREDIT

Some teachers ask collaborative writing groups to preface their final document with an acknowledgments page that explains who should get credit for what in the overall project. You should also acknowledge anyone outside your group who helped you on the project.

FINAL PRESENTATION

The final presentation of a collaborative project takes place when the document reaches its intended destination—whether it's the teacher, the Web, a politician or government official, or a community organization. You may want to schedule an oral presentation to go along with the delivery of the document.

ONLINE COLLABORATION

The new electronic communication technologies have created new ways for groups to work together, even when their members are far apart. It's no longer necessary to meet face-to-face to have the kind of exchange that gives a joint project energy and creativity. With the nearly instantaneous transmission of documents, commentary, and conversation, collaborators can now stay in touch, confer, argue, and refine their ideas with an immediacy that was unimaginable in the past.

Of course, group members don't need to be halfway around the world from each other to take advantage of the new technologies. Here are some good ways of how to use these technologies in collaborative writing projects:

- **Stay in touch with group members:** Ongoing communication among group members is one of the keys to successful group work. Setting up a listserv on email can help members to stay in touch in and out of class.

- **Consult with people everywhere:** Through email, newsgroups, and Web sites, your group can contact a wide range of people who are knowledgeable about your topic—to ask questions, get information, and try out ideas. Online communication can be much quicker and simpler than letters or phone calls.

- **Share working drafts:** To put together a successful collaboratively written document, coauthors need easy access to one another's working drafts. Drafts can be shared in ways that range from downloading files on email to state-of-the-art hypertext authoring systems.

- **Confer on drafts:** Online conferences make it easy for all group members to have input on drafts. New methods include "real-time" synchronous conferences facilitated by networking software.

REFLECTING ON YOUR WRITING

Consider a collaborative writing task you have completed. Explain why the particular situation seemed to call for a collaboratively written document instead of an individually written one. How did your group go about organizing and managing the writing task? What role or roles did you play in the group? What problems or issues did you confront and how did you handle them? What was the result of the group's work? From your own perspective, what do you see as the main differences between collaborative and individual writing? What do you see as the benefits and limits of each?

presenting

your work

© Dan Jaeger/stock.xchng. Image altered for design purposes.

5

INTRODUCTION: DELIVERING THE MESSAGE

Whether you are designing the manuscript of a critical essay or research paper, a fund-raising letter, a brochure, a Web site, or a PowerPoint presentation, the visual appearance of your work carries meanings and has its own rhetorical effects.

There are three main reasons to learn more about the visual design of page and screen and how the delivery of messages embodies writers' and designers' purposes:

- **To establish credibility with readers:** The reader's first impression of a print text or computer screen is likely to be influenced by its visual appearance. A sloppy manuscript or a Web site that's hard to navigate will raise doubts about the credibility of the person who prepared it. This in turn can undermine the rhetorical effectiveness of the message, no matter how interesting or insightful the content might be. Design is a means to establish the writer's ethos—by presenting the writer and the message as credible and authoritative.

- **To enhance readability:** One of the marks of effective page and screen design is that readers find the content easy to follow. Writers use visual cues such as paragraph breaks, white space, headings, and bulleted lists, while Web designers are concerned with the amount and size of text on a screen, the relationship between text and graphics, and the navigability of a Web site. In either case, the goal is to enable the reader to concentrate on the message by carefully designing its presentation.

- **To assist in planning:** As you have seen in earlier chapters, many genres of writing, such as letters, public documents, reports, and proposals, have a typical "look" that does more than make them immediately recognizable. The visual design of print and electronic documents also provides a scaffolding to help writers and designers organize and present their messages.

In the following chapters, you will find more information on how to design effective documents of various sorts. Chapter 19, "Visual Design," explores some of the purposes of visual communication and offers suggestions about designing such familiar documents as flyers, newsletters, and brochures. Chapter 20, "Web Design," offers a basic introduction to the rhetoric and design features of Web sites, while Chapter 21, "Oral Presentations," looks at how you can plan effective talks and use visuals such as PowerPoint. Chapter 22, "Essay Exams," offers suggestions about how to present your ideas when writing under pressure. Chapter 23, "Writing Portfolios," shows how you can design a portfolio of writing that presents and comments on the work you have done in your writing course.

chapter 19

visual design

There are two main reasons visual design belongs in a writing course. First, visual communication is playing an increasingly important role in the way information is designed and circulated. Second, writing itself is a form of visual communication that relies as much on graphic as verbal representation. Today, learning to write means learning how to produce well-designed print and digital texts—everything from academic papers, reports, and résumés to flyers, brochures, newsletters, posters, and Web sites. Throughout *The Call to Write,* we've examined what makes written texts persuasive and easy to follow. At this point, we turn to the visual dimension of writing and how the design of the page can contribute to readability and persuasion.

We start by considering how visual communication is used for purposes of identification, information, and persuasion. Next, we will see how you can create effective page designs and use type to enhance your message. Finally, we will look at visual-design projects as such as flyers, newsletters, and brochures.

HOW VISUAL DESIGN EMBODIES PURPOSES

In Chapter 17, "The Shape of the Essay," we looked at how written forms embody writers' purposes. In this section, we consider how visual forms embody designers' purposes in three ways:

- Identification
- Information
- Persuasion

IDENTIFICATION

A primary function of visual design is to identify things, places, publications, and organizations. Street and building signs, posters, flags, logos, trademarks, letterheads, package labels, and mastheads on newspapers and magazines are some of the typical visual forms used for identification.

531

United States Department of Transportation

One well-known example of designing for purposes of identification is the signage system the United States Department of Transportation commissioned the American Institute of Graphic Arts (AIGA) to create for transportation facilities and international events. Graphic designers Roger Cook and Don Shanosky designed 34 symbol signs in 1974, to which 16 additional images were added in 1979. The remarkable clarity and legibility of these now iconic images provided a means of visual communication to bridge language barriers and cultural differences. You will no doubt recognize immediately many or all of the 18 signs from the AIGA system of graphic identification reproduced here. Consider how the designers distilled complex messages into simple and consistent visual forms.

■ **EXERCISE**

Analyzing Posters, Logos, and Package Designs

1. Consider the three concert posters—for The White Stripes, TV on the Radio, and The Roots. How does the visual style identify the band? What aspects of the band's identity does the visual style emphasize? How does the poster use color, typeface, images, and design?

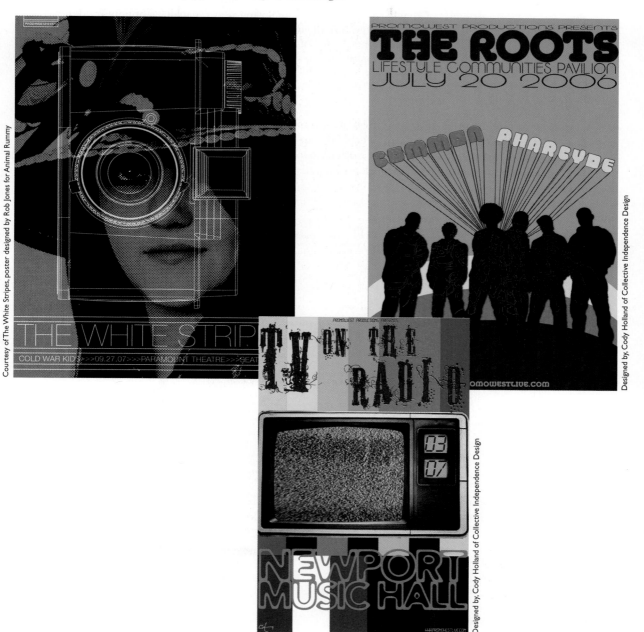

Courtesy of The White Stripes, poster designed by Rob Jones for Animal Rummy

Designed by, Cody Holland of Collective Independence Design

Designed by, Cody Holland of Collective Independence Design

2. Imagine you have been commissioned to create a logo for a particular company, product, organization, or institution. Read Bill Marsh's report on changing logo styles, "Warmer, Fuzzier: The Refreshed Logo," in Chapter 8, page 260. What image and identity will you project? What graphics, typeface, or overall design could you use to create this identity? Sketch one or more logos. Explain your design decisions.

3. Bring in three or four similar items you can buy in a grocery store. They could be jars of spaghetti sauce, bottles of spring water, packages of laundry detergent, or whatever. How does the design of the packaging—the brand name, logo, color of the label, fonts, shape of the product, or anything else that's notable—seek to create an identity for its product that distinguishes it from other products of its type?

INFORMATION

The purpose of information design is not simply to add visual interest to documents that are primarily verbal but to help readers visualize important processes, trends, and relationships. Notice how the visual display of information enhances the appearance of the page and makes the information easier to process.

orem ipsum dolor sit amet, vilputate consectetuer adipiscing elit, sed diam nonummy nibh euismod ipsum duis autem

CURRENT SNOOZE ALARM SALES

in vulputate velit esse molestie consequat, vel illum dolor e eu feugiat nulla facilisis at vero eros et acc umsan et iusto odio dignissim qui blandit pr aesent luptatum zzril delenit augue duis dolo re te feugait nulla facilisi. Lorem ipum dolor sit amet, consectuer adipiscing elit, sed diam

YEAR	$ UNTIS SOLD	$ RETAIL
1965	1,100	$ 12,000
1970	65,000	430,000
1975	220,000	2,800,000
1980	673,000	5,900,000
1985	1,220,000	11,670,000

nonummy nibh euismod tincidunt ut laoreet dolore magna aliquam erat volutpat dolore te feugait nulla facilisi. Duis autem vel eumle iriure dolor te feugait. aliquip ex ea commodo conse quat. Duis autem vel eum iriure dolor in hen drerit in vulputate velit esse molestie nulla facili sis at Lorem ipsum dolor sit amet, vilputate consectetuer adipiscing elit, sed diam nonummy nibh e dio dignissim qui blandit pr aesent luptatum zzril delenit augue duis dolo re te feugait nulla facilisi. Lorem ipum dolor sit amet, consectuer

Lorem ipsum dolor sit amet, vilputate consectetuer adipiscing elit, sed diam nonummy nibh euismod ipsum duor in hendrerit in vulputate velit esse molestie cois at vero eros et

PROJECTED TARDISNOOZ SALES

Lorem ipsum dolor sit amet, vilputate consectetuer adipiscing elit, sed diam nonummy nibh euismod ipsum duis autem vel eum iriure dolor in hendrerit in vulputate velit esse molestie consequat, vel illum dolor e eu feugiat nulla facilisis at vero eros et acc umsan et iusto odio dignissim qui blandit pr aesent luptatum zzril delenit augue duis

PROJECTED TARDISNOOZ SALES

YEAR	$ UNITS PROJECTED		$ RETAIL
1990	34,100		$ 430,000
1991	81,000		970,000
1992	239,000	(Break-even)	2,400,000
1993	310,000		3,700,000
1994	228,000	(Recession Projected)	2,200,000
1995	426,000		4,450,000

Lorem ipsum dolor sit amet, vilputate consectetuer adipiscing elit, sed diam nonummy nibh euismod ipsum duis autem vel eum iriure dolor in hendrerit

The visual display of information can be divided into three categories: textual, representational, and numerical.

Textual Graphics

Textual graphics organize and display information to emphasize key points and supplement the main text.

- **Sidebars and information boxes** add additional information to the main text and visual interest to the page layout. (See Mike Crouch's "Lost in a Smog" in Chapter 8 for examples.)

- **Tables** organize and display information that enables readers to make comparisons. (See Luis Ramirez's "Food Sources in South Providence" in Chapter 15 for examples.)

- **Time lines** list events on a horizontal axis to represent change over time.

- **Flowcharts and organizational charts** show processes, functions, and relationships. (See the Aristocracy organizational chart and the Research flowchart on the next page.)

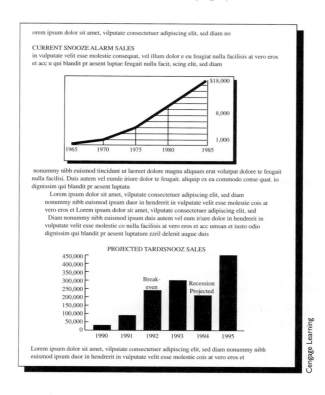

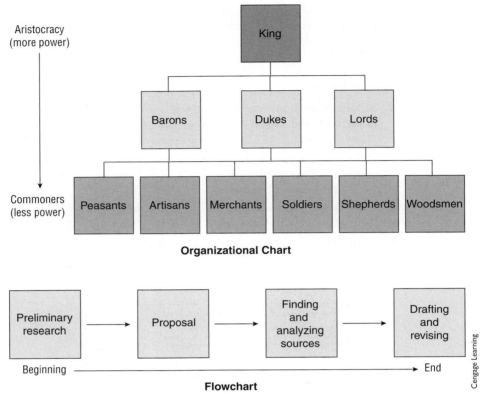

Organizational Chart

Flowchart

Notice that organizational charts are often hierarchical while flowcharts show processes.

Representational Graphics

Representational graphics use pictures to orient readers in time and space and to illustrate processes, relationships, and events.

- **Photographs, drawings, and other illustrations** enable readers to visualize the content of the written text.
- **Maps** often use color coding to help readers visualize the relative location of events or the distribution of a phenomenon.
- **Diagrams** use simplified representations to help readers visualize how processes take place.

Notice how the color coding on this map enables readers to visualize the extent of Israeli settlement in occupied areas of Palestine.

Numerical Graphics

Numerical graphics put the primary focus on quantitative data instead of words or diagrams. Numerical graphics enable writers to analyze the data they are working with and to represent trends and relationships.

- Tables are probably the simplest form of numerical graphic. While tables have the lowest visual interest of numerical graphics, they are useful when you have large amounts of information you want to organize and display in a logical and orderly way. Notice how the table titled Drug Offenders in State Prisons by Race/Ethnicity, 1999–2005 enables readers to see changes and comparisons.

TABLE 1: DRUG OFFENDERS IN STATE PRISON BY RACE/ETHNICITY, 1999–2005

	1999	2000	2001	2002	2003	2004	2005	Change 99–05
All drug offenders	251,200	251,100	246,100	265,000	250.900	249,400	253,300	0.8%
White #	50,700	58,200	57,300	64,500	64,800	65,900	72,300	42.6%
White %	20.2%	23.2%	23.3%	24.3%	25.9%	26.4%	28.5%	
Black #	144,700	145,300	139,700	126,000	133,100	112,500	113,500	–21.6%
Black %	57.6%	57.9%	56.8%	47.5%	53%	45.1%	44.8%	
Hispanic #	52,100	43,300	47,000	61,700	50,100	51,800	51,100	–1.9%
Hispanic %	20.7%	17.2%	19.1%	23.3%	20%	20.8%	20.2%	

From Marc Mauer, "The Changing Racial Dynamics of the War on Drugs." Copyright © The Sentencing Project. Reprinted with permission.

- **Line graphs** are used to show variation in the quantity of something over a period of time. By charting the number of cases on the vertical, or y, axis and the period of time on the horizontal, or x, axis, writers can establish trends. (See line graph on page 541.)
- **Pie charts** divide the whole of something into its parts, displaying the individual items that make up 100 percent of the whole. Pie charts help readers see the relative weight or importance of each slice in relation to the others. For this reason many graphic designers agree that, to avoid clutter and ensure readability, pie charts should use no more than six or seven slices.

More Than-One Third of Anchorage's Sports Participants Are Soccer Players

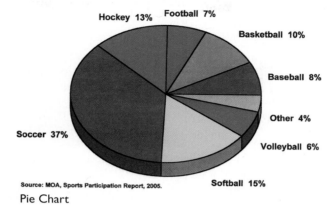

Source: MOA, Sports Participation Report, 2005.

Pie Chart

■ **Bar charts** enable writers to compare data and to emphasize contrasts among two or more items over time. Bar charts run along the horizontal axis from left to right. **Column charts** serve the same function as bar charts but run along the vertical axis, from down to up.

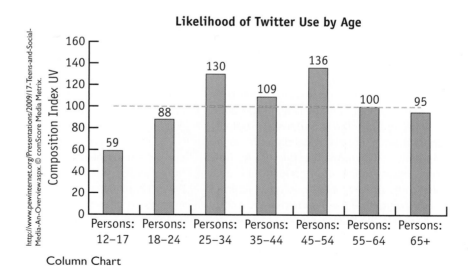

Column Chart

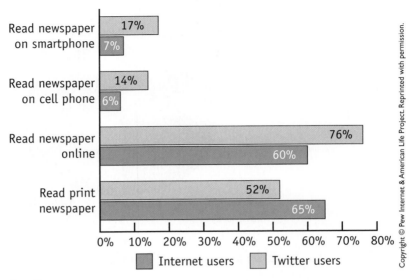

Bar Chart

ETHICS OF INFORMATION DESIGN

DATA DISTORTION

The information design expert Edward R. Tufte says that inept and misleading graphics are widespread in part because visual designers believe that statistical data are boring to readers and in need of jazzing up. As Tufte shows, however, instead of making the data more lively, graphic effects often misrepresent or exaggerate the meaning of the data.

Notice in the illustration on page 541, for example, that the numerical increase in "Fuel Economy Standards for Autos" from 1978 to 1985 is 53 percent—from 18 to 27.5 miles per gallon. As represented, however, the increase from the line representing 1978 standards, which is 0.6 inches, to the line representing 1985 standards, which is 5.3 inches, amounts to 783 percent—a huge distortion of the facts.

Moreover, by departing from the usual order of listing dates on an axis—either bottom to top or left to right—the new standards seem to be surging directly at us, exaggerating their effect.

Tufte redesigned this display of information with a simple graph, so that the size of the graphic matched the size of the data. As you can see, instead of the dramatic, ever-increasing change presented in the original, Tufte's redesign shows that the new standards start gradually, double the rate between 1980 and 1983, and then flatten out—a pattern disguised in the original display. Notice, finally, how the redesign includes a simple comparison of the expected average mileage of all cars on the road to the new car standards, another clarifying item of information missing from the original. ■

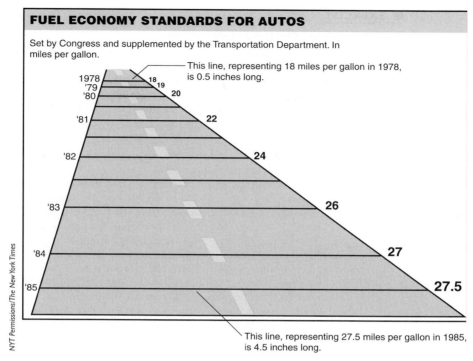

FUEL ECONOMY STANDARDS FOR AUTOS

Set by Congress and supplemented by the Transportation Department. In miles per gallon.

This line, representing 18 miles per gallon in 1978, is 0.5 inches long.

This line, representing 27.5 miles per gallon in 1985, is 4.5 inches long.

NYT Permissions/The New York Times

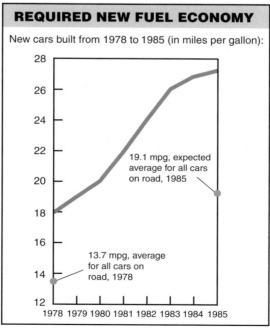

REQUIRED NEW FUEL ECONOMY

New cars built from 1978 to 1985 (in miles per gallon):

19.1 mpg, expected average for all cars on road, 1985

13.7 mpg, average for all cars on road, 1978

Line Graphs

■ EXERCISE

Analyzing Visual Display of Information

1. Look through some recent issues of magazines and newspapers to find three examples of the visual display of information to bring to class. Be prepared to explain how (or whether) your examples organize and display information in a way that complements the written text. Does the size of the graphic match the size of the data? If not, what is the effect?

2. The following situations present clusters of information that can be represented in visual form. In each case, decide whether a line graph, a bar chart, or a pie chart is the best choice to convey the information to readers. Make a sketch of your choice to display this information.

   a. You are preparing the annual report for a community service organization at your college. Part of your task is to explain how the organization has spent the annual budget of $7,500 it receives from the college. Expenditures are the following: $1,500 for printing leaflets, brochures, and the quarterly newsletter; $1,000 for speakers' fees; $500 for a workshop for members; $2,500 to send five members to a national conference on community service; $1,750 for donations to local community organizations; $250 for refreshments at meetings.

   b. Biology classes at your college are in high demand. No new faculty have been hired nor have any new courses been offered in the past ten years. With the rapid increase of biology majors, classes are overenrolled. In some cases, even majors can't register for the courses they need. You want to make the case that your college needs to hire more biology faculty and offer more courses. Here are the numbers of biology majors enrolled at the beginning of each academic year from 1997 to 2006: 1997—125; 1998—132; 1999—114; 2000—154; 2001—158; 2002—176; 2003—212; 2004—256; 2005—301; 2006—333.

   c. You are working for your college's office of alumni affairs and you are involved in a campaign to increase alumni donations. No one has ever researched whether donations vary depending on the major of alumni. To help plan the campaign, you are asked to find out how donation differs according to the major of alumni. You decide to look first at alumni who graduated between 1975 and 1984 and have established their careers. Here is the number of alumni who graduated in the ten-year period and the donations they gave in 1997 arranged by type of major: social sciences, 1,300 graduates—$158,000; humanities, 1,680 graduates—$98,000; business, 2,180 graduates—$326,000; engineering, 940 graduates—$126,000; sciences, 1,020 graduates—$112,000; fine arts, 720 graduates—$48,000; nursing and allied health, 680 graduates—$54,000.

3. In a group with two or three other students, choose one of the reading selections that appear in another chapter. Design a visual display of information to emphasize a main point, trend, relationship, or process in the reading. Be prepared to explain your design.

PERSUASION

You don't have to look very far to see how visual design is used for purposes of persuasion. Advertising, public service announcements, and advocacy campaigns contend for our visual attention.

Persuasion can address its readers in a number of ways. The famous Uncle Sam army recruitment poster of World War I, for example, took a direct approach to readers, staring them straight in the eye to deliver its command message: "I Want You." A British recruitment poster from the same era took a more indirect approach, putting readers in the role of spectators looking into a living room after the war where children ask their father, "Daddy, what did YOU do in the Great War?"

Notice, on the other hand, how the poster on page 544 from Men Can Stop Rape appeals not to shame but to positive self-image.

Persuasive Messages

MY STRENGTH IS NOT FOR HURTING.

So when she changed her mind, I STOPPED.

Men can stop rape.

Courtesy of Men Can Stop Rape/www.mencanstoprape.org

A Note on Reading and Seeing

Visual design draws on the use of sight in two distinct but related ways—reading and seeing. In some instances, these uses of sight operate separately. For example, when you look at an illustration in a book or a photo that accompanies a news report, you shift from being a reader to being a viewer. In other instances, however, visual designers put words and images together in ways that blur the activity of reading and seeing so that they happen as one event. Jean Carlu's poster promoting production during World War II is a good example of how reader-viewers take in at a single glance the powerful visual symbol of industrial mobilization, as text and image interlock to create one figure.

Notice how, in Amnesty International's appeal to free Ngawang Choephel, reading and seeing are integrated, with the column of text at the right running parallel to prison bars superimposed on Choephel's face.

The Library of Congress

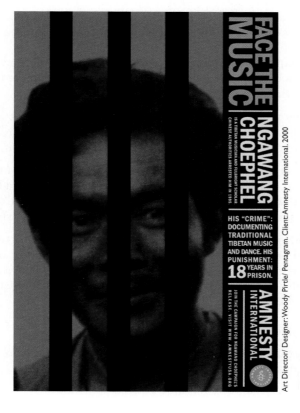

Art Director/ Designer: Woody Pirtle/ Pentagram. Client: Amnesty International. 2000

■ **EXERCISE**

Analyzing Persuasive Visual Design

1. Find a number of advertisements, public service announcements, or other forms of publicity that integrate words and images into a visual design. Try to get as wide a range as possible. Bring five or six to class. Work in a group with two or three other students. Pay attention to how each visual design addresses you as a viewer-reader. Is it direct address, where you feel someone is talking to you? Or are you positioned in the role of a spectator? Consider how these approaches—direct and indirect—embody the designer's purposes and the persuasive effects.

2. Use the same group of materials. This time analyze how seeing and reading work together and separately in the way you make sense of the message. What are the images you see? What are the words you read? How do they go together to form a message?

VISUAL DESIGN: FOUR BASIC PRINCIPLES

In this section we look at four basic principles that apply to virtually any document you may be called on to design. Each principle emphasizes a particular aspect of design, but all four overlap and mutually reinforce each other.

- **Group similar items together:** Grouping similar items creates visual units of attention on the page and thereby helps readers organize and remember information.

- **Align visual elements:** Alignment refers to the placement of visual elements on the page—whether you center them or align them left or right. Alignment enables readers to connect the visual elements on the page.

- **Use repetition and contrast to create consistent visual patterns:** *Repetition* unifies disparate visual elements and cues readers to where they can expect certain types of information to appear. *Contrast* is a way to emphasize certain visual elements—to make them stand out.

- **Add visual interest:** Visual design can follow the first three principles and still be a bit boring. Adding visual interest will not only make readers more likely to pay attention to your message. It also enhances your credibility as someone who knows how to make a sophisticated and stylish presentation.

USE THE FOUR PRINCIPLES TO REDESIGN DOCUMENTS

To see what the four principles look like in practice, here are examples of using them to redesign a résumé and a flyer.

Redesigning a Résumé

Groupings of information don't stand out.

Alignment is inconsistent— some headings are centered, some flush left.

No clear pattern established by repetition and contrast.

Martha Smith
143 Oakland Avenue
Philadelphia, PA 19122
(215) 555-2000

Education

Bachelor of Arts in English
Temple University, 2009

Experience

Journalism internship—*Philadelphia Inquirer*
2008–2009
  Covered and wrote by-lined articles on school board meetings
  Researched sex education K–12 for special report
  Assisted editor in preparing special education supplement

Public Relations Assistant—Trinity Repertory Theater, Camden, NJ
2007–2008
  Wrote advertising copy and designed promotional brochures
  Conducted focus groups
  Prepared instructional materials for Theater in the Schools

Writing Center Tutor—Temple University
2006–2009
  Tutored students on wide range of writing assignments
  Worked with international students
  Trained new tutors

Entertainment Editor—*Temple Daily News*
2007–2008
  Planned and assigned music, art, drama, and film reviews
  Edited reviews
  Led staff meetings

Related Skills
  Written and spoken fluency in Spanish, reading ability in French
  Feature Writing, Graphic Design, Editing, Photojournalism

Achievements/Activities:
  Dean's list (every semester)
  Member of Sigma Tau Delta, International English Honor Society
  Secretary of Amnesty International—Temple University chapter
  Varsity cross-country and indoor and outdoor track

References: Available upon request

Résumé (original)

Groupings are more distinct.

Visual elements are aligned in a consistent pattern.

Use of rules and boldface creates a pattern by repetition.

MARTHA SMITH

143 Oakland Avenue
Philadelphia, PA 19122
(215) 555-2000

Education

2009   Bachelor of Arts in English
Temple University

Experience

2008–2009   **Journalism internship** at *Philadelphia Inquirer*. Covered and wrote by-lined articles on school board meetings. Researched sex education K–12 for special report. Assisted editor in preparing special education supplement.

2007–2008   **Public Relations Assistant** at Trinity Theater, Camden, NJ. Wrote advertising copy and designed promotional brochures. Conducted focus groups. Prepared instructional materials for theater in the Schools.

2006–2009   **Writing Center Tutor** at Temple University. Tutored students on wide range of writing assignments. Worked with international students. Trained new tutors.

2007–2008   **Entertainment Editor** at *Temple Daily News*. Planned and assigned music, art, drama and film reviews. Edited reviews. Led staff meetings.

Related Skills

Written and spoken fluency in Spanish, reading ability in French. Course work in feature writing, graphic design, design, editing, and photojournalism.

Achievements/Activities

Dean's list (every semester)
Member of Sigma Tau Delta, International English Honor Society, Secretary of Amnesty International—Temple University chapter, Varsity cross-country, and indoor and outdoor track

References available upon request

Use of boldface and sans-serif headings creates a pattern by contrast.

Résumé (redesign)

Redesigning a Flyer

Centered
layout
makes
visual
elements
"float" on
the page

No consis-
tent color
scheme

No clear
pattern
of
informa-
tion
design

Wanna TRAVEL?

Join Emerson College's Travel Club!

This year our group will travel to the beautiful Arches National Park in Utah.
The trip costs $400 and includes:
airfare, lodging, food,
and admission to all activities!
To register, please visit our website at
emerson.edu, or talk to Dr. Brown in the Student Travel Office!

Steve Schirra

Flyer (original)

Groups
visual
elements

Aligns
visual
elements

Creates
coherent
visual
pattern by
grouping

Creates
contrast
by reverse
lettering

Uses con-
sistent
color
scheme

Creates
visual
interest

Wanna
travel?

Join
Emerson
College's
Travel Club!

To register, please visit our website
at emerson.edu, or talk to Dr. Brown
in the Student Travel Office!

This year our group will travel to the beautiful
Arches National Park in Utah.

The trip costs $400 and includes airfare,
lodging, food, and admission to all activities!

Steve Schirra Image copyright Foray, 2009. Used under license from Shutterstock.com

Flyer (redesign)

WORKING WITH TYPE

In the age of the personal computer, writers have access to literally hundreds of type fonts and can change their size and underline, italicize, or make them boldface with the click of a mouse. The vast range of possibilities now available, however, can be overwhelming. Writers need to understand what their options are in using type, and what kinds of effect their design decisions are likely to have on readers. Here are some basic suggestions about working with type:

- **Use white space as an active element in design:** White space is not simply the empty places on a page where no writing or visuals appear. White space plays an active role in creating the visual structure of a document and the relationship among its parts. Notice, for example, how white space makes headings more or less prominent by creating a hierarchy of levels:

  Level 1 heading (for titles)

  xxxxxxxxxxxxxxxxxxxxxxxxxxxxxxxxxxxxxxxxxxxxxxxxxxxxxxxxxxxxxx
  xxxxxxxxxxxxxxxxxxxxxxxxxxxxxxxxxxxxxxxxxxxxxxxxxxxxxxxxxxxxxx
  xxxxxxxxxxxxxxxxxxxxxxxxxxxxxxxxx.

  Level 2 heading (on separate line)

  xxxxxxxxxxxxxxxxxxxxxxxxxxxxxxxxxxxxxxxxxxxxxxxxxxxxxxxxxxxxxx
  xxxxxxxxxxxxxxxxxxxxxxxxxxxxxxxxxxxxxxxxxxxxxxxxxxxxxxxxxxxxxx
  xxxxxxxxxxxxxxxxxxxxxxxxxxxxxxxxxxxxxxxxxxxxxxxxxxxxxxxxxxxxxx
  xxxxxxxxxxxxxxxxxxxxxxxxxxxxxxxxxxxxxxxxxxxxxxxxxxxxxxxxxxxxxx
  xxxxxxxxxxxxxx.

  Level 3 heading (with text following) xxxxxxxxxxxxxxxxxxxxxxxxxxxxx
  xxxxxxxxxxxxxxxxxxxxxxxxxxxxxxxxxxxxxxxxxxxxxxxxxxxxxxxxxxxxxx
  xxxxxxxxxxxxxxxxxxxxxxxxxxxxxxxxxxxxxxxxxxxxxxxxxxxxxxxxxxxxxx
  xxxxxxxxxxxxxxxxxxxxxxxxxxxxxxxxxxxxxxxxxxxxxxxxxxxxxxxxxxxxxx
  xxxxxxxxxxxxxxxxxxxxxxxxxxxxxxxxxxxxxxxxxxxxxxxxxx.

- **Use leading appropriately:** Leading is the typographer's term for the white space that appears above and below a line of type. The basic guideline is that you need more leading—more space above and below type—when lines of print are long, less when they're short. A research paper, for example, is easier to read if it's double-spaced. On the other hand, in newsletters and other documents with columns, it's better to use less leading. Notice the difference between Column A and B:

  Column A

  For shorter lines, as in
  newsletters and other documents

  Column B

  For shorter lines, as in
  newsletters and other documents

with columns, use less leading. If there's too much white space, readers' eyes can drift when they leave one line and look for the start of the next.

- **Use uppercase and lowercase:** In general, the combination of uppercase and lowercase letters is easier to read than all uppercase.

  THIS IS BECAUSE UPPERCASE (OR CAPITAL) LETTERS ARE UNIFORM IN SIZE, MAKING THEM MORE DIFFICULT TO RECOGNIZE THAN LOWERCASE LETTERS, ESPECIALLY ON COMPUTER SCREENS OR SINGLE-SPACED OR ITALICIZED.

  The combination of uppercase and lowercase uses more white space, produces more visual variety, and thereby helps the eye track the lines of print.

- **Use appropriate typeface and fonts:** Typeface and fonts refer to the design of letters, numbers, and other characters. There are thousands of typefaces available. The visual appearance of typeface contributes to the personality or character of your document. Part of working with type is choosing the typeface that creates the right image and thereby sends the appropriate message to your readers.

SERIF AND SANS SERIF TYPEFACES

Typefaces are normally divided into two groups—serif and sans serif. Serif typefaces include horizontal lines—or serifs—added to the major strokes of a letter or a character such as a number. Sans serif typefaces, by contrast, do not have serifs. Notice the difference:

Serif	Sans Serif
New York	Geneva
Palatino	Arial
Times	Helvetica

The typical use and stylistic impact of the typefaces vary considerably. Serif typefaces are more traditional, conservative, and formal in appearance. By contrast, sans serif typefaces offer a more contemporary, progressive, and informal look. Accordingly, serif is often used for longer pieces of writing, such as novels and textbooks. It is also the best bet for college papers. The horizontal lines make serif easier to read, especially in dense passages, because they guide the reader's eyes from left to right across the page. On the other hand, technical writers often use sans serif for user's manuals and other documents because it evokes a more modern, high-tech look.

DISPLAY TYPEFACES

Display typefaces offer many options for creating the look you want in newsletter nameplates, organizational logos, invitations, posters, signs, advertisements, and other documents. Display typefaces can project the mood and image that's appropriate for an organization or occasion. The trick, of course, is finding the style that's right—that conveys the message you want to readers.

Notice the different images display type creates for Jetstream Printers. This type projects a sleek and contemporary look:

Jetstream

This type, however, is probably too staid and conservative, more appropriate, say, for a bank, stock brokerage company, or law firm:

JETSTREAM

On the other hand, this type is too light-hearted and informal. It's better suited for a restaurant or fashion boutique:

Jetstream

MIXING TYPEFACES

In some cases, combining different typefaces can enhance visual design. For example, it's common to use sans serif type for headlines or headings and serif for text. Make sure, however, that combinations of typefaces project a consistent image and that the styles used are compatible. (See the various design examples throughout this chapter.)

■ EXERCISE

Using Design Principles

Use the design principles we've just looked at to consider the changes Alex Schwartz has made to the following poster.

Warehouse State
FALL FILM SERIES
Classic Film Noir

All showings in Harrington Hall at 8:00 pm

Wednesday, September 14, 2001
Double Indemnity (1944)
Directed by Billy Wilder
With Fred MacMurray and Barbara Stanwyck

Wednesday, October 17, 2001
The Asphalt Jungle (1950)
Directed by John Huston
With Sterling Hayden and Marilyn Monroe

Wednesday, November 30, 2001
Touch of Evil (1958)
Directed by Orson Welles
With Orson Welles, Charlton Heston, and Janet Leigh

Original

Warehouse State
FALL FILM SERIES

All showings in Harrington Hall at 8 p.m.

CLASSIC FILM NOIR

Wedesday, Sept. 14
Double Indemnity (1944)
Directed by Billy Wilder
With Fred MacMurray and
Barbara Stanwyck

Wedesday, Oct. 17
The Asphalt Jungle (1950)
Directed by John Huston
With Sterling Hayden and
Marilyn Monroe

Wedesday, Nov. 30
Touch of Evil (1958)
Directed by Orson Welles
With Orson Welles, Charlton
Heston, and Janet Leigh

Steve Schirra

Redesign

VISUAL DESIGN PROJECTS

The following section looks at some of the considerations writers typically take into account when they design and produce documents such as flyers, newsletters, and brochures.

Preliminary Considerations

Like other writing tasks, design projects begin with a call to write—the felt need to send a message from an individual, group, or organization to prospective readers. Developing the design of a particular document will depend on answering questions such as these:

- What is the occasion that calls on you to design a document? What kind of document is most appropriate, given the circumstances (a flyer, leaflet, letter, brochure, or other format)? What is its purpose? Whose interests are involved? What is your relationship to the people who want the document produced and to those who will read it? What image should the document project?

- Who are your readers? What use will they make of the document? What do you want them to do after they have read the document? What tone and style are likely to be effective?

- What information will you be working with? How much of the document will be written text? What graphics do you have to use? How many sections do you foresee? In what order will they appear? Will you be doing all the writing? Some? Who else is involved?

- What technology do you have to work with? What does it enable you to do? What constraints does it put on the document?

- Are there any financial or time constraints you need to be aware of? Who will pay for the printing? When does the document need to be finished? Is this a realistic time frame?

By answering these questions, you can begin to make some basic decisions about the layout and other design features of your document. In particular, you will need to decide on the materials you will use in the document—whether you can use color, what type and color of ink, what type and color of paper, whether you plan to scan in illustrations or photos, what clip art, if any, you plan to use.

Working Sketches

The next step is to sketch a preliminary layout for the document. At this point, document designers often sketch a number of different arrangements. Such working sketches can help you identify potential problems you may face.

Flyers

Flyers are really small posters that can be passed out or posted on bulletin boards. They may announce upcoming meetings, events, and performances; advertise sales and other limited-time promotions; or urge people to do something. To be effective, flyers need to convey all the pertinent information at a glance. To do so, successful flyers combine seeing and reading with:

- Large headlines.
- Compact units of text.
- Attention-getting visuals and/or design features.

Newsletters

Newsletters are used by companies and organizations to communicate within the group and to the public. They run from a single page to eight pages or so, depending on their purpose and frequency. In many respects, they are like newspapers or little magazines. Key elements of a successful newsletter include:

- A distinctive nameplate and logo that identifies the newsletter.
- Clear identification of the sponsoring organization.
- Volume number, issue number, and date.
- Consistent design that maintains the identity of the newsletter from one issue to the next.
- Use of design features such as sidebars, boxes, pull quotes, photos, and illustrations to break up the text and add visual interest.

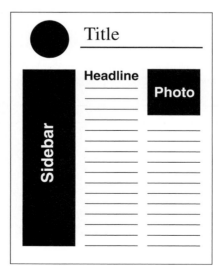

Newsletter Sketch

Brochures

Companies and organizations use brochures for promotional and informational purposes. Brochures usually include three or four panels. Here are some considerations to take into account when you're designing a brochure:

- Make the purpose of the brochure easy to identify. The front-cover headline should cue readers to the subject and purpose.

- The brochure should be easy to use. The outside panels—front, back, and middle—are often designed to be read separately. The inside panels should be designed as a continuous space.

- Make sure the brochure has all the information readers need—names, addresses, and phone numbers of organizations; maps to get to a store, museum, or historic district; bibliography; steps readers can take; answers to frequently asked questions; basic facts.

Brochure Sketch (inside)

Middle	Back	Front

Brochure Sketch (outside)

chapter 20

web design

This chapter presents a basic introduction to Web design. It doesn't explain the technical side of composing Web pages or putting them up on a server. That's beyond the scope of this book. Rather, we look at the rhetoric and design principles of Web sites.

This chapter can be used in a variety of ways. According to your instructor's directions, you can read it to learn more about the design of Web sites or you can use it to plan your own Web site. Whether you actually construct a Web site will depend in part on your instructor, your technical expertise, and the time and technical resources available. One option is to plan the Web site on paper as an exercise or writing assignment.

THE RHETORICAL PURPOSES OF WEB DESIGN

To examine what calls on individuals and organizations to design Web sites, we will use the same three purposes as in Chapter 19, "Visual Design"— identification, information, and persuasion—to see how Web sites embody their designers' purposes and how these purposes sometimes overlap.

IDENTIFICATION

Coco Fusco's Virtual Laboratory is a good example of how Web sites can project the identity of a particular person, in this case the performance artist and critic Coco Fusco. (See the page reproduced here.) The Web site contains a good deal of information and is at least implicitly persuasive in advertising her publications. Still, the dominant impression created by the Web site is to identify who Coco Fusco is and what she does.

Reprinted by permission of Coco Fusco

INFORMATION

"Dressed to the Nines: A History of the Baseball Uniform" is an online exhibit that is part of The National Baseball Hall of Fame and Museum Web site.

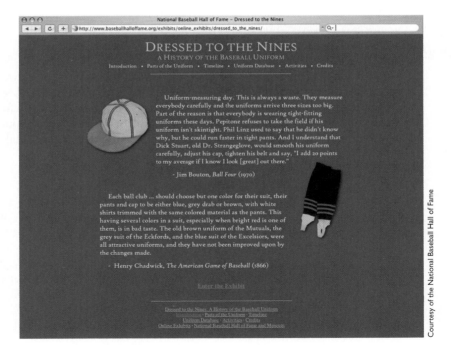

Courtesy of the National Baseball Hall of Fame

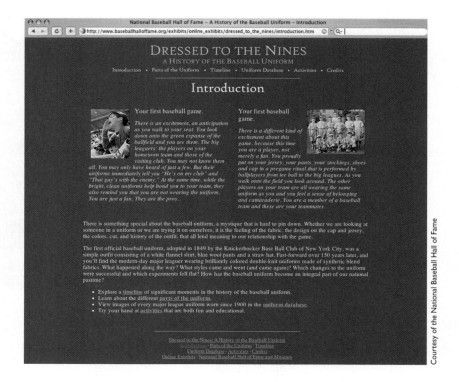

Courtesy of the National Baseball Hall of Fame

PERSUASION

Amnesty International is devoted to defending human rights worldwide. The Amnesty International Web site (see the page reproduced on page 561) is typical of advocacy group sites. It offers lots of information, in the form of reports and news updates, but it is also frankly partisan in its attempts to influence public opinion and get people involved in Amnesty International campaigns.

■ FOR CRITICAL INQUIRY

1. Visit Coco Fusco's Virtual Laboratory, www.thing.net/~cocofusco/. Consider it as a home page that projects the image and identity of a person. What dominant impression does it create about Coco Fusco and her works? How do the visuals add to that impression?

2. Visit the "Dressed to the Nines" online exhibit at exhibits.baseballhalloffame.org/ dressed_to_the_nines/index.htm. What range of information does it make available? What do you see as the purpose of this information? Who might use it? In what sense is this Web site like a museum?

Amnesty International

3. Visit Amnesty International's Web site, www.amnesty.org/. How does the site establish its credibility? What information does it provide? What does it call on visitors to do?

4. Now compare your experience visiting the three Web sites. How do the sites make their purposes clear? What features of the Web sites did you find particularly effective, useful, instructional, or entertaining? Were there features that didn't seem to work well? What generalizations might you draw about how visitors experience Web sites? What criteria can you begin to develop about what makes an effective Web site?

THE STRUCTURE OF WEB DESIGN

The structure of a Web site determines how pages are linked to each other and how visitors are thereby able to move from page to page. Web sites can have a **deep structure,** where visitors must click through a series of pages to get from the home page to a more remote destination.

In other cases, the Web site may have a **shallow structure,** where the home page presents enough options so that visitors can get to any destination in the site with only a click or two.

A **hypertext structure,** on the other hand, links pages to each other so that visitors can take different routes to get from the home page to a destination.

■ EXERCISE

Analyzing Web Structure

Work in a group of three or four. Analyze the structure of one of the three Web sites featured earlier in the chapter, a Web site that appears elsewhere in this book, or one that interests your group. Design a chart that shows how the

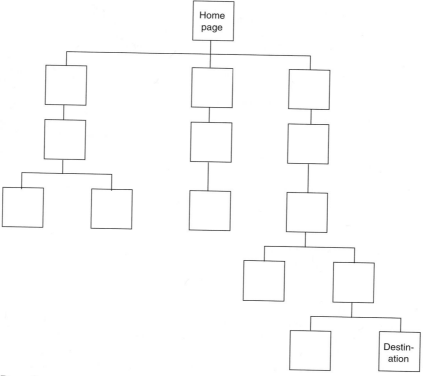

Deep Structure

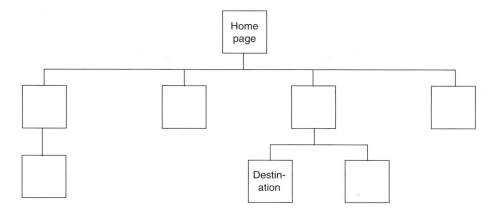

Shallow Structure

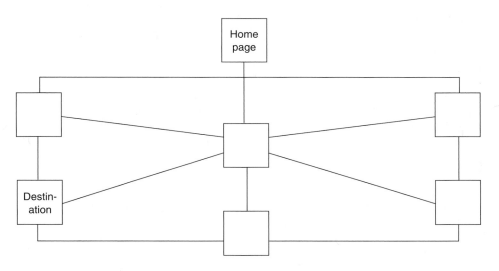

Hypertext Structure

pages are linked to each other, using the charts of deep, shallow, and hypertext structures as models. Consider how well the structure fits the purpose of the Web site and how easily you were able to move about the site. If time permits, your instructor may ask groups to present their findings and the class as a whole to draw conclusions about effective structures of Web design.

THE VISUAL DESIGN OF WEB SITES

All the principles presented in Chapter 19, "Visual Design," apply to Web sites as much as to printed material. Here are some visual-design considerations to take into account when you're planning a Web site:

- **Establish a consistent visual theme:** Home pages typically give an overview of the Web site by identifying its purpose and providing navigation tools. Just as important is that home pages also send a visual message about the site. Establishing a visual theme on the home page is crucial to the unity of a Web site and its credibility. Web designers consider how their choice of logo, images, background color, and font can best embody the site's purposes. As in other kinds of visual design, repetition and consistency are critical factors. Well-designed Web sites often use an identifying logo or header, the same background color, and the same placement of navigation tools on each page to create a consistent visual theme.

- **Make the navigation tools obvious and easy to use:** The navigation tools on a home page amount to a virtual table of contents that gives an overview of the Web site. Visitors should be able to see at a glance the main topics, even if the pages listed as navigation tools contain further links. There are various ways to set up navigation tools. You can use a navigation bar, icons, or buttons. In any case, keep the design, color, and placement consistent throughout the site. Visitors find it reassuring, for example, when the navigation tools are present on each page as a sidebar or at the top of the page. That helps them know where they are in the site and enables them to get back to the home page without clicking the back button on the browser. It's also helpful on longer pages to include a navigation bar at the bottom of the page so visitors don't have to scroll back to the top.

- **Resist clutter:** It can be tempting, particularly if you have the technical ability, to load up a Web site with such "bells and whistles" as animation, busy backgrounds, lurid colors, and lots of graphics. The danger, however, is that of cluttering the page with extraneous material and creating a chaotic effect. Visitors can become impatient rather quickly if the Web page they're trying to read is jam-packed, even if they are interested in the material. Whatever appears on the page should follow from the purpose of the Web site and not be simply decorative. Use white space creatively, as noted in Chapter 19, to enhance your design and focus the visitor's attention.

- **Create manageable chunks of information:** Despite the new and exciting multimedia features such as graphics, video, and sound, written text remains the key element of many Web sites. At the same time, using written text effectively is one of the major challenges of Web design because of the size of most people's computer screens and their reluctance to scroll through a long document or read written text that sprawls all the way across the page. (If they're really interested, they'll print it and read the hard copy.) This means that if you want people to read the pages on a Web site, you need to break up the written text into manageable chunks that can fit easily on a screen or require minimal scrolling. In many ways, this is a new approach to writing, which we'll look at more in the next section.

WRITING ASSIGNMENT

Planning a Web Site

In this assignment, you will encounter some of the decisions Web designers face in planning a Web site. As you'll see, they are similar in many respects to the decisions you've made in planning other kinds of writing. But, as just mentioned, there are also some important differences between writing print material and writing for the computer screen that you'll need to take into account.

Identifying the Call to Write

Planning a Web site begins, as other types of writing do, by identifying a call to write and clarifying your purposes. There are various situations that might call on you to design a Web site. You might believe there is an urgent issue on your campus, in your local community, or on the national or international scene. You might decide there is something people need to know about, or you may want to persuade them about your point of view. Or you may feel the desire to express yourself. As you've seen, Web design can embody the various and sometimes overlapping purposes of identification, information, and persuasion.

Here are some questions you might ask yourself at this point:

1. Why and how is a Web site a fitting response to the call to write? What can you do in a Web site that you can't do in other genres of writing?
2. What do you see as the main purpose of the Web site?
3. What personality and visual look do you imagine the Web site projecting?

Understanding Your Audience

One of the answers you may have given about choosing a Web site instead of another genre of writing is that it gives you a particular kind of access that connects you to readers online.

To help you plan your Web site, it's worth exploring that connection to online readers, the people who will visit your Web site:

1. Who do you imagine will visit your Web site? Are you planning the Web site for a specialized audience or for a more general one? What attitudes

and knowledge about the topic of your Web site do you think your intended visitors will have?

2. How will the design of the Web site indicate who your target audience is? Will your intended audience see that it's a site they would be interested in?

3. What do you want visitors to do when they get to the Web site? Is your purpose to have them navigate around your site, or do you plan to provide them with links to related Web sites?

Understanding the Genre

As already noted, one of the key differences between Web sites and many other genres of writing is that Web sites break up information into manageable chunks that can fit on the screen. Instead of giving readers written texts to read linearly, from beginning to end, Web sites link chunks of information together and give visitors navigation tools to determine their own paths from page to page. In this way, Web sites can create layers of information.

Designing Web Structure

Work through the following steps to design the structure of your Web site:

1. List as many topics as you can, taking into account what you think visitors need or want to know. Combine topics that overlap or are repetitive. Imagine that each topic will represent a separate Web page. The Web site you're designing might have anywhere between ten and twenty pages, including the home page. If you decide to include links to other Web sites, you can design a "Links" page or incorporate the links on your own pages where appropriate.

2. Select the topics you want to include on the Web site, and write each topic on a separate note card. Make sure to designate one note card for the home page.

3. Now arrange the note cards to try out designs for your Web site. Put the home page at the top as the entry point. Experiment with various arrangements of information. What topics should appear as navigation tools on the home page? What additional topics should be linked to these pages?

4. Draw a chart of the tentative structure of the Web site you're planning.

Drafting and Revising

Using your Web structure chart as a guide, write drafts of the individual Web pages. If you find some of the pages are too long, you may need to create new linked pages and revise the structure of the Web site. On the other hand, you may find you can combine planned pages into one. Whatever the case, each page should present a manageable chunk of information that will be easy to read on the computer screen and have a sensible place in the structure of your Web design. ■

REFLECTING ON YOUR WRITING

If you have created a Web site to put up on a server or designed a series of Web pages on paper, it's worth considering at this point how composing for the Web compares to composing for print media. What do you see as the main differences and similarities?

oral and PowerPoint presentations

A range of situations may require you to give a presentation. It's quite likely, for example, that you'll be asked to give an oral presentation in one or more of your courses. In addition, you may find yourself wanting to speak in a public forum, whether on campus or in your local community, to inform listeners about an issue that concerns you or to persuade them to share your point of view. Giving presentations is a standard feature of the workplace. And it is nearly certain that many presentations, no matter the setting, will call on you to use PowerPoint.

Planning a presentation has much in common with planning a piece of writing, but there are some key differences as well. Understanding these differences can help you use your knowledge of planning written texts to design presentations that use PowerPoint. We will first consider these differences. Then we'll see how you can plan, rehearse, and deliver an effective presentation.

UNDERSTANDING THE DIFFERENCES BETWEEN WRITTEN AND ORAL PRESENTATIONS

Depending on the occasion and the speaker's purposes, oral presentations pursue the same goals as written texts do: to inform, analyze, explain, and persuade. With a written presentation, however, readers have a text in front of them to refer to. They can read at their own pace—and reread sections as many times as necessary.

In oral presentations, however, listeners have to grasp the presenter's meanings as he or she is speaking. PowerPoint slides are helpful in focusing listeners on the speaker's message, but still there is no going back to an earlier section, as readers can do with written texts. The words evaporate as they are spoken and the slides change. In addition, research on adult attention spans indicates that even the most interested listeners can focus on a presentation for only twenty minutes or so (while the same person could read for a longer duration.

What's important is to understand that oral presentations put special demands on speakers to hold their audience's atttention and enable them to follow the talk and understand its main points.

DEVELOPING AN ORAL PRESENTATION

For our purposes here, we'll look at developing an oral presentation to give in one of your classes. These guidelines, however, are applicable to other situations that call on you to give an oral presentation.

PRELIMINARY CONSIDERATIONS

Consider how much time you have for your presentation. Listeners appreciate oral presentations that hold to their time limit. Such presentations require careful planning and rehearsal. Underprepared oral presentations tend to ramble in ways that listeners will find distracting.

Consider also how you will deliver the oral presentation. There is nothing quite so dull as speakers who read a paper to listeners, often with their heads down and eyes on the written text. Effective oral presentations are spoken, and preparation and rehearsal are the best way for you to establish eye contact with your listeners and give them the feeling you are speaking to them.

Some speakers write out their presentations and then memorize them. This can be risky, however, especially if you have a memory lapse during the presentation. A safer way is to develop an outline of main points and use it to practice until you can deliver your presentation without hesitation. If you're using PowerPoint slides, they can serve as a kind of outline to keep you on track.

PLANNING THE ORAL PRESENTATION

Identifying the Call to Write

Consider what makes the topic of your presentation interesting, important, controversial, or amusing. What do your listeners have to gain? Do you want to inform them, explain a concept, define a problem and propose a solution, evaluate a work or performance, advocate a point of view, or align yourself with others in a controversy?

Defining Your Audience

Who are your listeners? What interests do they have in the material you're presenting? What level of knowledge do they have about the topic? What do they need to know? How do you strike a balance between the needs of your instructor and the needs of your classmates?

Planning the Introduction

Introductions in oral presentations have two main purposes.

- First, you need to introduce the topic in a way that will suggest its significance and promote listeners' interest in what you have to say. An amusing anecdote, a telling example, a telling fact or statistic, or a controversial statement by an authority on the topic are possible opening strategies.

- Second, you need to help listeners follow your presentation by forecasting its organization as well as its content. At the beginning, tell your listeners what the purpose of your presentation is and provide them with an overview of its structure and the main points you'll be covering. PowerPoint slides can be particularly helpful to listeners in this regard, so they can visualize where the talk is going and stay oriented as it develops.

Arranging Your Material

A consistent scheme of organization is key to making your presentation easy to follow. Depending on your material, you can use a chronological, topical, or problem-and-solution type of organization.

Provide explicit transitions so that listeners can see how the parts of your presentation are related. For example, you might say, "Now that we've seen the scope of the problem of homelessness, we can turn to three proposals to deal with it." Help your listeners keep the "big picture" in mind by connecting the main points and omitting extraneous details. Some details may be interesting in their own right, but if they don't help lead your listeners through the main points of the material you're presenting, then you should resist the temptation to include them.

Planning the Ending

Cue your listeners that you are ending by saying something like "In closing, I want to emphasize . . ." or "To review the key points . . ." At the same time, you want to conclude with something more than a mere summary—such as an especially apt example that illustrates the crux of your talk, a troubling question that remains, or research that needs to be done. End on a strong note. Nothing undermines an ending like a nervous giggle or a shrug and "I guess that's it."

Being Prepared for Questions

One of the advantages of oral presentations is that the audience is present and can respond immediately with questions and comments. If your instructor wants a period of questions and responses after the presentation, pause for a moment after your ending and then say something like "I'd be happy to try to answer any questions you might have." If you are not sure you understand a question, ask the person who raised it for clarification. If you don't know the answer to a question, don't fake it or act defensively. Just say you don't know.

DESIGNING POWERPOINT SLIDES

PowerPoint slides not only offer a way to hold listeners' attention and help them remember key points; they can also help you plan your presentation, because the design of slides enables you to distill your material into its most essential elements. Think of visuals not as secondary sources to illustrate information at various points in the presentation but as a visualization of the structure of the presentation and each of its main points. If you've done a good job of designing your visuals, your audience should be able to grasp the main points of your presentation from reading the visuals you show.

Here are some suggestions for designing PowerPoint slides:

DESIGNING VISUALS

- **Design a slide for each main point in your presentation:** Once you have determined the main points in the presentation, write them out in a list. Now you can begin to consider how best to represent each point visually. In some cases, the visual will consist of an outline or key phrases. In other cases, the visuals may be a table, graph, or other type of illustration.

- **Keep text as concise as possible:** Slides with text should give the audience enough information to coordinate easily with what you are saying. Long or dense passages of text will distract the audience from the spoken presentation.

- **Use tables, graphs, or other illustrations selectively and accurately:** You may want to reproduce visuals directly from sources you've read, or you may design your own representation of information. Your selection should be keyed to the main points in your presentation. In either case, make sure your visuals render the information accurately—and that they provide your audience with a label of the information being presented and cite its source.

- **Use large type, clear fonts, and an appropriate color scheme:** Fourteen- to 24-point type size will usually give an easily readable projection on a PowerPoint presentation, depending on the size of the room where you'll be speaking. Don't use more than two different fonts (such as

Times New Roman and Helvetica) or more than two different styles (such as bold and italic) on a single slide. In general, use dark type on a light background. Light text on a dark background can look attractive but may not be easily readable, especially in a room with the lights on. Your visuals should have a clean and professional look. Avoid a visual presentation that will appear busy or unserious.

USING VISUAL AIDS IN A PRESENTATION

- **Use the slides but don't just read them:** As mentioned earlier, each slide should be linked to a key point in your presentation. Your audience can read the slide. Your task is to make the connection between what's on the slide and the line of thought in your presentation. You can refer to key words and terms on the slide but don't just read it verbatim.

- **Don't stand between your audience and the slide:** Your audience should be able to see both you and the screen where the slide is projected.

- **Look at your audience, not at the slide:** Maintaining eye contact with your audience is an important way of holding their attention and involving them in the presentation. You want them to feel that you are talking to them—not to the visual you are showing.

- **If appropriate, use a pointer to direct attention:** You can use either an old-fashioned pointer or a laser highlighter to stress particular aspects of a slide.

For more on PowerPoint, see Edward R. Tufte's "PowerPoint Is Evil" and Ellen Lupton's "Dos and Don'ts of PowerPoint" at the end of the chapter.

REHEARSING YOUR PRESENTATION

Even if you know your material well, you can undermine all your work unless you rehearse enough. No matter how intelligent the speaker, an audience will associate long pauses, mumbling, failure to make eye contact, awkward transitions, or fumbling with visual aids as evidence of the presenter's lack of familiarity with the topic and lack of planning. To make sure you don't send the wrong message, you've got to practice.

In fact, rehearsing your presentation is not just something you do once you've finished preparing it. Rehearsing can be an important way of developing and revising what you've got on paper. In many cases, it's only when a speaker practices that he or she becomes aware that more information is needed in a section of the talk or that the proper emphasis on main points isn't coming through effectively.

To get the most out of rehearsing, you need an audience. Some speakers practice in front of a mirror, but another person (or even better, a group of people) can provide you with kinds of feedback that may not occur to you. Or you may be able to record your presentation with a video camera, so that you can review it to determine what changes are called for. However you rehearse, though, you need some criteria to evaluate the presentation. Here are some suggestions about what to look for:

GUIDELINES FOR EVALUATING ORAL PRESENTATIONS

❑ Is the purpose of the presentation clear from the start?

❑ Is the presentation easy to follow? Do listeners know where they are at each point along the way?

❑ Do major points receive proper emphasis? Do they stand out clearly?

❑ Does the speaker use variation in tone, pitch, and loudness to emphasize major points? A monotone puts listeners to sleep, but verbal emphasis at inappropriate points will throw listeners off.

❑ Is the pace of the presentation appropriate? Too fast a pace makes an audience think the speaker is rushing through just to get it done, while going too slow can make them start to squirm.

❑ Does the speaker maintain effective eye contact with listeners?

❑ Does the speaker handle the visuals smoothly and effectively? Are the visuals well coordinated with the presentation? Are they easy to read?

❑ Does the speaker use gestures and body language effectively during the presentation?

❑ Does the presentation stay within the time allotted?

Answers to these questions can give you important information about how you need to change your presentation. Make sure you give yourself time to practice the revised version.

FURTHER THOUGHTS ON POWERPOINT

We present Edward R. Tufte's essay "PowerPoint Is Evil" and slides from Ellen Lupton's "PowerPoint Do's and Don'ts" to examine in greater depth the meaning and style of PowerPoint presentations. Edward R. Tufte is professor emeritus of political science, computer science and statistics, and graphic design at Yale University. He is also the author, designer, and publisher of three highly influential books on information design: The Visual Display of Quantitative Information *(1983),* Envisioning Information *(1990),* Visual Explanation *(1997), and* Beautiful Evidence *(2006). Ellen Lupton is a leading graphic designer, teacher, and theorist whose books include* Thinking with Type *(2004),* D.I.Y.: Design It Yourself *(2006), and* Graphic Design: The New Basics *(2008). You can find a PDF of the PowerPoint slides at www.elupton.com/index.php?id=52.*

POWERPOINT IS EVIL

EDWARD R. TUFTE

PowerPoint Is Evil
Power Corrupts.
PowerPoint Corrupts Absolutely.

Genevieve Lang

Imagine a widely used and expensive prescription drug that promised to make us beautiful but didn't. Instead the drug had frequent, serious side effects: It induced stupidity, turned everyone into bores, wasted time, and degraded the quality and credibility of communication. These side effects would rightly lead to a worldwide product recall.

Yet slideware—computer programs for presentations—is everywhere: in corporate America, in government bureaucracies, even in our schools. Several hundred million copies of Microsoft PowerPoint are churning out trillions of slides each year. Slideware may help speakers outline their talks, but convenience for the speaker can be punishing to both content and audience. The standard PowerPoint presentation elevates format over content, betraying an attitude of commercialism that turns everything into a sales pitch.

Of course, data-driven meetings are nothing new. Years before today's slideware, presentations at companies such as IBM and in the military used bullet lists shown by overhead projectors. But the format has become ubiquitous under PowerPoint, which was created in 1984 and later acquired by Microsoft. PowerPoint's pushy style seeks to set up a speaker's dominance over the audience. The speaker, after all, is making power points with bullets to followers. Could any metaphor be worse? Voicemail menu systems? Billboards? Television? Stalin?

Particularly disturbing is the adoption of the PowerPoint cognitive style in our schools. Rather than learning to write a report using sentences, children are being taught how to formulate client pitches and infomercials. Elementary school PowerPoint exercises (as seen in teacher guides and in student work posted on the Internet) typically consist of 10 to 20 words and a piece of clip art on each slide in a presentation of three to six slides—a total of perhaps 80 words (15 seconds of silent reading) for a week of work. Students would be better off if the schools simply closed down on those days and everyone went to the Exploratorium

or wrote an illustrated essay explaining something.

In a business setting, a PowerPoint slide typically shows 40 words, which is about eight seconds' worth of silent reading material. With so little information per slide, many, many slides are needed. Audiences consequently endure a relentless sequentiality, one damn slide after another. When information is stacked in time, it is difficult to understand context and evaluate relationships. Visual reasoning usually works more effectively when relevant information is shown side by side. Often, the more intense the detail, the greater the clarity and understanding. This is especially so for statistical data, where the fundamental analytical act is to make comparisons.

Consider an important and intriguing table of survival rates for those with cancer relative to those without cancer for the same time period. Some 196 numbers and 57 words describe survival rates and their standard errors for 24 cancers.

Applying the PowerPoint templates to this nice, straightforward table yields an analytical disaster. The data explodes into six separate chaotic slides, consuming 2.9 times the area of the table. Everything is wrong with these smarmy, incoherent graphs: the encoded legends, the meaningless color, the logo-type branding. They are uncomparative, indifferent to content and evidence, and so data-starved as to be almost pointless. Chartjunk is a clear sign of statistical stupidity. Poking a finger into the eye of thought, these data graphics would turn into a nasty travesty if used for a

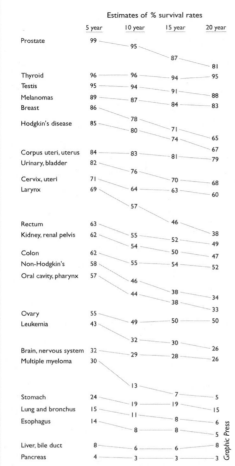

GOOD. A traditional table: rich, informative, clear.

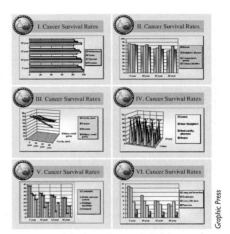

BAD. PowerPoint chartjunk: smarmy, chaotic, incoherent.

serious purpose, such as helping cancer patients assess their survival chances. To sell a product that messes up data with such systematic intensity, Microsoft abandons any pretense of statistical integrity and reasoning. Presentations largely stand or fall on the quality, relevance, and integrity of the content. If your numbers are boring, then you've got the wrong numbers. If your words or images are not on point, making them dance in color won't make them relevant. Audience boredom is usually a content failure, not a decoration failure.

At a minimum, a presentation format should do no harm. Yet the PowerPoint style routinely disrupts, dominates, and trivializes content. Thus PowerPoint presentations too often resemble a school play—very loud, very slow, and very simple.

The practical conclusions are clear. PowerPoint is a competent slide manager and projector. But rather than supplementing a presentation, it has become a substitute for it. Such misuse ignores the most important rule of speaking: Respect your audience.

POWERPOINT DOs AND DON'TS

ELLEN LUPTON

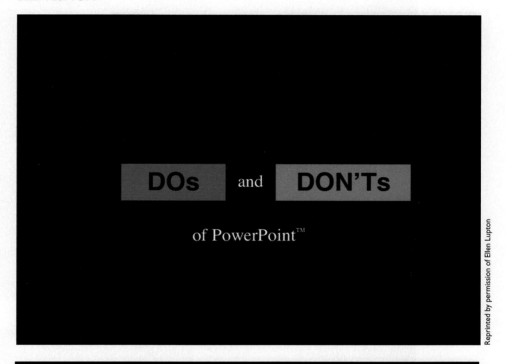

Reprinted by permission of Ellen Lupton

Reprinted by permission of Ellen Lupton

DO Break up your text into manageable chunks.

Respect your audience.

Write less. Use more space.

Reprinted by permission of Ellen Lupton

THIS IS TOO MUCH TEXT

PowerPoint has become a ubiquitous medium of business communication. At sales meetings, training seminars, and conferences, the audience has come to expect a PowerPoint slide show with every talk. This is not necessarily a good thing. Not only do people expect PowerPoint, they also expect it to be dull. PowerPoint has become associated with puffed-up presentations by paid consultants, corny "interactive" discussions led by professional facilitators, and any dull event where you get a free pencil. The fact is, everyone should learn PowerPoint. But you need to learn to use it well, and you need to know when not to use it at all.

Reprinted by permission of Ellen Lupton

BULLETS ARE NOT ENOUGH

• PowerPoint has become a ubiquitous medium of business communication.
• At sales meetings, training seminars, and conferences, the audience has come to expect a PowerPoint slide show.
• This is not necessarily a good thing.
• Not only do people expect PowerPoint, they expect it to be dull.
• PowerPoint has become associated with puffed-up presentations by paid consultants, corny "interactive" discussions led by professional facilitators, and any dull event where you get a free pencil.
• The fact is, everyone should learn PowerPoint.
• But you need to learn to use it well, and you need to know when not to use it at all.

Reprinted by permission of Ellen Lupton

WRITE LESS

USE MORE SPACE

Reprinted by permission of Ellen Lupton

DON'T Use design elements to create "interest."

If your content is boring, design can't save you.

Reprinted by permission of Ellen Lupton

EXCITING BACKGROUND. DULL CONTENT.

- PowerPoint has become a ubiquitous medium of business communication.
- At sales meetings, training seminars, and conferences, the audience has come to expect a PowerPoint slide show.
- This is not necessarily a good thing.
- Not only do people expect PowerPoint, they expect it to be dull.
- PowerPoint has become associated with puffed-up presentations by paid consultants, corny "interactive" discussions led by professional facilitators, and any dull event where you get a free pencil.
- The fact is, everyone should learn PowerPoint.
- But you need to learn to use it well, and you need to know when not to use it at all.

Reprinted by permission of Ellen Lupton

DO Use design elements to build or emphasize content.

Colors, boxes, bullets, and font variations CAN make your presentation more clear and meaningful.

Reprinted by permission of Ellen Lupton

USE A HIERARCHY OF FONT SIZES AND SHORT BULLET POINTS

People expect PowerPoint during

- puffed-up presentations by paid consultants
- corny meetings led by professional facilitators
- any event where you get a free pencil

Reprinted by permission of Ellen Lupton

Reprinted by permission of Ellen Lupton

Reprinted by permission of Ellen Lupton

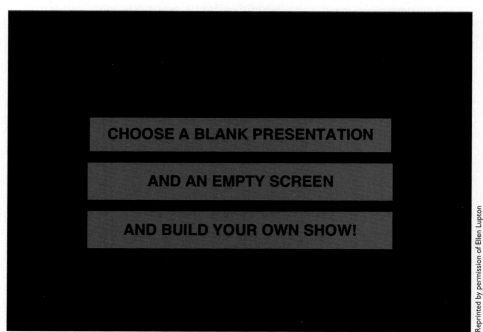

Reprinted by permission of Ellen Lupton

Reprinted by permission of Ellen Lupton

EXAMINING POWERPOINT

1. Edward R. Tufte says that PowerPoint has a particular "cognitive style" that is "disturbing" in schools. How would you define the "cognitive style" Tufte is pointing to? What does he see as the problem? How do the examples of "good" and "bad" PowerPoint design illustrate Tufte's point?

2. Compare Tufte's sense of "good" and "bad" PowerPoint design to Ellen Lupton's "Dos and Don'ts of PowerPoint." Do they seem to share similar assumptions about information design? What do you see as the main similarities and differences?

3. Consider Tufte's assertion that "PowerPoint's pushy style seeks to set up the speaker's dominance over the audience." Explain what Tufte is getting at. Take into account how he reinforces his point with the visual satire of the "totalitarian impact of presentation software."

4. Use Tufte's ideas, Lupton's advice, and your own sense of what PowerPoint can do well and not so well to design your own examples of "good" and "bad" PowerPoint slides. Imagine you are making a presentation to your class on a topic you know a lot about. Explain what makes the "good" slides "good" and the "bad" slides "bad."

chapter 22

essay exams

Essay examinations are challenging writing situations. Whether the exam consists of identification items, short-answer questions, full-length essays, or a combination, you have to write under pressure.

As many students can attest (and many teachers remember from their days as students), these pressures can be anxiety provoking. Small wonder. After all, something real is on the line, you can't know in advance exactly what will appear on the exam, and you have to produce on the spot, often by juggling multiple parts of a test. At the same time, writing under pressure can push you to new insights and unforeseen connections—when the course material seems to jell in ways you had not quite imagined.

The writing task you face on essay exams can be stated quite simply: you need to produce a good first draft in the time you're given. To do this, you'll need to develop an overall approach to writing essay exams. Developing a systematic strategy is your best bet to deal with the pressures of an essay exam and to maximize your performance. In the following sections, we'll look at three basic steps of successful exam writing:

1. Analyzing the format and questions of an exam.
2. Planning an answer.
3. Writing the essay exam.

ANALYZING ESSAY EXAMS

As you begin taking an essay exam, you can save yourself a lot of problems by paying close attention to the overall format of the exam and by reading each question carefully.

SURVEYING THE FORMAT

Before you start writing answers to exam questions, take time to survey the format of the exam. Notice how many questions there are, how many points each one carries, and any directions about how long an answer should be or how much space the exam allots to it.

Use this information to divide your time so that you'll be able to answer each question. Careful time management can keep you from running out of time.

As you survey the exam, make some tentative decisions about which questions to answer when choices are offered, and the order you will follow. You don't have to take the exam from start to finish. Students often find they do their best when they begin with the questions that seem the easiest to them. By doing the easiest questions first, you can build some confidence before tackling questions you find more difficult.

ANALYZING EXAM QUESTIONS

Analyzing exam questions is really a matter of recognizing the type of question and then clarifying what the question is calling on you to do. The three most common types of questions that call for written answers are identification items (often called IDs), short-answer questions, and essays. They differ in the length of writing called for and in the points they carry. Usually you can tell the type of question at a glance, according to its format, the directions it gives, and the amount of space provided for an answer.

Identification Items (IDs)

Identification items normally call for short statements that identify or define material from the course. You'll frequently get a series of items, and usually each item will carry only a few points.

Sample ID Items (from Media and Mass Communication)

Define each term in a sentence or two. (2 points each)

a. cognitive dissonance
b. agenda-setting
c. technological determinism
d. hot and cool media
e. gate-keepers

ID items such as these call on you to define course topics clearly and concisely. Most often, you'll have only a few minutes to spend on each item. For example,

a. Cognitive dissonance is a state of psychological discomfort that occurs when information a person receives is inconsistent with the person's already held attitudes.

Short-Answer Questions

Short-answer questions call for answers that can range from a sentence or two to a mini-essay. Typically short answers are a paragraph or two in length. Depending on the question, you'll have anywhere from a few minutes to ten minutes or so to write your answer.

Sample Short-Answer Questions (from General Chemistry)

Answer each question in a sentence or two. (5 points each)

1. Contrast *mass* and *weight.*
2. Define the word *molecule.*
3. Explain the relationships among the number of protons, neutrons, and electrons in an atom.
4. Compare *physical processes* with *chemical processes.*
5. Describe how a percent yield is calculated for a chemical reaction.

Note that a key term in each question—*contrast, define, explain, compare,* and *describe*—gives directions about what to do with course topics such as "mass," "weight," "molecule," and so on.

Sample Short-Answer Questions (from Early American History)

Write a paragraph or two on each of the following items. Define the term and explain why it is significant. (10 points each)

1. The Glorious Revolution
2. The Middle Passage
3. Virgin Soil Epidemics

Note that the key terms in this question call first for the recall of information about a particular course topic (*define*) and second for an elaboration of its significance (*explain*). For example,

1. The Glorious Revolution

In 1688, James II baptized his first son a Catholic, thereby perpetuating a Catholic monarchy in England. Fed up with James's arbitrary rule, parliamentary leaders responded by inviting James's Protestant daughter Mary and her husband William of Orange to take over as king and queen. James fled to France, and this bloodless change in the monarchy became known as the Glorious Revolution.

The Glorious Revolution had significant effects on the colonies. Colonists in Boston arrested the royal governor Sir Edward Andros and restored the colonial assembly he had tried to abolish. The Bill of Rights and Toleration Act passed by parliament in 1689 limited the power of rulers and guaranteed a degree of religious freedom. More importantly, the Glorious Revolution set a precedent for revolution against the king. John Locke's defense of the Glorious Revolution, *Two Treatises on Government* (1690), profoundly influenced political thinking in the colonies by arguing that when rulers violated the people's natural rights, they had the right to overthrow their government.

Essay Questions

Essay questions are usually allotted more time and more points on an exam than ID items and short-answer questions. You'll have more time to plan and write your response. Typically for essay questions you will be given anywhere from twenty minutes to an hour.

As is true of ID items and short-answer questions, the secret to writing effective exam essays is recognizing what the question calls on you to do.

■ WORKING TOGETHER

Analyzing Essay Questions

Working with two or three classmates, analyze the essay questions listed in the "Common Essay Exam Questions" box below. What key terms are given—directions and topics? What information would you need to answer the question successfully? What does each question call on students to do in their answers?

COMMON ESSAY EXAM QUESTIONS

❑ **Summarize main ideas.** Asks you to recall main ideas and present them clearly and accurately. Example from an anthropology course:

In their article "The Consequences of Literacy," Ian Watt and Jack Goody trace changes that occur with the rise of literacy. What do they see as the main differences between oral and literate cultures? In their view, what are the main consequences of literacy?

❑ **Explain significance.** Asks you to explain the importance of course material by giving reasons and examples. Example from a history of science course:

Watson's and Crick's discovery in 1953 of the double helical structure of DNA ushered in the "molecular revolution." What exactly did they discover? Explain the significance of their discovery to the field of biology. Give examples to illustrate the "molecular revolution" they initiated.

❑ **Apply concepts.** Asks you to apply concepts to works studied in the course or to your own experience. Example from an African American literature course:

The theme of "passing" as white appears in a number of important African American

novels. Analyze the theme of "passing" in at least three of the following novels we've read: Frances E.W. Harper's *Iola Leroy*, James P. Johnson's *Autobiography of an Ex-Coloured Man*, Jessie Faucett's *Plum Bun*, Nella Larsen's *Passing*. What do you see as the main differences and similarities in the treatment of this theme?

Example from a sociology course:

Define Erving Goffman's notion of "under-life" behavior. Explain how and why it takes place and in what contexts. Use the notion of "underlife" to explain behavior you have observed or read about.

❑ **Discuss a quotation.** Asks you to comment on a quotation you are seeing for the first time. Often written by your instructor, these quotations will typically raise a controversial point to discuss. Example from an American history course:

"The coming of the Civil War and the failures of Reconstruction have been seen by historians and others as failures of morality. This is wrong. The problems were actually political. Smarter politicians could have resolved these problems easily." How would you respond to this argument?

❏ **Compare and contrast.** Asks you to analyze similarities and differences between two works or ideas. Example from a Latin American literature course:

> Julia Alvarez's *How the Garcia Girls Lost Their Accents* and Cristina Garcia's *Dreaming in Cuban* both treat issues of immigration and acculturation. Compare and contrast the two novels' exploration of cultural identity and change.

❏ **Analyze causes.** Asks you to explain why and how something happened. Example from a film course:

> Explain the emergence of film noir in Hollywood films of the 1940s and 1950s. What values, beliefs, and ideologies of the time do these films embody?

> Example from a Russian history course:

> What factors led to Stalin's consolidation of control in the Soviet Union?

❏ **Evaluate.** Asks you to make a judgment about the strengths and weaknesses of one or more works or concepts. Example from a mass communication course:

> Evaluate the debate between Walter Lippmann in *The Phantom Public* and John Dewey in *The Public and Its Problems.* Explain the respective positions each thinker takes on the role of the public in political life. What do you see as the strengths and weaknesses of their arguments? Where do you stand in the debate?

❏ **Propose a course of action.** Asks you to analyze a problem and propose your own solution. Example from an education course:

> Briefly summarize the arguments for and against bilingual education. Then explain what you think should be done. Be specific in describing the kinds of programs you think can be successful.

❏ **Synthesize a number of sources.** Asks you to develop a coherent framework to pull together ideas and information from a number of sources. Example from a management course:

> You have read case studies of managerial strategies in a number of major companies—IBM, Nike, Harley Davidson, Apple, and General Motors. Based on these readings, explain what you see as the major challenges currently facing management. Use information from the case studies to illustrate your points.

PLANNING YOUR ANSWER

How you plan your exam answer depends largely on the type of question and the time and points allotted to it. Answering ID items, for example, should take you just a few seconds to recall the key information you need. For short-answer questions that call for a paragraph or two, you may want to underline key terms in the question or write down a few quick notes to help you organize your answer.

Full-length essays, of course, will require more planning time. In fact, it's not unusual to spend a quarter of the time allotted planning an answer. Here are some guidelines for planning:

■ Read the question carefully, noting key terms to clarify what your purpose should be. What kind of answer is the question calling for? What is the topic of the question? Are you being asked simply to define, describe, or summarize? To what extent are you asked to analyze, interpret, evaluate, or argue according to your own understanding of the material?

■ See if the question offers any organizational cues. If the question has multiple parts, consider whether these parts offer a possible scheme to arrange your answer. Often the parts consist of questions that lead logically from one to another.

■ Write a brief outline of key points. Begin with the main point—the response that answers the main question being asked. Then decide how to arrange supporting reasons, details, and examples.

■ Before you start writing, double-check your outline to make sure it answers what the question asks—not what you want it to say.

Notice how the brief outline below uses the essay question to organize an answer.

Sample Essay Question

You have read arguments for and against legislation to make English the official language in the United States. Write an essay that explains why this has become such a controversial issue. What is at stake for each side in the debate? Explain your own position, citing evidence to support it.

Sample Brief Outline

Main point: Demographic changes in the U.S. and the "new immigration" from Latin America and Asia have called national identity into question.
Pro: Desire for national unity
Anxiety about immigration
Belief that "old immigrants" (1890–1920) assimilated and learned English quickly
Con: U.S. as nation of immigrants
Value of many languages in global economy
Belief in multiculturalism
My position: Against English Only legislation
For increased language classes for recent immigrants

WRITING A GOOD ANSWER

Writing a good answer on an essay exam amounts to producing a good first draft. You can make additions and corrections, but you won't have the time to do thorough revisions. Here are some suggestions to help you write an effective answer:

■ Essay exams responses don't need introductions to set up the main point. State the main answer to the question in the opening paragraph. One good strategy is to use the question (or main question when there is a series) as the basis of your opening sentence. Answer the question as clearly as you can.

- Provide supporting evidence, reasons, details, and examples in the paragraphs that follow. Draw on material from lectures and readings, but don't pad with extraneous material. You don't need to show off how much you can recall. Instead, you need to show how you can relate supporting evidence to your main answer.

- Write an ending, even if you're running out of time. A sentence or two can tie together main points at the end.

- Make additions neatly. New ideas may occur to you as you're writing, and you should incorporate them if they fit into the main line of your thinking. You can add a sentence or two by writing neatly in the margins and using an arrow to show where they go in your answer.

- Write legibly and proofread when you've finished. You can make corrections by crossing out and replacing words and phrases. Do so as neatly as you can. A messy exam is hard to read and creates a negative impression.

- Watch the clock. If you're running out of time or need to go on to another question, it's best to list points from your outline. This way you can show where your essay is going, even if you can't finish it.

SAMPLE ESSAY ANSWERS

The following essay question appeared on an exam in a colonial Latin American history course.

Sample Essay Question

"Latin America's ruling elites maintained their position largely through ideological domination. Witness their ability to make patriarchy an unchallenged social assumption. Aside from such exceptional figures as Sor Juana, women at every level of society readily accepted their inferior status, along with the rigid gender conventions that called for female passivity, obedience, and sexual modesty." Discuss.

As you can see, the essay question is a quotation that takes a position on issues in the course, along with the direction "discuss." The key term *discuss* doesn't seem to provide a lot of guidance, but experienced students know that *discuss* really calls on them to offer their own interpretation of the quotation, along with reasons and supporting evidence from readings and lecture.

Two sample essay answers follow. The first is annotated. You can use the second one to sharpen your own sense of an effective essay answer.

SAMPLE ESSAY ANSWER A

Connects key terms in essay question to establish main focus of the answer

Although Latin American elites frequently used a policy of coercion to govern indigenous and African populations, they also used consent to maintain their position in colonial society through ideological domination. Colonial society was based on a hierarchical system of authority and dependence, in which the ruling elite established strong ties with the ruled through a shared ideology. Patriarchy, the social assumption that men were responsible for controlling the lives of women, was central to this shared ideology.

Explains key term "patriarchal ideology"

The colonial elite based its political and moral authority on the patriarchal ideology of men's superiority, masculinity, and honor and women's inferiority, modesty, and submission. Dignified men acquired their authority by controlling and protecting their dependents—women, servants, workers, and slaves. Women, on the other hand, were socialized to be modest and obedient and were regarded as dangerous and likely to succumb to temptations, instincts, and desires unless controlled by fathers and husbands.

Illustrates key term with details and an example

From father to husband, men had power over a woman's sexuality. Marriage was used by fathers to improve their status and make alliances with other families. Little consideration was given to a woman's own preferences. Once married, a woman was subordinate to her husband. The crime of rape, for example, was seen not as a crime against the woman but rather an assault on the honor of her father or husband. In cases of rape, fathers or husbands would publicly profess their shame, humiliation, and lack of honor for failing to protect a daughter or wife.

Notes exceptions and gives examples of exceptions

There were certain groups that posed exceptions to this gender ideology of male control and female dependence. Heiresses, nuns, and widows negotiated a certain amount of autonomy in specific circumstances. For example, the Condessa de Santiago inherited a fortune and became a powerful economic and political force—until she married and her power ended. Nuns such as Sor Juana found a limited space for self-expression in the convent, as demonstrated by the numerous literary works produced by nuns. Widows were the largest group of autonomous women. By law, dowries reverted to widows when their husbands died. However, women without husbands, especially widows, were suspected of immoral acts. The legend of La Florona, the "weeping widow," illustrates how autonomous women were seen as uncontrolled and threatening.

Analyzes role of patriarchal ideology among plebeian women

In the lower classes, there was a significant gap between the theory and practice of patriarchal ideology. Plebeian women were in the public sphere much more than elite women not because of their greater autonomy but because of financial necessity. The labor these women did as vendors, seamstresses, and domestic servants was hardly empowering, and they were often subjected to verbal, physical, and sexual abuse. In this way, they still adhered to the system of patriarchy and remained the dependents of their male employers.

Analyzes role of patriarchal ideology among plebeian men

For men, masculinity, honor, and social superiority were achieved by controlling dependents. By accepting such a patriarchal ideology, male plebeians, servants, and slaves were constantly reminded of their own position as dependents, with little economic or political authority over their lives. Lower-class and slave men could not exercise the type of patriarchal control and protect their women as the upper classes did. But because the lower classes believed in patriarchal control, they in effect consented to the moral and political leadership of the upper classes.

Ending ties key terms together

Morality, dignity, and honor, thus, were identified with the ruling elite in colonial society. This gender ideology reinforced the power of the ruling elite as both women and plebeian men consented to its patriarchal assumptions.

SAMPLE ESSAY ANSWER B

Depending on the circumstances, the ruling elite in colonial Latin America used force or consent to govern. For example, they routinely used military power against the Indian population and to suppress slave revolts. In addition, the Inquisition in Latin America used physical force, including torture to eliminate dissent.

Ideological domination was an important tool of the ruling elite, and patriarchy became one of the unchallenged social assumptions that reinforced the authority of the upper classes. The view was widely held by members of colonial society that men were the natural rulers and that women should be controlled by men. Men were considered authoritative, while women were supposed to be obedient.

Thus women in colonial society were excluded from both economic and political power. Excluded from the priesthood, higher education, and the professions, women were forced to remain in the home. This dependence reinforced male authority and kept women powerless and unable to challenge dominant social assumptions. Because women were the socializers of the family, they transferred this gender ideology to their children and thereby further reproduced the system.

If a woman misbehaved, she would dishonor her father or husband and her household. A stain on a woman's reputation tainted the reputation of her entire family. It was therefore a man's responsibility to control a woman and protect her against herself and keep her in the domestic sphere. Fathers decided the person a woman would marry or if she should become a nun. An unmarried woman in the presence of unmarried men was always accompanied by a chaperone to guard her virtue. Husbands controlled their wives and protected them. By engraining women with the dominant ideology of patriarchy, the elite were able to rule without opposition.

This gender ideology, however, did not transfer completely to the lower classes in colonial society because in order to be proper, women had to come from wealthy families. Single lower-class women often worked before they married, and this was considered threatening to their morals. Still, plebeian women did view males as authority figures. Once they married, they were subordinated to their husbands and restricted to the home. Women were considered devious and threatening and therefore needed to be protected and controlled by male authority.

Lower-class men, however, never achieved total patriarchal power and were in no position to challenge authority figures or social assumptions. While they accepted the rigid gender conventions of the dominant ideology, plebeian men remained dependents in relation to the upper classes. Due to their servile and economically insecure position in society, plebeians could not fully protect their women, which was one of the prerequisites of full manhood as colonial society understood it.

Nuns, heiresses, and widows were able in limited ways to evade patriarchal control. Except for priests, men were basically excluded from convents, and so to some extent the nuns could organize their own affairs. Heiresses might achieve a measure of autonomy by inheriting money, and widows received their dowries if their husbands died.

Overall, though, the gender ideology of patriarchy in colonial Latin America was very unfair to women in general and was used to keep lower-class men in their place.

■ **WORKING TOGETHER**

Analyzing an Essay Answer

In a group with two or three other students, follow these steps:

1. Look again at the sample essay question on page 591. What exactly does it call on students to do? Clarify for yourselves what seems to be the main writing task facing students who are taking this exam in colonial Latin American history.

2. Read the first sample essay answer and annotations. How well do you think it handles the writing task?

3. Read and analyze the second essay answer. Given your sense of what the writing task calls for and how well the first essay answer handles the task, what do you see as the strengths and weaknesses of the second answer? Be specific. What particular features of the essay work well or not so well?

writing portfolios

In a writing portfolio, students present a sample of their work as the culminating project of a writing class. Students typically select from among their various writing assignments and revise a limited number for their portfolios. This allows students to decide on the writing they want to present to the teacher for evaluation—and to show their teachers how they have handled different kinds of writing tasks. Portfolios also provide students with the opportunity to reflect on how they have developed as writers and to explain what the writing they've done means to them as students, learners, and people.

How teachers or writing programs ask students to put together portfolios varies. In this chapter, we present some options and examples of what might included in a writing portfolio.

SOME OPTIONS FOR A WRITING PORTFOLIO

Here are some types of writing often included in portfolios.

A REFLECTIVE LETTER

Almost all writing portfolios begin with a letter of reflection that introduces you and your portfolio. The purpose of such a letter is to persuade your instructor (or any other readers) that you have accomplished the goals of the course.

A reflective letter might discuss the choices you made in designing your portfolio, explain your development as a writer and the role of writing in your life, evaluate strengths and weaknesses in your writing, and discuss your experience as a writer and as a person in your writing class. The letter should provide readers with a sense of who you are. It might also indicate where you see yourself going next in developing your writing.

The writing you have done in response to the "Reflecting on Your Writing" assignments throughout the book can provide you with material for your reflective letter.

SAMPLE REFLECTIVE LETTER BY JENNIFER PRINCIPE

Dear Professor Trimbur:

Writing has always been an important form of expression for me. I have always had a hard time expressing myself verbally, and I feel that writing gives me a control over my words that I can't find anywhere else. Writing has almost become a form of medication for me, an objective ear always willing to listen. For as long as I can remember, I have kept a journal that I write in whenever there is something I want to straighten out in my life. My journal is one of the best ways I know to explore my thoughts and decide on a course of action to take. Writing forces me to slow down and really consider how I feel about something. It also creates a permanent record that I can go back to at any time.

Although I enjoy and rely on this sort of informal writing, I have felt for a long time that the formal writing I do in my courses could use improvement, and English 101 has definitely helped me to grow as a formal writer. In high school, my English teachers told me I had good ideas but that my writing was wordy and unfocused. I understood what they were saying, but unfortunately they never explained what I should do about my problem. This made writing a very frustrating experience for me.

In English 101, I think the most important thing I learned is that when I start writing I usually don't have a definite idea of where I am going. What I have found through the writing assignments and the peer commentaries is that my main ideas are often unclear at first, but as I get to the end of a draft they become much clearer. As I write more, I begin to focus on an idea and my essay begins to make more sense. In many cases, I could take ideas from the end of a draft and bring them up to my introduction to give me focus.

The writing samples included in my portfolio were chosen with several criteria in mind. First, I chose writing that I had strong personal feelings about because when I believe in a topic my writing tends to be more passionate and heartfelt, and thus more effective. For this reason, the writing samples that are included in this portfolio are strongly rooted in my personal beliefs. Second, I chose different kinds of writing so readers could see how I approached various writing assignments.

I chose to include the peer commentary I wrote for Joe Scherpa. I don't think this was necessarily the best commentary I did, but I was particularly happy about Joe's reaction to it. A week or so after I completed the commentary, Joe told me that my commentary helped him do a complete revision on that assignment. He seemed grateful for my suggestions and happy with the revised version of his work. Although I realize that my commentary was not the sole motivation for his revisions, I was happy to see that he felt it had made a difference in his writing.

In conclusion, I feel this class has been quite beneficial in my growth as a writer. I got lots of practice in different kinds of writing. I'm planning to major in chemical engineering, and I know that writing will be an important part of my upcoming career, as well as in my personal life. For my career, writing will be a tool that I will often need to get my point across. I feel that I need to work on knowing when to put personal opinions into my writing and when I should be more objective. Sometimes I get carried away by my feelings about a topic. This class has helped me to understand different writing situations, and I think I am now better able to see when the personal side is appropriate and when it's not.

REVISED WRITING ASSIGNMENTS

Portfolios usually include revised writing assignments. This gives you the opportunity to review the work you have done over the course of a term and to decide which writings you want to bring to final form and which best represent your abilities. It's a good idea to select a range of purposes and a range of genres. Your teacher will tell you how many to include.

A CASE STUDY

Some teachers ask for a case study of one of the writing assignments, including a working draft, peer commentary, and the final version, as well as your own explanation of how you worked on the piece of writing. Case studies look in detail at how you planned, drafted, and revised one particular piece of writing. Case studies offer you the opportunity to analyze the choices you made. Be specific by examining how you drafted and revised a key passage or two.

SAMPLE CASE STUDY BY JOHN URBAN

Introduction

I decided to present my profile of Professor Karen Jackson as a case study because it is the paper I revised the most and the one I got the most helpful peer commentary on. I have included the working draft of the essay, the peer commentary I received, and the final draft.

The peer commentary made me realize a couple of things. First, I hadn't created a good opening to introduce Prof. Jackson. In the revised version, I try to take readers into her lab and give the feeling of meeting her in person.

Second, I think the dominant impression was shaky in the first draft. I was trying to use the idea of putting life into biology as the organizing theme, but it wasn't working. The peer commentary gave me the idea of using the idea of "real reasons" instead. I think this gave a way to link the opening discussion of the premed program to her teaching and research.

Third, I realized the quote about Prof. Jackson's research is both too technical and too long. I tried here and in some other places to cut back on the amount of quoting and to use quotes more effectively.

WORKING DRAFT

Putting the Life Back into Premedical Education: A Profile of Karen Jackson

Given such daunting requirements as organic chemistry and a year of physics, premed students are assumed to be learning science to become better doctors. Sadly, the message of service often gets left behind in the process. "That's the most frustrating thing about directing the premed program. I assume two things when students tell me they want to go to medical school. First, they are saying 'I am good at science,' and second 'I like working with people.'"

As a professor of biology, department chair, and the director of the premed program at Warehouse State, Karen Jackson works a busy schedule. Between trips to oversee her research project at Memorial Hospital, authorizing department spending, and teaching the introductory biology course, Professor Jackson also advises students interested in medical careers. The hardest part about running the premed program, she says, is "finding students who are in it for the right reasons, and persuading those who aren't to be in it for the right reasons."

A key to Karen Jackson's beliefs about advising premed students comes from decisions she has made in her own life. Early in her career, she was strictly a researcher, focusing on metabolic biochemistry, but she did not feel she was doing enough. "I love research, but I found I also needed the intellectual stimulation and challenge that teaching has provided me." She attributes her success as a teacher to having "perspective."

In her introductory biology course for non-majors, you will not find a class ruled by textbooks, tests, and labs. In this course, there are also discussions on real-life current events in biology. "I have students fill out a survey to find out what interests them. I would rather talk about something they are interested in than sit there and lecture from a book. Biology is not in a textbook. Biology is real life."

As a teacher, Professor Jackson sees the need for more community involvement by students interested in medical careers, as well as by college students in general. "I think there should be a degree requirement of community service. I ask my advisees what they've done for community service, and something to the effect, well, my fraternity raised money for diabetes research.' There is a fundamental misunderstanding there. I am asking what *you* personally have done to help the community, not what your organization has done. Being a doctor is about helping those who most need it, not just raising a little money."

Karen Jackson received a Ph.D. in zoology from the University of Massachusetts. From there, she did a postdoctoral fellowship for the Multiple Sclerosis Foundation at the Medical College of Virginia. As a medical researcher, she has also seen the darker side of her area of expertise. She comments on changes in the health care system. "The business side of medicine is ugly. I'd like to see medicine get back to what is important: the patient. Medicine is a service, and that's exactly what it should do, *serve* the people."

She uses the example of her postdoctoral work, in which a team of researchers identified a gene that when expressed in diabetes patients caused heart defects. "We wanted to publish our work, to let colleagues know what we had discovered, but we were stopped by the company that funded the research because it wanted to patent the gene in hopes of making money in the future." Professor Jackson stressed the importance of focusing research not on profits but on the goal of improving the lives of people.

Karen Jackson continues her research on diabetes when she is not managing the department, running the premed office, and teaching. She looks at the problem of cellular metabolism in diabetes patients. "The general aim of my work is to identify differences in cellular metabolism between normal and diabetic individuals. We use a rat model to study the signal transduction pathway for insulin, which ultimately results in glucose being stored as glycogen. This function is impaired in people with diabetes. Even when provided with insulin, they are unable to activate the enzymes responsible for glycogen synthesis, and since it is a complex and poorly understood pathway, sorting it out in normal cells may give us a handle on what might be changed in the diabetic state."

Whether in the classroom, office, or lab, Professor Jackson is undoubtedly working to put the life back into biology.

John,

I enjoyed reading this and feel like I'm beginning to understand what a unique person Professor Jackson is. You've got a lot of good information here, but I think you can do more to create a dominant impression of her and her work.

The main impression I get is someone who is trying to put the life back in biology, and that comes across to a certain extent but I'm not always sure of what you mean.

For example, the title and opening make it seem like the profile is going to focus on her work as premed adviser when the profile you've written is broader. Also, it wasn't clear in the first paragraph who is speaking. You haven't identified Prof. Jackson as the subject of the profile. You could probably do more in the beginning by setting the scene and introducing readers to Prof. Jackson. What you write about her emphasis on community service is interesting, and I wonder if there are any details you could give to show exactly what she means.

I found it a bit confusing when you shift from discussing what Prof. Jackson sees as the "right reasons" for being a premed student to her teaching and research. I pretty much expected to hear more about her sense of "right reasons."

Finally, I think Prof. Jackson's description of her research is too technical and hard to understand.

"Real Reasons": The Many Missions of Karen Jackson
The door says 405C, and I walk into the newly remodeled lab of Professor Karen Jackson. New countertops, sinks, cabinets, and shelves stand glistening

and ready for use, with just a hint of dust left from construction. In the middle of the room, however, resides the hulking mass of an old, defective heating unit that had been replaced by more reliable temperature controls. Even before I catch my first glimpse of Professor Jackson, I hear her voice as she talks on the phone to the contractor who redesigned 405C. "What do you mean you don't normally remove old equipment?!? That thing needs to go, and you need to find a way to haul it out of here."

Then I see her, wearing a t-shirt with a "Stop Domestic Violence" sign, jeans, and sneakers. I fidget nervously, hoping I don't fit in the same category as the contractor. As she hangs up the phone, she becomes aware of my presence, smiles warmly, and says, "Drat these details. You're just the guy I wanted to see. Let's talk."

Karen Jackson is a woman on many missions, and she plays a range of roles at Warehouse State—as a diabetes researcher, biology professor, department chair, and director of the premed program. She admits right away that "I can make people nervous because I know how I feel and am not afraid to voice my opinion." She has seen many aspects of biomedicine, and she doesn't always like what she sees.

She tells me that a crucial part of medicine is often overlooked by premed students, the importance of being involved in the community. She believes there should be a community service requirement for premeds and for college students in general. "I ask my advisees what they've done for the community," she says, "and they normally say something to the effect, 'well, my fraternity raised money for diabetes research.' There is a fundamental misunderstanding there. I am asking what *you* personally have done to help the community, not what your organization has done. Being a doctor is about helping those who most need it, not just raising a little money."

To help premed and other students see what she means, Professor Jackson has set up a number of community service projects on domestic violence and health needs assessment of recent immigrants. She pulls out a copy of a report she and premed students wrote on the health situation of Cambodians who have settled in the Worcester area. Working on a project like this, Professor Jackson says, can help premeds understand the "right reasons" for pursuing a medical career.

According to Jackson, there are many "wrong reasons to become a doctor. Premeds tell me one of their parents is a doctor or doctors make a lot of money." The "right reasons," she says, are "being good at science" and "liking to work with people." As she sees it, her job as director of the premed program centers on "finding students who are in it for the right reasons and persuading those who aren't to be in it for the right reasons."

Another mission Professor Jackson has embarked on is to improve the introductory biology course for non-majors, and here the issue of "right reasons" comes in again. In her course, you will not find a class ruled by textbooks, tests, and labs. In this course, there are also discussions on real-life current events in biology. The "real reason" to study biology, she says, is to understand living organisms and how biologists go about investigating, not to memorize details. She has students fill out a survey to see what questions they have about biology, and she routinely integrates such current topics as genetically modified food, mad cow disease, and environmental toxins to illustrate principles of biology. She wants her students to see that "biology is not in a textbook" but a matter of "real life."

Not all of Karen Jackson's missions are solo sorties. In her current research on diabetes, she works with a team at Memorial Hospital to identify the differences in cellular metabolism between normal and diabetic individuals. She got started as a medical researcher at the University of Massachusetts, where she received a Ph.D. in zoology. From there, she did a postdoctoral fellowship for the Multiple Sclerosis Foundation at the Medical College of Virginia. As a medical researcher, she has seen the darker side of her area of expertise. She comments on changes in the health care system. "The business side of medicine is ugly. I'd like to see medicine get back to what is important: the patient. Medicine is a service, and that's exactly what it should do, *serve* the people."

She uses the example of her postdoctoral work to highlight the "right reasons" to do biomedical research. In this case, she was on a team of researchers who identified a gene that when expressed in diabetes patients caused heart defects. "We wanted to publish our work, to let colleagues know what we had discovered, but we were stopped by the company that funded the research because it wanted to patent the gene in hopes of making money in the future." Professor Jackson stresses the importance of focusing research not on profits but on the goal of improving the lives of people.

Whether it is on the frontlines of biomedical research, in the classroom, or in advising premed students, Karen Jackson is on a mission. Her inescapable personality and warm demeanor work to motivate those around her. She may make some people nervous, like the contractor who remodeled her lab. But she has taken on the mission of challenging people to see the "right reasons" for what they do. And that's the way she likes it.

PEER COMMENTARY

If you have written peer commentaries about other students' work, you may want to include a representative one, prefaced with an explanation of what you learned through the peer commentaries and what it was like for you to do them.

SAMPLE INTRODUCTION TO PEER COMMENTARY BY MARGARET KING

At first, it was difficult to criticize a classmate's work for fear of being too harsh and possibly offending them. But as the term progressed, it became easier because I learned what to look for and how to make helpful suggestions.

I realized that as a writer I wanted my classmates to give me honest feedback and that the best peer commentaries I got didn't try to judge my working draft but to give me suggestions about what to do with it. I tried to apply these ideas to the peer commentaries I wrote. I think the peer commentaries gave me insight as a writer and helped me to learn to read more critically and make choices in the revision process.

COMMENTARY ON COLLABORATIVE WRITING

If you were involved in a collaborative writing project, you might write a short commentary about your experience. What role did you play in the group's work? How does collaborative writing differ from individual writing? What is gained? What, if anything, is lost? Explain your thoughts and feelings about your involvement in producing a group-written project.

SAMPLE INTRODUCTION TO COLLABORATIVE WRITING BY DAVID SANCHEZ

To me, group projects have both good and bad points. Luckily, however, I believe the good points outweigh the bad points. In my opinion, the worst part about doing a group project is setting up meetings. With an abundant amount of other work, finding a time that everyone can meet sometimes becomes difficult. In addition, when the group finally meets, you usually end up talking about other things and basically just hanging out. It seems that for every hour or so of a meeting, only about thirty minutes of work is done.

On a good note, however, the actual project usually produces an interesting result. By having more than one person work on a project, especially a written one, a better result will usually come out. Each person adds a different view and also finds mistakes others have missed. As we have seen through our writing assignments, no one can write a perfect paper the first time. Through each peer commentary, many possible areas of improvement come to light and therefore a better final paper. The same is true of writing a paper with other people.

An additional drawback to writing a group paper, however, is that since it is written by more than one person, more than one idea is conveyed. Yes, as I said before, this is good in a way, but it also makes it harder to write a creative paper. Each person ends up having to modify their view in order to go along with everyone else.

Another bad thing, which can arise from some group projects, occurs when one or more people in the group do not do their parts. When this happens, the other people in the group end up doing too much work and get frustrated. I was happy to find that both John and Joe were willing to do the work. We first met a couple of times to decide on a topic for the project and to begin work. Next we all contributed to the collection of data for the survey. We then divided the paper into three sections, and each wrote one. Finally we had a meeting in order to bring the three parts together and to write an introduction and a conclusion.

Overall, I enjoyed doing the group project with John and Joe. Prior to doing it, I had not known either of them very well. Through this project, I can say that I have become friends with both of them. We all worked together quite well and produced a project I was happy with.

SAMPLES OF EXPLORATORY WRITING

If you have done exploratory writing, you could include a few samples that, for whatever reason, you like the most. Write an introduction that explains what it was like for you to do exploratory writing, what you learned, how this kind of writing differs from other writing assignments, the benefits you see, and so on.

SAMPLE INTRODUCTION TO EXPLORATORY WRITING BY JOHN HOGAN

Exploratory writing was one of my favorite things in this course. When doing this type of writing, I felt free to say what I wanted, any way I wanted. All of this freedom allowed me to put down on paper exactly what I was thinking. Usually when writing a more formal paper, I find that as I am writing I spend too much time making sure everything is structurally and grammatically correct. Many times I lose sight of some of my new ideas, as I try to perfect the previous ones. Here, there was no pattern or structure that had to be followed. When doing exploratory writing I simply wrote and did not worry about grammar, spelling, unity, or coherence.

MISCELLANEOUS

Depending on your teacher's directions, you may include a miscellany of writing done in or out of class—letters, notes, email, newsgroup dialog, poetry, fiction, posters, leaflets, flyers, and so on. Introduce these writings and explain what called on you to write them and how they differ from the other writing in your portfolio.

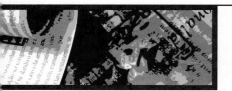

credits

TEXT CREDITS

Abraham, Verghese. Reprinted with the permission of Simon & Schuster Inc. and William Morris Endeavor Entertainment, LLC, on behalf of the author from *My Own Country: A Doctor's Story of a Town and Its People in the Age of AIDS* by Abraham Verghese. Copyright © 1994 by Abraham Verghese. All rights reserved.

Baldwin, James. "My Dungeon Shook: Letter to My Nephew on the One Hundredth Anniversary of the Emancipation," © 1962 by James Baldwin. Originally published in *The Progressive.* Collected in *The Fire Next Time,* published by Vintage Books. Copyright renewed. Reprinted by arrangement with the James Baldwin Estate.

Bartoy, Kevin M. *Stimulate the Economy – Forgive Student Loans,* Sponsored by: Kevin M. Bartoy.

Boxer, Sara. From "I Shop, Ergo I Am: The Mall as Society's Mirror," *New York Times,* March 28, 1998. © 1998 *The New York Times.* All rights reserved. Used by permission and protected by the Copyright Laws of the United States. The printing, copying, redistribution, or retransmission of the Material without express written permission is prohibited.

Braun, Lundy, PhD. "How to Fight the New Epidemics," *Providence Journal-Bulletin,* May 29, 1995. Reprinted by permission.

Butterfield, Fox. From "Studies of Mental Illness Show Links to Violence / New Finding Cites Role of Substance Abuse", *New York Times,* May 15, 1998. © 1998 *The New York Times.* All rights reserved. Used by permission and protected by the Copyright Laws of the United States. The printing, copying, redistribution, or retransmission of the Material without express written permission is prohibited.

"Call for a Moratorium on Executions," Fall 1999. Reprinted by permission of Equal Justice USA.

© comScore Media Metrix. http://www.pewinternet.org/Presentations/2009/17-Teens-and-Social-Media-An-Overview.aspx.

Cushman, Ellen. Reprinted by permission from *The Struggle and the Tools: Oral and Literate Strategies in an Inner City Community* by Ellen Cushman. The State University of New York Press, © 1998 State University of New York. All rights reserved.

Dargis, Manohla. From "Orphan's Lifeline Out of Hell Could Be a Game Show in Mumbai." *New York Times.* November 12, 2008. © 2008 *The New York Times.* All rights reserved. Used by permission and protected by the Copyright Laws of the United States. The printing, copying, redistribution, or retransmission of the Material without express written permission is prohibited.

Didion, Joan, "Los Angeles Notebook," from *Slouching Towards Bethlehem* by Joan Didion. Copyright © 1966, 1968, renewed 1996 by Joan Didion. Reprinted by permission of Farrar, Straus and Giroux LLC.

Dillard, Annie. From *An American Childhood,* Copyright © 1987 by Annie Dillard. Reprinted by permission of HarperCollins Publishers, Inc.

DiMartile, Katie. "Roadside Memorials." Reprinted with permission from the author.

Douglass, Frederick. From *Narrative of the Life of Frederick Douglass.* Yale University Press, 2001. Copyright © 2001 by Yale University Press. All rights reserved. Reproduced by permission.

Dreifus, Claudia. From "A Conversation with Pauline Wiessner: Where Gifts and Stories Are Crucial to Survival," *New York Times.* May 26, 2009. © 2009 *The New York Times.* All rights reserved. Used by permission and protected by the Copyright Laws of the United States. The printing, copying, redistribution, or retransmission of the Material without express written permission is prohibited.

Faludi, Susan. From "Shannon Faulkner's Strength in Numbers," Copyright © 1995 by Susan Faludi. First appeared in the *New York Times.* Reprinted by permission of the author and the Sandra Dijkstra Literary Agency.

Felson, Richard B., and Gmelch, George. "Uncertainty and the Use of Magic," *Current Anthropology* 20.3 (1979): 587–89. Copyright © 1979, Wenner-Gren Foundation for Anthropological Research. Reproduced by permission of University of Chicago Press.

Finders, Margaret. Reprinted by permission of the publisher. From Margaret Finders, *Just Girls: Hidden Literacies and life in Junior High.* New York: Teachers College Press. Copyright © 1997 by Teachers College, Columbia University. All rights reserved.

"First Things First Manifesto 2000" is being published in its entirety, with 33 signatories' names, in *Adbusters, Emigre,* and the *AIGA Journal* in North America, in *Eye* and *Blueprint* in Britain, in *Items* in the Netherlands, and *Form* in Germany. A poster version will be designed by *Adbusters* and dispatched to design schools around the world.

Frere-Jones, Sasha. *The Queen, Beyonce at last, The New Yorker,* February 9, 2009. © 2009 by Sasha Frere-Jones. Reprinted by permission.

Gmelch, George and Felson, Richard. "Can a Lucky Charm Get You Through Organic Chemistry?" *Psychology Today* (December 1980): 75–77. Reprinted with permission from Psychology Today Magazine, Copyright © 1980 Sussex Publishers, LLC.

Goodman, Ellen. "Minneapolis Pornography Ordinance," *Boston Globe,* 1984. © 1984, The Washington Post Writers Group. Reprinted with permission.

Gordon, Jennifer. From "Workers Without Borders." *New York Times* March 10, 2009. © 2008 *The New York Times*. All rights reserved. Used by permission and protected by the Copyright Laws of the United States. The printing, copying, redistribution, or retransmission of the Material without express written permission is prohibited.

© Greenpeace

Hari, Johann. "You've Been Lied to About the Pirates" in *The Independent* (UK). January 5, 2009. Copyright © 2009 *The Independent*. Reproduced by permission.

Heller, Andre. Letter and four page report, Doctors without borders. Reproduced by permission.

Hoard, Christian. "Review of "I Am Sasha Fierce" by Christian Hoard. © Rolling Stone LLC 2008. All Rights Reserved. Reprinted by permission.

Hoffman, Richard. From "The Ninth Letter of the Alphabet: First-Person Strategies in Nonfiction." Reprinted with permission from the author.

Ikle, Fred C. "Kill the Pirates" in *Washington Post*. April 13, 2009.

Lewis, David C., M.D. "Meth Science Not Stigma: Open Letter to the Media," July 25, 2005. Reprinted by permission of the author.

Liu, Eric. "Remember When Public Spaces Didn't Carry Brand Names?" *USA Today*, March 25, 1999. Reprinted by permission of the author.

Marsh, Bill. From "Warmer Fuzzier, the Refreshed Logo," *Sunday New York Times*, May 31, 2009, © 2008 *The New York Times*. All rights reserved. Used by permission and protected by the Copyright Laws of the United States. The printing, copying, redistribution, or retransmission of the Material without express written permission is prohibited.

Marsh, Dave. *Fortunate Son* by Dave Marsh, 1985. xv–xxvi. Copyright 1985 by Duke and Duchess Ventures, Inc. Reprinted with permission.

Mauer, Marc. From "The Changing Racial Dynamics of the War on Drugs." Copyright © *The Sentencing Project*. Reprinted with permission.

McGrath, Charles. "The Pleasures of the Text," *The New York Times Magazine*, January 22, 2006. Copyright © 2006 by Charles McGrath. Reprinted by permission of The New York Times Syndication Sales Corp.

"Mentally Ill People Aren't More Violent, Study Finds," as appeared in *Providence Journal-Bulletin*, May 14, 1995. Reprinted with permission of The Associated Press.

Montague, Julian. ©2009 Julian Montague. Used with permission

Ouellette, Laurie. Excerpt from "Building the Third Wave: Reflections from a Young Feminist." Reprinted by permission of *On the Issues: The Progressive Women's Quarterly*, Summer 1992, copyrighted by Merle Hoffman Enterprises, Ltd.

Passel, Jeffrey S., and Cohn, D'Vera. "A Portrait of Unauthorized Immigrants in the United States," Pew Hispanic Center. © 2009 Pew Hispanic Center. Reprinted with permission of Pew Hispanic Center, a Pew Research Center Project. http://pewhispanic.org/reports/report.php?ReportID=107

Patinkin, Mark. "Commit a crime, suffer the consequences," in *The Providence Journal-Bulletin*, April 19, 1994. Reprinted by permission.

PEN Center USA

Peters, Darcy and Boldt, Marcus. "Exchange of Letters Regarding a Readiness to Learn Family Learning Center." Copyright © Pew Internet & American Life Project. Reprinted with permission.

Petition "Call on Kenya to ease the suffering of Nairobi's 2 million slum dwellers," June 9, 2009, Amnesty International. All rights reserved. Reproduced by permission. Copyright © Pew Internet & American Life Project. Reprinted with permission.

© Phonak

Pierce, Jason L., Petition. "Tiger Woods—Stand Up for Equality—Augusta National Golf Club," from www.thepetitionsite.com

Powell, Kevin. "My Culture at the Crossroads." *Newsweek,* October 9, 2000. © Newsweek, Inc. All rights reserved. Reprinted by permission.

Quindlen, Anna. "Abortion Is Too Complex To Feel All One Way About" in *New York Times.* March 13, 1986. Reprinted by permission of International Creative Management, Inc. Copyright © 1986 by Anna Quindlen for *The New York Times.*

Quitadamo, Richard. "A Lawyer's Crusade Against Tobacco," Reprinted by permission of the author.

Rose, Mike. "Portraits of Thinking: An Account of a Common Laborer." Copyright © Mike Rose. Reprinted with permission.

Rose, Tricia. "Beware the Manipulation of the Funk" from *The Hip Hop Wars.* Basic Books, 2008. Copyright © 2008 by Basic Books. Reprinted by permission of Basic Books, a member of Perseus Books Group.

Satrapi, Marjane. "The Veil" from *Persepolis: The Story of Childhood* by Marjane Satrapi, translated by Mattia Ripa and Blake Feris. Copyright © 2003 by L'Association, Paris, France. Used by permission of Pantheon Books, a division of Random House, Inc.

Sengupta, Somini. From "An Empire for Poor Working Women, Guided by a Gandhian Approach." *New York Times.* March 6, 2009, © 2009 *The New York Times.* All rights reserved. Used by permission and protected by the Copyright Laws of the United States. The printing, copying, redistribution, or retransmission of the Material without express written permission is prohibited

Spiegelman, Art. From *In the Shadow of No Towers* by Art Spiegelman, copyright © 2004 by Art Spiegelman. Used by permission of Pantheon Books, a division of Random House, Inc. and Penguin Group UK.

Stanley, Michael. "My Town". Reprinted by permission of Sweet City Records Inc. and Michael Stanley Music.

Tardiff, Kristin. Letter to the Editor, *The Providence Journal-Bulletin,* May 3, 1994 reprinted by permission of the author.

Taylor, John N. Letter to the Editor, *The Providence Journal-Bulletin,* May 9, 1994 reprinted by permission of the author.

Tufte, Edward R. "PowerPoint is Evil." Reprinted by permission, Edward R. Tufte, *The Cognitive Style of PowerPoint* (Cheshire, CT: Graphics Press, 2003), as appeared in *Wired Magazine,* September 2003.

Watson, James and Crick, Francis. "A Structure for Deoxyribose Nucleic Acid," *Nature* Vol. 171, 25 April 1953: 737-738.

W.E.B. DuBois Institute, Harvard University. Reproduced with permission.

Weiner, Eric. From "Slum Visits: Tourism or Voyeurism." *New York Times,* March 9, 2009. © 2009 *The New York Times.* All rights reserved. Used by permission and protected by the Copyright Laws of the United States. The printing, copying, redistribution, or retransmission of the Material without express written permission is prohibited.

Welty, Eudora. Reprinted with permission of the publisher and Russell & Volkening as agents for the author from *One Writer's Beginnings* by Eudora Welty, pp. 32–33, Cambridge, Mass: Harvard University Press, Copyright © 1983, 1984 by Eudora Welty.

X, Malcolm. From *Malcolm X Speaks.* Copyright © 1965, 1989 by Betty Shabazz and Pathfinder Press. Reprinted by permission.

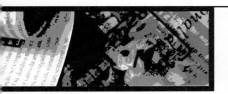

index

guide to reading selections

Readings found within the text are listed here by theme.